Leadership and Administration of Outdoor Pursuits

Design by Marilyn Shobaken
Cover Design by Sandra Sikorski
Editorial Assistance by Susan Lewis
Production Assistance by Bonnie Godbey
Typesetting by King Printing, State College, PA
Library of Congress Catalogue Card Number 85-51320
ISBN-0-910251-11-8

Other Books from Venture Publishing:

Recreation and Leisure: Issues in an Era of Change, Revised Edition, edited by Thomas L. Goodale and Peter A. Witt

Leisure in Your Life: An Exploration, Revised Edition, by Geoffrey Godbey

To Leisure: An Introduction, by John Neulinger

Recreation Planning and Management, edited by Stanley R. Lieber and Daniel R. Fesenmaier

Marketing Parks and Recreation, by the National Park Service

Vandalism Control Management for Parks and Recreation Areas, by Monty L. Christiansen

Winning Support for Parks and Recreation, by the National Park Service

Values and Leisure and Trends in Leisure Services, by the Academy of Leisure Sciences

Playing, Living, Learning — A Worldwide Perspective on Children's Opportunities to Play, by Cor Westland and Jane Knight

This book is dedicated to our parents, Wendell and Mary Ford and Bob and Jane Blanchard, who taught us to enjoy and respect the out-of-doors and to want to share it with others.

ACKNOWLEDGEMENTS

A book such as this cannot be written without the contributions and expertise shared by many people. We want to acknowledge the help and advice provided by Mel Jackson and Chuck Solin of the Eugene, Oregon, Department of Parks and Recreation; Keith Nelson, Bruce Mason, and Peggy Douthit of the University of Oregon Outdoor Program; and Bruce Ronning of the Mt. Bachelor (Oregon) Nordic Ski School.

Special thanks should be given to Steve Barron, Paul Green, Steve Hollenhorst, "B.J." Johnson, Lars McNaughton, Deb Nystrom, Simon Priest, Steve Selin, Mike Strong, Mike Swiderski, Mike Watkins, and other graduate assistants assigned to help lead in the University of Oregon Outdoor Pursuits Program. Thanks also goes to all the hard-working dedicated student leaders in the University of Oregon Outdoor Leadership Certification Program.

For help with specific sections of the book, we want to acknowledge the following:

Chapter 6: Steve Hollenhorst wrote the material on permits.

Chapter 7: Many ideas came from Mel Jackson who has staffed many programs of his own.

Chapter 11: Simon Priest provided the material on certification in Great Britain, Canada, Australia, and New Zealand.

We are also indebted to Anne Borland and Oscar Palmquist for their assistance in the selection and processing of photographs and to Diane Baxter, Dr. Michael Ellis, and Dean Celeste Ulrich of the University of Oregon for their understanding and encouragement throughout the entire process.

A final note of appreciation goes to our two typists: Dawne Daugherty of the University of Oregon and Marilue Von Bargen of Washington State University. They had to adjust to one of the authors moving from Oregon to Washington in the middle of the process and each one ended up typing unrelated sections of the manuscript without knowing what the other parts were about.

THE AUTHORS

PHYLLIS M. FORD

Phyllis Ford holds an appointment as Professor and Chair of the Department of Physical Education, Sport, and Leisure Studies at Washington State University. Dr. Ford earned a bachelor of science degree in Recreation from the University of Massachusetts, a master of arts degree in Education from Arizona State University in Tempe, and a doctorate in Recreation from Indiana University, where she also received the Garrett Eppley Alumni Award in 1976. She is the author of *Informal Recreation Activities* and *Principle and Practices of Outdoor/Environmental Education*, as well as co-author of *Camp Administration* and *Leadership In Recreation and Leisure Service Organizations*. She has written many articles and papers and has held program, leadership, supervisory, and administrative positions within youth agencies, resident and day camps, public schools, and universities. Dr. Ford was at the University of Oregon from 1961 to 1984, with the exception of 1969-71, when she served as Chairman of the Recreation Education Program at the University of Iowa. While at Oregon, she served as department head from 1971-1975, as department Graduate Student Coordinator, as a member of many university committees, and again as department head from 1981-1985.

Dr. Ford started camping at age four, and participated in her first backpack trip at age nine. She has hiked, camped, and/or climbed in the New England states, the Mid-West, the Northwest, and Canada. Her leadership experiences include Girl Scouts and climbing-club trips, high school and university courses. She is an avid amateur naturalist and has taught environmental interpretation, outdoor education, and recreation and natural resources on the university level.

With her major interests in outdoor/education/recreation, Dr. Ford has served as an officer for the American Camping Association both nationally and regionally. A life member of ACA, she received that organization's Hedley Dimock Award for contribution to the advancement of youth camping in 1973. She has served on one Bureau of Land Management and two U.S. Forest Service Advisory Committees, and has done volunteer work for the U.S. Forest Service.

JIM BLANCHARD

Jim Blanchard holds a bachelor of science degree in Geology and a master of science degree in Recreation and Park Management from the University of Oregon. He has held an appointment as Instructor and Coordinator of the Outdoor Pursuits Program of the Department of Physical Education at the University of Oregon since 1979. He has extensive experience in mountaineering, backpacking, and both Alpine and Nordic skiing, and has pursued these interests in Alaska, Canada, the western and eastern states, Mexico, Europe, and Asia. Since 1962, he has taught these activities for elementary and secondary schools, community colleges, universities, park districts and departments, Outward Bound, and many other private and public institutions. He has also directed his own Guide Service and Mountaineering School since 1967. As an expert in mountain rescue techniques, avalanches, and back-country first aid, he has maintained an active role as a mountain rescue team member since 1960. In 1965 he was President of the Mountain Rescue and Safety Council of Oregon. Through most of the '70's, he supplemented his teaching with work as a Forest Service Wilderness Ranger, developing a strongly biocentric philosophy and a sensitivity to the complex interactions of man and wilderness. He currently spends a portion of each summer leading backpacking and climbing trips in Japan and other Asian countries, and in Europe.

Contents

PART I
BACKGROUND

CHAPTER 1

INTRODUCTION

Between the late 1800's and the 1980's, people all over the world gradually moved to the out-of-doors for leisure-time experiences. Since World War II, the quantity of out-of-doors activities has increased astonishingly. In a veritable explosion of numbers, millions are backpacking, cross-country skiing, rafting, canoeing, bicycling, hiking, climbing, or caving. In short, millions are moving across land and water seeking enjoyment through physical exercise in primitive settings. Accompanying this rise in outdoor recreation have been predictable increases in environmentally related accidents, injuries and deaths, with a concomitant increase in environmental degradation.

Most of the participants in outdoor pursuits have had no formal or informal education addressing either care of the natural environment or care of themselves in that natural environment. Within the last decade, countless educational programs for users of outdoor areas have arisen throughout the United States, Canada, Europe, Australia, New Zealand and Japan. There are over 400 such educational programs in the United States alone. The leaders of these programs may have had some training and education as outdoor instructors but, until very recently, there have been few formal leadership courses offered by educational institutions. Since the mid 1970's four-year and two-year colleges have added courses to train outdoor leaders. It is recognized that the user needs to be educated in care of self and in stewardship of land and water resources. Those who are charged with educating users must, in turn, have been educated to teach them.

On the one hand we have the human element —people desiring experiences based on utilization of natural resources. On the other hand we have the non-human element—natural resources that can contribute to either successful or disastrous experiences. The connecting elements are the activity sponsor, resource-management consent and support, money, transportation and equipment all coordinated by a leader, who, it is assumed, has the knowledge and ability to make the transition efficiently and effectively.

This text is designed to meet the needs of outdoor leaders and administrators. While specifically addressed to potential leaders and instructors, this book should be of great benefit to administrators of outdoor programs as well. The managers of these educational and recreational programs are, with increasing frequency and urgency, being pressed to extend the scope of their programs to include outdoor pursuits. Yet few of them know enough about such activities to be able to select qualified leaders and to monitor and evaluate the development and implementation of the activities adequately. A better understanding by administrators of the specific demands of outdoor leadership should improve the process by which they select and supervise leaders, thus reducing non-quality programs and exposure to liability. Through the use of the material in this text, readers should become aware of the accepted standards, structures, controversies, principles, methods, and skills of leadership of outdoor activities. Readers should be able to plan, organize, and carry out safe and responsible programs for land or water-based activities in a natural setting. They should, further, be able to select, train and supervise outdoor leaders.

OUTDOOR ACTIVITIES

This book is primarily focused on activities perceived as outdoor recreation. The words "outdoor recreation" connote a wide variety of meanings. In its broadest sense, the terms were used by the U.S. Department of the Interior in its report, *The Recreation Imperative,* to the U.S. Senate in 1974. As a result of the 1962 Public Law 85-470, the Outdoor Recreation Resources Review Commission (ORRRC) was organized and mandated to review the outdoor recreation wants and needs of the American people in 1962 with projections for the years 1976 and 2000, and to inventory the available resources and recommend policies and programs to insure that the needs of the people would be met. In carrying out the charge, the commission defined outdoor recreation as follows:

"Outdoor recreation" is not defined by statute, legislative history, or administrative regulation. The Nationwide Plan, therefore, interprets the term broadly. For the purposes of the Nationwide Plan, outdoor recreation includes those activities that occur outdoors in an urban and man-made environment as well as those activities traditionally associated with the natural environment. With the advent of indoor-outdoor facilities, such as convertible skating rinks and swimming pools, an additional dimension has been added to the complex of areas and facilities encompassed in the term outdoor recreation.

As a result of this broad definition, and by surveying thousands of Americans, the list of the twenty-five most popular activities was generated, as shown in Table 1.1.

It is interesting to note that in 1984, the University of Maryland Research Center surveyed a sample of 5,757 people for the National Park Service in an attempt to update figures on participation in outdoor activities. Table 1.1 also shows the number of people participating in selected activities in the 1984 study. The rank order of activities by popularity is similar to that of the 1965 study, but the numbers of participants has grown dramatically.

This broad definition of outdoor recreation, encompassing urban and rural participants, includes more than most single books on outdoor activities are able to cover. Other definitions may be equally broad. The following definition, adapted from Reynold Carlson, is more limiting:

Outdoor recreation is any enjoyable leisure-time activity pursued outdoors or indoors involving knowledge, use, or appreciation of natural resources. (Reynold Carlson, Indiana University, lecture, 1960.)

The essence of Carlson's definition is the emphasis on "natural resources," thus eliminating facilities groomed to specifications which are artificial or developed and maintained through careful specifications. Carlson's definition, however, because of its inclusion of indoor activities involving use, knowledge, or appreciation of natural resources, is broader than many outdoor enthusiasts are willing to accept.

A third definition of outdoor recreation is proposed by Clawson and Knetsch in their

TABLE 1.1 OUTDOOR RECREATION
ACTIVITIES OF AMERICANS IN 1965 AND 1984

1965 Rank	Activity	1965 Participants	1984 Participants
1	Picnicking	114 Million	
2	Driving for Pleasure	110	
3	Swimming	104	
4	Sightseeing	100	
5	Pleasure Walking	77	
6	Attending Sporting Events	66	
7	Playing Outdoor Games or Sports	65	
8	Fishing	57	76.5 Million
9	General Boating	52	
10	*Bicycling	41	
11	Sledding	29	
12	Attending Concerts and Plays	26	
13	Nature Walking	25	
14	*Camping	25	54
15	*Day Hiking		31.5
16	Hunting	19	27
17	Ice Skating	17	
18	*Hiking with Pack	14	11.5
19	Water Skiing	10	
20	Bird Watching	9	
21	*Canoeing	6	
22	*Canoeing and Kayaking		18
23	Snow Skiing	6	
24	Downhill Skiing		13.5
25	*Cross-country Skiing		6.7
26	*Sailing	5	
27	Wildlife and Bird Photography	3	
28	*Mountain Climbing	1	

*Activities discussed in this book.

book, *Economics of Outdoor Recreation*. This definition is based on the premise that outdoor recreation occurs on large tracts of land and/or water located at considerable distances from the homes of the recreationists and, consequently, includes several phases. This multi-phased concept of outdoor recreation entails the activities, attitudes and economic values of anticipation (planning the event, including purchasing equipment, determining the route, and organizing the schedule), travel to the site, activities at the site (hiking, climbing, rafting), travel from the site, and recollection or reflection. While most outdoor leaders and their respective followers seem to be mainly concerned with activities at the site, it is clear that pre-trip planning and transportation, and post-trip evaluation are also integral parts of the leader's responsibility; thus the multi-phased concept of outdoor recreation has logical application for this book. These three definitions may serve to confuse or even annoy some outdoor enthusiasts who consider their personal outdoor recreational interest to be far removed from and even antithetical to the interests of others.

The authors of this book recognize, accordingly, that the terms used here will not be generally accepted by all outdoor leaders. For the sake of clarifying the contents of this book, the following discussion will serve to define outdoor pursuits as we see them. It is important to understand that, while the principles for activities pursued by *individuals* are basically the same as those for activities carried out by *groups,* this book focuses on administration and leadership functions that are carried out with and for *groups* of people. Further, it must be understood that the outdoor pursuits referred to here are usually those undertaken voluntarily for the sake of the activities themselves and with no gain in mind other than the intrinsic value of the activity. This, then, is a book on the administration and leadership of activities usually of a recreational nature.

Recreation is generally defined professionally as activities chosen voluntarily during leisure time for the sake of the activities themselves. Recreation as a process is more important than recreation as a product.

There are many definitions of recreation, but a statement from Jensen (1970) summarizes them most appropriately:

> Upon analysis of definitions it seems that many of them, even though stated differently, say essentially the same. The following elements are common to the several definitions.
> 1. Recreation directly involves the individual.
> 2. It is entered into voluntarily.
> 3. It occurs during leisure time.
> 4. The motivating force is enjoyment and satisfaction, as opposed to material gain.
> 5. Recreation is wholesome to the individual and his society.
>
> These common points distinguish recreation from work and other necessary activities; however, they do not give the term the strength it deserves. They do not *clearly distinguish* recreation from amusement, time-filling, or low-quality participation. They do not add a strong characteristic of *quality* to this meaning.
>
> The term "recreation" implies that the participant is recreated in some aspect — physically, psychologically, spiritually, or mentally; that he becomes refreshed and enriched; that he becomes revitalized and more ready to cope with his trials. In order to qualify as recreation, an activity must do something desirable to the participant. It must enrich him and add joy and satisfaction to an otherwise routine day. (*Outdoor Recreation in America,* 1970, pp. 8-9.)

Many outdoor scientific expeditions, i.e., climbing Mt. Everest, exploring the Mojave desert, or charting the Colorado River, entail the same skills and often identical leadership principles as recreational activities; however, the goals are specific about the accomplishment of the task, and the process often requires strict discipline, arduous functions, forced effort to succeed and even drudgery, hardship and deprivation — always with the accomplishment of the task in mind.

Recreational experiences may involve the same discipline, ardor, effort, drudgery, hardship, and discomfort; however, the end product is not the accomplishment of a required task, it is the accomplishment of an internal feeling of success, safe return, and joy of accomplishing something of personal value. While the goal of a funded expedition may be to reach the destination, the goal of recreation is personal satisfaction and a safe return with a chance to try again if desired.

It is a moot point to try to determine when an enjoyable outdoor recreation activity becomes an unpleasant bit of drudgery or a life-endangering crisis. Hopefully leaders and administrators who are aware of principles of group guidance and how to apply them will be able to prevent the drudgery and life-threatening crises which turn recreation into a goal-oriented torturous experience. The point to remember is that the major purpose of this book is to discuss the role and function of professional leaders who are paid employees or volunteers leading members of the general public in activities they choose voluntarily because of positive, enjoyable expectations.

The term "outdoor pursuits" is widely applied to those activities which entail moving across natural land and/or water resources by non-mechanized means of travel. In this context this book limits the scope of outdoor pursuits to non-mechanical and non-animal means of travel. Included in this perception of outdoor pursuits are such activities as hiking, backpacking, climbing (rock and snow), cross-country skiing, primitive camping (summer and winter), canoeing, rafting, caving, and snowshoeing. Specifically included are group activities based on land, snow, or water resources. Excluded are downhill skiing, car camping, motorboating, horseback riding, dogsledding, etc. The book is limited to non-mechanical group activities involving human judgment in areas remote from modern conveniences. The activities are based on the interrelationship of humans with the natural environment, particularly where that environment may present discomfort, danger, and unique situations.

The terms "outdoor adventure" or "adventure activity" are similar to but slightly different from "outdoor pursuits." Adventure activities would be those outdoor pursuits that, in addition to being based on the interrelationship of the human with the natural environment, apply stress to or challenge the participants *purposefully*. Skill, tenacity, stamina, and courage are elements added to usual outdoor pursuits that cause them to be termed "adventure acitivities." The point at which an outdoor pursuit becomes an "adventure activity" is often moot and may be determined by the participant who finds that skill, tenacity, stamina, and courage are more stressful than had been anticipated or more challenging in the initial experience with the activity than with a similar experience ten times later. The beginner in river rafting may *perceive* the experience as an outdoor adventure, but if the instructor does not apply stress purposefully, the activity, from the instructor's point of view, is an outdoor recreational pursuit.

It must be recognized, however, that many activities necessitating leadership in the outdoors are not perceived as recreation by the sponsors, leaders and/or participants. Classes required by various educational institutions, military training, referral programs for potential or adjudicated delinquents, and any program whose purpose is to develop self-concept, character, stamina, or other personal attribute cannot be labelled "recreation." Such programs should, nevertheless, follow the same leadership standards and principles as recreational programs. The purposes of each are different; however, the means of achieving those purposes differ little. Philosophically, it is believed that the attitude and technique of the leader can turn an otherwise unpleasant situation into an enjoyable one so that the purpose of the outing can be achieved more willingly, even with positive enthusiasm. Regardless of our ultimate goal, our leadership should never result in an antipathy toward the resources upon which the activities

are based, nor in anything other than an attitude of care for those resources.

It must further be understood that there is a fine line between voluntary and required activities. There are times when participants in required activities find themselves enjoying the experience and desiring to participate again. By the same token, there are times when the outdoor recreation enthusiast wishes only to get home and away from the activity. One of the authors recalls two friends who had climbed a glaciated peak in the sunshine and then descended in a cold rain. They subsequently tried to warm themselves over a miserably sputtering fire of wet sub-Alpine fir twigs. One turned to the other and asked, "Is this recreation?" With this in mind, the reader can understand that, regardless of the primary purpose of the outdoor event, the contents of this book can be used by every type of outdoor leader.

Hunting and fishing are excluded from this book, for they are basically sports with the goal of bringing back *something,* which is quite different from the recreational goal of bringing back an *experience.* (While one may bring back photographs, photography is considered concomitant to the experiential goal.) Further, rarely do people participate in hunting and fishing activities in a setting requiring group leadership.

Thus, regardless of the diversity of outdoor recreation definitions and the vast potential for definitions of outdoor pursuits, this book is focused mainly on the administration and leadership of voluntarily chosen non-mechanized outdoor activities undertaken in natural environments, remote from the city, for the purpose of enjoyment, self-realization and the intrinsic value of the experience itself.

Several things have brought about the need for highly qualified leaders of outdoor-pursuit activities. It goes without saying that an increase in participation probably brings on a correlating increase in accidents and deaths as well as degradation of the environment. Today, with instant news media, frequent high-value suits, and the popularity of outdoor pursuits, people expect all accidents to be the unnecessary fault of the leader. In earlier days, few people subjected themselves to outdoor activities for pleasure and those who succumbed to the elements or perished in falls or drownings may well have been considered brave heroes.

The increase in the use of natural resources for recreation are shown by the numbers of hikers completing the entire Appalachian Trail from Main to Georgia from 1936 to 1981, as shown on Table 1.2, and the number of boaters traveling in the Colorado River through the Grand Canyon from 1896 to 1972, as shown on Table 1.3. It is no wonder that travel on the Colorado River is now rationed!

TABLE 1.2 INCREASE IN HIKERS ON APPALACHIAN TRAIL

2000-Milers*

From 1936 to 1969 only 50 people hiked the entire A.T.

1970	10
1971	23
1972	35
1973	88
1974	71
1975	69
1976	92
1977	60
1978	77
1979	115
1980	118
1981	101

*Figures include only those hikers who reported their accomplishments to the Appalachian Train Conference. They reflect hikers who walked the Trail over a number of years as well as those who accomplished the feat in one season. 1981 figures are preliminary as it often takes up to six months for hikers to report the completion of their trip.

LOCATIONS FOR OUTDOOR PURSUITS

The sites for outdoor pursuits are many and include both natural outdoor areas and indoor instructional facilities using simulated natural resources for land sports (rock walls, climbing boards, etc.) and swimming pools for teaching initial boating and swimming skills. Indoors, the innovative leader may use walls for climbing, bleachers for practicing relaying techniques, beams for ascending and descending on Prussik slings or jumars. In pools one can teach rescue technique, entering and leaving water craft safely, use of paddles and oars, and kayak rolls. rolls.

Outdoor sites consist of millions of acres of land and lakes, miles of rivers, and countless caves. Forests, jungles, deserts, prairies, rocks, snow, ponds, streams, and beaches with accompanying challenges of weather, steepness, currents, cliffs, plants, and animals abound throughout the world. The lands are administered by various government agencies, youth-serving organizations, private businesses, timber companies, individuals, schools, and churches.

The resources for outdoor pursuits are made up of the land, water, plants, animals, air, and climate of the various areas. Within definable geographic boundaries, changing with either elevation or latitude, occur life zones or areas in which, because of identifiable climate, specific forms of plant and animal life exist. Basic life zones are Tropical, Lower Sonoran, Upper Sonoran, Moist Temperate, Dry Temperate, Canadian, Hudsonian, and Arctic-Alpine. The existence of life zones and accompanying different plant and animal species make the outdoor-pursuit acitivity more challenging, interesting, and varied. Since these climate zones change either as one moves south to north (or the reverse) and also as one climbs in elevation (or descends), it is important that the outdoor leader study and learn the conditions of all life zones into which the group will travel. The change in life zones in elevation is of importance to land pursuits such as hiking, backpacking, and climbing and, at times, to the river rafter when descending long distances.

Since species of plants and animals are different in different life zones, it stands to reason that the human being must make climatic allowances and adapt accordingly. Geographic areas of the world are so divided that knowledge of flora, fauna, geology, and weather are of vital importance to the adventurer who attempts outdoor recreation in more than one ecosystem. For the American to try backpacking, climbing, or river activities in New Zealand, Australia, the

TABLE 1.3 TRAVEL ON THE COLORADO RIVER THROUGH GRAND CANYON

Year or Years	Number of People	Year or Years	Number of People
1869-1940	44	1956	55
1941	4	1957	135
1942	8	1958	80
1943	0	1959	120
1944	0	1960	205
1945	0	1961	255
1946	0	1962	372
1947	4	1963-64*	44
1948	6	1965	547
1949	12	1966	1,067
1950	7	1967	2,099
1951	29	1968	3,609
1952	19	1969	6,019
1953	31	1970	9,935
1954	21	1971	10,942
1955	70	1972	16,428

NOTE: Data is compiled from records of individual expeditions and, after 1941, from the records of the Superintendent, Grand Canyon National Park. Penetration of the inner wilderness of the Grand Canyon began in 1869 with the pioneering descent of John Wesley Powell's expedition. Statistics from 1869 through 1955 are not exact (for example, repeat river-runners are not included for 1941-54), but the margin of error is very small.

*Travel on the Colorado River in these years was affected by the completion of Glen Canyon Dam and the resulting disruption of flow.

Orient, or Europe, it entails the ability to learn new things very rapidly. Drinking-water sources, obnoxious or even dangerous plants and animals, useful plants, emergency fuel sources, and changes in weather patterns are all important. By the same token, the New Englander who has spent years in the northern Appalachians is not automatically equipped to lead a group in Florida, New Mexico, the Washington rain forest, the glaciers of any state, or the high plains and prairies. Nor is any outdoor leader who is an expert in his or her own geographic area equipped to lead groups in any other area in the world without some preliminary examination of the plants, animals, weather, geology, and geography of the new area.

PARTICIPANTS

Many outdoor leaders perceive their followers to be similar to themselves, but such is rarely the case. Participants in outdoor pursuits might literally be defined as every type of person alive. Participants will vary in individual and group differences. Leaders would do well to consider some or all of the following as potential clients:

— Youngsters five years old, grandparents in their 80s;
— Families with parents in their late 30's or early 40's with children aged 14, 11 and 8;
— Participants who are deaf, partly or totally blind, physically disabled, mentally disturbed, or learning impaired;
— Minorities (blacks, Orientals, Chicanos in the USA);
— Students from elementary schools, high schools, colleges;
— Young men and women who find the outdoors their main source of personal challenge and gratifying recreation;
— Inner-city youth who find the outdoors frightening, alien, and even punitive;
— Several of the above combined into one group.

Leaders of outdoor pursuits must expect a wide range of participant ages, abilities, and backgrounds, many times in combination. While some activities should be limited to the very fit, most groups include a wide range of abilities, interests, and attitudes. The leader who is not willing and able to lead the slow, tired, frightened, or recalcitrant follower may do more damage than good. Leaders and administrators of outdoor programs often seem to assume that leadership is being offered to established groups whose interests and skills in the out-of-doors are the primary reasons for being there. This is more often *not* the case.

Usually participants are grouped with some common denominator as a tie. Regardless of ability, intelligence, income, or even equal liking for the activity, youth groups are tied together by their membership in a nationally sponsored organization with specified goals and behavior patterns. Boy Scouts, Girl Scouts, Camp Fire, YMCA, YWCA, and other similar groups are usually involved in outdoor programs as a sponsored group or troop. Each participant may have different reasons for being there. Social interaction, peer pressures, desire to excel, parental hopes, desire to earn an award, or other motivations may be stronger than a desire for any of the purposes of outdoor pursuits recognized by the leader.

Family groups may participate in outdoor programs for reasons primarily related to family cohesiveness. The main purpose may be to have a chance to interact on a recreational level in a new setting without the influence of outside factors. Here, as in the youth groups, the outdoor experience may be secondary to the family interaction. Leaders of two or three diverse families in a group may even find conflicting goals from one family to another and may need to make radical changes in the goals assumed for the occasion.

Mixed groups may attend outdoor-pursuit programs sponsored by municipal recreation departments, schools, or climbing clubs. Usually participants in such programs are there because of individual personal goals. Unlike the youth agency groups, they see no common denominator for belonging to the group and may not even be interested in being part of it. People who join city-sponsored programs, clubs, and college classes may be doing so because the desire to participate in the activity is primary and the temporary group association interest is only secondary or perhaps non-existent.

The physically or mentally disabled, the adjudicated delinquent, and the social misfit or miscreant are increasingly being programmed into outdoor pursuits for the purpose of developing self-confidence, experiencing success, learning to adjust to new situations, and experiencing group work. The physically disabled, including those with orthopedic, congenital, and neuro-muscular disabling conditions, can usually adjust to the environment and are usually in the program voluntarily with attitudes and skills as attainable (within the limitations of the disability) as any non-disabled person.

The mentally disabled may, on the other hand, not really know or understand why they are present or what they should do. Coping with problems caused by snow, danger, cold, rain, heavy loads, toileting, lack of comprehension, and length of time needed to perform tasks means a different approach to leadership.

The elderly may be in better shape mentally and physically than some people much younger. Yet they may need a slower pace, warmer clothes, more frequent rest, or other considerations. A totally mixed group could contain physical disabilities, mental impairment, the teenager, the retiree, young adults, and the middle-aged. In short, the outdoor-pursuit leader can anticipate responsibility for every category of person imaginable.

SPONSORING AGENCIES

Participants in outdoor pursuits are of two types: common adventures or proprietary groups. As common adventurers, they, in essence, sponsor themselves, all taking equal responsibility for cost, equipment, leadership, and success or failure of the event. Common adventure, also known as joint venture, assumes an undertaking wherein all participants have an equal voice in directing the conduct of the enterprise. In other words, common adventurers have no legally designated leader. They are a self-sponsored group with shared leadership responsibilities. They may be members of a college outdoor program, a private climbing club, a group of acquaintances, or a family.

While the principles of outdoor leadership may be applied sagaciously by groups of common adventurers, the major concern of this book lies with those proprietary groups operating under a sponsored program with a designated volunteer or employed leader. Proprietary groups may be discussed under seven headings: a) tax-supported programs, b) youth agencies, c) schools, d) churches, e) private-membership organizations, f) private businesses, and g) guide programs. Within each category leaders may be part-time or full-time volunteers, or part-time or full-time paid professionals. Examples of each group include but are not limited to:

a) Tax-supported Outdoor Programs
   municipal recreation programs
b) Youth-agency Outdoor Programs (Scouts, Campfire, YMCA, YWCA, YMHA, etc.)
   resident camps
   backpack trips
   day hikes
   canoe trips
c) School-sponsored Outdoor Programs
   outdoor-education programs
   wilderness-skill classes
   physical-education department courses
   natural-science field trips (geology, botany, zoology)
d) Church-sponsored Outdoor Programs
   SOLES (Suttle Outdoor Leadership Education — Methodist Church)
   LOM (Lutheran Outdoor Ministry)
e) Private-membership Programs
   Wilderness Society Trips
   Sierra Club
   local hiking clubs
   Federation of Western Outing Clubs
   Appalachian Mountain Club
f) Private Businesses
   National Outdoor Leadership Schools
   Minnesota Outward Bound
   Wilderness Users Education Association
g) Guiding Programs
   river guides
   trail guides
   horsepacker guides

OUTDOOR-PURSUIT LEADERS

Leaders of outdoor programs are almost as varied in personality and background as the participants. No two programs are identical, and the specific roles and responsibilities of leaders depend on countless variables. The only trait common to all outdoor leaders is an interest in the outdoors, and the only universal expectations of leaders is that they return with all participants in good health. Within these broad limits, almost anything is possible. While in most cases outdoor-pursuit leaders need considerable maturity, common sense, communication and leadership ability, and very specific skills and experience, there are situations wherein there are few qualifications for leadership. There is, however, great danger in underestimating the minimum qualifications of leaders. The wrong match of leader and program can result in dissatisfactions among participants, or even in their injury or death. The stakes are extremely high, ethically, morally, and economically. Unfortunately, such mismatches are common, usually because the administrator is not aware of the minimum qualifications for leaders of the activity or of the potential consequences if he/she uses less than fully qualified leaders. This is usually due to the administrator's lack of personal expertise in the activity, and may be compounded by temporal and/or economic constraints. Nevertheless, the selection of leaders is the responsibility of administrators. Later in this book we will attempt to provide practical, specific advice on the minimum qualifications of leaders for various activities, and on the number of such leaders needed for various group sizes and program formats. Administrators and leaders should pay careful attention to these suggestions as well as to the chapter on Liability and Risk Management.

Leaders of outdoor programs may include as many different types as there are types of participants with as many objectives. Many outdoor-pursuit leaders are *volunteers* — either helping youth or church groups or serving as leaders of membership outing clubs. They are usually willing members of an organization that has requested volunteer leaders. As such they are usually enthusiastic and members in good standing within the organization. They have had a wide variety of training and past experiences related to the outdoors and to group work. Some volunteer leaders are highly qualified as leaders of groups in the outdoors because others are unqualified in any way except willingness.

The *paid leaders* may or may not be better qualified than the volunteer leaders. Salaried outdoor-pursuit leaders may be employed full time or part time on an hourly basis or on a contract for each program. Salaried outdoor leaders may be found in tax-supported organizations, some youth-agency programs, private enterprises, packer-guide businesses, youth camps and educational programs such as Outward Bound, or the National Outdoor Leadership School. They may or may not be trained by the sponsoring organization; they may or may not be qualified by virtue of experience and knowledge. Usually the employed leader is responsible for a wider variety of groups and programs than the volunteer leader and may need to be more versatile. Certainly the leader employed full-time will need more long-range stamina and endurance than the leader who volunteers or is paid for a trip of short duration. Nevertheless, the strength, stamina, enthusiasm, knowledge, skills, attitudes and leadership-abilities prerequisite for any single trip *should* be the same for *all* leaders, as will be explained throughout this book. At the time of this writing, there are no universally agreed-upon standards for evaluating the qualifications of an outdoor-pursuit leader in the United States and no universally accepted outdoor-leader certification program although several different certification programs do exist.

Another type of leader involved in outdoor programs is one who may never meet the group or even venture onto the trail or river. Yet this leader is probably the one who is ultimately responsible for the success of the venture. The *administrator* who hires, supervises, evaluates, retains, and/or dismisses the trip leader plays a vital part in the outdoor-pursuit program. Usually this person is not a trained outdoor leader, yet the responsibility for the program and its leaders rests here.

Often administrators are reluctant to offer outdoor pursuit programs, particularly those that appear to be "dangerous" to them. They have three major concerns, the first of which is that they are, naturally, concerned about the possibility of participant injury or death. Remarkably, these same administrators usually offer programs in swimming, gymnastics, and other activities that appear to be equally "dangerous." This will be discussed later in the chapter on Liability and Risk Management.

Many others are concerned that the programs may not meet the needs of the participants, causing dissatisfaction and perhaps not adding to the total quality of life in terms of education. In this case, administrators are exhibiting a lack of trust or faith in the leaders. The third reason that some are not eager to start outdoor programs lies mainly with the land-resource administrators themselves. Quite rightfully these administrators fear damage to or loss of resources through participant carelessness or ignorance.

Any dissatisfaction with the outdoor-pursuit programs may lie with the inability of the administrator to recruit, hire, train, and evaluate good leaders. Inadequate leadership itself may be caused by many factors. Common factors that contribute to less-than-good leadership include: naivety (the leader simply doesn't know enough to be a good leader); fatigue; an attitude that the goal is to reach the destination—and no more; low standards for equipment, safety, personal decorum, or a myriad of things; faulty equipment; and inappropriate methods or techniques. All of these and other weaknesses in an outdoor program's leadership can be alleviated through leadership training and administrator supervision, as will be discussed.

THE VALUES OF OUTDOOR RECREATION

One might ask the question, "What good is outdoor recreation that we should spend so much time on it?" Or, "What are the values of outdoor pursuits?" One could spend much time relating the *economic* values of outdoor recreation in terms of money spent on equipment, transportation, guide service, and such amenities as photographic equipment, lightweight food and how-to-do-it books. This book, however, is about people and the benefits to the human being. Unfortunately, there is no documentation on the human benefits of outdoor pursuits except for some few studies on the benefits of outdoor activities for the mentally, socially, and/or physically disabled. These studies are done on disabled individuals whose disabilities are so severe that they are, indeed, handicapped and in need of special equipment and leaders. Whether anyone else has had actual benefits as a result of outdoor activity that could not be gained from some other type of leisure pursuit is quantitatively unknown.

In spite of the lack of quantitative data supporting the value of outdoor pursuits, there are *perceived* values that are undeniable. Human beings may be viewed holistically as a combination of mind, body, and spirit. Another way of looking at the holistic individual is as a complex organism whose non-biological essence is composed of knowledges, skills, and attitudes or emotions. The values of outdoor recreation may relate to each of those domains separately and in combination.

Physical Values

The physical values of outdoor recreation include the benefits of exercise, development of endurance, and increase in cardio-muscular function. With the increase in strength and endurance comes energy, an increase in muscle tone, an increase in the flow of oxygen to the brain, and a general feeling of well-being.

Mental Values

The knowledge gained from good-quality outdoor pursuits includes knowledge of self and self-concept, knowledge of safety measures and the need to follow them, and knowledge of skills that relate to the physical values. The knowledge of outdoor skills should be accompanied by the knowledge of the environment in which the activity takes place. Weather, flora, fauna, rock and soil formations, water quality, and changing ecosystems provide the individual with understandings of the world that can last throughout life and make other experiences more interesting.

Emotional Values

The emotions or attitudes one develops through outdoor pursuits may relate to the self, to others, to society, and to the environment. One can gain a sense of achievement, overcome stress, find relaxation, increase self concept, or just simply enjoy the experience. One may develop new attitudes toward the members of the group because of the closeness of the individuals in accomplishing difficult tasks. An appreciation for the natural environment and a commitment to save it from destruction may also emerge, a real concern for the survival of the planet after witnessing the results from acid rain, mining, blasting, burning, or herbicides when they are witnessed face to face in the seemingly untouched wildlands.

While the following passage was written during a 1954 workshop on recreation, it is interesting to note that the words are still valid today and have never been challenged. It may be, if the six objectives listed are met, that that in itself will be the greatest value of outdoor pursuits.

A first principle of recreation is that the experience must give satisfaction to the participant. This does not mean, however, that certain other values might not be derived. Neither does it mean that the leader and the organization or agency responsible for the activity should not have specific objectives. Objectives are generally stated in terms of values to the individual. Most of them, however, also have social significance, and programs are planned to meet social needs. The fostering of love of the land and pride in country, the understanding and practice of democracy, the strengthening of social institutions, and the development of conservation attitudes — these are values that might come from the participation in desirable outdoor recreation activities. Contributions of recreation to the health and happiness of people are themselves important social values.

The principal purpose of outdoor recreation is to provide for enjoyment, appreciation and use of the natural environment. Certain more specific objectives are the following:

1. To develop a sense of responsibility for the preservation, care and wise use of the natural environment;

2. To develop an awareness and understanding of the inter-relatedness of all nature, including man;
3. To develop an understanding and appreciation of man's heritage of outdoor living, skills, and pursuits;
4. To develop good outdoor citizenship;
5. To make a contribution to physical and mental health;
6. To develop resourcefulness, self-reliance, and adaptability. (*Athletic Institute*, 1954, p. 250.)

THE COMPONENTS OF A COURSE ON OUTDOOR LEADERSHIP

The contents of a course on outdoor leadership may be decided at the whim of the instructor. Usually they are based on the instructor's experiences plus the advice of friends and colleagues. In an attempt to identify the content of a college outdoor-leadership course, Green (1981) used a modification of the Delphi technique, a research method designed to gain consensus of opinions. Dr. Green is a member of the Outdoor Recreation faculty at Eastern Washington State University (Cheney).

The procedures utilized in a Delphi study are designed to record an individual's opinion without the psychological factors that are present in most face-to-face discussions: influence of dominant individuals, unwillingness to abandon expressed opinions, and group pressure for conformity.

It is difficult to know whose opinions should be elicited as being authoritative. While there is no validation that people in the field know exact answers, it must be assumed that active outdoor leaders have the best obtainable knowledge and should be closer to the truth than those from outside the field. In Green's study the leaders all came from the Pacific Northwest states of Idaho, Washington and Oregon, and the western part of Montana as far east as Bozeman, approximately the 111th meridian. Even though the consensus was limited to those from that fairly narrow geographic area, many of the respondents had participated in outdoor experiences throughout much of the rest of the world. It may be assumed that the contents of the leadership course developed by Green have some relevance to courses in other parts of the world.

In the first questionnaire of this study, respondents were asked to answer a series of demographic questions about age, experience, sex, and education. Table 1.4 shows a demographic profile of the 61 respondents who completed all of the questionnaires in the study. The majority of the 61 outdoor leaders were male (N=50), representing 82% of the total respondents. The age range was from 23 to 63, with an average of 36 years. By examination of the frequency distribution, it can be observed that 60% of the outdoor leaders were under 35 years old.

In regard to leading land-based outdoor pursuits, the outdoor leaders' experience range was from as few as 2 to as many as 25 years. The average experience of the respondents was 11 years. A majority (56%) of the leaders' experience ranged between 6 and 13 years.

Consensus was reached on 35 of the 176 topics which were generated and rated by the outdoor leaders. (The information is summarized on Table 1.5.) This consensus included those topics which had a mathematical mean rating of 3.25 or above. On a truncated four-point scale, the value 3.25 was represented as a response of "very important." The consensus includes 16 topics that cover participant safety and the protection of the natural resources. All five emergency medical topics were also included in the 35 consensus topics. The top 10 rated topics are as follows: 1) risk-management plans (minimizing risks, emergency plans, prevention); 2) judgment; 3) wilderness ethics; 4) first aid; 5) analyzing risks; 6) minimum-impact practices; 7) outdoor-leadership objectives; 8) hazards analysis: hypothermia; 9) back-country first aid; and 10) minimum-impact philosophy.

The outdoor leaders were also asked to select the 10 least important topics from a list of 31 that had received the lowest mean ratings on the second questionnaire. The 11 topics selected most often as the least important are as follows: 1) outdoor arts and crafts; 2) basic trap and snare techniques; 3) basic principles of anthropology; 4) outdoor songs; 5) transportation: automobile mechanics; 6) theories of personality; 7) transportation: driver's education (driving techniques); 8) photography; 9) humanistic psychology; 10) social psychology; and 11) philosophies of education.

Based on the findings of the study and within the delimitations set forth, the following conclusions were drawn by Green:

1. Outdoor leaders, regardless of age or years of experience, are in agreement on the most important topics (consensus) to be included in a college-level outdoor-leadership course for land-based outdoor pursuits in the Pacific Northwest;
2. Regardless of where in the Pacific Northwest the outdoor-leadership course is taught, the content should be the same or similar to the consensus topics in this study;
3. Knowledge of emergency medical techniques is important to outdoor leaders but *should be acquired prior to* an outdoor-leadership course;
4. Outdoor skills are required for leaders of land-based outdoor pursuits but should *also be acquired prior to* an outdoor-leadership course.

It is important to note that technical outdoor skills were not rated high in the final questionnaire. The ratings and the comments by the outdoor leaders indicated that skills are important but should be acquired *prior* to the outdoor-leadership course, either through experience or by completing a series of prerequisite courses. This allows more time for discussion and application of the most important topics in the outdoor-leadership course. An outdoor leader, however, must be knowledgeable and proficient in the technical skills required of the outdoor pursuit they are leading.

In addition to the technical outdoor skills, emergency medical techniques should also be acquired prior to taking the outdoor-leadership course. Although the emergency medical topics were rated very high, the consistent comments by the outdoor leaders and the investigator's experience indicates that these skills should be known *prior* to taking the outdoor-leadership course. From a practical point of view, more time could be allotted to the consensus topics in an outdoor leadership course if the participants were required to meet prerequisite criteria.

The application of the research based upon the rating of comments of the respondents was

TABLE 1.4 DEMOGRAPHIC PROFILE OF THE OUTDOOR LEADERS WHO RESPONDED TO THE COURSE-CONTENT QUESTIONNAIRES (N=61)

Demographic Categories	Number	Percent
Age (in Years)		
20-24	2	3.3
25-29	17	28.0
30-34	18	29.5
35-39	13	21.3
40-45	6	9.8
46-over	5	8.2
Experience (in Years)		
2-5	14	23.0
6-9	15	24.6
10-13	19	31.1
14-17	7	11.4
18-25	6	10.0
Sex		
Men	50	82.0
Women	11	18.0
Education (in Years)		
12-15	8	13.1
16-17	29	47.5
18-19	14	23.0
20-over	10	16.3
State of Residence		
Washington	26	42.6
Oregon	16	26.2
Idaho	11	18.0
Montana	8	13.1

TABLE 1.5 FINAL RANKING AND MEAN SCORES OF THE CONSENSUS TOPICS OF AN OUTDOOR-LEADERSHIP COURSE BY OUTDOOR LEADERS IN THE PACIFIC NORTHWEST

Rank	Mean	Topic
1	3.79	Risk-management Plans (minimizing risks, emergency plans, prevention)
2	3.78	Judgement
3	3.74	Wilderness Ethics
4	3.72	First Aid
5	3.72	Analyzing Risks
6	3.72	Minimum-impact Practices
7	3.71	Outdoor-leadership Objectives
8	3.71	Hazards Analysis: Hypothermia
9	3.66	Back-country First Aid
10	3.63	Minimum-impact Philosophy
11	3.57	Pre-trip Planning: Selection of Location
12	3.57	Liability Considerations
13	3.54	Outdoor Ethics
14	3.53	Outdoor-leadership Methods
15	3.48	Small-group Dynamics in the Outdoors
16	3.45	Teaching Methods and Techniques
17	3.44	Advanced First Aid
18	3.44	Hazards Analysis: Hyperthermia
19	3.44	Pre-trip Planning: Single and Multi-day or Week
20	3.41	Extended First Aid for Long Trips (professional help unavailable)
21	3.40	Assessment of Individual Capabilities
22	3.38	Pre-trip Planning: Travel Time, Length (Itinerary)
23	3.36	Map Reading and Interpretation
24	3.36	Small-group Dynamics
25	3.34	Decision-making
26	3.34	Program Goals
27	3.33	Teaching Principles for Leaders
28	3.33	Avalanche Awareness
29	3.32	Environmental Awareness Skills
30	3.31	Mountain Medicine
31	3.30	Assessment of Group Capabilities
32	3.29	Philosophy of Outdoor Leadership
33	3.27	Problem Solving, Analysis
34	3.26	Food Planning
35	3.25	Avalanche Safety

an outdoor-leadership course outline. The topical outline was recommended as a guideline for the content of a college-level outdoor-leadership course. It must be understood that these topics are based on opinions only. They may not *be* the best topics for such a course, but they are *opinions of what is best* and they are, further, the opinions of people currently involved in leading land-based outdoor pursuits. The prerequisites for the outdoor-leadership course should include emergency medical training and skill training associated with the outdoor pursuits. As a result, Green recommended the following course outline:

I. *Philosophy* - includes philosophy of outdoor leadership, objectives, and outdoor program goals
II. *Risk Management* - includes risk-management plans (minimizing risks, emergency plans, prevention), analyzing risks, and liability considerations, as well as assessment of individual and group capabilities
III. *Decision-Making* - includes judgment and problem-solving analysis
IV. *Outdoor Leadership Methods*
V. *Teaching Principles* - includes teaching methods and techniques for outdoor leaders
VI. *Small Group Dynamics in the Outdoors*
VII. *Environmental Awareness Skills* - includes wilderness and outdoor ethics, as well as minimum-impact philosophy and practices
VIII. *Pre-Trip Planning* - includes single and multi-day trips, selection of location, itinerary (travel time, length), and food planning
IX. *Hazards Analysis* - includes hypothermia, hyperthermia, and avalanche awareness and safety
X. *Map Reading and Interpretation*

The topics listed in the recommended outdoor leadership course outline were combined from several headings to include topics of similar or parallel content. Additionally, the topics were ordered to reflect a recommended sequence of presentation in the proposed outdoor-leadership course.

It is important to emphasize that the outdoor-leadership course outline is a guideline for the recreation educators teaching the college-level courses. Inasmuch as the topics generated by

Green's study are generic to any outdoor program, they will be included in this book, although in a different order. Nonetheless, all of Green's topics are covered here.

The remainder of this book consists of a series of progressive steps culminating with several recommended program models. Initially, in the section titled BACKGROUND, the discussion will cover the needs of humans and their survival requirements, followed by an examination of the environment and the conditions for its perpetuation.

In the pursuit of outdoor recreation, two parallel equal concerns must always be addressed even though the leader may, by virtue of interest, training, and philosophy, not be equally knowledgeable or skilled in each.

No outdoor-pursuit activity should be engaged in or lead without deliberate consideration for the care and safety of the land and human resources involved in the program. The quality of the outdoor experience as perceived by the participants depends upon the quality of the land, plants, wildlife, water, and air involved in it. Any lessening of the quality of the natural resource ultimately will reduce the quality of the experience and eventually preclude the possibility of having any at all.

Conversely, if the participants are injured, die, become permanently incapacitated, or return home dissatisfied, no matter how idyllic the setting or pure the water, the experience is unsuccessful.

It is impossible to say, like the chicken- or egg-first dilemma, which is more important — the care of the natural resources or the care of the human resources. They are interdependent and inseparable, but in spite of this, each may be discussed separately. The next sections of this book are devoted to a discussion of each separately; however, the reader is cautioned to treat each section equally and thoroughly, and to interrelate them.

The second section, ADMINISTRATIVE CONCERNS, deals with considerations to be covered prior to leaving town or embarking upon sponsoring an outdoor event. Part three, APPLIED KNOWLEDGE, deals with four basic skills required of every leader in the field: leading, first aid, map-and-compass, and search-and-rescue. The final section gives a step-by-step planning guide and a series of recommended model outdoor-pursuit programs.

SUMMARY

The principles of outdoor leadership are based on the need to assist those who desire outdoor experience to make a logical and safe transition from a generally sedentary indoor life to a usually active interaction with natural elements. This book is designed for outdoor leaders and administrators of both land and water-based outdoor activities. While mainly directed to leaders of recreational (voluntary) pursuits, the book also addresses leaders of required outdoor programs.

There are countless locations for outdoor pursuits, a wide variety of participants and both paid and volunteer leaders. Regardless of differences, basic standard leadership techniques are called for in every activity. Physical, mental, and emotional values have been identified for outdoor pursuits as well as values for the entire outdoor-recreation experience.

The inclusion of the topics in this book was determined from research done by Dr. Paul Green on the recommended components of an outdoor-leadership course. The remainder of the book is divided into progressive steps leading to a series of program models.

BIBLIOGRAPHY

Athletic Institute, *The Recreation Program*, Chicago: The Athletic Institute, 1954.

Brown, Christopher N., "New Handshake: Management Partners Along the Appalachian Trail," *Parks and Recreation*, National Recreation and Parks Association, June, 1982, pp. 36-42, 62.

Clawson, Marion, and Knetsch. Jack L., *Economics of Outdoor Recreation*, Baltimore: The Johns Hopkins Press, 1966.

Green, Paul J., "The Content of a College-Level Outdoor Leadership Course for Land-Based Outdoor Pursuits in the Pacific Northwest: A Delphi Consensus," unpublished doctoral dissertation, University of Oregon, 1981.

Jensen, Clayne, *Outdoor Recreation in America*, Minneapolis: Burgess Publishing Co., 1970.

Nash, Roderick, *Wilderness and the American Mind*, New Haven, CT: Yale University Press, 1973.

Swiderski, Michael J. "Outdoor Leadership Competencies Identified by Outdoor Leaders in Five Western Regions," unpublished doctoral dissertation, University of Oregon, 1981.

Yukic, T.S., *Fundamentals of Recreation*, New York: Harper & Row Publishers, 1963.

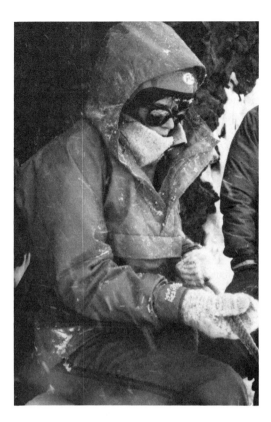

A STUDENT IN A BEGINNING MOUNTAINEERING CLASS WEARING LAYERS OF INSULATION, RAINWEAR AND SUNGLASSES
All are essential in providing an acceptable comfort level in Alpine environments. The helmet provides an additional margin of safety.

CHAPTER 2

HUMAN NEEDS

Leading people in outdoor pursuits entails knowledge and skill in two very diverse aspects of responsibility. The outdoor pursuits and their inherent skills may appear to be the major focal point of the program; however, a more important consideration is the second part of the responsibility: leading human beings in an adverse and often fragile environment. The needs of the environment as related to use by humans are discussed in Chapter 5; this chapter deals with the human needs themselves. In many ways, the activities, be they skiing, hiking, rafting, or any other, are a means to an end — that end being human growth and development. It is thus apparent that the leader of outdoor pursuits is really a leader of participants in outdoor pursuits and, as such, should be aware of the physiological and psychological needs of human beings.

The novice leader may be so over zealous about the outdoors and the activities in which the followers will participate that the needs of the followers may become secondary. The result can be frustration for the leader and reduction in the quality of the experience for the participant.

The major concern of all leaders — regardless of program — must be to meet at least the basic needs of each individual. Leader-determined goals and objectives are vital but must be secondary to individual requirements. If the needs of all individuals are met, at least partly, the chances of the group goals being reached become a reality. If the needs of one individual are not met at least minimally, the progress of the entire group could be deterred. There are, of course, times when meeting all the demands of one individual could create problems for the entire group, and compromises must be made to insure that the goals of *everyone* are met minimally but not optimally. People's needs can be categorized in several ways, but for the application of material in this text, the writers believe physiological and psychological/sociological groupings may be easily understood and applied.

One of the most widely quoted views on human needs is that of Abraham Maslow, who developed a hierarchy of needs, each based upon the fulfillment of the previous one. At the base of Maslow's hierarchy is the need for life-sustaining elements. This is a physiological demand — a demand for the things upon which life depends. In the human, life continuation depends upon adequate oxygen, maintenance of body warmth, adequate sleep, liquid, and food. (These will be discussed in greater depth later in this chapter.) After the physiological, Maslow identifies the psychological need for security and safety, which is basically the freedom from harassment. The third requirement is the requirement for belonging and acceptance which is manifested in the gregarious and caring nature of people. Following the need to belong is the need for self-respect and respect from others, like the group or groups to which one belongs. The fifth and final human need is the one for self-actualization, which Maslow feels is not possible to define sharply but is an "ongoing actualization of potentials, capacities and talents, as fulfillment of mission (or call, fate, destiny, or vocation), as a fuller knowledge of, and acceptance of, the person's own intrinsic nature, as an unceasing trend toward unity, integration or synergy within the person." (Maslow, Abraham, *Toward a Psychology of Being,* 1980, p. 25.)

Analysis of the foregoing descriptors reveals that self-actualization is closely related to the recognized goals of leisure experiences (see Chapter 1). It may be that it is through participation in leisure activities that self-actualization has its greatest potential. With Maslow's hierarchy in mind, analysis of physiological, and psychological/sociological needs can take place as they apply to outdoor pursuits.

PHYSIOLOGICAL NEEDS

Physiological needs, in terms of immediate survival, probably occur most often in the following order: adequate quality and quantity of fresh air; a body temperature controlled at or near approximately 98.6° F; shelter (from the elements of wind, precipitation, heat and/or cold); adequate drinking water; adequate rest/sleep; exercise of body organs and systems; and food and nourishment.

People need air, water, certain nutrients, and an environment that allows maintenance of body temperatures within narrow limits. In our normal, everyday lives we seldom consider these needs except momentarily when hunger or thirst compels us to seek food or drink. Setting out into the wilderness means leaving behind the warm and secure home, the supermarkets and the city water system, and asking our bodies to perform with great efficiency, sometimes in harsh weather at high altitude, sustained by whatever food and shelter can be carried in a pack, and by natural ground-water sources. On day excursions at modest altitudes in the summer, this is rarely a major problem. Most outdoor enthusiasts, however, want the option of trips of weekend length or longer, possibly at elevations above 5000 feet. Comfort, and in the long run safety, depend upon an understanding of basic physical needs and how to obtain them in back-country settings.

Air

Most people take air for granted, living at or near sea level. As one goes up in elevation, the presence of air, or at least an adequate supply of oxygen to body tissues, cannot be assumed as easily. The efficiency with which the body takes up oxygen has much to do with the pressure of the air we breathe. At 5000 feet, a common elevation for ski areas and trailheads, the percentage of oxygen in the air is essentially the same as at sea level, but the air pressure is significantly less (as may be noticed in a bulging water bottle). Most people experience the first signs of hypoxia, the inadequate profusion of oxygen, at about this altitude. For most, fortunately, the symptoms are barely noticeable, except for a lack of wind on heavy exertions. The most likely sensation is, in fact, one of exhilaration — that delightful mountain high that, like other "highs," is actually a function of mental impairment, in this case caused by an inadequate oxygen supply to the brain. As elevations increase, the effects of hypoxia increase and are compounded by other physiological responses to lowering pressure. By an elevation of about 8,000 feet, acute mountain sickness (AMS) will begin to become a problem, and at higher elevations high altitude pulmonary edema (HAPE) and cerebral edema (CE) can be life threatening. Anyone planning to travel above 6,000 or 7,000 feet should read one of the excellent books on the topic of altitude related illnesses. *Mountain Sickness* by Peter Hackett is a small, pocket-sized volume covering all aspects of diagnosis and modern care for these and other altitude-related medical problems.

Body Temperatures

The human body has a relatively small temperature range in which survival is possible. The internal body core of nearly everyone is maintained at a constant temperature of 98.6° F (plus or minus a few degrees). Should the body core rise above 105° or descend lower than 75°, serious physiological problems can occur with death the usual result.

Body temperature and related problems of hyperthermia and hypothermia, as well as equipment for protection from the elements of weather and some materials on water and food, are discussed in depth in Chapter 3, "Survival," and in Chapter 13, "First Aid."

Shelter

The need for shelter is related to the need to maintain a normal body core temperature. Wind, precipitation, and intense sun all can take their toll on the temperature of the body. Wind dessicates moisture with subsequential cooling; precipitation cools without dessication. Wind also promotes convective heat loss and accelerates evaporative loss, while precipitation contributes to evaporative losses and greatly reduces the efficiency of the insulation materials commonly used in clothing and bedding. Sun dessicates and can raise body temperature. Excessive solar radiation can contribute to hyperthermic conditions and, especially at higher elevations, can cause minor damage to the skin and eyes. Shelter from the elements is, then, a basic human requirement. This is also discussed in depth in Chapter 3.

Adequate Drinking Water

The amount of drinking water needed to sustain the human body varies with the individual and the situation. Large individuals who perspire freely upon exercising in hot weather need greater amounts of liquid than those small individuals who are bundled up and sitting rather statically while ice fishing. In spite of the variance, every leader should be sure every participant has access to drinking water at all times. It must be realized that water is basic to physiological need satisfaction and that without it people may die or, at best, only survive at the bottom of the needs hierarchy with little chance for having subsequently ordered needs met. This will be discussed further in Chapter 3, "Survival."

Adequate Rest/Sleep

The human being can go more hours without sleep than many think; however, a lack of sleep is accompanied by reduced muscle energy and reduced mental agility. A participant in outdoor pursuits must be alert and in top physical and mental condition to succeed (and in some cases to survive). In several cases of death or near disaster by hypothermia or exposure to the elements, there has been evidence that the victims were fatigued before the trip, a condition which may have been a contributing factor in subsequent unwise and life-threatening decisions.

It is recommended that all participants have extra sleep before a strenuous trip and that the leader insist on extra rest for him or herself. At least eight hours of sleep per 24-hour period is recommended for each adult, preferably for one to two weeks in advance of a trip lasting five or more days. On the trip itself, occasional long rests or even midday or mid-afternoon naps will help the body recover from fatiguing exercise and prepare it for more. A careful leader recognizes that a tired participant is a normal one at the end of a difficult stretch of terrain or water; however, a fatigued individual whose physiological need for sleep has not been met at the *beginning* of a trip — or even well into the trip — is an individual who may be a hazard to him or herself as well as to the rest of the group. While most leaders have no control over pre- and post-trip behaviors, part of pre-trip training should stress the responsibility of the individual to self and group for meeting personal physiological needs.

Food and Nourishment

For most people, but particularly for the outdoorsperson, food serves two functions: It is the source of both energy to fuel the mechanics of body activities and it is a prime builder and maintainer of morale. Inadequate, incomplete, or unbalanced meals create a problem in maintenance of strength and stamina, particularly in activities requiring heavy use of muscles and consequent use of energy. The palatable flavor of foods makes eating enjoyable and, while good energizing food provides the sagging muscles with necessary fuel, the psychological pleasure accompanying the "My, that's good!" expression brings a lift to sagging spirits. Because of taste pleasures, morale is lifted. It is common knowledge to most adults, however, that the morale boost provided by good flavor is not always accompanied by an immediate spurt of energy or a latent lasting boost to the muscles. The job of the trip leader is to understand the relationship between tasty food and food which provides energy to accomplish the recreational task at hand. Conversely, all energy-providing food is not tasty: some is not palatable.

Most people are much more concerned about what foods to take on an outing than about water supplies, although food is nowhere as vital. Remember the old adage that one can survive three minutes without air, three days without water, and three weeks without food. If anything, the limits for life without food are minimized here. Under most circumstances people can survive considerably longer than three weeks without eating.

Most outdoor activities are short term, from an afternoon hike or raft trip to a two- or three-day weekend backpack or climb. These short excursions should present few or no problems with regard to food, yet food-related discomforts are a primary complaint of outdoorspeople. Usually the problem is caused by taking along all sorts of high-energy or super-light foods because of anxiety over imagined extreme caloric needs, being lost for days on end, or

being crushed under an immensely heavy pack. All of these fears are unfounded on most outings. In fact it is hard to conceive of a three-day trip that would exceed the reserves stored in one's body. Certainly *some* food should be taken on even a short outing, especially when much of that cold stress and/or hard exercise are likely. Still, one doesn't need, and in fact will suffer from, great globs of "gorp" and freeze-dried beef stew.

A common mistake is to rationalize the purchase and consumption of great quantities of those delicious and expensive dried apricots, cashews, and double-fudge cream-filled mint balls that one would never eat in town. It is small wonder that so many hikers suffer gastrointestinal distress.

Food is comprised primarily of proteins, fats and carbohydrates (complex and simple) which are either stored in the body for later use or metabolized for immediate energy. Fats provide the most calories per unit weight (and usually volume as well), proteins next, carbohydrates next, and simple sugar least of all. Fats, however, are processed very slowly, while the rate of processing (metabolism) of the other categories increases through the list with simple sugar being metabolized very quickly.

Outdoor activities usually involve an increase in exertion levels above what is normal in everyday life, and this exertion often takes place at elevations substantially above sea level. Both the exertion levels and the elevation reduce ability to metabolize foods. While one may be able to digest salami at home, it is difficult to digest it at 7,000 feet.

Fats. Food fats are components which supply energy plus the fat-soluble vitamins A, B, E and K. The need for fat increases in the winter because of its high-calorie content and because the body burns more calories in the winter exercising and keeping warm. Fats build up in the body in the form of insulation. Fat on a trip can consist of that in cheese (especially cheddar), oleo (which keeps much long than butter and can be purchased in liquid form), nuts, salad oils, and oils in sardines and other canned fish. Like protein, fat may be difficult to pack and store for trip use. Most climbers find that very fatty foods, while essential on long, cold expeditions, are almost impossible to digest at higher altitudes.

Protein. The body needs protein containing amino acids (new protein) in order to fuel muscle action adequately. Meat, milk and cheese are considered "perfect" or complete proteins because they contain the necessary proportions and types of amino acids the body requires. While nuts and grains contain protein, they are "incomplete" because they lack the necessary quantity and some types of amino acids. The protein required by the body remains nearly constant, regardless of activity. For example, most people need 70 grams per day, half of which consists of complete or perfect protein. This factor presents a challenge to the leader who, on a trip of more than two days, must be sure all members of the group receive adequate "perfect" protein — even those who are vegetarians. Meat, milk and cheese are not always easy products to package and carry on a trip.

The combination of legumes and cereals necessary to provide adequate amino acids may be difficult to procure. Dried or freeze-dried meat is readily available, although expensive and not always reconstituted into palatable portions. Dried milk is plentiful, inexpensive, available with or without cream, unnoticeable in cooking or milkshakes, and very acceptable for drinking. Usually fortified with vitamins, it is a good item to take on a long trip.

Cheese is heavy, melts, is oily, and spoils; however, dried cheese is available. Processed cheese is less nutritious than natural cheeses such as cheddar, Jack, Jarlsberg, Swiss, etc.

Carbohydrates. Carbohydrates consist of readily usable energy from such foods as starches, sugars and cellulose that is not digestible but which provides roughage necessary for proper elimination. It is recommended that 50 to 65 percent of the daily intake of calories for outdoor active people be in the form of carbohydrates. The "carbos," as they are often called, need to be planned carefully for maximum energy. Rice, pastas, and dried potatoes are common trip staples with high carbo content. Breads and crackers vary in their nutrients. Finely processed flours lose out to whole grains in amount of energy by weight. Whole wheat,

graham, oatmeal, rye breads, or crackers reinforced with wheat germ, soy flour, and other grains are best. Heavy-grained bread reinforced with raisins and nuts may weigh a lot in comparison to other breads, but less is required to produce instant energy, and the flavor is considered by many to be far superior. Cereals provide carbohydrates; hot whole-grain cereals are better than cold flakes, and cold cereals may range in readily available amounts of energy from high-quality granola (oats, wheat germ, sesame seeds, pecans, brown sugar, and coconuts) to packaged flakes and sugared dry cereals. Recommended hot cereals are whole-grain varieties, while recommended cold cereals are granolas or meuslis with natural ingredients.

Candy is often overrated as an energy booster, for the energy produced is short-lived, often causing the body to draw on already depleted sources of stored energy. While sugars are consumed, they are metabolized rapidly, sending the blood sugar soaring. This is true of all of the simple sugars, from glucose to fructose. Honey and pure cane sugar have essentially the same effect on the blood-sugar levels. When the blood-sugar level goes up quickly, insulin levels also go up quickly to help move the sugar into the body cells. What usually happens is that the blood-sugar levels are then quickly reduced to levels that may be *less* than where they were prior to eating the sugar. The result is that all-too-familiar craving for more and more and more sugar. Another result of low blood sugar is tiredness and irritability. If your hiking partner is getting on your nerves, try sharing a candy bar! You'll probably get along a lot better, assuming one or both of you were suffering from low blood sugar. The problem is that the solution is only temporary, if you solve the problem with sugar. A much better and longer-lasting way to maintain blood-sugar levels is to eat more complex carbohydrates, like breads. Try sharing a bagel instead! Bread will be metabolized more slowly, so while insulin levels will go up, they won't skyrocket. You and your friend will probably feel good for an hour or so, instead of for just a few minutes. Good sources of natural sugar are dried fruits, coconut, fresh fruits such as grapes, and apples or peeled oranges. (Leave the peels at home. They are not biodegradeable except over very long periods of time and must be carried home.)

Candy in small quantities is an acceptable energy product if taken in combination with other foods.

A moderately large glucose challenge right before an endurance activity may actually impair subsequent performance. For example, the riding time of young men and women on a bicycle ergometer was reduced 19% when they consumed a 300-ml. solution containing 75 g. of glucose 30 minutes before exercise, compared to similar trials preceded by the same volume of water or a liquid meal of protein, fat, and carbohydrate. The mobilization of free fatty acids for energy was depressed throughout the glucose trial. The impaired use of fats for energy in endurance exercise reduces the carbohydrate-sparing effect of fat metabolism, thereby causing the glycogen stores in the muscles to be used more rapidly. This negative effect of glucose feeding is probably mediated by an increased insulin output following the glucose challenge and the inhibitory effects of insulin on fat mobilization. Thus, if large quantities of sugars are consumed prior to competition, sufficient time must be provided to permit assimilation of this nutrient and to permit re-establishment of metabolic and hormonal balance. (McArdle, William, et. al., *Exercise Physiology,* 1981, p. 45-46.)

The best general advice, then, is to carry with you foods that are as normal for you as possible. That is, carry with you what you normally eat, modified as follows:

1. Minimize fats.
2. Increase complex carbohydrates (breads, etc.).
3. Be conservative about simple sugars. (Take some, but eat *sparingly.* It's *sometimes* possible to size up a hill you're about to climb as "about 3 M & M's worth," eat the candy and burn up that sugar in perfect time, maintaining a good sugar balance all the while. It is much better to use bagels, crackers or bread.)
4. Avoid freeze-dried foods, unless you're quite used to them or have a special need, such as a very long trip on which you have to carry food for more than a week. Even then, plan to work into these foods slowly. Some freeze-dried foods are really good, but they are hard to get used to, very expensive, and the weight saved is insignificant for a trip of several days. Take what you are used to eating, emphasizing light-weight foods such as noodles and soup mixes from your local supermarket. They're much less expensive and aren't heavy (though for a weekend, canned beef stew is no problem in terms of total weight, if that's your particular culinary kink).

Food Planning

When planning food for the outing, one should consider high-carbohydrate foods, calories, and taste. The following material, written for athletes, is appropriate for outdoor-pursuit participants.

Why high-carbohydrate foods? Your precompetition meal should include moderate portions of high-carbohydrate foods because these take the least time to pass through your stomach. High-fat and high-protein foods stay in the stomach longer than high-carbohydrate foods. Foods which remain in the stomach during competition may cause indigestion, nausea, and even vomiting.

Most foods from the fruit-vegetable group and the grain group are excellent sources of carbohydrates and are digested quickly. High-protein foods, like lowfat dairy foods and lean meats (tuna, baked ham, broiled chicken), take longer to digest. However, these foods may be safely included in your pre-competition meal, as long as you eat them in moderate portions.

Pre-competition meals should avoid . . .

-- foods like hamburger, sausage, lunch meats, and peanut butter;
-- fried foods like doughnuts, chips, French fries, and fried fish or chicken;
-- condiments like mayonnaise and salad dressings.

Because these foods are high in fat, they take the longest time to pass through the stomach. If you include any of these foods in your precompetition meal, keep them to small amounts.

Why is carbohydrate important for performance? Fatigue is common after hard physical training day after day, especially when you work out twice a day. You might blame your exhaustion on a "bad day." But if you are always tired, it might be due to your diet.

When you exercise, you draw on energy stored as carbohydrate in muscles. This energy comes from the foods you have eaten. During a two-hour workout, you can easily use up all your stored carbohydrate. Unless you are eating enough foods high in carbohydrate, the carbohydrate level in your muscles will not be replenished for the next day's training.

Suppose you eat a diet low in carbohydrate. After just three days of two-hour workouts, your muscle carbohydrate can be nearly used up. You are a candidate for fatigue. However, on a high-carbohydrate diet after the same workouts, your muscle carbohydrate level can be almost as high as it was before you began training. So you can have the energy to train and compete at your top performance level by eating a diet high in carbohydrate throughout the season.

Calories. The use of calories varies with the amount of energy and type of exercise. Table 2.1 shows the differences in calorie use from sedentary to active activities.

TABLE 2.1 APPROXIMATE CALORIES USED FOR EVERY 15 MINUTES: 150-LB. PERSON

Sunbathing	20
Sitting around campfire	25
Working at picnic site	45
Walking a nature trail (2½ mph)	53
Bicycling (5½ mph)	53
Ice skating	60
Swimming (¼ mph)	75
Canoeing	83
Playing volleyball	90
Water skiing	130
Cross-country skiing	145
Jogging (5 mph)	165

Other necessities. Other food necessities include vitamins which provide the enzymes to help break down the food into usable or stored energy. Vitamins are found naturally in most foods and a well-balanced menu should preclude need for supplementary vitamins.

On long trips (several weeks) evidence has been found that vitamin deficiency can cause irritability, mental depression, or night blindness. For this reason, leaders of long trips might consider recommending supplementary vitamins or carrying a complementary supply. Minerals needed by the human are water soluble and found in adequate amounts in meats, vegetables, and fruits. Like vitamins, however, it may be wise to carry a supplementary supply on trips lasting several weeks.

Because of the taste factor and need for enjoyable eating experiences, condiments are considered necessary additions to the menu. Individuals preparing their own meals or groups cooking together can decide on garlic, paprika, oregano, lemon pepper, dried green pepper, dried onions, onion salt, bullion, or a myriad others, each of which enhances flavor but each of which is not equally appreciated by all people. The indiscriminate use of curry in a casserole may create a range of emotions from anger and disgust to pure ecstacy. While condiments are important, wise selection and use is of greater importance.

The frequency and size of meals is something the leader can plan, advise, implement and control for the benefit of the group. Several rules of thumb may help.

1. Eat small portions of carbohydrates frequently (several times a day). They supply immediate energy. Carbohydrates usually leave the stomach in about two hours. Eat twice as many energy units of carbohydrates as all other foods combined.
2. Eat proteins and fats at night. They break down slowly. Fats take up to six hours to leave the stomach, then one tends to feel empty.

Good Health

A final physiological need directly related to success in outdoor pursuits is good health which is defined simplistically as absence from disease or illness. Neither participant nor leader should embark on a strenuous or lengthy trip (in distance or duration) with any sign of illness. Colds and flu are especially common and debilitating, yet shrugged off as "minor." The reduction in participant or leader stamina caused by a cold could be just enough to endanger a trip. When there is a need to move rapidly or continuously, a problem is created by having to wait for one whose normal energy has already been sapped before the trip started.

Safe, enjoyable, and worthwhile trips can be run for any level of fitness. It's important for the leader to ascertain the fitness levels of all participants prior to an outing so that the program and route can be tuned to this level. Mixed levels can create dissatisfaction among participants and create a substantial challenge to the creativity and patience of the leader. Fitness provides an important margin of safety in backcountry travel, and an entire group can be compromised by one unfit participant. Fitness tests are often employed by leaders in an attempt to eliminate or reduce problems in the field related to inadequate fitness or widely disparate fitness levels within the group.

Exercise

It goes without saying that under ordinary circumstances, leaders need not concern themselves with the human physiological need for exercise, for every outdoor pursuit requires the use of many muscles, including the heart. In the case of a group stranded in a storm, holed up in a tent, snow cave or crevasse, and in the case of injury and the long wait to be rescued, the human body will suffer from lack of exercise. Use of muscles increases circulation and respiration as well as developing and maintaining strength. A leader should not expect participants of any age to "sit still" very long. In cramped quarters there must be opportunity for exercise. Isotonic exercises (muscle stretching and tensing) can be done while the participant is lying in a sleeping bag, but they may be boring and thus are not desirable over prolonged periods of time. It is incumbent upon the leader to understand the need for exercise and develop a series of activities to maintain muscle tone as well as cardio-vascular efficiency.

Without exercise, muscles atrophy quickly, and lose their elasticity and strength. Persons who are weak after a long illness are often weak because of lack of muscle use, not from the illness itself. Campers waiting out a long storm in a small tent must exercise their muscles or they too can weaken.

A prolonged period of inactivity compounded by dehydration can be extremely dangerous, since such circumstances predispose people to the formation of blood clots. An all-too-common result is clotting in the leg veins (thrombo phlebitis), which has afflicted many expeditionary climbers and individuals in survival situations. This condition can lead to death if a clot breaks loose and lodges in the lungs (pulmonary embolism) or brain (cerebral embolism).

Summary

It is thus the leader's responsibility to help assure that participants' physiological or life-sustaining needs are met. Good quality and quantity of fresh air, a body temperature controlled near 98.6° F, shelter from inclement weather, adequate drinking water, adequate rest and sleep, adequate and proper exercise, and adequate and proper nourishment are all on the first or bottom level of human needs. Without these requirements being minimally met, one will probably not be able to meet the next level, either.

In outdoor pursuits people need strength, endurance, and mental agility for success in what may be or become harsh environments. And only the human resources of mind and body can overcome these difficulties. Therefore, leaders should be first and foremost dedicated to assuring that basic human physiological needs are met before and during the trip.

PSYCHOLOGICAL NEEDS

If we utilize Maslow's hierarchy as a base and recognize that the first level consists of physiological needs, it will be seen that level two, the need for security and safety, is the first psychological need an outdoor leader must address.

Security

While Maslow initially referred to security as freedom from harassment, meaning freedom from having to look over one's shoulder to spot oppressors, the need for security also means a feeling that no one in the group to which one wishes to belong will harass, ridicule, or outcast. Individuals need first to feel secure and safe with themselves and then with the members of the group.

One of the characteristics of many participants in new ventures, particularly those ventures containing elements of risk, adventure, suspense, and development of technical skills is insecurity. People may feel insecure within themselves (lack a positive self-concept) because they are unsure of their skills, their stamina, their ability to perform adequately, the appropriateness and adequacy of their equipment, or getting along in the group. People who are insecure may perceive the rest of the group to be opposed to them on every move. It may be difficult to visualize harassment actually occurring in a recreational or educational event, but it does occur among those of all ages. The imagined (or real) harassment takes the form of teasing, ridicule, avoidance, or jokes. An insecure person may react to innocent teasing as if it were total harassment. Being alone in a group, being unskilled, or being teased all lead to feelings of insecurity and potentially to elements of fear. It is important for leaders to understand that meeting the need for security within the self includes dispelling imagined (or real) harassment. Vindictive teasing, ridicule, or harassing behavior can take place in an outdoor situation if the group has a wide variety of skills and knowledge, but this can be prevented if the leader makes an effort to be sure that all feel secure. The leader must be confident that all participants will be able to execute the skills necessary for the activity. This means that he or she has some pre-trip responsibilities to the individuals. They must learn, practice, and become adept at skills needed for the trip. They must have physical conditioning to develop strength and stamina. They must develop a feeling of personal security *prior* to embarking on the journey. People who are confident in their own ability tend to act secure, thus tending not to harass others or to perceive harassment coming at them.

In addition to feeling insecure because of inferior ability, participants may feel insecure because they appear as single individuals in a group of strangers. One of the first things a leader should do when meeting a group for the first time is to welcome them warmly and not only to learn everyone's name but to expedite the process by which everyone learns everyone else's name and something about everyone which will help subsequent conversations. Learning people's names and being able to carry on conversations with each other not only helps each participant feel secure, it helps the leader develop a closeness with each individual in the group.

Relative to the need for security is one of the most common psychological problems, fear. Symptoms of fear include:

1. Increase in the pulse rate;
2. Muscular tension — even inability to move in extreme cases;
3. Perspiration of palms and soles of the feet;
4. Dryness in the mouth;
5. Feelings of "butterflies" in the stomach.

Fear of the unknown, fear of discomfort, and fear of the result of personal weakness all seem to be apparent in outdoor recreational situations. *Fear of the unknown* is that experience of anxiety found among people in job interviews, students prior to examinations, and any outdoor participant about to tackle a new challenge. In the outdoors, *fear of the unknown* is seen in the fear of being alone (no companions, no voices, no help), fear of darkness (inability to see), and fear of animals (imagined attacks). It is also the fear of "what lies ahead" (unknown terrain, weather, hardships, route and environment). It tends to be more severe in some people than in others and in some circumstances rather than others. It affects people differently, as some are obviously frightened and show it in open-eyed, open-mouthed, white-faced staring while others internalize the fear or even disguise it with bravado. The leaders should assume a degree of fear of the unknown is present in every member and take steps to lessen it.

The *fear of discomfort* or of suffering includes fear of no relief from cold, heat, thirst, or hunger as well as fear of anticipated or real pain. *Fear of discomfort* can usually be controlled through proper equipment. The fear of cold or dampness may be alleviated by the feeling of security given by carrying sweaters and rain gear, proper shelter, sleeping bags, and ground cover. The fear of hunger and thirst may be alleviated by feeling secure that adequate and proper nourishment and water are available. It is the responsibility of the leader to realize that such fear of discomfort usually does not develop until the participant is a long way from home and the environmental conditions have deteriorated to a point of potential hardship. If the participant has not brought adequate food, liquid, source of heat, clothing, shelter, and rain gear, there is little the leader can do to prevent this fear. This underscores a need for adequate clothing and equipment.

In the case where, in spite of every precaution, the leader realizes one or more people fear discomfort, there is a need to assess whether the potential discomfort is imagined or real. If it is imagined, the positive attitude of other members of the group may be effective in changing the person's mind. If it is a real possibility, the leader's responsibility is to take precautions to prevent it by improvising, borrowing, or changing plans.

Fear of personal weakness includes a fear of death and its immanent inconvenience to family and loved ones as well as the natural fear of the unknown. It also includes a fear of society through loss of face, ridicule, admitting failure, guilt, and reprisal.

Fear of one's own weakness is a reality usually brought about by lack of any or adequate practice or conditioning prior to the trip, or as a result of a debilitating injury. "I can't make it" generally means, "I don't think I have the strength or stamina" (a fear of weakness). If the participants have been in a long-term conditioning course, they will realize they have developed strength and stamina. Activities such as running, jogging, bicycling, weight lifting, jazzercise, and many others develop strength and stamina if performed continuously, regularly, and for 30 minutes or more daily or even twice daily. Adequate rest and nutrition, of course, must accompany the program so no one starts a trip without adequate rest, nourishment, or conditioning exercise.

Belonging

The third need recognized by Maslow is the need to belong and to be accepted. Fulfillment of this need is a particularly important aspect of the outdoor-pursuit leader for outdoor-recreation leadership implies groups and is recognized as leadership of social groups involved in outdoor skills. Even the most well-skilled, well-equipped, and well-conditioned member of the group needs to feel accepted by others and must have psychological barriers to acceptance broken down. Some excellent activities for developing group security and group trust are described in the books, *New Games* by Terry Orlick, and *Cowstails and Cobras* by Project Adventure. These activities, initiative tasks, and cooperative games are designed to bring about group continuity, a sense of group cohesiveness, and the indoctrination of attitudes which recognize the need for a total group effort to accomplish difficult tasks. Through pre-trip participation in initiative tasks, each person can start to understand how members of the group need each other, can help each other, and can work together for the success of the unit regardless of size, age, sex, or any other variable.

Learning people's names, and being able to carry on a conversation with each participant not only helps the participant to feel a sense of belonging but helps the leader know the participants' interests and experiences.

The sense of belonging may follow rapidly upon completion of group-building skills, for the participants may gain it as part of the participation. That feeling must persist throughout the activity. One way to help participants feel they belong is also to make them feel needed or important. In some sponsored outings, it is the practice for leaders to cook, clean up, and pack up. Participants who share in these tasks gain a feeling of cohesiveness to the group and a sense of being needed — hence belonging.

Respect for Self and Respect from Others

The need to feel respected follows the need to belong and may certainly appear as a concurrent need. Belonging to a group in which one feels secure from harassment is basic to belonging to a group in which one feels an element of respect. People want to feel good about themselves and want others to respect them. The two are probably never mutually exclusive, for self-respect seems to grow with the increase of group respect. The outdoor leader is in a position of encouraging people's interactions and potential for this. It need not be a respect directly related to the activity at hand. Group members can respect knowledge of plants, accurate weather predictions, ability to tell jokes, strength, humor, or any other human skill, knowledge, or attitude if the leader facilitates the process by demonstrating respect first. Since one of the leader's roles is to facilitate all aspects of the program, each leader should purposefully facilitate the process of developing mutual respect.

Self-Actualization

Self-actualization is an ongoing process through which individuals grow toward their own unique capabilities, potentials, or talents. It is the process in which, because all other needs have been met, one is free to develop one's talents and capabilities to their fullest. The need for self-actualization may be the same in each person; however, because each person is a unique individual, no two people will move toward it identically. Since self-actualization is a process, it has no ending; consequently, it is never attained.

The challenge to the leader here is to understand the uniqueness of each participant with accompanying differences in goals, skills, capabilities, motivations, perceived and real barriers, and a host of other factors that contribute to individual differences. Individuals have been influenced by their own physical and mental ability, by their own body structures and their physical and intellectual fitness levels, by race, family, economic or geographic factors, as a result of local customs and mores, because of educational factors and many less obvious forces.

For some, climbing a 4,000-foot mountain or canoeing through a series of short riffles is a big step in the self-actualization process. Others may need a glacier climb or a 12,000 footer, a trek across 150 miles of desert or a 200-mile raft trip on a roaring river. For some, the self-actualizing process reaches to the point where they are helpers, teachers, and sharers. Maslow describes healthy people as those with the following 13 clinically observable traits (Maslow, p. 26).

1. Superior perception of reality;
2. Increased acceptance of self, of others, and of nature;
3. Increased spontaneity;
4. Increase in problem-centering;
5. Increased detachment and desire for privacy;
6. Increased autonomy and resistance to enculturation;
7. Greater freshness of appreciation and richness of emotional reaction;
8. Higher frequency of peak experiences;
9. Increased identification with the human species;
10. Changed (the clinician would say, improved) interpersonal relations;
11. More democratic character structure;
12. Greatly increased creativeness;
13. Certain changes in the value system.

Individual Differences

It is an accepted fact that participants have many moods or emotional reactions to various situations. We can assume that the moods of one participant will not be the same as those of others in the group. The moods of a person who is generally optimistic will differ from those of a typically pessimistic person, and the leader can accept the idea that the moods of the group as a whole reflect the average of all moods of the group members.

It is not generally understood that both individual and group moods change at different phases of the activity, thus making it difficult to lead with the same group emotions in mind throughout the activity. Even the moods of the leader may change as a trip progresses from elation to fatigue to peaceful to powerful depending upon the stage of the trip.

Three studies have been completed on mood changes in outdoor experiences. In each case, eleven mood factors were analyzed at each of the five phases of an outdoor recreation activity, identified by Clawson and Knetsch, a) planning, b) travel to, c) participation on the site, d) travel from, and e) recollection. The first study involved college botany students on a field trip; the second study took place on a winter camping experience on Mt. Hood in Oregon by a class training to be outdoor leaders; and the third took place with sixth graders attending a one-week residential outdoor school near the Pacific Ocean in the northwest in May. Each group was different in age, size, location, and purpose of trip. The weather was clear in Tennessee, mixed rain and snow on Mt. Hood, and three days of rain and two days of sunshine in the outdoor school.

It was not expected that the moods or mood changes would be the same from group to group. The eleven moods studied through a paper-and-pencil questionnaire are shown in Table 2.2

The mean and standard deviations of scores from the college winter-camping class and the sixth-grade outdoor-education program are shown in Table 2.3.

Each mood was measured during each of the five phases of the experience and the means and standard deviations computed and analyzed for significant differences through analysis of variance tested at the .05 level of confidence. It may be seen that, as the experience progressed for the college group, significant mood changes occurred in social affection, fatigue, concentration, anxiety, aggression, vigor, skepticism, and sadness. The sixth graders, however, showed significant mood changes for elation, aggression, sadness, and egotism. Further perusal of the table shows that overall, the sixth graders appeared to be more friendly (social affection) and elated throughout (Ford and Cloninger, 1982-83). In the case of the college students, the mood changes might have been caused by the

TABLE 2.2 MOOD FACTORS AND THEIR COMPONENTS

1. Social Affection
   friendly
   kindly
   warmhearted
2. Fatigue
   drowsy
   sluggish
   tired
3. Concentration
   thinking (engaged in thought)
   serious (intent)
   concentrating
4. Elation
   happy (elated)
   overjoyed
   pleased
5. Surgency
   playful
   carefree
   witty
6. Anxiety
   jittery
   fearful
   uptight (clutched up)
7. Aggression
   defiant
   angry
   rebellious
8. Vigor
   active
   full of pep (energetic)
   avigorous
9. Skepticism
   doubtful (dubious)
   unsure (skeptical)
   suspicious
10. Sadness
    regretful
    sad
    sorry
11. Egotism
    self-centered
    boastful
    selfish (egotistic)

TABLE 2.3 MEANS AND STANDARD DEVIATIONS FOR ELEVEN MOOD FACTORS FOR TWO GROUPS AT EACH OF A FIVE-PHASE OUTDOOR EXPERIENCE

	Anticipation		Travel to		On Site		Travel From		Reflection	
	M	SD	M	SD	M	SD	M	SD	M	SD
1. Social Affection										
6th Graders	10.2	1.28	10.04	1.51	10.03	1.58	10.43	1.36	10.04	1.66
*College students	9.23	2.05	7.42	2.43	7.39	1.85	6.67	2.46	6.48	2.20
2. Fatigue										
6th Graders	5.48	2.31	5.88	2.53	5.56	2.63	7.36	2.62	5.43	2.46
*College students	6.00	3.11	4.42	2.84	7.15	3.00	8.83	2.41	5.52	2.71
3. Concentration										
6th Graders	9.06	2.03	8.29	2.12	8.59	2.18	8.61	2.39	8.49	2.18
*College students	9.69	1.55	7.58	2.54	8.54	2.22	5.75	2.09	7.12	2.24
4. Elation										
*6th Graders	10.06	1.91	10.37	1.46	9.38	2.41	10.05	2.00	9.41	1.77
College students	7.92	2.33	8.08	2.07	6.77	2.65	7.58	1.38	7.48	2.24
5. Surgency										
6th Graders	8.06	1.73	8.86	1.58	8.11	1.86	8.43	1.94	8.50	1.76
College students	7.54	1.86	6.67	1.37	7.39	2.18	7.08	2.43	6.64	2.33
6. Anxiety										
6th Graders	5.34	2.13	5.16	2.10	4.89	2.21	4.84	2.17	4.66	1.93
*College students	5.77	2.74	5.92	2.50	5.08	2.06	3.25	0.45	3.60	0.87
7. Aggression										
*6th Graders	4.86	1.65	5.69	1.68	5.73	1.55	5.82	1.74	5.35	1.66
*College students	4.15	1.86	3.33	0.65	5.31	2.32	3.58	1.17	3.96	1.72
8. Vigor										
6th Graders	9.08	1.77	8.55	1.75	8.32	2.26	8.77	1.94	8.68	1.90
*College students	9.31	2.43	9.08	2.19	7.54	2.50	4.92	2.31	6.52	2.71
9. Skepticism										
6th Graders	5.66	2.27	5.67	2.29	5.53	2.11	5.30	2.03	5.19	2.05
College students	5.92	2.25	4.83	2.33	6.00	2.04	3.75	1.42	4.16	1.75
10. Sadness										
*6th Graders	4.20	1.71	4.80	2.16	5.29	2.55	5.36	2.47	4.04	1.59
*College students	4.62	1.33	3.58	1.00	5.00	2.00	3.42	1.00	3.68	1.95
11. Egotism										
*6th Graders	4.38	1.85	5.04	1.55	5.00	1.91	5.56	1.96	4.80	1.80
College students	4.85	2.08	3.92	1.24	4.85	2.27	5.42	2.43	4.80	1.78

*Significant at the .05 level of confidence

miserable weather they encountered, causing wet tents and sleeping bags and presumably a decreasing enthusiasm for the experience. It is also interesting to note that the sixth graders started their outdoor experience feeling much more elation than the college students.

For the prospective leader, these two studies demonstrate the fact that people's needs, emotions, and attitudes differ at various phases during a trip and differ among groups. It may be conjectured that similar differences may be demonstrated for every possible group in every possible situation. This means the leaders cannot have set expectations for the emotional make-up of any group at any time and must be prepared for and expect changes in the group attitudes from time to time. It becomes obvious that meeting the psychological needs of people is a complex matter which cannot be over-simplified by being purely aware of Maslow's hierarchy.

The outdoor-pursuit leader cannot afford to be just a leader of outdoor pursuits. He or she is always a leader of people, all of whom are different. Beyond the basic physiological and psychological needs are specific needs that may have an impact on the basic needs. The inexperienced person whose glasses are broken has a different fear and security problem than does the experienced person who carries an extra pair (and who, incidentally, may not remember the frightening experience that caused him or her to pack an extra pair regardless of the situation). The hypoglycemic person (low blood sugar) has different dietary needs from others and needs more frequent snacks of protein (dried meats, nuts) and fats (cheeses) than others. The person over 65 years of age may have a slower pace than a 25-year-old but may also have a higher tolerance for long hours of exercise. Older people usually have more endurance while younger people have more speed. A 45-year-old man cannot imitate all the actions of a 10-year-old boy without wearing out first. The 10-year-old boy, however, requires more rest, and has shorter bursts of pep at those high-energy activities. He may be taking a two-hour nap while the adult can go at his or her own pace tirelessly for eight hours or more.

Other individual differences that have an impact on basic human needs include:

-- Age - outdoor pursuits are participated in by people aged 2 to 102;
-- Intelligence - trainable retardates, educable retardates, normal folks, geniuses;
-- Fitness - ill, out of shape, of average fitness, athletes, highly fit persons;
-- Sex - male, female;
-- Physical ability - strength, endurance, speed;
-- Physical skill - ability to ski, swim, rappel;
-- Physiological differences - heart rate, blood pressure, metabolism;
-- Prior experience;
-- Reason for being there;
-- Socio-economic background;
-- Others.

It is easy to see that, while basic physiological and psychological differences are the same, individual differences have such an impact that no two people can be said to have the same "amounts" of any needs. Each person's needs are similar but in dissimilar proportions. Only the leader who understands this phenomenon can be an excellent one. Those who can put the individual above the activity are also true leaders, for leaders have followers. Since an activity is never a follower, the "leader of outdoor pursuits" is really only a myth. It is "leaders of outdoor-pursuit *participants*" that interest us here.

SUMMARY

The leader of outdoor pursuits needs to understand the physiological and psychological needs of participants. Physiological needs include adequate quantity and quality of air for breathing, a body temperature near to or at 98.6° F, shelter from harsh elements, drinking water, rest, exercise, food, and good health. Psychological needs, based on the hierarchy proposed by Abraham Maslow, include security, belonging, respect for self and others, and self-actualization.

Leaders should be cognizant of both kinds of needs and methods to help participants attain them. Since each person differs in each differing situation, the meeting of individual needs in a group experience in the out-of-doors becomes a complex and challenging responsibility.

BIBLIOGRAPHY

Buell, Larry, *Leader's Guide to the 24-Hour Experience,* Greenfield, Mass.: Environmental Awareness Publications, 1978; St. Louis Dairy Council, 1980.

Clawson, M. and Knetsch, J.L., *Economics of Outdoor Recreation,* Baltimore: Johns Hopkins Press, 1966.

Fear, Eugene, *Outdoor Living: Problems, Solutions, Guidelines,* Tacoma, WA: Mountain Rescue Council, no date.

Ford, Phyllis and Cloninger, Karl, "Multi-Phasic Mood Changes in a Five-Day Residential Outdoor Education Experience," *The Journal of Environmental Education,* Vol. 14, No. 2, Winter 1982-83.

Maslow, Abraham, *Toward a Psychology of Being,* 2nd edition, New York: D. Van Nostrand Co., 1980.

McArdel, William D., Katch, Frank I., and Katch, Victor L., *Exercise Physiology,* Philadelphia: Lea and Febiger, 1981.

Winterburn, David, "Participation Mood During Each Phase of Clawsen's Multi-Phase Theory of Outdoor Recreation," unpublished master's thesis, University of Oregon, 1979.

A STUDENT JUMPING A SMALL CREVASSE
Mountaineering is a tremendously rewarding
experience but demands a significant investment of
time, energy and equipment. Good leadership of
mountaineering classes requires meticulous attention
to myriad details of planning, logistics, and
procedures.

CHAPTER 3

SURVIVAL

To some people, it may seem unnecessary to
discuss survival in a leadership book because it
is usually assumed that an outdoor leader would
be very knowledgeable in the art of surviving in
the out-of-doors. Most outdoor leaders do seem
to understand and practice the skills of living in
the outdoors but have never been in a situation
that calls for survival of the *wilderness emergency situation.*

Because the outdoor leader has never been
called upon to exhibit the skills of emergency
survival it is difficult for the program administrator to judge the competence of a prospective
or even a veteran employee. Possessing the
presence of mind and using the "right" judgment to make the "right" decision is the
ultimate characteristic of a competent leader.
Fortunately, most leaders never have to prove
their ability to survive and to guide a group to
survive under emergency conditions. Unfortunately, when the rare survival situation occurs,
some participants, some leaders, and some
entire groups fail the ultimate test.

In this chapter, we are not concerned with the
usual day-to-day living in the out-of-doors. We
are concerned with surviving the unexpected
emergency. Further, we are concerned with the
responsibilities and actions of the leader to
ensure that the participants survive the emergency.

POSSIBLE EMERGENCY
SITUATIONS

The unexpected emergency situation is usually a
situation that is a distinct possibility, yet of low
probability. The situation may be related to the
participants themselves or may be related to
environmental factors. Most emergency situations may be identified and planned for *even
though they are not anticipated.*

Emergency survival conditions involving
individuals or a group are usually classified as
being *personal* or *situational. Personal* conditions that necessitate survival techniques include

those where one or more of the members of the group become ill, fatigued, or injured. The *situational* conditions are those related to one or more people getting lost or stranded. Being stranded is often the result of environmental factors, although it may be the result of poor judgment, accident, or (*very* rarely) faulty equipment. (Rather than *faulty* equipment, stranding is usually the result of inadequate, incorrect, or insufficient equipment.) In other words, it is often the result of poor judgment in the planning stage.

Environmentally related emergency survival situations include the following:

1. Weather conditions
   Rapid changes, macro vs. microclimatology, specific conditions: lightning, whiteouts, hail, winds, etc.
2. Temperature-related trauma
   Hypothermia, frostbite and other cold injuries, heat exhaustion, heat stroke.
3. Sun-related trauma
   Sunburn, sunblindness, allergy.
4. Snow and ice hazards
   Deep snow, avalanches, cornices, bridges, crevasses, snow and ice falling from trees, etc.
5. Dangerous terrain
   Steep slopes, rivers, brush and vegetation, swamps.
6. Water hazards
   Floods, high tides, swollen streams.
7. Mountaineering hazards
   Altitude effects, rock fall, exposure, and responses.
8. Nightfall
   Inability to see, fear of darkness.
9. Wildlife
   Big game hazards and distribution, rodents and birds, poisonous snakes, spiders, scorpions, and insects.
10. Poisonous plants
    Contact irritants and ingested poisons.

In all cases we need to understand the survival needs of people, the survival equipment needed, and techniques for survival. Since this is not a book on techniques, we will not discuss building fires, building shelters, making a solar still, etc. It is assumed that aspiring leaders have those skills just as it is assumed they have a knowledge of basic campcraft, knots, cooking, climbing, etc.

PLANNING FOR SURVIVAL

It was said earlier that survival situations are related to either the individual or the environment. Understanding potential emergency situations and planning for them is probably the best way to prevent them. Much of this prevention can come about long before the trip starts.

Planning for Individual Emergency Situations

Before an individual packs for an outing, a list of individual requirements can be made and checked. For example:

-- Has my diet been one of good nutrition?
-- Am I in good physical shape? Free from a cold?
-- Am I rested?
-- Where am I going? When am I expected to return?
-- Who knows?
-- Do I have the right equipment?
-- Are there enough of us in the group?

Planning for Environmental Emergency Situations

Every environmental condition should be considered and planned for. For example:

-- Am I prepared for rain? (In mountainous areas or fall, winter, and spring the question is, "Am I prepared for snow?")
-- Am I prepared for sun? Glasses, shelter, sun screen?
-- Are my boots/shoes well broken in? Waterproof?
-- May there be insects? Thorns, poisonous plants, snakes?
-- Am I prepared for wind? for perspiring? for temperature changes?
-- What about: avalanches, high tides, flood conditions, etc.?

The leader must answer these questions as an individual and must be sure participants have answered them, too. If the answers to any are "no," or "I don't know," the leader should make the decision not to lead or not to permit that participant to go on the outing. This is the first step in preventing an emergency situation.

BASIC SURVIVAL NEEDS

In Chapter 2, the basic needs of individuals were discussed in terms of physiological and psychological needs. Survival needs are identical to the basic needs of all humans; however, the order and intensity of the needs may change. Most important for survival is a psychological state that is even more basic than those described by Abraham Maslow (Chapter 2). It is the *will to live* — the challenge to stay alive. Thus survival priorities and the length of possible survival are often listed as:

1. Will to live (depends on the individual)
2. Oxygen or air (three minutes)
3. Shelter from temperature extremes (three to four hours)
4. Water (three days)
5. Food (three weeks or more)

The chance of survival without any one of the above may be decreased by the state of mental health, injuries, lowered (or raised) body temperature, and diseases that affect the body's defense mechanisms. Chances of survival may be increased through knowledge, equipment, planning, and mental and physical health.

THE WILL TO LIVE

There is no way we can predict how strong a person's will to live is, but we know that death comes hard to those who struggle against it. It goes without saying that it is the leader who needs to provide the example of stick-to-itiveness. It is the leader who must instill hope into the minds of the participants. If they are prepared and know it, there is a better hope for survival than if there is inadequate or insufficient equipment or knowledge. The leader has a twofold responsibility: maintaining a personal will

to live and encouraging the will to live among the participants. It is easier to have the will to live if there is hope. Knowing all necessary survival plans have been made in advance offers a great deal of it.

SHELTER, CLOTHING, AND EQUIPMENT

If we were still roaming the savannah in search of edible plants and small game, this written material wouldn't be necessary, or at least would be mercifully brief. Having long ago wandered far from those regions where we were adequately protected by our own organs, we are now faced with the necessity of clothing and equipment. Perhaps the only exceptions to this would be the occasional opportunity for a little skinny dipping at a particularly favorable time and place. Our complex cultural development has increased our dependence upon external interfaces with nature, as most of the world's populations, even those still inhabiting physically "friendly" environments, have long since lost the skills necessary for survival without technological intervention. In outdoor pursuits we now delight in the exploration of extremely hostile environments and in the performance of physical activities that demand extensive and often highly specialized gear. We can't seem to "get away from it all" without taking a great deal of "it" with us. Here we will explore some of the philosophic implications of the use of clothing and equipment as well as the practical aspects of gear requirements, access to necessary items, and means of assuring that what is required is actually with your group when you head up the trail or push off from shore.

Philosophical Implications

As leaders, we can expect to have to discuss, debate, and justify the requirements we set for participants. Let's look at some basic issues. Why do we take so much stuff with us? After all, one of the reasons most often cited for participation in outdoor pursuits is the opportunity for escape from the frustrations of everyday life. For many people, one of the more frustrating aspects of life in our society is our dependence upon material goods and technological support to accomplish even the most mundane tasks. In most "advanced" countries we spend much of our life energy in accumulating, sorting, stacking, polishing, re-sorting, cataloguing, and protecting vast piles of stuff. We like comforts, but we rebel against dependence. We want to interface more directly with the natural world, to see the world unfettered by man's inventions; yet we are by nature inventors, tool makers. We carry 65 pounds of gear on a weekend backpacking trip, see clearly for a moment the price we pay for comfort, then return home, set the thermostat for 65-72°F, and complain if stores, banks, postal service, telephones, transportation systems, and other providers of comfort and security fail to perform at peak efficiency. Tools provide comfort, and with comfort comes both security and dependence.

There is no one solution, no perfect kit. For any given outing the complex interactions of any number of variables will define a range of possibilities. While there are no absolutes, the leader bears the responsibility of assessing the consequences of whatever clothing and equipment is utilized on the outing and, conversely, what is omitted and cannot be utilized.

Certainly there are sound and compelling reasons for requiring specific gear for each individual and each group engaged in certain outdoor-pursuit activities. We will discuss those in a moment. First, let's look at the issue from a different perspective. For every individual concerned about the consequence of taking too much equipment on an outing, there is another individual who can't wait to try out the latest technological advance, or at least his or her latest acquisition. "Gear-freaks" permeate every outdoor pursuit. Most of us know at least one individual who is marvelously equipped with the latest and best goods for some activity — all shiny and new, of course, and likely to stay that way since the individual rarely does anything requiring the gear! Gear acquisition, and sometimes designs, constructions, or modifications, is a common avocation in its own right. Many people enjoy the process of putting together assemblages of equipment, as much or more for the sake of the equipment as for the activity itself. Participation in the sport may be primarily for the sake of showing off the superb

kit, and/or for keeping up with the latest innovations. Many outdoor-pursuit participants take great pride in and thoroughly enjoy the process of putting together efficient life-support or mobility systems. While these individuals probably know dozens of good mobile-home or caravan jokes, they are really doing just what the travel-trailer folks do, except that the trailer folks have a bigger box on wheels. As outdoor leaders, should we encourage or even condone this interest?

The obsession with gear isn't at all surprising, and is probably inevitable. We all seek comfort, and we have, at least in the technologically and economically advanced countries, large amounts of discretionary time and money. Given the time and the means, we produce and accumulate devices to keep us comfortable. We can camp for years in complete satisfaction, but inevitably we will recognize opportunities for increased comfort. (The tarp seems all one could ask for until the pretty little yellow tent is set up in the campsite across the creek. Just think . . . five fewer mosquito bites in the morning, and maybe a few degrees warmer.) We seek out all of the potential benefits; we're inventors, aggressors. The negative factors of cost, weight, size, maintenance, and isolation from the very environment you have worked so hard to get to are discounted. It's not in our nature to look first at the limitations. Almost inevitably, the tent, or one like it, is assimilated into the kit. The process of acquiring it provides countless hours of entertainment, gathering catalogues, visiting shops, talking to friends, and finally buying the tent. Then we bring it home and stake it out on the living room floor to be crawled around in by kids, dogs, and us. Later, sometimes much later, and often as somewhat of an anticlimax, we fit this rather large, heavy, and unwieldy object into our pack and stagger out into the woods to actually use it. Chances are that on that very trip we will see a great little stove in use by another set of campers. Their soup is ready almost *ten minutes* before ours is! And on it goes. Is the new tent owner really enjoying his or her experience? Probably so. More than when just the tarp was being used? Probably not.

Hike someday through an area used by both the hunting and fishing crowd and the "hardcore" backpackers and climbers. Let's assume that both groups are safely equipped; that is, both groups have sufficient clothing and equipment to safely survive the worst reasonably foreseeable weather. Chances are that these hunters and fishermen are wearing sturdy cottons and carrying wool and inexpensive "low-tech" rain gear and low-cost, high-weight camping gear. The backpackers and climbers are probably wearing lugsole boots and clothing of sophisticated design and high-tech fabrics, and are carrying rainwear of Goretex or some other wonder fabric, expensive, super-strong carbon fiber-wanded tents, thermostat pads, and blast furnace stoves. Who is having the most fun? Does it have anything to do with the equipment or clothing choices?

What seems clear to us is that any use of gear beyond that which is truly needed to maintain adequate comfort and security should be considered very carefully. The penalties for excessive gear use go beyond the obvious elements of cost, weight, and interference with the quality of an individual's interaction with the environment. Excessive amounts of gear, especially certain high-technology items, put unneeded strain on an already overtaxed ecosystem. Over-consumption of material goods, a chronic problem in most of the Western world, seems especially out of place in a wilderness or back-country setting.

The foregoing concerns are important and should be considered carefully, but must be balanced against the consequences of inadequate clothing and equipment. While requiring too much gear may eliminate potential participants due to cost barriers, perpetuate dependence upon material goods, and otherwise degrade the experience, requiring too little may have far more serious consequences.

Participants rightfully expect to return home healthy, well, and happy. The leader must anticipate and require sufficient gear to insure not only survival, but reasonable comfort as well. This isn't easy to do since the environment is unpredictable and each individual has physical and psychological tolerances that vary in response to myriad variables. Those who contest the leader's responsibility to require adequate gear cite the personal responsibility of individuals and the advantage of learning by experience. The argument with regard to individual responsibility, while generally valid, assumes that each individual involved is fully knowl-edgeable about equipment and clothing demands of the particular outing and activity, fully aware of the implications of taking or not taking each item, and willing and able to come prepared in a manner consistent with the goals and philosophy of the group. These are major assumptions that can rarely be made even on professional expeditions!

No one is likely to contest the advantages of learning by experience. Many of us who now manage outdoor schools and programs learned in this way, through many years of alternative success and failure. Unguided experiential learning is a fine way to learn, if one survives the process and if the resource base can withstand the abuse of the learners. But guidance can reduce the risk of injury to the participants and to the resources during and following the experience. Comfortable participants are more observant and receptive learners and are far more likely to be considerate of resources.

Practical Considerations

How do you as a leader determine what clothing and equipment to take? What do you require, and what do you simply suggest? In this section we will show a system for arriving at a concise list for any outing you may be planning. Keep in mind, as you apply the process to your planning, that despite all of the philosophical considerations in the foregoing section, you are ultimately responsible for seeing that adequate clothing and equipment are taken on the outing. In a positive light, conscientious effort at this point in your planning process can greatly facilitate the attainment of your objectives for the trip. In a "worst-case" scenario, where an injury or accident occurs, you may find yourself in more than just a moral dilemma if your requirements weren't adequate. In a legal action you may be asked to explain and justify any variance between your gear requirements and those endorsed by other professionals conducting similar activities. It's nice to be positive about all this, but a touch of paranoia may be healthy here. Gear planning is largely a matter of prediction, and the accuracy of your prediction depends upon your understanding of the environment in which the activity will take place, the demands of the activity itself, and the needs and expectations of the participants. The quality of the final list depends upon the leader's ability to predict needs and the leader's judgment in balancing the costs and benefits of each item. Uncertainty is inevitable. Therefore, once a list is determined, it would be wise to compare it to that of established and respected operators of similar programs. Since no two lists are likely to be identical, this comparison can provide insights, ideas, and an opportunity to alter your list.

We should consider what causes a rise or fall in body temperature. If we understand what causes these temperature fluctuations, we may understand the need for so many clothes. To maintain the heat of the body, the effect of five elements must be considered and appropriate measures taken to provide shelter against them. Rain is a serious concern because it can occur suddenly at virtually any place on earth. Many people seem to be optimistic and assume that if it isn't raining when they leave home it won't rain before they return. As a result, raingear is left behind. *Rain* can rob clothing of 90 percent of its insulation value. Even wool (advertised as warm when wet), polypropylene (advertised as warmer than wool), and 60/40 cloth (advertised as water *repellent* — not waterproof) are of minimal and usually little value if worn in the rain very long.

Wind can blow heat away from the body faster than the body can produce more heat. Coupled with rain, winds of speeds even as little as five miles per hour can drive away heat and cause hypothermia in temperatures as warm as 45°F. *Still cold air* can cause body-heat loss through radiation. *Immersion in water* (falling in a river or stream) causes rapid cooling of the body with an accompanying need for rapid drying and warming. The *sun* causes the reverse problem: a loss of energy due to heat gain or dehydration from sweating.

Let's look at the process of assembling a comprehensive clothing and equipment list for a specific outing or event. Assume that the site, the program, and the participants have been determined in advance. There are several reasons for generating gear lists. The leader needs a list as a tool for organizing and comparing options, and as a reminder during the packing process. Participants need lists in order to know what to bring. A method of listing that works well is to construct three lists: one for participants, one for leaders and staff, and one for group gear. The "staff" and "group" lists usually need only be single listings of items, since the purpose of these lists is to serve as reminders. The "participant" list usually needs to be more detailed and perhaps annotated, since the users of the list presumably have less experience in the activity. Look at the sample lists. Clothing and equipment are listed separately, and the required and optional portions of the lists are clearly defined.

The actual listing process can be confusing and inefficient if no logical order is applied. People might develop a complete and appropriate gear list starting with sunglasses, then the cooking pot, then the sweater, etc. The simplest way we know to list clothing is to start at the ground and work up: boots first, then sox, underwear, pants, rainpants, and so on to the hood over the hat. An equipment list can also be started this way, beginning with the ground and working through waxes, skis, or whatever meets the ground, and ending with helmet, headlamp, or whatever is likely to be on top. A complete equipment list can be generated through the latter process; then, following a chronological sequence through the entire program — for example, thinking through the camping process — you can elicit a list of items in the order in which they might be used.

Once a basic list has been generated by the above process, it is time to review the list in terms of safety. Be a pessimist! Consider everything that might go wrong, and how the clothing and equipment requirements might affect the outcome of the situation. Experience and good judgment are essential here. The leader's obligation is to consider any and all reasonably foreseeable problems. Changes in the weather, injuries or illness, and the possibility of an individual or the group becoming lost are all "reasonably foreseeable" in virtually all outdoor pursuits, yet the relative importance of each will vary with each outing.

While it is certainly possible to conceive of a situation in which an individual participant in the program is lost and seriously injured during a period of foul weather, the usual practice among professional leaders is to discourage such possibilities. Though the likelihood is low, especially if the leader modifies the program in the event of foul weather, such a situation could develop. Most experienced leaders require clothing and equipment adequate for 1) reasonable individual comfort in all temperatures and weather likely to be encountered, 2) group survival for several days in the case of highly unlikely but possible situations such as extremes of weather or the group becoming lost, 3) individual survival in the event of separation from the group for one or two nights, and 4) treatment of serious injuries or minor illnesses in a group setting, including overnight care, and 5) evacuations of an incapacitated individual if uncertainty exists with regard to the ability of rescue services.

In the case of a one-day trip, item 1 is usually satisfied rather easily. Some pessimism about the weather is always called for, of course. Since weather is in fact hard to predict, the list should probably be issued well in advance of the outing, and a little extra gear isn't nearly as inconvenient as having to change plans due to lack of equipment. Because leaders are typically skilled, fit, and used to needing very little insulation, they need to be especially sensitive to the considerably greater needs of participants. Concern number 2, group survival, requires some form of group shelter and some provision for obtaining an adequate water supply. In most cases this means at least a very large tarp, means of starting a fire, and a cooking pot for boiling water supplemented by a stove and fuel where fires would not be feasible. Food is potentially useful here, though rarely absolutely essential. Item 3, individual survival, assumes that a single individual loses track of the group and must survive independently for two or more days before being found or finding his/her way to assistance. Since the weather can change considerably in a period of several days, the gear list has to assume the worst and provide adequate insulation and weatherproofness. Minimum requirements generally include a personal shelter, water, matches, and sufficient insulation to protect against the coldest nights the individual would be likely to encounter. These items complement the group-survival items suggested above. Item 4, injuries or illnesses, implies the need for first-aid equipment and for adequate shelter and insulation to protect the injured person. The group tarp provides the shelter, although additional insulation may

be necessary in the form of extra parkas or perhaps a sleeping bag. In snow-covered terrains, especially above the timberline, one or more insulating pads may be necessary. Item 5, a means of evacuation, could consist of a climbing rope or several pack frames — provided, of course, that someone in the group knows how to construct effective litters from these items.

Items of equipment are listed in the appendices, starting with Appendix A, Hiking. Notice that the list for participants is briefly annotated to help insure that appropriate items are brought to the outing. Also note that the required items are simply described, while the optimal items are in some cases discussed at greater length. The reason for this is that participants have a choice to make on *optimal* items. The extent to which annotation is useful depends on the experience level of the participants and upon the extent to which the clothing and equipment requirements have been explained to them. If at least one substantive pre-trip meeting is held well in advance of the outing, the list may not need annotation. It's usually worthwhile, though, given the limitations of verbal communication and the potentially serious consequences of inadequate gear.

WATER

The human body is approximately 80% liquid. Intake and output of liquids are necessary for life processes and the normal functions of the vital organs. When water loss exceeds intake, dehydration takes place. Dehydration of 6% to 8% of the body weight will result in decreased body efficiency; uncorrected it will end in complete collapse.

Humans lose water three ways: perspiration, breathing, and urination. Excess body heat must be dissipated by evaporation of perspiration on the skin. Sweating uses salt; salt deficiency causes disruption of body chemistry (muscle cramps, headaches, nausea). Adequate salt intake will also help retain moisture in the system. When hiking it is wise to drink 3 to 4 quarts of water or juice per day to prevent dehydration.

For a person whose water supply is limited, the problem is to ration water loss rather than intake of water. Conserve the water in the body by reducing the body's basic needs for water. Drink available water until your thirst is satisfied, instead of attempting to stretch the supply.

Problems relating to the consumption of water probably cause more distress than the sum total of all other concerns discussed in this chapter on human needs. We think so little about water in everyday life! It's readily available, fresh from the kitchen tap, filtered and otherwise purified by the city. Furthermore, we don't really need to drink very much plain water in town since our foods tend to be high in water content, and we tend to consume a lot of other "fancy" waters from cans, bottles, tea cups, and cartons. Since, during an average day of light work in town, we lose about two liters of water through urination, perspiration, and respiration, we must replace that amount. The average diet contains about 750 mls. of water as liquid water, and we gain another 250 ml. through the metabolism of foods, water being one of the end products of that process. That leaves about 1000 ml. (one liter) to replace each day. That's only about four cups, not much when you add up all the sips from the drinking fountain, cokes, and other sources of a typical day.

So what happens when we head for the hills? First, if we do actually go up, the increase in elevation (and resulting lowered air pressure) results in a more rapid loss of water. Several other factors can also increase water losses. Low humidity, high temperature, and wind all contribute. Increasing the level of exertion, something almost universally true in outdoor pursuits, dramatically increases the losses. Overall, one is probably going to lose at *least* three liters of water per day. It is common in hot, dry or strenuous circumstances to lose four or more liters per day, and one of the authors once had to abandon a climb in Mexico when 10 liters per day proved insufficient.

In the short run, a little unreplaced water is not of much concern. If one goes out for a day of ski touring, replaces only a liter of water, and returns at the end of the day a liter behind, one isn't likely to feel it, except for being a little less energetic and more sensitive to cold than might be otherwise. Chances are that thirst will inspire replacement of part of the deficit before returning for the night, and a couple of glasses of water in the morning will complete the job.

But what if one is out for several days? Here is where the trouble begins. You are not only losing water at a much higher rate than usual, but the food you carry tends to contain less water and water may be hard to find. In the winter or in cool conditions the situation is further complicated by a lack of interest in drinking something cold, a true lack of thirst caused by mild hypothermia, the freezing of water bottles, or frozen water sources requiring slow and fuel-consumptive stops to melt ice. A common result is dehydration, and a surprising number of hikers, climbers, skiers, and river runners suffer from this condition, attributing their symptoms to all sorts of maladies. One widespread myth is that if you needed water, you would be thirsty. The thirst mechanism works quite well for small deficiencies, but unfortunately tends to sound an alarm only intermittently, and is easily silenced by a small amount of water. Thus one can gradually become more and more seriously dehydrated without feeling constantly thirsty. The occasional sip of water, every half hour or so, usually eliminates almost all sensation of thirst.

What happens when you get behind on your water supply? Aside from weighing less (the one result that some people seem to enjoy), one is likely to feel weak and sometimes nauseated. It is well known among Wilderness Rangers and others who deal with large numbers of backwoods travelers that the overwhelming majority of complaints of illness among these travelers involve feelings of weakness and slight nausea, and that almost all of these people respond almost miraculously to a substantial dose of water and a little rest. AMS may be involved as well in Alpine areas, but the role and frequency of dehydration seem clear. Beyond simple discomfort, dehydration can have some very serious consequences. Perhaps most important is the reduction of metabolic efficiency. In dehydration, blood volume is decreased, and though concentrations of vital components of the blood are thus somewhat increased, the overall oxygen-carrying capacity and other functions of the blood are impaired. This accounts not only for the weakness, but the limits in the body's ability to produce heat. In a winter environment this is an especially serious problem since for the reasons listed above you are more likely to go without water in the very environment wherein good metabolic heat production is essential. Other effects include a predisposition to thrombo-phlebitis as a result of the thickening of the blood. Thrombo-phlebitis is blood clotting, usually in the leg, which can result in a coronary or pulmonary thrombosis should a clot break lose and travel to the heart or lungs. Dehydration also upsets the body's electrolyte balance and hinders elimination of acid wastes.

How can dehydration be recognized? One of the first things to be aware of is anyone with eyes a bit sunken and the beginnings of dark circles. Look at the hikers and climbers leaving a popular area on Sunday evening, or wait at the end of a marathon. Chances are that these people are to some degree dehydrated, and a good-sized dose of water is unlikely to harm them. Another well-known sign to most climbers is urine color. If the urine noticeably decreases in volume, becomes darker or more intense in color, or begins to cause a burning sensation, one should suspect dehydration.

Prevention of dehydration is not as easy as it might seem. Your thirst mechanism, as we said earlier, doesn't do a very good job of reminding you of your needs since a small quantity of water consumed at a water break is likely to subdue your thirst for awhile, even if it wasn't enough intake to re-establish a normal level of hydration. That's why climbers and others frequently threatened by dehydration say to "drink what you feel like drinking, then drink another equal amount." The extra amount can be hard to swallow, but is well worth the effort. This practice should be modified if you find yourself having to urinate excessively. Women should be especially careful to maintain good hygiene and a substantial normal-to-somewhat-clear urine volume since they are especially susceptible to bladder infections — a common and frustrating condition caused or at least predisposed to by dehydration.

Even if you are aware of the danger of dehydration, obtaining the necessary water can be difficult. In dry areas water may be hard to find, and in the winter the price of water may be high in terms of fuel consumption and time. Under either of these conditions the problem

can be avoided by carrying water from town if you're only going to be out for a day. On longer trips the weight of the needed water (or the problem of freezing your supply) usually makes carrying water impractical. Since you will probably be relying at least in part on natural local ground-water supplies, you should carefully study your map and consult guide books and knowledgeable users of the area before departure. Keep in mind that: 1) maps are approximations based on interpretations of aerial photographs with *some* on the ground; 2) water supplies vary widely with the seasons — that lake on the map may be a meadow in the dry season; and 3) the creek that the local guide has been drinking from for twenty years may be heavily polluted now. Water pollution is variable and is very hard to predict, and the local guide may be immune or asymptomatic to local pollutants (or just very lucky). There are many potential pollutants in back-country water supplies, from soaps and detergents to a range of organisms and from virus to bacteria to flagellates like Giardia Lambdia and Entamorba Histolytica.

Here is a little test. Which of the following sources would you consider to be the safest?

A. A deep-source spring.

B. A section of creek five miles downstream from the spring, below three miles of rapids and falls.

C. A small warm shallow pond with a fair abundance of frogs and other life forms. No inlets or outlets.

D. A big lake, perhaps a mile long, with several small mountain streams entering and an exit stream.

If you assume that we're in a back-country or wilderness area in the mid-latitudes (in most of the U.S.A. except perhaps the southernmost portions), then "A" is the answer. Chances are you guessed correctly, assuming, of course, that the spring source is not polluted. Figure 3.1 shows a spring in a wilderness area in the northwest. It's a popular water source, but a risky one. Little do users know that they're drinking "Boy Scout soap." Still, if they are careful to assess the source of water at a spring, this is usually the best choice. We are definitely *not* saying that all springs are safe. The only way to be safe with any natural water supply is to purify it yourself. The second choice is less obvious, "C". Yes, "C". To understand why, you need to understand what it is you are trying to avoid. As a human, you are trying to avoid human diseases. These diseases are, with a few exceptions, transmitted via the fecal tract of humans or in some cases of domestic or wild animals. The organisms, mainly bacteria and virus, do just fine in the dark and special environment of the fecal track. The pond is often free of human disease because 1) with no incoming stream, fecal contamination is unlikely, 2) what contamination does reach the pond will be subjected to intense isolation (sunlight) and will likely be killed, 3) surviving organisms face a lot of competition in the pond and will likely be consumed in the active food chain there, and 4) since the pond is relatively warm, the few surviving "bad guys" will grow (that is, move through their life cycles) faster than in colder waters. This is good, since while they "age" faster, reproduction is inhibited in this strange environment, so *"die off"* occurs more quickly. The overall process is called the "reservoir effect," and has been known and used for centuries as a means of purifying water. Certainly there are parts of the world where some nasty little organisms may infest the pond, and even at our latitudes you want to be sure that people or dogs haven't been in or near the pond. Purification, as we said before, is always the safest course. If you can't purify your water, though, such a pond is a fairly safe bet. You may have to suck the water through your teeth to hold back the frog eggs, but then a little protein in your drink shouldn't hurt.

The next best choice is the big lake, "D". Here, you may be lucky and be able to find water that has been in the lake long enough for the reservoir effect to have reduced the level of contamination. On the other hand, you may find highly polluted waters if the complex hydraulics of the lake brings you water fresh from the incoming surface streams or seepage from a lakeside campsite. Being colder and

deeper, the lake reduces competition, growth rates, and the effects of sunlight.

The last choice, always highly suspect, is "B" the surface stream. One of the hardest myths to destroy is that a mile of rapidly flowing stream purifies the water. A number of studies have shown that only slight improvement results from the effects of even miles of rapids and falls, especially when the water is very cold. In cold water the "bad guys" live a long time, and if the stream is fast, they go a *long* way. You *may* have a dilution factor in your favor, but at best it's Russian roulette.

The only way to be *sure* of the water supply, unless you are melting clean fresh snow, is to purify it yourself. There are several methods in common use among backpackers, yet all seem to be rather poorly understood — or at least inadequately utilized. Boiling will provide one with safe drinking water, assuming the pollutants are living organisms. The usual mistake made in this process is failure to boil the water for an adequate length of time. Too often, people seem to think that boiling the water (as a purification process) means bringing the water to a boil, watching it bubble for a few minutes, and calling it sterile. While at sea level one may be justified in feeling confident in 10 minutes, at 5000 feet one needs to boil the water for at least 20 minutes to achieve the same effect, since at 5000 feet the water will boil at only 203°F. Another common mistake is failure to decontaminate all containers. Some people empty their water bottles into a big pot, boil it for awhile, and then pour it back into the same bottles without boiling the bottles. Certainly it's an odds game that depends upon how much risk you're willing to take, You might, however, want to watch how carefully a past victim of Giardia or of the explosive trots treats his/her water supply. *Very* carefully.

Many people prefer to use halogens, iodine crystals, or a bromine or chlorine compound such as Halazone or common bleach. These methods also work, and will even evidently kill Giardia cysts *if* used properly. They rarely are added, partly, again, due to impatience. While altitude lengthens the boiling time, cold water, commonly found in most back-country areas,

FIGURE 3.1 Possible Sources of Water

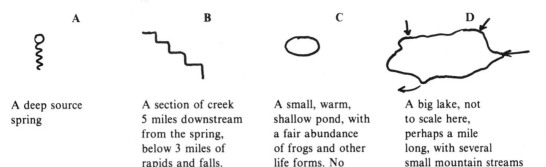

A	B	C	D
A deep source spring	A section of creek 5 miles downstream from the spring, below 3 miles of rapids and falls.	A small, warm, shallow pond, with a fair abundance of frogs and other life forms. No inlets or outlets.	A big lake, not to scale here, perhaps a mile long, with several small mountain streams entering and an exit stream.

lengthens the necessary treatment times. The labels on the bottles are misleading; they assume you're using 70° or room-temperature water and clear water. Water containing silt or visible organic material may require both additional treatment time and additional quantities of the chemical. Typical treatment times for 30° spring water are about 30 minutes. Be patient!

A third and increasingly popular method is filtration. Here again, the method is often misunderstood and misused. Most of the filters that have recently appeared on the market employ a combination of filtration and chemical (usually iodine) treatment and claim to deliver perfectly safe water. This statement is deceptive and dangerous since most of the filters in these devices are not small enough to catch Giardio cysts. Some units do have filters small enough (6u), but those units are sometimes painfully slow. By far the best we've found is the Ratadyne pump. It's been around for a long time and does the job fairly quickly, though it's a bit heavy and quite costly.

One last thought on water sources about a few possible pollutants we haven't discussed. If you are hiking in an area where streams or spring sources could include agricultural or timber harvesting areas, be very careful. A terrifying array of deadly sprays are used in these areas. Those who use such chemicals may not bend over backwards to identify all possible contamination of water supplies. The danger continues all year long, as high water and rains

flood contaminants into the waterways, while low flow may result in less dilution.

A common problem in the higher elevations is red algae. In the snowfields, you all know not to eat yellow snow. Don't eat the red either, or drink from streams or ponds draining from snowfields splotched with the watermelon-pink algaelbloom. It's a common sight all over North America, and from Japan to Austria. The problem is that the pretty pink color comes from phenopthalein, a powerful laxative which is in fact the active ingredient in commercial laxatives. A small amount of this algae is present in most Alpine water supplies in late spring and early summer, and probably contributes to the mild diarrhea that is so common in hikers at this time of the year.

FOOD

When selecting foods for a trip of less than a week, it is probably not necessary to maintain a well-balanced diet. Nevertheless, you will be most comfortable if your diet closely approximates your normal diet, with the following exceptions:

1. Be reasonable about weight. A can or two of beef stew won't hurt, but in general it's best to buy those foods that weigh less, such as dried soups or macaroni. Freeze-dried foods are very light, but very expensive and less palatable if you aren't used to them.

2. Shift your diet away from fats and toward breads and other easily digestible carbohydrates. Fats are harder to digest at higher elevations.

3. Avoid excessive amounts of "gorp," candy, nuts, dried fruit, and other high-energy, low-bulk goodies. These are often consumed in large quantities by backpackers, with predictable (and unpleasant) results. Plan on a few more of these goodies than in your usual diet, but *not* a lot more. As space or emergency rations, these foods are fine.

4. Avoid foods that spoil quickly (such as fresh meats) or that take a long time to cook. There are suggestions for outdoor menus in many backpacking books, and most experienced backpackers have several favorite recipes to share.

The following list may be taken on a three-day outing. It can be varied a little each time, with substitutions and additions from the "alternatives" list.

BASIC LIST

2 macaroni-&-cheese dinners or equivalent (rice)
12 bagels or a loaf of sour-dough French bread
   or whole-wheat bread
1 lb. of crackers — whole wheat, rye
6 oz. of cheddar or other hard cheese
hard-boiled eggs
granola
beef jerky
4 oz. of cream cheese, cheddar, Jarlsberg, or
   Swiss
4-6 oz. of peanut butter
4 pks. (to make 4 cups) cocoa
2 oz. milk powder
2 oz. sugar
6 oz. cereal (cold) or oatmeal
4-8 oz. candy (M & M's, Hershey's, "gorp,"
   good old raisins and peanuts
½ oz. salt
4 tea bags

ALTERNATIVES AND EXTRAS

iced-tea mix
Wylers drinks
orange juice concentrate (heavy but good)
fresh fruit (oranges and green grapes last
   longest)
applesauce
frozen strawberries (heavy, but good on the
   cheesecake!)
dried fruit (raisins, apples, etc.)

jelly, preserves, or marmalade
jello (good as a hot drink)
pie or other baked goods (banana bread is
   great!)
jello instant cheesecake mix (good!)
nuts & seeds
soup mix

FOOD SELECTION

Six guidelines can be given for food selection after the basic menu plan has been developed.

1. Aim for simplicity. Use supermarket readily available items when possible.

2. Remember the condiments (seasonings).

3. Add a few choice delicacies (freeze-dried ice cream has a high carbohydrate content and is a good boost to conversation. A box of cookies or a pound cake tucked away for the middle of the trip boosts morale. A few bits of choice fruit or candies help. And in hot weather a watermelon cooling in a creek at the end of a trip does miracles for ending on a happy note.)

4. Pack enjoyable foods — ones that people like *at home* that are also enjoyable to carry (lightweight and compact).

5. Choose packable non-perishable foods (Green grapes are marvelous for the first day out — perched on top of the pack — but are difficult to put inside unless in a bulky hard-sided container. Melons keep well but are heavy and it's hard to dispose of the rinds, which one must carry to the trip's home destination).

6. Plan a master list of foods and utensils. For example:

   a. Individual responsibilities
      Breakfast
      Snacks (enough for one to four times a
         day)
      Lunch (consider two small lunches per
         day)
      Dinner
      Cup, water bottle, knife, fork, spoon,
         small pan?

   b. Group responsibilities
      May be the same items as individuals if
         decided that way.
      Add special items, vitamins, minerals.

c. Group *use* items
   Condiments
   Coffee/tea
   Snacks (if control is deemed desirable)

Guidelines for Preparation

1. Breakfast:
   Cereal and quick snack for early energy
   Eggs and/or meat for *later* energy only
2. Snacks:
   Immediate energy between meals
      (carbohydrates)
3. Lunch:
   Carbohydrates for energy, snacks; light
      protein for later energy
4. Dinner:
   The *big* meal; protein for slow breakdown
      and fuel storage during rest or sleep

Plans for Water

1. Always carry some.
2. Upon arrival at lunch, dinner, rest, or campsite, procure a supply of water. When snow
   must be melted, it is faster to start with water
   poured from the water bottle into the pot to
   which snow is then added. After drinking
   from a water bottle, replace the water with
   snow, which will usually melt from body or
   pack heat to replenish the amount drunk.
3. Drink often.
   A good rule of thumb is to anticipate your
   needs. If you are hungry or thirsty, your
   body is signalling a depletion. When using
   much energy, the fuel supply must be con-
   stanly available; therefore, in order to maintain a constant fuel supply the following
   advice is recommended:

EAT BEFORE YOU ARE HUNGRY.

DRINK BEFORE YOU ARE THIRSTY.

Menu Planning

Menu planning consists of more than a list of
what one plans to eat. A menu checklist
includes:

1. Number of meals to be prepared (for a Fri-
   day/Saturday/Sunday trip, two breakfasts,
   three lunches, two dinners, six snacks)
2. Number of people at each meal (usually the
   number in the group)
3. Where the meals are to be prepared (in
   camp, on snow, in the mountains in a snow
   cave, on the water, beside the river, in the
   desert, etc.)
4. How the food is to be transported (individual
   packs, food boxes)
5. How the food is to be packaged (all meals
   individually complete, all dinner ingredients
   together for choice, packages of eight servings, individual servings, all canned goods
   distributed equally, etc.)
   a. What is combined? All oils, dry ingre-
      dients, canned goods, seasonings, all
      meats, all of one day's meals?
6. Total weight per person (in rafts it may go
   as high as 100 pounds, on the back it is
   usually 25% of the load of one person.)
7. Utensils needed (pots, servers, stirrers,
   spatulas, stoves, reflector ovens, dutch ovens,
   grills, griddles)
8. Packaging material, zip-lock bags, color-
   coding devices (red = seasonings, etc.), mesh
   bags to see what is inside

Food Preservation and Preparation

1. Food for the first day may be frozen,
   wrapped in watertight plastic and newspaper
   and stored in the middle of the pack. On a
   very warm day, steak, hamburger, chicken,
   fish, etc. may taste good on the first night
   out if the participants are not used to hiking,
   rafting, cross-country skiing, etc. It is heavy,
   but a lighter pack the next day is anticipated
   eagerly (though it may not even be noticeable). Half-way through the day the food
   should be checked to see if it is actually
   thawing fast enough to be ready for dinner.
   It may need to be moved closer to the surface in the summer, or closer to body heat in
   the winter.
2. Preparing the basic part of breakfast the
   night before helps speed up the preparation
   stage, allowing groups to make optimum use
   of early daylight hours. Dried fruits can be

reconstituted in advance. Dry ingredients for baking can be pre-mixed at home.

3. Carry garbage inside several thicknesses of heavy bags. This can't be over-stressed. Foil can be dried and crumpled tightly. Cans must be washed, dried and crushed, garbage is burned where practicable and feasible and the residue carried out. Some garbage may not be burned because of the location of the trip (See Chapter V, "Care of the Environment") and must be carried intact. Only sturdy leak-proof bags carried without chance of puncture will suffice.

Questions to Ask When Purchasing Foods

1. How long will it keep?
2. How ample are the proportions? Will a "4-man" portion feed four hungry men or will it barely feed two hungry women? Try it out at home first!
3. How is it wrapped? It is waterproof? Insect proof? Immune to rough handling or being stuffed in a pack without further wrapping?
4. Is it sufficient in itself? Or must other ingredients, condiments, bulk, or nutrition be needed?
5. What are the "tricks" to preparing it? Soaking? Boiling? Mixing?
6. What utensils are needed and how many?
7. How can you save an unused portion for a later meal? Or can you?
8. What is the cost per person per serving? Can something just as nutritious, tasty, lightweight, and convenient cost less?

SURVIVAL KITS

Many are the lists of equipment necessary for survival and many are the people who purchase such kits and take them on every trip with little or no knowledge of why some items are included or how to use them. Fishing hooks, nylon lines, and waterproof matches are of no use to the lost camper in the desert or in the snowy mountains. They are also of little use to the non-fisherman next to a trout stream in July. The service an outdoor leader can perform related to survival kits is to be certain the participants know what should be taken on *every* trip and how to use each item.

Many times we read of the "10 Essentials" and find several different essentials, or 11 essentials, or ten plus two, or something else. Some of the items in the "10 essentials" are not "essential" but are matters of common sense. (Toilet paper is often called "the 11th essential.")

The following is a recommended survival kit:

1. Advance planning to survive — personal condition, equipment, and communication on where you are going;
2. Adequate shelter, clothing, and equipment for the worst possible conditions of that area and that time of year;
3. Ample water and knowledge of how to get more (plus equipment to do it);
4. Food — high-energy carbohydrates plus a small amount of sweets for morale boosters. Instant soups, broth, nuts, crackers, cheese;
5. Common-sense articles to help the above:
   a. Stove, fuel, matches (matches alone only if adequate supply of dry fuel is guaranteed), and the knowledge of how to operate them
   b. Sunglasses — a *must* in snow or desert travel
   c. Sun screen to ward off ultraviolet rays (a must in snow or desert.)
   d. A knife — a must as a single *tool*, a pocket knife with two blades, an awl, screwdriver, and can opener (The knife with over six blades requires a large hand to use it safely!)
   e. Personal first-aid kit with Band-Aids and moleskin or similar material
   f. Maps and compass ONLY IF THE PARTICIPANT KNOWS HOW TO USE THEM (A map and/or a compass is of NO USE unless one knows how to use them.)

The important parts of the survival kit are:

ADVANCED PLANNING
WILL TO LIVE
SHELTER
WATER

The leader must supply a group first-aid kit.

Knowing edible plants and how to trap, skin, and cook wild animals may be fun to learn about but has little application for surviving most emergencies. Chances are the plants and animals you learn about won't be indigenous to the area where your emergency occurs and are never available during the season of your emergency.

TEACHING FOR SURVIVAL

It is incumbent upon the leader to prepare the participants to plan for their own survival. As was said earlier, part of this is planning in advance for survival. The leader should make the advance plans and teach them to the participants so that they, in turn, will follow the same patterns of behavior when they are on their own. The advance plans may be as follows:

1. Know where you are going. Gather as much information about the area as possible. Seek information on trail or water conditions from management agencies and people who have been there recently. Check on all conditions en route to the site and at it: roads, snow, water levels, etc.
2. Make a list of equipment. Follow the list and check it before leaving. Many experienced outdoorspeople keep standard checklists of day-trip, backpacking, cross-country-ski-trip and climbing or water-travel equipment where they store it. No trip is ever taken without checking the appropriate list. Old-timers who seem to pack their gear by second nature have been known to forget such vital gear as sleeping bags or extra jackets because they packed automatically rather than by plan.
3. Tell someone (friend, family, supervisor) where you are going, what time you are leaving, and when you plan to return. Be sure to call them when you *do* return. If you are not back by a designated time they will look for your vehicle first and then you where you said you'd be. This means the next point is important.
4. Stick to your plans. (Or inform people where an alternate route might be.) If you plan to run Silver Creek or climb Haystack Peak and tell people, that is where they'll look for you.

If you change your mind and go down White River or up Old Baldy, no one will think of looking for you there! Do not alter your plans.

5. In case someone in the group becomes separated from the others and is lost, that person should know what to do. If everything discussed so far has been followed, there is really only one thing to do. STAY PUT. Given the fact that the lost member has adequate gear, there is no need to move. The search party will be able to locate a lost person easily if the person doesn't roam further astray and become "loster."

A program for lost children, called "Hug-A-Tree" might be taught to adults as well as children. The plan was derived as the result of the tragic death of a lost nine-year-old. The story is told here as a tribute to the volunteers who developed the program.

In February of 1981, three brothers were together on Palomar Mountain, 60 miles from San Diego. They were walking on a popular nature trail a half mile from the camp where their parents were fixing lunch. Suddenly, there were only two brothers together; the nine-year-old had vanished. The weather was warm and sunny, and there were many hours remaining before sundown. The family spent two hours searching on their own, then contacted the County Sheriff, who is responsible for conducting searches for missing persons. By mid-afternoon, the Sheriff's Reserve Search and Rescue Unit was on the scene, along with the ASTREA helicopter unit and the San Diego Mountain Rescue Team. The official search began and quickly rolled into high gear as the afternoon and, later, the night went on.

February is a month of change along the Pacific Coast. Cold wet storms often follow several days of mild spring-like weather. By the next morning it was cold, wet, and foggy. One by one, the fine tools of the search-and-rescue specialists lost effectiveness. The helicopters couldn't see in the fog that shrouded the mountaintop, and had to fly below the cloud ceiling when it lifted enough to take off. Despite a good knowledge of the area where the boy had last been seen, it was impossible to locate and follow his track. The wind and rain had neutralized his scent track, so dogs were of no use. The only hope was to systematically search the entire area and pray for a sign of the boy.

Tuesday morning the weather broke and the sun came out. There were about 400 searchers on the scene, including 200 Marines. That afternoon the boy's jacket and one shoe were recovered and his direction of travel was finally established. When they reached his body, though, he was already dead from exposure to the cold.

Many of the searchers felt a great anguish for the lost boy and his family. It was a deep and personal feeling that you could see in many faces on the mountain for months afterward. There was grief for a young boy who had lost his life, and also a feeling that a great wrong had occurred with nobody to blame. It just wasn't right.

This feeling was the beginning of Hug-A-Tree. It brought together people of different and necessary abilities and enabled them to work together as one on a project of great meaning. The goal was to prevent the loss of any child in San Diego County and insure his survival if he did get lost.

Three factors were identified that had played a major part in the tragedy. Two were that the weather and the terrain had been out of the control of any man. The third was that perhaps the boy's actions in response to his situation could have been modified; he could have been educated so that he would have known what to do. Thus children could be taught how not to get lost, how to stay safe and comfortable if they did get lost, and how to attract the attention of searchers.

While teaching children seemed like the best approach, it was not a new one. A movement has been underway for some years in California to make survival education mandatory in the schools. Wheels truly turn slow, so the people who started Hug-A-Tree decided to bypass the bureaucracy and put together an assembly program. A shooting script was written and a mock search conducted so that over a thousand photographic slides could be shot. Every search-and-rescue organization in the county participated. After processing and editing, the pictures seemed to tell a story by themselves. This story was written down in a script so that any demonstrator could get through the program in good

shape. A sound track was recorded to acquaint the children with noises they may hear at night if lost and a handout was written for the children to take home.

Once the program was put together, it was presented to a group of fifth graders at Marvin Elementary School who shared their candid comments and criticisms. Several slides were eliminated at their urging and the script rewritten. Three weeks after this discussion about the project, it was approved for presentation in San Diego schools. The first few presentations were followed up by critiques from students, teachers, and principals, and their suggestions incorporated. The result was a polished and effective program.

Demonstrators were then recruited from local search-and-rescue organizations. In addition to an expert knowledge of search and rescue, the ability to relate to children and speak in public was important. The demonstrators had been on the search on Palomar Mountain, and their dedication has been remarkable.

From the beginning, schools have been anxious to make this program available to their children, and a full calendar has been the rule. The 9th District PTA was approached for assistance, and one of their volunteers became the scheduler. Additionally, they have helped with the printing of the handouts and with letting their local units know of the availability and value of the program.

The local media, both broadcast and print, have also helped spread the word to parents and school personnel about the program. Following an article in a national women's magazine, over 1500 letters were received requesting further information about the program and expansion to their areas.

Hug-A-Tree has definite needs if this program is to continue. It is non-profit, incorporated, and currently in the process of acquiring a tax exemption. The wheels continue to turn slowly, however, and we would welcome assistance in acquiring this exemption. Second, funding is needed. These funds would provide projectors and repairs so that demonstrators could have reliable equipment. While demonstrators donate their time and expertise, insurance, telephone bills, office supplies, and seemingly a hundred other necessities are also draining off the capital faster than it comes in. Third, there is a definite need for assistance in the administration and day-to-day operation of the program. These tasks are currently resting on a very few, very tired shoulders.

Those who have worked with this program have a deep feeling of accomplishment and dedication, and hope to continue indefinitely. With assistance in surmounting the obstacles facing them, they can continue in their heart-felt goal until every child has been reached and the schools incorporate the material into the curriculum.

Hug-A-Tree Has Six Basic Steps To Remember

1. ALWAYS CARRY A TRASH BAG AND WHISTLE ON A PICNIC, HIKE, OR CAMPING TRIP. By making a hole in the bag for the face (without this hole, there is a danger of suffocation) and putting it on over the head, it will keep you dry and warm. The whistle will carry farther than the voice, and takes less energy to use.

2. HUG A TREE ONCE YOU KNOW YOU ARE LOST. One of the greatest fears a person of any age can have is of being alone. Hugging a tree and even talking to it calms one down and prevents panic. By staying in one place, the person is found far more quickly and can't be injured in a fall.

3. NO ONE WILL BE ANGRY AT YOU. Time and again, people (especially children and the mentally disabled or learning impaired) have avoided searchers because they were ashamed of getting lost and afraid of punishment. Anyone can get lost, adult or child. If they knew a happy reunion filled with love was awaiting, they would have been less frightened, less prone to panic, and worked hard to be found.

4. MAKE YOURSELF BIG. From helicopters, people are hard to see when they are standing up, when they are in a group of trees, or when they are wearing dark and drab clothing. Find your tree to hug near a small clearing if possible. Wear a red or orange jacket when you go near the woods or desert. Lie down when the helicopter flies over. If it is cool and you are rested, make crosses or "SOS" in broken shrubbery or rocks, or by dragging your foot in the dirt.

5. THERE ARE NO ANIMALS OUT THERE THAT CAN HURT YOU. If you hear a noise at night, yell at it. If it is an animal it will run away. If it is a searcher you are found. Fear of the dark and of "lions and tigers and bears" are a big factor in panicking children and others into running. They need strong reassurance to stay put and be safe.

6. YOU HAVE 200 FRIENDS LOOKING FOR YOU. We have had children in the area of a search tell us, "My parents would never spend the money to search for me with all these people." Of course, search personnel are professionals and volunteers who charge nothing and do it because they care. Many children who are lost don't realize that if they sit down and stay put, one of a few hundred people will find them. Some are afraid of strangers or men in uniform, don't respond to yells, and have actually hidden from searchers they knew were looking for them.

SUMMARY

If advance plans have been made for water, shelter, and equipment, and if the times and routes have been communicated, a group in an emergency situation should be able to wait until help comes or send for help. (That is covered in the chapter on search and rescue.) Even if the group or individual must wait several days for help to survive, survival should be a definite possibility. A well-skilled leader enhances the chances by being able to get more water and build shelters and fires. While it is hoped the leaders have such skills, they will go to waste if the initial survival shelter and water are not available or if no one knows where to start looking for a missing group.

BIBLIOGRAPHY

Darst, Paul W. and Armstrong, George P., *Outdoor Adventure Activities for School and Recreation Programs,* Minneapolis: Burgess Publishing Co., 1980.

Fear, Daniel, *Surviving the Unexpected,* Tacoma, WA: See-Hear Communications, 1971.

Fear, Eugene, Simac, John, and Lasher, Everett (Eds.), *Guidelines for Outdoor Living,* Tacoma, WA: Mountain Rescue Council, no date.

Fear, Gene. *Surviving the Unexpected Wilderness Emergency,* Tacoma, WA: Survival Educational Association, 1972.

Heet, Jacqueline, *Hug-a-Tree and Survive,* 6465 Lance Way, San Diego, Calif., 1984.

Merrill, Bill, *The Survival Book,* New York: Arco Publishing Co., Inc., 1974.

Merrill, W. K., *Getting Out of Outdoor Trouble,* Harrisburg, PA: Stackpole Books, 1965.

Province of British Columbia, *Outdoor Safety and Survival,* British Columbia Forest Service Information Branch, 1979.

Risk, Paul, *Outdoor Safety and Survival,* New York: John Wiley & Sons, 1983.

Stoffel, Robert and LaValla, Patrick, *Survival Sense for Pilots,* Tacoma, WA: Survival Education Association, 1980.

THE NORTH SISTER, A 10,000 FOOT PEAK IN THE CENTRAL OREGON CASCADES
These two pictures were taken just before and just after a storm in August. Clouds came in
soon after the first picture was taken, and snow fell from late afternoon through the evening of
the following day. The second picture was taken soon after clear weather arrived the next morning.

CHAPTER 4

THE NATURAL ENVIRONMENT

To many people, the natural environment is an undifferentiated mass of plants, animals, dirt, heat, cold, rain, and things that go bump (or worse) in the night. To others it is a super-abundance of fresh water, fish, trees, fresh air, and open space. To still more it represents a challenge that must be overcome or conquered or a vehicle to be utilized for self-aggrandizement. One of the responsibilities inherent in the job of outdoor leader is making outing participants understand and feel comfortable in the natural environment, regardless where it may be. We are not talking about comfort in terms of the physical but in terms of psychological at-homeness.

What is "out there" is basically the same no matter what part of the world you are in. The natural environment is comprised of two parts — living (biotic) and non-living (abiotic) components. Non-living components are the air, soil, and water, and the living ones are the animals and plants. The initials of these items spell "a swap" — easy to remember when we realize that when we exchange our urban life for life in the outdoors we experience "a swap" — an exchange of things with which we are familiar for things with which we are not. Air, soil, water, animals, and plants . . . what basic facts should participants know about each in order to feel at home? There is more to be versed in about any one part of that list than any one person could ever learn; yet some universal facts about these can be applied throughout the world. What we need to know are basics that make us feel comfortable, but aware of potential dangers.

ENVIRONMENTAL AWARENESS

As in any other subject, outdoor teaching has various levels of difficulty, starting with programs for the beginner and leading to advanced activities. Many people, adults as well as children, are not ready to learn about natural resources because the out-of-doors does not interest them or because they are ill at ease or because they are so absorbed in staring wide-eyed at the endless and confusing variety of life outdoors that their minds cannot focus on one thing. A child in a new school needs to know about new friends, the cafeteria, recess, the playground, the gymnasium, teachers, rest rooms, and new books and seating arrangements before becoming involved in the daily lesson. So it is with outdoor teaching. People need a progression of activities to acclimate them to the outdoors before they start becoming familiar with concepts about nature and learning necessary skills.

Three simple awareness concepts, *art, analogies,* and *sensory involvement,* are basic to familiarity with the out-of-doors and feeling comfort and understanding. The average person in today's society does not feel at home or secure in an outdoor setting, and resulting expressions and emotions include fear, shyness, bravado (with no foundation), indifference, raised voices, and silliness. People who are not ready to learn will not learn at all or ineffectively. Those who are ill at ease with any topic cannot concentrate, for their attention focuses only on ways to become more comfortable.

Using the three concepts of outdoor awareness presented here you can stimulate at-homeness, interest, and initial confidence in both the knowledge and skills required in outdoor settings. These three concepts are of importance to all, regardless of the level of the learner. It is axiomatic that one must learn walking before running and standing before walking. So it is with teaching in the out-of-doors. Every learner progresses through the same steps regardless of age or mental acuity.

The more mature, more sophisticated, and more intelligent will progress at greater speed, in greater depth, and through much more complicated processes than those at more elementary levels. Nevertheless, each of the three basic stages of outdoor teaching must be undertaken for optimal value. As in any field, advanced levels can be completely comprehended only if the basic fundamentals are well-learned. The mentally disabled must spend much time working with art, analogies, and sensory awareness, and some will not progress beyond a beginning level. Hours and days may be spent in repetitious activities based on the three concepts. Children and adults of typical intelligence may learn faster; however, they may review the concepts in greater depth and with greater mental stimulation throughout life. Attaining knowledge of ecological principles best occurs after the learner feels at home in the outdoor setting and has developed a curiosity towards it.

Art Forms

It is difficult to make a clean break between the definitions of the three awareness levels; however, they can be clearly segregated. The *art form* level of outdoor learning is designed to develop a degree of appreciation, sensitivity, awareness, and discrimination toward the visual environment. It draws on the learner's ability to recognize basic art forms found in the urban setting (home, school, city, church, library, etc.) and to seek visual evidence of similar forms in the natural world. Seven art forms can be identified in the natural setting by visual perception. Recognizing and identifying these is the initial step in feeling at home in nature.

Line. The following list illustrates the types of lines one can find in art, the urban setting, and the outdoor setting.

Line		Urban	Natural
Horizontal Lines	☰	the horizon; clapboards on a house; rows of bricks	the horizon; branches of some trees; branches lying on the ground
Vertical Lines	‖‖‖	fences; sides of buildings	tree trunks; grasses; veins in iris leaves
Diagonal Lines	/// \\\	ramps; roof lines	some branches; hills
Intersecting Lines	+	crossroads; church crucifix; telephone poles	branches; flower petals
Circles	O	glasses; drinking straws; oranges	stems; trunks; stumps; the moon
Spirals	⧢	circular stairs; springs	snail shell; seeds on a sunflower; scales on a cone (in actuality, all plants grow in spirals)

One can experiment further with combinations like half circles, wavy lines, and a line collage.

Shape and Form. Shape is two-dimensional while form is three-dimensional. Naturally participants in outdoor experiences should be able to differentiate these; however, during night hikes objects can only be viewed two-dimensionally, so basic shapes must be learned. Examples are:

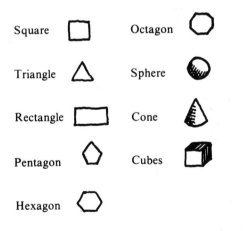

Square — Octagon
Triangle — Sphere
Rectangle — Cone
Pentagon — Cubes
Hexagon

Color. Intensity (the brightness or dullness of a color), value (the lightness or darkness of a color), and hue (the name of the color) are all observable in the natural world, although persons who are color blind will have less success identifying these than those who are normal-sighted. People who are bored driving across long expanses of desert or forest often find the trip more pleasing after they have learned to analyze the various hues as well as the intensity of each one. The person who feels the woods are "all green" also soon learns that there is a great variety of color to be seen.

Texture. Texture is the tactile quality of an object and is best understood in the natural world through activities involving sensory awareness. Until the beginner is coached in the value of touch, his or her understanding of the natural world must be through the visual sense and the imagination. Such tactile describers as rough, smooth, fuzzy, prickly, soft, hard, etc. can be comprehended by the viewer, however, even though texture cannot be verified without experience.

Balance. In both art and nature, balance refers to symmetry. Formal (symmetrical) balance has identical objects on each side of an imaginary line, while informal (asymmetrical) non-balance has different sized or shaped objects in one area than in another. Examples of formal balance in nature are:

--The opposite branching patterns of maples, ashes, and dogwoods;
--The sepals of dogwood blossoms;
--The arrangement of petals on a daisy;
--The placement of fins on a fish.

Examples of assymmetry in nature would be:

--A rock worn smooth by water on one side but not on the other;
--The arrangement of petals on a violet, lady's slipper, or monk's hood;
--The mitten-shaped sassafras leaf;
--The different sized and shaped main claws of the fiddler crab.

Contrast. Contrast refers to light and dark areas. In nature, dark areas are often caused by shadows that change visual perception of the environment. Understanding shadows and thus contrast helps those who are insecure in the depths of an unknown forest. Further, an ability to adjust to the changes from light to dark at twilight aids participants in making the psychological transition from day to night.

Patterns, Repetitions. Once you have identified lines, forms, colors, textures, balance, and contrast, it is time to notice any continuity in design created by a pattern, or a series of repeated lines or objects. Seeing the repeated zigzag on conifers against the skyline or the repetition of the half circle of the tops of deciduous trees helps people perceive nature as something other than a "mass of sticks and weeds."

Acquiring the ability to recognize and identify the foregoing "art forms" in nature is a logical first step toward the next level of the outdoor-learning hierarchy.

Analogies

One way to help people feel at home in a natural setting is to have them relate to nature in terms of items which are familiar to them. An analogy is a resemblance between the attributes, circumstances, or effects of two things. Through mental analogies, people can find that the unfamiliar reminds them of the familiar. Partici-pants must be cautioned, however, that an analogy does not make the item *identical* to its partner.

To introduce people to a natural community (i.e. pond, woods, meadow, stream), discuss and identify the analogous components of the community from which the group comes. Generally, through brainstorming, participants list inhabitants, factories, jobs, residences, trans-portation systems, water supply systems, garbage collectors, alarm systems, stores, schools, etc. Further discussion will show that they can expect to find a resemblance in some particulars between communities otherwise unalike: those in the Southwest and those in the Northwest; urban and rural communities; a community of Chinese and a community of Norwegians; and so forth.

Following a discussion of the components of the human (man-made) community, one can ask the group to observe a natural community to locate similar components. For each of the components in the previous list, there are analogous items to be located in a natural setting. A second way to utilize analogies in learning about the natural environment is by describing new things in familiar terms to which everyone can relate.

Utilizing analogies helps people form pictures in their minds, and these mental images are more easily retained than plain descriptions. Nearly all outdoor leaders use a few — some to the point of making them almost universal.

Commonly used American analogies include:

--The top of the hemlock tree looks like a tired boy's farewell, or a debutante's farewell, or a buggy whip;
--The five main veins of the maple leaf are like the five fingers of a hand;
--The red tips on the sepals of the dogwood are like drops of blood on the crucifix;
--The needles of the Douglas fir are like the bristles of a bottle brush;
--The shape of an elm is a vase (or a feather duster);
--Cirro-cumulus clouds look like the mackerel scales or buttermilk.

Sensory Involvement

In order to understand the natural world, people must have a readiness to learn, and this comes about through successful first-hand experiences that whet intellectual appetites for information. Most individuals seem to approach inspection of the out-of-doors in the same position as they would approach the inspection of a new home — i.e. erect. But in inspecting the new home their position might change from upright to one more conducive to analyzing a house. They might kneel down and feel the carpet, stretch up and feel the top book shelves, sniff the air and notice the odor of newness. In short, looking over a new home could involve several senses at various levels.

Investigating a forest or meadow should entail similar behavior, yet because of insecurity, self-consciousness, or indifference, people seem to look at a forest or field from a standing position, hands in the pocket and head down, chin on chest. Everything is viewed through eyes held five to six feet above the ground without utilizing all senses effectively; however, the other senses can be heightened through practice, and enjoyment of the world can increase correspondingly.

In a pamphlet entitled, *Forest Lands in Management* the U.S. Forest Service states that, in terms of the total use of the five senses, 87% is sight, 7% is hearing, 3.5% is smell, 1.5% is touch and 1.0% is taste. Even with these percentages, though, far less is actually perceived correctly. We look but do not really see. A person examining the seed of an elm tree might notice an oval but probably fails to see that it has a clear indentation in one end. And how many people looking at trees realize that branch placement is opposite in some species and alternating in others? People can see aspen leaves quiver and quake; however, few look closely or touch to discern the reason for the action. We should learn to see colors, shapes, and patterns in the world around us.

When learning to see, the first imperative is that we look at various levels. Some things are best observed while the viewer kneels or lies down. Certain plants are even referred to as "belly" plants because of the prone position that must be assumed by the viewer. Some items are best viewed by climbing, others by looking at an opposite side. (Whenever the viewer needs to move an object for better study, it is mandatory that it be replaced exactly as it was found. Rocks harbor larva homes, and disturbing them is tantamount to destroying them.)

Even people with good hearing need instruction in listening. We tend to block out superfluous sounds in our everyday lives, for we find traffic, air conditioning, elevators, footfalls, and other noises distracting. Some people use radios constantly, either to provide or to block out background noise. Such sound tends to destroy our ability to discriminate various other ones because it's meant to be a sound *masker*. Thus people in the out-of-doors must be taught to listen discriminately to background noise or they will not hear it because of their conscious effort to shut it out in the past.

When listening in the outdoors, we may successfully hear sounds of the wind or rain. But if we have been concentrating on a low tone, such as the buzzing of bees, we may not be able to hear a high one, such as a cricket. People must train themselves to "listen high" or "listen low" and to focus their attention on background noises. Bird watchers have been known to pick out songs of migrating birds above traffic noise or the music of an orchestra. The true knack of listening also enables a person to carry on a conversation intently as both a listener and a speaker, at the same time being able to interrupt and call attention to a bird singing in the nearby shurb or the footfall of an approaching animal.

Seeing and hearing are simple and safe activities, and, for the most part, so is the sense of smell. There are times when one may find a good strong inhalation results in gagging and nausea; ammonia is tolerable if sniffed gently and obnoxious if inhaled strongly. Keeping ammonia in mind, one can learn to practice smelling everything as if it *might* be unpleasant, gently at first, then more strongly until the odor is clear.

Smelling objects enhances appreciation. Roses are known for their fragrance as well as their form; honeysuckle is appreciated for its aroma as much as for its greenery. Most people develop an increased appreciation for the Ponderosa pine when they realize that in the heat of the summer the pines living in their native habitat give off a distinct vanilla odor from crevices in the bark. This smell is absent in the winter or rain. The millipede's protective device consists of an ability to curl its hard body into a circle while releasing a chemical odor resembling that of peach or cherry pits (prussic acid). In the winter the millipede's odor often resembles a miner's or climber's lamp (carbolic acid). Picking up the insect and smelling the exuding chemical odor thus helps you to understand the protective device better than just hearing about it.

Incidentally, poison-ivy flowers are extremely fragrant, and where they grow profusely they may be detected at a ten-foot distance without harm! Things are also sniffed more easily in the mist than in dry or cold air. (Foxes and coyotes lick their noses to enhance their ability to smell.)

The sense of touch is another one easily used; however, people seem to be conditioned not to touch and are reluctant to take their hands from their pockets to learn about things through feeling them. Of course, touch can have more serious consequences than smelling if burns, cuts, rashes, etc. result. But you can learn to touch gently at first with the pads of the finger-tips, then with more pressure. Large areas may be touched with the palm — especially sand, moss, bark, or rocks. The form of some objects will even be more evident through feeling than through sight; the triangular stems of the sedge and the diamond shape of spruce needles, for example, are best understood through sense of touch (attempting to roll each between the thumb and index finger). And through tactile sensations we can understand how rain and snow slide off the spruce and why it consequently grows in adverse conditions.

For understanding the extreme smoothness of some items, parts of the face are used. Only through touching it to the cheek, for instance, can one fully appreciate the texture of a rose. And only through learning to use sense of touch can one appreciate the meaning of any texture.

Perhaps the reason that taste is the least used of all our senses is because unpleasant tastes and poisonous items come to mind. Certainly this sense must be developed with great care and probably only in persons over six years of age and with normal intelligence. Everyone must be aware of plants which should not be sampled because of deleterious effects, i.e. poison ivy,

poison sumac, etc. Tasting is best done under careful supervision of a leader who knows plants thoroughly, or one who discriminates against plants that are *not* known.

Techniques for tasting involve several steps and the knowledge that it is done with the *tongue.* Certain things are savored on the tip of the tongue and a few at the back. At no time should tasting necessitate swallowing. The steps are:

1. Touch the tip of the tongue against the object.
2. If no flavor is evident, bite the object gently with the incisor teeth, then touch the tip of the tongue to it.
3. If you still can't taste anything, chew some of the material and spit it out.
4. If no taste is evident after this, go no further.

There are only four tastes: sweet, sour, bitter, and salt. Certain items of interest for taste experiments are: any of the sour grasses or wood sorrel, peppermints, spearmints, inner bark of wild cherry in the spring, sassafrass bark, wild grape, blackberries, and blueberries.

Some words of caution for tasters. Plan on leaving all white berries alone. They tend to be poisonous and any swallowed could mean trouble.

UNDERSTANDING ECOLOGY

The word "ecology" comes from two Greek words meaning the study of the home. The home in this case is the place where we live and the biosphere or life-supporting part of the earth. It consists of the earth's soil, water, and air and a vertical arrangement of this matter beyond which no life can exist, an area from a few feet down into the soil to the upper atmosphere. The invention of the word "ecology" is credited to a German zoologist who coined it in 1866, although it wasn't until the early 1900's that it was widely accepted. When ecology became a household word in the 1960's and 1970's, its meaning became lost in the excitement over the cause known as the "ecology movement."

Ecology is the study of the interrelationships of all parts of the biosphere. Simply put, it is the study of the interrelationship of all living and non-living components. In the study of ecology, reference is made to ecosystems which are major identifiable segments of the biosphere. The components of the ecosystem are similar to the building blocks of a human dwelling or a human body.

At its lowest level, an ecosystem is protoplasm combined into cells. Groups of cells become tissues and similar tissues make up organs (heart, kidney, lungs). Organs are combined into organ systems (cardiovascular, urino-genitary) and these systems make up organisms or individuals. Individuals of like kind make up populations; a group of populations becomes a community and several communities become an ecosystem.

In any ecosystem there will be many different kinds of individuals. All the individuals of any one species become a population of that species. All the dogs in a city are the dog population; all the mice make up the mouse population; and all the people make up the human population. These combined populations are a community. In an urban setting this may be primarily human, but also cat, dog, mouse, canary, goldfish and others. In a forest community there are virtually hundreds of populations: oak, hickory, redbud, maidenhair fern, hepatica, lady's slipper, red-headed woodpecker, scarlet tanager, cardinal, mouse, squirrel, mosquito, snake, beetle, ant, mushroom, grass, and on and on. Recognition is also given to those who pass into and out of the area, such as a non-indigenous animal. We identify forest communities, meadow communities, grassland communities, marshland communities and others. When reference is made to an ecosystem, it means a community and its non-living elements (all the plants and animals plus air, water, soil and minerals). Another name for ecosystem is biome (home for life). Commonly studied ecosystems include oceans, salt-water estuaries, sea shores, streams, rivers, lakes, ponds, marshes, deserts, tundras, grasslands, and forests.

Components of an Ecosystem

People involved in outdoor activities work, play and learn in one or more ecosystems and are vitally involved with all its components. They can develop a basic understanding of what is going on around them by learning and remembering a few basic facts and concepts about ecosystems. There are four components of any ecosystem with specific and different functions.

Abiotic Substances. The basic non-living parts of an ecosystem consist of elements and their compounds. In outdoor activities, this means concern with soil, water, and air. Their quality and quantity are vital to life, and within each are chemical elements which either enhance or retard it.

Producers. In any ecosystem, there must be producers that are capable of manufacturing food; in a natural ecosystem these are largely the green plants. A prime characteristic of green plants is that they are autotrophic; that is, they are self-nourishing. Green plants can fix light energy and manufacture food from simple inorganic substances. This function is made possible because of the chlorophyl that acts as a catalyst to aid in the process of photosynthesis (synthesizing light into energy).

Plant life derives the raw materials for building its own substance from two sources, air and water. Within the green leaves of plants is an agent for combining the elements so procured into carbohydrates, from which all food matter is derived. From the air are derived oxygen and its compound, carbon dioxide (CO_2), while from the soil the roots draw up water, H_2O. In addition, small quantities of nitrogen, phosphorous, potassium, calcium, and magnesium are needed by a plant. And besides the elements of hydrogen and oxygen derived from the water, water itself must be present in sufficient quantities, along with sunlight, to furnish the energy to bring about the combining of the raw materials. The process known as photosynthesis is at the basis of all food production.

All other organisms are dependent upon plants for their source of food, thus the rationale behind the saying, "Have you thanked a green plant today?" In the ecosystem the green plants are considered *dominants*.

Consumers. Consumers, obviously, are organisms that depend upon the plants for their energy. They are heterotrophic (other-nourishing) and utilize, rearrange, and decompose the complex materials synthesized by the autotrophs.

Consumers are categorized into several levels. The *plant eaters* (herbivores) are made up of very small to very large animals. While most people think of the cow eating grass as a prime example of an herbivore, the largest amount of plant consumption is done by the plant-sucking and chewing insects. Insects and rodents, which are considered of minor interest (or great bother) to many outdoor people, are, nevertheless, "key-industry" animals since they support the predators that depend on them for food.

After the herbivores are the *first-level carnivores*. These feed on the key-industry animals, and like the herbivores, they range in size from very small to very large. Lady-bird beetles eating aphids, coyotes eating mice, birds eating insects or worms, and lions feeding on antelopes are all examples of first-level carnivores.

Second-level carnivores are those animals that prey on and eat the first-level carnivores. They tend to be larger, more fierce, and fewer in number (within each species) than the first-level carnivores.

Two other types of consumers complete the list. *Parasites* live off but do not kill their hosts (though their host may die eventually from weakness) and *scavengers* eat dead, decaying animals. There are, then, five consumers to remember: plant eaters, first-level carnivores, second-level carnivores, parasites, and scavengers. Combinations such as the omnivore and third- and fourth-level carnivores are also present, but the basic consumers are the five explained, the *macro-consumers* (large eaters). **Decomposers.** *Micro-consumers* are those organisms such as bacteria, fungi, and algae which break down the dead plant and animal material into chemical (abiotic) elements. These chemical elements subsequently become the ingredients for the food manufactured by the green plants.

Food Chains

A linking of the "eating-eaten" relationship is known as a food chain. Generally there are three-link chains of organisms; however, many-linked food chains also exist as shown below:

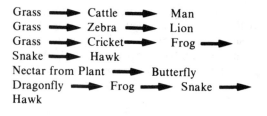

Grass ➜ Cattle ➜ Man
Grass ➜ Zebra ➜ Lion
Grass ➜ Cricket ➜ Frog ➜
Snake ➜ Hawk
Nectar from Plant ➜ Butterfly
Dragonfly ➜ Frog ➜ Snake ➜
Hawk

Many-linked chains also appear in the ocean:

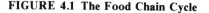

Photoplankton ➜ Zooplankton ➜ Shrimp
Herring ➜ Salmon ➜
Sea Lion

Each chain is a cycle revolving through the producers, consumers, decomposers, and abiotic elements and powered by the energy-giving sun. (See Figure 4.1.)

FIGURE 4.1 The Food Chain Cycle

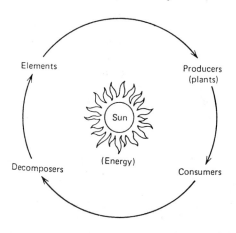

The food chain, if left alone, always produces enough for the consumers, though most organisms are eaten before they reach the adult stage. Each link in the food chain has more food energy than the one before it and usually supports fewer numbers. For example, an animal gains only 10 percent of the energy of the plant it eats. Ninety percent is lost to heat. That animal is eaten by another animal which gains only 10 percent of the energy of its prey as ninety percent is again lost to heat.

It is often said that it takes 100 cottontails to feed ten coyotes to feed one eagle. This is confusing because the number of animals eaten is irrelevant. It takes 100 *energy units* of cotton-tails to make 10 *energy units* of coyotes to make one *energy unit* of eagle. This energy-loss to heat is called the food pyramid, best illustrated in correct dimensions but rarely done so because of lack of space.

Limiting Factors

The four items upon which each organism depends for life are basically sunlight, air, water and soil. These can be identified by their first letters as the limiting LAWS. It is the multitude of varying combinations of these four items that creates different ecosystems and helps us under-stand the distribution of vegetation and animal life all over the world. Less and less water creates a desert, more water creates a marsh; less sunlight results in different species of trees and shrubs; poor soil supports only certain plants; rich soil produces greater growth; pure air helps growth; polluted air retards or stops it.

Ecological Forces

The abiotic constituents of the ecosystem are the soil, water, air, and their components. But other non-living factors affect each ecosystem and make it different, like temperature, wind, humidity, fire, gravity (landslides, avalanches), earthquakes, volcanism, and even the basic topography of the land.

Summary

In summary, an ecosystem is made up of abiotic substances, producers, consumers, and decom-posers. These interact in a continuous cycle called the food chain. Ecosystems differ because of varying amounts and qualities of sunlight, air, water, and soil and because of the effect of other non-living forces. Anyone involved in outdoor activities can understand or at least appreciate the different types of floral regions through which he or she travels if these basic facts are understood. The answer to the question, "Why is this area unlike another?" is found in knowledge, understanding, and analysis of these facts.

ECOLOGICAL CONCEPTS

Knowing the basic components of an ecosystem leads to learning about basic ecological con-cepts. While these are many and different authors recommend different lists there appear to be five ideas basic to comprehending the natural world and easily expressed in lay terms. The five explained here are taken from several sources, but appear to be the essence of the majority of beginning outdoor education pro-grams that teach awareness of ecosystems.

1. The sun is the source of all energy.
2. Everything is connected to everything else.
3. Everything must fit how and where it lives.
4. Everything is going somewhere and becoming something else.
5. There is no free lunch.

Learning these five concepts is easy, and analyzing them simplifies understanding of what is going on in any natural area.

1. The sun is the source of all energy and affects the four basic constituents of any ecosystem and the function of the producers. The saying "Have you thanked a green plant today?" is a good reminder of this idea, for plants are able to synthesize sun energy into food for those who cannot manufacture their own.

   Energy is essential for ecosystems to sur-vive since it is required by all biotic and abiotic components. When an animal eats a plant or another animal, energy passes from the eaten to the eater. Energy is also respon-sible for wind, tides, the water cycle, and other vital ecological cycles.
2. Everything is connected to everything else. Another way of saying this is, "All living things interact with other things in their surroundings." This concept may be the most important one, for only through appreciation of the interrelatedness and interdependance of all living and non-living components of the universe can one become truly objective about nature.

   Historically, humans have egocentrically asked "What good is it?" "What good is poison ivy?" "What good are mosquitoes?" "What good are dandelions?" The questions always imply an unspoken "to me" at the end. Understanding that all items are inter-related and affect more than just humans answers these questions. Every plant and animal has a niche, a reason for being, a role to play.

Mosquitoes are related to water purification (some larva eat coliform bacteria) and the control of plant life (the adults suck plant juices for sustenance). Most insects keep the otherwise over-production of leaves on trees, shrubs, and grasses under control. Without plant-eating insects, every leaf would grow to its maximum size and too much shade would result, stifling younger plant growth.

3. Everything must fit how and where it lives. Adaptation is a fitting word for this idea since a species must fit in with its environment or it will not be able to survive. The ecological principle involved is known as the DAM LAW, an acronym meaning that, under adverse conditions, organisms will **D**ie, **A**dapt, or **M**ove. Plants adapt more readily than they move; animals seem to do one or the other. Those which neither adapt nor move will die.

The dandelion, brought to this country by early settlers, is a green pot-herb raised in Europe as a vegetable. When allowed to grow naturally, it sends its leaves up into the air six to eight inches. In suburban American lawns, it adapts to the passing lawn mower and sends leaves out flat against the ground. The kangaroo rat of the southwestern desert has adapted to its need to utilize every precious drop of water it ingests and has no liquid urine — only a hard pebble of solid waste. Such adaptation is easily recognized, but other forms which have become permanent over the centuries are less well understood.

4. Everything is going somewhere and becoming something else. An ecosystem is dynamic; it must change. There is no such thing as static in nature. Within this movement life and death occurs, among other things. In death there is no waste since matter is continually recycled among biotic and/or abiotic components. This can be seen in the food chain and the cycle from producers to abiotic elements; the building materials of life must be used over and over.

Rocks are worn down to become soil; soil is utilized, changed, moved, leeched, com-pacted to become other forms of rock, etc. Plants come to life, bloom, bear seeds, die, decompose, and are utilized for nutrients for more plants. Understanding this concept helps people understand that a forest, a pond or a meadow cannot be preserved. Meadows, if left alone, generally become forests; ponds may become marshes; and rivers change their courses. Everything is in a constant state of change.

5. There is no free lunch. For every action there is a reaction. For every event, there is a consequence. The delicate balance of nature is a result of a definite interrelationship between producers and consumers that allows both to exist. If the interrelationship becomes and remains unbalanced, one and/or both members will die. Plants and animals live together in areas which meet their special needs. One animal's needs may be met through the life of another. When an animal eats well, its offspring are many and healthy. When those young eat their prey, the population of the prey declines so that there are not enough to feed the many progeny of the well-fed predator. The result is a loss of health, sometimes death, and always smaller, weaker ensuing generations that remain small until the prey has been able to build up its numbers again. At this point, of course, the predator becomes well-fed again and the delicate seesawing balance continues — each paying for its success with its life.

There is no free lunch is thus a way of stating simply that for every action there must be a reaction.

The ecological concepts presented here may be taught to help participants understand all components of a forest, meadow, pond and stream, or plants, animals, soil, and water. These five concepts are basic and elementary, but there are many more.

Air

The most important part of the natural environment that participants must understand for their own safety is the weather. This means the interaction of wind, sun, precipitation, humidity, and air pressure over a short period of time.

Next to daylight and darkness, weather has the most significant effect on your experience in the outdoors. If you ask most people what the weather is like, they will look out the window and let you know, usually adding a forecast based on last night's TV news. Many outdoorspeople are only slightly more sophisticated. While they generally pay a bit more attention to the predictions, they are often painfully unaware of the differences between valley and mountain or desert weather, and lack any ability to forecast weather for themselves.

Nothing can replace the careful review of a good meteorology text, and local guidebooks and other resources should always be tapped for insights into specific weather hazards and conditions in your area. There are, however, several general principles to keep in mind. Like the sun that drives it, our weather follows patterns. While never so precisely predictable as sun movements, weather *can* be forecast with some degree of accuracy. Government and private broadcasts over the news media usually attempt twenty-four hour and longer estimates based on computer models and a wealth of information from hundreds of stations, and we all know minor errors are frequent, major errors not uncommon. Yet believe it or not, you can probably do better yourself given the basic ideas we will list below — if you change the rules a bit. First, don't try to pin things down too closely. If you predict an eighty percent chance of rain by 10:00 a.m., you will likely blow it. "It will probably rain by lunch" is a safer statement. Keep in mind that all you really want to be able to do is to decide whether or not to modify your trip plans; you know you can't possibly reach one hundred percent assurance, so you travel prepared for anything anyway. Your predictions *can* help you decide when and where to camp, whether or not tomorrow will be a good day for picture taking, for climbing, or for hanging out in the tent all day. Keeping one eye *always* on the weather is characteristic of all experienced outdoor people since surprises can be unpleasant or even deadly. Second, do not try to predict too far into the future. Take it four to six hours at a time. You can usually forecast tomorrow morning's weather, but if you

try before late evening, don't bet your last monster cookie on it.

Ask the typical hiker what the weather is likely to do, and, in the absence of recalling the last forecast off the car radio, he will likely look up . . . then maybe east, then maybe north, then consult his partner for a bit. "Rain . . . maybe . . . ." You can do better than that!

So what do we mean by *weather* anyway? What we are mainly concerned about here is *bad* weather — storms, winds, rain and snow. Such conditions are usually associated with low-pressure areas, generated at the interfaces of major air masses and moving from west to east like giant pinwheels. These lows rotate counter-clockwise in the Northern Hemisphere and actually consist of a set of fronts. Fronts are boundaries between elements of the air masses that originally rubbed together to form the low. Figure 4.2 shows cross sections indicating the cloud and weather sequences typical of cold and warm fronts, respectively.

Figure 4.2

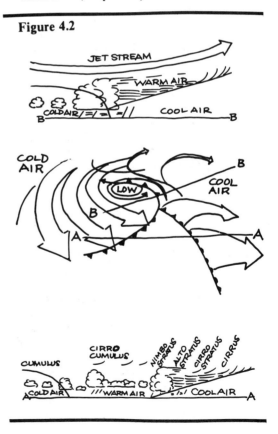

63

Note that the vertical scales in the sketches are very much exaggerated. The entire low pressure system is thinner in proportion than a pancake. Note also that what you might experience at a given point on the ground depends on many factors, including where the storm is relative to you, how fast the storm is moving, and wind velocities, temperatures and humidities within each air mass. You can, however, make some pretty fair guesses. Some useful considerations are listed below.

1. Storms (lows) generally move from west to east. You should check locally to find out what is normal for each season in your area. In most areas the storm will approach from somewhere between the southwest and the northwest. Along the southern and south-eastern coast, however, hurricanes can be a significant exception. Know where your weather comes from, and pay attention.

2. Storms (lows) move at varying speeds, usually from twenty to thirty miles an hour. They speed up and slow down, but generally progress at about twenty-five miles per hour.

3. Cirrus clouds, with their distinctive "mare's tales" of tiny hexagonal snow crystals, usually precede warm fronts by about twelve hours. If you see these clouds, watch to see what happens next. If the warm air behind the front is unstable, you are likely to get cirrocumulous (or "mackerel" clouds), followed by turbulent build-up of cumulous clouds and quite possibly lightening. If the warm air is stable, you should see a thickening and lowering of the clouds, with alto-stratus changing to stratocumulus, nimbo-stratus and stratus — i.e., drizzle and steady rain or snow. Cirrus clouds in the late after-noon? You had better stake out your tent fly, even though the evening will likely be dry.

4. Look to the west or southwest, northwest, or wherever *your* weather comes from to make long-term (three-and-a-half hour) forecasts. If you see that characteristic low grev line in an approaching storm coming over the horizon, estimate how long it will be before it gets to you. In rolling low hills you may be able to see only fifty or sixty miles, or about two or three hours into the future. In the desert, or if you are in the mountains with a good view to the west, you may be able to see well for a hundred and twenty miles, or as much as two hours into the future. Remember that if you are facing an oncoming low, with its counter-closewise circulation, the winds will actually be coming from forty-five degrees or more to the left. To make a shorter range forecast, perhaps up to an hour or two, look into the wind and see what is coming.

For example, in the Pacific Northwest experienced backwoods travelers frequently scan the horizon, starting in the south/south-east to be sure to catch the short-term fore-cast, then passing around to the northwest to see what might happen several hours later.

5. Some of the nastiest weather is not always related to fronts. Thunderstorms are a parti-cular problem, and while many backpacking and mountaineering texts give advice on what to do if you are caught in one, few mention predictions. Those thunderstorms that build up unrelated to frontal distur-bances usually do so in reasonably predic-table fashion — unstable air is uplifted due to strong heating of the ground or sharp differ-ences in ground temperature. The points to remember are 1) that it is common for huge, active storms to develop within an hour from clear sky (thirty minutes is not unusual), and 2) that cumulonimbus clouds tend to form in certain predictable areas and usually drift in directions characteristic of the region. In the Oregon Cascades, for instance, storms almost always drift slowly toward the north/north-east. There is no excuse during hot, humid and unstable weather, when thunderstorms are a possibility, for not keeping a careful eye in the direction of likely buildup. Thun-derstorms are serious business.

6. Do not forget the effects of elevation. In clear air, expect temperatures to drop by about five-and-a-half degrees F for every 1,000 feet of elevation gain. If condensation (cloudiness) is occurring, the rate of cooling drops to about two-and-a-half degrees F per 1,000 feet. A figure often used for estimates, when predictions aren't known, is about three-and-a-half degrees F. Thus a good guess would be that that mountain campsite at 8,000 feet is at least twenty-eight degrees cooler than your sea-level home town. This means that freezing temperatures are not at

TABLE 4.1 Clouds

	Name of Cloud	Forecast
HIGH CLOUDS —	These clouds are composed of tiny ice crystals and found at elevations of 20,000 to 40,000 feet.	
	Cirrus — thin, wispy, and feathery; sometimes called "Mares Tails."	Blue sky: fair, Grey-blue sky: warm front.
	Cirrostratus — thin and patchy; rarely seen.	Fair weather.
	Cirrocumulus — small, white flakes or round masses that cause them to appear as ripples.	Fair weather.
MIDDLE CLOUDS —	These clouds occur from 6,000 to 20,000 feet above the earth. They can bring either fair weather or rain.	
	Altostratus — Layers or sheets of gray or blue. They look slightly striped. The sun looks as if it is being seen through frosted glass.	Warm front; Rain.
	Altocumulus — Patches or layers of puffy or roll-like clouds; whitish gray.	Possible weather change.
LOW CLOUDS —	These clouds occur from near the earth up to 6,500 feet. They are rain clouds.	
	Stratus — Low and like fog. Only a tiny drizzle can fall from these clouds.	Fine drizzle.
	Nimbostratus — True rain clouds. They have a wet look and often there are streaks of rain extending to the ground.	Rain.
	Stratocumulus — Odd-shaped masses spreading out in a rolling or puffy layer; gray with darker shadings.	Won't produce rain.
TOWERING CLOUDS —	These form at almost any altitude.	
	Cumulonimbus — These are thunderheads; great air movement; very tall, almost touch the ground; lightening.	Thunderstorms and cloudbursts of rain.
	Cumulus — Puffy and cauliflower-like. The shapes constantly change.	Fair weather.

TABLE 4.2 Beaufort Scale of Wind Force

Beaufort Number Symbol	Specifications for Use on Land	Miles Per Hour	U.S. Weather Bureau Forecast Terms
0	Calm; smoke rises vertically.	Less than 1	Light
1	Direction of wind shown by smoke drift but not by wind vanes.	1-3	Light
2	Wind felt on face; leaves rustle; ordinary vane moved by wind.	4-7	Light
3	Leaves and small twigs in constant motion; wind extends light flag.	8-12	Gentle
4	Raises dust and loose paper; small branches are moved.	13-18	Moderate
5	Small trees in leaf begin to sway; created wavelets form on inland waters.	19-24	Fresh
6	Large branches in motion; whistling heard in telegraph wires; umbrellas used with difficulty.	25-31	Strong
7	Whole trees in motion; inconvenience felt in walking against wind.	32-38	Strong
8	Breaks twigs off trees; generally impedes progress.	39-46	Gale
9	Slight structural damage occurs.	47-54	Gale
10	Seldom experienced inland; trees uprooted; considerable structural damage occurs.	55-63	Whole Gale
11	Very rarely experienced; accompanied by much damage.	64-75	Whole Gale
12	Heavy damage.	above 75	Hurricane

all uncommon even in mid-summer in most of our mountainous regions. A cool sixty-degree summer evening at sea level could mean freezing temperatures at just over 5,000 feet.

7. When the sun rises, the mountains begin to heat up and do so faster than the sea. As a result, once the sun has begun to "cook" the land, morning winds tend to blow inland and upstream. The reverse happens at night. These winds can be a frustration for hikers and river runners since paddling plans often revolve around predictions of their direction.

On or near the high mountains, the effects can be very severe on otherwise cool, clear nights. Radiant cooling of the surface of exposed high-elevation rock and snow can send torrents of very cold air flowing down gullies and streams. Usually the primary effects are poolings of often sub-freezing air in lake and meadow basins, and gentle but frosty breezes icing the sleeping bags of those careless enough to sleep near creeks. Occasionally these winds come rushing down with great force, often with a strange pulsing rhythm that stops almost completely for a few minutes, nearly shredding tents.

8. You should be aware of the effects of mountain ranges or weather, especially precipitation. (See Figure 4.2.) When moisture-laden air is forced upward by mountains, it is cooled, and cool air cannot hold as much moisture as warmer air. Condensation often results, forming clouds and perhaps precipitation. Notice that since the general motion of storms is from west to east, the west side of mountain ranges usually receives much more moisture than equivalent elevations on the downwind or eastern side of the range.

Soil

The story of soil formation begins with solid rock. For thousands and often millions of years, solid rock has been broken into smaller pieces by many kinds of processes: the freezing and thawing of water; pressure from growing roots; moving ice, water, and wind; and chemical reactions with the rock minerals. Through the ages, these and other processes have formed the few inches of topsoil which support life.

Soil is formed from bedrock and parent material. We can tell soil types and characteristics if we know something of the rocks it comes from. According to how they are formed, there are three classes of rocks:

Igneous Rocks: These have been cooled from molten masses from within the earth's crust and on the surface. Many of these rocks come from volcanoes. Pumice, obsidian, granite, tuff and basalt are examples of igneous rocks.

Sedimentary Rocks. These are formed by deposited sediments from mud, chemical, and organic residues. When compressed into hard layers, these deposits are called sedimentary rocks. Shale, sandstone, and conglomerate are examples of sedimentary rocks.

Metamorphic Rocks. These are derived from existing rocks affected by heat, pressure, or water to cause changes in their minerals or texture. Examples of metamorphic rocks are: shale changed into slate; sandstone into quartzite; limestone into marble; conglomerate into schist; and soft coal into hard coal.

Darker topsoil (A Horizon) is built up gradually from the subsoil or parent material by the addition of humus from decaying plants and animals. Rain water washes fine particles and dissolved chemicals out of the topsoil and leaves them in the parent material below the topsoil to form subsoil (B Horizon). These layers are usually lighter colored and contain less decayed plant material. They are more compact, feel smooth and sticky (clay texture), and air and water may not penetrate them as rapidly. In dry climates, they may contain many salty chemicals and become hard like concrete. Subsoil is thus not as favorable to the growth of plants as topsoil. Between the lowest subsoil and solid rock is a horizon of parent material consisting mostly of raw rock fragments and minerals that are poor for plant use.

Each soil has a profile, or cross section, that is made up of several layers called horizons. These differ in depth, color, feel, and chemical composition. (See Figure 4.3.)

As you look around the field-of-study area, you may find soils of different colors, soils with more sand or clay than others, soils with stones on the surface, etc. These differences can be caused by a variation in the kinds of rocks and plants that have formed them. Topography, temperature, rainfall, and the age of the soil may also make it different from others.

If you dig below the surface of the ground, you may also see how earthworms and other small animals help to grind up materials into finer particles as they eat their way through the soil.

The capable outdoor leader must be able to distinguish between the types and qualities of rocks on which or up which participants are climbing. A knowledge of "rotten" rock in volcanic country is paramount for understanding safe — even lifesaving — climbing techniques. It is assumed that the leader knows the rock thoroughly, and it is his or her responsibility to convey this knowledge to participants. Learning to climb on a rock with no knowledge of the rock itself is analogous to learning to canoe with no knowledge of water conditions. Skills must be adjusted to known environmental conditions.

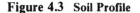

Figure 4.3 Soil Profile

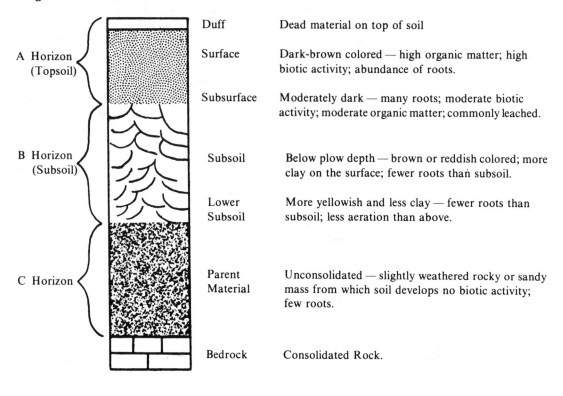

		Duff	Dead material on top of soil
A Horizon (Topsoil)		Surface	Dark-brown colored — high organic matter; high biotic activity; abundance of roots.
		Subsurface	Moderately dark — many roots; moderate biotic activity; moderate organic matter; commonly leached.
B Horizon (Subsoil)		Subsoil	Below plow depth — brown or reddish colored; more clay on the surface; fewer roots than subsoil.
		Lower Subsoil	More yellowish and less clay — fewer roots than subsoil; less aeration than above.
C Horizon		Parent Material	Unconsolidated — slightly weathered rocky or sandy mass from which soil develops no biotic activity; few roots.
		Bedrock	Consolidated Rock.

Water

Most people seem to take water for granted, giving it little thought as long as it is clear and cool. Yet water is probably our most important resource. Like sunshine, air, and soil, it is necessary for life, and all forms of life are dependent upon it. Humans use water for consumption, industry, irrigation, fish hatcheries and recreation. The freezing and thawing of water also help break rocks into smaller particles that eventually become soil, then water helps leach nutrients down into the soil so plant roots can use them. Some of the water that plants use is lost through the leaves by a process called transpiration, analogous to perspiration in people. Water in the soil is additionally used by plants to manufacture food, and wildlife needs it in order to live.

Water repeats itself through the water cycle. The elements that make up the weather (heat, pressure, wind, and moisture) cause precipitation, evaporation, and condensation in an endless cycle. Because of heat, water in lakes and oceans evaporates and rises into the atmosphere. Here it cools and condenses, forming clouds which are blown by the wind. When the clouds get too full of moisture, it starts to rain. As the rain falls to the ground, some of it soaks into the ground and is stored in underground streams, caverns, or air spaces between soil particles. Underground streams form springs when they reach the surface of the earth, a welcome sight to the hiker. Water that does not soak into the ground runs off into streams, lakes, and oceans, where some of it evaporates and returns to the air to form clouds again. Thus the cycle repeats itself. (See Chart 4.1.)

The following characteristics distinguish water from other substances that make up our world:

1. In its pure form, it is colorless, odorless, and tasteless.
2. It exists as a liquid (water), a solid (ice), and a gas (water vapor or steam).
3. It is an extremely good solvent.
4. It exhibits a definite surface tension. (Hence we can boat and swim.)

Participants on an outdoor trip are usually aware of water in streams and rivers, but may not understand why dew condenses on grass (and sleeping bags), in meadows, or on spider webs. They may also not notice rocks broken apart by water freezing and expanding in cracks and crevices. And they may be interested in knowing that fast-moving water does *not* purify itself as was once believed, and that the quality of water differs with different uses.

Municipal water in the USA is of uniform quality, and that used for drinking, washing, flushing the toilet, and watering the garden all comes from the same pipe. In some countries, water used for washing, flushing, and watering the garden is of less pure quality than that used for drinking — hence two different sources.

Industrial water may need to be free from sediments or mineral deposits that would not harm people drinking it, like water used in breweries and automobile batteries. Water from glaciers may seem to be fine for irrigating crops, but, in some cases, the finely ground mountain rocks called "glacial flour" or "glacial milk" can eat through the best irrigation equipment in a

CHART 4.1 Water Cycle

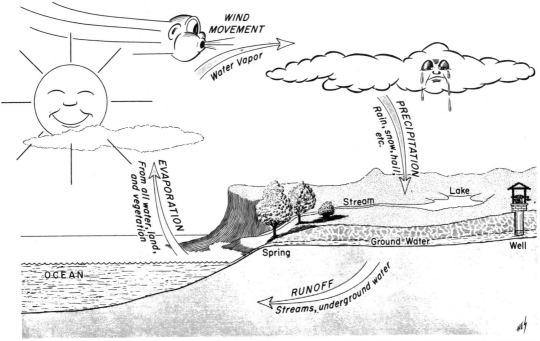

WATER COMES AND GOES FROM EARTH TO SKY IN AN ENDLESS CYCLE

U S DEPARTMENT OF AGRICULTURE SOIL CONSERVATION SERVICE   M-3321

7-0-16664-L

matter of days. Water for fish hatcheries must be cold and clean, while recreation water needed in large amounts for swimming and boating must have a temperature between sixty-five and eighty degrees Fahrenheit and be aesthetically clear.

If the outdoor enthusiast understands the water cycle, he or she may be better able to predict the weather and better prepared to appreciate the plants and animals that depend upon water.

Animals and Plants

There are literally millions of species of animals and plants in the world and no one could possibly know them all. Still, we can understand something of the similarities and differences with a few helpful hints. The following series of outlines represents a brief summary of the biological facts a leader can start on to accumulate the basic knowledge of all flora and fauna. The outlines can serve as a starting point for investigating and learning more. (Source: Audubon Camp of the West. 1970)

Understanding Plants and Animals

These are the four living kingdoms, with emphasis on components easily interpreted in analysis of ecosystems to the general public.

I. MONERANS
  A. Phylum Schizophyta — *Bacteria*
    1. produce decay
    2. produce nitrogen
    3. produce disease
  B. Phylum Cyanophyta — *Blue-green Algae*
    1. single-celled — may form colonies
    2. photosynthesis
    3. blue-green pigment — often hidden by other pigments
    4. food for aquatic animals

II. PROTISTAS
  A. Red Algae
  B. Brown Algae
  C. Green Algae
  D. Fungi (absorb food from living or dead organisms)
  E. 4 others
  F. Slime molds
  G. Ciliates
  H. Flagellates
  I. 2 others
  J. Algal
  K. Protozoan

III. PLANTS
  A. Bryophtes
    1. mosses — no true roots
    2. liverworts — no true leaves
    3. hornworts — no true stems
  B. Tracheophytes
    1. Ferns and fern allies
    2. Gymnosperms (naked seeds) — cone bearers
    3. Angiosperms (seeds in jars)
      a. Monocots
        — Liliacae = lilies
        — Gramineae = grasses
        — Iridaceae = iris
        — Orchideae = orchids
        — Others
      b. Dicots
        — Ranunculaceae = buttercup, crowfoot
        — Rosaceae = rose
        — Umbelliferae = parsley
        — Leguminosae = pea
        — Compositae = sunflower (largest family)
        — Cruciferae = mustard
        — Solanaceae = nightshade
        — Labiatae = mint
        — Scrophulariaceae = figworts, foxglove
        — Ericaceae = heath
        — Aceraceae = maple
        — Betulaceae = birch
        — Salicaceae = willow
        — Others

IV. ANIMALS 26 phyla — 4 listed below
  A. Mollusca (6 classes)
    — calcareous shell, mantle of tissue
    — ventral muscular foot
    — gut with 2 openings
    — body cavity
    1. Apphineura (chitons)
    2. Gastropoda (snails)
    3. Pelecypoda (bivalves)
    4. Cephalopoda (octopus)
    5. 2 others

B. Echinodermata (5 classes)
— internal skeleton
— radial symmetry
— gut with 2 openings
  1. Asteroidea (sea stars)
  2. 4 others
C. Arthropoda (7 classes)
— chitonous skeleton
— jointed legs
— segmented body
  1. Arachnids (spiders)
  2. Crustaceans (shrimp, crab, barnacles)
  3. Chilopoda (centipede)
  4. Diplopoda (millipede)
  5. Insecta (insects) about 1,000,000 species, 29 orders
    — Odonata = dragonflies
    — Onthoptera = grasshoppers
    — Isoptera = termites
    — Hemiptera = true bug
  5. Insecta
    — Homoptera = cicadas
    — Neuroptera = lace wings
    — Lepidoptera = butterflies
    — Diptera = flies
    — Hymenoptera = wasps
    — Coleoptera = beetles
    — 19 others
D. Chordata (3 sub-phyla, 1 is Vertebrate)
Vertebrate (5 classes)
— flexible supporting rod
— hollow dorsal nerve tube
— gut with 2 openings
— gill slits
  1. Fishes
  2. Amphibians
  3. Reptiles
  4. Birds (27 orders)
    — Passeriformes (song birds)
    — Anseriformes (ducks, geese)
    — Falconiformes (hawks)
    — Strigyformes (owls)
    — Apodiformes (hummingbirds)
    — Galliformes (quail)
    — Piciformes (woodpeckers)
    — Charadruformes (gulls, sandpipers)
    — Gaviiformes (loons)
    — Podicipediformes (grebes)
    — Pelecamformes (cormorants)
    — Ciconiformes (herons)
    — Gruiformes (rails)
    — Columbiformes (pigeons)
    — Others
  5. Mammals (18 orders)
    — Lagomopha (rabbits)
    — Rodentia (rodents)
    — Carnivora (bear, skunk, raccoons)
    — Artiodactyla (deer)
    — 14 others

GENERAL INFORMATION ABOUT VERTEBRATES

Vertebrates — the most advanced of all animals — are so known because of their spinal column of vertebrae bones that protect the nerve cord, an extension of their highly developed brain.

Vertebrates include the following *Classes:*

Pisces —	Fishes (17,000 species)
Amphibia —	Frogs, Toads & Salamanders (2,500 species)
Reptilia —	Snakes, Lizards, Turtles & Crocodilians (6,000 species)
Aves —	Birds (9,000 species)
Mammalia —	Mammals (4,400 species)

From fish to birds and mammals, vertebrates display great diversity and efficiency with their adaptations to many environments.

Following is a list of structural characteristics that give vertebrates biological supremacy:
1. Internal skeleton of bone.
2. A body consisting of head (skull), trunk, and, in some, a neck and tail.
3. Limbs in the form of fins, legs, wings or flippers — never more than two pair.
4. Major sense organs (eyes, ears, nose) on the head.
5. The following specialized *systems:*
   a. Integumentary — the body covering, such as scales, feathers, or hair for protection.
   b. Muscular — muscles to move bones, pump blood, transport blood, and digest food.
   c. Skeletal — bones and cartilage for a body framework.
   d. Digestive — preparation of food for use by body tissues.
   e. Respiratory — gills or lungs to exchange gases between the organism and its external environment.

f. Circulatory — a ventral heart with blood vessels containing blood to nourish body tissues and carry away wastes.

g. Excretory — the removal of waste.

h. Endocrine — glands that produce necessary secretions for normal function of body systems.

i. Nervous — the brain, spinal cord, nerves, and sense organs to coordinate environmental stimuli.

j. Reproductive — to continue the species.

In vertebrates, the highly developed sense organs and brain provide the basis for complex *behavior.* Much of the activity of an animal is inborn or inherited *innate behavior.* The most interesting and the least understood of the innate responses are those we call instincts. Self-preservation (flight or fight) is a basic instinct. *Species preservation* instinct directs animal reproduction and care of the young. *Learned behavior,* or conditioned reaction, is common among vertebrates. *Intelligent behavior* involving problem-solving and decision-making is a higher, more complicated level of nervous activity that *birds* and *mammals* exhibit to a limited degree — but man is supreme among vertebrates in this respect. Therefore, we need to study, respect, and make careful decisions concerning our wildlife.

CHARACTERISTICS UNIQUE TO EACH VERTEBRATE GROUP

FISH

Habitat — fresh, brackish, or salt water.

Skin — with many mucous glands (slime) and usually scales.

Fins — for limbs.

Gills — for respiration; covered by an operculum.

Body temperature — variable, dependent upon environment (poikilothermic).

Reproduction — males with sperm or milt; females with eggs that are spawned (oviparous).

Food — most are predaceous upon small invertebrates or other fishes. A few eat aquatic vegetation.

Enemies — other fish, water snakes, some turtles, alligators, birds, and mammals.

AMPHIBIANS

Habitat — fresh water (aquatic) and land (terrestrial).

Skin — moist and glandular, no scales.

Limbs — legs for walking or swimming; 4-5 toes.

Nostrils — with valves connected to mouth.

Gills, lungs and *skin* — for respiration.

Body change — (metamorphosis) from tadpole larva to adult stage.

Body temperature — variable.

Reproduction — oviparous.

Food — small invertebrates (insects), fishes, mammals as adults; algae as larvae.

Enemies — turtles, snakes, birds, raccoons, large fish. Toads are protected by bitter mucous.

REPTILES

Habitat — dry land areas, and moist tropical regions below 7,000 feet.

Skin — dry and scaly.

Limbs — two pair with 5 toes or none; suited for rapid locomotion.

Lungs — for respiration.

Body temperature — variable.

Reproduction — oviparous with a shelled egg; some retain fertile eggs for development within.

Food — most feed on animals; some lizards and land tortoises eat vegetation.

Enemies — other reptiles, birds, and mammals.

BIRDS

Habitat — land, sea, and air.

Skin — covered by feathers.

Limbs — anterior pair modified into wings; posterior pair adapted for perching, walking, or swimming.

Lungs — compact and with air sacs between internal organs.

Voice box (syrinx) — at base of windpipe.

Body temperature — regulated (homoiothermic).

Reproduction — females usually with only left ovary; eggs covered with hard shell are deposited externally for incubation.

Food — because of their high metabolism rate, birds have large food requirements. Vegetation, seeds, flower nectar, all animals and carrion

have food potential according to
species.

Enemies — various parasites, man,
house cats, weasels.

MAMMALS

Habitat — Mostly terrestrial; some
aquatic and marine.

Skin — usually covered by hair; oil,
sweat, scent, and mammary glands.

Dentition — well developed and
structured to food habits.

Limbs — for walking, running,
climbing, burrowing, swimming, or
flying.

Respiration — by lungs only.

Vocal cords — well-developed, variety
of sounds.

Body temperature — regulated
(homoiothermic).

Reproduction — embryo retained for
development within female, then
born (viviparous). Young nourished
after birth.

Food — vegetation (herbivorous),
other animals (carnivorous), either
plant or animal (omnivorous),
insects only (insectivorous).

Enemies — man and other animals are
predatory; most have some parasites.

INVERTEBRATES

I. MAJOR GROUPS OF INVERTEBRATE ANIMALS

Phylum Protozoa, one-celled animals:
Marine and freshwater predators and
scavengers; also some symbionts and parasites in higher forms. Some form glass and
lime shells. Occur in sediments over 600
million years old. Predators, parasites,
scavengers (c. 30,000).

Phylum Porifera, freshwater sponges:
Considered to be the most primitive multicellular animals. Most are marine and yellow
or green irregular masses; coin to fist-sized
on underwater objects; predators (c. 5,000).

*Phylum Coelenterata, jellyfish, sea anemones,
corals:* Mainly marine, with a few freshwater
species; predators (c. 9,000).

*Phylum Platyhelminthes, flatworms —
tapeworms, flukes, planaria:* Some of the
most common parasitic worms, but there
are also a few free-living forms; scavengers
(c. 5,500).

*Phylum Aschelminthes, (nematoda) round-
worms:* Marine, aquatic, and terrestrial.
Many are parasites on plant roots, others in
animals; some are herbivores and some
predators (c. 12,000).

Phylum Mollusca, mollusks: Includes such
diverse forms as snails, clams, and octopuses.
This is one of the most familiar of all the
large-animal groups. Inhabit all waters and
land; herbivores and predators (c. 132,000).

*Phylum Annelida, segmented worms —
earthworms, tubifex, and leeches:* Found on
many marine shores; some aquatic, a few
terrestrial. Herbivores, scavengers, predators,
and parasites (c. 7,000).

Phylum Arthropoda — Arthropods: Animals
with a jointed external skeleton, arthropods
make up about 80% of all known animals.
They include the largest of all animal classes,
the insects, as well as the various crustaceans
centipedes, and millipedes and the arachnids,
spiders, and king crabs. The external skeleton of chitin is shed periodically and a new
one secreted to allow body growth — a
process called molting. Arthropods are
found almost everywhere on earth. They fill
a wide variety of ecological niches.

Class Arachnida: Animals with 8 legs,
antennae lacking (c. 65,000).
   Spiders — body of 2 regions, head-
   thorax and abdomen; land and freshwater; all predators.
   Ticks — body of one region, flattened;
   blood parasites on land mammals.
   Mites — minute to pea-size; land and
   freshwater; parasites.
   Scorpions — large pincers, elongated
   tail with stinger; terrestrial; predators.
   Harvestmen — no pincers; spiderlike
   but with what appears to be only one
   body region; terrestrial; scavengers.

Class Crustacea: Crustaceans are animals
with many legs, two pairs of antennae,

CLASSIFICATION CHART

Realm Life								
*K	Plant	Animal	Animal	Animal	Animal	Animal	Animal	Animal
P	Spermatophyta	Arthropoda	Chordata	Chordata	Chordata	Chordata	Chordata	Chordata
C	Angiospermae	Insecta	Aves	Mammalia	Mammalia	Mammalia	Mammalia	Mammalia
O	Asterales	Lepidoptera	Passerfformex	Ungulata	Carnivora	Carnivora	Carnivora	Primate
F	Compositae	Danaaidae	Ploceridae	Equidae	Felidae	Canidae	Canidae	Hominidae
G	*Helianthus*	*Danais*	*Passer*	*Equus*	*Felis*	*Vulpes*	*Cania*	*Homo*
S	*annuus*	*menippe*	*domesticus*	*caballus*	*domesticus*	*fulva*	*latrans*	*sapiens*
CN	Sunflower	Monarch Butterfly	English Sparrow	Horse	House Cat	Red Fox	Coyote	Man

RULES:
1. Write the genus name first and species name second.
2. Capitalize the genus name only.
3. Underline both the genus and species name, or italicize in print.
4. All higher levels of classification are capitalized but not underlined.
5. Animal family names end in the letters: *idae* (notice).
6. Plant family names usually end in: *aceae* or just *ae*.
   Examples:
   Lily family — Liliceae
   Pine family — Pinaceae
   Rose family — Rosaceae
   Pea family — Leguminosae

*K - kingdom
P - phylum
C - class
O - order
F - family
G - genus
S - species
CN - common name

Scientific classification is termed "taxonomy." The double-name system for scientific names is termed "binomial nomenclature."

The rules for taxonomy and binomial nomenclature are absolutely maintained by two organizations of biologists — The International Congress for Zoological Nomenclature and The International Congress for Botanical Nomenclature. These organizations meet at intervals of several years to recommend changes or corrections in scientific names.

some with a solid shell over head and thorax. Abundant in most seas, some inhabit freshwater and land. They are largely scavengers or feed on plants, but some are predators, others parasites (c. 30,000).

Fairy shrimps — no carapace but shrimplike, with stalk eyes; freshwater.

Clam shrimps — carapace of two valves or shells, clamlike but with 10-28 pairs of appendages, filter feeders.

Sowbugs — no carapace; segmented, flattened, terrestrial scavengers and herbivores.

Scuds — no carapace, flattened from side to side; freshwater; mostly scavengers.

Ostracods (mussel shrimp) — carapace bivalved; very small; 3 pairs of appendages; mostly bottom forms but active swimmers; filter feeders on micro-organisms.

Class Diplododa: Millipedes — two pairs of legs per body segment; slow, wormlike, round body; terrestrial predators (c. 8,000).

Class Chilopoda: Centipedes — one pair of legs per body segment; fast, somewhat flattened and wormlike; terrestrial; poisonous predators (c. 5,000).

Class Insecta: Insects — largest of all animal classes, they compose over three-quarters of all described species of animals living today. They have adapted to all known habitats on earth. The class is divided into 29 orders but even within each order there may be great diversity; beetles may be leaf eaters, wood borers, leaf miners, fungus eaters, flower feeders, grain eaters, scavengers, parasites, and predators.

All insects have one pair of antennae, a body divided into three body regions (head, thorax, and abdomen), and six legs. Other distinctive features are compound eyes, a powerful sense of smell, tremendous reproductive powers, and a hormone system that responds to environmental factors and controls stages in the life cycle (c. 800,000).

Phylum Echinodermata, spiny-skinned animals — *sea stars, sea urchins, sea cucumbers:* Radial symmetry; no head; entirely marine bottom dwellers as herbivores, scavengers, predators, and filter feeders (c. 6,000). (In the phylum to which man and the other vertebrates belong there are only 42,000 species.)

II. INSECT LIFE CYCLES

A. Direct Developmen—egg—miniature
adult—adult.

Order Thysanura — bristletails and
silverfish (land scavengers).

Order Collembola — springtails (land
scavengers or herbivores).

B. Gradual or Incomplete Metamorphosis
— egg—nymph—adult.

Order Orthoptera — grasshoppers,
crickets, roaches, walking sticks, mantids
(nymphs and adults are land scavengers
or predators; many destructive types).

Order Dermaptera — earwigs (nymphs
and adults on land; mostly scavengers,
also predators and herbivores).

Order Plecoptera — stoneflies (nymphs
aquatic, adults land; both mostly herbivorous, some are insect predators, some
adults never feed).

Order Isoptera — termites (nymphs and
adults on land; adult caste system of
reproductives, supplementary reproductives, workers, soldiers, adults [repro-
ductive workers] and nasuti; wood eaters
owing to flagellate mutualism).

Order Hemiptera — bugs (nymphs
aquatic or land, adults land; mostly
predators, some blood sucking or plant
sucking; disease carriers).

Order Homoptera — cicadas, hoppers,
scale insects, aphids, white flies, plant
lice (nymphs and adults on land, mostly
herbivorous; many carry plant diseases).

Order Ephemeroptera — mayflies
(nymphs aquatic, adults on land; nymphs
herbivorous, adults do not feed).

Order Odonata — dragonflies and
damselflies (nymphs aquatic, adults on
land; predators).

C. Complex or Complete Metamorphosis —
egg—larva—pupa-adult.

Order Neuroptera — Dobson flies,
alderflies, snakeflies, mantidflies, lace-
wings, ant lions (larvae and adults in
water or on land; insect predators).

Order Trichoptera — caddice flies (larvae
aquatic and often case-making, scavengers or predators; adults poor fliers on
land, usually feed on liquids).

Order Lepidoptera — butterflies, skippers
moths (larvae on land, herbivorous, often
are destructive to plants, or are scavengers; adults on land as nectar feeders
and valuable pollinators of plants).

Order Coleoptera — beetles (larvae and
adults in water or on land; great variation in food habits).

Order Hymenoptera — sawflies, horntails,
bees, ants, and wasps (larvae and adults
on land; great variation in food habits).

Order Diptera — flies (larvae in water or
on land; adults on land; great variation
in food habits).

Order Siphonaptera — fleas (larvae and
adults parasitic, adults only periodically
so on birds and mammals).

HOW TO KNOW THE ORDERS OF ADULT INSECTS

Key to the Orders of Insects
1. Winged insects;
   Wingless insects.
2. Fore wings horny, leathery or parchment-
   like, at least at the base; hind wings
   membranous or absent;
   Wings membranous.
3. Fore wings veined or hind wings not folded
   crossways when under fore wings;
   Fore wings uniformly horny and veinless;
   hind wings, if present, folded crossways
   and lengthwise when under forewings.
4. Mouthparts a jointed beak for piercing and
   sucking;
   Mandibles move laterally; mouthparts
   chewing.
5. Mouthparts (beak) arising from front part
   of head; fore wings usually leathery at the
   base and membranous at the tip, the tips

generally overlapping when at rest; (Bugs) HEMIPTERA

Beak arising from back part of head, often appearing to arise from base of front legs; fore wings of uniform texture throughout, the tips not or only slightly overlapping when at rest. (Hoppers) HOMOPTERA

6. Wings similar in size, shape, and venation, not folded; social forms living in colonies. (Termites) ISOPTERA

Hind wings folded and broader than fore wings. ORTHOPTERA

7. Abdomen terminated by pincers. (Earwigs) DERMAPTERA

Abdomen not terminated by pincers. (Beetles) COLEOPTERA

8. With two wings;
With four wings.

9. Body grasshopper-like;
Body not grasshopper-like. ORTHOPTERA

10. Abdomen without thread-like or style-like tails; (Flies) DIPTERA

Abdomen with thread-like or style-like tails.

11. Hind wings represented by minute hook-like structures; antennae long and conspicuous; minute, usually under 5 mm. long; (Scale Insects) HOMOPTERA

No hind wing representation; antennae short; usually over 5 mm. long (Mayflies) EPHEMEROPTERA

12. Wings mostly or entirely covered with scales; mouthparts for sucking, usually in the form of a coiled projection; LEPIDOPTERA

Wings transparent or thinly clothed with hairs.

13. Wings long and narrow, the margins fringed with long hairs; (Thrips) THYSANOPTERA

Wings not as above; if wings are somewhat linear, then the tarsi have more than two segments.

14. Hind wings smaller and with fewer veins than fore wings;

Hind wings as large or larger and with as many or more veins than fore wings.

15. Fore wings with many cross veins and cells; antennae short and bristle-like; abdomen with two or three long thread-like tails; (Mayflies) EPHEMEROPTERA

Fore wings with few cross veins and cells; no thread-like tails if antennae are short.

16. Tarsi of two or three segments;
Tarsi of four or five segments, usually five.

17. Mouthparts arising from back of head, often appearing to arise from base of front legs; sucking; HOMOPTERA

Mouthparts normally situated at the front of the head; chewing. CORRODENTIA

18. Wings noticeably hairy; wing venation similar; TRICHOPTERA

Wings not visibly hairy; fewer veins and cells in hind wings. HYMENOPTERA

19. Tarsi of three or four segments;
Tarsi of five segments.

20. Antennae inconspicuous, small, short, bristle-like; ODONATA

Antennae long and conspicuous.

21. Tarsi of front legs enlarged; males; EMBIOPTERA

Tarsi of front legs normal.

22. Wings of similar size, shape and venation; ISOPTERA

Hind wings larger than fore wings. PLECOPTERA

23. Front margin of fore wings with numerous cross veins; NEUROPTERA

Front margin of fore wings with one or two cross veins. MECOPTERA

24. Free-living; body usually neither flattened nor leathery;

Usually external parasites of birds or mammals; body essentially leathery and flattened.

25. Abdomen provided with a spring; not more than six abdominal segments visible; COLLEMBOLA

Abdomen not provided with a spring; abdomen with more than six visible segments.

26. Abdomen with three terminal, bristle-like appendages; THYSANURA

Abdomen without three terminal, bristle-like appendages.

27. Mouthparts drawn into head and not apparent; abdomen with at least nine segments, some containing style-like appendages; THYSANURA

Mouthparts distinctly chewing or sucking; no style-like appendages.

28. Abdomen constricted at the base;   (Ants, Wasps) HYMENOPTERA

Abdomen not constricted at the base, nearly as broad as thorax.

29. Tarsi three-segmented, basal segment of front tarsus swollen;   EMBIOPTERA

Tarsi if three segments, does not have basal segment swollen.

30. Body covered with scales;   (Wingless Moths) LEPIDOPTERA

Body not covered with scales.

31. Mouthparts sucking with elongated beak extending backwards from head or cone-shaped and directed downward;

Mouthparts chewing; when present beak is fairly long and directed down.

32. Minute insects with long and narrow bodies; beak cone-shaped;   THYSANOPTERA

Body usually more or less oval; size variable.

33. Beak arising from front part of head; HEMIPTERA

Beak arising from back part of head. HOMOPTERA

34. Abdomen terminated by pincers; DERMAPTERA

Abdomen without pincer-like cerci.

35. Mouthparts a downward-directed beak; MECOPTERA

Mouthparts not in the form of a beak.

36. Small crawling and running louselike insects; external skeleton soft or tough; prothorax small and inconspicuous; CORRODENTIA

Not louselike; external skeleton generally hard; prothorax large.

37. Hind legs enlarged for jumping; ORTHOPTERA

Hind legs not enlarged for jumping.

38. Tarsi of four segments; whitish, soft-bodied;   ISOPTERA

Tarsi of five segments;   ORTHOPTERA

39. Mouthparts chewing;

Mouthparts sucking, sometimes the piercing parts are withdrawn.

40. Antennae of five or fewer segments; tarsi with 1 (mammal parasites) or 2 (bird parasites) claws;   (Chewing Lice) MALLOPHAGA

Antennae more than five segments; not parasites.   CORRODENTIA

41. Body compressed from side to side; jumping insects;   SIPHONAPTERA

Body compressed from top to bottom; do not jump.

42. Antennae hidden from above in groove beneath the head;   (Louse Flies) DIPTERA

Antennae not hidden from above, usually conspicuous.

43. Beak elongated, extending back below body;   HEMIPTERA

No beak, short anterior projecting snout;   ANOPLEURA

EIGHT COMMON INSECT ORDERS

Phylum: *Arthopoda*   Class: *Insecta*

LEPIDOPTERA — Butterflies & Moths (scale wing)

antennae

butterfly

moth

coiled sucking mouthparts

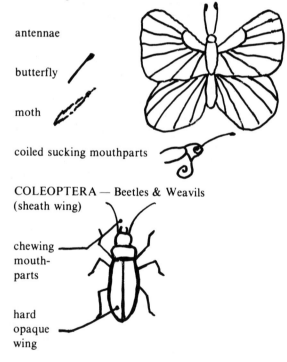

COLEOPTERA — Beetles & Weavils (sheath wing)

chewing mouth-parts

hard opaque wing

ODONATA — Dragonflies & Damselflies
(with tooth)

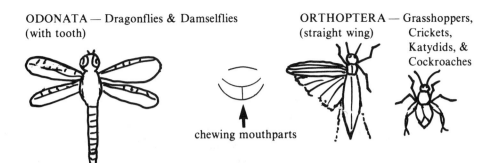

↑
chewing mouthparts

ORTHOPTERA — Grasshoppers,
(straight wing) Crickets,
Katydids, &
Cockroaches

DIPTERA — Flies, Gnats, & Mosquitoes
(two-winged)

sucking &
lapping mouth-
parts

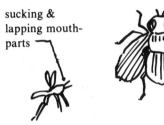

HEMIPTERA — True Bugs
(half-winged)

opaque

clear

head

piercing & sucking
mouthparts

HYMENOPTERA — Bees, Wasps, & Ants
(membrane-winged)

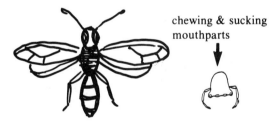

chewing & sucking
mouthparts

↓

HOMOPTERA — Leafhoppers,
(same-winged) Aphids, Cicadas &
Spittlebugs

piercing &
sucking
mouthparts
as in
Hemiptera

HOW TO LOOK AT A FLOWERING PLANT

1. *Look at its stem;* is it
   woody or herbaceous (not woody)?
   one or many?
   erect or prostrate?
   with or without leaves?
   smooth, hairy, sticky, or thorny?
   round or angled?
   solid or hollow?

2. *Look at its leaves;* are they
   simple or compound?
   alternate, opposite, whorled, or basal?
   with or without a leaf-stem (petiole)?
   thick (often evergreen) or thin (often deciduous)? odor? stipules?
   linear, lanceolate, ovate, oblong, oval, round, or other (sketch) in shape?
   parallel, palmate, pinnate, or netted in veination?
   sticky, waxy, hairy, glandular or smooth in texture?
   smooth, toothed, incised, or lobed in margin?

3. *Look at the flower arrangement* (inflorescence)

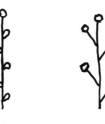

spike   raceme

   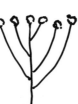

panicle   corymb

Special types of inflorescence:
   umbel (parsley); head (dandelion); catkin (willow); spadix (calla)

Other (make a sketch):

4. *Look at the flower!* Beautiful?

   About sepals: are they
   present or absent?
   many?
   separate or united?
   persistent or deciduous (after flowering)?
   green or petal-like?
   straight or reflexed?

   About petals: are they
   present or absent?
   many?
   separate or united?
   persistent or deciduous (after flowering)?
   colorful? What odor?
   distinctive in outline or appendages?

   About the corolla: is it
   regular or irregular?
   If petals are united, is the corolla cylindrical, bell-shaped, funnel-shaped, rotate, salverform or other?

   About stamens: are they
   present or absent?
   many? any sterile?
   separate, united to each other or to corolla?
   equal or unequal in length?
   longer or shorter than corolla?

   About the pistil: is it
   present or absent?
   more than one?

   stigma: single or divided?
   style: present/absent? single/ divided?
   ovary: above (superior)/ below (inferior) point of attachment of sepals;
   how many compartments (locules)?
   how many seeds (ovules)?

This is how to look at a flower if you want its name to stick. The sequence (1 to 4) is from the most variable to the most consistent; that is, the least to most reliable of the characteristics used in classifying flowering plants. You'll find infinite variation and combinations.

Besides examining the individual plant, look around. What month does it bloom? Where is it found (wet or dry habitat; rocky, sandy, or composted soil; exposed or sheltered situation)? With what other trees, shrubs, or flowers does it grow? What is the habit of its growth (tall slender tree, compact shrub, low plant)?

SUMMARY

Understanding the natural environment seems to be a very complex task to most people. With knowledge of a few basic facts and skills, however, you can enhance the possibility of every participant enjoying the natural surroundings and feeling comfortable in every ecosystem.

Becoming aware of the world around you through observation of simple art forms and analogies is a beginning to environmental awareness. Use of sight, touch, sound, smell, and odor can make people even more aware of their surroundings. These skills help make people feel at home. Understanding ecology and ecological concepts helps you know about what is happening "out there." Basic knowledge of air, soil, water, animals, and plants is the final step. Beyond this, participants can branch out and expand their own interests in special or general topics.

BIBLIOGRAPHY

Buchsbaum, Ralph and Mildred, *Basic Ecology,* Pittsburgh: The Boxwood Press, 1957.

Ford, Phyllis, *Principles and Practices of Outdoor/ Environmental Education,* New York: John Wiley and Sons, Publisher, 1980.

Odum, Eugene, P., *Fundamentals of Ecology,* Philadelphia: W. B. Saunders, Co., 1959.

U.S. Forest Service, *Forest Lands in Management,* Washington, D.C.: Department of Agriculture, no date.

(Also miscellaneous handouts from the Audubon Camp of the West, National Audubon Society.)

USING A SMALL STICK FIRE
Fires are either illegal or environmentally detrimental in most Alpine and sub-Alpine regions, and along some popular rivers. In areas where fires *are* reasonable and legal, this type of fire provides quick, easy cooking heat using very little fuel. Site damage and fire danger is minimal and restoration is simple.

CHAPTER 5

CARE OF THE ENVIRONMENT

For tens of thousands of years man was a minor or even trivial component of the delicate web of life on earth. Our connections to the system were clear, at least pragmatically. Survival itself depended upon relative stability in the environment. Primitive tools were inefficient and populations were small and mobile, so if one site was temporarily overtaxed another pristine site could be found nearby. Resource limits were approached only rarely and in limited contexts.

Now, of course, the situation has changed. We have vast populations and an ever-expanding tool kit giving us almost unlimited power to affect our environment. Unfortunately, our innate drives haven't changed much over the centuries. We still seek to gather unto ourselves as much as we can from the world around us and to do so with the aid of ever more efficient tools and techniques. More, more, more. The

more we know, the faster we learn. The more we have, the more we want. The cycle is hypnotic and captivating, playing upon our most basic urges.

Few people appreciate or have any need in their immediate personal lives to even think about the ecosystem upon which the entire game depends. The environment filters through to us by media channels. Only when the wheels of the car spin in the snow or the precious electric power is cut by an ice storm do we momentarily acknowledge our relationship to the natural world. The problem is that we are, on a global scale, no less dependent on the ecosystem than we were in the beginning, yet we continue to abuse the system in even more profound ways. The environment to which we and our societies are so finely tuned is only the current equilibrium state in an ongoing process of adjustment and readjustment, and shifts in this equilibrium can threaten every aspect of the human experience.

Wearing blinders of ignorance, religions, or faith in technology, we forge ahead in pursuit of our personal goals. Meanwhile, populations already absurdly large continue to grow as the earth's natural resources are gobbled up at accelerating rates by the industrialized nations. Clearly, the current path can lead only to disaster for the ecosystem, of which we are a part. It is hard to be optimistic! Nevertheless, there's no point in giving up. Outdoor-pursuit leaders and administrators are in an exceptionally favorable position to help.

What can we do to alter the seemingly inexorable course of events significantly? Plenty! Outdoor pursuits can provide an opportunity to sensitize participants to the environment, the first and essential step on the path toward increased understanding of environmental processes, increased understanding of our place in and dependence upon the ecosystem, and finally to action on behalf of the environment. The environmentally conscious outdoor administrator can recognize sensitization as a major program goal and encourage appropriate outings and leadership techniques. And leaders can accelerate the environmental development of participants in several ways.

Perhaps most important for leaders is a good basic understanding of the physical and biological characteristics of the area to be visited. Leaders should at the very least know enough about the area to identify major geologic and geographic features, and the more common plants and animals. Ideally, leaders should know a lot more than just the names of features, plants, or animals, yet names alone are often valuable in helping participants gain an appreciation of the environment. Labels allows us to catalogue, sort out, and remember things, and the very process of pointing out objects causes people to notice what they may otherwise have missed. Photography can similarly enhance perceptions as people aggressively seek out new, interesting subjects. Interesting bits of information about what is being observed can help focus attention while moving the observers toward a better understanding of the interrelationships of all the components of the system. This points to the value of leaders having a good comprehension of basic physical and natural science. The leader who understands basic physical, geological, meterological, and biological principles and processes can take his or her participants much farther along the path

toward enlightened action. If this leader is also excited by and about environmental issues, and is an effective and personable teacher, he or she can induce major and long-lasting changes in participant attitudes and behaviors, even on a short excursion.

Clearly, one essential characteristic of a leader, if he or she is to accomplish anything environmentally substantive, is personal behavior consistent with that desired among participants. If the leader shows excitement, interest, and appreciation vis-a-vis the environment, so will most of the participants. If the leader modifies his or her behavior as needed to minimize impacts on the environment, so will others. If the leader stops to pick up litter in the parking lot before setting out on the trail or stream, most of the group will notice, a few will actually help, and even the most thoughtless and inconsiderate individuals are likely to think twice before littering, at least on this outing.

The opportunities for environmental education in outdoor-pursuit activities are the result of direct contact with the natural world. This contact also results in real or potential damage to the environment and major challenges for the outdoor leaders. Any activity, anywhere at any time, has consequences. The hike or canoe trip that is invaluable in sensitizing participants to our environment and its problems also leaves its mark, wearing hard on what may be especially fragile or overused lands.

CARRYING CAPACITY

Carrying capacity — the ability of the land to carry the impact of human use without perceptibly decreasing in quality — is a relatively new concept in education and recreation land use. The notion of recreational carrying capacity is a carry-over from the use of the term for rangeland and livestock. The number of acres needed to feed certain kinds of stock at certain rates of growth is known, as are the rates of rejuvenation of the land after so many animals have grazed on it for a specified period of time. The term "carrying capacity" is adequate for range and stock.

But the term is inadequate for the education/recreation field. Stock presumably have no opinion as to what, perhaps irreversible, damage their foraging, trampling, and littering does to the land. Humans, however, do have an opinion as to how they want their natural land to look and what their outdoor experiences should be like. People have definite expectations and anticipations when they embark on an outdoor experience, and this complicates things enormously, especially where carrying capacity is concerned.

The original term "carrying capacity" does not provide for the feelings and attitudes of human beings. Recreational/educational carrying capacity is no longer measurable in terms of biological-ecosystem rejuvenation only, but comprises other factors dealing with our subjective concept of how much is too much. In most of the literature, carrying capacity is used in relation to wilderness; however, that is only because the majority of the literature on the topic is in response to the question of wilderness management. Carrying capacity, as defined today, refers to any land used for human purposes.

Roderick Nash (1967) defines wilderness carrying capacity simply as "the ability of an environment to absorb human influences and still retain its wildness" (p.255). Stankey and Lime (1971) state it more abstractly: "The recreational carrying capacity is the character of use that can be supported over a specified time by an area developed at a certain level without causing excessive damage to either the physical environment or the experience for the visitor" (p. 175). In determining carrying capacity, both the physical resources of an area and the attitudes of the users must be weighed, along with management objectives. Stankey calls these "ecological and sociological components of carrying capacity," whereas Nash divides them into biological, physical, and psychological components. In each case the conclusions are about the same, although the nomenclature differs.

Physical Impact

Physical carrying capacity here refers to the capability of the land to accommodate people without destruction or diminished quality of the physical features such as rocks, soil, water, air, and topographic features. Where there are too many roads, trails, drainage fields, and the like, the physical features of the land are either destroyed or changed beyond necessity.

Soil Abrasion

Certain soils, especially when very wet or very dry, are subject to disturbance and erosion when walked on, especially by lug-soled boots. Leaders can help here by suggesting or requesting the use of shoes with less stiff and abrasive soles, at least in and around camp.

Soil Compaction

Some soils, even those soils which at other times might be easily abraded, are compressed and hardened when stepped on. This process is one of the most common ways in which people have an impact on the wilderness and is most difficult to reverse. Compaction prevents normal permutation of water into the soil, resulting in the death of many kinds of plants. Compaction also promotes erosion when water on a slope, unable to sink in and no longer slowed by plant life, runs along the surface and gains energy until some uncompacted normal soil is reached. The high-speed, high-energy water then washes away the weaker and more vulnerable normal soil. Compaction damage is a quiet, slow, cumulative process but one that is almost impossible to reverse.

Water Quality

A third type of alteration of the physical environment relates to how we may change the quality of the water. Washing dishes, bodies, or clothes in otherwise natural lakes, rivers, and streams alters both the purity and visual quality of the water. Soap and food residues are unpleasant to view and unpleasant to ingest when invisible. The bacterial count of high-altitude lakes may be higher than that permitted by municipal sanitarians when tested in the middle of the summer after hordes of hikers have used the area for swimming, bathing, and cooking.

Biological Impact

Biological carrying capacity refers to the ability

of the flora and fauna to withstand constant contact with the humans who visit the area. How many pairs of trampling feet can a meadow tolerate in March? May? July? November? In sun, rain, snow, or drought? How many people crossing through grazing land will it take to drive the deer away permanently? These things are unknown, yet when the biological carrying capacity is surpassed, the quality of the environment diminishes as well as the opportunity for optimal enjoyment.

Disturbance of Plants

Plant life is especially vulnerable to human impact. Abrasion and compaction combine to destroy countless plants each season, from tiny microspecies to giant forest trees. Some plants will die if stepped on only once. Most will be stepped on repeatedly. At low elevations (generally below about 3000′ (1000 meters) at mid-latitudes, the growing season is relatively long, many species flourish, and the ecosystem is quite resilient. As elevation increases, the growing conditions become less favorable. As a result, higher elevations mean both fewer species and fewer members of each species, and an ecosystem that is much more easily disturbed. After being walked on by a group of hikers, a low-elevation field might, if left undisturbed, return to near normal within a few weeks, while a high Alpine meadow might wear visible signs for many years.

Many sub-Alpine and Alpine plants do give the impression of being tough and able to withstand the fiercest storm or abuse when in reality quite the opposite is often true. These plants may be, in fact, just barely hanging on, just barely able to maintain themselves under the harsh conditions and extremely sensitive to damage by abrasions or compaction. Heather, for instance, a widespread and hardy-looking sub-Alpine plant, gives the impression of great durability yet has been shown to succumb to only a few passages by people in lug-sole boots. As another example, hundreds of wilderness trees are lost each year in campsites. When soil profiles are lowered by abrasion and compaction, the roots of the trees become exposed and abraded, inviting disease and impairing their functions.

Often more critical is the reduction in the amount of water reaching the deeper roots, caused by the hardened top layer of soil which sheds the water rather than allowing it to permeate downwards. Leaders can do much to prevent unnecessary damage to vegetation by abrasion and compaction. Here are some suggestions. Following them should reduce the immediate impact of the group and, perhaps even more important in the long run, introduce participants to environmentally sound practices.

Disturbance of Animal Life

People affect animal life in many ways, yet a group of hikers may see no obvious signs disturbance. There is no good equivalent in the animal kingdom to the axe-scarred abused old tree that stands for years as testament to its mistreatment. Animals respond to disturbance by changing populations, by changing locations, or both. Individuals rarely exhibit obvious signs of abuse. Whatever our hikers see will likely be taken as "normal" for the area, unless they are informed otherwise. Actually, of course, there are few places on earth where animal populations haven't been profoundly disturbed by man. "Normally" is an elusive concept in this case. Hunting- and fishing- and game-management policies have altered the populations and distributions of virtually every large animal on earth. Those animals not affected by these processes have often been affected, if not eliminated altogether, by agricultural or industrial pressures on limited resources — even in formally designated wilderness areas where the norm is hard to define and even though these areas are supposedly intended to serve as "biologic baselines."

How natural and undisturbed can one expect the animal population to be in the typical wilderness area? The land is often encroached on along all sides by logging and farming, and it abounds with deer and other game enjoying the good eating typical of farm and clearcut. Since control programs have all but destroyed the old balance provided by predators, these populations, unchecked and well-fed, in no way resemble their natural state. Inside the wilderness area, the balance is typically shifted in the other direction, except where the abnormally high adjacent populations temporarily intrude. Fire suppression over the last fifty years or so has greatly reduced the rate at which new meadows are cleared by fire, causing meadows to grow dense with trees and choke out the vital food plants that grow only in full sun.

Another major disruption is centered on wilderness and back-country lakes. Thousands of these lakes, virtually every lake that doesn't freeze to the bottom in every wilderness area, are stocked each year for the amusement of fishermen. Almost all of the stocked lakes are naturally devoid of fish, so adding them totally changes the water's ecosystem and has major effects on a wide range of animals outside of the lake, including a variety of predators. Just as permanent or popular campsites lure and provide sustenance for increased populations of rodents, birds, and predators of rodents and birds, so stocked lakes become focal points for new or expanded populations.

Sociological Impact

Ecological carrying capacity deals with the physical/biological changes brought about by natural processes and human or recreational impacts on these processes. It is the ability of a biotic community to survive under use. Any use creates some change, so unless we disallow it, we must be able to accept change. Most studies on carrying capacity have dealt with the ecological aspect and have included such things as present vegetation, importing hardier ground cover, soil compaction, erosion, wildlife census and behavior patterns, coliform count in streams, watershed runoff patterns, air quality, fire history in an area, and climate. Perhaps most of the focus has been on the effects of ecological carrying capacity rather than on the complex, nebulous area of the social consequences of increasing use pressures because ecological carrying capacity can be more easily measured and because the rates and types of change must be known before management can implement its objectives.

The sociological component of carrying capacity deals primarily with the attitude of the user

towards the wilderness experience. Many factors make up and influence this attitude, and the user may not be aware of all of them. They are subjective and changeable opinions and are difficult to measure in terms of acceptable limits of change. The sociological component also asks whether there are accepted norms that govern wilderness behavior and to what extent violations of these norms affect others. The three primary influences are: 1) recreational-use influences, 2) environmentally related influences, and 3) management-related influences, all leading to a loss of quality experience.

1. Recreational-use influences. Stankey (1972) gives four categories under this heading.
   a. Intensity of use — when the user's perception of solitude is exceeded by too many encounters.
   b. Character of the encounter — conflict between types of use, such as meeting large groups or those going under their own steam (hikers, canoeists, snowshoers, skiers), versus those being carried by horsepower (on horseback, in motorboats, snowmobiles, or recreational vehicles).
   c. Spatial aspects — the location of the encounter, whether at the trail head, on the trail, or at the campsite.
   d. Destructive visitor behavior — evidence of littering, vandalism, and campsite overuse.
2. Environmentally related influences. One example is the perception of the resource quality, including biological components of carrying capacity.
3. Management-related influences. This includes Nash's physical component of carrying capacity. It is in part the resource's capacity to " 'absorb' constructed trails, bridges, roads, signs, and other man-made features" (Nash, 1967, p. 267).

The tolerance level of these factors in combination with such others as mental attitude, belief systems, physical condition of the area, and, especially, expectations determines for one individual at a given moment what a quality experience will be. One way to determine quality experience and therefore sociological carrying capacity is to find out what value the user puts on each of these factors and what the user is willing to give up to attain and enjoy them. Thus supply and demand, or the economics of recreation, may determine what kind of recreational experience the visitor will have. Supply and demand on scarce resources should be balanced in the most fair and beneficial of ways. How much a user is willing to give up for a quality experience may be stated in non-dollar terms, and there are three non-dollar costs to the user, according to David Greist (1975):

1. Decreased chances of entry if use limits are imposed;
2. For solitude seekers, decreased satisfaction due to high-use levels;
3. For those who seek undisturbed natural environments, decreased satisfaction due to environmental change associated with high-use levels.

The carrying capacity could also be stated as the use level demanded by users after they consider costs. Frissell and Stankey (1972) call this the "limits of acceptable change," focusing most of their attention on the users' perception of this change.

In relation to outdoor recreation, the aesthetic or psychological carrying capacity affects the amount of space a person needs for privacy and an absence of a feeling of crowdedness. At the same time, it also affects the need for human proximity to dispel loneliness, fear, and isolation. This feeling of space is different for different people at different times.

Other aesthetic features of land include noise, wind, vistas (both long and short), diversity in plant life, topography, color, shadow, openness, and so on. Some people like open forests, some like dense stands of trees; most find the sound of running water soothing, yet some find it tiring. No known formula has been devised for calculating the aesthetic quality of land. At times, however, it seems obvious that because of noise or confusion, or the sight of building after building, the aesthetic quality of the land has been diminished by too many people. Littering, personal sanitation, and other habits all have an impact on sociological carrying capacity.

Littering

All of the foregoing impacts we've discussed have both physical and social significance,

though the social effects are relatively less important. In the case of littering, the physical is relatively small compared to the social. Litter is unsightly and highly disturbing to all but the most insensitive observers, yet is the only impact we've discussed so far that is easily reversed in most instances. Except for the growing problem of small bits of wind- and animal-dispersed litter, most can simply be picked up and removed. In comparison to the difficulties of reversing the effects of compaction or other abuses of the ecosystem, littering is a minor issue.

Fortunately, most outdoor enthusiasts are conscientious about not leaving their tracks behind. Unfortunately, litter continues to accumulate wherever people go. Some of the debris is accidentally dropped — bits of gum wrapper or foil intended for the pocket. Most is left by people who are insensitive, inconsiderate, uncaring, and/or sloppy. Some of these people can be educated, and the behavior of certain others can be modified by coercion; that is, by the intimidating power of regulations and the threat of fines. Still, much littering will probably continue, and most of the debris will have to be picked up by more considerate and caring users. Few resource managers have budgets sufficient to fund enough rangers and garbage men to clean up, so leaders have an opportunity here to help the environment and raise consciousness of the issue among participants.

Sanitation

The disposal of human wastes is primarily a social concern. The physical impacts of human waste disposal are rarely significant, except in certain exceptionally fragile or overused sites where water supplies may be sensitive to excessive input of nutrients. Social problems relate to both health and aesthetics; many diseases are carried by feces, contaminated insects, or water supplies, and aesthetic concerns range from odors and unpleasant sights to the delights of finding oneself walking through a "mine field" near a camp.

The extent of the potential problem seems to be determined mainly by the degree of use and the elevation of the site. Higher-elevation sites have simpler ecosystems, wherein biodegradation typically proceeds at a much slower pace than at lower elevations. At sea level or even up to elevations as high as 3,000 feet (1,000 meters), biodegradation of organic matter such as fecal wastes is relatively rapid. At higher elevations this is not the case. At a middle altitude of 6,000 feet (1,900 meters), for example, organic material may take ten times longer to decompose than at sea level. At 10,000 feet (3,000 meters) the rate may be ten times slower yet. Unfortunately, the most popular of many of our wilderness areas are at relatively high elevations. High rates of use and a slow rate of degradation of the wastes result in build-ups that all too often reach water supplies or food. Outhouses and chemical toilets are rarely adequate solutions, since outhouses inevitably drain into water supplies and because both facilities usually end up being filled more with garbage than with sewage. In addition, such facilities are only used by a few people — when they are very close at hand or when there are so many people they become essential for privacy. When camping out in the back country, how far will you go out of your way to use an outhouse? How far if it's dark and no one's around and the outhouse is full of creepy crawling things and an odor that clings to your clothes for hours?

There are a few other sociological considerations to allow for when leading people on trips away from urban settings.

Noise

Leaders should be aware that the noise of one group may disturb another. Raucous talk may decrease the quality of the experience of another group, for example, when they are watching a rainbow. Late-night singing, use of battery-powered radios and televisions, and loud conversations can also disturb people camping in nearby campsites. Leaders should show concern and support for one another by ensuring that their groups are considerate of this factor.

Visual Disturbance

In a primitive natural setting used for backpacking, bright, obtrusive shades are disturbing to those who came to "get away from it all." To many, bright represents the busy, neon-lit urban environment left behind and is antithetical to the greens and blues and browns of the natural world. When possible, campers today should buy and use tents and tarps in earth tones so as not to disturb others with incongruent colors. In addition, litter, broken branches, and other evidence of disregard for the natural environment can impair the visual harmony of the outdoor setting. The leader should ensure that his or her group leaves the environment as they found it.

Animal Problems

Dogs and horses are not loved equally by all. Generally, hiking and pack-horse trips do not mix, and people understand that. Yet for some unknown reason, it is not as obvious that dogs should not be permitted on trips sponsored by agencies or organizations. Families or private groups make their own policies and may agree to take their pets; however, groups with paid or appointed leaders should refrain from doing this. Dogs tend to run ahead and then back to their owners, weaving in and out between the legs of a line of hikers. Several dogs on a trail usually result in a fracas. Leaders should take a firm stand and state, "No pets."

MINIMIZING IMPACT

Since it is obvious that the human alters the state of the environment with every sortie, what can we do to make sure the impact is kept to a minimum? Land managers recommend "minimum-impact camping," "no-trace camping," or "low-impact camping." Each means camping or hiking or boating or engaging in any outdoor pursuit in a manner that leaves little or no trace of human evidence on the land or water.

The recommendations are many, yet if followed become an ingrained environmental 'ethic and to some an irreprochable way of life. Following these recommendations will make a difference in the quality of the outdoor experiences both now and for years to come.

MINIMIZING PHYSICAL IMPACT

The following steps should help keep physical impact to a minimum:

When Travelling

1. When possible, use existing trails and footwear that is no more abusive to the soil than necessary. Lug-sole boots are often the worst. The deeper the lugs and stiffer the sole, the greater the damage to certain types of soil.
2. Avoid widening the trail. This means not stepping on the shoulder of the trail but walking right in the middle of it instead. Don't form multiple trails by walking alongside a water- or weed-filled path. Instead, if you must stay out of the water or away from dew-covered plants, have the group fan out to avoid creating a second parallel trail.
3. Don't cut corners or switchbacks! Follow the trail around the corner even if less considerate hikers have worn a shoulder path. If you can spare the time, take a minute or two to place barriers to reduce further damage! Getting participants involved in trail repair focuses their attention on the problem and makes it unlikely that they will cause similar problems elsewhere.
4. When you come to a damaged section of trail, trees, or limbs, try to repair the damage or to at least clear a path through the debris. Making a path around the obstacle causes unnecessary damage, magnified by hikers and game that follow. Most trail-maintenance programs are poorly funded, and even the best can't get to every problem site in time. Doing minor maintenance is one way in which organized groups can, in a sense, compensate for the greater.
5. When travelling off-trail, don't create new paths! Every attempt should be made to avoid leaving any sign of passing. The most sensitive areas are hillsides and meadows. In either case, single-file travel by a group should be avoided. Fanning out reduces the impact at any one point, but individuals on hillsides should also walk in a zigzag pattern if the soils are soft to prevent starting a little stream course down the hill. At first

leaders have to be strongly assertive until participants get used to the idea of finding their own way. No one wants to put out any extra energy, especially on hillsides where people may get a bit tired. The easiest path, often that taken by the leader, is therefore the route everyone wants to take. It helps to stop before such sensitive areas, explain the problem and course of action, and then start people across the area from separate points. Even so, frequent reminders may be necessary along the way to prevent people from converging onto common paths.

6. When travelling off-trail, use snow or rock when possible. Here again, minimizing impact may require people to put out a little bit of extra energy, and the leader may need to provide both control and encouragement while setting a good example.
7. Also when travelling off the marked trail, don't mark your route with flagging or rock piles (cairns, ducks, or birds) unless there is a real need to follow the exact route again, in which case all markings should be removed on the last passage over the route. Old unneeded plastic flagging left by less considerate pathfinders should be removed as well. Marked routes encourage concentrated use, and plenty of marked routes exist already. It should go without saying that in no case should trees be blazed (notches cut in the bark) to mark a route.

When Camping

1. Select campsites carefully! Good choices for durability include river or shore sands, glaciated rock surfaces, areas of deep fir or pine-needle duff, and previously hardened campsites. When using a site that is already beaten down to a hard and nearly vegetation-free surface, be sure to limit activity to well within the existing limits of the site. Don't expand the site by allowing too many people to camp in it, or by allowing tent placements or activities that wear on the surrounding ground cover. Never camp on the fragile grasses of meadows or near bodies of water, except on maintained or developed campsites. These sites are not only extremely subject to abrasion and compaction, but are

very poor choices for a number of other reasons as well.

2. Control the foot-traffic patterns in the camp area so that new trails aren't formed between camps or to viewpoints, latrines, or water sources. This is important even when the campsite will only be used for a day or two.

3. Encourage the use of camp shoes with soft or smooth soles.

4. Never cut trenches or otherwise modify a site. Modern tents have floors, thus eliminating the need to dig drainage trenches around them. Show participants how to choose a good site and how to use it effectively without resorting to disturbance of the soil.

5. If sticks and stones are moved to make a bed or campsite, put them back before you leave!

When Building Fires

Compaction and abrasion are by no means the only ways in which hikers directly affect vegetation in the back country. Several very significant types of damage relate to the use of campfires. The most obvious is wildfire damage caused by escaping fires. Leaders can prevent most of these problems by:

1. Digging a trench down to mineral soil around the fire site;
2. Putting the fire out completely.

Most people make some effort to extinguish their fires, yet most fail to do so completely. The usual reason for failure is that most of the applied water runs off or sinks into the soil, and what is left is baked out of the ashes by residual heat in the ashes and soil. If a fire ring of stones has been used, the heat in the stones finishes the job so that in a few hours the fuels are totally dry. All it takes is one tiny spark to restart the fire, and many embers usually remain protected under the stones of the fire ring. Another common reason for fires continuing to burn after attempts to extinguish them is that roots and other underground vegetable matter may smoulder far away from the confines of the fire ring if the trench was not dug down to mineral soil. The fire can spread a long way, not uncommonly springing up on the surface fifty feet or more away from the original fire site. Wilder-

ness rangers tell tales of amazingly long escapes, up to 100 yards or so, and of extensive areas of underground smouldering fires lasting through entire winter seasons under the snowpack. These fires can be extremely hard to control, requiring tedious hands-and-knees digging and a lot of damage to the soil surface.

Selecting the Fire Site

Leaders need to supervise the selection of campfire sites to be sure that the sites are free of nearby or overhanging combustibles, that there are no opportunities for wind-driven sparks to set fires elsewhere, and that the duff layer, the layer of organized material on top of the mineral soil, is not too thick. If rocks are to be used, leaders should suggest the use of only one or two, rather than a whole ring — just enough to support a pot and perhaps provide a little wind protection. This will help make it easier to put out the fire later. Large existing fire rings should always be dismantled down to a minimal number of rocks, and the unneeded rocks should be carried back to their original location. With luck, this may help reduce the risk of future fires by making it easier for future campers to put out their fires as well.

Participants should be shown how to prepare the site by digging a trench around the outside of the fire ring to mineral soil. If the group consists of adults, the leader can usually expect them to put the fire out properly; that is, to stir in lots of water with a stick, roll the rock back, and feel the site with bare hands for hot spots. If the group consists of children, then this chore usually falls on the leader, although the children should certainly be involved. In either case, regardless of the ages of the participants, the leader needs to check each fire site by hand, feeling carefully throughout the fire bed, rock sites, and trench for any signs of remaining or escaping fire.

Campfires produce a lot of heat focused on a small area. The result is sterilization of the soil at the site combined with an increase in certain minerals left over from combustion of the wood — and nearly permanent scars. These scars range from charcoal debris in sand and carbon stains on rock to ugly blackened spots on meadows. Leaders can help by pointing out such scars to participants while hiking, and by guiding the site selection process if fires will be used. Man-made concrete or metal fire sites should always be used if possible. If not, try to find a site that will show the least damage. This may be an existing site, but should in no case be a meadow. A once-popular technique to avoid is that of cutting out a complete disk of grass and topsoil and replacing it after having used the mineral soil for the fire. The replaced ring may look great when set in with care, but within a few days it begins to die. At best, the result is a funny-looking sometimes-raised and sometimes-depressed circle of sickly grasses, occasionally fringed or spiked with invading plant species seeking the fire-concentrated minerals beneath.

Using Wood for Fuel

Perhaps the most significant impact of camp-fires is on the consumption of natural fuels. Problems resulting from overuse plague managers of wilderness and back-country resources around the world. Popular misconceptions and outdated habits abound among users of our wilderness lands and waters, adding to the difficulty of resolving the problem. Fire-makers burn the woody parts of trees and other plants.

Whether or not a problem exists depends upon how much potential fuel is produced by the site, how much of the potential fuel must remain in place for the health of the ecosystem, the amount of fuel consumed, and the method of gathering the fuel. Generally speaking, high-elevation sites produce less fuel than low-elevation sites. For example, a forest in the Pacific Northwest of the United States might produce nearly a hundred times more fuel per acre at 2,000 feet (650 meters) than at 6,500 feet (2,100 meters). Unfortunately, consumption often exceeds production even in the low-elevation sites yielding large quantities of fuel. Outdoor pursuits are increasingly popular, activity is typically concentrated along rivers and trails, and the environmental consciousness-raising of the last decades hasn't significantly diminished the appeal of the campfire. The result is thousands of seriously overtaxed sites nestled within forests otherwise well-endowed with burnable woody debris.

In many wilderness and back-country areas the problem is compounded by the tendency of

hikers to favor the high-elevation trails and campsites. Anyone who has wandered through the Alpine wilderness area of the United States or Canada over the last fifteen or twenty years can testify to the recent ravages of fuel-hungry campers who lay waste to countless trees of all ages, including the spectacular silver-grey gnarled snags that once were so common. Many acres now prohibit campfires altogether, usually after consumption of almost all of the accumulated fuels and many living trees. But in most areas the option of whether or not to have a fire is still left open. The choice is up to the individual, who unfortunately may lack either adequate understanding of or sincere concern for the environment, or both. Sites where options exist are a valuable opportunity for leaders. Given an option, the leader can help the participants decide whether or not to have a fire. Working the participants through the decision process will make them aware of the immediate site-specific concerns related to fire and should provide a basis for their future decisions vis-a-vis campfires.

These concerns need to be addressed before deciding to use a campfire:

1. The first consideration should be the overall concentration of fuel materials near the site. Careful observation of vegetation and ground cover in areas well away from the site should show the normal amount and distribution of these. Often the most accurate sense of a normal state comes from observations made along the trail during the day's hike because disruption of normal fuel supplies may extend a half mile out from the camps in popular areas. Unless fire suppression or other artificial means have altered natural patterns, the amount of potential fuel material on the ground should approximate the normal and healthy balance for that site at that time.

2. Look, next, at the site itself and at the area immediately surrounding it. Is the amount of fuel at and near the site close to normal? Has the site been partly stripped of "dead and down" wood? Have trees or branches been cut for fuel? A common pattern in popular areas is for there to be no fuel left on the ground within fifty feet (fifteen meters) or so of the fire ring. Signs of minor damage to

trees extends even farther. In a heavily abused site, broken-off limbs and axe and saw scars near the fire site usually indicate a lack of dead and down wood nearby since most people gather these fuels out to a radius of a hundred feet or more before hacking into standing wood. If the site appears to have nearly a normal fuel distribution close at hand, then a fire may be a reasonable option if fuels are gathered over a wide area and not lazily scavenged from the closest possible site. There are still a few more things to consider, however.

Other Considerations

Some other considerations should be obvious.

1. Are fires allowed?
2. Can the fire be safely contained and extinguished?
3. Will the site be scarred by the fire?
4. Is there sufficient air movement to carry the smoke away? Many lake basins have serious pollution problems caused by campfire smoke.
5. If you decide to build a fire, gather fuels over a wide area and don't use axes or saws. These tools leave permanent ugly scars and are totally unnecessary at almost all sites.
6. Consider using a tiny little stick fire consisting of two small rocks and pencil-sized fuel. This sized fire is fast and easy to cook with, uses little fuel and produces little smoke. Usually the site can also be returned to a near-perfect state in a couple of minutes. Those who use these fires seldom go back to the chimney and problematic old rock-ring design.
7. Leaders may want to point out that a campfire makes a group's presence obvious to any wildlife or other campers within a wide area due to noise (wood gathering and chopping or breaking), visual impact (smoke during the day and firelight at night), and smell (often noticeable miles downwind). The result is greater disturbance of the lives of local animals as well as less privacy and possible disruption of the experiences of other campers who may be seeking some sense of solitude.
8. Don't forget to consider those nifty little burn holes in tents, and clothing that smells permanently of wood smoke.
9. Finally, consider, too, that fires also tend to mask the sights and sounds and smells of the woods at night, as campers sit transfixed by the flames.

Final Thoughts

All of this is by no means intended as a blanket condemnation of backwoods campfires. The intent has been to point out some concerns that might not be obvious and to offset what, especially in America, amounts almost to campfire-mania. Leaders concerned about the effects of fires should study the matter carefully to gain an understanding of the role of fire in the ecosystem, and to understand the difference between natural fires burning fuels in place and campfires fueled by collected materials. It's also important to recognize that in many parts of the world forest fuel accumulations are far higher than normal because of fire suppression by land managers. This is in many regards just as hard on the system as excessive building of campfires, since it precludes natural processes necessary to the maintenance of open lands. Open lands, like fire-caused meadows, are vital to a host of plant and animal species. In areas of excessive fuel buildup, it should be remembered that the fire damage may be extremely high and that more campfires aren't the solution. The only way to return such areas to normal is to let nature take its course.

Minimizing Biological Impact

So what can leaders do to reduce group impact on animal life? Here are some suggestions:

1. Check with the resource management agency and/or local wildlife manager to find out what particular problems or concerns may exist in the area of your proposed route. Adjust your route and activities accordingly.
2. Travel quietly, camp away and preferably downwind from meadows and feeding areas, and keep children and dogs under control at all times.

3. Leave a clean camp. Food wastes should be either carried out or burned. It takes only a little debris from each camping party to begin attracting rodents and other scavengers into camp, along with the snakes and predators for which they themselves are food.
4. Keep all foods, shampoos, other soaps, detergents, toothpaste, insect repellents, and sunscreen products out of the water supply!

Food, soaps, and detergents in amazingly small quantities can add enough nutrients to lakes and streams to cause major shifts in both plant and animal populations. Consider not taking any soap or detergent at all! Many experienced backpackers make do very well with moss, sand, or fir cones for scrubbing, followed by a hot-water rinse. Swimmers should be careful to rinse off repellents and lotions well away from lakes and streams, especially in sub-Alpine or Alpine regions. Even dyes and soap residues can harm these fragile waters, so clothing, if it must be worn in the water, should be carefully rinsed as well. The idea here is to distribute the toxic residues on the more resistant land-based life forms, sparing more sensitive waters.

Minimizing impact on plant life starts with following the steps for lessening physical impact. In addition are the obvious considerations to not pick wild flowers, no matter how plentiful, and not cut down or into living shrubs or trees.

Those who like to identify species will be much more successful if they take small field guides with them to the outdoor site than if they try to preserve bits and pieces of picked flowers to identify upon their return home.

Minimizing Sociological Impact

Several suggestions are in order for minimizing sociological impact:

Littering

1. Take a few minutes at the trail head or put-in point to pick up the litter in the area, with the help of participants. The site will look better, you and the participants will feel good, and the amount of litter left by partici-

pants will be reduced. A person who has spent some time cleaning up litter isn't likely to remain part of the problem. Also have cigarette smokers pick up all the cigarette butts! Maybe that will convince them that stepping on them doesn't make them vanish!
2. Set a good example by picking up any and all litter found along the trail. Some leaders of kids like to use an incentive program with prizes for those who find the most litter. This may work for some groups, although praise and a sense of pride may be better than material rewards.
3. Provide litter bags so each person overcomes initial reluctance based on fears of getting their pockets or gear dirty.
4. Never bury trash. Set a good example and carry it out. Trash pits result in unnecessary damage to the soil, and are usually uncovered by foraging bears and other animals who then scatter the debris. Even if burial is successful, the trash is still there and will take an extremely long time to decompose if it contains plastic, aluminum, or glass. Carry it out!
5. Consider repackaging foods and other supplies before heading out to minimize or eliminate unnecessary packaging.
6. If a fire is used, don't try to burn plastics or metal — especially aluminum cans or foil. It's far, far easier to put empty plastic, aluminum, and foil wrappers and containers into a trash bag and carry them out. If foil-lined wrappers are burned, the foil remains in the fire. Initially blackened, it's hard to see and messy to retrieve and carry out. After one or two rainstorms, scorched foil is washed clean and shiny, then blown by winds out into the surrounding area to accumulate as part of a permanent legacy of debris.
7. Consider stopping by the office of the land-management agency on the way back from the outing to present the trash your group has collected. If this isn't convenient, you might send in a few shots of the group and the bags of litter you've collected. Organized groups are often criticized by individuals and small private parties because of real or imagined overuse of certain resources, so this is a purely political gesture designed to better

the image of organized groups in the eyes of managers and the public.

Sanitation

Here are some suggestions for minimizing health risks and aesthetic problems related to sanitation.

1. When possible, minimize the amount of fecal waste and urine deposited in the wilderness. This doesn't mean teaching techniques of self control — what we have in mind is using the facilities at home or at trailheads, considering day hikes or shorter visits to sensitive areas, and keeping food intake moderate on longer outings.
2. Reduce impact on sensitive sites by taking appropriate stops outside of the sensitive areas and at lower or higher sites.
3. Carefully assess the possibility of contamination of water supplies, and issue clear directions to participants. Remember that in many areas, especially at high elevations or in glacially scoured areas, the bedrock may be near the surface. Rain or spring-snow melt can easily wash water into the water supplies, so note drainage patterns!
4. Select campsites that are near desirable toilet sites and well away from bodies of water. Some land managers specify 200 feet (65 meters) or more. This is because it's well known that in the middle of the night most campers are not going to stumble 200 feet off into the bushes. If tent partners are tolerant, they are more likely to take about two giant steps away from the tent. It is necessary, therefore, to place the camp itself in a safe place vis-a-vis sanitation.
5. Discuss procedures clearly and openly with all participants. If a latrine is used, explain how to find it and how to use it. Usually, however, latrines are not a good idea unless the site is at low elevation, has a very thick (2-3 foot) duff layer, and does not drain into any water supplies. Catholes are generally superior and are almost always the best solution at high elevations. Like a cat, scratch a shallow depression no more than a few inches into the duff. This insures that the fecal matter will be within the upper level where biologic activity can begin the process

of biodegration. Cover the spot with scratched-out material. Small logs or rocks can also be temporarily moved and the space beneath used. This is a considerate way to do it in places where others may walk later. Toilet paper, if brought along, should be used sparingly, then ignited. The unused portions will burn, and the rest will be disposed of by insects and other decomposers. *Be sure that the duff isn't ignited too.* Snow and moss both work as well as toilet paper and aren't as uncomfortable as they may sound.

THE RIVER — A SPECIAL CASE

The river is a special environment with travel taking place on the water and eating and sleeping taking place on the land, often right next to the water. The entire topic of minimum impact on the river is thus presented in this section.

Whether you are enjoying the peaceful solitude of a lazy day on the river or challenging yourself with a new section of white water, river running is a very satisfying outdoor experience. As more and more folks of all ages turn to rafting, kayaking, drifting, and canoeing, environmental damage in and along the river increases, including: lost equipment, fire damage to soil and vegetation, human waste, water waste, and litter.

Minimizing environmental impact on river trips begins during the planning stage. A good place to start is with the literature available in libraries, the Forest Service, and the Bureau of Land Management Offices, or the Outdoor Program room at colleges and universities. Each river has a different management plan. Check the information on the river you plan to run. The *River Information Digest* published by Interagency White-water Committee is a good source of information for specific river regulations and includes addresses and phone numbers of the management agencies if additional information is needed. Most river regulations center around campfire use, human waste, waste water, and garbage disposal.

Repackaging or containerizing foodstuffs is another step to consider before you get on the water. Properly packaged food will minimize spoilage and loss as well as confusion. Plastic containers are lightweight, reusable, and water-tight and prevent cut feet and equipment damage. Most food items can be containerized with poly bottles. Eggs are best stored in Styrofoam cartons or special containers available from camping-equipment stores, and aluminum cans are superior to glass containers. Remember that you'll have to pack it out, so look for containers that are lightweight, nonbreakable, and waterproof. Aluminum and plastic fit this description.

Once on the river it's important to pack the craft well and secure all equipment from loss. Personal equipment and camera gear are best packed at the bow for easy access. Using spring clips is a fast and easy method to secure gear. Lash equipment down well and check, particularly before entering white-water rapids. The food cooler fits well at the stern, again fastened with handy spring clips. To prevent injury in white water, the rocket box porta-potty, fire pan, and grill, and raft-repair kit are best stored in the stern.

Campfire Use

The use of fire in the outdoors is always the most potentially hazardous environmental impact. Many rafters find stoves to be the fastest, easiest, and cleanest method of cooking. In fact, some rivers such as the Colorado *require* the use of stoves. Fire pans are the next best option for minimizing fire damage. Fire pans are required on the Salmon and Owyhee Rivers, recommended on the Rogue and Selway, and even provided for rafters on the Green. Fire pans can be a garbage-can lid or the bottom of a charcoal pan. Necessary equipment includes fire pan, grill, small shovel, and water container for fire control. To use the fire pan:

1. Locate it below the high-water mark so that any coals that may spill out will be washed away.
2. Douse the area and set the fire pan on rocks to prevent scorching the substrate and destroying soil microorganisms.
3. Small sticks burn hot and break down into small ashes. Large logs burn slowly and sometimes never burn completely.

4. Keep a bail bucket or other container of water nearby for fire control.
5. Once you've enjoyed the meal, moisten the ashes until they are cool and shovel them into an ammo can, purchased from a surplus or outdoor store.
6. At the next camp empty the ashes into the fire to break them down finer as the trip progresses.
7. When finished, it's a good idea to douse the area again to prevent burned feet.

Human Waste

1. When in a small group on rivers with no regulations regarding human waste, urinate or defecate above the high-water mark and at least 100 feet away from the river.
2. Use a small shovel or trowel to dig a hole 6-8 inches deep. Decomposition takes place fastest in the top layers of soil.
3. Carefully cover up the hole when finished.
4. Carry the toilet paper out in a plastic bag.

Use of the rocket-box-porta-potty method is best for large groups. The rocket box is a large surplus ammo can and is sufficient for twelve people on a five-to-six-day trip.

Other equipment includes a toilet seat, large heavy-duty plastic bags, a chemical deodorant or chlorine bleach to prevent methane gas production, toilet paper, and hand-washing bucket. To use the rocket box porta-potty:

1. Line the box with two layers of plastic bags, and fold over the edge.
2. Pour in the deodorant.
3. Place toilet paper, tampons, and sanitary napkins in the toilet.
4. Keep the hand-washing bucket nearby. Cover the entire operation with another bag if flies are a problem.
5. To dismantle after a day's use, squeeze out excess air. An efficient way to do this is to immerse in a bucket of water and tie off.
6. Place this bag in another large plastic bag. As other bags are used, store them in the same kitchen bag.
7. Store the whole thing in the rocket box, ready for future use.

Waste Water

For meals with numerous plates, cups, silverware, and pots, the best dishwashing procedure is the three-bucket wash method:

1. In the first bucket add very hot water and some biodegradeable dishwashing soap.
2. Use second bucket for rinsing.
3. In the third bucket add a capful of chlorine bleach to disinfect the dishes.

To dispose of the waste water, dig a hole above the high-water mark and at least 100 feet away from the river. Carefully remove the sod. Use a collander or cheesecloth to strain off food particles and dispose of in the garbage. Toothbrushing waste can also be disposed of in the waste-water hole.

When you leave the site, carefully replace the sod and stamp it down. If you must shower with soap, use it sparingly. Have a friend rinse you off well away from the river. Never put soap in side streams or in the river.

Garbage

Large plastic bags are good for garbage. Burn the burnable if you are using a fire pan. Do not burn plastic, Styrofoam, or aluminum foil. The rest of the garbage should be segregated into recyclable and non-recyclable. Both can be placed in a reinforced bag such as a feedbag or gunny sack to prevent puncture and loss, then tied securely to the craft.

As the trip progresses and food supplies diminish, the garbage sack can be stored in an empty cooler. With an awareness of potential environmental impacts, the right equipment, and the proper techniques you, too, can minimize environmental damage on river trips.

So what, one might ask. Leaders should be prepared to respond to such comments, since it really isn't obvious why we should be concerned about such changes.

Most participants will begin to appreciate the issues if they are clearly explained. A good point to discuss might be the value of biological baselines. Another point worth attention is that only a relatively tiny part of the earth now remains in anything resembling a pristine state.

In the United States, for instance, designated wilderness areas in the continuous 48 states include only about 1% of that land mass, an acreage roughly equivalent to that under asphalt and concrete in the same 48 states! Surely we can afford to be a bit fussy about such a special resource.

One (perhaps the most important) outcome of outdoor recreation is the development of a sense of stewardship, a sense of caring for the land, and a commitment to protecting the land from damage. Because no one knows how to determine the fine line between land of good quality and land of poor quality, the outdoor leader must be careful not to approach the peak of carrying capacity. Evidence of change in quality and return to a state of quality is difficult if not impossible to measure.

SUMMARY

It is the responsibility of the outdoor-pursuit leader to practice a strong environmental ethic and to teach participants to do likewise. Caring for the natural environment includes understanding the concept of carrying capacity from the biological, physical, and sociological point of view, and practicing minimum-impact camping techniques.

Participants need to understand how to prevent soil compaction and abrasion, how to avoid altering the quality of water resources, how to care for human waste, garbage, and litter, and how to leave the natural environment as nearly natural as possible. Developing an attitude of stewardship for the land is one of the major goals of outdoor leaders.

BIBLIOGRAPHY

Frissell, Sidney, and Stankey, George H., *Wilderness Environmental Quality: Search for Social and Ecological Harmony,* Paper presented at the annual meeting, Society of American Foresters, Hot Springs, Ark., Oct. 4, 1972.

Greist, David A., "Risk Zoning: A Recreation Management System and Method of Measuring Carrying Capacity," *Journal of Forestry,* 1975, 73: 11, pp. 711-714.

Greist, David A., "The Carrying Capacity of Public Wild Land Recreation Areas: Evaluation of Alternative Measures," *Journal of Leisure Research,* 1976, 8(2), pp. 123-128.

Hendee, John C., Stankey, George H., and Lucas, Robert C., *Wilderness Management,* Washington, D.C.: U.S. Department of Agriculture, 1978.

Leopold, Aldo, *Sand County Almanac and Sketches from Here and There,* London: Oxford University Press, 1966.

Lime, David W., and Stankey, George H., "Carrying Capacity: Maintaining Outdoor Recreation Quality," *Forest Recreation Proceedings,* Upper Darby, PA: Northeast Range and Experiment Station, 1971.

Lucas, Robert C., "Wilderness: A Management Framework," *Journal of Soil and Water Conservation,* 1973, 28(4), pp. 150-154.

Manning, Harvey, *Backpacking, One Step at a Time,* Seattle: The REI Press, 1972.

Nash, Roderick, *Wilderness and the American Mind,* New Haven, CT: Yale University Press, 1973.

Stankey, George H., "A Strategy for the Definition and Management of Wilderness Quality," *Natural Environment: Studies in Theoretical and Applied Analysis,* John V. Krutilla, editor, Baltimore: The Johns Hopkins University Press, 1972, pp. 88-114.

Stankey, George H., *Visitor Perception of Wilderness Recreation Carrying Capacity,* USDA Forest Service Research Paper, Inc., 1973, p. 142.

Stankey, George H., "Wilderness: Carrying Capacity and Quality," *Naturalist,* 1971, 22(3), pp. 7-13.

A SHELTERED BACK-COUNTRY CAMPSITE
The tent is situated within the needle-fall zone of conifers and near the edge of a very small clearing. The needle bed is durable (resistant to compaction), and the trees provide a visual screen that reduces the visual impact of the site while assuring privacy. The site is also about 100 yards from the nearest water, a sanitary advantage.

CHAPTER 6

LAND-MANAGEMENT AGENCIES

Often these questions arise: "Where can we go?" "Where are the sites for outdoor pursuits?" "Who can use them?" In the United States, there are so many outdoor-pursuit areas and so many agencies administering them that choosing one can be confusing. Before looking at the agencies that manage outdoor areas, then, it might be wise to look at the methods by which recreational lands are classified.

LAND CLASSIFICATION FOR RECREATION

It is possible to classify land by many methods. Commonly used systems include those categorizing by forest types, life zones, hunting zones, water districts, agricultural soils, minerals, climate zones, topographic areas, and recreational uses. In 1962, however, the Outdoor Recreation Resources Review Commission, in its study of available resources for outdoor recreation, recommended a land classification system based on recreational uses. This system has now been adopted worldwide and has become the single land classification system of value in understanding the *recreational uses* of large areas that often serve other purposes. Table 6.1 indicates the five classifications (always identified by Roman numerals), examples of each, and available activities. The greatest amount of outdoor-pursuit activity takes place on Class III lands, partly because this category includes the largest number of acres and partly because it includes thousands of miles of trails and rivers for hiking and boating. Class II and Class V lands each are frequented by large numbers of outdoor enthusiasts, yet they are of far different types. There may be fine camping sites and many miles of trails or rivers in Class II land, which is usually part of a park with fairly well-developed facilities, telephones, and close emergency aid — good for beginners or novices. Class V lands are usually utilized by those who expect no amenities other than trails, and maybe not even those. Included in Class V are legally designated wilderness areas, roadless areas, and many others that have no legal designation but are remote, primitive, and lacking any development. It is important that leaders recognize the impropriety of conducting outdoor activities near Class IV or VI lands and the impracticality of utilizing Class I and much of the Class II lands. It is also important for outdoor-pursuit leaders to be aware that natural land is used for activities other than recreation.

Outdoor-recreation land managers and users also designate many land areas by their legally accepted terms. In addition to the classification system that defines recreational limits and gives guidelines for appropriate management, certain lands are designated by law for specific uses. Wild and scenic rivers, scenic trails, and wilderness paths are all titles of land or water specifically managed similarly no matter which agency owns and maintains the lands on which they exist. The following definitions clarify these differences.

Wild, Scenic, and Recreational Rivers

Wild rivers are truly primitive on at least four counts. They are unpolluted, inaccessible except by trail, free of impoundments, and have primitive shorelines or watersheds. River management focuses on preservation and enhancement of primitive qualities as the dominant priority, and no facilities for recreation, except trails, are provided.

Scenic rivers or river sections are free of impoundments and have largely primitive watersheds and undeveloped shorelines, but are accessible by road in places. Management emphasizes maintenance of a natural, though somewhat modified, environment, and a modest range of facilities for recreation is allowed.

Recreational rivers may have been much more affected by man but are still essentially free-flowing. Some past impoundment or diversion is permissible, but usually such activities are precluded in the future. Shoreline development

TABLE 6.1 Recreational Land Classifications

Class	Examples	Activities
I High-density recreation areas	Coulter Bay in Grand Teton National Park; Yosemite Valley; Huntington Beach, CA; Jones Beach, NY.	Sports, games, sight-seeing; use of many man-made facilities, marinas, etc.
II General outdoor-recreation areas	State parks; county parks; large city parks.	Picnicking, camping, hiking, biking, skiing, water sports, fishing, ball playing; many man-made facilities.
III Natural environment areas	Parts of National Forests, National Parks, large land holdings.	Hiking, camping, boating, fishing, hunting, almost exclusively; many trails, some picnic facilities, some pit privies
IV Unique natural areas	Old Faithful, Yosemite Falls, Bristle Cone Natural Area in the Inyo National Forest	Sight-seeing, nature study
V Primitive areas	Legally designated wilderness areas, (Boundary Waters Canoe Area, Lostine Wilderness), roadless areas, primitive areas.	Canoeing, hiking, climbing; some trails — no other manmade amenities
VI Historic or cultural sites	Valley Forge, Casa Grande Ruins, Mesa Verde.	Sight-seeing, studying history or culture.

TABLE 6.2 Components of the National Wild and Scenic River System

River Segments, State	Lengths		Year
	km.	mi.	Establ.*
Middle Fork Clearwater, ID	298	185	1968
Eleven Point, MO	72	44	1968
Feather, CA	150	93	1968
Rio Grande, NM, TX	393	53,191	1968,78
Rogue, OR	138	85	1968
St. Croix, MN, WI	406	200,27,25	1968,72,76
Salmon, ID	396	104,125	1968,80
Wolf, WI	40	25	1968
Allagash, ME	153	95	1970
Little Miami, OH	151	66,28	1973,80
Chattooga, NC, SC, GA	92	57	1974
Little Beaver, OH	53	33	1975
Snake ID, OR	108	67	1975
Rapid, ID	39	24	1975
New, NC	43	26	1976
MS, MT, NE, SD	335	149,59	1976,78
Flathead, MT	353	219	1976
Obed, TN	73	45	1976
Pere Marquette, MI	107	66	1978
Sakgit, WA	254	158	1978
Delaware, NY, PA, NJ	178	75,35	1978
American, N. Fork, CA	62	38	1978
St. Joe, ID	117	73	1978
Alaska Rivers:			
13 segments (N.P.S.)	2,037	1,265	1980
(Alagnak, Alatna, Aniakchak, Charley, Chilikadrotna, John, Kobuk, Mulchatna, Koyukuk, Noatak, Salmon, Tinayguk, Tlikakila)			
7 segments (F.W.S.)	1,876	1,165	1980
(Andreafsky, Ivishak, Nowitna, Selawik, Sheenjek, Wind, Beaver Creek)			
5 segments (B.L.M.)	935	581	1980
(Birch Creek, Delta, Fortymile, Gulkana, Unalakleet)			
Klamath, CA	460	286	1981
Trinity, CA	327	203	1981
Eel, CA	634	394	1981
American, CA	37	23	1981
Smith, CA	530	329	1981

*Some streams have more than one designated segment; these are indicated by more than one mileage and date.

and pollution may be present, but roads and railroads are nearby, providing easy accessibility.

Management of recreational rivers is strongly oriented toward providing for the visitor but maintaining an aesthetically pleasing environment. Recreational river areas usually provide a wide range of readily accessible recreational opportunities, more elaborate and numerous than in the other classifications. The environment may reflect substantial evidence of man's activity, however.

Classifications are also applied to segments of streams, labeling the first part of a designated segment wild, the second recreational, and the third scenic, or any combination of these. Few streams in the system are of one classification only, and an entire segment must be at least 25 miles long to be categorized. (See Table 6.2.)

National Scenic Trails

National scenic trails are major cross-country trails administered by the Secretary of the Department of Agriculture or the Department of the Interior. They provide opportunities for extended trips on foot or horseback. These trails may cross through lands administered by the U.S. Forest Service, National Park Service, Bureau of Land Management, Bureau of Indian Affairs, and other federal agencies, as well as lands owned by states, counties, and private individuals and corporations. None of the trails is entirely complete, and all users should inquire about and procure all necessary permits before attempting to travel on them. Table 6.3 lists the national scenic trails.

TABLE 6.3 National Scenic Trails

National Scenic Trails	Length		Admin.
	km.	mi.	
Appalachian	3,300	2,050	NPS
Pacific Crest	3,700	2,300	USFS
Continental Divide	4,990	3,100	USFS
North Country	5,200	3,200	NPS
Ice Age	1,600	1,000	Wi.DNR
Potomac Heritage	1,126	704	NPS
Natchez Trace	1,110	694	NPS
Florida	2,080	1,300	USFS

Wilderness

The term "wilderness" holds different meanings for different people. Psychologically, wilderness connotes a primitive, pristine, often remote and adventurous area. To some, the woods on the edge of a large city, the forested areas of a state park, or any area with a hiking trail can be perceived as a wilderness. On the other extreme, some people regard it as only those areas that have no obvious mark of humanity — no trails, no signs, no fire rings, not even any vestiges of earlier human occupation or travel. This is often referred to as the *sociological* or the *psychological* definition.

Legally designated wilderness, however, is land set aside by Congress and defined in the Wilderness Act of 1964:

> A wilderness, in contrast with those areas where man and his own works dominate the landscape, is hereby recognized as an area where the earth and its community of life are untrammeled by man, where man himself is a visitor who does not remain. An area of wilderness is further defined to mean in this Act an area of undeveloped Federal land retaining its primeval character and influence, without permanent improvements or human habitation, which is protected and managed so as to preserve its natural conditions and which (1) generally appears to have been affected primarily by the forces of nature, with the imprint of man's work substantially unnoticeable; (2) has outstanding opportunities for solitude or a primitive and unconfined type of recreation; (3) has at least five thousand acres of land or is of sufficient size as to make practicable its preservation and use in an unimpaired condition; and (4) may also contain ecological, geological, or other features of scientific, educational, scenic, or historical value.

The word "untrammeled" is defined as untouched, unaltered, or unhampered.

This Act, then, provided special areas managed for preservation and available for recreation by those seeking natural settings. As with most resources, the preservation of this environment is dependent upon the behavior of the visitor, though most are sensitive to the environmental quality, ecological factors, and psychological benefits of primitive areas.

WILDERNESS PERMITS

A problem arising is that a greater number of people are starting to seek the benefits mentioned above. As these numbers increase, improper behavior by some threatens the environmental value and quality of the wilderness resource, creating a need to control its use. Therefore the US Forest Service has adopted a permit system *which may be used* to regulate visitors *as the need arises.* The permit system also helps the USFS obtain important data about visitors which can be used to improve wilderness management.

The US Forest Service issues numerous types of permits such as special use, camp and day use, and outfitter guide. As outdoor recreationists and users of wilderness areas, we come in contact with the single-use wilderness permit often. To obtain one, you must give information on a form about yourself and other visitors, starting and finishing dates for the trip, location of entry and exit, primary method of travel, number of people, pack or saddle stock in the group, and number of watercrafts. The permit also requires a list of all camp areas in which your group is planning to spend the night.

The wilderness permit may actually be thought of as a "permission slip" to travel through or camp in a designated wilderness area. In the Pacific Northwest this "permission" is almost always granted. In other states, where the concentration of population has necessitated regulation of high-use areas, permission may be denied. If a permit must be obtained, even free of charge, it means there is a possibility that such permit may be refused.

Who must obtain a permit? All those individuals who plan to travel through or spend an evening in a wilderness area must. The single-use permit may be filled out by the individual or the informal group leader and be carried at all times during the stay within the wilderness area. This permit is designed for individual and/or family and friends who are pursuing an outdoor recreational adventure. On the other hand, an instructor or professional guide leading a group must obtain a special-use outfitters-guide permit, available through the District Forest Service Offices.

Where are permits issued? Individuals or small groups may obtain self-issuing wilderness permits at many of the trailheads in the Pacific Northwest region. Individuals, larger groups or pack-stock groups may also obtain permits from Ranger stations and field offices near the point of entry. If a trip extends through more than one National Forest or through both a National Forest and a National Park, permits should be obtained from the Forest or Park where the trip starts. One issued by the National Forest for a trip originating in the Forest Wilderness and ending in a National Park is valid in both places, and the reverse situation is also valid.

How are permits issued? Wilderness permits are issued free of charge by mail, in person, or by telephone. They are issued by mail at least fifteen days in advance by writing to the District Office or Ranger Station nearest the point of entry. They may also be obtained in person at trailheads, as mentioned earlier, or by visiting the Ranger Station nearest the point of entry during office hours. Information may be secured by telephone or, in some areas, arranged with the same phone call. Reservations are even available for a few wilderness areas which have capacity or trailhead limits.

Just as an elevator has capacity limits or a motel vacancies, the wilderness can only handle a limited number of visitors if destruction is to be avoided. Thus each area is divided into travel zones where computerized data from the permits is analyzed. To avoid overuse and overcrowding in some places in the United States, the number of people allowed in each travel zone per day is controlled by limiting either the number of permits issued or the number of people allowed to enter at a related trailhead. Controls are added or removed as environmental conditions change.

Why is a permit needed? Before 1940, wilderness travel in the high country was rare; therefore, natural resources remained in their natural state. Little information was needed about the back-country traveler. In some areas, registration cards were designed merely to "count heads," but these were rarely filled out by wilderness enthusiasts. Today this registration system exists only in certain areas. With the increase in back-country and wilderness travel, preservation of these areas has become a problem, and the wilderness permit has become an important management tool — particularly in those areas mentioned above where the impact of visitor use is endangering natural and wildlife resources.

According to the literature and certain administrative officials at the US Forest Service, census and control are still the main reasons for issuing wilderness permits. The former, for statistical analysis, collects information from the permit on visitor characteristics, number of visitors, and distribution of use. Then this raw date is keypunched and processed according to region. Computer programs compile and translate the permit data for management planning and administrative decisions, thus giving the US Forest Service information as to *how* many wilderness seekers are traveling into *which* popular areas for *what* length of time. After analyzing this data, distribution of visitors may be regulated to maintain a high-quality wilderness resource and to aesthetically protect the wilderness experience.

According to the USFS manual, the wilderness management plan considers all appropriate and compatible methods to distribute use within the capacity of the area. The second reason for issuing wilderness permits, therefore, is to assist the Forest Service with visitor distribution. Methods of visitor distribution may include:

1. regulating the use of saddle horses and pack stock;
2. restricting specific areas for certain forms of visitor travel;
3. informing visitors about less congested areas;
4. limiting the number of people in parties or the number permitted to stay overnight at specific locations;
5. limiting the number of users;
6. distributing information to encourage visits to lightly used or relatively unknown areas;
7. stressing the experience and value to be found outside the peak-use period.

In some states this method of distribution is now being used and will eventually serve more as a control factor in the Pacific Northwest

Region. California, Colorado, and certain areas in Arizona actually deny wilderness travelers "permission" to enter high-use areas to prevent physical destruction of the wilderness ecology from the impact of too many people in a given area at one time. This method of distribution and restriction is also on the planning table in the Pacific Northwest. Mount Jefferson and Three Sisters Wilderness Areas are being closely and seriously analyzed because of high use, though it will take approximately three years to implement this method of regulation. First the public must be educated in this problem area and then be willing to accept restrictions. This is what takes time.

A third reason for wilderness permits is to maintain the valuable spiritual aspects of a quality wilderness experience. According to ecologist Raymond Dasmann, man needs this. Without the wild country there will be no space left for that last wild thing, the free human spirit. Clinical evidence shows the spiritual benefits of wilderness to man's mental health. Sociologists agree that camping under primitive conditions provides people with a rare opportunity to release their hidden qualities and establish their identities. Therefore, the US Forest Service assumes responsibility to avoid creating the noise, crowding, deterioration, etc. that are typical of modern day high-speed living — and from which the wilderness visitor seeks to escape.

The fourth reason for issuing permits is to improve behavior through educational contact between the user and the Forest Ranger. User awareness of the proper "Rules of Behavior" helps to protect fragile features, and this personal contact may be an important educational link between wilderness conservation practice and visitor habits.

The wilderness permit offers many benefits to our wilderness resources and to us, the outdoor recreationists. It also assists the USFS in terms of administrative decisions, regulation of high-use wilderness areas, educational contacts, and the preservation of natural resources. Unfortunately it also creates many problems, which may be classified as administrative or philosophical. One current administrative problem is that of uniformity in distributing permits; methods of issuing are inconsistent within the Pacific Northwest Region. Some people have now become familiar with the self-issuing permit system, for example. They may decide to travel, upon a later date, into another area where permits are issued at the Ranger Station nearest the trailhead. The problem here is that people are confused as to which areas supply self-issuing permits and which require personal contact with the Ranger while obtaining the permit at the Ranger Station. Further, some wilderness areas do not even require a permit.

Within the Pacific Northwest Region, plans are being implemented to unify wilderness-permit distribution methods. The self-issuing method is working well within the Willamette National Forest, but not in the remainder of the Pacific Northwest Region because of incorrect data from permits or no permit use at all in some areas outside Willamette. Therefore the US Forest Service is planning to eliminate the self-issuing method and revert solely to agency issue (mail) and Ranger Station issue (in person). This means more staffing at Ranger Stations, more paper work at District and Regional Offices, and more enforcement in the field.

In some regions advanced reservations are available, such as the Mt. Rainier and Olympic Wilderness Areas. Advanced reservations pose another problem, however. For instance, the carrying capacity within Yosemite's travel zones is closely regulated. Wilderness permits for fifty percent of the carrying capacity may be obtained through "advanced reservations," while the remaining permits are issued on a "first-come-first-served" basis. The problem here is that individuals and groups may reserve three and four areas in advance, then make a choice as to which "reserved" wilderness area and permit they will use depending upon weather, travel distance, etc. As a result, the quota in some zones is not filled, but there is no way to predict the number of "no shows" to balance the quota with "first-come-first-served" permits.

A third administrative problem is that of regulating high-use areas. Computed data obtained from permits shows that while no terrible problem exists now, visitor use of the wilderness areas within the Pacific Northwest Region will eventually have to be regulated. This means that some wilderness enthusiasts will not be allowed into the area they wanted to visit and advised to change itinerary and travel zones because the requested area will be full.

With regulations and restrictions being imposed upon visitors, philosophical problems arise. Right now many people do not like the idea of wilderness permits at all and merely filling out the regimented form produces resentment; the wilderness permit imposes implied restrictions contrary to wilderness philosophy. Then enforcement becomes a problem. Even with a minimum requirement of forty hours of law-enforcement training to authorize an individual to issue citations, officers are an unwelcome sight to people in the wilderness. What kind of quality experience does a visitor receive if he or she encounters a policing agent while in the back country?

Philosophical problems tend to create ill feelings, and Roderick Nash expresses them very well in *Wilderness and the American Mind:*

> . . . the idea of the intense control that quota systems entail is difficult to square with the meaning of wilderness. Essentially a man-managed wilderness is a contradiction because wilderness necessitates an "absence" of civilization's ordering influence. The quality of freedom so frequently associated with wilderness is diminished, if not destroyed, by regulation. Campgrounds become sleeping-bag motels with defined capacities and check-out times. (p. 273)

Philosophical controversies and administrative problems are numerous regarding wilderness regulations and enforcement methods. Thus pressure is being put on the US Forest Service from both sides and they are caught in the middle — working for the preservation of natural resources while assisting with advancements in public outdoor recreation. "Damned" by angry wilderness users if they regulate high-use areas and "damned" if they don't, the USFS is also "cursed" by preservationists if they open up an area for free access and "cursed" if they close it. Problems will continue to exist until all those involved on both sides of the issue are happy. (Table 6.4 delineates the impact of alternative rationing systems.)

In summary, we can say that the wilderness permit acts as a management tool on which to base moral decisions in order to serve the public and protect the wilderness.

TABLE 6.4 Summary of Impacts and Consequences of Alternative Rationing Systems

| Rationing system | User Evaluation Criteria | | | |
	Clientele group benefited by system	Clientele group adversely affected by system	Experience to date with use of system in wilderness	Acceptability of system to wilderness users[1]
Request (Reservation)	Those able and/or willing to plan ahead; i.e., persons with structured life styles.	Those unable or unwilling to plan ahead; i.e., persons with occupations that do not permit long-range planning, including many professionals.	Main type of rationing system used in both National Forest and National Park wilderness.	Generally high. Good acceptance in areas where used. Seen as best way to ration by users in areas not currently rationed.
Lottery (Chance)	No one identifiable group benefited. Those who examine probabilities of success at different areas have better chance.	No one identifiable group discriminated against. Can discriminate against the unsuccessful applicant to whom wilderness is very important.	None. However, is a common method for allocating big-game hunting permits.	Low.
Queuing (First-come, first-served)	Those with low opportunity cost for their time (e.g., unemployed). Also favors users who live nearby.	Those persons with high opportunity cost for time. Also those persons who live some distance from areas. The cost of time is not recovered by anyone.	Used in conjunction with reservation system in San Jacinto Wilderness. Also used in some National Park Wildernesses.	Low to moderate.
Pricing (fee)	Those able or willing to pay entry costs.	Those unwilling or unable to pay entry costs.	None.	Low to moderate.
Merit (Skill and knowledge)	Those able or willing to invest time and effort to meet requirements.	Those unable or unwilling to invest time and effort to meet requirements.	None. Merit is used to allocate use for some related activities such as technical mountain climbing and river running.	Not clearly known. Could vary considerably depending on level of training required to attain necessary proficiency and knowledge level.

[1]Based upon actual field experience as well as upon evidence reported in visitor studies (Stankey 1973).

[2]This criterion is designed to measure how the different rationing systems would directly affect the behavior of wilderness users (e.g., where they go, when they go, how they behave, etc.).

(Source: *USDA Wilderness Management, p. 329*)

	Administrative Evaluation Criteria			
Rationing system	Difficulty for administrators	Efficiency—extent to which system can minimize problems of suboptimization	Principal way in which use impact is controlled	How system affects user behavior[2]
Request (Reservation)	Moderately difficult. Requires extra staffing, expanded hours. Record-keeping can be substantial.	Low to moderate. Under-utilization can occur because of no shows, thus denying entry to others. Allocation of permits to applicants has little relationship to value of the experience as judged by the applicant.	Reducing visitor numbers. Controlling distribution of use in space and time by varying number of permits available at different trailheads or at different times.	Affects both spatial and temporal behavior.
Lottery (Chance)	Difficult to moderately difficult. Allocating permits over an entire use season could be very cumbersome.	Low. Because permits are assigned randomly, persons who place little value on wilderness stand equal chance of gaining entry with those who place high value on the opportunity.	Reducing visitor numbers. Controlling distribution of use in space and time by number of permits available at different places or times.	Affects both spatial and temporal behavior.
Queuing (First-come, first-served)	Difficulty low to moderate. Could require development of facilities to support visitors waiting in line.	Moderate. Because system rations primarily through a cost of time, it requires some measure of worth by participants.	Reducing visitor numbers. Controlling distribution of use in space and time by number of persons permitted to enter at different places or times.	Affects both spatial and temporal behavior. User must consider cost of time and of waiting in line.
Pricing (Fee)	Moderate difficulty. Possibly some legal questions about imposing a fee for wilderness entry.	Moderate to high. Imposing a fee requires user to judge value of experience against costs. Uncertain as to how well use could be fine tuned with price.	Reducing visitor numbers. Controlling distribution of use in space and time by using differential prices.	Affects both temporal and spatial behavior. User must consider cost in dollars.
Merit (Skill and knowledge)	Difficult to moderately difficult. Initial investments to establish licensing program could be substantial.	Moderate to high. Requires users to make expenditures of time and effort (maybe dollars) to gain entry.	Some reduction in numbers as well as shifts in time and space. Major reduction in per capita impact.	Affects style of camping behavior.

FEDERAL LAND MANAGERS

In the United States, land and water utilized for outdoor pursuits consists of large holdings by the federal government, states, countries, and cities, as well as those owned and managed privately. Privately owned land useful for outdoor activities includes timber areas, farms, ranches, and nature preserves.

Table 6.5 delineates the acreage owned and managed by six federal agencies. Perusing the table will help you understand that most of the federal acreage is in states west of the Mississippi River, but that every one of the fifty states contains at least some federal land. As will be discussed later, most outdoor recreation occurs in USFS-administered areas. To learn more about who manages the federal lands, it may help you to study Table 6.6, which delineates the major federal organizations that hold the land used for outdoor pursuits. We can see that three federal departments administer most of these regions.

The Department of Agriculture

In the United States, the greatest amount of outdoor recreation takes place on land managed by the US Forest Service, a division of the Department of Agriculture. Forest Service lands are considered agricultural lands because of the timber crop that is planted, managed, and harvested there. The Forest Service, unlike the single-purpose National Park Service, performs a variety of functions. These are, simply, to manage:

Timber — the greatest amount of American lumber is harvested on National Forest lands;

Forage — grazing for domestic and native animals such as cattle, deer, antelope, moose;

Wildlife — most wild animals of all kinds, but particularly large species, reside within National Forest boundaries;

Water — much city water comes from the western half of the USA, stored in water tables deep under the carpeted floors of the national forests. It falls as snow or rain and eventually trickles through the soil to rivers, streams, and reservoirs;

Recreation — most American hunting, fishing, boating, hiking, camping, skiing, climbing, etc. occurs on US Forest Service land.

For the most part, outdoor activities are held on Class III and V lands. As of 1978, Forest Service facilities for these included:

1. 100,000 miles of trails for hiking, skiing, and snowmobiling;
2. 262 winter-sports sites, with over two million linear feet of ski lifts on 165 downhill ski areas;
3. Most of the National Wilderness Preservation System outside Alaska;
4. 128,000 miles of fishing streams;
5. Two million acres of lakes;
6. One third of the big-game animals in the nation;
7. 4,500 campgrounds with a capacity to handle more than 460,000 persons at one time;
8. 1,500 picnic grounds;
9. 660 interpretive sites, 52 of which are major interpretive centers;
10. 1,500 recreational special-use residential areas;
11. Seven National Recreation Areas.

The Department of the Interior

America's Department of the Interior has often been nicknamed the Department of Natural Resources, for it manages national parks, wildlife refuges, flood plains, mining, oil, gas, and several other resources. Within the Department of the Interior are four divisions managing the large amounts of acreage used for outdoor pursuits. The purpose of each component of the Department of Interior is different, as are their policies for recreation. The user is advised to be familiar with the differences in the agencies and their policies before considering their land for recreation.

The National Park Service

The National Parks of America may be referred to as living museums of natural and cultural resources. Included in the over 79 million acres administered by the National Park Service are national historic sites, battlefields, cemeteries, memorials, parkways, and the White House and National Visitor Center, none of which are available for outdoor pursuits. Nearly 55 million acres of national park land exist in the State of Alaska, and over 24 million acres in the contiguous 48 states and Hawaii.

It has been said that the National Park idea is one of the few cultural creations given to the rest of the world by the USA, though it was actually conceived by Indian painter George Catlin and implemented by Congress with the establishment of Yellowstone National Park in 1872. Today there are parks in 120 nations, including Canada, Russia, Germany, Australia, Kenya, Zaire, Zambia, Tanzania, and Switzerland.

The US National Park Service, formed in 1916, was charged with the administration of national parks and national monuments:

> The service thus established shall promote and regulate the use of the Federal areas known as national parks, monuments, and reservations hereinafter specified by such means and measures as conform to the fundamental purpose of said parks, monuments, and reservations, which purpose is to conserve the scenery and the natural and historic objects and the wildlife therein and to provide for the enjoyment of the same in such manner and by such means as will leave them unimpaired for the enjoyment of future generations. (Tolson, Hillary, "Laws Relating to the National Park Service, the National Parks and Monuments," U.S. Government Printing Office, Washington, D.C. 1933.)

Analyzing the purpose of the parks shows that their management must be a balance between preservation and use. This may appear paradoxical to many until they learn that national parks are not playgrounds and that any recreation there must be appropriate to the setting. National parks are basically single-purpose lands — lands to preserve unique national resources.

The back country of most national parks offers excellent opportunities for outdoor

pursuits, if carried out according to park regulations. Because national parks are to be treated as biological entities, hunting, fishing, and campfires are often prohibited, and areas for boating, hiking, climbing, etc. are carefully monitored. In some parks such activities are allowed only with a permit, qualified guides, or approved equipment. The National Park Service reported over 2.3 million overnight stays in back country areas in 1975, with about 1.8 million of these occurring on lands in wilderness or near wilderness.

Before taking a group (or going as an individual) into national park back country, be it designated wilderness or not, you should obtain user regulations and the proper permit for that park. As each may have different regulations, information should be obtained directly from the superintendent of the specific park in question. Further, anyone pursuing back-country recreation should learn about the uniqueness of the area and try to understand and practice camping and traveling skills compatible with management policies.

The Bureau of Land Management

The Bureau of Land Management (BLM) manages approximately 20 percent of the land in the USA, most of the Mississippi River. The agency is not well understood by most people, and Knudson describes it succinctly as follows:

The Bureau of Land Management has a longer history and broader jurisdiction than almost any other federal government land agency. One of the agency's predecessors was formed in 1792, five years after the Constitution was signed; the General Land Office was the official holder, recorder, and dispenser of public lands in the expanding United States. This is the group that administered the Homestead Act, gave lands to the railroads to open the West, and took title to Alaska, Oregon, and most other western states. Today it handles drilling on the outer continental shelf and federal lands.

The GLO's former functions were inherited by the Bureau of Land Management, formed in 1946 by a merger of the General Land Office and the Grazing Service, which had been established in 1934 by the Taylor Grazing Act. The BLM combined the duties of custodian and

TABLE 6.5 Acreage of Recreation Land Administered by Four Federal Agencies, 1983

State	USFS[1]	NPS[2]	C of E[3]	USFWS[4]	Bureau[6] of L.M.
Alabama	644,378	7,376		49,889	3,100
Alaska	23,043,437	54,667,615	44,412	76,061,834	166,984,847
Arizona	11,219,462	2,825,995	9,878	1,593,075	11,881,773
Arkansas	2,477,280	104,772	535,745	202,934	1,820
California	20,403,803	5,006,693	103,377	270,545	18,001,527
Colorado	13,818,593	595,715	18,050	56,857	8,346,472
Connecticut		4,181	7,457	183	
Delaware		25,380			
Florida	1,098,558	2,330,330	61,442	472,018	2,332
Georgia	861,364	63,184	338,838	468,438	
Hawaii		270,154		255,823	
Idaho	20,382,867	87,142	55,504	85,070	11,906,669
Illinois	253,240	12	154,682	118,063	28
Indiana	187,280	12,944	115,374	7,763	
Iowa		1,661	178,375	73,598	
Kansas	108,177	735	325,251	51,443	728
Kentucky	528,932	94,268	352,642	2,174	
Louisiana	597,839	20,000	44,131	290,433	3,962
Maine	41,833	64,662	17,028	30,883	
Maryland		65,241	8,126	26,077	
Massachusetts		49,982	17,028	12,220	
Michigan	2,753,544	715,709		108,537	766
Minnesota	2,710,546	241,220	31,383	442,124	61,275
Mississippi	1,143,688	119,602	708	113,173	627
Missouri	1,452,901	82,840	493,838	55,570	400
Montana	16,765,671	1,273,001	595,392	1,144,135	8,125,262
Nebraska	257,257	6,247	41,207	157,101	8,581
Nevada	5,150,088	702,927		2,360,924	48,281,508
New Hampshire	686,790	8,709	18,824	2,229	
New Jersey		50,095		39,721	
New Mexico	9,297,647	266,888	27,698	382,166	12,718,948
New York		90,784	5,895	23,522	
North Carolina	1,214,912	283,234	87,271	136,236	
North Dakota		72,081	475,322	1,263,462	68,206
Ohio	176,694	32,714	85,343	8,690	120

Oklahoma	248,085	9,536	746,173	140,927	6,988
Oregon	15,511,258	174,915	163,669	509,291	13,573,655
Pennsylvania	510,393	105,733	104,137	9,173	
Rhode Island		5		1,240	
South Carolina	609,329	20,981	150,245	189,487	
South Dakota	1,134,225	274,146	601,220	490,773	277,212
Tennessee	625,250	364,837	183,212	84,071	
Texas	665,082	1,149,709	814,090	290,615	22,750,844
Utah	7,989,521	2,096,866		101,815	
Vermont	294,023	4,365	6,077	5,755	
Virginia	1,632,307	325,597	123,720	105,193	
Washington	9,053,419	1,936,675	81,103	179,683	310,675
West Virginia	966,736	64,894	122,768	300	
Wisconsin	1,503,316	123,806		221,075	589
Wyoming	8,682,014	2,396,862		74,569	18,416,333
Territories	27,846	22,599		143,456	
TOTAL	162,619,803	79,392,206	7,689,403	88,939,713	341,059,245

[1]Source — US Department of Agriculture *Land Areas of the National Forest System as of September 30, 1983.*

[2]Source — US Department of the Interior, NPS Correspondence, March 5, 1984.

[3]Source — Department of the Army, Correspondence, April 2, 1984.

[4]Source — US Department of the Interior, *Annual Report of Lands Under Control of the US Fish and Wildlife Service as of September 30, 1983.*

[5]Source — US Department of the Interior, *Summary Statistics — Water, Land, and Related Data, 1982.*

[6]Source — Bureau of Land Management, personal telephone call, June 3, 1985.

TABLE 6.6   Departmental Location of Federal Land Management Agencies

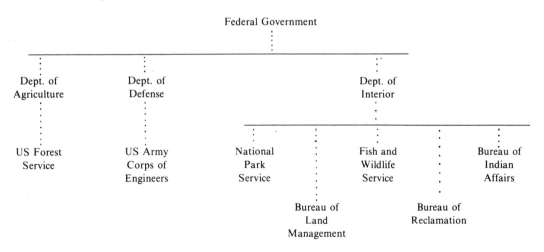

manager for grasslands, forests, deserts, and tundra that had not been claimed by the Forest Service, National Park Service, school grants, railroad grants, homesteaders, ranchers, speculators, miners, or states and their subdivisions. Now the Bureau of Land Management is responsible for the remainder of America's rich land bounty, though most of it looks like residue with some spectacularly notable exceptions. These include the highly productive timber lands of the reverted Oregon and California Railroad Grant, as well as beautiful mountain, desert, and arctic scenery.

This agency is not well known among the general public, especially east of the Mississippi. Until recently, its major constituents have been ranchers who graze their cattle on public lands for nominal fees, miners who prospect and stake claims there, and a dwindling supply of homesteaders and settlers. (Knudson, *Outdoor Recreation,* 1981, p. 256.)

In recent years, recreationists have discovered the beauty of BLM lands as well as many other attributes conducive to outdoor pursuits. The BLM identifies special resources for the purpose

BLM identifies special resources for this purpose, including:

thirty special recreation areas covering 3.1 million acres;
the California Desert Conservation Area, within 12 million acres of federal lands;
45 recreational and whitewater rivers suitable for outdoor pursuits, covering 2,500 river miles with four designated in the National Wild and Scenic River system and sixteen others being considered;
216 miles of National Recreation Trails and 5000 additional miles of trails;
250 developed recreation areas, including 4000 campsites and over 250 primitive campgrounds;
King Range National Conservation Area, covering 41,000 acres plus thirty miles of Pacific beach and two new conservation areas in Alaska;
A rapidly growing collection of wilderness areas.

The Bureau of Reclamation

The Bureau of Reclamation, like other federal agencies, was not created to provide recreation but by public demand and then by law. The Reclamation Act of 1902 empowered the Bureau of Reclamation to build dams for irrigation and hydroelectric power in seventeen western states, though many of the rivers dammed by the Bureau of Reclamation are now used for rafting, floating, kyacking, etc. This agency usually contracts the US Forest Service, the National Park Service, the Fish and Wildlife Service, or state and local agencies to develop and manage camping sites and sanitary stations along the routes.

The Bureau of Indian Affairs

Within the Department of the Interior is the Bureau of Indian Affairs. Unfortunately, many people assume that tribal holdings comprise part of the United States' "public" lands because the National Park Service, Bureau of Land Management, and Fish and Wildlife Service are "public" lands. It must be made clear that the approximately 51,000,000 acres of land granted to various Indian tribes by government treaty are *private* lands administered by tribal councils with assistance from the Bureau of Indian Affairs.

For all recreational activities conducted on tribal lands, permission must be granted by the tribal councils of the various reservations. Many National Forests and National Parks have boundaries contiguous to reservations, and often trails and rivers pass through Indian land. Part of the Pacific Crest National Scenic Trail in the southern half of California is a good example, as is part of the Mount Jefferson Wilderness Area in Oregon.

There are times that hikers and boaters cross over Indian land by circumstances of their routes. But any good leader will recognize boundaries designated on maps and respect the property as being private. Any time a journey of any length (i.e. several nights) includes camping on tribal lands, permission should be gained — just as on any other private land.

The United States Fish and Wildlife Service

Another Department of the Interior agency that manages large amounts of land with limited facilities for outdoor pursuits is the US Fish and Wildlife Service. Of the almost 89 million acres administered by this service, about 718 thousand acres have been designated as wilderness. This may be misleading to anyone who perceives wilderness as a legally designated area for camping. In fact, Fish and Wildlife Service areas are set aside as portions of the National Wildlife Refuge System for the main purpose of protecting rare, endangered, and/or migratory animals. Recreation on refuges therefore consists primarily of wildlife observation, photography, sight-seeing, and nature walking (82 percent in 1985). Of over 32 million visits in 1975 only three percent were devoted to camping — and that was by special arrangement.

Participants in the outdoor pursuits discussed in this book should never plan to use wildlife refuges for overnight trips or climbing. In some areas day trips for hiking, cross-country skiing, and boating practice are allowed with permission. Boat trips for those wishing to experience the solitude of the Okefenokie National Wildlife Refuge are conducted by licensed guides who have been granted permission to enter the wildlife refuge for a short distance. But they are part of a private non-profit organization that has leased adjacent land from the State of Georgia to carry out this activity — a rare use of wildlife refuges.

The Department of Defense

The Federal Government regulates commerce in the United States; consequently, it has the power to keep navigable streams and rivers open and free and to legislate relative to building or prohibiting dams. The Secretary of the Army has the primary responsibility for regulating navigable streams and also for studying and controlling floods. As a result, the US Army Corps of Engineers manages the largest water-resource recreation program in the country — nearly 8,000,000 acres of land and 3,000,000 acres of water.

For the most part, the Corps shares the management of lands adjacent to its water resources with state and county or other federal agencies. Further, most of the visitors to Corps of Engineers' water resources are daily or weekend guests who use facilities developed for camping, picnicking, boating, or swimming. Nevertheless, because of increasing demand for hiking trails, the Corps and its co-managers have started to encourage more non-facility-based recreation.

While not usually considered the ideal location for outdoor pursuits away from the amenities of civilization, Corps of Engineers' waterways do make excellent training areas for water skills needed in primitive settings.

The same may be said for the 600,000 lakes managed by the Tennessee Valley Authority, created in the 1930's, and the Land Between the Lakes area, created in western Tennessee and eastern Kentucky in 1964. Outdoor activities popular on these lands and waters include boating, fishing, and camping in developed campgrounds, yet opportunities for developing skills for other lands and waters are immeasurable.

PRIVATELY OWNED LANDS

In much of the USA, particularly east of the Mississippi River, privately owned outdoor-recreation land is available for the outdoor enthusiast. Generally, private land may be categorized as that belonging to timber companies, ranchers, or farmers. Since 65 percent of the marketable timber in America grows on privately owned land, there is much potential for outdoor pursuits here. Permission may be obtained from landowners to cross private land and to camp there from river or trail travel. In each case the individual land owner must be contacted for permission. Usually the landowner will be cooperative if some assurance can be given for minimum impact on soil, plants, and animals and if respect for property boundaries, fences, and gates is guaranteed.

LEADERS' PERMITS

Federal agencies in the United States are responsible for assuring use of government land on an equal basis to all citizens regardless of race, religious faith, creed, or national origin. Further, the government has developed a set of regulations designed to ensure that paid leaders charge fees that are fair to all, carry adequate insurance, conduct specifically approved activities, and care for natural resources appropriately. The various federal agencies administer leader permits differently and change from time to time. Table 6.7 is an outline of permit requirements for four federal agencies. Since these data are subject to periodic change, leaders are advised to check with the proper authorities before taking a group onto federal property.

Table 6.8 is a sample of the first page of an Outfitter/Guide Permit issued to an individual private leader who, on a private-for-hire basis, offered cross-country skiing lessons and backpacking and hiking in three national forests in Oregon between November 22, 1981, and June 15, 1982. It is included here to show that even in winter months outfitter/guide permits are required.

Following Table 6.8 are the first thirteen general provisions standardly required on all outfitter/guide permits. Provisions 14-27 are special and specific to the activities approved under this permit.

TABLE 6.7   Leader Permits Required For Use of Lands and Waters Under Federal Jurisdiction

Agency	Type of Group	Permits Required
I. US Forest Service	A. Clubs or youth groups with voluntary leaders	A. No permits required of leaders
(Use permits required of every group in a wilderness area.)	B. Youth agencies with paid leaders	B. Outfitters permit required
	C. Park-and-recreation departments	C. Outfitters permit required
	D. Schools and universities	
	1. Instructional program	1. No permits required of leaders
	2. Extra-curricular, extra-fee program	2. Outfitters permit required
	E. Private/commercial programs	E. Outfitters permit required
	F. Youth camp	F. Special-use term permits required

NOTE: All leaders have a legal responsibility for fire restrictions. Outfitter/guide permits require the itinerary, participants, dates, and a leader resume, as well as evidence of public liability insurance.

TABLE 6.7 CONT'D

II. National Park Service	Permits are issued on a case-by-case basis	All groups are advised to procure back-country permits

NOTE: Certain parks have a limited number of permits because of a need to protect fragile ecosystems from overuse.

III. US Fish and Wildlife Service	A. All groups	A. No camping permitted in any federal wildlife refuge
	B. Day-use groups	B. No permit needed; Refuge should be notified and permission for day-use requested
IV. Bureau of Land Management	A. Land-based activities	A. Usually no permits required (exception is for areas with potential environment damage)
	B. Water-based activities	
	1. Groups with volunteer leaders	1. Certain rivers require use permits for *all* groups
	2. Private/commercial groups	2. Certain rivers require use permits *with fees* for private/ commercial groups

TABLE 6.8 Outfitter/Guide Permit

U.S. Department of Agriculture
Forest Service
OUTFITTER/GUIDE
PERMIT
Land Use - Grazing

Authority: Act: June 4, 1897

Instructions: FSM 2700. Original to permittee, 1st carbon to S.O., 2nd carbon E.D.

a. Record No. (1-2)	b. Region (3-4)	c. Forest (5-6)
7 0	0 6	01, 07, 12, 18

d. District (7-8) Willamette	e. User No. (9-12)	f. Kind of use (13-15)
01, 04, 07, 08	— — — —	153

g. State (16-17)	h. County (18-20)	k. Card no. (21)
41	039, 043, 047	1

(Name)   *(Post Office Address and Zip Code)*

(hereafter called the permittee) is hereby authorized to use National Forest lands, as indicated below, in connection with outfitter and guide operations within the Willamette, Deschutes, Ochoco & Siuslaw National Forest at the locations stated, subject to the **General Provisions** on the reverse and to the **Special Provisions and Requirements,** items 14 to 27 on page(s) 3 to 5, attached hereto and made a part of this permit. The location of camps, routes of travel, and grazing areas (where applicable) are shown on the attached map(s), which is (are) a part of this permit.

TABLE 6.8 CONT'D

1. Camp Use:

Campsite Name or Number	Period of Use From	To	Maximum Use Days	Improvements
See attached itinerary.	11/22/81	6/15/82	709 Service Days	

2. Grazing Use:

Livestock Number	Kind	Period of Use From	To	Maximum Use Animal Mo.	Grazing Allotments

For this use from November 22, 1981 to June 15, 1982, the permittee shall pay to the Forest Service, U.S. Department of Agriculture, the sum of One Hundred Seventy-Five and no/00 dollars ($175.00).

This Permit is Accepted as Stated.

_____

(Permittee's Signature)   *(Date)*

Date: _____ Issuing Officer's Signature: _____ Title: _____

1. The permittee shall deposit his fee payment for land use and grazing with the designated Forest Service collection officer not later than the date specified in the Bill for Collection. The permittee shall not use the camps or permit his livestock to enter upon Forest Service administered lands until the permit is validated by paying the fees specified on the Bill for Collection.
2. Development plans, layout plans, construction, reconstruction, or alteration of improvements; or revision of layout or construction plans associated with this use must be approved in advance and in writing by the Forest Service.
3. This permit is subject to all valid claims.
4. The permittee, in exercising the privileges authorized by this permit, shall comply with the regulations of the Department of Agriculture and all federal, state, county, and municipal laws, ordinances, or regulations which are applicable to the area or operations covered by this permit.
5. The permittee, his agents and employees, and his contractors and subcontractors shall take all reasonable precautions to prevent, make diligent effort to suppress, and report promptly all fires on or endangering Forest Service administered land. No material shall be disposed of by burning in open fires during the closed season established by law or regulation without a written permit from the Forest Officer in charge.
6. The permittee shall exercise diligence in protecting from damage the land and property of the United

States covered by and used in connection with this permit, and shall pay the United States for any damage resulting from negligence or from the violation of the terms of this permit or any law or regulation applicable to the National Forest by the permittee, by his agents and employees when acting within the scope of their employment, or by his contractors and subcontractors.

7. The permittee shall fully repair all damage, other than ordinary wear and tear, to National Forest roads and trails caused in the exercise of the privilege authorized by this permit.
8. No Member of or Delegate to Congress or Resident Commissioner shall be admitted to any share or part of this agreement or to any benefit that may arise herefrom unless it is made with a corporation for its general benefit.
9. Upon abandonment, termination, revocation, or cancellation of this permit, the permittee shall remove within a reasonable time all structures and improvements except those owned by the United States, and shall restore the site, unless otherwise agreed upon in writing or in this permit. If the permittee fails to remove all such structures or improvements within a reasonable period, they shall become the property of the United States, but that will not relieve the permittee of liability for the cost of their removal and restoration of the site.
10. This permit is not transferable.
11. The permittee shall not sublet or enter into any third-party agreements involving the privileges authorized by this permit.

12. This permit may be terminated upon breach of any of the conditions herein or at the discretion of the regional forester or the Chief, Forest Service.

13. In the event of any conflict between any of the preceding printed clauses or any provision thereof and any of the following clauses or any provision thereof, the following clauses will control.

14. This permit is issued for the purpose of conducting a service defined as follows: teach cross-country skiing, backpacking, and hiking.

15. A late-payment charge in addition to the regular fees shall be made for failure to meet the fee payment due date or any of the dates specified for submission of statements required for fee calculation. The late payment charge shall be $15, or an amount calculated by applying the current rate prescribed by Treasury Fiscal Requirements Manual Bulletins to the overdue amount for each 30-day period or fraction thereof that the payment is overdue, whichever is greater. If the due date falls on a non-workday, the late-payment charge will not apply until the end of the next workday.

16. By accepting this permit, the permittee hereby agrees to comply with Title VI of the Civil Rights Act of 1964 and all requirements imposed by or pursuant to the Regulation of the United States Department of Agriculture (7 CFR, part 15) issued pursuant to that Act, and hereby assures in the operation and performance of this permit to take immediately any measures necessary to effectuate this requirement. If any real property or structure thereon is provided or improved with the aid of Federal financial assistance extended to a permittee by the United States Department of Agriculture, this assurance shall obligate the permittee, or in case of any transfer of such property, any transferee, for the period during which the real property or structure is used for a purpose for which the Federal financial assistance is extended or for another purpose involving the provision of similar services or benefits. If any personal property is so provided, this assurance shall obligate the permittee for the period during which he retains ownership or possession of the property. In all other cases, this assurance shall obligate the permittee for the period during which the Federal financial assistance is extended to him by this permit. This assurance is given in consideration of the Federal financial assistance extended in this permit to the permittee by the United States Department of Agriculture. The permittee recognizes and agrees that such federal financial assistance will be extended in reliance on the representations and agreements made in this assurance. The permittee further agrees that the United States, in addition to any other rights and remedies provided by this assurance, the Civil Rights act of 1964, or the regulations issued thereunder, shall have the right to enforce this agreement by suit for specific performance or by any other available remedy under the laws of the United States or the State in which the breach or violation occurs. Signs setting forth this policy of nondiscrimination, to be furnished by the Forest Service, will be conspicuously displayed at the public entrance to the premises, and at other exterior or interior locations as directed by the Forest Service.

17. The permittee shall indemnify the United States against any liability for damage to life or property arising from the occupancy or use of National Forest lands under this permit.

18. The permittee shall have in force public liability insurance covering: (1) property damage in the amount of Ten Thousand Dollars ($10,000), and (2) damage to persons in the minimum of Three Hundred Thousand Dollars ($300,000) in the event of death or injury to one individual and the minimum amount of Three Hundred Thousand Dollars ($300,000) in the event of death or injury to more than one individual. The coverage shall extend to property damage, bodily injury, or death arising out of the permittee's activities under the permit including, but not limited to, the occupancy or use of the land and the construction, maintenance, and operation of the structures, facilities, or equipment authorized by this permit. Such insurance shall also name the United States as additional insured and provide for specific coverage of the permittee's contractually assumed obligation to indemnify the United States. The permittee shall require the insurance company to send an authenticated copy of its insurance policy to the Forest Service immediately upon issuance of the policy. The policy shall also contain a specific provision or rider to the effect that the policy will not be canceled or its provision changed or deleted before thirty (30) days written notice to the Forest Supervisor, P.O. Box 10607, Eugene, Oregon 97440, by the insurance company.

19. Avalanches, rising waters, high winds, falling limbs or trees, and other hazards are natural phenomena in the forest that present risks which the permittee assumes. The permittee has the responsibility of inspecting his site, lot, right-of-way, and immediate adjoining area for dangerous trees, hanging limbs, and other evidence of hazardous conditions and, after securing permission from the Forest Service, of removing such hazards.

20. The permittee shall pack out or otherwise remove from National Forest land all unburnable refuse resulting from operations under this permit.

21. The Forest Service shall have the authority to check and regulate the adequacy and type of services provided the public and to require that such services conform to satisfactory standards. The permittee may be required to furnish the Forest Service a schedule of prices for sales and services authorized by the permit. Such prices and services may be regulated by the Forest Service *provided* that the permittee shall not be required to charge prices lower than those charged by comparable or competing enterprises.

22. The permittee, in his advertisements, signs, circulars, brochures, letterheads, and like materials, as well as orally, shall not misrepresent in any way either the accommodations provided, the status of this permit, or the area covered by it or tributary thereto. The fact that the permitted area is located on the Willamette, Deschutes, Ochoco, and Siuslaw National Forests shall be made apparent in all of the permittee's brochures and advertising regarding use and management of the area and facilities under permit.

23. Damaging trees and shrubbery is prohibited. Trees may not be hacked, cut, or damaged in any manner, nor may signs, wires, or other materials be nailed to trees.

24. The permittee shall maintain and operate ski-touring classes on the permit area. The director for said school shall be qualified to the satisfaction of the Forest Supervisor to give instruction and to direct others in giving instruction in all degrees of skiing proficiency required. Ski safety shall be emphasized in all instructions.

25. The permittee shall conduct the operations authorized by this permit with full recognition of the need for public safety. In furtherance of this requirement, the permittee shall prepare a safety plan designed to provide adequate safety to the users of the permitted area and facilities. The plan shall have the written approval of the Forest Supervisor prior to operation. The plan shall include, but shall not be limited to, avalanche identification and rescue equipment and procedures.

26. The permittee shall protect, in place, all Cultural Resources including, but not limited to (1) historic sites, buildings, ruins of buildings or cabins, and other structures such as corrals, water troughs, and fences; (2) historic artifacts or relics such as coins, cans, bottles, tools and all other historic items; (3) prehistoric sites, burial sites, rock art, Indian middens and all other evidences of pre-historic Indians; (4) Indian artifacts or relics such as arrowheads, spear points, stone tools, beads and all other prehistoric items. This responsibility includes the obligation to prevent the permittee's customers and guests from disturbing, injuring, destroying, looting, or collecting any cultural resource. Nothing in this clause shall be interpreted to prohibit permittee from showing or explaining cultural resources to such customers or guests. If the permittee discovers previously unidentified cultural resources, discovers a site or deposit is disturbed, or observes any person disturbing, injuring, destroying, looting, or collecting any cultural resource, the permittee shall notify a forest officer as soon as possible.

27. Unless sooner terminated or revoked by the regional forester in accordance with the provisions of the permit, this permit shall expire and become void on June 15, 1982, but a new permit to occupy and use the same National Forest land may be granted provided the permittee will comply with the then-existing laws and regulations governing the occupancy and use of National Forest lands and shall have notified the forest supervisor not less than one month prior to said date that such new permit is desired.

OTHER PERMITS

In many states, all camping groups are required to obtain and obey permits for campfires and individual licenses for fishing and hunting. Those hiking the National Scenic Trails may be able to procure permits to cover wilderness and fire use for the entire trip.

SUMMARY

The purpose of this chapter is not to educate leaders in the details of government and private lands and their management. Rather, it is to help the leader understand the responsibilities inherent in using such lands for outdoor pursuits. Thus the leader has several responsibilities when planning any trip on land or water. These include:

1. Determining who has jurisdiction over the land or water to be traveled;
2. Ascertaining a list of policies or regulations for using the land or water;
3. Obtaining necessary permits or permission to use the land or water for recreation;
4. Following the regulatory policies precisely.

It should be further pointed out that any time a group is lead by a person or organization that charges for the service, a use permit may be necessary.

BIBLIOGRAPHY

Brockman, C. Frank, and Meriam, Lawrence C., *Recreational Use of Wild Lands,* New York: McGraw-Hill Book Company, 1979.

Dasman, Raymond, *The Destruction of California,* New York, 1966, pp. 197, 199.

Hart, John, *Walking Softly in the Wilderness,* San Francisco: Sierra Club Books, 1977.

Hendee, John C., et al, *Wilderness Management,* Misc. Publication No. 1365, Washington, D.C.: Forest Service, U.S. Department of Agriculture, 1978.

Hendee, John C., Stankey, George H., and Lucas, Robert C., *Wilderness Management,* Washington, D.C.: Forest Service, U.S. Department of Agriculture, 1978.

Jensen, Clayne R., *Outdoor Recreation in America,* (fourth edition), Minneapolis: Burgess Publishing Co., 1985.

Knudson, Douglas, *Outdoor Recreation,* New York: MacMillan Publishing Company, 1984.

Look, Dennis, *Joy of Backpacking,* Sacramento: Jalmar Press, Inc., 1976.

Menninger, Karl, "Planning for Increasing Leisure," *Architectural Records,* 126, 1959, p. 198.

Nash, Roderick, *Wilderness and the American Mind,* Yale University, 1978, p. 273.

"Permits for Commercial Outdoor Recreational Facilities and Services," Publication No. 95-52, Washington, D.C.: U.S. Government Printing Office, 1977.

Personal interviews with Gale Burwell, Public Information Specialist, USFS: Jesse Waldstein, Applications Examiner, USFS; Ed Graham, Assistant in Recreational and Wildlife Management, USFS.

Stankey, George H., and Baden, John, "Rationing Wilderness Use: Methods, Problems, and Guidelines," USDA Forest Service Research Paper, INT-192, July 1977.

Stankey, George H., "Visitor Perception of Wilderness Recreation Carrying Capacity," USDA Forest Service Research Paper, INT-142, November 1973.

Stone, Gregory P., and Taves, Marvin J., "Research Into the Human Element in Wilderness Use," *Proceedings of the Society of American Foresters,* 1956, pp. 26-32.

Tolson, Hillary, "Laws Relating to the National Park Service, the National Parks and Monuments," Washington, D.C.: U.S. Government Printing Office, 1933.

US Department of Agriculture, *United States Forest Service Form 2300-30,* Washington, D.C.: USDA, (no date).

US Department of Agriculture, *United States Forest Service Manual,* Section 2323.12b, Washington, D.C.: USDA, (no date).

US Department of Agriculture, *Land Uses of the National Forest Systems as of September 30, 1983,* Washington, D.C.: USDA, 1983.

US Department of the Army, Correspondence, April 2, 1984.

US Department of the Interior, *Annual Report of Lands Under Control of the US Fish and Wildlife Service as of September 30, 1984,* Washington, D.C.: USDI, 1984.

US Department of the Interior, Correspondence, April 1, 1984.

US Department of the Interior, *Summary Statistics - Water, Land, and Related Data, Bureau of Reclamation,* Washington, D.C.: USDI, 1984.

PART II

ADMINISTRATIVE CONCERNS

CHAPTER 7

STAFFING OUTDOOR PURSUIT PROGRAMS

One of the biggest challenges for program administrators is staffing the outdoor component of the agency. How to locate, interview, and select capable leaders is a difficult task — particularly in the United States where there are no rosters of qualified leaders. How to train, supervise, and retain leaders once they are employed adds pressure to the challenge. An inability to locate and hire leaders in whom the administrators have the utmost confidence is possibly the biggest deterent to the initiation of outdoor-pursuit programs. In some places certification programs are available for those leading wilderness and climbing groups. Occasionally there are training programs for leaders of youth groups on weekend to ten-day trips on well-marked trails or rivers. In some countries there are certification programs for leaders of advanced skills.

GLOBAL PERSPECTIVES OF OUTDOOR LEADERSHIP

Five English-speaking nations are presently engaged in preparing outdoor leaders to provide for the needs and experiences of a population who actively involve themselves in exciting, adventurous activities. The current approaches for each country differ somewhat, but historically their origins can be traced to a common source: The British Mountain Leadership Certificate System. The program, begun over a quarter of a century ago, has served as the basis of similar programs in Australia and New Zealand, and has provided a reference for some North American programs.

United Kingdom

The United Kingdom was the first nation to institute a formal training program for outdoor leaders. In 1969 the Scottish Mountain Leadership Board, on behalf of the three outdoor-leadership training agencies in the United Kingdom, published *Mountain Leadership* by Eric Langmuir. Revised in 1973 and reprinted in 1976, this book provides much of the groundwork for candidates attempting to obtain leadership training and receive a Mountain Leadership Certificate.

Within the United Kingdom, a Mountain Leadership Certificate is accepted as proof of having achieved a minimum standard of proficiency in those skills important to teachers and other leaders in charge of children participating in high-risk outdoor activities. There are four levels of certification within the outdoor-leadership training scheme: Mountain Leadership (summer), Mountain Leadership (winter), Mountaineering Instruction, and Advanced Mountaineering Instruction.

The summer certification program deals only with the basic skills necessary to safely care for a group on walking and camping trips in the British mountains under normal summer conditions. The winter certificate is a more technical version of the summer certificate, oriented toward winter conditions most prevalent in Scotland. In England, Wales, and Northern Ireland, the two certificates are not differentiated and are simply referred to as a (combined) Mountain Leadership Certificate.

The Mountaineering Instructor's Certificate and the Mountaineering Instructor's Advanced Certificate are two technical qualifications intended for individuals wishing to teach mountaineering and climbing skills to school students and youth groups. The chief difference between the two is that the advanced certificate is seen as more appropriate for full-time leaders and instructors employed at British outdoor-pursuit centers. Both certificates are more of a professional requirement and deal primarily with teaching strategies and learning progressions. Recent projections have seen these two certificates joined.

Leadership certificates are awarded to candidates who meet the necessary prerequisites, fulfill the requirements set forth by the Mountain Leadership Training Board, and pass the assessment procedures that take place at an approved outdoor-pursuit center. The only prerequisites are a genuine interest in leading others in the outdoors and a minimum age of eighteen years upon entry in the program and twenty years by the time certificates are awarded.

Applicants who are accepted to the Mountain Leadership Certificate scheme undergo a residency of at least one week or a non-residential course of four full weekend outings. During this period the candidate receives instruction in the following areas: map and compass, route planning, walking skills, personal equipment, camping equipment, camp craft, security on steep ground, river crossing, special mountain hazards, weather, accident procedures, information on clubs and guidebooks, responsibilities of party leader, and related interests.

A period of at least one year of practical training follows, where the candidate puts into practice the technical skills learned during the basic training period. The experience from a minimum of sixteen days spent in mountainous country is entered into a log book that serves as a record of candidates' climbs and related experiences. During this period the candidate must also obtain a British Red Cross Certificate of Basic First Aid prior to his or her advancement to the assessment procedure.

The assessment takes place during a one-week residency held at an approved mountain or other outdoor-pursuit center. A written report and recommendations are made on the basis of examined knowledge, and observed performance is evaluated by a field assessor who accompanies the candidate on a scheduled expedition. The report and recommendations are forwarded to the Mountain Leadership Training Board for final approval before a certificate is granted.

In 1971, an unfortunate accident, referred to as the "Cairngorms Disaster" occurred. A teacher in charge of a party of school students was caught out in bad weather and five children froze to death in the mountainous Cairngorms region. In the years following this tragedy, The Hunt Committee on Mountain Training examined the mountain leadership certification scheme and made sweeping recommendations that focused on doing away with the certificate but retaining the training courses. In time a schism grew, with separate factions representing educators and climbers. The educators maintained that the certificate was necessary to provide a guaranteed standard of leadership care, and the climbers felt that abolition of the certificate would dispel the belief it assured competence on the part of all teachers and leaders.

Some important points were raised by the Hunt Report. The Mountain Leadership Certificate was seen as having an inflated value and appearing to attract the wrong people ("paper chasers") for the wrong reasons (interest in securing another "ticket"). The emphasis placed on safety in the training program was seen as excessive and destructive of the spirit of the adventure. The outcome was a lengthy political debate involving the sport's governing bodies and the Mountain Leadership Training Board. Changes were slow to occur, but the report was closely examined by leadership organizations in other countries.

One positive outcome of the tragedy was a massive influx of money into mountain-leadership training. Programs were improved and facilities were upgraded. By 1976, well over three hundred outdoor-pursuit centers run by individual school boards had been created in Great Britain. At the same time, almost every school board or educational authority had some form of outdoor-pursuit program in their educational curriculum. Certified leaders found employment in this multitude of programs.

Today, faced with dwindling finances, many schools have children attend some of the larger outdoor centers such as Plas y Brenin in North Wales; Plas y Deri, also in North Wales; Glenmore Lodge in Scotland; Brathay Hall in Cumbria; and Eskdale (the Outward Bound School), also in Cumbria. As the mountain-leadership certification scheme evolved, offshoot programs developed within the context of formal academic training institutes. Several colleges now offer diplomas and degrees in outdoor pursuits with congruent leadership certification. Examples include I.M. Marsh College of Physical Education in Liverpool, Charlotte Mason College of Education in Cumbria, Bingley College of Education in Yorkshire, Moray House College of Education in Edinburgh, and Bangor Normal College of Education and University College of North Wales, both in Bangor, North Wales.

The scope of *Mountain Leadership* by Eric Langmuir has had a far-reaching impact. As the Mountain Leadership Certificate grew to be the normal requirement for school teachers responsible for children involved in hill-walking or mountain-climbing activities, this related textbook became the standard authority throughout the United Kingdom, was used extensively in other European countries, and was further adapted by such commonwealth countries as Australia and New Zealand.

Australia

Of the seven Australian states, three actively involve themselves in the training of outdoor leaders. South Australia, Victoria, and Tasmania all offer certification programs in "Mountain and Bushwalking Leadership." The Victoria program was the first of the three, created in response to the concern that heavy use of outdoor teaching environments might lead to accidents and fatalities. The South Australian program is very similar to Victoria's, but concentrates primarily on training school teachers to care for children involved in outdoor-adventure activities. The Tasmanian program takes the Victoria system one step further by incorporating a unique experimental component, aiming more at commercial operators than at school teachers.

Historically, the Australian outdoor-leadership movement began with the first Victorian course offered in May of 1969. The program format at that time was heavily modeled on the British Mountain Leadership Certificate scheme currently used in the United Kingdom. Training materials were obtained from U.K. advisory training boards and the content adapted to suit local bush settings such as those which might be encountered in the Snowy Mountains region. Over the years that followed, many alterations were made as it became apparent that there were a few shortcomings in the British system of leadership development. These changes included the application of advisor and assessor panels and the introduction of preliminary appraisal sessions.

Today, a typical program for leadership applicants begins with an initial week-long residential course during which the technical and safety skills of each applicant are appraised and recommendations on their potential for leadership ability are made. If the applicants are lacking any major skills, they are refused acceptance to the training program and additional experience or outside training are suggested. Should they lack competence in only one area, such as first aid, they are accepted on probation to the candidate stage and directed to improve that skill with the appropriate training.

Once they have been recommended for leadership, candidates are assigned established, experienced leaders as advisors for one or two years. During this interim training period, they experience a wide variety of leadership roles with many different groups in a range of settings. These intensive and extensive experiences are recorded in a log book, then the candidates meet with their advisor to discuss the log. Once the candidates have collectively put in a minimum number of days as experienced apprentice leaders, they are once again appraised and recommended for advancement to the assessment stage.

The assessment stage begins with individual four-day trips with each candidate taking full leadership responsibility. An advisor attends as back-up leader, and members of an assessment panel go along to critique each candidate's leadership performance. If satisfactory performance is demonstrated on this trip, the candidates are advanced to a final, week-long residential-assessment course. During this time, a panel of advisors and judges observe and evaluate the leadership performance of several of them under a wide selection of actual and simulated situations. At the conclusion of the assessment period, candidates who meet the criteria for advancement are recommended for a leadership certificate. At any time during this process, any candidate who fails to meet a criterion has the option of withdrawing from the program or returning to repeat that stage of training.

Both the South Australian and Tasmanian programs follow this scheme, but with a few exceptions. The South Australian program, oriented toward outdoor-education teachers, concentrates heavily on the instructional capabilities of their candidates. Thus the program focuses on teaching strategies, instructional aids, and lesson planning.

In Tasmania, the rugged island state which lies south of Victoria, more emphasis is placed on safety skills such as accident response, route finding, weather interpretation, and search-and-rescue. The Tasmanian program also has more stringent application prerequisites than the other two programs. Applicants must be highly experienced in bush and mountain travel before they will even be considered as candidates. The result is a leadership-trainee group at an advanced technical-skill level that can concentrate on the more critical aspects of leadership development like group dynamics, decision making, and problem solving.

All three states make use of the manual *Bushwalking and Mountaincraft Leadership,* published in 1978 by the Victoria Bushwalking and Mountaincraft Advisory Board. The manual details six areas of concern for the leadership candidate: the leader, trip planning, the walk, food, the elements, and emergencies.

Appendices list further readings, equipment, food menus, outdoor shops, outdoor clubs, leadership skills, and general knowledge. As the program evolved, however, organizers realized that there was more to leadership than the technical skills covered in the manual. In time a series of informational papers specific to each state were prepared to compliment the course notes. These cover such topics as: conflict resolution, party morale, leadership style, group dynamics, decision-making, and environmental ethics.

One unique experimental component of the Tasmanian program is an attempt to adapt present leadership theories from the world of education, the military, and business to group-leading in the outdoors. Currently the program looks closely at the Vroom and Yetton Decision-making Tree, the Fiedler Contingency Theory, and several models proposed by Hershey & Blanchard, Valenzi & Bass, and Green & Mitchell. Participants in these study sessions are given written theories to read and assimilate. These are then demonstrated through simulated practice cases. Actual experience is gained by attempting to apply the theories on field trips, and course organizers feel the models presented by Fiedler and Vroom and Yetton have greatest application in outdoor-leadership situations. Their investigations, however, are quite new, and they are the first to admit that much more study is needed in this area.

No outdoor-pursuit centers in Australia offer formal courses in outdoor-leadership, but training boards do use some centers to operate the residential component of their leadership courses. Some training is also available within a tertiary education framework; Bendigo College in Victoria and several Colleges of Advanced Education throughout the country offer diplomas in outdoor education that are heavily oriented toward outdoor pursuits.

New Zealand

In 1977 the provisional Outdoor Training Advisory Board (OTAB) was formed to examine a national outdoor-leadership training system for New Zealand. The "Hunt Report" had recently been published in the U. K., advocating sweeping alterations to the British Mountain Leadership Certificate Scheme. OTAB's recommendations for outdoor-leadership development at home were based heavily upon the changes occuring overseas.

After lengthy and difficult discussion, OTAB formed a policy to approach outdoor-leadership training from a new and fresh perspective. They agreed to adopt an open-ended development scheme that did not present a certificate, thus implying that a candidate should continue to seek lifelong learning opportunities in outdoor-leadership training. A modular approach was also used that allowed the system to be flexible enough to meet an individual's unique needs, to be applicable to many levels of skill or experience, and to be available to potential leaders from many outdoor-pursuit areas and organizations. In addition, OTAB decided upon self assessment, rather than evaluation by a panel of board members, as a means to encourage leaders to take responsibility for their own training and development.

OTAB is designed to be an advisory agency. At present they assist other associations with outdoor-leader training programs at a "grass roots" level rather than dictating a mandatory series of courses for all leaders in general. They also operate a resource-and-information clearing-house based in the capital city of Wellington, and have two major publications of note: a self-assessment *Logbook* and an *Outdoor Training Guide*.

Authors of the *Logbook* are quick to state that entries should not be interpreted as a guarantee of leadership competence and that the responsibility for useful accuracy lies with the writer. The log has space for personal particulars, equipment checklists, training sources, and further information. New experiences can be recorded under three categories: Course Experience, for noting any new skills learned; General Experience, for listing personal trips; and Experience of Leading, for entering the details of trips where a responsible role was played. The Self-assessment section provides the opportunity to evaluate one's leadership capacity in fourteen core modules adapted from the *Outdoor Training Guide*. Such assessment, made from time to time, should be graded on a scale of 1 to 5, and *Logbook* owners are cautioned to be wary of overestimating their skills and knowledge.

The *Outdoor Training Guide* (interim edition, 1980) suggests suitable guidelines for leadership development and assessment. It details fourteen areas of leadership knowledge and skill, including: leadership theory, human growth and development, environmental issues, planning and organization, legal and moral issues, finance and administration, food and hygiene, clothing and equipment, weather, land navigation, interpreting the environment, first aid, emergency procedures, water safety.

Designed to provide a means for leaders, instructors, and course coordinators to analyze their personal strengths and weaknesses, and to respond by seeking an appropriate educational source, the publication also lists reading references and resource associations as sources available to all leaders.

Only one residential center in the country of New Zealand has any kind of involvement in the outdoor-leadership training; the Outdoor-Pursuit Center of New Zealand, located near the North Island volcanos, offers a yearly course based upon OTAB content that focuses on group-management skills more than mere technical-activity skills. The New Zealand

Outward Bound School on the South Island does not offer any formal outdoor-leadership development courses, but several teachers' colleges in major cities such as Auckland, Christchurch, Dunedin, Palmerston North, and Wellington do.

Canada

Canada is relatively new at the work of developing outdoor leaders. No recognized program exists nationally, but at the provincial level a few currently operate and others are under consideration.

The first to flourish in Canada was the Nova Scotia Outdoor Leadership Development Program, which serves three functions: as a clearing house for information on outdoor leadership, as a service program providing outdoor-leadership resources and class instructors, and as the sponsor of a basic course in leadership training. Willing applicants attend an introductory leadership school to obtain a groundwork in some of the more important leadership skills. As candidates, they apprentice in an experiential leadership role and then attend a leadership assessment school. Once they complete this program a certificate is *not* granted; instead graduates are encouraged to continue their training, self-assessment, and development as outdoor leaders.

The stream of leadership training follows a modular pattern. Introductory and assessment schools deal with teaching methods, problem solving, group dynamics, trip planning, and expedition behavior.

On their own, candidates must obtain the specialized technical skills in the adventure activities where they expect to lead parties and the necessary core skills of navigation, survival, campcraft, environmental ethics, and emergency procedures.

Many small outdoor-leadership training programs exist within tertiary educational frameworks in British Columbia, Alberta, Ontario, Quebec, and Nova Scotia. Some include Outdoor Recreation Management at Capilano College in British Columbia; Outdoor Pursuits at the University of Calgary, and Outdoor Education at Camrose Lutheran College in Alberta; Outdoor Adventure at Laurentian University; and Outdoor Recreation at Lakehead University in Ontario.

One important Canadian publication presents a most noteworthy and thoughtful approach to outdoor-leadership development. *Leading to Share; Sharing to Lead* was written by Bob Rogers for the Council of Outdoor Educators of Ontario. In his monograph, Rogers outlines the essential components of the adventure experience, lists the building blocks to outdoor leadership, explains that objective judgment is the clay for molding outdoor leaders, and presents a model of the development process. Environmental behavior, personal growth, technical skills, and safety are considered to be the essential components of any adventure experience. Rogers also defines objective judgment as being able to see beyond the excitement of the adventure and to evaluate the non-technical forces that act on the experience. Objective judgment holds together the many building blocks of outdoor leadership, which he groups under five headings:

1. Physiological Forces (micro & macro climates, first aid, hypothermia and hyperthermia, physical fitness);
2. Social-psychological Forces (human behavior, personal interaction, small-group dynamics, valuing);
3. Environmental Forces (weather, ecology, environmental land ethic);
4. Safety Forces (accident and emergency procedures, group security, special hazards, search and rescue); and
5. Technical Forces (navigation, program planning, route planning and expedition planning, group travel, personal and group equipment, wilderness skills, legal liabilities, outdoor clubs and community opportunities).

Roger's model for leadership development calls for prerequisites and evaluates training needs. Practical experience prior to assessment plays a major role in the scheme. The unique aspect of the model is the suggestion that outdoor leadership is not just certified training, but lifelong learning. Rogers is also quick to point out that certification of technical activity and motor skills should take place concurrently yet outside the training scheme.

Two centers in Alberta offer outdoor-leadership training programs dealing primarily with technical outdoor-living skills. The Yamnuska Mountain School, run by the Rocky Mountain YMCA near Banff, offers a wilderness-travel leadership course in conjunction with the Alberta Camping Association for persons wishing to lead back-country hiking and camping trips. The Blue Lake Center in Northern Alberta offers courses in everything from archery to wilderness nature crafts. This center is funded by the provincial Ministry of Recreation and Parks, and conducts outdoor-skills courses with leadership development in mind.

Three additional and quite notable outdoor centers operate in Canada, but none offer programs totally oriented toward outdoor-leadership development. Outward Bound Canada has two schools: a mountain school in the dry interior of British Columbia and a wilderness school in the lakes area of northern Ontario. The Strathcona Outdoor Education Society also has a water-based outdoor program on Vancouver Island in British Columbia.

United States

The United States of America has no nationally recognized outdoor-leadership development scheme. However, two private organizations train and certify outdoor leaders on a large scale. The National Outdoor Leadership School in Wyoming operates an outdoor center which administers a wide variety of outdoor-skills courses, including specialized courses for outdoor leaders and instructors. The Wilderness Education Association offers a number of leadership certification programs within many higher-education degree programs in physical education and recreation. Both these organizations were founded through the drive and initiative of Paul Petzoldt, a former Outward Bound instructor.

One publication closely related to outdoor leadership in the United States is *The Wilderness Handbook* by Paul Petzoldt. Though the author only devotes one short chapter to leadership, in which he touches upon the qualities and duties of an outdoor leader, the book also outlines his philosophy, on which the National

Outdoor Leadership School and Wilderness Education Association were established.

At the National Outdoor Leadership School (NOLS), the emphasis in leadership training is placed upon teaching capability and technical skills. Certificates at three levels are given: outdoor educator, outdoor leader, and NOLS instructor. The outdoor-educator certificate is awarded to skills-program graduates who demonstrate an ability to teach "no trace" outdoor skills; the outdoor-leader certificate is awarded to graduates of longer courses who demonstrate the ability to lead groups in the outdoors; and the NOLS instructor certificate is given to outdoor leaders who pass the specialized instructor course, apprentice for one season, and effectively carry out the philosophy of the National Outdoor Leadership School.

The Wilderness Education Association (WEA) was founded in 1976 with the aim of preparing outdoor leaders to safely lead others in enjoyable outdoor experiences, to make sound decisions under a variety of conditions, and to conserve the beauty and natural resources of the wilderness. WEA offers the National Standard Program for Outdoor Leadership Certification, geared toward developing quality judgment and decision-making ability in outdoor leaders. The curriculum includes expedition behavior, environmental ethics, expedition planning, group-handling skills, recognizing abilities and limitations, enjoyment (of the wild outdoors), safety systems, and rescue and evacuation techniques.

In an attempt to decrease liability insurance costs, the national office of Outward Bound has directed each individual school to develop a certification scheme for Outward Bound instructors. The North Carolina school has recently responded with the Kurt Hahn Leadership Center for Outdoor Educators; the other four schools are expected to follow suit in the near future.

Many universities and colleges in the United States offer academic credit for participation in outdoor-skills programs run by such organizations as NOLS, WEA and Outward Bound. Several more offer similar programs of their own in technical outdoor-skill areas. Some are the University of Oregon, the University of Minnesota, the University of Montana, Idaho

State University, Central Washington University, Eastern Washington State University, Brigham Young University in Utah, and Unity College in Maine.

A plethora of tertiary education institutes offer single outdoor-pursuit courses and call them outdoor-leadership training, but in fact they cover only one aspect of the leadership development process: activity safety skills. These courses are an appropriate start to outdoor-leadership development, but, as is apparent from the lists of curricula from around the world, there is more to outdoor leadership than technical proficiency, including organizational ability, instructional capabilities, group-dynamics facilitation, and experience-based judgment.

More often than not, the term "outdoor leadership" has been used as a buzzword to describe learning about different aspects of outdoor pursuits in North America. This misuse of the term has led to heated debate over what constitutes outdoor leadership and whether or not the capacity for it can actually be certified based on the manner in which technical skill proficiency is currently evaluated.

THE CERTIFICATION ISSUE

One may wonder why the United States has not developed a nationally agreed-upon certification system. Several reasons can be cited for this gap in leadership standards, and some are interrelated.

1. If certification were required of all outdoor-pursuit leaders, there would be no universally agreed-upon set of prerequisite skills and knowledge. Outdoor pursuits in the USA take place in forests, deserts, jungles, prairies, glacier-covered mountains, and rocky spires, and on immense lakes, roaring rivers, flat ponds, and countless other settings. No one has conjectured whether leaders should be certified for one, some, most, or all those areas.
2. If certification were required, who or what would be the certifying agency? A survey by Senosk in 1972 found that outdoor leaders did not want the federal government to be

the certifying body, but had no suggestions concerning who it *should be*.
3. For what activities would a certified leader be required? Americans are independent folks who wish to try things on their own. A non-sponsored activity or an activity pursued by a group of common adventurers would not warrant certified leaders. At what point could certified leaders be utilized? A scout group on a weekend outing? A college class on a weekend outing? A private climbing club?

   Some people feel that certified leaders should be required for any group going into the woods or onto the rivers. Others feel only those offering wilderness trips for a fee should be certified.
4. What does certification do? What are its advantages? Certainly outdoor pursuit certification does not guarantee that the leader will run a safe program anymore than a driver's license guarantees the holder will drive safely.
5. If the advantages of certification are a guarantee that the holder of the certificate has attended and passed a training session, who should sponsor the training session and what should the contents be?

Thus we come full circle, back to the question on skills and knowledge. Regardless of how each individual thinks about the subject, the fact remains that there is no widely agreed-upon certification program in the United States; why have one, what should it consist of, and who should bear the responsibility for it? In the absence of certification, the administrator can do several things to assure the hiring of a reasonably capable staff.

HIRING THE LEADER

Before seeking a leader, it is best to develop a job description that outlines the leader's duties and qualifications, and the agency to whom he or she will be responsible. Job descriptions vary a great deal from job to job and should be written specifically for each situation. Figures 7.1 and 7.2 are examples of job descriptions developed for a supervisor and for a leader in a community recreation department.

FIGURE 7.1 Job Description of Outdoor Supervisor

SUPERVISOR POSITION

MAIN FUNCTION:
Work with the Outdoor/Environmental Coordinator in planning, organizing, and supervising a total outdoor/environmental program.

EDUCATION:
A college degree in recreation management or a related field.

EXPERIENCE:
At least two years of experience in a variety of outdoor activities. (Leadership and supervisory qualities are important.)

DUTIES:
1. Plan, organize, and direct a year-round program in outdoor recreation and environmental education.
2. Provide face-to-face leadership as needed.
3. Assist in budgeting and finance control.
4. Promote outdoor/environmental programming through basic media and by speaking to various groups.
5. Supervise part-time and volunteer leaders and assist in training sessions.
6. Participate with other outdoor/environmental groups in various areas of consultation and assistance.
7. Promote outdoor safety.
8. Relate outdoor/environmental potentials to other activity areas within the department such as community centers, handicapped, senior citizens, and youth.
9. Assist the Outdoor/Environmental Coordinator in keeping adequate department records such as attendance reports, equipment inventories, and staff and program evaluation.
10. In general, assist the Outdoor/Environmental Coordinator in developing better outdoor and environmental programs.

RESPONSIBLE TO:
Outdoor/Environmental Coordinator.

FIGURE 7.2 Job Description of a Short-Term Outing Leader

LEADER POSITION

MAIN FUNCTION:
To lead an outdoor-oriented activity.

EXPERIENCE:
Display knowledge, skills, and abilities which will qualify for leadership in a specifically designated activity. Actual successful leadership is important.

ADDITIONAL QUALIFICATIONS:
Hold a certificate (if a certification program exists) in the area of the specific activity.

DUTIES:
1. Develop a program of specific interest in cooperation with the Outdoor/Environmental staff.
2. Act as the primary leader for this program.
3. Accept responsibilities for planning and directing some of the support activities for programs such as transportation, publicity, food, equipment, and pre-trip meetings.
4. Provide a program report when the program is completed.
5. Other duties as assigned.

RESPONSIBLE TO:
Outdoor/Environmental staff.

EXAMPLES:
Leadership positions related to this job description include mountain-climbing outing, canoe trip, backpack program, Alpine school, environmental workshop, cleanup program, day hike, fishing workshop.

EXPLANATION:
This is a short-term program position where a leader, paid or volunteer, conducts a specific activity such as a workshop or an outing.

Where to Find Outdoor Leaders

One must be on the lookout for new leaders constantly and maintain a file of potential leaders for future needs. Many potential out-door leaders may be available in every community.

Possible sources are the following:

1. The general population of the community. Most have persons interested in and qualified to supervise certain outdoor activities. Boaters, backpackers, campers, skiers, or climbers may be interested in being trained to use their skills as leaders. They may be located by making telephone calls to people who know other people and so on until potential leaders are located. All will not be interested; however, some may be.
2. Local clubs or organizations formed to perpetuate outdoor activities and interests. Many times club members are highly skilled and may already possess good leadership skills. They may be very willing to train to become paid leaders. There is also the possibility of forming a co-sponsorship with an organization such as this, and good public relations for both your organization and this group may result. Many times local outing clubs may have special equipment, facilities, safety programs, etc., which can also save a great deal of time and energy in implementing your program.
3. College and university classes. College and university students work in well in summer paid positions. Many higher-education institutions have outdoor programs that train students while they participate. Also, several colleges and universities offer degrees in outdoor recreation and outdoor education, and students who have enrolled in this curriculum can offer your program valuable leadership. Workstudy and fieldwork students may be willing to help at little or no cost as well. Students can add the excitement and ideals of youth to your programs; their enthusiasm can at times outweigh their lack of experience.
4. Build your own leadership corps. Select some potential leaders, starting with from 3 to 8 and ending with no more than 10. Bring in an expert to operate a leadership school; even if you must pay this person it will be worth the money. With a core group trained and ready, your leadership needs can be solved.

5. Full-time personnel. There are times when full-time personnel already employed by your agency will have an outdoor specialty that they are willing to share. This method works well in the early stages of outdoor programming.

There are several other potential leadership sources that should be investigated. Governmental agencies in forestry, soils, water, wildlife, etc. have experts in their fields whom you can draw on as resource personnel.

Leadership Selection

When selecting the leaders for the program, there are some basic qualities to look for. The following is *not* in order of importance, however.

1. Enthusiasm. An important quality because this is the dynamic force which is contagious. Enthusiasm is difficult to teach.
2. Ability. This is the basic ability to guide people in an activity, like being able to operate a canoe to lead a canoe program. This quality is best evaluated in a practical test or an actual situation.
3. Experience. This is a valuable quality that comes with year after year of active participation. The saying "experience is the best teacher" is very true; experience builds up a valuable frame of reference which can be classed as knowledge about what will work, how it will work, and when it will work.
4. Judgment. This is the quality of control which is vital to any leader. One can have 100% of every other quality, but without judgment he or she will be a liability to your program. This is very difficult to discover during an interview; thus after the leader is hired a certain amount of close supervision will be necessary until you can be confident in his or her judgment.
5. Appreciation of the out-of-doors. This is becoming an increasingly important quality because of the necessity to create an enjoyment and appreciation in the participants. There are certain values, structures, balances, and beauties that must be recognized.
6. Enjoyment of the outdoors. A genuine enjoy-

ment of the outdoors and the activities therein is a solid quality which is very necessary. It is difficult to fake, for any length of time, true enjoyment — especially when you're confronted with some of the more diverse situations of weather, time, and inconvenience. An acceptance of good and bad, a smile, and high morale regardless of the crosscurrents of the situation are signs of a good leader.

The Application. The written application is a very useful tool if it is used properly. Most agencies have standard forms, but an additional one may be useful when the program becomes large and employs many people. It is time-consuming for everyone involved to do priority listing by application; this is especially true when there are 100 applicants for 10 positions. Thus, when hiring for outdoor jobs, you should look for some indication of the potential leader's qualifications in outdoor recreation — at least enough to separate those with none from those who should be interviewed.

If a new application is being printed, some consideration should be given to the information below. The shape and order of the blanks or questions are important only if they include this information:

Name,
Address & Zip Code,
Telephone,
Age,
Position applied for,
Minimum acceptable salary,
Time preferred (evenings?),
Height,
Weight,

Marital status (single?),
Number of dependents (maybe ages),
Own home or renting,
Membership,
Typing or shorthand speed,
Own car or bicycle,
Certificates,
Military Service (dates of duty),
Employment discharge history,
Police record,
Medical history,
Physical limitations,
Driving record,
Education (leave blanks for school names,
    dates, and course study),
Machine/equipment skills, and
Employment information (should be detailed).

An additional page listing any outdoor-activity skills should be attached to the application for outdoor positions. Candidates should list a broad variety of activities plus his/her own specialty in several blanks. It may be helpful to add a self-rating system such as: 1) would indicate interest but no actual participation; 2) could mean novice participation; 3) shows informal education; 4) shows formal education; 5) could equal a "have taught" background. This should be set up to give you some idea of their proficiency in any activity; however, it should be followed up with some practical testing or evaluating to be positive that the individual is being realistic about his or her abilities if he or she is hired as a leader. See Figure 7.3.

FIGURE 7.3 Outdoor-Leader Skills Checklist

Name _____

*Rate your learning priorities on a scale of 1 to 5:

1 - Must know
2 - Need to know
3 - Desirable to know
4 - Optional skills
5 - No interest

	Can teach others confidently	Can assist teaching	Limited personal experience	No knowledge or experience	*Learning priorities
BASIC MOUNTAIN BACKPACKING SKILLS					
Equipment care and selection					
Packing a pack					
Clothing care & selection					
Campsite selection					
Tent & tarp rigging					
Camp stoves — care & maintenance					
Food planning					
Camp cooking					
Sanitation & personal hygiene					
First Aid					
Breathing/bleeding					
Cardiac arrest/shock					
Sprains, fractures, dislocations					
Heat exhaustion					
Hypothermia					
Head and back injuries					
Evacuation procedures					

Map & compass

Route planning
MINIMUM-IMPACT CAMPING SKILLS

Hiking — group organizing & control

Expedition planning
ENVIRONMENTAL INTERPRETATION

Geology

Weather

Astronomy

Conservation

Fishing

Plant life
MOUNTAINEERING SKILLS

Basic knots

Rope handling

Belaying

Free climbing

Snow climbing

Crevasse rescue

Self-arrest

Rappelling
WINTER SKILLS

Avalanche forecasting

Avalanche rescue

Skiing, downhill

Skiing, cross-country

Snowshoeing

Winter camping — snow shelters

Winter survival

WATER SKILLS

Canoeing					
White-water rafting					
White-water canoeing					
Sailing small boats					
Drownproofing					
Lifesaving					
Swimming					
Rubber-raft repair					

Examinations. A written examination can show applicants' basic knowledge. Following are 49 questions which could be asked as part of such an exam. This two-hour written test can be of assistance in determining what, at least on paper, the applicant knows about outdoor activities. A great many of these questions have common-sense answers, but outdoor leadership involves a great deal of this.

1. How would you identify poison oak? (or poison ivy and poison sumac where indigenous.)
2. What is a bowline knot used for?
3. What does biodegradable mean?
4. List four methods of purifying water.
5. What is carrying capacity?
6. List four restrictions which apply to a wilderness area.
7. How can you tell the difference between a sprain and a broken bone?
8. What treatment should be given for a bee sting?
9. What is declination?
10. When would you or would you not cut boughs for a bed?
11. Explain hypothermia.
12. List ten outdoor games.
13. Describe a safe place in a lightning storm.
14. What is the effect of chocolate bars on tired hikers?
15. What would you do if a camper had brought drugs on one of your outings?
16. What is the approximate wind-chill temperature equivalent of 40 degrees F at 30 mph?
17. List ten "essentials" to bring on an outing.
18. What is the single most important item of equipment?
19. What is the ground-to-air signal for "all is well"?
20. When does a person need a license to operate a C.B. radio?
21. List seven outdoor crafts.
22. How many miles per hour will a group of thirteen-year-old girls average on a six-hour day?
23. What is a good material for outdoor clothing? Why?
24. What is an increment bore?
25. Make a list of minimum equipment for a two-day trip in May.
26. What is coliform?
27. What is a fall line?
28. How do you tell the difference between a Noble Fir and a Douglas Fir?
29. Why is it a good rule to keep people roped together on a glacier?
30. Plan a menu for three days.
31. How does a reflector oven work?
32. What kind of a cloud is a cumulonimbus?
33. What is meant by a low-pressure area? What kind of weather is involved?
34. Explain how to build a snow shelter.
35. What is a carabiner?

36. How do you tell the bow of a canoe from the stern?
37. What is the best insulating material?
38. Why is dehydration an important factor in outdoor recreation?
39. What is a topog (topographical) map?
40. What is tertiary treatment of water?
41. Explain the difference between cross-country skis and downhill skis.
42. In backpacking, what is the maximum weight a 180-pound man should carry?
43. What is a belay?
44. Name ten edible plants.
45. What is the treatment for a heel blister?
46. Name ten poisonous plants.
47. What causes food poisoning in the outdoors?
48. If you need search or rescue, what agency should you call?
49. Why is a clear night cooler than a cloudy night?

The following examination has been used to test those who applied to a college course for outdoor leaders:

Entrance Exam

Social Security No: _____

PART 1
True (+) and False (0)   (2 points apiece)

Place a + by each correct statement and 0 by each incorrect statement in the appropriate space.

1. _____ Our maps are oriented to true north.
2. _____ Contour lines point up gullies.
3. _____ A fifteen-minute-series map gives less detail than a seven-and-a-half minute-series map.
4. _____ Successive contour lines very close together indicate a gentle slope.
5. _____ The word "nimbus" means rain cloud and is added to the names of clouds which typically produce rain or snow.
6. _____ Increasing pressure or a climbing barometer often announce an approaching storm.
7. _____ In the western United States, southerly or southwesterly winds usually precede and accompany most storms.
8. _____ In a fall of any distance the first aider should suspect neck or back injury.

9. _____ The most concentrated source of energy is protein.
10. _____ The body will not store carbohydrates for future use.
11. _____ Heat stroke is more dangerous than heat exhaustion.
12. _____ Protein builds and repairs all body tissue while supplying energy.
13. _____ To properly bury human waste in the back country, dig a small hole in the earth, 6-8" deep, so that bacteria and insects may convert the feces into soil.
14. _____ Fats are relatively easy to digest.
15. _____ The energy from protein is released quickly after consumption.
16. _____ The preferred treatment for frostbite is rapid rewarming.
17. _____ Walking on a frozen foot produces more damage than inadequate warming or warming in circumstances in which the victim's entire body cannot be rewarmed.
18. _____ After initial frostbite treatment, give the patient complete rest and a diet high in protein.

PART 2
Short Answers and Fill Ins (2 points apiece)

1. List one advantage and one disadvantage of a cartridge backpacking stove.

   Advantage_____

   Disadvantage _____

2. What is one of the advantages of a frame pack over a frameless pack?

   _____

   _____

3. Why do we require people to bring wool clothing that covers the entire body on all our outdoor trips?

   _____

   _____

4. On maps, every 4th or 5th contour line is darkened for easier reading.

   These are called _____

137

5. What is meant by coalescence and how does it occur?

_____

_____

_____

6. What conditions must exist for snow to fall?

a) _____

b) _____

c) _____

7. List three (3) visible initial symptoms or signs of hypothermia (exposure).

a) _____

b) _____

c) _____

8. What steps would you take if someone in your backpacking group showed the initial signs or symptoms of hypothermia?

a) _____

b) _____

c) _____

9. What are three areas of the body where frostbite predominantly occurs?

a) _____

b) _____

c) _____

10. How may frostbite be prevented? _____

_____

11. If the bearing to a point is 126 degrees, how would you take a back bearing?

_____

_____

12. Good sources of fat are butter, _____

and _____

13. Good sources of protein are cheese, _____

and _____

14. Good sources of carbohydrates are breads,

_____ and _____

15. The difference between magnetic north and true north is called: _____

16. You are near the Pacific coastline standing atop a 2480 ft. peak with your USGS topo map of the area (80-ft. contour intervals). The polar icecap has partially melted and the Pacific shoreline has risen. The rising water stopped at Joe's Fruit Stand just east of Florence, Oregon. You can see Joe's Fruit Stand and you know its elevation is 640 ft. on your map. How many contour lines are between you and the new Pacific shoreline according to your map?

_____

17. Using your compass to walk a bearing in the field, you place the number of degrees you would like to travel on "Read Bearing Here." Now, to orient your compass in the field, you would turn your body and compass until the red magnetic needle points to:

_____

18. The distance in vertical height between contour lines is called the _____

19. If five contour lines merge (contour interval — 80 ft.) what does the map indicate?

_____

20. Closed-circle contour lines indicate a _____,

or _____ .

PART 3
Clouds and Weather (3 points apiece)

Please fill in the *numbered* blank spaces according to
the format given below:

Family	Cloud Type	Description	Weather Forecast
High Cloud	1) _____	forms a halo around the sun and/or moon	
2) _____	3) _____	marestails, wispy feather strands	4) _____ _____ _____ _____
Middle Cloud	Altostratus	5) _____	
Low Cloud	6) _____	dull gray, uniform sheet like fog	*may* produce fine drizzle but not rain
7) _____	8) _____	true rain clouds with streaks of rain extending to ground	rain approaching
	Cumulonimbus	9) _____ _____ _____	10) _____ _____ _____
	11) _____	puffy cauliflower with constant changing shape	12) _____ _____ _____

PART 4 (3 points apiece)

Use your Three Sisters Wilderness Map and Silva compass to fill in the empty boxes. Use summits and lake centers where appropriate.

FROM:	TO:	TRUE BEARING:	HORIZONTAL DISTANCE:	YOU GO UP (+) DOWN (-)	ELEVATION DIFFERENCE IN FEET:
1. Lucky Butte— S27, T19S, R73	Williamson Mtn. S18, T19S, R8E				
2. Northern Peak of Pack-saddle Mtn.— S20, T19S, R E		206°	1-1/8 mi		
3.	Lookout Lake— S33, T18S R7E	57°	3 mi		
4. Horse Lake (North Tip) S22, T18S		51°		+1310'	

140

PART 5
Matching (1 point apiece)

Place the letter of the most appropriate answer in the designated space. Use a letter only once.

1. _____ dew

2. _____ dehydration

3. _____ radiation

4. _____ conduction

5. _____ convection

6. _____ evaporation

7. _____ respiration

8. _____ wind chill

9. _____ triangulation

10. _____ frostbite

11. _____ constriction of
blood vessels

12. _____ hypothermia

a. loss of body heat by contacting anything cooler than skin temperature

b. production of heat by oxidation of food

c. vital body organs do not function properly because the inner body cools below the normal temperature

d. loss of body heat by inhaling cool air and exhaling warm air

e. this phenomenon occurs when body water loss exceeds water intake

f. parallel trails often created during wet spring conditions

g. loss of body heat by sweating and moisture vaporizing to control body temperature

h. this bodily phenomenon reduces circulation at skin layers, thus keeping blood nearer to the central core of the body

i. leading cause of body heat loss, especially with an uncovered head

j. a bodily injury produced by cold in which tissues freeze

k. water vapor that condenses on solid surfaces

l. loss of body heat by cold air passing the body and decreasing warmth

m. increased wind velocity which intensifies the cold

n. the proper distance from water sources in which to camp, cook, and relieve oneself

o. the calculated intersection of two straight bearing lines on a map from two known points

The Interview

Most interviews really tell potential employers very little about the applicant. The usual questions about where you have worked, what schools you have attended, etc. usually can be answered by reading the application. Maybe a practical test interview could help employers make more objective choices. Some examples:

1. Provide a piece of rope and ask them to tie several knots.
2. Provide several different musical instruments (harmonica, guitar, drum, or other) and ask them to make a choice and play a tune. (Not only do the interviewers find out if they can play, but also how well.)
3. Let them splint a simulated broken leg or give first aid for some other type of injury.
4. Hand them a map and compass and ask them some direct questions about reconnoitering.
5. Show them ten different types of leaves and ask them to tell something about the trees they grew on.
6. Have them tell a story.

What about having a full weekend interview? Taking all qualified applicants out on an overnight outing would enable the interviewer to check their skills, techniques, and attitudes.

Training the Leaders

Staff training may possibly be the most important program of the year. This provides the opportunity to show leaders of the programs what really needs to be done. Methods, techniques, ideas, and details of the program period should be covered thoroughly. You'll also get to know the leaders better, and they can learn from each other. Enthusiasm and practical material are the keys to making it worthwhile.

There are five general areas that should be covered in a training session, but the portions of these that you cover depend on what you feel is important.

1. Basic take-care-of-yourself abilities are an important part of outdoor leadership. A good knowledge backed up by some experience in actual outdoor living are fundamental to being an adequate leader. A leader who cannot take good care of him or herself cannot be expected to be able to help anyone else in the outdoors. Outdoor living, survival equipment, keeping warm and dry, and other skills should be tested.
2. Outdoor programming techniques can be learned through a well-organized leader training program. Menu planning, storytelling, arts and crafts, nature games, and other actual programming activities should be included. Leadership efficiency and time-saving expertise can be increased, and most of this activity is tangible and can be measured.
3. Teaching techniques are important because a large amount of outdoor activity is based on improving the skills and abilities of participants. Educators trained in methods of material presentation and learning processes make excellent leaders. For this reason a training session for outdoor leaders should include techniques of teaching.
4. Leadership techniques and skills are the most difficult to learn or teach in a training session. These are qualities like sensitivity to people, responsibility, maturity, charisma, decision-making, wisdom, and judgment. Sometimes a potential leader either has it or doesn't, and there is not much a training session can do either way; these qualities are difficult to measure and more difficult to teach. A training session does, however, give the supervisory staff an opportunity to observe leaders in action and should give an insight into each one's character.
5. Department needs are best covered in the training session when leaders are together, and they include filling out timesheets, reports, forms, and policies, and doing other paperwork. Outdoor leaders usually like this part of the program the least, but if they are to understand that this is part of the program, they will accept an hour or two with a minimum amount of grumbling.

The best staff training session is an actual outdoor experience which involves pertinent parts of the above five areas. A great deal can be learned in three to four concentrated days under good leadership. Furnish the food and pay them for half the time (example: in a four-day session, leaders volunteer for two days and get paid for two days at their regular salary). If the group is small, there is time for much practical learning plus some fun. Hold the session far away from the city to minimize the staff's desires to return to other obligations. Actual situations using the group as an outdoor party provide the best learning situations.

Staff training should continue throughout the work period. Administrative and supervisory personnel should use any opportunity, good or bad, to help the program staff become better leaders. New ideas, improved methods, and constructive criticism are tools for better programming.

Ratio of Leaders to Participants

It seems that the number of participants allowed to participate, as well as the leader-participant ratio, are deciding factors in the number of problems accrued on an activity. Enjoyment and learning experiences of the individual participant also fluctuate to a greater extent. Since this ratio and an enlarged party make such a difference in reaching our objectives (enjoyment and development are major objectives), we should, therefore, establish a list of fundamentally sound and economically justifiable standards for the number of participants per trip and the number of participants per leader. These standards should be based on the following factors:

1. LEADERSHIP. Leaders vary in ability, interest, experience, and dependability. Some leaders can handle a larger group with greater skill.
2. VOLUNTEERS (Part of leadership). Depending on the number and capabilities of the volunteers, they can take loads of responsibility off the leaders.

3. AGE OF PARTICIPANTS. It is a simple fact that six-year-olds take more supervision than adults. But there are other factors to consider than age.
4. TYPE OF PARTICIPANT. Handicapped, delinquent, and hyperactive individuals will require more direction.
5. AREA. Some areas are easier to supervise than others.
6. ACTIVITY. Mountaineering requires more leadership than does a day hike. Use instructors rather than supervisors.
7. LENGTH OF ACTIVITY. Constant pressure is difficult for the leader to withstand. A break is also pleasant for the participants.
8. EQUIPMENT. More supervisors are needed to control the use of special equipment. Three rafts equals three leaders; six rafts equals six leaders.

Standards can be set for numbers of participants per activity quite easily. Decide on the number which is most feasible and limit the sign-up. No wilderness-type program should have more than fifteen participants. Fifteen persons need two leaders, thus that is settled (assuming that participants are "normal" individuals). One rule of thumb says one leader per eight hikers plus one extra leader for an emergency.

All standards should be set with the following in mind:

1. Quality of program,
2. Safety margin,
3. Leadership efficiency,
4. Efficient programming.

Standards for participant/leader ratio are also quite simple to set, and the same four considerations should be given these decisions.

The chart below shows a very loose set of standards that varies by many conditions. Families, man-wife combinations, competent participants, and proper supervision can decrease the need for leadership. Special programs, participant problems, and hazardous activities can increase the need for leadership.

Age	Participants	Leaders Plus 1 extra for emergency	
5 and under	----	----	Should be in parental custody; outdoor programming minimal.
6 to 8	6	1	
9 to 10	7	1	
11 to 12	7	1	Co-educational programs should have men and women leaders.
13 to 15	6	1	
16 to 18	8	1	Depending on maturity, should be treated like adults.
Adult	10	1	Educational programs could need more leaders.
Senior Citizens	8	1	
Handicapped	2 or 1	1	5 of every 6 leaders can be volunteers.

There are two other considerations to make:

1. Allow the program to gain merit for quality, not quantity. Too many people decrease the value of the activity. It is far better to provide a great and rewarding experience for fifteen participants than to program chaos for twenty-five persons.
2. Allow the leadership the opportunity to be leaders, not simply policemen attempting to direct a mob.

Leader Compensation

There is always a need to compensate leaders for the time they spend working with programs. Many times we think of pay in terms of money (and that is a major item); however, one should be aware of the other types of remuneration.

Payment in money is the most widespread method of compensation. This can be done by the hour, month, or job. In determining the amount to be paid there should be great latitude to be sure the leader receives what he should.

The best way to pay leaders is by the job. Conditions that vary the amount are program difficulty, number of participants, and time commitment. This method of payment is excellent for one-time activities such as a weekend outing or a workshop. A flat rate for a special-interest program may be financed by participant fees; decide what leading the program is worth and figure out what the program will support. Then ask the leader what he will charge and come to an agreement that best satisfies everyone involved.

Equipment provided for the leaders' use can also be thought of as compensation. Furnishing rain parkas, hard hats, tents, or packs helps the leader conserve his personal gear.

Food is usually provided for leaders. Participant fees cover the cost if the food is part of a group program, or if the department gives a $5 to $10 food allowance to the leader if everyone is to purchase his or her own food.

Insurance for leader accidents should be covered by the sponsoring agency. For full-timers there is also 24-hour medical insurance and social-retirement insurance available.

Training opportunity is a reason for working because leaders who supervise can gain a great amount of expertise and background. This may be the number-one compensation for volunteers.

Variation of the work assignments gives a leader a more interesting schedule. This also creates more opportunities to learn skills and methods.

Overtime pay is nearly non-existent. Outdoor leaders must expect to put in hours beyond the call of the paycheck. If a task takes a little longer than expected or a program is late in returning, it is considered just "one of those opportunities" available to outdoor personnel. Compensatory time is also treated quite informally.

Privileges to use certain equipment is also a borderline compensation. This must be handled very carefully; for example: you could allow the staff to borrow a canoe on their days off to run a river, if they were exploring it for a possible trip.

Recognition for work in excess of paid hours is certainly a compensation. Official recognition for a "job well done" from the administration or an article in the newspaper about the program compensates a little for extra effort.

Volunteers

In an outdoor program efficient use of volunteers is very important. Before financing is available to hire staff, volunteer leaders may well carry the full load, and there are several factors to remember:

1. Look at the volunteer's motives and ask yourself, "Why is he or she volunteering the time?" Motives such as the desire to show others the out-of-doors you enjoy is a good one.
2. Have a need before accepting volunteer workers. Nothing is worse than having a group of good people wasting their time wanting to do something but having nothing to do. And, they may volunteer only once.
3. Do not put great loads of responsibility on volunteers. Select tasks that they can perform easily and do not work them to death.
4. Give a specific end-of-duty when they are accepted. Try not to have a flock of people (ex-useful volunteers) hanging around the area.
5. Pay? Remember that volunteers get paid, but not in money. It is also very difficult to pay some and not others for the same job.
6. Insurance coverage should especially include liability. Volunteers can have medical/ accident coverage on the same plan as the participants.

7. Supervising volunteers takes more skill than supervising paid personnel. Paid personnel are motivated by money most of the time, and this is very coersive. Volunteers are there because they want to be; if you keep them happy they will stay.
8. Recognition is very important to volunteers, so reward them with plaques, letters, dinners, or in other ways to help them understand how much the program depends on them.

Most agencies do not take full advantage of the volunteers in their communities. Most public recreation agencies could take a lesson in "volunteerism" from the Boy Scouts or the YMCA.

Leader Problems

Sometimes there are leader problems, but remember that leaders are only human. Listed here are a few of the typical shortcomings of program leaders.

1. *Tardiness.* With literally hundreds of things to do before a trip, leaders are sometimes late. A good Leader/Supervisor talk about the subject will help.
2. *Poor supervision of participants.* This may be the result of other problems, but it is serious and should be corrected immediately.
3. *Poor judgment.* Good judgment is the most important quality of leadership. Dismissal should be forthcoming if bad judgment continues or accidents will force action on the part of the supervisor.
4. *Dress and Grooming.* Most of the time dress and grooming codes for outdoor leaders can be a little less stringent. Long hair is okay as is rough and rugged clothing. Dirty bodies are not.
5. *Sex.* Boy/girl combinations in the outdoors always raise eyebrows, but what happens outdoors usually happens in the city, too. The problems occur when young participants come home with stories about the leaders' behavior, stories which may be exaggerated.
6. *Alcohol and Drugs.* Public outdoor recreation programs have a single, simple rule — NONE.

7. *Police Record.* It is the policy in some programs to run a check on each new employee. This is not done secretly; applicants are told about the procedure.
8. *Taking Advantage.* Supervision of outdoor programs is difficult, and there are a few leaders who take advantage of being far away from any societal control. Word will get back to the supervisors, however, and they will apply the control later.
9. *Staleness.* Almost anyone in a leadership role will develop faster than the program. Be aware of this development ratio since leaders who surpass the program too rapidly become stale very quickly.
10. *Technical Skills.* Because of the great variety of technical skills needed for outdoor recreation programming, leaders should not be expected to get involved in specialized areas when they are not trained in those skills. Leader difficulty caused by this type of problem should be blamed on the supervisory personnel.
11. *Gossip.* Idle, sometimes untrue gossip can cause staff problems. There is usually an underlying cause and open information channels are the best cure.
12. *Hostilities.* When choosing a staff, attempt to select good team workers. Staff who are fighting among themselves are not good leaders. Separating the hostile ones is usually the answer; or maybe you can select a new team.
13. *Money Hunger.* Some attention should be given to a leader who becomes money hungry. When the first thing a prospective employee asks is "how much," begin to doubt the strengths of their other motives.

Most outdoor personnel want to do a good job, and ninety percent of the problems can be solved if the leaders know the details of what is to be done. Better communication between supervisor and leader can act like oil to a squeaking wheel, so talk about problems when they are small.

Scheduling the Leader

One of the intricate tasks of supervising and administrating an outdoor program is scheduling (or assisting in scheduling) the leadership. Poor scheduling can cause a great waste of manpower and related agency resources. For this reason, leadership scheduling should be done by task. Know the job that must be done and schedule the needed time to complete it. This sounds very elementary, but usually it is done in reverse, with tasks added to the schedule.

There are times when the leadership (especially experienced leadership) knows more about the tasks which need to be done than do the supervisors or the administrators. Some of the best schedules allow the leaders to fill in the time-block tasks.

Begin scheduling with a list of activities to be led. Then set up a task pattern for each activity. (One should have some idea of how long each task will take to complete. It usually takes longer than you thought.) Assign a schedule to the tasks and a leader to the schedule and the schedule is complete.

Scheduling should be based on task completion; if not, it opposes leadership needs. (There are leaders who will attempt to fit the program schedule into their own personal schedule, and even though some flexibility should be allowed, the program schedule must come first.)

It is important to schedule free time into a leader's day to give him or her the opportunity to get away from participants for an hour or two. Free weekends and days off should be part of all personnel schedules. A full schedule with back-to-back programs may be acceptable for short periods; however, it begins to show quickly on leadership efficiency.

Many times in outdoor recreation, a leader's day actually covers 24 hours. Payment for this length of time is of course impossible; program/hour schedules are different from pay/hour schedules. Since pay is usually given for eight hours in any 24-hour day, leaders should be made well aware of this policy before they begin work.

Listed below are some of the tasks that should be included in the schedule:

1. *Planning.* Someone must come up with the details of the trip in the beginning.
2. *Pre-trip checkout.* This may take as long as a full day. (8 hrs.)
3. *Pre-trip meeting.* One evening should be sufficient. (3 hrs.)
4. *Program schedule and equipment lists.* (3 hrs.)
5. *Food planning and purchase.* Time can vary depending on the date of the trip. (4 hrs.)
6. *Transportation organization.* (vehicles, gas, tire chains, spare tires) (1 hr.)
7. *Equipment preparation.* (ropes, tarps, packs, tents, canoes, car racks) (2 hrs.)
8. *Personal gear.* This should be done on the leaders' own time — 3-6 hours.
9. *Registration checkout, telephone calls, and participant needs.* (2 hrs.)
10. *Emergency preparedness, first aid, call lists.* (2 hrs.)
11. *Last-minute decisions.* These are based on weather, road conditions, and river conditions. (1 hr.)
12. *Paperwork.* (trip reports, forms, timesheets) (1 hr.)
13. *Post-trip tasks.* (clean-up, storage lost/found, equipment return) (2 hrs.)
14. *Actual trip.* Figure on eight hours for each 24-hour period. (24 hrs. for 3 days)

(53 hrs.)

Some of these tasks can be completed simultaneously, and some can be done by the supervisor, but usually the leaders commit more hours to a program than they think. Pay should be allotted for about four hours of preparation time, so a three-day trip accumulates 28 paid hours.

ADMINISTRATION'S EFFECT ON LEADERSHIP

Leadership is probably the single most important factor in the success of an outdoor recreation program. For this reason an outdoor-recreation administrator should spend the majority of his time working with and for the leaders of the program.

Leaders are a resource, and what a program receives from this resource may depend entirely on the administration and the supervisor. To get the most from leaders, they must have:

1. confidence in the administration;
2. proper implementation of the program (this means site, publicity, equipment, etc. — all the basic needs);
3. interested supervision (someone they can talk to);
4. adequate salary and compensation (including any fringe benefits);
5. pride in the program and the operating agency;
6. opportunities for advancement;
7. recognition for endeavors;
8. pleasant and safe working conditions;
9. satisfaction that their job is important.

The key to making most of the above list a reality is supervision — good supervision. Many times it seems that a supervisor in actuality becomes a snoopervisor, which in general fouls communications and inadvertently has a bad effect on the program. Among all personnel, rapport should be such that there is little change in the program (or the leader's feelings) when supervisory/administrative persons are at the site. Too many times supervisors are looking for what is wrong rather than what is right.

In an age when nearly all agencies have "administration pollution," there are always persons who must (in an effort to show their importance) question each small facet of a program. This action, commonly called "nit-picking," is one of the best ways of robbing leadership of the enthusiasm and resourcefulness which are so necessary to outdoor programming.

By nature, outdoor leaders are individualists. This is good. In the outdoors these leaders have learned to be self-reliant; they have tasted the freedom and naturalness of the non-synthetic world. When a leader is confronted by a so-called administrator who talks like the books he learned from, the leader loses his or her drive and enthusiasm about the program very quickly.

If a person is hired to do a job, let him do it. Give him the support and supervision he needs, then stay out of the way.

SUMMARY

While certification programs exist in several English speaking countries, there is no nationally accepted certification of outdoor leaders in the USA. In the absence of certified leaders, administrators must locate, hire, and train their own.

Applicants for outdoor-pursuit programs may be asked to complete written examinations, demonstrate skills, and even participate in outdoor trips as part of their selection process. Outdoor-pursuit leaders can expect long hours and weekend work and should be paid for preparation time as well as for time on the trail or river.

ADDITIONAL FURTHER READING

Bushwalking and Mountaincraft Leadership, Victorian Bushwalking and Mountaincraft Training Advisory Board, Youth, Sport, and Recreation Branch, 570 Bourke Street, Melbourne, Victoria, 3000, Australia, 1979.

Jackson, Mel, *Outdoor Leadership and Programs,* City of Eugene, Oregon (Unpublished Manuscript).

Logbook, New Zealand Outdoor Training Advisory Board, Private Bag, Symonds Street, Auckland, N.Z., 1981.

Mountain Leadership, Scottish Sports Council, 1 St. Colme Street, Edinburgh, Scotland, EH36AA, 1976.

Outdoor Training Guide, New Zealand Outdoor Training Advisory Board, Box 5122, Wellington, N.Z., 1980.

Petzoldt, Paul, *The Wilderness Handbook,* New York: W.W. Norton and Company, Inc., 1974.

Robert J. Rogers, *Leading to Share; Sharing to Lead,* Council of Outdoor Educators of Ontario, Ministry of Culture and Recreation, 77 Bloor St. West, Toronto, Ontario, 1979.

CROSSING A COLD, FAST STREAM USING A POLE FOR SUPPORT
Some hazards are not so obvious. There is, of course, some danger of being swept away by the current at any temperature. The great danger here, if "Tyrolean" and side rope security are used, is the cold water. Legs become useless and rubbery in a matter of minutes in very cold, fast-moving water.

CHAPTER 8

RISK MANAGEMENT

"MISSING MOUNT HOOD CLIMBERS SURVIVE FREEZING NIGHT, WALK TO SAFETY."

Timberline Lodge — Three climbers missing on Mount Hood since an unexpected snowstorm hit Sunday afternoon walked out to Timberline Lodge 25 hours later, tired and hungry but unharmed, after spending the night in a stone shelter at Paradise Park.

None of the missing climbers was prepared for spending a night in weather that dipped to 24 degrees at Timberline Lodge. Three to five inches of snow fell overnight and another three inches fell Monday. Each climber was wearing hiking boots, jacket, and hiking clothes. While the rest of their group returned safely to Timberline Lodge, the three apparently veered west of the trail downslope. They thought they were far east of the lodge, but actually were about two miles west.

When the companions thought they had arrived at the lodge, they climbed a canyon wall to find themselves at the Paradise Park shelter, a low stone structure with a large front door.

They used ice axes to chop their way into the shelter and clear a space in its 12 by 12 foot interior. Scrounging wood, they managed to build a fire.

"Luckily, Steve had a little pot, so we were able to boil some snow," Miss _____ said. "I had some chicken-noodle soup, Giggle Soup, and we made that. That helped warm us up. But we really watered it down."

The three fashioned a bed from rain slickers and a foam rubber mat that one had packed.

"I never thought three people could sleep on one of those," _____ said. "We slept right next to each other for the warmth. We took turns sleeping in the middle. We put on all the clothes we had, but it was still cold. We didn't sleep much."

At first light Monday, they cooked the last of their soup and headed for the lodge. Throughout the day, a storm swirled around the mountain, with winds of up to 30 mph. in exposed areas whipping the snow into 10-foot drifts.

The search started early Monday at the direction of the Clackamas County sheriff's department. Mountain-rescue specialists from Benton, Marion, and Hood River counties assisted

The three climbers said Sunday's climb was their first ascent of Mount Hood. While each had some outdoor camping experience, none had any expertise in mountain climbing.

"SEARCHERS COMB RIVER FOR TEEN"

Grants Pass (AP) — Deputies and volunteers searched Saturday for a 17-year-old girl who they say may have drowned after she fell out of a raft near _____ Creek on the _____ River.

Deputies said the girl apparently was one of four people in two rafts on the river when she fell out. Deputies found a life jacket she had been holding on her lap.

The teenager's identity was not disclosed.

One of the primary reasons that administrators, sponsors, and/or leaders are often reluctant to offer outdoor-pursuit programs appears to be related to the concern for accidents causing injury or even death. There is currently no precise information on the number of outdoor-pursuit related accidents, yet all available sources tell us that incidence is minimal. In discussing accidents, injuries and fatalities, three things must be kept in mind:

1. The incidence of fatal accidents in vehicles in the United States is higher than the known rate for outdoor-pursuit accidents. It is believed by one authority that there is a fatality rate of .7 per million hours of exposure to driving an automobile and .5 per million student hours of exposure to adventure programs. It is also believed that the most dangerous aspect of the outdoor-pursuit program is the transportation to and from the site of the activity, not the activity itself. There is no evidence that outdoor activities are inherently dangerous. As a matter of fact, there are no dangerous *activities*. It is *people* who cause the accidents — people in wrong places at wrong times with wrong equipment making wrong decisions.

2. People are risk-takers. Individuals like to test their skills, try new challenges, and have adventures. Risk-taking is found in all sorts of situations. Actually, there is probably less risk in terms of mental health on a whitewater raft trip than in accepting a new job. There is probably less physical risk in mountain climbing than in riding a motorcycle.

   The word "eustress" is used by the Canadian psychiatrist Hans Selye to define a positive form of stress — stress that is self-imposed because of its positive effect on release of boredom and increase in joy of living. With more opportunity for outdoor pursuits, more people expose themselves to risk for the pure joy of it. For many of these people (in spite of the availability of time, equipment, natural resources, and a sense of adventure) the positiveness of eustress becomes the agony of negative stress and resulting misadventure, accident, and even death. Since we recognize that people *are* risk takers, it should be our responsibility as leaders to conduct activities wherein the risks are minimized; where self-imposed, positive eustress remains just that.

3. In any outdoor program, as in any situation, we as leaders are never guaranteers or ensurers of safety. Unforeseen conditions, improper decisions, and/or behaviors on the part of the participant preclude guaranteed safety.

With the above three things in mind, we have as our task the goal of managing risks and minimizing the possibility of accidents. A risk is a chance of encountering harm, injury, loss, hazard, or danger. Management refers to the act of controlling something, thus risk management is a control of injury, hazard, loss, or danger. A risk-management plan is a set of regulations, policies, and procedures for conducting an activity with inherent peril involved.

Risk management is the responsibility of the leader of every program in which there are active participants. While some activities have more potential for accidents than others and must be planned with extreme caution, there are potential hazards inherent in nearly every program. The injury of a participant in the collapse of a chair during a pre-trip training session is of no less importance than the injury of a skier who breaks a leg in a fall. As a matter of fact, in the former case the responsibility was probably entirely that of the sponsoring agency that provided faulty equipment, while in the case of the skier it might be claimed that he or she contributed partly to the accident through poor execution of learned skills.

The management of risks is based on the premise that people should pursue their natural inclinations in activities involving risk; however, the likelihood of resulting accidents should be lessened through plans to control them. It must be realized that leaders of outdoor activities are never ensurers of safety. We cannot guarantee unqualified freedom from accident or injury; it would be impossible to do so. It is also philosophically wrong to deny a participant the right to participate in an activity of potential yet controlled risk. People want to test themselves, to move faster, to climb higher, to perform more difficult figures, to attempt the unattempted. No program should deny the participant the chance to succeed at what was not attempted or performed before, and everyone has the right to try a sponsored activity and to fail. Inherent in that right is the right to fail without serious physical, mental, or emotional consequences and the right to try again. Achieving a goal is a positive experience. If the participant returns home unscathed and able to try again, it is relatively unimportant that the summit was not reached.

Risk-management planning is an integral and vital aspect of the overall planning of outdoor-pursuit activities. Comprehensive risk management includes the identification of threats significant to the health and safety of all individuals potentially affected by the activity, and the development of policies and directions to minimize identified risks. In addition, risk-management plans should identify and set policy and directions in regard to any significant potential for damage to or loss of property or resource values. Finally, risk-management plans must be compiled in a clear, concise, and accessible document.

Risk management should be understood as a process of information gathering, assessment, and policy making, and not as an attempt to eliminate all risks from the activity. In fact, such a goal is probably neither realistic nor compatible with the objectives of most outdoor-pursuit programs. It should also be understood that virtually all risks in outdoor pursuits stem from human activity. There is rarely anything inherently hazardous about the environments in which the activities take place! Problems arise only when people are in the wrong place at the wrong time or act inappropriately. Exceptions to this rule are exceedingly uncommon and are even then generally limited to small geographic areas. Reasonably safe activities can be conducted almost anywhere, except perhaps on certain Alpine or river sites where volcanic or gravitational forces create no-man's land.

"Comprehensive risk-management planning" takes into account all aspects or elements of the activity, and results in clear concise policies and directions for dealing with all foreseeable risks. These may result from individual elements or from the interaction of these elements. Of concern in a typical outdoor-pursuit activity are resource lands and facilities, the weather, access routes, transportation modes, group and individual equipment, and several categories of people who are directly or indirectly affected by the activity. These people include the public at large (via taxes, insurance rates, associations with individuals directly involved in the activity, or an obligation to respond to an emergency, i.e. search-and-rescue teams), the public directly involved (co-users of the area or facility), land or facility managers, administrators and officials of the sponsoring agency, the staff and leaders of the activity, and, of course, the participants.

When people and resources interact, potential problems are created. The list of these is virtually endless, although most can be contained adequately in three categories, 1) injuries or health problems, 2) damage or loss to property or resources, or 3) failure to meet participant expectations. Accurate identification of potential problems and assessment of risks requires a thorough understanding of the site(s), the facilities and possible weather conditions, the activity to be pursued, and (too often minimized) the goals, objectives, and limitations of the program, the leaders, and the participants. Developing effective policies and procedures for containing and minimizing these risks demands, in addition, an awareness of applicable management regulations and laws and a sensitivity to social and legal conventions.

In order to assure concern for the welfare of each participant, the risk-management plan should also be developed so that it gives evidence of an attempt to follow a "standard of care."

STANDARD OF CARE

All outdoor leaders are assumed to be competent to lead their respective activities. Defining this term may appear to be difficult; however, in the courts of law in the United States, competency means a *reasonable and prudent professional utilizing the best and most current professional practices.* This comparison to a reasonable and prudent (or careful) professional is known as a standard of care. In cases where litigation occurs and the leader, administrator, or director is sued, the defense states that the best standard of care was followed. In other words, in order to be adjudicated as competent, the leader must show that a standard of care comparable with that of the best professional practices was followed.

A standard of care adheres to the points made in the outline below:

I. Supervision
   A. General Supervision
     1. Supervisory plan and number and location of supervisors
     2. Awareness of dangerous conditions
     3. First-aid knowledge
   B. Specific Supervision
     1. Communication at level of participant
     2. Participant understands and adheres to safety practices
     3. Attention to changing conditions
II. Conducting the Activity
   A. Adequate instructions and progressions

   B. Understanding the participants
     1. Age and size
     2. Skill and maturity
     3. Special conditions (mental, physical, etc.)
   C. Warning of dangers and required use of protective devices
III. Understanding the Environment
   A. Equipment checked
   B. Conditions checked
     1. Man-made structures
     2. Natural hazards
   C. Layout and design checked.

If each of the above items is carefully monitored, the leader has a better chance of being competent than if there is no evidence that an attempt was made to follow them. How to go about doing this is shown below:

Supervision. Supervision is divided into *general* and *specific* categories. *General supervision* requires three considerations:

1. *Supervisory plan.* The leader should plan to have an adequate number of supervisors and an indication of where they can be located. For example, on a hike there should probably always be two people designated as leaders. The one in front should stay in front and allow no one in the group to pass him or her. The second leader should serve as the "tail" and permit no one to stray behind. Two group members may be designated as leader and tailer and the rest informed that they must stay in between these two people. In white-water rafting the raft carrying safety and rescue equipment should always be the last one down the river. If the group wants to go swimming, the main leader may decline to permit that activity because there is no one with a current lifesaving certificate present. If it is a youth group, there should be one water-safety instructor plus one lifesaver per every 25 swimmers and an additional "watcher" to make up a total ratio of 1 to 10 swimmers. If a group of *adults* is swimming in a lake after climbing a mountain and the leader is not qualified to assume the responsibility of lifeguarding, the group must know that swimming is at their own risk. A *sponsored* group

must have an adequate number and placement of qualified lifeguards if the activity is sponsored as part of the outing or else a standard of care cannot be proven for the swimming activity.

Regardless of the outdoor pursuit, the leader has the responsibility to ascertain in advance the number and qualifications of all needed supervisors and to make it known to everyone in the group where they will be. Generally this need not be put in writing; however, it should be made clear to all the members of the group.

2. *Awareness of dangerous conditions.* The leader must show that there was thought and planning put into the trip for whatever could normally be considered possible dangerous conditions. Naturally one is not expected to fantasize about the remote earthquake in a non-earthquake zone; however, much else can be:

   a. conditions of the road when driving to and from the trip (ice, rain, dust, detours, etc.);
   b. conditions of the trail (mud, snow, covered by snow, washed out) and the river (high water, low water, rocks, etc.);
   c. weather. (Obviously different plans are made in winter than in summer, but what plans should be made for thunderstorms, blizzards, etc.?)

All leaders must be able to recognize dangerous conditions or signs of trouble and be able to report them correctly. Storms, shivering, fear, fatigue, unsafe practices, and tasks which are too advanced for the participant are but some of the conditions all leaders and leader-helpers must be able to see and report.

3. *First-aid knowledge.* The chapter on first aid covers the knowledge needed by leaders of people venturing into back-country or remote areas. The leader also has the responsibility of knowing instinctively how to administer immediate first aid. There can be no time for looking things up in the book or guessing or hoping to remember. A standard of care assumes that the leader will have immediate recall of what is needed for situations unique to the activity. The hike leader, for instance,

may not be expected to remember immediately what to do in case of burns from industrial lye, for there would be none expected on the trip. However, he or she *is* expected to know immediate first aid for a wide variety of minor and serious accidents since they can occur on an outing far away from the amenities of civilization. Cuts, bruises, broken bones, and contusions are probably the most frequent injuries. But a river guide must also have the ability to perform drowning resuscitation correctly and immediately. And the leader who does nothing may be as negligent as the one who acts rapidly but incorrectly.

Under *Specific Supervision,* there are also three categories of care:

1. *Communicating at the level of the participant.* This means that the leader must be able to relate to the age and intelligence of the participant. Younger people, beginners, and frightened people may need to have longer or briefer explanations than those given to advanced groups. They may need to hear things several times and may need a simpler vocabulary. It is the responsibility of the leader to be sure that everyone in the group understands what is said, and it should be clear that afterwards individuals in the group will consistently act on what they heard.

   Furthermore, the leader must not ask the participant to do anything unreasonable and imprudent, or to undertake any obvious risk or exposure to foreseeable harm.

2. *Participant understands and adheres to safety practices.* This means that the participant must understand what the safety practices are and why they are practiced the way they are. A participant may put on a life jacket because it is the rule, but if he or she doesn't understand why the jacket is worn and why it must be correctly fastened, then he or she doesn't understand the practice. Climbers may be told to wear hard hats and not follow the policy because it seems silly to wear a hard hat on a snowy ridge or on a smooth rock face. They must know what the safety practice is and why it is that way, and then they must follow it. Many participants do not understand why they must bring wool

clothing instead of polyester. As a result they may not follow the practice and put the leader and the rest of the group in a precarious position when the weather turns cold and damp.

3. *Being alert to changing conditions.* This refers to changing conditions in the environment and in the participant. The leader needs to recognize fatigue, fear, the onset of hypothermia, etc. Plans need to be made in advance for frequent rests, early stops, and changes in route if the participants' conditions indicate such is wise. Psychological, physical, and climatic conditions change often without warning; the leader should be aware of all possibilities and make plans accordingly.

Conducting the Activity. In conducting the activity, three sub-divisions are recognized:

1. *Adequate instructions and progressions* mean that the instructor must know not only how to perform the skill to be taught, but how to analyze the skill in terms of its components in order to help the participant move from the simple to the complex, from the basic to the advanced, along logical lines which are within his or her capacity. A ten-year-old child may progress rapidly in canoeing skills (perhaps more rapidly than an adult), for example, but there are skill progressions recommended by all experts on canoeing, and every leader should follow these recommended progressions. This applies to almost every activity requiring highly executed skills. Leaders should be familiar with the literature of their field to keep current with the latest thinking on the teaching of these.

   Not only must the leader be able to teach skills in logical progression, he or she must be able to modify plans to meet the age, skill, experience, and maturity of the participant.

2. *Understanding the participants* means understanding age and size, skill and maturity, and special conditions in everyone. The tall leader needs to realize that the short follower cannot place his or her feet on the same rocks as the leader can. The very young may have much more initial energy than the elderly, who may in turn have more endurance than the young. Words of encouragement used for the young will also differ from those used with the elderly. And the obese participant may not have the energy to move as rapidly as those who have less weight to carry. As is pointed out in Chapter 11, "Outdoor Leadership," the maturity of the participant means maturity in terms of the activity. Those who are beginners are less mature in the activity than the advanced participant and, regardless of age, can't be expected to act in the same way. But beginners must also be made to feel that they are able to learn new skills regardless of age. There is a different plan of leadership to be undertaken with the novice and the expert, too. Children do not use the same judgment as mature adults; the inexperienced do not perform like the experienced; the disabled, either physically or mentally, need a longer period of conditioning and training and may need more supervision than other participants. The leader who forgets that the task is to teach people — not activities — is not acting as a reasonable and prudent professional.

3. *The leader must warn the group of dangers and mandate the use of protective devices and practices.* Participants may not know the dangers of crossing a stream, the risk of sitting incorrectly in a canoe, or the need for care in crossing a glacier with hidden crevasses. He or she may not know about the presence of poison ivy, the construction of a proper shelter in a blizzard, the necessity to get off the water or off a peak in a thunderstorm, and many other practices. It is the responsibility of the leader to explain these things in a clear manner and insist on proper behavior in the followers.

   Wool may be made mandatory clothing for winter outings; hard hats should be compulsory equipment for climbing; life jackets should be required for boating. Again, the leader may need to be autocratic and make no exceptions, even refusing to permit those without proper equipment to participate. In the interest of performing at an acceptable standard of care, he or she is justified in excluding those without proper equipment from participating in the activity.

Understanding the environment. This refers to both the natural and the altered environment:

1. *Equipment checks* must be made on vehicles used for transportation, on rafts, canoes, ropes, crampons, paddles, stoves, bridges, life jackets, and all man-made equipment. In essence, everything should be checked for good condition before it is used. Equipment must also be appropriate for the *size* and *experience* of the participant.
2. *Conditions checked* are man-made facilities such as roads, and the natural hazards expected. What is the weather report? What weather is possible? Ice, snow, mud, rapids, hidden rocks, poison plants, animals, broken ice, freezing rain, etc. must be anticipated.
3. *Checking the layout or design* in outdoor pursuits means checking the trails, the route, the points of egress and exit. It means checking the source of emergency help from various points along the route of the trip. It means locating telephones, ranger stations, and sources of aid, and knowing the alternate routes that may be taken. In short it means checking not only the conditions of the chosen trail, but all surrounding areas.

THE RISK-MANAGEMENT PLAN

So how do we begin, now that a seemingly overwhelming task has been outlined? Assume that at the moment you are simply pondering an idea. Perhaps you perceive a need among your constituency for some of the benefits associated with an outdoor-pursuit activity, and have decided to explore the possibility of providing an outing experience. At this point the situation is quite simple; no responsibility has been assumed and no activity-related risks exist. *Now* is the time to begin the risk-management planning process. From the very beginning you should be attentive to all potential hazards. Again, there is no need for anything approaching paranoia since the *elimination* of risk is not intended. What is required is a conscientious and consistent review of each aspect or element of the proposed event. The first order of business is of course to "rough out" the idea, to satisfy yourself as to the accessibility of the

essential ingredients, land or water resources, suitable participants, capable leaders, and those "connections" between resources and people, dollars, transportation options, and clothing and equipment. As you conduct this initial survey you should also be identifying potential problems, and satisfying yourself, if possible, that all the risks you identify are either 1) inherently low enough to be acceptable or 2) capable of being rendered acceptably low by some reasonable modification of the activity. Finally, assuming that all of the "ingredients" are accessible and that no unacceptable and unavoidable risks exist, you are ready to plan the details of the activity itself. (Once again, "activity" refers to a set of one or more pre-trip meetings and outlines within a larger "educational or recreational program.")

It is at this point that written expression of the full and detailed risk-management plan should begin. Keep in mind that the people responsible for implementing the activity will need easy access to the information, policies and directions in the plan. One method of presenting the material is to follow a topical order so that staff or leaders can locate needed information quickly by following a logical time-ordered sequence. A typical sequence might begin with program goals and policies, then consider activity goals and objectives, pre-trip events, equipment and clothing requirements, transportation, sites, and routes, and end with the actual conduct of the activity in the field. Each of these topics can be used as a section heading. The use of subheadings (an "outline" format) can further increase the ease of information recovery from the completed documents. Suggestions and comments are given below for each recommended section.

Following this standard of care may seem to encompass a ponderous amount of work and planning, but it can be done easily by following the risk-management plan recommended in Figure 8.1. This plan takes into consideration all the components of the standard-of-care outline. It is recommended that risk-management plans such as the one presented be followed on every outing and used to indicate the extent to which the leader followed the standard of care. (The standard-of-care outline is incorporated into the risk-management outline.)

Figure 8.1 Components of a Risk-Management Plan for Outdoor Pursuits

EVENT _____ DATE(S) and TIME(S)_____

PURPOSE

A. Goals of Sponsor _____

B. Goals for Activity _____

LOCATION _____

Route	Possible Conditions	
Travel to _____	_____	VEHICLES CHECKED____
In Field _____	_____	DRIVERS CHECKED____
Travel from _____	_____	PERMITS PROCURED __

PARTICIPANTS

Number males_____ Number females _____ Total_____

Age Range_____ Experiences _____

Special characteristics _____

I. Activity

By designating the program and the activity, the leader starts to form a picture of the types of risks to be managed. A cross-country ski trip involves different risks than a canoeing class, yet each contains potential accidents. A group rappelling down a cliff brings to mind a possible high-energy physical activity under controlled circumstances, while winter camping brings to mind a different activity with less obvious control and an entirely different set of risks. Each activity must be examined on its own merit in terms of the characteristics of the participant, the site, and the degree of difficulty in executing the skill.

Activities may be classified as high, medium, and low risk. However, these labels may not accurately reflect the risk involved in some activities, for this can fluctuate depending upon environmental conditions and participant characteristics. A swimming instructor demonstrating a skill in the shallow end of an indoor pool is involving the group in a low-risk activity compared to a senior citizen attempting the rough-mile race in the ocean, yet each is participating in a swimming activity.

II. Date(s) and Time(s)

It seems obvious why the dates of a program are stated on the risk-management plan; risk management for an activity conducted in the summer might be considerably different from one conducted in the winter. The reasons for stating the times of the activity may be less obvious, but if an outdoor activity takes place in the winter, one needs to think of the time

LEADERS

Name	Age	Certificate	Qualifications

EQUIPMENT SUPPLIED (Attach List)

Type	Number	Condition	Owned _____
			Leased _____
			Borrowed _____

EQUIPMENT REQUIRED PER PERSON (Attach List)

POLICIES (Attach)

very carefully. The number of hours of daylight in the winter are fewer than in the summer. A program that may be held in the summer between 6:00 a.m. and 9:00 p.m. could not be held in the winter when daylight lasts from only 8:00 a.m. to 4:00 p.m. or even fewer hours if it is cloudy or stormy. A second reason for listing the number of hours is in consideration for the working time of leaders and the possible set-in of fatigue. A leader of a rafting or hiking trip 100 miles away from the city may be very fatigued if he or she is in charge of driving, guiding, chaperoning, lunch hour, and all other responsibilities with no break in a twelve-hour day. There are times when more leaders may be required in order to give ample relief time for those in charge.

III. Purpose

A. Sponsor goals and policies

The sponsor's goals are stressed here because they are too often left out of risk-managment plans for specific activities; yet they are, in fact, of considerable importance. Goals are vital to program coherence and thus effectiveness, giving purpose and direction to the activities and allowing estimation of acceptable (and justifiable) risk levels. Program policies with regard to employment and fund distribution directly affect program quality and safety. (Risk-management planning is of little value without adequate support from the program, agency, and/or individuals in charge!)

B. Activity Goals and Objectives. Clearly, the goals and objectives of the activity need to be understood not just by the initiator of the event, but also by leaders and participants. Written concise goals and objectives allow valuable scrutiny, helping to insure that they at least are reasonable. Too often, disaster or at least disappointment is built into an event right from the start!

IV. Location and Facility

The location of an event will necessitate preventing very different types of potential accidents. The conditions that exist at the location will also affect the potential for risks.

A. Indoor. The first thing a leader should do when using an indoor facility is to check automatically for building components that may be needed in case of emergency: light switches, heat controls, electrical outlets, water faucets, drinking water, fire extinguishers, first-aid kits, telephones, numbers for police and ambulance, closets for mops and brooms, and wastebaskets for litter. The competent leader knows where each of the foregoing is located and how to use anything that may be needed in an emergency.

B. Outdoor. The outdoor leader may conduct activities in a city park, a play area or the vastness of a national forest wilderness area. In the city, broken glass, holes, and dangerous street crossings must be checked each time the site is used. In the outdoors, hazards range from certain poisonous plants and annoying animals to topographical and geographical hazards. In any case, the site must be checked and the possible natural hazards listed.

C. Conditions. Conditions under which an activity is conducted are weather and climate, both seasonal and potential. Hiking on a dark and stormy night, picnicking on a predicted warm day in May, camping in tornado season, and rafting on white water in November in Idaho each bring to mind conditions that may require the management of specific risks that would not be found in other situations. Certainly the conditions for snowshoe trips will differ early, mid-way through, or at the end of the season. The risk-management plan should consider the worst circumstances foreseeable at the given time of the event being planned.

D. Transportation. The transportation of staff and participants to and from the site is often the most dangerous portion of the entire program. The responsibility for reaching the field may rest with the program, the participants, a contracting agency or everyone. Whatever the case, the responsibilities of the program should be clearly delineated in the risk-management plan. In the case of transportation, if the program bears responsibility, policies and directions must clearly provide for reliable safety-checked vehicles and for competent drivers. A thorough plan will include specific reference to common-sense (but too often ignored) issues such as the use of seat belts, drinking and drugs, speeding, and compliance with traffic laws. The plan must also anticipate accidents, injuries, breakdowns and getting lost, and provide clear directions for resolving these situations. Another concern usually addressed in this section of the plan is the return of participants to town and/or their homes. The plan should address the exceptional potential for accidents caused by tired drivers at the end of the outing (especially when long days, long drives, or multiple-day outings are involved).

E. Routes and Sites. Routes and sites must also be considered in the plan, with specificity adequate to minimize any site- or route-related hazards. The plan should evaluate and identify all of the potential hazards of the site, although this process is usually limited to a general statement or two regarding the most "typical," with elaboration only of exceptional or unusual hazards. Acceptable accuracy usually requires both direct experience on the site and competency in map interpretation that in turn assumes good current maps. The plan should also identify alternative routes, escape routes, and potential travel or other difficulties that might be caused by adverse weather. Exact routes should be specified, although it may be wise to specify acceptable and unacceptable options and conditions should a change of plan occur.

V. Participants

The precautions one takes in managing risks starts with an identification of several characteristics of the participants.

A. Number. How many will be involved? What is the maximum and minimum number for a safe program? This may depend on other variables. A 36-passenger bus means a maximum of 36, including leaders. A financial policy may dictate a minimum number without which the activity will be cancelled.

B. Sex. The sex of group members should be noted. It may be approximate in number but the ratio of males to females is often needed when planning for chaperones, activities needing strength, and other events. When both sexes go on certain field trips, it may be necessary to have some male and some female leaders to supervise young children using restroom or overnight facilities.

C. Specific characteristics. How activities are held depends upon the characteristics of the group members. Senior citizens, sixth graders, high-school joggers, and mentally disabled adults all require a different set of guidelines for managing risks, and even within these categories one will find differences. Activities for older adults from 65 to 95 vary greatly; those who still enjoy fishing are probably unlike those who climb mountains. Some sixth graders may be physically limited and some high-school athletes may have injured knees. Mentally disabled people may be institutionalized or mainstreamed. Thus every possible variable must be considered because every participant expects to be included with thought and care on the part of the leader. Experience may also differ, and events may be held for the beginner, intermediate, or advanced participant. In short, all special charac-teristics must be recognized and considered in the planning of a safe event.

VI. Leaders

Policies and procedures for the activity should be based partly on the ability of the leader(s) to carry them out in terms of age, number, and qualifications. Age is usually important only at the lower limits, but various activities require or suggest mature leaders for a positive effect (not a guaranteed corollary). Drivers' licenses are issued at minimum ages set individually by each state; chauffeurs' licenses generally require older drivers. The American Camping Association recommends a minimum age of 25 for camp directors because it is felt that the experience gained up to that age may make a real difference in the quality of the program offered to children. A thirty-year-old leading a ten-day backpacking trip would be considered to be more mature and to have potentially better judgment than a twenty-year-old would.

The number of leaders is likewise a serious consideration. There must be two leaders for most programs and some require ratios of leaders to participants. A swimming program might require one leader per 25 swimmers in a pool, while on a lake more might be required; a hike for children aged ten to twelve should have one leader per eight children plus one extra for emergencies; a bus trip should have, in addition to the driver, one leader per fifteen participants if they are children, yet one leader is considered adequate for 35 senior adults. Senior citizens require fewer leaders for control but more highly trained ones in terms of first aid and knowledge of the needs of older adults. No standards exist for the ratio of leaders to groups in most activities, but good judgment is always to be assumed in planning for the event. The names of *all* leaders should be listed on the plan.

Leader qualifications are the third consideration in this category. One needs to know what training the leader has had in order to determine whether he or she is qualified for the activity. Certainly leaders with *current* certification in first aid, water-safety instruction, and boating programs are desirable for some activities. Special training through college-degree programs, workshops, in-service seminars, etc. also add to his or her qualifications in most activities. The leader's age, previous experience, and any other special characteristics that might help make the program safer should be recorded on the risk-management plan.

VII. Equipment

Every activity has special requirements. The risk-management plan must provide clear and concise policy and directions to assure that whatever is necessary is available at the right time and place. It must consider all reasonable contingencies, such as lost or injured people, equipment-failure possibilities, and changes in the weather. And it should specify the means by which compliance with requirements will be evaluated, what will be done if compliance is not complete, procedures for resolving the condition of safety gear, and, of course, who is to be responsible for what items. The plan should also specify policy with regard to the use and control of safety gear (such as who is to use group first-aid kits and the number to be carried by each independent-travel group in the field). While perhaps outside the proper scope of risk management, this is a convenient point at which to clarify equipment control (check-out, clean-up and check-in) procedures.

Analysis of equipment is usually necessary for proper programming and is mandatory for managing risks. Equipment must be considered in terms of type, number, and condition. A list of mandatory and optional group and individual equipment should be attached to the plan.

A. Type. Every risk-management program should list the type of equipment to be provided by individuals and by the organization. For example, canoeing class may utilize canoes, paddles, and life jackets provided by the agency and clothes provided by the individual. While this seems simple enough, a three-day backpacking trip may require food provided by individuals and stoves by the agency, followed by a long list of equipment that is mandatory and provided by one or the other. Here we need to know much more information. How much food? What kind? How to be prepared? How to be packaged? What weight? What of stoves, fuel, weight, and amount needed? Some programs will necessitate

lists of mandatory and optional equipment duplicated and given to each participant as part of the program itself.

B. Number. Recording the number of pieces of equipment may be a simple matter of stating, for example, that the agency will provide three canoes. It might also be much more complex. On the backpacking trip, the list might read one tent per two people, one stove per four people, one climbing rope for three people, and one first-aid kit for the entire group.

C. Condition. The condition of all equipment must be checked before, during, and after each event. Any breaks, tears, weaknesses, etc. must be reported at once. Any equipment being returned after an event should be returned in excellent and clean condition or be reported and sent for repairs before it is shelved. The recommended risk-management plan checklist has a space to record equipment that was found to be in need of repair and how it was reported.

VIII. Emergency Numbers

No group should leave on a trip without listing in advance and *carrying with them* a list of numbers to call in case of emergencies. These may include but not be limited to the following:

A. State Police or County Sheriff (or agency in charge of search and rescue);

B. Ambulance or medical assistance;

C. Director of sponsoring agency; and

D. Emergency numbers for participants.

IX. Policies

The final portion of the risk-management plan requires a list of policies and procedures under which risks are managed. These policies are developed from the material listed at the beginning of the form and are dependent on those facts. The event, participants, leaders, and equipment are prime considerations in developing the plan for managing risks, and policies may be the same for many activities, particularly those that are deemed as "low" or "medium" risk. In these cases, there may be standard procedures for the operation of many similar activities, along with standard emergency numbers, accident forms to fill in, and procedures for checking equipment.

This final section of the plan should include everything taking place, from arrival to the trailhead to return to the trailhead. (For convenience' sake, the final transportation phase was included in the section on transportation.) Many concerns must be addressed here, and again a time sequence seems the most logical ordering system. While every outing will require a special set of policies and directions, the following considerations apply to most. For each some provision must be made for reducing the implied risk.

1. *Roll or attendance keeping.* (Who is there, and how will you keep track during the outing?);
2. *Issuance of warnings and basic instructions.* (What are the dangers of injury, becoming lost, or causing environmental damage, and what should participants do to minimize risks?);
3. *Informing participants of plans.* (What's going to happen? Who is responsible for what, to whom, and for whom?);
4. *Rechecking health status of staff and participants.* (Is everybody really ready for this?);
5. *Rechecking gear, clothing, and equipment.* (Is everything in order? Does everybody have the needed equipment?);
6. *Securing the vehicle.* (Will vehicles be safe, secure, and usable upon return, and are keys safe and accessible?);
7. *Staff ratios and group control.* (How much staff per student, what skills need be present in each independent-travel group, and how will the groups conduct themselves to avoid losing staff or participants?);
8. *Injury or illness.* (What qualifications, if any, are required of the person who treats the victims or of the types of treatment allowed, and what provisions have been made for transporting the person to medical aid?);
9. *Lost or missing person(s).* (What will be the procedure if someone is missing?);
10. *Teaching strategies.* (What will be taught, what progressions and methods will be used, and are they appropriate for the participants? Will standard and currently accepted techniques be employed in the conduct of the activity?).

The suggestions given above should provide an adequate framework upon which to build comprehensive and effective risk-management plans for most outdoor-pursuit activities. Very few serious problems will arise if the planning process is conscientiously attended to, since the great majority of problems are caused by lack of adequate foresight or preparation.

Be thoughtful and thorough, and you will have every reason to be optimistic.

SUMMARY

There must always be the hope and chance for success; therefore, the goal of the leader must be to prevent accidents or injuries so that participants have a chance for success or a chance to fail without serious consequences.

As human caring leaders, we are morally and ethically bound to manage risks so that few accidents occur and that those which do occur are minor. The welfare of participants is our primary concern. We must take care, therefore, that they are unscathed physically and psychologically through our leadership. From a pragmatic point of view, risk management, by preventing or minimizing accidents, can prevent or minimize lawsuits and financial loss. It can be especially effective in preventing these due to negligence. In addition, those programs with few or no accidents may be eligible for better insurance rates. An agency literally cannot afford *not* to require risk-management plans.

LEGAL MATTERS

In the United States, the practice of suing to recover money for actual damages is a practice that causes concern to those offering activities that may appear to encompass an element of risk. Thus it is appropriate that the matter of legal liability be discussed here. At the onset, it must be reiterated that our philosophical concern is the welfare of the human beings entrusted to our care in an environment foreign to that usually experienced by most people. We must recognize, however, that in addition to our concern for the individual there is another reason why we must be very careful to practice appropriate care. The possibility of a lawsuit is a worrisome idea at the least. Certainly, if we follow a risk-management plan, the chance of accidents can be lessened. With fewer accidents, it follows that there will be fewer lawsuits and, subsequently, fewer suits lost and less money due in damages. If a person looks at risk management as wise fiscal management, that person cannot be faulted. It is the position of the authors, however, that it is philosophically correct to consider risk management a necessity — first because of a concern for human welfare and second because of a concern for fiscal stability. Be that as it may, the elements of legal liability should be understood by all who undertake to lead others.

The type of legal liability of most concern to the outdoor-pursuit leader is "tort." Tort is wrongdoing against a person who suffers damages as a result. While there are intentional torts (assault, fraud, slander, misrepresentation, etc.) our concern here is with *unintentional* tort. Unintentional tort is a wrongdoing based on negligence, and the actual damages may be paid by the wrongdoer to the one who was wronged.

In a court of law, the plaintiff must prove four points in order to show that negligence occurred. It must first be illustrated that the person in charge had the duty or responsibility to provide the participant a safe environment. In a common adventurers program, no one assumes the sponsored leadership, for there are no sponsors. In any program with a leader designated by the administration sponsoring the program, though, there is a responsibility to provide a safe environment. This means a safe environment under normal conditions. One can never guarantee there will not be unforeseen circumstances, but this assumes that the area will be as secure as predictable. A leader camping in a recognizable avalanche path, for example, is not providing a safe environment; even if it is not avalanche weather, there is the potential for one. Thus we can usually assume that there is a responsibility to provide a safe environment in any program sponsored by any organization. Second, the plaintiff must show that the duty to provide secure surroundings was breached by the leader since he or she

didn't offer the standard of care explained in the previous section. In such a case, the leader must show that the participant was not exposed to unreasonable risk and that there was no foreseeable danger. If it can be shown that there was, in fact, a duty to provide a safe environment and that the leader did not follow a standard of care, the plaintiff must then show that this failure was the proximate cause of the injury and that the injury was actually manifested in actual damage of a nature warranting recovery of funds. If those four facts can be proven, then a person may be found guilty of negligence. In many cases a jury decides the verdict.

LIABILITY WAIVERS

Many people feel that a liability waiver, signed by a participant, will preclude that participant suing for negligence. That misconception deserves consideration here. The majority of American courts have ruled that those agencies providing services to the public cannot contract to absolve themselves of liability to the public to whom they render services. Private enterprises *may* not be considered under the same legal opinions. Regardless, there is a tendency for courts not to enforce liability waivers. That being the case, why might an outdoor-pursuit leader insist that part of risk-management planning is the use of such forms?

Basically, liability waivers may discourage injured parties from suing, but more important, probably, is the fact that liability waivers can help indicate an important element of standard of care. The properly executed waiver can increase the participant's awareness of the program risks and can give evidence that the leader is not only aware of the risks, but also shows a concern for the welfare of the participants by informing them.

Often a liability waiver for a minor is signed by one or both parents (or legal guardians), who state they will not sue for negligence. Administrators and leaders should be aware of the fact that, while the parents may indeed not sue, no parent has the right to sign away a *child's* right to sue. While minors cannot do this, states recognize the child's right to take legal action upon reaching the age of majority up to a legally determined statutory limitation. (This varies from state to state. In some states it is two years beyond the age of majority, in others it may be more. Readers are advised to investigate the statutory limitations in their own states.)

Figures 8.2, 8.3, and 8.4 show examples of liability waivers. Notice that each contains the following information:

1. Identification of the sponsoring group;
2. Information concerning the risks of the activity;
3. Signature of participant acknowledging the activity risks and waiving rights or claims for damages.

Figure 8.3 was recommended by an attorney for a specific program. The other two have been used by university departments offering trips and outdoor courses. Figure 8.5 is an example of a health-report form that all participants are advised to complete before any outing. This practice alerts the leader to possible medical problems that could occur on a trip and allows adequate time to record them on the risk-management plan under section V.C. — special characteristics.

Figure 8.6 is simply informative and is given to students as advice.

FIGURE 8.2 Sample Liability Waiver

University of Oregon
Department of Physical Education
Outdoor-Pursuit Program

SAFETY INFORMATION

Our program involves activities in rugged terrain in all extremes of weather, far from any professional medical or emergency services. You will be exposed to real risks or injury or even death, from such hazards as falls, rock falls, avalanches, lightning, river crossings, hypothermia, and cold injuries. Be aware that rescues usually take more than 24 hours and that any and all medical rescue costs are your personal responsibility. Our leaders are well trained but are not "supermen" or "superwomen," and they will sometimes make mistakes and may be unable to solve problems for you. Your safety is your personal responsibility. We encourage you to develop a questioning attitude and to ask your leaders to explain any decisions with which you are uncomfortable. You can reduce risks by paying careful attention to the safety rules and procedures presented in class, exercising good common sense, staying constantly alert, participating only in activities well within your physical abilities, and by having and using proper equipment.

I have read the above statement and agree that I am personally responsible for my actions and safety.

Signature _____

Date _____

FIGURE 8.3 Legally Executed Liability Waiver

FORCE 12 PROGRAM
AGREEMENT UNDER SEAL (Requires
Notary Public Seal)

WHEREAS, the undersigned (the "Applicant") wishes to be accepted for participation in a *FORCE-12* trip to be organized and conducted by the faculty of Newton North High School; and, in consideration of Newton North High School's action in allowing the Applicant to participate in such a trip:

The undersigned acknowledge(s) the said *FORCE-12* trip will necessarily subject the Applicant to certain stresses and hazards, not all of which can be foreseen. It is fully understood that the Applicant may spend several nights outdoors. *Reasonable precautions will be taken to protect the student. It is understood that unforeseen circumstances may occur in trips such as are proposed, for which the instructor or Newton North High School cannot be held responsible.*

The undersigned assumes all of the ordinary risks normally incidental to the nature of the trip, including risks which are not specifically foreseeable.

The undersigned applicant hereby releases Newton North High School, its faculty and agents from all liability of any nature for loss or damage to personal property. The undersigned applicant further releases Newton North High School, its faculty and agents from all liability for personal injury resulting from the failure of the undersigned applicant or other students on the trip to obey safety regulations and directions of the trip leader, or resulting from the exercise of judgment by the trip leader in good faith in response to emergencies and exigencies which occur on the trip; provided, however, that

nothing contained herein shall excuse any member of the faculty or person assigned to be a trip leader by a member of the faculty from the responsibility to act with reasonable care for the safety of the undersigned applicant during the course of the trip appropriate to the circumstances.

It is the intention of the undersigned that this agreement will be governed by the laws of the Commonwealth of Massachusetts.

Executed this   day of   , 198
under seal:

_____
Applicant

_____
Parent or Guardian
(if student is under 19)

_____
Witness (Notary Public)

Student's Name -
    Address -
    Phone -

Source: Mr. Chris Jones
         Newton North High School
         360 Lowell Avenue
         Newtonville, MA 02160

FIGURE 8.4 Liability Waiver for a University Class

UNIVERSITY OF OREGON
Department of Leisure Studies and Services

WHEREAS, the undersigned ("Applicant") wishes to be accepted for participation in a trip to be organized and conducted by the faculty of the Department of Leisure Studies and Services at the University of Oregon; and, in consideration of Leisure Studies and Services' action in allowing the Applicant to participate in such trip:

The undersigned acknowledge(s) the said trip will necessarily subject the Applicant to certain stresses and hazards, not all of which can be foreseen. It is fully understood that the Applicant may spend several nights outdoors. *Reasonable precautions will be taken to protect the student. It is understood that unforeseen circumstances may occur in trips such as are proposed, for which the instructor or the Department of Leisure Studies and Services cannot be held responsible.*

The undersigned assumes all of the ordinary risks normally incidental to the nature of the trip, including risks which are not specifically foreseeable.

The undersigned applicant hereby releases the University of Oregon, its faculty and agents from all liability of any nature for loss or damage to personal property. The undersigned applicant further releases the University of Oregon, its faculty and agents, from all liability for personal injury resulting from the failure of the undersigned applicant or other students on the trip to obey safety regulations and directions of the trip leader, or resulting from the exercise of judgment by the trip leader in good faith in response to emergencies and exigencies which occur on the trip; provided, however, that nothing contained herein shall excuse any member of the faculty or person assigned to be a trip leader by a member of the faculty from the responsibility to act with reasonable care for the safety of the undersigned applicant during the course of the trip appropriate to the circumstances.

It is the intention of the undersigned that this agreement will be governed by the laws of the State of Oregon.

Executed this   day of   , 198   :

_____
Applicant

_____
Parent or Guardian
(if student is under 19)

FIGURE 8.5 Health Information Form

University of Oregon
Department of Physical Education
Outdoor-Pursuit Program

Name _____

Outing _____

Term _____ Year _____

HEALTH INFORMATION
Describe any illness or injury, current or past, that might affect your ability to participate fully and safely in this course, including but not limited to back or knee problems, cardiac or respiratory ailments, diabetes, allergies, migraines, fear of heights, or sensitivity to cold. _____

_____

_____

_____

List any drugs or medications you are currently taking: _____

_____

Contact Information:

Yourself _____
          (address)   (city)   (state)   (phone)

Local contact _____
          (address)   (city)   (state)   (phone)

Parents or relatives _____
          (address)   (city)   (state)   (phone)

Physician _____
          (address)   (city)   (state)   (phone)

Social Security No. _____ ____ _____ Driver's License & State _____

General Information

Have you taken classes in this activity before, or do you have prior experience? Describe briefly ____

_____

Do you have first-aid or medical training? Describe _____

_____

Medical insurance is your responsibility. We suggest you obtain appropriate insurance.

FIGURE 8.6 Responsibilities of Students and Faculty in Activity Courses

RESPONSIBILITIES OF STUDENTS AND FACULTY IN ACTIVITY COURSES

The courses in which you have elected to participate are either required as part of your major or elected.

Regardless of the case, you must realize that there is a certain assumption of risk which you engender when you participate in activity classes such as these. *You must be aware of this assumption.*

Throughout the conduct of each class you will receive competent, progressive, sequential instruction and proper supervision. Every effort will be made to keep all facilities and equipment in good, safe, workable condition.

You will not be asked to do anything which is inconsistent with the activity or is in any way not reasonable and prudent.

However, the entire responsibility is not the instructor's. You, too, have a responsibility. For your own safe participation, and that of your fellow students, you must call to the attention of the instructor any situation which you perceive to be a potential danger to you or your fellow students. This would include, but should not be limited to:

— equipment that has broken or is in need of repair;
— when you are not feeling well or are unduly fatigued;
— when you have unusual difficulty in performing a skill.

Also, you are obligated to follow the rules and regulations set down by the instructor for your safety. This includes the proper dress, such as tennis shoes and protective equipment, e.g., eyeglass guards. If you choose not to use such protective equipment provided or requested, you must realize that you are doing so at your own peril and that injury might occur.

We all want a safe environment, but it must be recognized that accidents do occur in active participation. We want vigorous participation, but all of us (instructor, you, and fellow students) must use good judgment and work together for safe participation.

Should an injury be incurred during participation in this class, the instructor will make arrangements for transportation to the University Health Center.

The injured party is responsible for all financial obligations incurred in this process and subsequent treatment necessitated by the injury. Because of this, students are encouraged to carry some form of health-care insurance. Please discuss with your instructor any known physical problems which may limit your participation in any class. *This should be done by the second class session.* It is important to do this inasmuch as a medical examination is no longer a requirement for admission to the University.

Should you have any questions regarding this statement, please contact your instructor.

RECOMMENDED POLICIES

In order to assist leaders in developing the policies section of the risk-management plan, examples of what might be implemented are found at the end of this chapter. These policies could be repeated for each subsequent similar outing, thus precluding the necessity to draw up new ones for each risk plan.

SUMMARY

The management of risk is based on the premise that participants have natural inclinations to pursue activities involving the potential for accident. While program sponsors cannot guarantee freedom from accident, risks can be managed so that the likelihood of accidents is lessened. Every outdoor leader should perform like a reasonable and prudent professional following the best and most current professional practices. Such performance is known as practicing a standard of care.

A standard of care adheres to specific points related to supervising, conducting the activity, and understanding the environment. One way to practice a standard of care is to develop and follow a risk-management plan that identifies potential dangers and outlines how the activity may be managed to lessen the risk.

BIBLIOGRAPHY

American Alpine Club, "Accidents in North American Mountaineering," Volume 4, Number 2, Issue 32, The American Alpine Club, New York, 1979.

Edginton, Christopher, and Ford, Phyllis, *Leadership for Recreation and Leisure Service Organizations,* New York: John Wiley and Sons, 1985.

Hart, John, *Walking Softly in the Wilderness,* San Francisco: Sierra Club Books, 1977.

Kaiser, Ronald A., "Program Liability Waivers," *Journal of Physical Education Recreation and Dance,* A.A.H.P.E.R.D., August, 1984.

Knudson, Douglas M., *Outdoor Recreation,* New York: MacMillan Publishing Co., Inc., 1980.

Howard, Gordon E., "Hiking and Mountaineering," *Safety in Outdoor Recreational Activities,* Washington, D.C.: A.A.H.P.E.R.D., 1977.

Meier, Joel, Morash, Talmage, and Welton, George, *High Adventure Outdoor Pursuits,* Salt Lake City: Brighton Publishing Co., 1980.

Meyer, Dan, "The Management of Risk," *The Journal of Experiential Education,* Fall, 1979.

SAFETY POLICIES AND PROCEDURES

I. The following policies and procedures are designed to maximize participant safety during an outdoor-pursuit program. Strict and uncompromising compliance is expected. Any exceptions should be authorized in writing by the coordinator of the program.

A. Planning
   The instructor must provide, in advance of the activity, specific plans, including:
   1. A teaching progression designed to provide safe, responsible attainment of course objectives. The progression must provide for the presentation of all safety-related skills and knowledge in a logical, ordered sequence and in a manner suited to the learning ability and experience level of the participants.
   2. Alternative plans in the event of changes in the weather, unexpected travel difficulties, injury or accident, or incapacitation of the instructor.
   3. A provision for explaining to participants the general level of risk inherent in the activity, the major specific risks of the activity and the unpredictable nature of the environmental hazards to be encountered, and the need to carefully examine their personal insurance coverage.

B. First-aid Qualifications and Policies
   1. All leaders of field outings must possess a current first-aid card. This must be an American Red Cross Advanced First Aid card unless an exception has been approved by the coordinator and the supervisor.
   2. Leaders of water-based courses must possess a current lifesaving card or equivalent certification or experience approved by the Head of the Service Course Division, or have a lifeguard present during water sessions.
   3. All students in the basic course are required to read the ARC Advanced First Aid Book, receive a two-hour first-aid lecture on hypothermia and other specific outdoor first-aid concerns, and cover assigned related readings.
   4. All preparation classes must include a reminder of potential hazards that could result in a need for first-aid skills, and a review of the appropriate procedures.
   5. Each vehicle used for transporting students must include at least one individual with the qualifications in item 1 above. Only state vehicles may be used to transport students.

6. Every independent field group must include at least one individual with the qualifications in item 1 above, and must carry a first-aid kit approved by the coordinator.
7. All participants and staff on field outings must be informed as to who in the group is qualified in first aid, and as to the location of the first-aid kits.
8. *Any* use of the first-aid kits must be reported immediately to the course instructor and, upon return to campus, to the coordinator. Kits that have been opened must be clearly marked for inspection and resupply.
9. *All* accidents or injuries, even if minor, must be reported to the coordinator of the outdoor-pursuit program upon return to campus.

C. Field Leadership Ratios
   Leaders are those individuals assigned to the outing because there is evidence they understand their responsibilities, are capable of carrying out their responsibilities, and freely consent to the acceptance of their responsibilities. An independent group, for the purposes of the program, is defined as any group out of contact with the remainder of the party for more than a few hours at a time. Specifically:
   1. At least two leaders must accompany each field group.
   2. Groups or individuals travelling out of contact with the remainder of the party for short (2- to 4-hour) periods of time may, with the consent of the instructor, be accompanied by only one leader.
   3. Groups or individuals may not travel unaccompanied by a leader except with the instructor's consent, in special situations involving short periods of separation (less than a few hours) and safe, absolutely unmistakable terrain (or other) barriers, and terrain well within the ability, experience levels, fitness, and equipment of the participants.

D. Field-group Sizes
   Group sizes must never exceed the instructor's estimation of the maximum safe size for a given activity.
   1. Group sizes, including leaders, must not exceed management agency guidelines (8 to 20 people, depending on jurisdictions).
   2. Group size should not exceed eight people, including leaders, in areas of heavy use, high fragility, or potential for conflict with the interests of other users.

E. Equipment owned or rented by the Department
  1. No department equipment or other equipment the department rented is to be used for other than regularly scheduled activities within the department.
  2. Any equipment suspected of being in unsafe condition is to be removed from use immediately and reported to the supervisor.

F. Participant Clothing and Equipment
  Strict adherence to clothing and equipment requirements is essential in terms of participant safety and program liability, and serves to remind participants of the importance of proper gear.
  1. All participants must be given a complete list of the required clothing and equipment for their outing at the first preparation meeting, and reminded of the requirement that *ALL* items be brought on the outing.
  2. No participant is to be allowed to participate in an outing without all of the items on the required list for that outing.
  3. All participant clothing and equipment on the required list is to be checked prior to departure from town. The gear may be checked at the last meeting prior to the time of departure, or (preferably) at the assembly point immediately prior to departure. The gear must be checked in one of the following ways: a) visually, by having each person show the items satisfying each requirement or b) verbally, by having each participant *describe* the items satisfying each requirement. (Questions to the class such as "Did anyone forget raingear?" or "Do you all have raingear?" will not suffice. Specific identification of each item by each person is necessary.)
  4. Participants must be advised prior to the outing of the fact that extra clothing or other items left in the vehicles at trailheads are not insured by the department and that such storage is entirely at their own risk.

G. Participation in Outings
  In order to participate in an outing a person must be enrolled in the activity or be a leader.
  1. All participants must meet the fitness requirements of the activity, such as a running test, prior to and within the term of the outing. Minimum recommended running standards include a two-mile run in twenty minutes for backpacking, ski touring, and snow-camping outings, and two miles in eighteen minutes for mountaineering and all advanced-level wilderness and back-country outings.
  2. All fitness requirements must be met prior to participation. This includes a 200-yard swim test prior to all water-based courses.
  3. All participants must read and sign the waiver form prior to departure.
  4. No participant may meet an outing at other than the regular assembly point without the approval of the leader.
  5. Any person leaving an outing before the end of the program must be accompanied back to the point of departure by the instructor or a leader assigned by the instructor.

H. Transportation
  There is probably no more hazardous component of an outdoor trip than transportation of the leader, staff and participants to and from the trailhead. Special care must be focused on this aspect of the outing. Safety must *always* come before cost or convenience.
  1. All participants are to meet in one place and be transported to and from the trailhead in approved vehicles only.
  2. Only approved drivers are to drive the vehicles.
  3. No vehicle is to be driven by a person who is, in the opinion of the instructor, unable for any reason to function in a normal, alert, and safe manner.
  4. All applicable motor vehicle laws are to be obeyed explicitly.
  5. *All* occupants of *all* vehicles are to wear seat belts at *all* times. *No seat belt, no passenger.*
  6. No alcoholic beverages or intoxicating substances of any kind are to be used by any participants during the outing. This includes the entire period from group assembly before departure to formal dismissal of the group following return. No exceptions can be made for the transportation phase of the outing, including stops enroute.
  7. Do not compromise on vehicle conditions. Check all safety-related functions of the vehicle, and if anything is questionable get it fixed *before* transporting participants.

I. Emergency Response
  If a participant must be taken home from an outing due to illness or other problems, the instructor is to consider carefully the implications of the transportation of the participant in terms of the potential effects on both the individual and the group. The instructor must determine whether outside assistance (search-and-rescue teams), evacuation by the group, or walking out by one or two individuals is appro-

priate, and whether or not an ambulance is required. In any case:

1. The person to be evacuated should be involved in and consent to all decisions, if this is possible under the circumstances.
2. The instructor or a responsible assistant is to accompany the individual until the individual is in the care of medical personnel (if needed) or safely at home with roommates or relatives.
3. The administrator of the program is to be informed immediately of any situation requiring evaluation for illness or injury, and of any search that is ongoing or involves outside-agency assistance.
4. In the event of an incident involving the press or other agencies, all questions should be referred to the administrator, unless your immediate response is needed to maximize the health and safety of your students.

J. Climbing
The choice of general and specific routes must be made conservatively.

1. All climbing above class 3 will involve upper belays of all participants unless specifically approved by the trip coordinator.
2. Hard hats will be used by all instructors and all participants during the entire activity portion of rock-climbing classes.
3. Hard hats will be used by staff and participants at any time during mountain climbs when: 1) falls or rock falls are reasonable possibilities or 2) the use of hard hats is common practice, as in all self-arrest and glissading sessions.
4. Any anchor-knot, tie-in, or rappel system which is significant in terms of safety must be checked by the instructor or his/her qualified representative.
5. All rappels are to be belayed, and hard hats worn at all times. Standard and conservative mountaineering practices must be adhered to strictly at all times.
6. Participants are not to lead rock or snow climbs.

K. Canoeing
Prerequisite: each participant must pass a swim test *prior* to on-the-water sessions. This must include a minimum of a 200-yard swim (any stroke).

Equipment Requirements:
1. *Every* participant must wear a Coast Guard-approved Type II or III Personal Flotation Device during *all* on-the-water sessions.

2. Canoes must be equipped with adequate flotation.
3. On day trips at least one rescue rope must accompany the group.
4. All participants and staff must provide the personal gear and clothing specified in the required equipment lists for the class, and wear no less than the clothing and equipment specified by the course instructor when on the water.
5. Under no conditions should one canoe split off from the group.
6. At least two leaders must accompany each day outing.

Class Procedure:
1. *All* participants must take part in a rescue session prior to any day outing.
2. Course content must follow an accepted progression by the American Red Cross or American Canoe Association.
3. On day-trip outings, each participant must bring an extra change of clothes.
4. Under no circumstances should more than two persons be in one canoe.
5. All paddlers must *kneel* in canoes at all times.
6. The American White-water Association (AWA) Safety Code must be adhered to at all times (see 4 above).

L. White-water Canoeing

Prerequisites:
1. Each participant must pass a swim test prior to on-the-water sessions. This must include a minimum of a 200-yd. swim (any stroke).
2. Each participant must have a minimum level of entry skill, specifically:
   a. The student should have taken a basic canoeing class through the Red Cross, American Canoe Association, or some other organization.

If not, the student:

   b. *must* show a working knowledge of canoe nomenclature;
   c. *must* demonstrate the ability to paddle in a straight line with a dependable rudder stroke or, preferably, a j-stroke;
   d. *must* demonstrate the ability to turn the canoe in a full 360-degree turn using appropriate maneuvering strokes: draw, sweep, crossdraw, pry;
   e. *must* have had 10 hours minimum time on flat water, and *should* have some moving-water experience.

Equipment Requirements

1. *Every* participant must wear an approved Coast Guard Type II or III Personal Flotation device during *all* on-the-water sessions.
2. The canoe must be equipped with extra flotation (over and above that built into the canoe).
3. At least two rescue ropes must accompany every river trip.
4. All participants and staff must provide the personal gear and clothing specified in the required equipment lists for the class, and wear no less than the clothing and equipment specified by the course instructor when on the water.

Group Size, Instructor Ratio:

1. Lake sessions and river trips must not exceed nine canoes at any one time.
2. Under no circumstances should a single canoe split off from the group.
3. At least two leaders must paddle different canoes with each field trip.
4. A leader must occupy the lead and sweep boat on any river trip.

Class Procedure:

1. *All* participants must participate in a rescue session prior to any day outing.
2. Course content must follow an accepted format approved by the American Red Cross or American Canoe Association.
3. If the combined air temperature and water temperature is less than 120 degrees F, all participants must wear a wet suit on river trips.
4. River difficulty will not exceed Class III level, with the majority of teaching sites being Class I-II.
5. Group leaders *must* follow the AWA Safety Code at all times (see 4 above).
6. Under no circumstances should any canoe paddle over a man-made weir or dam.

M. Rafting

Prerequisite:

Each participant must pass a swim test prior to the on-the-water session. This must include a minimum of a 200-yard swim (any stroke).

Equipment Requirements:

1. All participants and staff must provide the personal gear and clothing specified in the required equipment lists for the class, and wear no less than the clothing and equipment specified by the course instructor while on the water. *All* required gear *must* be checked before leaving town.
2. All participants, including staff, must wear a Coast Guard approved Type 3 or better lifejacket at all times when on or in the water or watercraft.
3. Each raft must carry an approved throw rope and one extra lifejacket.
4. Each rafting group (up to three rafts) must carry a comealong, two pulleys, 120′ of appropriate line for rescue purposes, an approved raft-repair kit, a pump with suitable fittings, an ensolite or similar sleeping pad, a sleeping bag or half-bag, and an approved first-aid kit.

Group Size, Instructor Ratio:

1. Rafts must carry no more than the maximum number of people recommended by the manufacturer, the Coast Guard, or other applicable standards, whichever is *least*.
2. Rafting parties may not exceed four rafts or twenty people per river per day.
3. All state or federal managing agencies and the other major institutional and commercial users of a river must be contacted well in advance of the outing to insure compliance with regulations and permit requirements, and to minimize conflicts with other users.
4. Every raft must have an experienced leader.
5. Every rafting party must have at least one leader who has run the section of river at least twice.

Class Procedure:

1. All regulations of agencies having authority over watercraft use and campsite use must be strictly adhered to.
2. Every effort must be made to minimize real or potential conflict with the river or riverbank users.
3. At the launch site and before rafting, all safety-related skills, procedures, and policies must be thoroughly reviewed for all participants and staff.
4. Paddle signals must be established prior to launching.
5. No raft may be out of sight of *all* of the other rafts and other craft in the party for more than five (5) minutes or one-quarter (¼) mile, whichever is least!
6. The raft carrying the rescue and safety equipment must travel last down the river at all times.

N. Wind Surfing

Prerequisites:
1. Each student must pass a swim test prior to on-the-water sessions. This must include a minimum of a 200-yd. swim (any stroke).

Equipment Requirements:
1. *Every* participant must wear a Coast Guard approved Type II or III Personal Flotation Device during *all* on-the-water sessions.
2. At least one rescue rope must be located at the instructional site.
3. All participants and staff must provide the personal gear and clothing specified in the required equipment lists for the class, and wear no less than the clothing and equipment specified by the course instructor when on the water.

Group Size, Instructor Ratio:
1. Lake sessions must not exceed twenty participants.
2. At any one time, boards on the water will not exceed fourteen.
3. The instructor-student ratio will not exceed 1:5 at any one time.

Class Procedure:
1. Class format must follow accepted progression by Windsurfer Schools.
2. If combined air temperature and water temperature is less then 120 degrees F, participants must wear a wet suit.
3. *Every* participant must participate in a rescue session prior to lake experience.
4. Instruction site for basic class *must* include a sand beach with gentle drop off, and every effort must be made to find an on-shore breeze.

SAFETY CODE OF THE AMERICAN WHITE-WATER AFFILIATION

Personal Preparedness and Responsibility:

1. *Never Boat Alone.* The preferred minimum is three boats. (Two of these boats should be paddled by individuals who have demonstrated their ability to paddle in rivers with a classification equal to or greater than the river you will run.)
2. *Always Wear a Life Jacket.* You never know when you will capsize. Minimum flotation should be fifteen lbs. for adults and twelve lbs. for children under 100 lbs.

3. *Wear a Crash Helmet in Class 3 or Greater Rivers.* Your head is the most valuable asset you have; protect it in heavy water.
4. *Have a Realistic Knowledge of Your Boating Ability.* Don't attempt rivers beyond your ability — that is, two or more class levels above what you have already mastered.
5. *Know and Respect River Classification.* Know what the classification is of rivers you have mastered and of the river you are attempting. Remember that most river classifications increase at high-water level.
6. *Be Practiced in Rescue and Self-rescue Procedures.* Remember that it is more difficult to perform a rescue or self rescue in higher-classification rivers. Be competent to judge whether you are the best available person to do the rescue. If not, stay clear for someone who can and perhaps you can rescue any stray equipment.
7. *Beware of Cold Water and Weather Extremes.* Rubber wet suits, wool clothing, a dry change of clothes, etc., may be essential for safety as well as comfort.
8. *Try to Learn to Swim.* Everyone can learn to swim if they try hard enough. If you can't swim or have a fear of the water or river that you are on, let the trip leader know and make sure you have a buddy or two in other boats who can keep an eye out for you.
9. *Support and Inform your Leader.* Respect the leader's authority and experience. If you are running a river for the first time and/or of a higher classification — tell the leader so he/she can help and watch you.

Boat Preparedness and Equipment:

1. *Test New and Unfamiliar Equipment.* Don't tackle difficult rivers with untested and unfamiliar equipment. At the most critical time, the equipment may fail you.
2. *Use Flotation Devices.* Flotation devices should be securely fixed and designed to displace as much water from the boat as possible. A minimum of one cubic foot at each end is recommended.
3. *Have Bow and Stern Lines.* Use ⅜″ diameter rope eight to fifteen feet long. Fasten it securely to the boat at one end and the other end should release if tugged. For kayaks, grab loops at both ends; a six-foot stern line makes rescuing a lot easier.
4. *Use Spray Cover Wherever Required.* Be sure cover release is instant and foolproof.
5. *Be Sure Craft is in Good Repair.* Inspect your equipment often and replace when worn or broken. It is difficult to make repairs on a trip.

Group Equipment:

1. *Throw Lines.* 50' to 100' of ⅛" rope;
2. *Spare Paddles.* At least one paddle for each type of boat;
3. *Repair Kit.* Roll of duct tape and paper or towelling to dry the boat;
4. *First-aid Kit.* Supplied with fresh and adequate supplies, including waterproof matches, and stored in a watertight container that will float.

Organizer's Responsibility:

1. *Know the River.* Know how the river changes classification with water level. Be prepared to change plans to meet the existing conditions.
2. *Know Who is New on the River.* Be prepared to give instructions to the inexperienced on how to navigate the river. Assign an experienced paddler to each inexperienced one to help and/or watch them at each difficult point on the trip.
3. *Recommend Paddlers Not Participate if It Is Beyond Their Ability.* If in the leader's judgment an individual will be attempting a river that is beyond his/her ability and that could jeopardize the group's safety or the individual's safety, the leader should recommend that the individual not participate or at least portage difficult stretches. If the individual does participate, be sure to alert *all* of the experienced paddlers to the situation so they can assist in making the trip as safe as possible.
4. *Designate Lead Boat and Rear Guard (Sweep Boat).* Lead boat should know the river. Rear guard is equipped and trained for rescue.
5. *Keep Party Compact.* If the party is too big, divide them into independent teams with separate trip leaders, lead boats, and rear guards.
6. *Organize a Shuttle.* Determine when the shuttle should be run and make plans for someone to do the return shuttle.
7. *Know the Current Condition of Weather, Visibility and Water.* The leader should inform the group of these conditions and make decisions on the basis of the related dangers.

On The River:

1. *Each Paddler Must Know:* group plans, hazards expected, location of special equipment, and signals to be used.
2. *Lead Boat:* knows the river, sets the course, and is never passed.
3. *Rear Guard:* is equipped and trained for rescue and is always in the rear.
4. *Each Boat is Responsible for the Boat Behind:* Each boat passes on signals, indicates obstacles, and sees the boat behind it through bad spots.
5. *Keep Party Compact.* Divide into independent teams if party is too big.

If You Spill:

1. *Be Aware of Your Responsibility to Assist Your Partner.* For canoes and C-2's.
2. *Hold on to Your Boat.* It has flotation and is easy for rescuers to spot. Get to the upstream end so that it cannot crush you on any rocks. If possible, grab your paddle and boat loop in one hand, leaving the other hand free to grab a rescuer's boat.
3. *Follow Rescuer's Instructions.* The rescuer is in a better position than you are to know what you should do and is trying to help — try to cooperate.
4. *Leave Your Boat if This Improves Your Safety.* Your personal safety must come first. If rescue is not imminent and the water is numbing cold or worse rapids follow, then head for the nearest shore. Author's note: "We might add that proper swimming posture is important to the boater's safety. Float on your back and keep your feet up, pointed downstream. Never try to stand up in rapids; foot entrapment is a real danger. A backwards sculling motion with the hands may be used to move toward shore."
5. *Stay on the Upstream End of Your Boat.* In other positions you risk being pinned against an obstacle; in waves you may be pushed under the water.
6. *Be Calm.* Help will come, but don't become too complacent.

If Others Spill:

1. *Go After the Boater.* First make sure the boater is safe.
2. *Try to Rescue the Boat.* Do this only if you are qualified and will not jeopardize your own safety.

CHAPTER 9

TRANSPORTATION AND FINANCES

The challenge of transporting participants and financing their trips are matters of concern to both administrators and leaders. Each requires a considerable amount of detailed planning and specific data, and the knowledge and skills involved in each are not at all akin to those used in the actual outdoor activities. Each is presented in this chapter with recommendations that must be studied and then modified for specific local conditions.

TRANSPORTATION

Because most outdoor pursuits are not held within walking distance of participants' homes or the facilities of the sponsoring agency, transportation becomes a major factor in planning and implementing a successful outdoor venture. Some administrators may be reluctant to offer programs away from their own facilities because of concerns about injuries, accidents, subsequent litigation, and potential liability. Certainly all the best planning for successful experience in the field is of no value unless participants arrive at the site and return home safely. Just as certainly, there *are* real risks associated with transportation. Yet with careful planning and effective management control, these risks can be reduced to acceptable levels.

Resources for Transportation

It goes without saying that modern transportation necessitates motorized travel, i.e., train, plane, bus, or automobile. Using trains and planes to transport participants to appropriate sites for outdoor pursuits will, in all likelihood, also entail cars and/or buses to move people from the depot or airport to the location of the activity. It is with this in mind that much of this material concerns automotive transportation.

Selection of vehicles for transporting participants may seem simple until one examines the pros and cons of several alternatives. Private cars, participant owned and operated cars, agency (sponsor) owned vehicles, school buses, chartered buses, public buses, and several less obvious sources such as military reserve-unit vehicles are all potential ways of taking participants to their recreational destinations.

Private Cars. Recruiting volunteers to use their personal vehicles for conveyance from agency facilities to the outdoor site appears to be a simple solution to the transportation dilemma. Car pools are often viewed as a cost-saving measure, but only in a limited sense and usually at the expense of the car's owner/driver. While most passengers in a car pool seem to expect only to share in the cost of gasoline, most car owners know that gas is but a small part of the cost of operating a vehicle. More equitable systems of compensation can be complex and frustrating to apply, and still not be fair for all drivers. The best and most popular of these systems is a flat rate per mile, shared by the entire group rather than just the two people in one pickup truck or the five in one sedan. Automobiles owned by non-participants (parents, friends, or relatives) and driven by their owners should be utilized only as a last resort and should probably never be used by some agencies. The cost of using the vehicle would be relatively low (gas and oil reimbursement); the drivers would not be fatigued from the exercise of the outdoor activity; and the drivers could deliver their passengers directly to their own homes — yet none of these conveniences could cancel the risk involved.

When one uses volunteered private vehicles and drivers, one has little or no control over what happens. Speeding, reckless driving, consuming alcoholic beverages, failure to require and/or enforce the use of seat belts, or any other undesirable conduct may occur. A leader or administrator accepting volunteer help can insist that the driver follow certain policies, but he or she has limited ability to supervise the situation or to enforce the policies. One can insist that the group stay together, stop at one

restaurant rather than another, stop for periodic rests, take alternate routes, or take any other action; unfortunately, through sincere mistakes or simple disobedience, time-consuming mishaps are frequent. In any program, the leader is responsible for maintaining control. In a car pool situation, it is at best extremely difficult to do so. As a leader one should remember that loss of control does not necessarily free one from responsibility or liability. When a leader doesn't have control of *all* the transportation, there is really no program since travel to and from the site is an integral part of it.

It must be recognized that many volunteer drivers are extremely conscientious and drive carefully and defensively. But many do not want to risk having an accident while transporting strangers or friends, thus oftentimes the most qualified and careful drivers are unavailable because they refuse to volunteer.

Despite the limitations and risks, youth agencies and church groups frequently use volunteers for transporting people involved in their programs. In these cases, which vary throughout the world, there are various methods of insuring the drivers and passengers — even when drivers are reimbursed for expenses. A local agency may carry special insurance, a non-owner policy may be procured for every vehicle not owned by the sponsoring organization, or participants may be insured by the sponsor. The situation varies so much that any enterprise utilizing or reimbursing volunteers should seek counsel from its own insurance agency. Most municipal and private businesses probably should not consider these drivers, and youth agencies and churches should investigate the situation thoroughly before choosing this potentially frustrating and hazardous option.

Participant cars. Using cars owned and driven by outing participants is little, if any, better than using non-participant cars and drivers. Control is still limited although those taking part in the outing may tend to be more cooperative than those who do not.

There could also be insurance problems for participant operators who transport passengers. Even though these drivers are not salaried, if passengers have paid for the program then the sponsoring agency may be liable for accidents or injuries incurred during the trip. If the passengers pay the driver, then the vehicle is again being used for business purposes. Drivers should be reminded that no money should change hands until *after* all passengers are safely back in town, and that even discussing a plan for compensation can result in drivers being viewed as commercial carriers. When car pools are used, many organizations leave the transportation to the participants and meet them at the trailhead or river. For this system it is important to be very clear (preferably in writing) that the program *begins* and *ends* at the meeting point at the trailhead or launch site; the sponsor incurs no responsibility for any members of the group prior to or after arrival at the trailhead.

Leader-owned Vehicles. Rarely is it advisable that a leader use his/her own vehicle to transport participants for the agency which employs him/her. Insurance on a private-use vehicle does not cover it as a car for hire. Youth camps may need to use private cars or trucks for errands or emergency transportation and may incorporate non-owner vehicle policies in their insurance coverage; however, such insurance may not cover transporting children for program activities.

Agency-owned, rented, or leased vehicles. The most highly recommended method of transportation for small groups is by agency-owned vehicles. Station wagons, twelve- or fifteen-passenger vans, and minibuses are recommended. A twelve- or fifteen-passenger (8-12 mpg.) van may cost more in terms of gas mileage than three five-passenger (15-30 mpg.) automobiles; however, insurance, depreciation, maintenance, and salaries for two extra drivers may make the three vehicles more expensive in the long run than the vans. It's also much easier to control one van than two or three smaller vehicles.

Purchasing vans or other vehicles is the most expensive method of transportation, yet controlling the situation may be important enough to offset the shock of the initial expense. It is possible that owning agency vehicles is the only way to acquire insurance coverage for the program. And in some cases vans and other vehicles can be rented or leased from private enterprises or parent organizations. Govern-

ment agencies often have access to motor-pool vehicles for which usage charges are usually slightly less than for equivalent commercially rented vehicles. In either case, the advantages of having no capital investment or maintenance costs, lower insurance costs, and flexibility may well exceed the advantages of complete control over the vehicle(s).

Agencies also gain more control of the transportation phase of the total program by having staff drivers for all vehicles. The only drawback to this is that a driver who is already tired from a strenuous outing has to continue to remain alert on what may be a long, difficult drive home. An alternative is to employ an extra staff person to drive the participants to the trailhead, return the vehicle to town, and go out again for them, doubling gas mileage but resting the driver. Yet there may be a problem with a group ending up at a spot other than the one where they started (intentionally or unintentionally) and having no vehicle there. Thus several suggestions may help in cases where qualified participating group leaders or other participants drive:

1. Day hike — same exit as entrance; leaders drive.
2. Day hike — different exit from entrance; leaders drive two vehicles but shuttle one vehicle to trail end. Upon arrival at trip destination, one drives that vehicle back to the trailhead to get the other vehicle. When only two leaders are assigned to the group, however, this leaves the group unattended during the moving of the shuttle vehicles, resulting in supervisory problems.
3. Provide alternative drivers so that each vehicle has at least two qualified drivers who can alternate.
4. Allow time for drivers to stop for rest and refreshment at least every two hours. (The passengers need this too!)
5. Delegate field activities, assignments, and responsibilities in such a way as to maximize the physical and mental states of the drivers when they return to the trailhead.

If non-participant drivers are used, the following suggestions may help:

1. Overnight to several days — either 1) or 2) above or: drivers (non-participants) transport group to trailhead (or boat ramp) and return to town. Drivers return to trailhead (or take-out site) to drive group and equipment home.
2. A major and often prohibitive *disadvantage* of returning vehicles to town is that when this is done no escape vehicles are left at the trailheads. Unless the trailhead has phone service and/or positive access to emergency assistance, a vehicle with a key location known to the group must be left at the trailhead and may need to be left at a key escape-route point.

The logistics of a shuttle may present a challenge. If the group and gear are to be dropped off at point X and picked up at point Y, which may be many miles from X, getting a vehicle to point Y may be difficult, particularly if the driver is a group leader. Many times juggling cars and drivers creates additional mileage, which in turn affects the cost of the trip.

A trailer or pickup truck for gear is often an economical way to conserve on space and allow passengers to ride more comfortably as well as more safely. Great carrying capacity can be added to a van if a rack is added to the top. Such a rack does more than just increase the number of potential passengers — it also reduces risk by removing gear from the inside of the van. Packs, skis, and other items stored inside the vehicle can be lethal in an accident, and can also block egress should rapid escape be necessary.

Care must be taken, however, to avoid over-loading the vehicle, causing structural damage or unsafe handling conditions. Either problem can easily result from too much weight inside the van or on *top*, which causes a dangerous high center of gravity. Fifteen adult passengers, each with fifty-pound packs, will weigh about 3000 pounds, assuming a mix of male and female passengers. That is beyond the limits of safety in many models.

In review, considerations for transportation by automobile or van include:

1. Insurance of vehicles, drivers, and participants;
2. Condition of vehicles, including proper emergency equipment;
3. Qualifications and supervision of drivers;
4. Distance to be driven;
5. Location of start and end points of the outing;
6. Ratio of leaders and of drivers to participants;
7. Availability of drivers;
8. Need for a shuttle;
9. Need for a vehicle for equipment;
10. Possible fatigue in drivers.

Buses. For trips involving thirty or more participants, owned or leased buses provide good possibilities for transportation. Chartered buses, while relatively expensive, have the advantage of professional drivers, licensing by the Interstate Commerce Commission, strict safety inspections, relative comfort in seating and air temperature, and, often, restroom facilities. "Dead heading," the practice of driving people to a destination and returning empty to the home base, is considerably expensive, so chartered buses are usually not engaged to transport groups to trailheads or boat-landing sites. However, it is hard to think of any program other than a day camp or ski school which would necessitate transportation for as many as thirty participants in one vehicle.

School or church buses may be investigated as possibilities, particularly for day camps, one-day sight-seeing tours, or short distances, but their lack of comfort may outweigh their economy on long trips.

Transportation Safety

The following is a set of recommended guidelines for safe driving. In many cases, an administrator may be able to adopt some or all of them without alteration. In other situations, mainly because of warmer climates, some administrators may find a need to alter them. Regardless, it is highly recommended that these or other policies covering the same precautions be an integral part of every risk-management plan and consequently a mandatory segment of the leader's responsibilities.

CENTER OUTDOOR PROGRAM
DRIVER INFORMATION

All drivers (employees, contractors, and volunteers) must have a current motor-vehicle driver's license which is valid in this state in order to participate in our *drivers testing process*. All drivers must complete and submit the attached release form to authorize us for access and review of your driving record. Drivers must further possess a current and valid chauffeur's license in this state before being permitted to drive for the program.

_____

I, the undersigned, authorize the review of my driving record.

Driver's License No. _____ State _____

_____

Signature

_____

Printed Name

_____

Address

Sample Driver Check-out Form

The following form may be used by program supervisors, administrators, or other designated persons to evaluate the driving of a potential trip driver on a road test.

Driver Check-out Form

Driver: _____

Observer: _____

Date: _____

DRIVING SKILLS

Before leaving, check lights, signals, flashers, tires, first-aid kit, fire extinguisher, jumper cables, chains, tools, flares, oil pressure, ammeter, gas gauge, safely secured load rack, and adequate seat belts.

Passengers instructed to use seat belts as driver buckles up.

Vehicle started in PARK, not neutral (manual transmissions, start in gear).

Lights on at all times when driving. (This may vary depending on geographic and legal situations.)

Sample On-the-Road Check-Out

Uses mirror and signals for all lane changes.

Smooth starts and stops.

Smooth and controlled panic stop from 35 mph.

Use of right foot only (automatic transmissions only).

Stop at sidewalk *and* curb when entering streets from alleys, driveways.

Safely park and start on steep hills.

Verbalizes safe procedures for turning around on a narrow road with unguarded drop-off on one side, facing danger.

Use of horn before backing.

Back in a straight line using mirrors only.

Demonstrate to tester an awareness of defensive driving attitude by verbalizing hazards she/he sees as driving during part of test period.

Demonstrates a courteous and considerate driving attitude during the test period towards other drivers, pedestrians, bicyclists, animals, etc.

Knows (verbalizes) and practices the functions and shifting procedures of automatic shift gears:

PARK — for starting, parking; not to be engaged if vehicle is moving.

D — for all normal driving at all speeds.

1 — for steep or difficult terrain at speeds less than 30 mph.

2 — for steep grades, heavy loads at speeds less than 45 mph.

Mountain-road skills demonstrating turnarounds and horn signals on blind corners.

Knows (verbalizes) and practices the function and shifting procedures for manual shift.

Knows (verbalizes) and practices use of correct gear(s) when stopped (parked) on hills.

Able to stop by using emergency brake.

Does not take eyes from road or turn head when conversing to passenger in front seat.

Maintains vehicle in consistently safe lane position.

Does not cross center line on turns.

Observes all speed limits.

The following form may be used by an agency to evaluate a driver's ability to handle a vehicle safely on snow and ice.

Driver: _____

Observer: _____

Date: _____

Able to securely strap down a load in the van rack.

Knows how to safely perform a battery jump start.

Knows how to start a cold or flooded engine.

Demonstrates an ability to mount and dismount tire chains.

Knows speed limits for driving with chains.

Recovers from a skid in chained and unchained van.

Makes a controlled, no-skid stop in a chained and unchained van.

Able to make an emergency stop from 20 miles per hour using the emergency brake on a chained and unchained van.

Drives with lights on. (Varies with conditions.)

Slows down before approaching curves.

Shows a high level of caution, awareness, and safety habits while driving.

EVALUATION

How would you rate this winter driver training? _____

_____

Do you think the training prepared you for winter driving challenges? _____

_____

Do you feel at ease with chaining? _____

_____

What were your impressions of the leaders' presentations, testing, and guidance? _____

_____

How do you feel about the time commitment for this training? _____

_____

What subject areas should be included in the next training? _____

_____

Responsibilities of the driver. Each driver should be supplied with a responsibility list which should be viewed as an integral part of the job.

Driver Responsibilities

VAN PROCEDURES

1. A driver's first responsibility is to the safety and welfare of the participants. The driver *must not drive* if his or her ability to drive safely is limited in any way by tiredness, drugs, illness, injury, or any other cause. Personal or program expense or inconvenience does not justify any compromise of driving safety.

2. City vehicles are to be used for city business only.

3. All drivers must be approved by supervisory staff; authorized drivers *cannot* sub-delegate or authorize anyone else to drive the vehicle. Winter driving requires special authorization.

4. Drivers should have a participant list with emergency phone numbers and/or permission slips. A copy should also be left at program facility.

5. The driver must check the following items before the start of each trip:

   --Headlights, low/high beams;
   --Taillights;
   --Turn signals and emergency flashers;
   --Brake lights;
   --General tire condition;
   --Fuel gauge (after starting);
   --Oil-pressure gauge (after starting);
   --Horn;
   --Windshield wipers and windshield-washing solution;
   --Mirror position.

6. Each van must be equipped appropriately. The driver must check for the following gear:

   --Functional seat belts for driver and all passengers (in place and ready to use *before* loading passengers);
   --Fire extinguisher (is it functional?);
   --Aproved first-aid kit (supplies fully stocked, cleaned and dry?);
   --Flashlight (fresh batteries?);
   --Emergency flares;
   --Jumper cables;

--Chains and tighteners (in season, and with chain repair kit);

--Snow shovel (in season);

--Ice scraper (in season);

--Vehicle accident forms, emergency call lists, and credit cards.

7. No gear shall be packed above seat level unless fully restricted from any forward motion. Side exit doors must not be blocked by equipment. Gear loaded on the rack must be secured with adequate tie-downs. No objects or parts of the body shall be allowed to extend through the window.

8. Accidents, moving violations, or failure to adhere to van policies while driving shall be grounds for disciplinary action.

9. Drivers and participants shall wear seat belts when the van is in motion.

10. Games, songs, or activities shall not interfere with the driver's concentration.

11. Emergency key locations shall be known by all staff.

12. Drivers are to take into consideration possible adverse public relations regarding where vehicles are parked and actions or activities taking place near or within them.

13. In the case of an emergency, see to the immediate needs of the participants first, and contact the necessary police or emergency services. Then use the emergency call list to contact your supervisor or a city representative for additional help in parent/guardian contact, transportation aid, and possible public-statement guidelines. Circumstances in which you should use the call list include, but are not limited to, the following:

--serious illness or injury;

--lost person(s);

--van breakdown;

--significant delay.

Emergency call lists are available from your supervisor. Make sure you get one. You are required to have it in your possession on any program trip.

Vehicle Breakdown

If a vehicle should become immobilized through mechanical breakdown or running out of gas, *the first responsibility of the leader is for the safety and welfare of the participants.*

If the vehicle is in a hazardous position, passengers should be moved from the vehicle to a safe location.

The vehicle should be marked so as not to be a hazard to other drivers.

(Each sponsoring agency should here insert the practices to be followed in case of: repairs, towing, citations, inoperable vehicle.)

Vehicle Accident

A driver's first responsibility is to the safety and welfare of the participants. Administer first aid, and contact emergency services in the event of injuries. Most jurisdictions require that the police be contacted if the accident was on public roads or if injuries or property damage occurred.

No statement of liability shall be made by the driver or any participant.

The accident must be reported to your supervisor immediately.

A "Vehicle Accident Report" form must be completed at the scene and given to your supervisor. Copies should be in the van glove box. An example is also in this packet.

In the event of injuries a "Personal Injury/Accident Form" must be completed for each injuried person. The completed form should be given to your supervisor.

Emergency Action. Drivers may be supplied with material similar to the following that explains how to meet driving emergencies.

Meeting Driving Emergencies

COMMON TYPES OF DRIVING EMERGENCIES AND CORRECTIVE ACTION

The quality of driver reactions usually determines the difference between a close call and a collision. The many variations and complications of emergency situations make it difficult to prepare for every one. The following emergencies have been selected to stimulate thought and assist in preparing for decisions:

1. Driving on Snow and Ice
    --Drive at reduced speed;
    --Make no sudden changes in speed or direction;
    --To slow down, pump brake pedal lightly two or three times per second;
    --In starting, accelerate gradually for optimum traction;

--Try to anticipate icy spots and slow down *before* you come to them.

2. Recovering From a Skid
    --Avoid braking on icy pavement;
    --Steer in the direction in which the rear end of the vehicle is skidding.

3. Running Off Pavement
    --Release accelerator pedal;
    --Keep firm grip on steering wheel;
    --*Resist urge* to return to pavement immediately;
    --Straddle pavement edge until vehicle is *moving slowly;*
    --Turn sharply back onto pavement where pavement is nearly level with shoulder.

4. Deep Ruts and/or Holes in Road
    --Reduce speed;
    --Try to avoid ruts and holes if such action can be done safely;
    --Before wheel drops in rut or hole, let up on brakes so wheel will turn;
    --Maintain firm grip on steering wheel.

5. Animals on the Road
    --Avoid hitting an animal only if you can safely do so by braking and steering. Do not swerve so drastically as to lose control. It may be better to strike the animal.

6. Bee in Vehicle
    --Ignore while driving;
    --Stop on shoulder and *then* remove bee.

7. Physical Emergencies Affecting the Driver
    --For dirt in eye, violent coughing and sneezing attack, signal, slow down, and stop, until condition is corrected;
    --For dropped articles, do not try to retrieve anything from the floor of vehicle while vehicle is moving. Stop, then recover or dispose of dropped item.

8. Blinding Lights
    --Dim lights even though other driver does not;
    --Look at the right edge of the road;
    --Slow down.

9. Tire Blowouts
    --Keep firm grip on steering wheel;
    --Keep wheels as straight as possible;
    --Gradually release accelerator pedal;
    --Pump brakes lightly;
    --Reduce speed to 15 mph or less before pulling off onto shoulder;
    --Have vehicle well off the road to change tire.

10. Brake Failure
    --Take foot off accelerator pedal;
    --Pump brake pedal repeatedly;
    --Shift to lower gear;
    --Engage parking brake;
    --Turn off ignition;
    --Rub tire against curbing if on a steep city hill;

--Rub fender against cliff or run into bushes before picking up speed if on a mountain road.

11. Steering Failure
    --If hard steering develops, pull off road and check for low tire or broken power-steering belt;
    --Complete failure: apply brakes moderately to prevent skidding.

12. Lights Fail
    --Try other lights such as high or low beam, turning signal, parking lights, fog lights, brake lights, as the problem may be in one of the switches.

13. Accelerator Sticks
    --Pump accelerator pedal with several sharp jabs to release;
    --Turn off ignition;
    --Apply brakes and pull off highway.

14. Flooding of Carburetor
    --Hold accelerator pedal against floor (Do not pump pedal);
    --Engage starter for 20 to 30 seconds, let starter motor cool, and repeat if necessary.

15. Hood Flies Up
    --Look ahead out of left window;
    --Decelerate as rapidly as can safely be done;
    --Do not cross center line;
    --Pull off road as soon as possible.

16. Stalling on Railroad Tracks
    --If train is coming, leave vehicle;
    --Leave area of impact and go in direction train is approaching;
    --If train is not coming, place gear shift on standard transmission. With lever in low or reverse, engage clutch and engage starter, push. For automatic transmission, place in neutral and push or pull with another vehicle.

17. Submerged Vehicle
    --Escape through open window, before water reaches window level, if possible;
    --Most vehicles will float for several minutes;
    --If vehicle sinks too rapidly, move to the rear of passenger compartment to breathe trapped air while planning to escape;
    --Open side window or knock out back window;
    --Open door when water pressure is equalized.

18. Vehicle Catches on Fire
    --Evacuate passengers immediately (toxic fumes, gasoline);
    --Cut off electrical power if possible;
    --Carry and use an approved fire extinguisher;
    --Throw mud, dirt, or snow on blaze.

19. Rear-end Collision Imminent
    --Position your body across seat or slump down so your head is supported by back of seat. In this unusual case (rear-end impact that is sufficiently predictable), this would help. In the

broader perspective it is too often used as a rationale against seat belts!

--Use your arm to support the back of your head and neck, or slump down so your head hits the back of the seat, and encourage riders to do the same.

20. When an Accident is Imminent (Head-on or front-corner impact)

--Steer until accident is unavoidable;

--Stay in vehicle;

--Immediately before impact, driver should cross arms over face and press head and arms against steering wheel.

Driving Tips. Sometimes agencies provide all drivers with checklists of what to do before and during use of vehicles. The following checklist is given to all drivers approved to drive vehicles owned by the city of Eugene, Oregon. The list should be used each time a driver takes a group of participants on an outing.

Driving Tips

Eugene, Oregon, Parks and Recreation — Outdoor Program

This may be the most important five minutes of your job! The driver *must check the following items* before the start of each trip.

Under the Hood

--Radiator water level (antifreeze);

--Battery water level;

--Battery connections;

--Oil level (correct weight);

--Automatic-transmission fluid level (if applicable);

--Windshield-washer fluid level (and washing solution).

In the Car

--Windshield-washer operation;

--Windshield-wiper operation and effectiveness;

--Horn;

--Emergency brake;

--Seat belts for everyone (in place and ready to use);

--Indicator (idiot) lights for oil, amps, high beam, etc.;

--Fuel gauge (and know what kind of gas the vehicle uses!);

--First-aid kit (fully stocked, clean, and dry!);

--Jumper cables;

--Ice scraper (in season);

--Snow shovel (in season);

--Flashlight (fresh batteries!);

--Emergency flares;

--Emergency call list;

--Vehicle accident forms;

--Credit cards;

--Maps (if needed);

--Jack/handle/lug wrench (good idea to see if you are able to loosen lug nuts with wrench provided);

--Tire chains (that you *know* fit) and tighteners.

Out of the Car

--Headlights (high/low beams all working);

--Taillights;

--Turn signals (front and rear);

--Brake lights;

--Emergency flashers;

--Tire-tread depth (should be excellent) and wear;

--Spare tire (inflated);

--Mirror position.

COMMON PROBLEMS

Engine will not start (or starter clicks rapidly). Check for loose battery connections. Check battery water level. Make sure all lights or unnecessary power-consuming circuits are switched off.

Flooded engine. Hold gas pedal down fully; do not pump gas pedal; try to start engine (do not hold starter on for more than 5 seconds, giving the battery at least ten seconds of rest between tries). Engine should start within 10 tries. Or just let engine sit for ten to twenty minutes without attempting to start it.

Jump starting. Jump only twelve- to twelve-volt systems. Jump only alternator to alternator, generator to generator systems. If different, remove battery cable from good battery to protect donor's system. Connect one jumper cable (red) from positive side of donor's battery to positive (+) side of ineffective battery. Connect the other (black) cable from the negative (-) side of the donor's battery to suitable ground on the nonstarting engine. Start engine and remove cables — in reverse order (negative first). *Do not* make the final connection at the battery! Hydrogen gas is present and may explode if ignited by the spark, blowing the battery apart and possibly blowing you with acid. Connect the final negative (ground) terminal to some part of the engine or frame away from the battery!

ACCIDENT PROCEDURES

If you are involved in an accident, you must render aid to other individuals also involved.

1. If danger of spilled gasoline, or vehicle severely damaged, turn off ignition. Do not allow anyone

to smoke anywhere in the vicinity of the vehicle! Vapors travel a long way.

2. Render first aid and *send for professional help.*
3. *Warn other drivers* — place flares to warn traffic in both directions. Place at least two flares about 150 ft. (50 yds.) and 250 ft. (85 yds.) behind accident. Place at least one flare 150 ft. ahead of accident. These are bare minimums! Remember, it takes 125 ft. for a car to stop on *good dry pavement* when going 40 mph. Protect yourself and others; *warn other drivers far enough away that they will be able to stop safely if they have to.* Snow and/or ice can easily *triple* stopped distances!
4. Protect yourself and others from the environment; stay warm and dry.
5. Be cautious about accepting *towing* help from non-professional passers-by. They may do more harm than good and cost you more than a professional.

If you are not involved but decide to stop at an accident scene:

1. Have a reason for stopping. No sight-seers, please!
2. Drive past the accident and stop/park in a safe place.
3. *Warn other drivers* — place flares, add additional ones, or replace dying ones.
4. Do not attempt to pull out a snowbound vehicle without realizing the extreme dangers you place yourself and others in. *Towing is best left to the professionals.* You must not cause other accidents. *You may be held liable for any problems that arise.*

If you are unable to stop, you can often help by tossing out a few flares (unlighted) as you drive slowly by.

Friendly Advice: Problems with tire chains and driving too fast are the major cause of accidents in the mountains. Practice putting your chains on before you venture into the mountains. The better you are at it, the easier it will be out in the rain and slush. Slow down. Driving at 60 mph. rather than 45 mph. would only save about fifteen minutes on a sixty-mile trip. Is it really worth the risk? Remember — *cars don't "go out of control," drivers lose control.* Have a safe and enjoyable trip.

Miscellaneous policies should be written to cover various contingencies along the following lines:
The number of people per vehicle. "No vehicle shall contain more people than the manufacturer's intended maximum" (i.e., six passengers, five passengers, etc.).
Starting time. Vehicles shall leave early enough to

reach the destination (site or home) before dark if possible.
Relief. Drivers should be relieved by a rest or change of drivers every 100 miles.
Payment. Who pays and by what means for:

a. Vehicular breakdown repairs and/or towing en route?
b. Moving-vehicle violation fines (speeding)?
c. Non-moving vehicle violation fines (parking)?
d. Meals en route?
e. Emergency items (windshield wipers, light bulbs, etc.)?

Winter-Driving Tips. The following two sets of aids were developed for helping drivers put on tire chains. They are each presented here so that the readers can see both consistency and variety in this type of material and develop their own driving tips to fit their own situations.

Winter Driving Tips

Driving under winter conditions presents many hazards that are unfamiliar to the summer driver. Packed snow, "black ice," white-outs, blizzards, and blocked traffic are only a few of the problems drivers should be prepared to cope with. Of any winter outdoor activity, driving to and from the recreation site is probably the most dangerous aspect of the outing. Proper preparation of your vehicle and knowledge of winter driving techniques can help insure safe and enjoyable excursions. The following notes, hints, and suggestions are compiled from personal experiences and information supplied by state-police, auto-club, and highway-department personnel.

CHAINS

Although snow tires and studded tires offer somewhat better traction than regular tires, they do not replace the need for tire chains. Cars without tire chains may be cited by police when chains are required, even if they have studded tires. In many states studded snow tires are prohibited.

--Carry tire chains that fit the car's tires. Try them on at home to make sure they fit and are in good condition. "Cables," "strap," and other recent innovations are almost never as good as old-fashioned steel-link chains. Be a cautious consumer.

--Carry a few repair links (and pliers to put them on).

--If rubber chain tighteners are used, most normal operation only requires that they be hooked at three points, forming a triangle. Putting them on too tight can cause excessive wear on the sidewalls of the tires.

--If possible, avoid jacking up the car to put chains on. Do not crawl under a jacked-up car.

--An inexpensive rainsuit and gloves make chaining up somewhat comfortable.

--Park in a plowed turnout, never blocking traffic or on a blind turn or steep grade.

--Chain up *before* you have to. Getting pulled out of a snow bank is more costly and time consuming than chaining up early.

--Check chains after a few miles of driving or sooner if you hear signs of looseness.

--Chains offer better traction but not necessarily better control (steering). *Slow down!*

--It should take a total time of *less than ten minutes* to chain up a car or van using this system:

1. Park safely off the road!
2. Lay the chains out behind the rear wheels (front wheels on front-wheel-drive vehicles) with ice bar down, the inside hook on the inside next to the tire, and the outside latch on the outside next to the tire.
3. Back onto the chains until the hook and latch ends are accessible, just in front of the tire (about a foot of chain should be loose).
4. Flop the chain up and over the tire and hook the inside hook.
5. Vigorously pull the chain tight on the outside and latch it.
6. Add the tighteners (rubber loops with hooks).

PARKING

--Park only in plowed turnouts, as far from the roadway as possible.

--Park in the direction you wish to leave from (or downhill); and, if it is snowing or a storm is pending, put your chains on before you leave on your excursion (especially overnights).

--Do not block other cars from getting out.

--If engaged, your emergency brake can freeze ON. Park in gear.

--If parking overnight, mark your car with a flag on the antenna to avoid being crunched by a snowplow when your car becomes covered by snow.

DRIVING

Knowing how to drive a car on ice and snow requires judgment, good instruction and experience. Make sure your vehicle is in good operating condition: wipers, lights, brakes, steering, tires, etc.

--Slow down, but remember large vehicles such as trucks must maintain their momentum to retain traction. Try not to impede traffic. It is required by state law that you pull over and allow traffic to pass if more than five cars are close behind you. Maximum speed when using chains is recommended to be 30 mph.

--Drive with lights and seat belts ON!

--Driving when tired and sleepy is doubly dangerous on slippery roads. Let someone else drive or pull off and refresh with fresh air, sleep, or coffee.

--Allow plenty of time to make the trip. Don't try to make up time on the road. "Better late than never."

--If conditions are slippery, use your gears to slow down. Use brakes with extreme caution. Pump lightly to slow down.

--Start with an easy foot on the accelerator and slip the clutch. Don't spin the wheels. Traction is greatest just before the wheels spin.

--If the wheels spin, try rocking the car forward and backward. Also try sand, gravel, or traction mats to get out of a pocket.

--Once underway, try to keep up your momentum. When approaching a hill, keep far enough behind the next vehicle so you will not have to slow down or stop.

--Icy surfaces make steering difficult. Slow down *before* reaching curves. It is very difficult to judge the exact speed at which to make a corner. If the corner is perfectly flat (unbanked), the concern is only that the car may go too fast and slide toward the outside. If the road is banked, then going too *slowly* may cause the vehicle to slide into the inside of the corner. Either mistake can send the car off the road or into oncoming traffic.

--If the rear of the car starts skidding, release the accelerator and steer the front of the car in the direction the rear is skidding. As the car starts to straighten out, straighten the front wheels. Don't oversteer.

--On a winter day when the road surface is clear, watch for icy patches in shaded areas beneath overpasses and on bridges. These can easily cause a skid if you are going too fast.

EQUIPMENT LIST

Sunglasses;
Appropriate clothing;
Blanket;
First-aid kit;
Fire extinguisher;
Tire lug wrench and jack;
Battery jumper cables;
Shovel;
Tow rope or chain;
Flashlight (good batteries);
Windshield deicer/cleaning solution;
Old towel for cleaning windows *and lights;*
Thermos with hot beverage for return trip;
Twenty-minute highway flares (at least six or more);
Extra food for emergencies;

Tire chains and repair links, wire, and pliers;
Rubber chain tighteners;
Antifreeze in your radiator;
Windshield scraper;
Tool kit.

SOME ADDITIONAL DRIVING NOTES

1. If driving conditions are extremely bad, perhaps it would be better to stay home. Call state police for road report.
2. Gasoline may be difficult to get in some areas. Be aware that you should not carry extra gas in the passenger compartment of any vehicle. It is extremely dangerous.
3. Before leaving vehicle, check to make sure lights are turned off. They are often left on in the excitement of getting "up the hill' or "on the slope."
4. Don't venture into the mountains with a car that you "think" will "just" make it.
5. Plan ahead when stopping. Distances needed to stop safely are greatly increased by wet or icy roads.
6. If conditions are marginal, don't *assume* you will have a clear road ahead and "won't need chains if I can just keep moving." There is probably someone else off the road or blocking the road around the next turn who thought the same. Chain up early.

Tire Chains

Eugene Parks and Recreation Department

Cars without chains, or with incorrectly mounted chains, are a major cause of accidents and delays on the mountain passes each winter. If you *practice* the method suggested below, you'll find chaining up quick, simple, and easy.

First, get your chains ready. Drag those rusty chains out of that soggy box or bag and spread them out neatly. Carefully check over each link of the side chains and cross chains for cracks (a very common cause of chain failure). If you clean them up, this will all be easier. Now, with them spread out neatly again, make sure there are no twists in the side chains. With the side chains pulled out straight, the links should alternate at right angles to each other. If you find a twist, you should carefully unthread it by pulling one end of the tire chains through the space between the cross links where the twist was found. This can be a somewhat frustrating operation, but don't get discouraged. With luck, you'll never have to do it again. (See Diagram 1.)

Now, look at the latches. Figure out how to use them and check them for damage. Some chains will have a latch on one side and a "quick hook" on the other. If you have hard-to-use latches, you can purchase and install different ones, or even "quick hooks." Make up a repair kit for your chains from pliers, some soft wire, an *extra* set of chain tighteners, repair links, and an extra cross link or two. When you put your chains away, a light spray of oil will help prevent rusting. Hold up one end of the chain and lower it into the bag or box, leaving an end of each chain on top, ready to pull out.

PUTTING THEM ON

The best place to check out this procedure is in your driveway or on a nice dry parking lot. Practice will really pay off when you're out in the slush and slop of a turnout. Remember, if you drive past a "Chains Required" sign and don't put on your chains and *then* cause an accident or block the road, you could be cited for reckless driving (not a pleasant thought)! So practice this, and you'll be able to chain up effortlessly (well, almost). A plastic garbage bag to kneel on and an old towel to wipe your hands afterward are deluxe additions to your chain-up kit.

Here goes! In three simple steps:

STEP ONE.

Lay the chain over the top of the tire. The cross chain toward the front of the car should be tucked neatly under the front of the tire. (See Diagram 2.) If you have "quick hooks," the hook side goes on the inside of the tire.

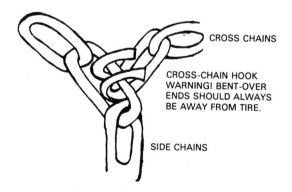

CROSS CHAINS

CROSS-CHAIN HOOK
WARNING! BENT-OVER
ENDS SHOULD ALWAYS
BE AWAY FROM TIRE.

SIDE CHAINS

STEP TWO.

Drive forward *slowly* until the rear end of the chain is even with the center of the tire (the axle).

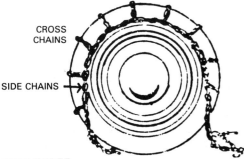

CROSS CHAINS

SIDE CHAINS

STEP THREE.

Latch the *inside* first, then take up all the slack possible and latch the outside. Any extra links can be held down by the chain tighteners when you put them on. Chains should be on firmly, but if they are too tight, they will damage the sidewall of your tires. Do not use rubber tighteners on *cable* chains.

HINTS and THOUGHTS

1. If you pull out at the beginning of a chain-up turnout and chain up there, you can then drive the length of the turnout to check your chains. If they need adjustment, you can do it then without having to drive all the way to the next turnout while your car is battered by a loose chain.
2. When driving with chains, remember that your traction is improved, but your steering is not. Be careful and don't get overconfident. Also, studded snow tires do not replace the need for chains. While they will improve handling over regular street tires, they do not come close to giving the security of chains.
3. A car with front-wheel drive needs to have the front wheels chained up.
4. Always put your chains on in a turnout plowed for that purpose. Just pulling to the side of the road is not only an invitation to a ticket, but can be disastrous!

Summary

Transportation of groups from their urban communities to the sites of outdoor pursuits is an integral part of all trip planning. Careful transportation planning and driving can reduce risks of accidents considerably. Administrators and leaders must consider resources for transportation and transportation safety. The former include vehicles owned and operated by volunteers, employees, and professionals while the latter includes such items as evaluating drivers and informing drivers relative to driving practices, meeting emergencies, public relations, and winter driving.

FINANCING

Gone is the day of John Muir, who could hike through Sierra Mountain snowstorms with only an overcoat and an occasional blanket to keep him warm through the night. No longer do outdoor people, as Muir did, exist on boiled tea and hard bread broken from the stale loaf by kicks of the boot while walking along a rocky trail. The writings of John Muir, founder of the Sierra Club, may gloss over potential discomfort, frostbite, exposure to inclement weather, and other outdoor hazards and invite the novice outdoorsperson to emulate his style; however, in truth, Muir's trips were not taken in the worst of conditions, for he hiked only when and where his fancy lead him, not being limited to weekends, not being interested in testing himself in difficult situations or inclement weather, and being driven by scientific investigations, not the drive to pit himself against nature.

Today's outdoor enthusiasts seldom possess the skills and the mental and physical conditioning necessary for such marginally equipped adventures. Participants now expect to minimize both discomfort and risk by utilizing the readily available and ever-improving clothing and equipment designed especially for outdoor pursuits. For some, equipment is necessary for simple comfort; for others it becomes a means for survival on ventures into elements where the human is pitted against nature. Because of the relative lack of conditioning for inclement weather or harsh environments, coupled with the desire to test oneself in increasingly difficult situations, today's outdoor advocate takes along equipment to ward off adverse elements. Lightweight, sturdy, fashionable equipment can be found in hundreds of catalogs and stores. It is difficult to recommend a specific budget for equipment for one, let alone several, outdoor-pursuit activities since the costs vary widely even for basic items considered essential for each. In some cases, low-budget options are available, however.

Ideally, equipment and clothing should be purchased with only two things in mind: need and function. Thus this material on finances is written with the assumption that costs are for sturdy, functional, and necessary items. Expenses may be divided into individual equipment, clothing, and trip costs.

Individual Equipment

Financing clothing and equipment for an outing requires effort and commitment, whether one is providing for personal needs or for those of an entire group and/or program. Probably only those who have been personally involved in an activity can fully appreciate the importance of proper equipment. It is common, for instance, for prospective participants to complain loudly about the costs of a good set of raingear; however, when it rains on the outing, those with good raingear would not be willing to part with it for many times the price.

The important point here is that the administration, leaders, and participants must understand the need for equipment in order to be committed to the financial stress of obtaining it. With this in mind, one should be familiar with the material on environment, clothing, and equipment in this book as well as a complete description of the area in which one will travel before deciding how much should be allocated to purchasing or renting equipment.

As a leader, one is expected to require no less clothing or equipment than is generally considered minimum by other practicing professionals in that geographic area. To be on the safe side, financial planning should include sufficient funds for the amount and condition of equipment utilized by reputable organizations in that area. Lack of funds is not a good defense in court if a defendant is asked why the organization did not provide the same quantity and quality of equipment as other groups. (The same goes for equipment maintenance.) One is never required to follow anyone else's patterns, but it is difficult to offer a defensible reason for allowing standards lower than those considered prudent by others in the same locale.

Depending on the nature of the activity, the cost of individual equipment for outdoor pursuits can range from $50 to $5,000 per person, with the typical being close to $200. In initial instruction, planning, or orientation meetings participants should be warned that "any old clothes" will not suffice for safely executed outdoor pursuits; however, secondhand stores and Army/Navy clothing stores sell excellent wool trousers and sweaters which, while not particularly attractive or stylish, can serve as comfortable and inexpensive outdoor clothing.

Each individual should consider the lists of basic equipment itemized in the appendices, starting with Appendix A, Hiking.

Trip Costs

The costs of the trip itself borne by the sponsoring agency include group equipment, travel expenses, the salaries of the leaders, insurance permit, and special-use fees and some miscellaneous items.

Group equipment provided by the sponsor may include:
1. Food (which could be individual)
2. Stoves and fuel
3. Cooking utensils
4. Shelter
5. Group-sized first-aid kit
6. Boats, paddles, life jackets
7. Climbing gear
8. Skiing equipment
9. Others

Sponsors Expenses include many possible expenditures. A possible list of considerations for trip expenses may appear like the one below.

Possible Trip Expenses for Agency Consideration

Salaries
--Full-time employees
--Part-time employees
--Contracted staff
Taxes, Insurance, FICA for employees
Transportation
--Rental
--Insurance
--Gas
--Oil
--Servicing
--Safety equipment
--Labor (Maintenance)
--Parts (Maintenance)
--Road Service
--Parking
--Tolls
--Public transportation
Accommodations
--Campsite fees
--User fees
--En-route lodging
--Resource access costs (permits, etc.)
Equipment
--Purchased
--Rental
--Maintenance
--Repairs
Food supplied by agency
--En route
--On trip
Insurance
--Staff
--Participant
Office Supplies
--Telephone
--Postage
--Printing
--Information packets
Pre/post Trip Meetings
--Leaders wages
--Building rentals
Miscellaneous
--Maps
--Books
--Guides
--Promotion
Administration
--Employees
--Lawyer/CPA
--Computer services
--Volunteers

A budget-planning sheet used by a municipal recreation department is shown in Figure 9.1. This example does *not* consider full-time employees or their personal expenses, agency utilities, etc., but is a planning sheet to calculate how much should be charged participants to cover expenses over and above those funded by the tax base. Because the potential for unexpected expenses is high, this sample planning budget includes a built-in contingency amount of 7%. In this case excess funds usually pay for the promotion of the next trip.

In figuring the cost of a trip using Figure 9.1, several explanations are in order: Payment of part-time (contracted) staff only is considered here since, in this case, their salaries are included in the tax-base budget. In the case of a contracted person, such employee pays his or her own income tax, social security (FICA), and insurance and is hired (contracted) as a private consultant or specialist.

These contracted leaders may receive an hourly rate based on minimum wage laws or may be contracted for each program at a pre-established fee. In the above case, outdoor leaders who are responsible for overnight or long-range trips were paid an hourly rate for a maximum of ten hours per day even though they were officially in charge when asleep.

FIGURE 9.1 Outdoor Adventure/Education Program

BUDGET SHEET/FINANCIAL SUMMARY

Activity: _____   Pre-Trip Date: _____

Activity Date: _____   Location: _____

	EXPENDITURES	Pre-Trip	Actual

Salaries:
    Leader _____ hrs x $ _____ rate x _____ days $ _____ $ _____

    Leader _____ hrs x $ _____ rate x _____ days $ _____ $ _____

Transportation:
    Pre-Trip: _____ miles x _____ ¢/mile $ _____

    Actual: _____ miles x _____ ¢/mile $ _____

Insurance:
    Pre-Trip: _____ participants x _____ ¢/day x _____ days $ _____

    Actual: _____ participants x _____ ¢/day x _____ days $ _____

Refunds:
    _____ x $ _____ $ _____

Equipment Rental:
    Pre-Trip: _____ participants x $ _____/day x _____ days $ _____

    Actual: _____ participants x $ _____/day x _____ days $ _____

Other:

    1._____ $ _____ $ _____

    2._____ $ _____ $ _____

    3._____ $ _____ $ _____

    4._____ $ _____ $ _____

TOTAL EXPENDITURES .... $ _____ $ _____

FEES

Based on $ _____ Total Expenditures divided by _____ minimum participants $ _____

Based on $ _____ Total Expenditures divided by _____ maximum participants $ _____

INCOME

_____ participants x $ _____ participant $ _____

Other:

    1._____ $ _____

    2._____ $ _____

TOTAL INCOME

    Total Income $ _____

Less: Total Actual Expenditures   ($_____)

    RESERVE FUND........ $ _____

    DEFICIT .... $ _____

SUMMARY

Transportation of participants to an outing site entails planning for the vehicles and the skill of the drivers. Carefully thought out steps for driving safely should be followed by each driver every time people are entrusted to his or her care. Many items and procedures should be checked before leaving the place where the vehicles are stored. By the same token, financing an outing includes many items besides the equipment, which may in itself be the most costly portion of the program.

BIBLIOGRAPHY

Eugene, Oregon, Park and Recreation Department.

Spokane, Washington, Park and Recreation Department.

Buell, Larry, *Leader's Guide to the 24-Hour Experience,* Greenfield, MA: Environmental Awareness Publications, 1978.

CHAPTER 10

PROGRAMMING AND PUBLIC RELATIONS

One may wonder why public relations and programming go hand in hand. Actually, public relations is an inherent element of every outdoor-pursuit administration. It is with the actual program itself, however, that one is most likely to plan for promotion.

In reality, the program is everything — planned and unplanned — that affects the participants. By the same token, public relations is everything — planned and unplanned — that affects public attitude toward the program. In theory, this should be a planned effort to influence the opinions of the public in a favorable, positive direction. If, because of lack of a plan to direct feelings, the public derives a negative attitude toward an enterprise, we assume "poor public relations!"

A simple example of the interrelations of program and public relations follows:

A group is caught unprepared in a hailstorm. People are cold and shivering. At the end of the trip an assistant leader announces, "Nearly everyone had hypothermia!" Two errors occur here: One, the program is poorly planned, resulting in a lack of protective equipment, and two, there seems to be no consideration of the results of thoughtless (and probably incorrect) remarks from what may be an untrained assistant leader. With this example in mind, we turn to a discussion of program principles followed by public-relations principles.

THE PROGRAM

An outdoor program may be assessed as being a practical translation of the sponsoring organization's goals and objectives. In other words, the program is the vehicle through which an organization meets its goals. Consequently, before a program is planned, one should understand the objectives of the agency, which are often very dissimilar. This may be better understood if we realize how different a military training unit, an institution for the mentally ill, a college recreation program, a community center, and a youth agency are, and how the purposes of their outdoor-pursuit programs must differ.

Regardless of ultimate goals, program planning principles should recognize both the group and the individual within the group. The type, length, and content of the program should be based on these considerations. Principles may be defined as guiding rules for action or beliefs on which action is based.

Group-centered Principles

The principles to be considered here will vary according to the type of group you are working with. Groups consisting of single categories of individuals (i.e., Boy Scouts) will be less affected by some guidelines than groups made up of a wide range of individuals (i.e., participants at a community center.) Accordingly, the following ten principles do not apply equally to all groups; yet each should be considered.

1. The program must focus on the needs and interests of the group, plus available leadership and equipment.
2. The program should be planned for age ranges and abilities within the group. For example, a youth group may range from ages ten to sixteen, include beginners and experts, and consist of both able-bodied and disabled members. A college class may consist of males and females of all abilities, conditions, and interests who range in age from seventeen to thirty. A community-center group consists of all ages, all abilities, all socio-economic levels, and all interests. Obviously the municipal outdoor programmer has a much more diversified clientele than does the planner of a program for the ROTC or the inmates of a detention facility for males.
3. The program should offer a majority of activities within the financial budgets of all potential participants. If some members of the target group cannot afford the program,

either the program should be altered or expenses should be somehow defrayed (through scholarships, donations, borrowing, renting, improvising).
4. Conditions under which the program is conducted must be safe so that participants will understand that optimal precautions are necessary when they operate on their own. It is better to turn back and refund some money than to risk loss of life. It is also better to have the group decide to turn back as if they did not have the expertise of the leader to rely on. The next time they may be going out on their own anyway.
5. Most programs should offer the continuity of year-round operation. Courses about care and repair of equipment, first aid, meteorology, geology, map and compass, etc. all contribute to the overall outdoor program and can be offered during what is often called the "off-season."
6. The program should provide activities of a progressive nature (not a repeat of the same old trips to the same old places).
7. The program should be a supplement to what is already offered and available within the community.
8. The program should involve some long-range planning to ensure future leadership, finances, facilities, and equipment.
9. The program should be based on the standards developed by national agencies or research studies. (Ratio of leaders to participants, leader competencies, progressions, equipment, etc.).
10. The program should follow the best practices known in the field.

Individual-centered Principles

At the same time as they plan a program for a group, leaders need to consider each individual and keep the following principles in mind:

1. The program should provide the individual with an outlet for expressing skills and interests.
2. The individual should be provided with a wide range of individual choices in a variety of activities. This will vary with different groups since a prescribed outdoor program

will have fewer choices than one sponsored by a municipal recreation department. Nevertheless, individual differences should be recognized and programmed accordingly.

3. Every program should provide the opportunity for social interaction and fellowship.
4. Every program should create and develop an interest in self-leadership, self-sufficiency, and self-reliance. The program that makes groups and individuals reliant on the leader is missing one of the goals of outdoor pursuits — that of self-reliance.
5. The program should involve the participant in the planning process and, to some extent, in the decision-making process.
6. The program should provide the opportunity for creative expression. Singing, storytelling, menu making, cooking, and joking are all forms of self-expression.
7. The program should provide the opportunity for adventure and new experience. Even though the leader has been there and done something a hundred times, it must be treated as a new and wonderous adventure to the beginner. Instead of belittling a climb with, "Oh, I've done that route lots of times," a leader could say, "Isn't the view from the ridge spectacular," or "What did you think of the steep pitch just before the summit?"

To Start A Program

Programs are initiated for a variety of reasons, depending upon the type of sponsoring agency. Basic to any program, however, are the needs of the potential participant. The interest, enthusiasm, and goal of the leader notwithstanding, no program will go beyond the conceptual stage unless everyone wants to participate. It is not within the scope of this book to discuss needs assessment or marketing, but some program planning guides are appropriate. Figure 10.1 is an example of a program planning form that may be used as an initiator. It is basic to any organization, school, youth agency, recreation department, private enterprise, etc.

Writing down objectives is another step inherent in the planning of any program. Basically, these answer the questions, "What do you plan to do?" and "What do you hope to accomplish?" Objectives should be attainable and measurable in any given program, and there should be at least some verification that they were met. The following guidelines may help in forming objectives.

Each objective should:

1. Start with the word "to" followed by an action verb.
2. Specify a single result to be accomplished.
3. Specify a target date for the accomplishment.
4. Be as specific and quantitative (hence measurable and verifiable) as possible.
5. Specify only the "what" and "when." Avoid the "why" and "how."
6. Relate directly to higher-level goals of the organization.
7. Be readily understandable by those who will be contributing to its attainment.
8. Be realistic and attainable, but represent a significant challenge.
9. Be consistent with the resources available or anticipated.
10. Be consistent with the basic policies and practices of the organization.
11. Be willingly agreed to by all parties without undue pressure or coercion.
    Examples:
    a. To organize and implement an eight-week canoeing class for sixteen participants which develops their ability to travel by canoe on flat water for two days.
    b. To teach basic canoeing skills to beginning paddlers.
    c. To teach group cooperation through a two-day and one-night canoe trip on Flatwater Lake.

Program Contents

The diversity of programming with land- and water-based outdoor foci is surprising if one wishes to consider all the possibilities. Programs may be developed around several different categories, and the following list shows only a few. While the major part of this book centers on land and water-based activities carried out in the natural environment away from the comforts and security of the urban environment, the following may be included as integral parts

FIGURE 10.1 Program Planning Form

EMPLOYEE: _____   PROGRAM DATE:_____

ACTIVITY:_____   LOCATION: _____
               (Descriptive Title)   (Facility Name and Street Address)

TYPE OF PROGRAM: JUSTIFICATION OF NEED:
_____ Continuous   _____ Carryover from previous activity
_____ Special   _____ Expansion of previous activity
_____ Annual   _____ Survey
_____ Other   _____ Availability of Expert Leadership
                               _____ Speculation Due to Area Served
                               _____ Other — Specify

PROGRAM OBJECTIVES:

1. _____

_____

2. _____

_____

3. _____

_____

4. _____

_____

(Continue on Separate Page If Needed — Be Specific)

ACTION STEPS:

1. _____

_____

2. _____

_____

3. _____

_____

ACTION STEPS (Continued):

4. _____

_____

5. _____

_____

6. _____

_____

7. _____

_____

(Be specific — detail exactly what has to be done to plan and implement the program, step-by-step, including a detailed outline of what activities are to occur, when, and who would be in charge. Use separate page if needed.)

METHODS OF PUBLICITY:
_____ Newspaper Advertisement
_____ Press Release
_____ Photographs
_____ Brochures
_____ Special Emblem
_____ Exhibition
_____ Displays
_____ Demonstrations
_____ Buttons, Decals, Banners, etc.
_____ Word of Mouth
_____ Flyers
_____ Bulletin Boards
_____ Posters and Signs
_____ Radio and Television
_____ Film and Slide Presentations

PARTICIPANTS: ESTIMATED NUMBER
_____ Male
_____ Female
_____ Adults - Specify ages _____
_____ Youth - Specify ages _____
_____ Special Characteristics

FACILITY REQUIREMENTS:

_____

_____

_____

_____

(Physical Set-up — Arrangements)

PARTICIPANT SAFETY:
_____ Abilities, qualifications, experiences of participants.
_____ Special policies?
_____ Permission slips for participants
_____ Identifiable hazards
_____ Emergency services and telephone numbers
_____ Staff preparation/training
_____ Permission from authorities?

LEADERSHIP:

_____ Staff members (names)
_____ Volunteers (names)
_____ Paid Officials (names)
_____ Others — Specify

_____
_____
_____
_____

TRANSPORTATION REQUIRED:

_____
_____
_____

(Distance to location)

EQUIPMENT, SUPPLIES, AND OTHER
ITEMS NEEDED:

_____
_____
_____
_____

CLEARANCE AND/OR COORDINATION:

_____ Supervisor
_____ Facility
_____ Parent Permission
_____ Scheduling
_____ Other — Specify

PROGRAM COSTS:

$_____ Leadership
$_____ Facility
$_____ Equipment
$_____ Transportation
$_____ Supplies
$_____ Promotion
$_____ Other — Specify
$_____ TOTAL COST

---

of such programs. Such activities may be carried out during pre-trip training, on the trip, or at post-trip review sessions. Or they may be used as programs offered to complement and/or supplement the outdoor-pursuit offering.

Competitive Events:
  Orienteering contests;
  Tent-pitching races;
  Softball on snowshoes;
  Plant identification (or rock, bird, etc.) contests;
  Outdoor cooking-for-taste contests.

Drop-In (unsupervised self-interest activities):
  Map-reading practice;
  Knot-tying boards;
  Reading reference books.

Interest groups:
  Clubs;
  Lectures;
  Slide shows;
  Films.

Special Events:
  Winter carnival;
  Pot lucks;
  Progressive cookouts;
  Award programs;
  Recognition nights;
  Litter clean-up trips;
  Trail-building trips;
  Fund-raisers (sponsoring hikers or boaters for $.50 or $1.00 per mile).

Classes:
  First aid;
  Weather;
  Map-and-compass;
  Plant identification;
  Meterology;
  Geology;
  Outdoor-cooking;
  Swimming;
  Photography;
  Astronomy;
  Animal-tracks;
  Bird-watching;
  Care and repair of equipment;
  Making and remodeling equipment.

Programs can be developed for age and skill levels, and should be organized by season, month, and sometimes week. All outdoor-pursuit leadership does not occur on a trail or river; some may happen indoors, in town, and in structured lectures.

Registration

Registration is also a public-relations part of the program. Methods and personnel involved certainly give the participant his or her first impression of the program. Thus several items should be considered when setting up a registration procedure. Remember that during registration participants make their first contact with your agency. If the contact is not good, it may well be their last.

Points of consideration include these methods:
1. Telephone;
2. In person;
3. By mail.

For registration all of the above may be used. This allows the procedures to fit the convenience of the participant or the participant's parents. Certain standards must also be conformed to with each method to keep registration from becoming chaotic.

Registration *by telephone* is very easy, many times so easy that participants forget that they are registered. Thus registration by telephone should simply save a place until the proper forms are completed and the fees paid.

Registration *in person* is actually the best method; however, it is also the most inconvenient for participants. If they come in person, the forms can be filled out, the fees paid, the information picked up, and questions answered with one contact.

By *the mail,* registration is convenient if the participant gives complete information. But it is very difficult to close a program when forms keep arriving in the mail after the limit is filled.

Conducting registration by any method can be summed up in one sentence: Make it efficient and simple. To avert the hosts of problems which come from sloppy registration, use these hints to set up better procedures:

1. Registering personnel must have total information about the program, plus total information about the procedures of registration. Most problems originate because desk or phone personnel lack needed information.
2. An information sheet must be available to participants and should provide the following:

Program;	Meeting Place;
Date;	Meeting Time;
Time;	Return Time
Place;	(usually an estimate);
Age, Grade,	Tentative Schedule;
or Group;	Limited Number of
Prerequisite	Participants;
(experience);	Insurance;
Equipment;	Last Date for
Food;	Registration;
Leadership;	Telephone Number for
Transportation;	Further Information.
Cost;	

3. Registration forms should include blanks for name, age, address, phone, program desired, and fee paid. Parent/guardian release forms and permission sheets should also be provided. Be positive that, if the registration form is on a brochure, participants can detach and mail it back without returning the program information.
4. A registration master book should be kept with the following information about each participant: name, address, phone, age, fee paid, information received, and program desired. This book should not leave the office; needed lists of participants can be hand-copied or xeroxed.

In a mass-registration situation such as a workshop or cross-country ski lessons, procedures must be simple for registration personnel or soon there are long lines of impatient people. For workshops, make up pads which have blanks for name, address, etc., and include a list of workshops. To register, participants simply fill out the proper blanks and circle the workshops of their choice, then hand the form to a secretary. Or, by telephoning, an organization secretary can fill in the blanks and circle choices. At the end of the day someone can put these into the master book, a simple process. A ski program which registers as many as forty participants per day can be handled exactly the same way on peak days.

For a smaller-sized program such as a wilderness backpacking trip, the master book is filled out by the person registering. Seldom is there more than one person doing this at one time, so when the program is filled it is known immediately. This is the prime reason for using one master book.

Alternates. Out of fifteen registrants, one person will usually not participate. Thus, an alternate list should be kept. Be positive that these alternates understand their position (that they can not go unless they are called), otherwise they may show up and there will be four to five too many, causing much disappointment for the alternate.

Keep registration procedures efficient and simple.

Scheduling

A detailed schedule is sometimes difficult to follow and there are outdoor leaders who do not like things to be scheduled; however, some scheduling is necessary to: 1) inform the participants what is to happen, and 2) keep the leaders up-to-date about what should be done. The following is an actual schedule for an adult skills camp in which one of the major objectives was to learn outdoor methods and techniques.

(This program went very near to schedule, most of the education was completed, and participants obtained some valuable skills. Without a schedule it would have been difficult to remember all the material that was to be covered or the order to follow. This schedule was mailed to each participant two weeks prior to camp time, allowing them to prepare for some of what was expected of them.)

Sample Schedule

July 26 (Monday)
9:00 am — Meet — figure logistics; packing and preparation
11:00 am — Depart for Willamette Pass
2:00 pm — Arrive Willamette Pass
4:00 pm — Set up base camp

5:00 pm — Meal, food & cooking
7:00 pm — Equipment selection & use of campfire

July 27 (Tuesday)
7:00 am — Breakfast
8:00 am — Map & compass; initiative tasks
10:00 am — Fire-building
12:00 pm — Lunch
1:00 pm — Free time
2:00 pm — Survival shelters
4:00 pm — Read and review
5:00 pm — Meal
7:00 pm — First aid; campfire

July 28 (Wednesday)
6:00 am — Arise, breakfast, pack, begin hike to Rosary Lakes
11:00 am — Arrive, make camp; lunch
1:30 pm — Rock-climbing technique
7:00 pm — Meal, free time
9:00 pm — Attitude, campfire

July 29 (Thursday)
8:00 am — Breakfast
9:00 am — Staying warm and dry; insulation
10:00 am — Emergencies, evacuation, search and rescue
12:30 pm — Lunch, free time, clean-up
2:00 pm — Open time (group needs)
5:00 pm — Meal
7:00 pm — Pack for hike out; campfire — star study
11:00 pm — Night-hike out
3:00 am — Arrive at base camp

July 30 (Friday)
Morning — Sleep late
9:00 am — Breakfast
10:00 am — Map/compass review
11:00 am — Hazards, dangers, water programs, lunch
2:30 pm — Route-finding
4:00 pm — Carrying-capacity, meal
6:30 pm — Review of the program
7:30 pm — Cold injury: frostbite, hypothermia
9:00 pm — Campfire

July 31 (Saturday)
8:00 am — Breakfast
9:00 am — Conservation & ecology, food chains
11:00 am — Evaluation of program; meal; pack for trip home; clean camp
12:30 pm — Leave base camp

2:30 pm — Start home drive; stop,
        Oakridge — snack
5:00 pm — Arrive Sheldon Center; store
        gear

Program reunion — August 12, 7:30 pm. Bring family, show pictures, & renew friendships.

One knot learned and practiced after each meal.

Insurance

There is an increasing need for adequate insurance coverage on outings. Protection is needed in four areas: 1) liability for the agency; 2) liability for the leaders; 3) participant accident, and 4) personnel accident.

Liability insurance coverage for the agency and the leaders is a must. As cautious as administrators are, eventually someone will think they have a case and take everyone involved to court. No program should be planned until the insurance angles are resolved.

Individual leaders are urged to purchase a personal liability policy of their own. It does not cost much and it does provide protection. (Suggested coverage is $100,000.) Be positive, if your program uses volunteers, that they are covered. You may need to put volunteers on the payroll just to do this.

Participant accident insurance is really a service and does not protect the programming agency, but it is inexpensive. The cost of the coverage can be included in the fee for the program. For outdoor programs this may be $.20 per day per participant, and for this amount, the insured (no matter what age) receives a $2500 medical or death benefit. This is not a great deal, but it will pay for a broken arm or sutured foot, the type of accident it is designed to cover.

Program Evaluation

We can not tell whether the participant liked or disliked the program unless we evaluate it. The main purpose of an evaluation is action — to change what might be handled differently and enforce what seems to be working well. There are many types of written evaluation forms, and it is recommended that each agency develop one

with short answers that is easy to complete and to use. Figures 10.2 and 10.3 are examples of two different evaluation forms. One is from a city recreation department; the other is from a university that sponsors both outings and instructional programs through its student recreational organization.

PUBLIC RELATIONS

As stated earlier, public relations should be the planned effort to steer public opinion in a favorable direction. In other words, public relations implies a concerted *effort* in the *direction* of developing *positive opinion*. There are several "publics" to which we refer.

The first and most immediate public is, of course, the participant. This person receives first-hand experience, thus developing opinions related to the program as an individual. The parents or families are the second public to concern us. Their opinions are formed by hearing about the experience from either the participants or someone else (leader, supervisor, news reporter, or emergency personnel) telling them what happened. A third public is the other potential participants, members of the immediate community who may or may not be planning to participate in a similar venture. Regardless of interest in the particular program in question, these people may form an opinion of the entire enterprise. A fourth public is the public at large, who may form an opinion of the operation from television or news broadcasts, or from the behavior of a group eating hamburgers at a rest stop en route to or from an outing. A final group that may be influenced is, of course, the administration of the program. Sometimes outdoor programs are curtailed because administrators develop negative opinions of their value or safety. A wise administrator, by developing and adhering to risk-management plans and public-relations plans, can help the program be successful. A naive or laissez-faire administrator is as much a contributor to the problem of poor public relations as a poor leader is.

FIGURE 10.2 Outdoor Recreation Participant Evaluation Form

Activity: _____

Date: _____

We appreciate your comments. With your help and input, we can make improvements in our program.

1. Did you enjoy the program?   Yes _____ No _____
   Comments: _____
   _____
   _____

2. Did the program fulfill your expectations?   Yes _____ No _____
   Comments: _____
   _____
   _____

3. Please indicate your responses below:

	Excellent	Good	Poor
Leader's knowledge of the material covered:			
Attitude of the leader:			
Location of activity:			
Pace or speed of activity:			
Length of program:			

   Comments: _____
   _____
   _____
   _____
   _____

4. How did you hear about this program? _____
   _____

5. Would you recommend this program to a friend?   Yes _____ No _____
   Because: _____
   _____
   _____

6. Other comments: _____
   _____
   _____

7. Ideas for future trips? _____

_____

_____

Portland, Oregon, Bureau of Parks and Recreation

FIGURE 10.3   Outing/Clinic Evaluation Form

TRIP NAME: _____   DATE: _____

CLASS LEVEL: FR   SOPH   JR   SR   GRAD   FAC   STAFF

MAJOR: _____   SEX: M _____ F _____

Please help to improve the quality of our program by filling out and turning in the evaluation to a staff member. Thank you.

Please rate the program from Excellent (1) to Poor (5)   1   2   3   4   5

Instructors/
Leaders Coordinators

	1	2	3	4	5
Organization of trip leaders					
Quality of instruction/administration					
Competency of staff					
Attitudes towards participants					
Overall rating of leaders					

Comments: _____

_____

	1	2	3	4	5
Outing/Clinic Pretrip information and arrangements					
Travel arrangements					
Accommodations					
Outing/clinic organization					
Adequacy of outing/clinic description					
Overall rating of outing/clinic					

Comments: _____

_____

_____

Did this outing/clinic meet your expectations?   yes   no
Would you be interested in taking a future outing/clinic
    of this nature?   yes   no
Would you be willing to recommend this outing/clinic
    to friends?   yes   no
How would you improve this outing/clinic?

1) _____

2) _____

Principles of Public Relations

In order to achieve maximum benefit from a
public-relations program, leaders and
administrators might well understand and follow
three principles:

1. The public-relations program should be
   continuous. This means that planning and
   implementation should be part of every
   program and an everyday occurrence. Every
   time the program and its sponsor are
   mentioned, by word of mouth or in print,
   opinions may be formed or altered. A public-
   relations program *after* the fact is too late.
2. Public relations should be honest. In spite of
   the fact that one purpose of such a program
   is to arouse favorable opinion, the truth
   should never be stretched or altered to
   achieve this goal. An administrator who
   promotes a program through brochures that
   show photographs of areas not utilized in the
   program is dishonest. A brochure that
   identifies leader qualifications that do not
   exist is dishonest. Written *intentions* do not
   suffice for honest facts.
3. Public relations should be all-encompassing
   and comprehensive. The public needs to
   know the entire story. An organization that
   offers a "memorable canoe trip" interprets
   the outing incompletely unless the public is
   led to understand it occurs on a slow-moving
   river past spectacular scenery or on white
   water pouring through immense canyons.

Public-relations Media

If one interprets public relations as being all
activities which influence public opinion, the
public-relations media would be "everything." It
is, however, possible to discuss these media in
four logical categories.

Human Channels. Being a people-oriented
business, the outdoor-pursuit program can make
optimal use of the human element in public
relations. Probably the best tool for this is the
group itself. Part of participant-created public
opinion comes after the outing when participants
are at home relating the joys (or panic) or their
experiences to family and friends. Another part
comes while the group is enroute to or from the
outing site. How they look and talk in
restaurants and gas stations directs public
opinion. While they are on the trail, lake, or
river, they can also influence the opinion of
those who see and/or hear them.

The leader is included in all the preceding
situations and can exert an even greater
influence on public awareness of the program.
Whenever the leader discusses his or her
experiences and/or appears among those who
are aware of the programs, opinions are formed.
He or she represents the sponsoring organization,
and the reputation of the various programs
offered by that organization may rise or fall
because of the effect of the leader's behavior in
hundreds of situations unrelated to the site or
the activity.

Printed Materials. Every program uses the
printed word for one or more purposes.
Promotion flyers, sign-up sheets, equipment
lists, report forms, instruction sheets, and
numerous other printed materials are used to
convey information. Needless to say, the quality
of the material can be judged by both
appearance and content. Gone is the day of
smudgy mimeographed flyers or faint, illegible

spirit-duplicator copies. New types of office machines capable of producing clear, crisp copies have left inferior ones far behind. No one can afford sloppy-looking material anymore.

The content of the printed material must likewise be precise. Incorrect language use and spelling reflect on the intelligence of the sponsor and thus create negative opinions of the entire program. Even the signature on written letters should be legible; an illegible scrawl may be interpreted as a sign of one who is pompous about his or her importance and doesn't care for the reader enough to take the time to sign a name legibly.

Visual Media. Many times the sponsor of a program will use a slide show to promote it. More often the leader will use slides to illustrate topics under discussion at pre-trip training. Sometimes the sponsor or leader is so enthusiastic about the merits of the topic discussed that poor, fuzzy, or out-of-date pictures are shown as if the audience will imagine what good shots would look like. Until there are enough good slides to cover 100 percent of the program, no slide show should be given. Further, no slides should be shown unless they are authentically related to the topic at hand. Older adults are not usually convinced of the ease of a trip if all they see are Boy Scouts. Nor would the Scouts be convinced of the necessity for being in top shape if all they saw were older people at rest.

Mass Media. Ordinarily, one does not think of mass media as a prime method for generating public opinion about an outdoor-pursuit program. Mass media includes newspapers, radio, and television, which are available to the majority of the general public. Rarely do these give much space to the positive attributes of outing trips. Certainly there are weekly columns written by outdoors people, schedules of trips and where to get more information, and occasional articles and photographs related to successful ventures. These rarely, if ever, rate front-page space and are more likely relegated to the family section or hidden inside the paper as fillers. But if an accident or tragedy occurs, it is front-page and prime-time news.

It is at such times that there needs to be a carefully thought-out plan for public relations.

Such a plan might include: what to do at the scene of the accident, the role of the program administration, how to notify the victim's family, how to relate to the news media, and how to record the details of the accident.

The Scene of the Accident

What is done at the scene of an accident affects the reporting of the incident as well as the opinions of participants and their friends and families. After first aid is given, the events must be recorded immediately, so the leader must be prepared with a notebook and pencil. (Ink smears and smudges in dampness — where most accidents seem to occur.) Every accident-related item must be written down. Don't trust your memory, since this changes in time. Only those events written down right after the accident occurred may be correct. Even better than a notebook is a copy of an accident form (see figure 10.4). Notice that who, what, when, where, and how are listed. Diagrams are important as are photographs if someone thinks to take them. Photographs of people, injuries, vehicles, and even the weather is helpful. Maps, conditions, and equipment lists are also of value. Get the names, addresses, and telephone numbers of witnesses, and ask them to verify the accident report by signing it.

Try to analyze the situation to understand why the accident occurred. By writing this down you may get a jump on a future lawsuit by acting as a reasonable and prudent professional. Get a list of as many people involved as possible. Names, addresses, phone numbers, age, previous experience, where each person was, and why are all important. If you do this, those who were not witnesses because they were around a bend, looking in another direction, or whatever, will not become witnesses in six weeks or six months due to a change in memory. You might also note the condition of the witnesses, i.e., calm, exhausted, incoherent, etc.

Between the administrator and the leader there must be an understanding of who is to be the spokesperson. Since witnesses may all remember things differently, they need to know that one person is the spokesperson and all questions should be directed to that person. The spokesperson is usually the one who has written

FIGURE 10.4 **Accident Form**

CENTERVILLE RECREATION DEPARTMENT

ACCIDENT REPORT FORM

Name _____ Date of Birth _____
     Last   First   Middle

                                                      Sex _____

Address _____ Telephone _____
     Number   Street

City   State   Zip Code

Name of Parents _____ How Notified? _____ When? ____

Address (if different)

_____

Date of Injury _____ Hour _____ AM   Weather_____
                                       PM

Place of Injury _____
                        (Include equipment involved)

Describe Injury & Circumstances _____

_____

_____

First Aid Given _____ By _____

_____ When _____

_____

Disposition of Patient: Home _____ Hospital _____ Continued Activity _____

WITNESSES

Name _____ Address _____ Telephone _____

Name _____ Address _____ Telephone _____

Name _____ Address _____ Telephone _____

On back explain risk management plan, how accident might have been prevented, and relevant details.

Submitted by _____ Date _____

everything down, and participants should understand that the written word is probably correct and certainly consistent. If too many different views of what happened are given orally, the public may tend to disbelieve them all.

The administrator should be contacted immediately following an accident, injury, or missing-person report. Usually he or she then calls the victim's family since the leader is probably involved with the remaining participants, the media, or the search-and-rescue group. It is vital that the victim's family be notified by one of the program staff — preferably the administrator — before the name is broadcast by the news media. A leader may withhold the name of the victim until the family has been notified.

Public-relations action continues after the accident. A follow-up call and visit to the family, followed by another contact, is always a good idea. Evidence that the leader and sponsoring organization care also helps defray negative emotions. Of course, good insurance coverage that helps with medical expenses is a positive force, too.

The following is an example of an emergency procedure established by the Eugene, Oregon, Parks and Recreation Department. It encompasses a good public-relations plan because it shows in detail how to work with various publics in a caring, calm, and honest manner.

Some Thoughts on Public Relations Following a Serious Accident

The public relations aspect of any serious accidents are in many ways very much like day-to-day contact with the public. Your "image" can be no better than the job you are doing. You must be honest, accurate, and reasonable. You must also be prudent due to legal factors.

If your negligence has contributed to the accident, you will have an extremely difficult situation, personally and professionally.

However, if there was no negligence and you respond swiftly and efficiently, your supervisor should be able to maintain public confidence by explaining the circumstances and response to the situation. Litigation is sometimes necessary to determine whether negligence was involved, and this possibility makes prudence essential.

Regardless of whether a situation was an accident or involved negligence, there are several things to keep in mind that could simplify the ramifications. The items listed below represent the public-relations point of view; however, the staff should be well aware that public relations cannot be the only consideration at this point.

1. The welfare of the injured party comes first. This may seem like a simplistic statement, but it is an important part of how the public will evaluate what has happened. Included in the protection of the injured party is keeping bystanders and/or witnesses calm and in control from the outset. Someone needs to assume authority so that you don't have too much unwelcome help or interference.

2. After the injured person has been cared for with first aid or other medical attention as needed, be sure that the family is notified immediately with as clear an evaluation of the present status of the injury as is possible. The family certainly has the right to know the situation before any information is released to the news media and before the information can reach them in a distorted form through second-hand sources.

   Common sense dictates that it is important to communicate the actual seriousness of the situation, but be sure to present the information calmly and without dramatic interpretations of a "great rescue effort." At least in the initial announcement, the family does not need and probably does not want to know the shocking or graphic details of the injury, or any unfounded rumors or speculation in the event of a search. Rather, you should tell them the important facts, giving only useful information about the injury, illness, or search.

3. Be sure that your supervisors or other parties likely to be contacted about the accident are well informed about the incident immediately!

4. If possible, anticipate inquiries from the media. Prepare a written statement for them if time permits, or at least be prepared to give the pertinent information as you know it, but do not release it without talking to the

information coordinator or your supervisor. Of course, if the media is beating down your door, you cannot say "I have got to wait to let the information coordinator give you this."

Such information might include: the name of the injured person and, if under age 18, parent or guardian, age, address, time, circumstances, location of incident, and that address. If possible, the supervisor should handle all media inquiries to avoid the confusion of contradictory stories. That person should be very well informed and, if possible, be the most knowledgeable about the incident.

A word of caution — if litigation seems possible or probable, be wary of people who call and "just ask questions" or who identify themselves by name only and not by agency. People have been known to ask leading questions of those informed and not informed in order to establish a legal case. There is no need to be rude, but it is completely appropriate to ask why they need the information. A reasonable answer to that question can help you provide more useful information for legitimate inquiries, protect the privacy of the injured party, and sort out those who really should have information from those who should not.

If questions are obviously aimed at a legal problem or insurance coverage, or if you are not sure, refer the questioner to your supervisor.

5. Cooperation with the press and public in providing the best information possible is important at this point. Try to accentuate the positive when you can. For example: "Although the girl fell backward off the diving platform, *the doctor indicated* she has probably suffered only a minor concussion. She was able to move all her limbs and to speak clearly before she was transported to the hospital."

Unless you have a medical source to quote regarding the condition of the injured, be very careful about evaluation. Clearly refer them to a hospital or a doctor for confirmation and clarification of the condition.

6. Despite the need and desire to inform the media and the public about the actual

occurrence, be careful about giving out information which might jeopardize the rights of either the agency or the individual should a legal suit result from the accident. No statements regarding fault or liability shall be made.

This is a very touchy area. *If there is any question, it is better to defer public comment until contact has been made, by your supervisor, with an attorney for your agency. The more serious the accident, and/or the more likelihood of responsibility by the agency, the more important this aspect becomes.*

When approached in this kind of situation, give some sort of "bare bones" statement if possible. For example, you might say that the patient has been taken to the hospital and a report on the incident is being prepared which will be available at a later time. It would also be appropriate to suggest what person to contact and an approximate time to do so. In some cases, it is better to give no statement. These types of situations should be discussed beforehand by all supervisors and staffs.

7. The most important thing you can do is also the most difficult; *stay calm!* This is especially important if your actions and statements might affect the welfare of the victims. Your ability to make prudent decisions and statements under stress is vitally important. Anxiety, overexcitement, or loss of firm control of your behavior can very seriously alter both the actual and the publically perceived outcomes of the incident. Work through scenarios in your head and with your supervisor before you encounter a real emergency. Talk to people who work in emergency services and/or in public relations, and develop your skills and confidence by reviewing past incidents.

8. Follow through after the emergency stage. Let the family know that you are concerned for the outcome of the patient. Follow through if you can provide additional information on the incident. Let your staff and supervisors know anything you find out, so they, too, can answer questions which are likely to be asked by the public.

If photos are necessary for insurance or legal purposes, have your supervisor contact the information coordinator as soon as possible.

Contact the information coordinator and/or your supervisor day, night, or weekend if necessary to help you — it's part of their job.

Emergency Procedure
Eugene, Oregon, Parks and Recreation Department.

I. Give basic first aid.
II. If the ambulance is needed, call one.
  A. Before the ambulance is dispatched, they will need the following information:
    1. The location of the accident or emergency.
    2. Directions, if needed, to the site and where someone will meet the ambulance to guide it and/or the crew to the victim.
    3. What happened (victim feel and hit head, etc.)
    4. What seem to be the results (unconsciousness and irregular breathing).
    5. At this point, you will be told to hold while the ambulance is dispatched.
  B. They will then need the following:
    1. Your name.
    2. That you are an employee of the City of Eugene Parks and Recreation Department.
    3. The number of the phone you are calling from and, if the number is different, where you can be reached if they call back.
    4. The victim's doctor's name, if known.
    5. What you have done for the victim, who has done it, and advice as to what to do until the ambulance arrives, if needed. (If you must know this before giving the four items above, say so.)
III. Call the parents, guardians, friends, relatives, or people that the victim is staying with if it is possible.
  A. Do not alarm them. Give them only the information that you know for sure, do not make a diagnosis, and do not give them any unnecessary information that may upset them.
  B. Tell them the ambulance is on the way *just in case it is needed.* This is to reassure them that it may not be too serious but that you are not taking any chances, and that they are not going to be stuck with the bill. (If it is not needed and there is a charge, the City will take care of it.)
  C. Give them your location, your name, or who they should contact on arrival if they are coming.
  D. Find out what hospital they want the victim taken to (to be given to ambulance crew).
  E. Find out the name of the victim's doctor (to be given to ambulance crew).
  F. If relatives need a ride to the place of the accident or the hospital and it is possible for a staff member to give them one, offer them the service.
  G. Relatives may also want to call their doctor. If they do not, the ambulance service will do so as soon as they know the doctor's name.
IV. Call the victim's doctor and give him the needed information.
V. The police do not need to be called unless it is an accident that involves traffic, assault, or some other activity that involves an illegal act or possible liability.
VI. If it is found that the ambulance is not needed, call back immediately and let them know.
VII. If you are not sure if an ambulance will be needed, get them there anyway and they will give the victim needed care and then advise you, as well as the parents or guardian, about what should be done.
VIII. We want to be safe first; we will worry about cost later.
IX. Fill out accident report. This must be done in case of illness that requires action on our part as well as accidents.
X. In the case of follow-up by a lawyer, all interviews with the staff must be arranged through our Finance Department.
XI. If there are police involved, they will make out a complete report and get those

reports to the various places they need to go. This does not excuse the staff person from his or her responsibility to fill out our departmental accident report and any other reports required by the situation.

XII. We do not want staff transporting people who have been injured, even if the injury is minor, in their own personal cars or even in City vehicles unless it is a last resort. The first would be the ambulance if there is a need for that type of transportation; if the ambulance is not needed, the first should be the victim's parents, relatives, or friends; if no one is available, then call the police. The last resort should be our staff, transporting either in City cars or their own vehicles.

ADVERTISING AND PUBLICITY

The importance of advertising and publicity is often underestimated. People must know a program is being offered before they can participate. Usually some end up saying, "I sure would have liked to go with you on that outing, but I didn't hear about it."

An outdoor program must use all available media to promote activities; we are in a competitive business and must accept this as a fact and compete.

Methods used:

1. **Newspaper.** The newspaper is probably one of the best methods of publicizing a program. There are several ways this can be done.
   a. Regular news stories. Giving basic information is a regular method of newspaper publicity. The agency tells the newspaper what, where, how, etc., and they write the story.
   b. Display ad which is purchased by the programming agency. This is a great method but the problem is cost: from $2.65 to $3.50 per column inch, which is expensive but varies with different newspapers.
   c. A tabloid section, which is also purchased, is as effective and expensive as the display ad. One greater advantage

is that the tabloid may be removed from the paper and saved as a schedule.
   d. **Column.** If a newspaper is interested in an outdoor-recreation column, maybe someone associated with your agency can write the copy. This can serve to educate the public as well as publicize program opportunities.
   e. **Co-sponsorship with a newspaper.** Some departments cooperate with local newspapers to provide various outdoor programs. They take care of the publicity and we provide the programs, which are usually filled on the first day of registration.

2. **Television.** Television is an increasingly effective method of publicizing outdoor programs. Rapidly shown, thirty-second programs with a telephone number at the end are very effective. Thirty-minute programs are also available. There are commercial enterprises that should be approached to purchase this program for you, and they can advertise. Talk shows, public service programs, plus the regular paid advertising are available, too.

3. **Radio.** Most radio stations are willing to assist in promoting programs. Write the information on a card and mail. All information is more readily accepted if it is mailed to a specific individual who is approached personally prior to mailings.

4. **Posters.** The poster in a store window does attract small amount of attention. Posters, when used, should be well done and kept up-to-date. They can be expensive, however, and at times a mimeographed sheet on a bulletin board to announce a specific activity will get as good a result ratio as expensive posters.

5. **Brochures.** The printed program that can be handed out or mailed is a useful promotional tool. It should be informative, with details about what, where, how, etc. Flyers, a single-sheet condensed version of the brochure, are valuable as handouts when talking to general interest groups. Both brochures and flyers should be printed at a minimum cost.

6. **Newsletter.** A monthly or bi-monthly newsletter that is sent to a general mailing list is a good method of promoting a program. This method should be used as an educational tool and promote all types of outdoor programs. The largest cost is postage; bulk mail for over 200 will cost approximately four cents per copy.

7. **Word of mouth.** The most potent of all publicity is person-to-person, commonly known as word of mouth. When a participant enjoys a program, he or she will tell others. It should be remembered that others will also be told if he or she does not have a good time.

8. **Presentations (slides, lectures, movies).** This area of promotion is usually neglected because it is time consuming to present as well as put together. This method does have results because it adds a personal touch from the person who presents the program. Give them a brochure after the program and they may sign up.

9. **Cooperative Organizations.** Much like a newspaper co-sponsorship, other groups will handle or assist with the publicity if they co-sponsor the program. For example, local service clubs can promote an activity a great deal. This allows someone else to blow your horn for awhile, and it costs little for this kind of publicity.

10. **Door to door.** A door-to-door neighborhood promotion will get results, especially if a couple of people in the community are already participants in the program. Simply ring the doorbell and chat about the opportunities in outdoor recreation. Leave a program, too. This is a time-consuming method, but it gets results.

11. **Schools.** There is usually an opportunity to promote programs through schools using several of the aforementioned methods (brochures, flyers, presentations, posters). Here you'll find a concentration of interested potential participants. Call any of your local media. They will help you with your publicity problem.

Marketing and Promotion

Look in the back of any outdoor magazine, in the flyers of many city or county recreation departments, in school and college papers and catalogues, in club bulletins, and on the wall of any outdoor-equipment store, and you will see ads for all sorts of outings and classes. Unfortunately, a large percentage of the activities don't take place due to insufficient participation.

Promotion of an outing or class requires an understanding of what prompts people to participate and an understanding of what stands in the way of participation. Motivation may be positive or it may be compelled by internal or external processes. Examples of positive motivation are interests in fitness enhancement or skill development, scientific or aesthetic interest in the environment, or the improvement of mental health via relaxation and recreation. Other possible advantages of taking part in outdoor pursuits have been discussed earlier in Chapter 1. Equally powerful motivation can come about through pressure to conform, as when spouses, close friends, or others in a peer group urge participation in an activity. Sometimes the participant really has little choice, as is often the case with children, students, and military personnel.

When promoting an outing, keep the goals and objectives clearly in mind yet be willing to at least consider modification as you become more familiar with the potential group. Typically, the organizer of an outing or class is a devotee of the activity, and finds great satisfaction in it. It's easy to forget that the great majority of people have no comparable interest in the activity, no matter how exciting it may seem to the organizer. Before formulating the marketing scheme, look carefully at the group of people which you hope to attract! Try to understand *their* view of the activity. People absorb new ideas very slowly, so unless lots of time and money are available for massive educational promotion, it's best to present the activity in a way that is consistent with the expectations of potential participants. People see what they *expect* to see. If your institution typically offers a certain kind of program and usually promotes programs in a certain way, an argument can be made for following this pattern if it has been successful in the past. If successful marketing channels already exist, it is best to fit the old format as much as possible since it usually saves money to plug into well-worn systems. It is certainly possible to create wholly new types of programs and to use new and eye-catching promotional techniques. The problem is that this usually involves a very high start-up cost, and outdoor-pursuit activities are usually very low-budget operations.

When designing the layout of advertisements, several points should be kept in mind.

1. **Keep it simple.** In most cases people will not read, or cannot read, very much. Simply tell what, when, where, and how much it costs, with at most a sentence or two extolling the virtues of the activity. Especially when seeking participants for an introductory or beginning-level experience, it's important to mention the key benefits of the program. People are usually much more interested in these (skills, thrills, relaxation, or whatever) than in place and details other than time and cost. Remember that name, address, and phone number are usually worth including, for people will write them down. Think about the posters you see. What do you look for and remember? A good flyer leaves the viewer eager for more information and aware of the name of the contact agency.

2. **Use sketches or photos if possible.** As with the written portion, keep illustrations clear and simple. Most flyers, magazine ads, and other printed messages are only glanced at for a few seconds at most. When selecting or designing the illustration, try to find or create one that inspires curiosity. Photographs tend to do this, as the viewer may at least be curious as to when and where the picture was taken. You want the person passing along the flyer or thumbing through the magazine to be drawn to the advertisement, and to stay fixed for a few seconds. Skiers tend to spot and fix attention on skiers, climbers on climbers, kayakers on kayakers, and so on. Be sure that body position, equipment, or technique in the illustration is appropriate and correct! Beginners may not notice errors, but devotees and experts do and often make fun of the illustration, damaging the image of the program. When trying to attract beginners, it is a good idea to elaborate on some

aspect of the activity that may be especially appealing to them, even if it is not an especially important part of the sport for avid participants. A rock-climbing course, for example, might use an illustration of a rappel, taking care, of course, not to illustrate anything *too* scary. Most people seek a bit of excitement in outdoor pursuits, but also like to think of themselves as growing old with all limbs still attached. A beginning ski-class poster should show some appealing aspect of learning how to ski, not someone on the lunatic fringe descending an icy sixty-degree chute!

When deciding when and where to place ads or flyers, try to find those publications or places with a high volume of likely clientele. Specialty magazines, club newsletters, and specialty sporting-goods shops work well for intermediate and advanced programs in most activities, and may attract a few beginners, too. If the intent is to bring new people into an activity, say backpacking or canoeing, it may be best to focus on schools, general sporting-goods stores, hunting or fishing establishments, and fitness-oriented organizations such as the YM or YMCA and health spas.

When designing the promotional scheme, and in fact the program itself, it's a good idea to bear in mind the reasons why people *don't* sign up for outdoor pursuits. For example, one common reason is the perception that great physical prowess and/or youth is a prerequisite to participation. When real barriers don't exist, the promotional scheme should include elements designed to break down these misconceptions. Good photographs can be invaluable in getting this sort of message across. Another and all-too-often valid concern is the cost. What may seem a worthwhile expense to a devotee of outdoor pursuits may not seem worthwhile to one not yet hooked. This concern points up the importance of emphasizing personal benefits in promotional materials. Time is another major concern. Never forget that most people don't see themselves as having much discretionary time. Weekends seem to be consumed by lawn mowing, cleaning house, washing the car, or other chores, and by voluntary or obligatory visits with friends or relatives.

Promoting an outdoor program is not just a matter of attracting people from some vacuous limbo. The program has to be seen as sufficiently rewarding to overcome the real or perceived constraints of everyday life. A good promotional campaign should simultaneously extol the virtues of the activity and attempt to reduce the effects of these constraints. This is especially important when dealing with potential entrants, that is, true beginners, and argues for short duration, easy access, low cost, low-obligation experiences. A person who might never commit to a weekend of high Alpine backpacking, no matter how easy and no matter how fabulous the scenery, may well sign up for a half- or full-day hike, especially if it is cheap and the kids can come along. A warning here . . . this technique can be highly successful as a means of "indoctrination" and getting people involved, or it can be a total failure if not adequately promoted. Most people, especially people trying something new, need a lot of time to think about it first. New experiences are usually preceded by a thorough mental "walk-through," which may be inspired by friends relating their experiences, by television or other mass media, or by repeated exposure to program flyers. It is not uncommon, when trying to recruit new people into an activity, to see few or no results for one or two seasons or even for a couple of years. Many programs are abandoned only to have a number of inquiries in the following year from people who have finally decided to get involved.

Another concern to be dealt with is the distaste many people have for any commitment of time. This is easy to appreciate since most working people and many students have so much of their lives structured that they are hesitant to sign up for an event unless it seems especially worthwhile. This is a problem even when promoting events like short hikes or single-day excursions. Unless those events are perceived as exceptionally exciting, potential participants will prefer having the day free; unless the activity obviously requires instruction or other assistance, many people prefer to maintain control over their time. Some suggestions for overcoming concerns about time commitment are:

1. Check the calendar carefully to avoid any conflicts (athletic events, etc.).
2. Promote well in advance (a month or more) since people are much more likely to commit themselves to a distant date. A day a month

in the future seems much less significant than one next weekend when the lawn needs mowing and the car needs washing, especially if it has been a hard week already.
3. Try to combine a *perception* of low commitment with a real commitment of money. A fee schedule that gives a substantial break for early payment but that disallows refund of part or all of the fee is usually perceived as fair, especially if the amount is small. Such a schedule helps minimize budget worries, and also tends to reduce the number of dropouts.
4. Counter the concern directly by pointing out the advantages of commitment to a program. Many people appreciate being obligated to go on an outing, since they recognize the mental and physical advantages of participation but have difficulty justifying involvement when faced with short-term internal or external pressures.

SUMMARY

Program is everything that affects the participants, and public relations is everything that affects public attitudes about the program. Each should be planned carefully and completely. Program planners should keep in mind both the group and the individual; the program starts long before the actual activity because of the need to develop objectives, content, registration, insurance, and evaluation. Public relations includes a continuous, honest, comprehensive scheme to influence the public in a favorable manner. Leaders need to keep in mind how to react in case of emergency as well as how to promote the program.

BIBLIOGRAPHY

Buell, Larry, *Leader's Guide to the 24-Hour Experience,* Greenfield, MA: Environmental Awareness Publications, 1978.
Edginton, Christopher and Ford, Phyllis, *Leadership of Recreation and Leisure Service Organizations,* New York: John Wiley and Sons, 1985.
Rodney, Lynn, and Ford, Phyllis, *Camp Administration,* New York: Ronald Press, 1971.

CHAPTER 11

OUTDOOR LEADERSHIP

What is a leader? How does one become a leader? What makes some people leaders in title only, while others become leaders without officially sanctioned authority? This topic has filled many books and given rise to many theories, models, and studies. In this chapter, the relevance of modern leadership theory to outdoor pursuits will be discussed.

Before discussing leaders, it may be best to discuss followers, for no one can last as a leader without one or more of these. One of the best practices for becoming a leader is to serve as a follower and analyze the components of leadership from that standpoint. In a theoretical sense, you can do that by participating in the following exercise.

Imagine yourself signing up for an outdoor-pursuit exercise. It does not matter what the activity is or where it will take place as long as you envision an experience that will hold the potential for a degree of enjoyment, excitement, challenge, and/or adventure. Since the idea is to put yourself in the place of the typical participant or student, you may want to think about some activity with which you are not familiar or that tends to be intimidating to you. If your forte is not fast-water canoeing, imagine you have just signed up for a three-day river trip. If you are an ice climber, imagine a trip to the desert or vice versa. If you are really set on imagining your own favorite pastime, imagine signing up for a very advanced lesson or clinic.

Now try to imagine what expectations you would have for the imaginary leader of your program. If you have been a leader or teacher for many years, it may be difficult to imagine a role reversal. If you are unable to put yourself into the position (imaginary or real) of being a follower (particularly one of your own followers) you may not have what it takes to be a good leader.

What would you expect of your leader? Of the total experience? Can you generate a list of your expectations? First, you probably expect the individual to be friendly, reasonably easy to get along with, and interested in, even excited about, the program. Of no less importance is the maturity and evident good sense of the person. These qualities are often considered the primary criteria for leadership of any sort although they are extremely difficult to assess. What else do you have a right to expect? You *should* expect the person to have a good basic understanding of the terrain, the weather, and the potential hazards of the locale chosen for the activity. You should also expect the leader to be sufficiently concerned about and aware of environmental issues and accepted practices to minimize your group's impact on the land and water. Certainly you expect your leader to understand basic human physical and psychological needs, and to know how to meet these needs in the environment and context of your activity. You also should expect high levels of knowledge, skill, and experience in the activity, plus familiarity with back-country first aid and search-and-rescue or other appropriate skills so he or she can handle any reasonably foreseen emergency.

Of course you do not and should not expect Superman or Superwoman, and you do expect to retain much personal responsibility for what happens to you on the trip. Nevertheless, it is not at all unreasonable to want your leader to be a competent and up-to-date practitioner of the activity.

You have a right to certain expectations in at least two other areas. The leader should be willing and able to *control* and *lead* the group adequately. This is by no means assured by the satisfaction of any or all of the foregoing qualities. A similar statement might be made for *teaching*.

Does the foregoing list mean that you, as a leader, need to anticipate and to meet all of these expectations? The general answer is, of course, yes. Characteristics on our list now include friendliness, maturity, sense of humor; knowledge of weather, hazards, environmental issues, and practice; knowledge of people's physical and psychological needs and how to meet those needs; a high level of skill; first aid, search-and-rescue techniques, group control; and teaching and leading ability. And we don't even know if these expectations have been verified by anyone other than our own selves reacting in a moment of challenge to imagine what we want in our leaders.

Generally though, the expectations imagined above are probably the same as those of both adults and parents whose children we may lead. To some extent, the leader is controlled by the hopes of people served. If the expectations of the followers are not met, there may be dissatisfaction and accompanying participant drop-out at least, or, in serious cases, substantial liability and risk of litigation. The imagined situation is a good one for understanding how we might feel as participants.

THE PARTICIPANTS

As mentioned, in all leadership situations there must be followers. Thus before analyzing the outdoor leader's characteristics, it is best to understand the people who seek the organized outdoor-pursuit experience. Initially, the leader should recognize the fact that outdoor participants are *groups* of people bound by the constraints of time (pre-trip, trip, and post-trip) and by space (the location of the event).

The group will develop an identification as "members," a sense of purpose, a pattern of interaction, and some commonly agreed-upon system of order. Members of outdoor-pursuit groups are undoubtedly also members of *social* groups and interact accordingly. They call each other by their first names, and derive much of their satisfaction from group interaction, including talking, eating, and sharing the exigencies of the outdoor environment. They are aware of being group members and identify with the group by cohesiveness in working together, a sense of shared purpose, and a need for and acceptance of others in the group.

An outdoor group may consist of several *primary* groups such as families, siblings, or scout troops, but it is probably more often identified as a *secondary* group. A *primary* group is a lasting group that shapes personalities and emotional character while a *secondary* group is usually one that meets for a short time only and allows us to achieve, gain recognition, meet basic social needs, and polish our behavior. An outdoor-pursuit activity may consist of several groups, i.e., families, meeting as a secondary group. People's behavior in primary groups differs from their behavior in secondary groups.

Properties of Groups

Sessoms and Stevenson (1981) have identified nine properties of groups that may be explained in terms of outdoor pursuits as follows:

Purpose. The main purpose of the outdoor-pursuit group is identical to that of the sponsoring agency. All wish to complete the goal established. Common purposes are, for example:

To climb Baldtop Mountain;
To learn to cross-country ski;
To travel 100 miles by canoe;
To explore Limestone Cave.

Such goals are self-evident. There are also, however, three tacit goals for all outdoor pursuits. They may not be verbalized; however, they are of greater importance, in the long run, than destination goals. We refer to the following:

To return unharmed;
To maintain the environment in its natural condition;
To have an enjoyable or at least personally rewarding experience.

It may be assumed that those are the main group and leader goals of all outdoor experiences.

Tone or Social Atmosphere. The group as a whole will have an identifiable social atmosphere. It may be up to the leader to set the tone so that the group is optimistic, careful, friendly, and supportive of each other. A hostile, careless, disgruntled, or frightened member can "set the tone" for the entire group if the leader is less than adequate, and he or she must influence the interaction of the entire group.

Cohesion. The tone of the group may well be influenced by group cohesion. If the group is divided on what route to follow, what action to take, whether to go on or to turn back, or even which menu to follow, there is no cohesion and this can lead to breakdown in social atmosphere. The leader must have the ability to maintain a cohesive group.

Organizational Structure. Some groups are organized on a formal basis, as in a classroom, while others are informally organized, as in a discussion group. The organizational structure of an outdoor-pursuit group may vary within one event or may be entirely formal or informal. The group needs to know who is in charge, what the positional hierarchy is, and when formal or informal procedures will occur. Formal organization is needed when a lot of beginners participate in an overnight cross-country skiing trip, but the organization will be less formal during the evening meal and maybe on the trip home. Lessons, activities performed in high-risk situations, and events involving young children are usually formally organized.

Patterns of Communication. Every group develops a system for receiving and sending messages consisting of specialized vocabulary, body language, and facial expressions. Outdoor-pursuit groups have their own unique communication systems. Such terms as "high-tech gear," "skid lid," "60/40," "polyprop," "Class III," "on belay," and many others are included. Hikers and river runners alike can understand body and hand language that indicates cold, heat, rain, sleep, fatigue, etc.

Patterns of Interaction. Watch any group and interaction patterns will become evident. Who speaks to whom? Who speaks the most? How are responses made? Who seems to have seniority? Who never speaks? These are patterns of interaction. A good leader should not monopolize the discussion, should try to involve everyone (but not force those who are by nature and/or preference reticent). A good social group usually has a fairly evenly distributed level of interaction.

Procedures. Groups have definite ways of getting things done. How is the raft packed each day? What goes in first? last? Who packs what? How is the campfire ring returned to its natural state? Who leads on the trail? For how long? Such patterns are identifiable characteristics of all outdoor groups.

Internal Commitment. All members of the group may not be equally committed to the goal of the event. Some individuals may not really care if the summit is reached and some may be terribly disappointed and get angry at a leader who turns back in deference to group safety. The leader has the unenviable responsibility of trying to unify commitment even if it means changing the goals. If the group itself is involved in setting or modifying these, however, chances are that commitment will be more unified than if the leader makes an arbitrary, automatic suggestion.

Group History. Each group may be made up of individuals with a history of similar experiences in that group or individuals with previous experience together, some with previous experience only with other groups and some with no similar background. Individuals who have traveled together before may exhibit certain behavior and patterns of interaction that preclude socialization with others new to the group. The group made up of participants who have no group history may be the easiest to lead once procedures are defined. The group with a long history together may be the next easiest to lead (although not always), and the mixed group may challenge the leader to achieve a new goal — bringing old and new members into a cohesive unit.

These properties give each group its own special identity. No two exhibit identical characteristics, and understanding these properties helps the leader to mold his or her style to meet the needs of his followers.

Reasons for Following

Why do some people never want to be leaders while others never sign up with a sponsored group, preferring to join a group of common adventurers where the leadership may be shared or everyone may be an autonomous individual? Sessoms and Stevenson (1981) have proposed three reasons why people want to be followers, or why they desire to have leaders.

These reasons, simply, are *efficiency, satisfaction,* and *experience. Efficiency* means that individuals want leaders when they are involved in situations where they are unwilling to undertake certain responsibilities themselves and find it easier to be followers. Many individuals discover that the most efficient and effective way of achieving their goals is through delegating responsibility for that achievement to someone else — the leader. In the outdoors this reason for being a follower is particularly relevant. If one wishes to climb a mountain or run a river for the first time, it is much easier to achieve that goal by following a leader who knows the route than to chart all potential routes and head forth without first-hand knowledge of what lies ahead. Many people would find the achievement of outdoor goals so difficult without a leader that the activities would never get started in the first place; they would find themselves on serious expeditions, not recreational events.

Satisfaction refers to the fact that if people are already followers and are satisfied with the way things are going, they tend to continue to follow the current leader. In many outdoor situations where participants could take on minor leadership roles (i.e., preparation of meals, teaching minimum-impact techniques, demonstrating rafting skills), they prefer to continue to be followers because they are completely at ease and satisfied with the leader's style and accomplishments.

Experience means that many people have not had the experience of being a leader, thus they remain as followers. Many people are comfortable and secure in the familiar role of follower. The idea of becoming a first-time leader brings a fear of the unknown which is overcome easily by reverting to this familiar role.

Thus many people are followers because it is efficient, satisfying, and comfortable. That is not to say, however, that *everyone* wants this role. Many wish to assume command, but for most the preceding lists of reasons give us a basis for understanding our function as leaders.

Why Do People Need Leaders?

Unlike early mankind, for whom an intimate awareness of the subtle interplay of the land, sun, weather, water, and all living things was clearly necessary for survival, the vast majority of outdoorspeople today confront the environment recreationally. And even this contact is muted and modified through the intervention of quantities of sophisticated equipment and apparel. Outdoorspeople immerse themselves in the "wildness," but usually only on weekends (preferably sunny ones) and surrounded by a buffer of technological gear created to shelter them from the very environment they set out to enjoy.

In actuality thousands know very little about natural hazards, yet have no problem surviving. The urban dweller can duck into stores or subways if caught in a storm with inadequate protection. Those who are hiking may be lucky enough not to get caught, or may rely on the equipment and skills of their companions to help them out. As a matter of fact, thousands survive day- or week-long hikes or rafting trips unscathed without proper gear and with little or no knowledge of the environment.

If this is so, why should one bother to acquire so much knowledge before setting out? There are two good reasons:

1. The first, most often expressed by those familiar with the outdoors, is that knowledge of the area, its weather patterns, its hazards, its pathways, and the physiological needs it creates materially affect a person's safety. While this appears to make sense, it is difficult to substantiate through empirical research. Nevertheless, the ill-prepared, unknowing, summer-day hiker on a five-mile mountain-trail hike might be compared to a driver going ninety miles per hour on a freeway for three hours. Things can go wrong! The consequences can be painful and costly for the individual, family, friends, those who render first aid, and environment. The chance of something going wrong on a short hike or on a short drive at high speeds may be very low, but the results are too serious not to be considered. It stands to reason that a substantial reduction in risk occurs among those who have learned about the environment and its relation to their activities.

2. The second reason for learning about the environment and its demands on human energy, for being well-skilled and well-equipped, is also not proven statistically yet is nevertheless compelling. The more one knows and the better the skills and adequacy of the equipment, the greater the chance for enjoyment. There are, of course, limits to this since too *much* equipment can easily reduce one's enjoyment, particularly when back-packing. It is generally true, though, that the better prepared one is in terms of knowledge, skills, fitness, and equipment, the more options one has — hence greater control over the experience.

Combining these two reasons for learning, one can understand that safety and enjoyment relate specifically to the goals of the outdoor experience. In a sentence: Preparedness produces pleasure. There is no danger in overlearning or overpreparing to the point of reducing the delights of discovery. The seemingly least diverse and simplistic landscapes are in reality so complex and varied that each defies total comprehension. The more one knows, the more one sees, and the process accelerates.

Boredom is not related to the scenery; it stems from a lack of understanding and unhoned perceptions.

Forces Affecting Participants

Inasmuch as the outdoor-pursuit leader is leading people, it is important to understand as much about the participants as possible. While you cannot predict behaviors, reactions, attitudes or understandings, it is possible to understand the wide range of forces that have an impact on individuals and groups. Forces that influence people may be obvious, visible, and recognizable *external* forces, or they may be subtle, unspoken, invisible *internal* forces. Sessoms and Stevenson (1981) have discussed the influences of external and internal forces on participants in typical societal urban settings such as committees, planning sessions, municipal recreation activities, etc. Their list has been adapted here to demonstrate how external and internal forces affect the outdoor-pursuit participant.

External Forces. Each of the following has an impact on every participant. Some possible reactions are listed beside each external force.

1. Time
   a. When will we get there?
   b. What time do we eat?
   c. Why must we get up so early?
   d. I wish today would never end.
   e. I've always wanted to see a wilderness sunrise.
2. Space
   a. This tent is too crowded.
   b. You can see forever.
   c. This cave goes on and on.
   d. It must be 2,000 feet straight down!
   e. How come *they* are camping at *our* lake?
3. Lighting
   a. It's dark out.
   b. What fascinating shadows.
   c. I should have brought my darker sunglasses.
   d. Thank heaven the sun is coming up.
   e. Hold the candle still. I can't see a thing in here.
4. Acoustics
   a. What a great echo.
   b. Speak up, I can't hear you above the waterfall.
   c. That darn stream won't shut up and let me sleep.
   d. It is so still here I feel peaceful.
   e. It is so still here I feel lonesome.
5. Isolation
   a. I miss my family.
   b. Boy, is it good to be away.
   c. How close is emergency help?
   d. What news am I missing?
   e. There's nothing out there.
6. Extended time from home
   a. I wonder if they're all right.
   b. Bet my desk is piled high when I return.
   c. What if Henry called and couldn't reach me?
   d. Did I turn off the stove?
   e. I can hardly wait for a hot shower, fresh milk, and a soft bed.

7. Food
   a. This is so easy to prepare.
   b. I really don't care for beef stew.
   c. I don't think we've brought enough.
   d. I'm hungry.
   e. How will we cook the trout?
8. Primitive toilet facilities
   a. How inconvenient.
   b. What do you do when you are roped up on a steep glacier?
   c. What do you do on the river?
   d. Is this really private?
   e. It takes longer when you are constipated.

The reader can imagine reactions to other external forces. People respond differently to temperature; height; personal privacy (sleeping, dressing); speed; environmental factors such as vast deserts; deep forests, swamps or snowdrifts; and many other factors. When you analyze the myriad external forces that have an impact on all participants and the accompanying potential reactions, you can see that outdoor leadership entails a great capacity for understanding people.

Internal Forces. External forces can be observed and are actually easy to see, but internal forces often come from within a person and are not observable. Internal forces are also those within the group itself, and they can affect the dynamics of the group and individual members within it.

1. Group size
   a. Eight is just right.
   b. We need one more strong person.
   c. There are too many people here.
2. Dress
   a. Everyone is prepared with wool and Goretex.
   b. I wish I had boots like those.
   c. I didn't know I'd need a hat.
3. Sex
   a. Too many women . . .
   b. I wonder if he's married.
   c. There's no privacy.
4. Age
   a. Look at that old guy go!
   b. Kids have no sense.
   c. I'm too old for this group.

5. Skills
   a. I've run this river fifteen times.
   b. I think I can; I think I can.
   c. I never learned to tie a bowline.
6. Physical characteristics
   a. What does he mean, step on those rocks? He's 6'4" and I'm only 5'2"!
   b. Hope my "trick knee" holds out.
   c. I'm small but tough.

The above list of forces exists within every group, and the possible reactions are only a sample. Other, less obvious, internal forces include:

1. Motivation — What makes different people participate?
2. Perceived status — How does each person view his or her status in the group?
3. Group norms — Certain behaviors are "expected" among outdoor participants (for example, low-impact camping.)
4. Homogeneity/heterogeneity — Is the group made up of similar or dissimilar people in regard to age, experience, backgrounds, education, etc.?
5. Group Atmosphere — A pessimistic atmosphere imparts pessimism to individuals. This group force must be controlled by the leader.
6. Personal feelings and attitudes — Some people bring with them openness or prejudice, courage or cowardice, an innate love for the outdoors or a trepidation about insects, reptiles, and even many mammals.

Responsibilities of Group Members

In spite of the fact that all group participants expect guidance and safety from the leader, they are not without considerable responsibility to themselves and each other. These responsibilities include judging personal skills, abilities, and fitness.

The individual who signs up for a trip without the appropriate and/or required physical conditioning and/or skills may be as much at fault for going as the agency or leader is for permitting him or her to go. The person who slows down because of inadequate personal preparation may endanger the entire group and thus may contribute to the discomfort, accident, or injury of others.

Knowledge of the Trip, Its Location, Schedule, Required Skills and Equipment. The participant who shows up without mandatory equipment should, in most cases, not be permitted to accompany the group. The person who doesn't attend required training meetings should not go either. Failure to bring a correct map or proper footwear; arriving at the departure point late or requesting to leave the group early; bringing a guest or a pet; or carrying firearms, alcoholic beverages, fireworks, hallucinogens, and other prohibited items are all irresponsible acts.

Knowing the Leader's Qualifications. It is the participant's responsibility to verify the leader's qualifications, certifications, references, abilities, and reputation. A participant signing up for a wilderness or river trip with someone whose brochure guarantees an exciting trip through fabulous country may get more excitement than he or she desired. Anyone who fails to know more than that about a leader's qualifications may be a contributing factor to his or her own accident or injury if the leader turns out to be unqualified, irresponsible, or incompetent.

Leader-Follower Relationships

Like communication, leading and following is a two-way street. Without positive relations and interaction from one to another, the leader/follower relationship may break down and dissolve entirely. Edginton and Ford (1984) have identified a set of eight desirable relationships between leaders and followers. Adapting the list to outdoor-pursuit activities, we have used the following examples:

Shared Expectations. Some participants may come to the pre-trip meeting expecting the trip to be a guided tour with much of the everyday routine of cooking and cleaning up done by the leader and "assistants." Another may perceive the trip to be completely "roughing it" with a diet of native nuts and berries. The leader's hopes may fall somewhere between these two extremes, but until the expectations of all are congruent, the chance of a successful trip for anyone is diminished. Expectations must be shared and a consensus reached before any progress can be made in positive relationships.

Trust. A level of trust must exist between leader and participant in order to produce a satisfying experience. The follower must trust the leader's judgment and the leader must trust the follower to act according to plan.

Effective Communication. Each leader and follower must develop both speaking and listening skills with opportunity for input and feedback.

Shared Decision-making. In spite of the fact that on many occasions the leader must make autocratic decisions for the welfare of the group, sometimes followers can share in the decision-making process during outdoor activities. When to eat, a choice of routes where practical, a choice of activities, and even a determination to turn back or go on can be made by sharing the facts and the risks.

Cooperation. There must be a willingness on the part of the follower to cooperate with the directions given by the leader. By the same token, the leader must be willing to cooperate with the follower so that his/her needs may be met.

Sense of Risk and Spontaneity. Participants appreciate spontaneity, for it creates an illusion of freedom and, to some extent, a sense of unpredictability. The leader must, however, share with the group an awareness of true or existing and perceived risks. As discussed in Chapter 8, risk does not necessarily imply danger. A spontaneous decision on the part of a troop of Girl Scouts, all of whom are strong swimmers, to go skinny dipping in a mountain lake is "risky" in terms of propriety, but not dangerous. The shared sense of risk and the spontaneity of the situation bring leader and followers closer together.

Positive Reinforcement. Leaders must encourage followers and usually do so by giving positive reinforcement as the followers progress. Participants, in turn, can reinforce the leader. One says, "You certainly are catching on fast." The other says, "Thanks, I've wanted to learn to do this since I was a little kid." Social and emotional bond. . .

The leader must show interest in each participant in terms of warmth, humor, and under-standing. The follower will, in turn, show respect and admiration. Usually this relationship is initiated by the leader, with the result that participants respond positively and develop a social bond in return.

It is obvious that outdoor leadership and "followership" are strongest when both groups interrelate positively. You cannot expect followers to understand the forementioned eight interactive relations, yet leaders must not only understand them but take steps to initiate them.

THE LEADER

Having discussed some reasons why people want leaders and what they expect of them, we can now turn to the topic of leadership itself. A leader may be defined as one who influences the behavior of others and helps them reach their common goals. He or she may direct or guide people into action with a resulting improvement in knowledge, skill, or attitude.

How Are Leaders Selected?

According to Shivers (1980) there are four possible ways in which leaders attain their positions. These may be related to outdoor situations as follows:

Appointment. Leaders are appointed by a person in a superior position. In leisure settings they are hired and assigned specific duties and responsibilities. In volunteer work they may be selected by a chairperson or council president.

Election. Teams or countries may elect leaders. Outdoor clubs may elect officers, trip chair-persons, climbing coordinators, or river guides.

Emergence. An emergent leader is one who, while not initially chosen, comes out of the group to assume leadership roles when the "right" (often unpredicted) situation occurs. The quiet follower who takes charge of leading the evacuation from a burning forest, the housewife who directs first-aid care following a landslide, or the teenager with the ability to whistle loudly through the fingers who "leads" the rescue party through the fog to the scene of the accident are all leaders who emerge from unusual situations.

This type of leader usually assumes that role because he or she possesses and can use special skills, knowledge, or abilities that complement those of the appointed leader in existing and unusual situations.

Charisma. Charisma is an indefinable power to draw others to oneself. Highly attractive, intangible, and often enigmatic qualities combine to cause people to fall under this power. Because of personal demeanor, the charismatic leader may have a devoted following. In fact, it is because of charisma that some people become leaders.

Leadership and Power

Many people believe leadership is synonymous with power. In this case power usually refers to such terms as influence, control, authority, and strength. The outdoor leader actually does exert this force, and a brief discussion of the types of authority he or she possesses is in order. French and Raven (1984) have identified five sources from which power emanates. *Legitimate* power is that coming from the assignment of the leadership role to a specific person as well as that derived from the laws, regulations, and rules that the leader follows.

Reward power comes from the leader's ability to reward specific behavior. A shoulder patch awarded for the ascent of designated peaks, a first-aid certificate, and a scout badge are examples of tangible rewards, while recognition in the form of praise, testimonies, a pat on the back, a thumbs-up signal, or applause are examples of intangible rewards. It is within the leader's authority to offer these rewards.

Coercive power derives its source from the leader's ability to withhold or withdraw a privilege. This type may seem negative and even threatening, yet it may well be used when safety is the greater issue. "No one will be permitted on this trip without every one of the items of required equipment," or "No raft will proceed until every person aboard is wearing a properly secured life jacket," are examples of acceptable and appropriate use of coercive power, particularly when used along with a proper explanation of the reasons why these things are being required.

Referent power is simply derived from the leader's ability to attract. Charisma is a nebulous, yet forceful trait that draws people to a certain individual. Some leaders are influential by virtue of the "halo" effect and can do no wrong in the eyes of their followers. The wise leader does not let adulation go to his or her head, but tempers it with humbleness and discretion. *Expert* power probably is derived from the fact that the leader was hired due to his or her skill in the particular outdoor pursuit being offered.

The prudent leader understands that these five types of power are tools to be used carefully and responsibly in helping the participant meet his or her own needs. They are not to be used for the self-aggrandizement of the leader.

Leadership Traits

Many studies done since the early 1900's have postulated that successful leaders have identifiable traits or characteristics, and countless lists of leader traits have been generated. Describing these has some merit in terms of helping prospective leaders understand what followers feel are desirable characteristics. Participation in the exercise at the beginning of this chapter was one way of looking at leadership characteristics. You probably generated your own list in addition to the one we recommended you to imagine. The following lists show personal and leadership qualities (to which we might add knowledge, skill, a sense of humor, enthusiasm and others) that have been modified from items identified by Larry Buell (1978) as integral in the preparation, training, and experience of quality outdoor leaders.

Personal Qualities	Leadership Qualities
Poise; bearing	Realizes objectives
Cooperative attitude	Understands participants' needs
Self-discipline	Gets along with participants
Tolerance	Shows originality
Patience	Demonstrates resourcefulness
Concern for others	Gains confidence of participants
Appearance; neatness	Is able to analyze problems

Physical fitness
Dependability

Willingness to learn
Pleasing voice

Effective speech
Integrity

Promptness
Self-confidence

Enthusiasm

Can adapt to situations
Has ability to arouse and
  develop interests
Leads without dominating
Handles disciplinary
  problems effectively
Can inspire others
Can lead informally as
  well as formally
Shows initiative
Encourages participant
  leadership
Has ability to plan and
  organize
Observes rules and
  regulations
Takes proper care of
  equipment
Contributes to staff
  meetings
Uses time advantageously

Certainly no one would doubt the value of such traits, but having these or others in any combination and quantity does not guarantee a good leader. Unless he or she can act holistically, using his or her own unique characteristics appropriately in a wide variety of situations, the possession of them is of no value. We can always study lists of recommended traits, try to strengthen those we already think we possess and develop those we do not, but always with the realization that it is how the traits and qualities are combined and utilized that defines the leadership ability.

It seems clear that the leader should acquire a combination of skills, knowledge, and attitudes that can be interfaced with personal characteristics. Figure 11.1 shows a composite of leadership qualifications.

FIGURE 11.1 Composite of Outdoor Leadership Traits

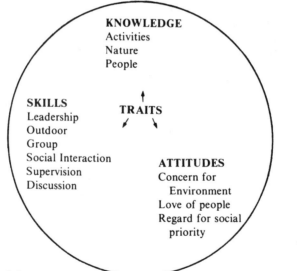

Leadership Model

A logical question at this point is "How does leadership work?" What works in one situation and not in another?

The literature on leadership contains at least eleven explanations of the role and function of leadership (Edginton and Ford, 1985), ranging from the very simple to the complex combination of several simple functions. Rather than analyze all eleven of these, the authors have elected to discuss a tri-dimensional model developed by Hersey and Blanchard (1977) and relate it to the outdoor experience. The "tri-

dimensional leadership effectiveness model" is based on two previously recommended ones. One of them (Ohio State study) defines leadership as a continuum between processes that are concerned with human relations in the accomplishment of a task. The other model (Reddin) suggests that certain styles are effective at times and ineffective at other times. Hersey and Blanchard tell us that on the continuum between human relationships and the accomplishment of tasks, one's leadership style will vary according to two variables: the *level of maturity* of the group of followers and the *demands of the situation.* They propose that the leader should determine his or her *style* of leadership *after* diagnosing the maturity of the group and the demands of the situation. This leadership model is particularly relevant to the leader of outdoor pursuits, as will be explained.

Maturity, according to Hersey and Blanchard, occurs on a continuum that is not necessarily related to age. A mature group member in an outdoor pursuit has considerable experience and education relative to the tasks to be performed, is capable of setting high but attainable goals, and possesses the willingness and ability to take responsibility. Immature group members lack *all* of those characteristics, while those on the continuum between the extremes lack some of them. (Figure 11.2 shows this maturity continuum.) A group of well-trained, experienced Eagle Scouts may be more mature as outdoor-pursuit followers than a group of parents who are novices — even though the parents may be assumed to be mature in other areas. The parents, because of lack of skill and knowledge, may not set attainable goals, and may lack the ability to be responsible for their own welfare. A group of very young beginners would probably lack skills, realistic goal-setting abilities and a degree of personal responsibility. They may "feel" they can raft for eight hours on an unknown river, yet in actuality, if they do, they will experience the need to call for help in all likelihood. They cannot take responsibility for their choices and actions.

The *demands of the situation* relate to the task to be accomplished. In outdoor pursuits, the situation may range from formal to informal, tense to relaxed, dangerous to safe. It may demand a great amount of leader control or little or no control. Figure 11.3 explains this.

In crossing the roaring mountain stream, the leader may need to be very pedantic — even autocratic and not on an equal basis with the participants. In the case of dabbling feet in a small creek, resting, eating, talking, etc., the situation is such that the leader may, indeed, appear as one of the group.

Combining the maturity of the group with the demands of the situation, we find the three-dimensional leadership model proposed by Hersey and Blanchard wherein they propose that styles of leadership change accordingly. Telling, selling, participating, and delegating are the styles of leadership they define as the two continua of maturity and situation overlap. (Figure 11.4 portrays this model.)

In the case of the leader teaching beginning rock climbing, the style would be pedantic, direct, and even autocratic *(telling)*. In a situation where the participants are somewhat or very well-skilled and the leader tries to convince them of the necessity for carrying the correct type and amount of food, we find the technique is *selling*. If the leader wants a close relationship with participants and the task to be performed requires little direction, i.e., cooking dinner with skilled adult participants, this component is *participating*. Or the task to be accomplished is minimal, as is the need for leader intervention (gathering kindling, group singing, picking berries, or dabbling feet in the creek), and the technique to use is *delegating*.

FIGURE 11.2 Maturity Continuum

IMMATURE	SOMEWHAT MATURE	MATURE
Unskilled	Lacks in one or more elements of maturity	Skilled
Unknowing		Knowledgeable
Sets no goals or unrealistic goals		Sets realistic goals
Unable to take responsibility		Takes responsibility

FIGURE 11.3 Demands of the Situation

SITUATION DEMANDS LITTLE LEADER CONTROL	SITUATION NEEDS SOME LEADER CONTROL	SITUATION DEMANDS COMPLETE LEADER CONTROL
Dabbling feet in small creek	Crossing slow creek at waist height	Crossing roaring, steep mountain stream

FIGURE 11.4 Situational Leadership

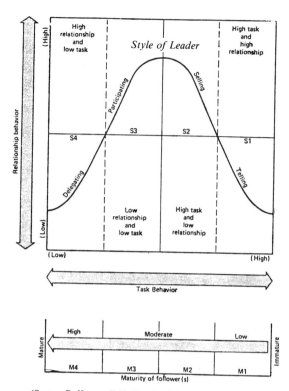

(*Source:* P. Hersey, K.H. Blanchard, *Management of Organizational Behavior: Utilizing Human Resources,* 3d ed., © 1977, p. 170. Reprinted by permission of Prentice-Hall, Inc., Englewood Cliffs, NJ.)

It is obvious that with a mature group, picking berries can be delegated entirely; however, with youth, who may get disoriented and become lost, some leadership is necessary. Whether it be telling, selling, or participating will depend upon the group maturity and the environmental situation. Thus we see that the style of leadership depends upon the maturity of the group and the demands of the situation, as is explained below.

High Task Orientation, Low Relationship (with Followers). When teaching of complex skills such as rappelling or raft guiding to beginners, you must explain the necessity of wearing completely fastened life jackets or taking wool clothing on the trip. Here the leader's style is one of organizing, directing, telling, evaluating, initiating, finalizing. The situation is demanding and the maturity level low, and the leader has a very impersonal relationship with the group.

High Task Orientation, High Relationship. The leader here is concerned with a very important task to be accomplished such as planning nutritious meals, but, because of the skill, knowledge and responsibility of the group, works *with* them, not *for* them. The leader may participate, interact, motivate, suggest, or integrate, and consequently serve as an ennabler with this advanced group.

High Relationship, Low Task. In this case the leader *participates* in the preparation of the evening meal with an experienced group through techniques involving trust, listening, acceptance, advice, and encouragement. He or she relates to everyone as an equal in a situation when no one really cares if the soup boils over.

Low Task, Low Relationship. In this case, whether the task is accomplished well or at all is unimportant, nor is the strength of the leader's influence. When picking berries recreationally, the leader may just set out some time and area limitations, then sit back and wait for the task to be accomplished.

Superimposing situational demands over the continuum of maturity tells us that the leader's *style* will change depending on the *task/relationship* orientation as well as *group maturity.*

To further illustrate the four dimensions above, assume a group of adults is starting their first white-water rafting class or winter-mountaineering excursion. As a whole, the group's knowledge, skills, and ability to take responsibility for themselves is very limited or lacking (immature), and safety is a prime concern of the leader who would use a directive task-oriented approach with little interaction with the learners. The leadership style would change to the point where it might even be participative as the learners become as adept as their leader.

Role of the Leader

The role of the leader is to guide, influence, and direct the participant toward what should be mutually agreed-upon goals compatible with the philosophy and goals of the sponsoring agency. As mentioned several times in this book, the three fundamental goals of outdoor pursuits are; a safe return, care of the natural environment, and an emotionally rewarding experience. Other than those, participants may have one or more of the following reasons for attending outdoor pursuits:

1. exploration;
2. self-discovery;
3. creativity;
4. mental health;
5. social relationships;
6. intellectual growth;
7. physical fitness;
8. self-determination;
9. independence;
10. wise use of leisure;
11. family unity;
12. enjoyment;
13. concern for the environment;
14. cooperation;
15. desire for new skills;
16. good conservation practices;
17. interest in nature; and even
18. only to reach the destination.

With such a diverse list of potential purposes to help meet, the leader's first role is challenging. Beyond the challenge of helping followers to meet their goals, outdoor leaders may perform the following functions:

1. Helping to build group cohesiveness;
2. Helping participants to identify and work for goals common to all;
3. Planning the procedures by which group goals can be met;
4. Organizing the participants according to their abilities so that the planned procedures can be carried out;
5. Motivating the participants to carry out the plans, energizing them, encouraging them, and demonstrating behavior conducive to goal attainment;
6. Evaluating the attainment of the goals and the reasons for non-attainment;
7. Serving as spokesperson for the group, representing the group and the sponsoring agency (especially in times of accident or

injury), being the contact with government officials, and composing any official communication;
8. Helping participants to learn, grow, and improve in knowledge, skills, and attitudes and encouraging self-development;
9. Serving as the catalyst for establishing group climate or atmosphere.

There may be many more roles for outdoor leaders to play; however, these are role expectations we have for all leaders.

RECOMMENDED COMPETENCIES FOR LEADERS

With the foregoing material in mind, one might well ask the question, "What competencies should outdoor leaders possess?" or "What abilities do outdoor leaders need to develop?" The knowledge, skills, and attitudes needed for success as an outdoor leader are not universally agreed upon. In fact, there is no way to substantiate without doubt just what make up the qualities and qualifications of the adequate leader. They might be described as "best guess."

When the options of professional leaders are collected and analyzed, the average of the high scores of these potential actions becomes the recommended standard. Yet no one can prove that these highly agreed upon opinions are actually the most accurate answers. They are purely opinions which become the (best guess) recommended standard. These standards remain in effect until overtaken by new ideas. It is assumed that opinions are gained through experience, objective analysis, or real situations and a reasonably consistent degree of knowledge, skill, and attitude.

Two studies on the competencies needed by outdoor leaders are of particular interest here. By competency, we refer to measurable proficiencies of skill, knowledge, experience, and attitudes in outdoor pursuits. They are all deemed necessary for being qualified as a capable outdoor leader, instructor, supervisor, and/or administrator.

Cousineau, in a 1977 study of outdoor-pursuit leaders in Ontario, Canada, related to the advisability of certification for outdoor leaders, found that his 113 respondents agreed that, in order to be certified as competent outdoor leaders, each should be examined in the following areas of competence:

1. Recognized level of achievement in specific outdoor skills such as canoe tripping, rock climbing, sailing, orienteering, caving, winter camping, cross-country skiing, white-water canoeing, and kayaking;
2. Successful completion of courses and work-shops in outdoor skills;
3. Experience as a participant and leader in outdoor pursuits;
4. Desirable personality traits for outdoor leadership;
5. Establishment of a minimum age;
6. Physical fitness and health (judged essential);
7. Skill in wilderness first aid, lifesaving, and rescue techniques;
8. Skill in aquatic lifesaving.

In 1981, Swiderski conducted a survey of 282 outdoor leaders in five western regions of the United States Forest Service to determine opinions on the importance of fifty outdoor-leadership skills.

The United States Forest Service has divided the United States into nine working regions according to location of national forests, national grasslands, land-utilization projects, and field offices. For the purpose of surveying outdoor leaders in this study, the five western regions were selected. These were chosen for this study based on considerations of climate, terrain, natural environment, vegetation patterns and land-based outdoor pursuits, and because no other geographical divisions seemed as logical. Respondents were asked to give their opinions on the importance of each of the fifty skills of land-based outdoor leaders and responses were received from 148.

A six-point Likert-type scale was used for measuring the responses. For each skill area, respondents circled the number on the continuum that best indicated their opinion on the importance of that competency.

A statistical mean for each competency statement was used to determine their rank order. This weighting resulted in the highest mean yielding the highest rank of 6.00. The lowest mean yielded the lowest rank of 1.00. The

higher the mean, the higher it was ranked. All non-responses were listed at a median score of 3.5.

After reviewing each region's rank order, it was found that there were six competencies which appeared in the top ten of all five of the western regions. These six competencies were:

1. Exercise good judgment and common sense while performing duties as a leader under stress and pressure.
2. Handle situations which pose potential safety problems.
3. Foresee and be prepared for situations in which problems and accidents might occur.
4. Prevent illness or injury, but if either occurs recognize and apply proper procedures and controls to stabilize or improve the ill or injured person's condition.
5. Teach causes, prevention, symptoms, and physiological effects of environmentally related injuries and illness which may include but not be limited to hypothermia, frostbite, heat exhaustion, heat stroke, high altitude, and fluid intake.
6. Follow a personal ethic which displays sensitivity and concern for the wilderness, reflected in everyday practices and consistent with accepted and sound environmental values.

As a result of this high mean ranking within each region, these six competencies were ranked one through six respectively in order of importance for the total group as shown in Table 11.1.

An analysis of variance was conducted for each of the 50 competencies as well as an analysis of variance for the combined means of all competencies to determine if significant differences existed among the five western regions. The analysis of variance conducted over the combined means of all competencies resulted in no significant differences among regions. In the analysis of variance conducted on each of the 50 competencies, five of the competency statements were significantly different among regions. When significant differences were found, a post-hoc comparison was conducted using Duncan's test to indicate where the differences occurred.

What Cousineau's and Swiderski's studies tell us is that outdoor leaders can agree upon the

TABLE 11.1 Rank Order of Importance of Means of Outdoor Leadership Competencies, Total Group (N - 148)

Rank	Competency Statement	Sum of Scores	Mean Score*
	EXTREMELY IMPORTANT — MANDATORY		
1	Exercise good judgment and common sense while performing duties as a leader under stress and pressure.	854.50	5.77
2	Handle situations which pose potential safety problems.	842.00	5.69
3	Foresee and be prepared for situations in which problems and accidents might occur.	840.50	5.68
4	Prevent illness or injury, but if either occurs recognize and apply proper procedures and controls to stabilize or improve the ill or injured person's condition.	836.50	5.65
5	Teach causes, prevention, symptoms, and physiological effects of environmentally related injuries and illnesses which may include but not be limited to hypothermia, frostbite, heat exhaustion, heat stroke, high altitude, and fluid intake.	823.50	5.56
6	Follow a personal ethic which displays sensitivity and concern for the wilderness, reflected in everyday practices consistent with accepted and sound environmental values.	817.00	5.52
7	Generate respect, interest, humor, enthusiasm, confidence, and commitment through actions, feelings, and demonstrations.	797.00	5.39
8	Demonstrate minimum-impact off-trail campsite selection and differentiate between low- and high-impact area.	791.50	5.35
9	Recognize and assess own limitations, plan group activities accordingly, and seek to improve abilities.	785.00	5.30
10	Recognize the indicators of potential physiological and psychological problems.	771.50	5.21
11	Demonstrate off-trail route finding and navigation which may include but not be limited to route selection, triangulation, navigation with map only, route finding in poor visibility, and calculation of speed over varied terrain.	766.50	5.18
12	Follow effective lifesaving and water-rescue procedures in emergency situations.	765.50	5.17
13	Clarify the importance of the appropriate method of solid-waste disposal.	765.00	5.17
14.5	Evaluate and assess physical, mental, and emotional strengths and weaknesses of individuals and groups which may include but not be limited to physical handicaps, medical problems, physical conditions, skill levels, personalities, and desires.	764.00	5.16
14.5	Maintain control of the group with emphasis on noise, sanitation, littering, and inter-group conflicts.	764.00	5.16

Rank	Competency Statement	Sum of Scores	Mean Score*
16	Maintain excellent personal physical and mental condition.	755.00	5.10
17	Demonstrate proficiencies in teaching knowledge, skills, and attitudes to others.	749.00	5.06
18	Demonstrate how to read a map and use a compass, and teach these skills which may include but not be limited to map scales, contours, descriptions of ground from topographical features on map, walking a bearing, plotting a course, and measurement of distances.	741.00	5.01
19	Demonstrate compliance with land-management regulations.	740.00	5.00
20	Employ good judgment in aquatic safety procedures which may include but not be limited to when and where to ford rivers, river-crossing and stream crossing techniques.	739.00	4.99
21	Display a proficiency in organizational skills.	734.00	4.96
22	Demonstrate when and how to treat water for drinking purposes.	732.50	4.95
23	Employ appropriate emergency survival skills which may include but not be limited to shelter construction, water procurement, fire building, improvising navigational instruments, and food gathering.	728.50	4.92
24	Clarify the importance of proper equipment and clothing which may include but not be limited to selection, cost, care, repair, improvising, storage, use, qualities, and style.	727.00	4.91
25	Interpret weather phenomena and implications of the effects of weather on the comfort and safety of the group which may include but not be limited to reading signs of changing weather, regional patterns, seasonal variations, and mountain influences.	726.50	4.91
26	Apply principles of group management and security while traveling.	722.00	4.88
27	Demonstrate healthful menu planning on the basis of nutrition, taste, bulk, weight, storage properties, packaging, cost, and ease of preparation.	717.50	4.85
28	Utilize communication and listening skills to enhance teaching and leading capabilities.	706.00	4.77
29	Illustrate awareness and knowledge of avalanche hazards and forecasting which may include but not be limited to terrain and weather factors, and avalanche survival.	702.00	4.74
30	Demonstrate safe driving procedures and maintain a safe driving record.	701.00	4.74
31	Demonstrate safe use of backpacking stoves for cooking in all types of weather.	693.00	4.68
32	Follow mountain rescue procedures which may include but not be limited to ground searches, crevasse rescue, and avalanche search and recovery.	691.50	4.67

Rank	Competency Statement	Sum of Scores	Mean Score*
33	Analyze the dynamics of group problem-solving and initiate group decision-making.	684.00	4.62
34	Practice proper trail-walking technique which may include but not be limited to pace, breathing, foot placement, courtesy, conservation of energy, and balance.	683.00	4.61

OF MODERATE IMPORTANCE

35	Illustrate correct principles of packing and carrying one or more types of packs which may include but not be limited to size, balance, weight, and displacement.	656.50	4.44
36	Practice resourcefulness and economical consumption of firewood.	643.00	4.34
37	Interpret ecosystems, geology, history, culture, flora, fauna, and wildlife of the area of travel.	617.00	4.17
38	Practice snow/ice techniques which may include but not be limited to uses of the ice axe and crampons.	615.50	4.16
39	Construct shelters in an emergency using materials such as tree limbs, boughs, and ground cover.	611.00	4.13
40	Practice snow-travel techniques which may include but not be limited to cross-country skiing and snowshoeing.	609.50	4.12
41	Illustrate awareness and knowledge of crevasse hazards.	602.00	4.07
42	Teach rope handling which may include but not be limited to coiling, tossing, and knot tying.	601.00	4.06
43	Demonstrate procedures in rappelling and setting anchor systems which may include but not be limited to dulfersitz, carabiner brake, multiple rappels, natural and artificial anchors.	599.00	4.05
44	Teach climbing signals and belaying procedures.	590.50	3.99
45	Construct snow shelters for enjoyment and survival which may include but not be limited to trenches, igloos, and caves.	586.00	3.96
46	Demonstrate proper bouldering techniques which may include but not be limited to three points of contact, low center of gravity, and friction principles.	560.50	3.79
47	Illustrate the capability of cooking over an open fire.	525.50	3.55
48	Demonstrate the proper use of campcraft tools such as the axe or saw.	487.00	3.29

Rank	Competency Statement	Sum of Scores	Mean Score*
	NOT IMPORTANT — NOT NEEDED		
49	Introduce and teach fishing techniques to outing participants.	399.00	2.70
50	Demonstrate proficiencies in teaching hunting and trapping techniques and the care and preparation of wild game.	331.00	2.24

*Higher mean value = higher importance ranking.

competencies they see as necessary in all outdoor leaders, and their opinions should be heeded, for who can better assess the needed qualifications for outdoor leadership than outdoor leaders themselves. Swiderski's study, though, tells us that, while there may be an identifiable core of competencies that should be mandatory for all, leaders in different areas of western portions of the United States do not agree on all competencies. It may be concluded from Swiderski's study that, beyond the fact that some competencies can be agreed upon by the majority, some are so regionally specific because of terrain, weather, climate, resource base, or other reasons that there are statistically significant differences in how the competencies are evaluated from region to region.

This gives the outdoor leader a challenge. Which are the *minimum* competencies for his or her region and what *additional* competencies are recommended? In this book it will be assumed that *minimum* competencies for all leaders, regardless of area, are the first six on Swiderski's list. The other competencies on his list and many regionally necessary ones not mentioned are *recommended*. It behooves the leader in each part of the world to develop competencies beyond the six minimum ones suggested here and beyond or instead of the next 28 listed as mandatory.

SUMMARY

Outdoor leadership is a complex combination of understanding the participants and the role and function of leadership. Participants are members of groups that possess all the properties of all other groups. They have reasons for being followers and needs for having leaders, and are affected by many external and internal forces. Every group member has specific responsibilities for him or herself and all groups have identifiable leader/follower relationships.

Leaders may be selected in several ways, and all leaders exert several types of power on the followers. Outdoor leaders may have certain recognizable traits, but no list guarantees that the possessor will be an effective or adequate leader. The four-dimensional model of leadership tells us that leadership style depends upon the level of maturity of the group as it relates to the demands of the task to be performed.

Outdoor leaders can agree on the mandatory importance of some competencies; however, regional and activity differences make it necessary to develop additional competencies that may be mandatory in one situation and inappropriate in others.

The outdoor-pursuit leader needs to understand the interrelationships of participant and group characteristics, leadership theory, and leader competencies before embarking with a group anywhere.

BIBLIOGRAPHY

Buell, Larry, *Leader's Guide to the 24-Hour Experience,* Greenfield, MA: Environmental Awareness Publications, 1978.

Cousineau, Claude, *A Delphi Consensus on a Set of Principles for the Development of a Certification System for Education in the Outdoor Adventure Programs,* unpublished doctoral dissertation, University of Northern Colorado, 1971.

Edginton, Christopher and Ford, Phyllis, *Leadership of Recreation and Leisure Service Organizations,* New York: John Wiley and Sons, 1985.

Hersey, P., and Blanchard, K. H., *Management of Organizational Behavior: Utilizing Human Resources,* 3rd edition, Englewood Cliffs, NJ: Prentice-Hall, Inc., 1977.

Sessoms, H. Douglas, and Stevenson, Jack L., *Leadership and Group Dynamics in Recreation Services,* Boston: Allyn and Bacom, Inc., 1981.

Shivers, Jay S., *Recreational Leadership,* Princeton, NJ: Princeton Book Company, 1980.

Swiderski, Michael J. *Outdoor Leadership Competencies Identified by Outdoor Leaders in Five Western Regions,* unpublished doctoral dissertation, University of Oregon, 1981.

CHAPTER 12

LEADING IN THE OUTDOORS

It is probably an endless task to itemize, step by step, the process a leader undergoes to take a group on a planned outing into the natural environment. Nevertheless, this chapter covers some of the more important parts of this process to understand and address prior to any outdoor venture.

RESPONSIBILITIES OF LEADERS

Leaders of outdoor activities should recognize that they are responsible for the actions, health, and safety of all participants in an outing from the time they leave to the time they return. Also, the burden of the responsibility for the well-being and conduct of the group increases in proportion to time and distance away from help and weather conditions. In the outdoors there is no back-up support, medical aid, telephone, written policies for emergency procedure, or chain of command found back in the confines of the building that houses the sponsoring agency.

Many people are reluctant to become outdoor leaders because of this all-encompassing responsibility; others are oblivious to it and lead on with their heads in the proverbial clouds. Yet planning, forethought, preparedness, and adherence to set rules generally lessen the threat of problems. First, leaders must be aware that any assistance other than that from their group may be hours and days away. Hence the need for planning and preparation for emergencies of all types — even minor aches and pains. Second, people attempting to teach in the field must realize that participant control and attention are much different than in the controlled environment of a classroom. Many factors may alter even the most ideal teaching situation, but participant personal comfort is the key here. If a learner is too cold, too warm, too tired, too thirsty, or too hungry, or has a need to relieve body waste pressures, he or she will not be attentive or responsive. Aches, pains, or miseries from any source distract the learner and cause disregard for general rules of safety and conduct.

Planning and forethought can remedy these undesirable teaching problems. Participants can be dressed properly for the outdoor teaching environment — or the teaching environment can be changed to a more comfortable weather area. Then the group can be controlled by planning and rules and set procedures. To achieve this state, leaders and assistant group leaders should scout the proposed teaching sites in advance and become familiar with hazards, escape routes, and alternate teaching sites in the event the chosen site becomes dangerous or uncomfortable from weather. Teaching in the natural environment is thus a challenge that demands considerable thought and a search for suitable natural materials.

You should also remember that when any undisciplined group of people leaves their accustomed habitat and the *known rules and regulations* governing them, they tend to shed all responsibility for their conduct and actions. Fear of reprimands deceases and spontaneous action becomes the rule, hence the need for specific leadership guidelines. When a group leaves the sponsoring agency, they should, in fact, take it with them in the form of a leader representative who becomes just as responsible as the administrators they left behind. The safari to the out-of-doors may start at the agency headquarters, but represents it throughout the activity. Conduct on the trip to the site reflects upon the agency and is remembered by those who read and note the name on the bus or the T-shirts. Conduct away from the vehicles used for transportation also reflects on it; litter left behind, flora and fauna damage, noise, inconsiderate actions, injuries, inconveniences, and obviously dangerous actions or individuals all expose the inadequacy of adult supervision and leadership of those responsible for the outing. This is true of agencies, clubs, churches, or any sponsoring organization.

PARTICIPANT BEHAVIOR

Participant behavior varies depending upon settings and leaders should recognize this. The *individual alone* may exhibit behavior indicative of his or her true personality, but rarely does a leader see a participant as a lone individual. There are several settings in which the individual must react with one other person; the *experience of two* in a mountain tent or a canoe calls for different behavior. While it is often desirable for each to be of approximately the same age and skill, that is not always possible. The two must tolerate and understand each other's needs, however, and should each be reasonably neat and organized with their personal possessions and equipment. They may need to share the responsibilities of cooking, packing, carrying equipment, and caring for it.

Leaders should also recognize the responsibility of *each individual to the entire group*. We expect everyone to be on time and not delay the group, to be organized about their own gear, to be neat, and to dress and act "appropriately." Further, each individual is expected not to offend the group by offensive personal habits, bragging, or complaining. A leader can teach trail etiquette: don't follow too closely, avoid letting branches snap back into the next hiker's face, step off the trail when stopping to adjust equipment, etc. But naturally he or she can't change long-time personal behavior. Thus leaders can humor, guide, and even remove some individuals from the group to "take them under the wing" person to person.

On the other hand, the *group is obligated to the individual*. Even if the majority rules, the needs of each person should be met. Leaders who side with the majority to the detriment of the minority are not acting responsibly. When seven in a group of eight want to press on and one is in pain or exhausted or close to hypothermia, the group should be made to understand why they must change their goal and respect the needs of this individual.

The group itself has a *responsibility to other groups*. Trail and river courtesy dictates privacy, quiet, and overt contact. Slow groups should let faster ones pass, and groups arriving second at camping sites should move away from those who arrived first — regardless of the attributes of a neighboring site.

Groups also have responsibilities to the land- or water-management agencies. They must have the proper permits and know agency restrictions. They must know the restrictions on fires, horses, pets, firearms, fireworks, fishing, etc. Further, the group has a *responsibility to the local populace.* How the group looks and acts on the way to and from the trail or river; behavior at restaurants and rest stops; pitch and content of conversations; respect for livestock, fences, and private property; and group interaction are all part of group responsibility to the general public.

Knowing the foregoing material and anticipating a variety of interactive behavior will help the leader relate to each member of the group empathetically and humanistically.

TEACHING VS. LEADING

The differences between teaching and leading are not always clear. Perhaps it is simplest to define teaching as learning from an instructor and leading as facilitating self-taught learning. On the other hand, there are many times when the outdoor leader teaches and the teacher leads. Much of this depends on the experience or maturity of the group and the tasks to be accomplished (see Chapter 11). We prefer not to differentiate but rather to discuss teacher-directed and self-directed programs separately.

While theories of leadership may be applied broadly to many situations, the *techniques* of leadership usually relate to specific activities in which one person — the leader — organizes, directs, influences, instructs, or otherwise affects the behavior of others — the followers. The techniques utilized by leaders of outdoor pursuits may often be automatic and unacceptable for other types of human effort. Inherent in outdoor pursuits, however, is an element of risk, danger, and even death. Accordingly, an outdoor leader may use firmness, non-democratic methods, and unilateral decisions. It is difficult to know at what point to be firm and autocratic, particularly since most leadership training pro-

grams emphasize group dynamics and leadership by consensus. Before discussing how the leader arrives at decisions, then, it may be wise to examine the inherently different expectations that mature and immature people have for the leaders of their programs.

Teacher-Directed vs. Self-Directed Programs

Most leaders remember how they were taught as children and tend to emulate the techniques of their teachers. This is fine when followers are children or youth; however, we have learned that adults learn differently than children and require different teaching strategies. Webster's Dictionary defines an adult as a "mature, *self-directing* individual." This means that adults do not always need the teacher-directed programs of youth. Going back to Chapter 11, "Outdoor Leadership," we remember that leadership style varies with the *maturity* of the group; there seems to be a difference in the way immature and mature participants learn, summed up in the following four points adapted from Edginton and Ford's *Leadership of Recreation and Leisure Service Organizations.*

1. The immature are dependent learners. As individuals grow they move from dependency to self direction. People who have reached maturity need to be recognized as self directing and given the opportunity to choose their own methods of learning.
2. The immature lack experience, or cannot generalize based on previous situations. Mature learners benefit more from learning conditions in which they can tie in some of their previous experiences.
3. Both immature and mature learners have teachable moments. For many these coincide with a stage the individual faces in a specific role. Thus the timing of learning experiences becomes as important as knowing at what stage a group or individual may be.
4. The immature beginner has many basics to become familiar with while the mature or advanced person is interested in a problem-

centered approach to learning. The receptivity of the mature learner peaks when the issue being studied is of immediate concern and not just an abstract theory.

Table 12.1 delineates the differences between our understanding of immature and mature behavior in five different areas. It should be understood that this dichotomy is really based on a continuum, not an either-or situation. In groups individuals may be at various points on the continuum and you should not categorically assume that immature and mature behavior is entirely separated. The dotted line on the table means that there is not a clear demarcation between these two; on the whole, the immature are more likely to be to the left and the mature to the right. (The beginning climber is not very self-directed compared to the veteran of 200 climbs.) The less mature the individual, the more pedagogical (leader-oriented) the approach should be. Learners with intermediate skills may exhibit both immature and mature behaviors, so it is possible to say that they would likely fall within a wide area in the middle of the continuum.

Because of their lack of maturity, limited experiences, interest in the present and lack of ability to be self directing, most children are assumed to be immature while most adults are assumed to be mature. Some adults, however, may select leader-directed leisure experiences similar to those for children because of an interest in a specific topic or activity, a desire for an extrinsic reward, a lack of earlier experience, or situational immaturity.

In terms of our *perception of the participant*, leaders should generally view the immature as being dependent on others and the mature as being self-motivated. In a leader-directed

TABLE 12.1   Continuum of Immature and Mature Learners

Assumptions About:	Immature (Beginner)	Mature (Advanced)
1. Perception of the participant	Dependent upon others	Self-motivated individual
2. Status of participants' experience	Built on progression of earlier experiences leading to selected outcomes	Based on own past experiences with chance to grow
3. Readiness for new experiences and new learning	Varies with maturity	Based on life problems and life tasks
4. Orientation to learning-time perspective	Topic or activity centered for future use	Task- or problem-oriented; solutions based on current need; focus on *now*
5. Motivation	Extrinsic award (ribbons, badges, trophies) and intrinsic rewards (praise, winning, peer acceptance)	Intrinsic incentives (personal growth, self-actualization, self-esteem, belonging, fulfilling curiosity)

(immature) situation, the participant is viewed as being dependent upon the leader, while in a self-directed (mature) experience the participant is self-motivated and self-directed.

In terms of experience, leaders should develop progressive programs to meet the needs of the immature based on earlier programs for beginners, who also need *leader-selected* outcomes. The mature participant is generally viewed as being able to participate in activities that draw from past experience and knowledge with a chance to grow through individually selected goals. With beginners there is usually one-way communication since the leader is the primary resource for the learning. With the mature, leaders and participants engage in transactional communication where everyone's experience is valued as a resource for learning.

Leader-directed (pedagogical) techniques may be utilized in situations involving children, adults, and groups of all ages — whenever people are beginners or immature in experience. Self-directed (andragogical) leadership is generally practiced in settings with adults or experienced participants. The process of each technique is compared in Table 12.2. Here *setting* refers to the physical, interpersonal, and organizational climates under which the program is conducted. In leader-directed programs (for beginners), the setting is formal, organized with predetermined locations for participants, equipment, and so on. The leader and often the sponsoring organization establish the format for the setting, as can be seen with many youth agency badge programs. There is little interpersonal communication.

In self-directed programs (for the advanced learner), the setting is informal. Participants and leader share an equal status wherein the leader is a facilitator rather than a director. Time is devoted to getting acquainted, sharing ideas, and socializing, and the organization is viewed as being cooperative and supportive in establishing group comfort. For example, the site is usually decided by consensus rather than by the leader.

The process of *organization and planning* under leader-directed settings is almost always implemented by the leader, who plans and organizes what activities will be undertaken. In self-directed programs, program organization occurs with participant involvement in the decision-making process. Examples of leader-directed leisure programs would be a canoeing lesson, a climbing lesson, or a backpacking trip sponsored by a municipality, where the leader structures the format. In a self-directed program, planning is done mutually with the leader involved as a participant. Examples would be club programs, common adventurer outings, and advanced trips sponsored by a municipality.

Assessing interests, needs, and values of a leader-directed program is a primary function of the leader. An overnight hike for ten-year-olds, for instance, is usually planned according to his or her perception of participant interests and needs and his or her own values. If this were not the case, ten-year-olds might plan to hike too long a distance, to bring a mixture of indigestible food, and perhaps even to engage in dangerous activities or those which would annoy other campers. Self-directed programs involve the participants in assessing their own interests, needs, and values in agreement with the group.

In leader-directed settings, *goals and outcomes* are primarily established by the leader, while in self-directed programs, they are created by group negotiations with consensus. The leader might set a twelve-mile hike as a goal, which the participants meet, in a leader-directed program, while in a self-directed program, participants might discuss various hike lengths and reach an agreement based on consensus of group members.

In planning the *sequence of events and activities,* the leader of a leader-directed experience will plan purposefully, in a logical sequence, the order in which events are to occur. An example of this is a leading plan where the event may be divided into specific units, each of which contributes to the integral whole. For example, hiking, cooking, map and compass, survival and environmental ethics are often taught separately before the trip. This sequence of events is planned so that each one builds purposefully on previously learned skills, knowledge, and attitudes.

In self-directed programs, events and activities are conducted according to the desires of the group, assuming everyone already has a foundation of basic skills on which to build and can undertake projects at any stage needed to reach the goal. As a matter of fact, because of the wide variety of individual readiness levels in

TABLE 12.2   A Comparison of Processes of Leader-Directed and Self-Directed Programs

Elements	Leader-Directed Program	Self-Directed Program
	CONTINUUM	
1. Setting	Formal, organized, competitive leader-oriented, judgmental	Informal, equal status, cooperative, supportive, agreement by consensus. Leader facilitated
2. Organization and planning	Primarily by the leader	Through participant decision-making process
3. Assessing interests, needs, and values	Primarily by the leader	By consensus or agreement
4. Goals, outcomes	Primarily leader set	By negotiation with consensus
5. Planning the sequence of events and activities	By units, part vs. whole, logical sequence, building purposefully from past events	By project sequencing (whole vs. part) in terms of personal desire and individual readiness
6. Implementing leisure activities	Techniques, rules, format, transmitted by leaders; practice drills, assigned steps, and projects for earning awards.	Independent activities, group projects, discussions, sharing; experiential
7. Evaluation	Primarily by the leader	By mutual group consent through self-gathered data and completion of projects

self-directed programs, different events and activities may be conducted by part of the group rather than having everyone perform every step. In a canoe trip that is self-directed, for example, the group may start out, travel for a while, then go ashore and analyze how to do things more efficiently.

Implementing activities requires two different processes. In leader-directed activities, techniques, rules, and format are transmitted to the participants by the leader, who may assign practice drills or designate specific steps and projects to be followed for earning badges or awards. In self-directed activities, the program is often conducted independently of the leader's goals and wishes. The group may plan a variety of activities for independent participation by different people, rather than have everyone doing the same thing. The program might be implemented through discussion, sharing, and experimental involvement, with the leader being a facilitator rather than a director.

Evaluation of leader-directed programs is conducted primarily by the leader. It may be in terms of "You did well," "You have made a lot of improvement," "You had the best time," or "You have earned your badge." In a self-directed program, evaluation occurs through mutual group consent, with members stating, "we did well," or "we succeeded," They also gather data that support group evaluation of individual portions of the project, parts of which may be assessed as being better than others. Here the final result or product isn't evaluated as much as the process the group went through to complete the project. No person loses or fails because of a leader or any other one individual making that decision, and any individual or project deemed successful merits this praise on the basis of group consensus. Success in the self-directed process is measured in terms of group or individual expectations, not those of the leader. In the andragogical process, evaluation is not a dead end, but moving on to assessing more or different needs and finding ways to meet them. Rather than a single-minded orientation toward judgment and comparison with past events or scores, it focuses on changing the situation to bring about success in the future. In the andragogical process, each individual is measured in terms of his or her own ability, not against others in the group. As long as this person contributes to group goals with his or her own unique abilities, his or her achievement can be assessed highly. Through this process each individual makes the enterprise successful.

Because of situation, circumstance, type of program, age, or ability of participants, one can never assume that every program will be either entirely leader-directed or self-directed. A leader-directed (formal) setting may be used in a self-directed activity with the group helping to plan, assess, and create goals. On the other hand, the self-directed group may, through consensus or agreement, plan a very logical and purposeful sequence of events and implement precise techniques, rules, and assignments for completing them. The point here is that much adult outdoor leadership occurs in self-directed

groups; the prudent leader should understand that he or she may need to make some modifications in the leadership process to meet the goals of the self-directed group. Even in what may appear to be a leader-directed program with an identifiable progression, some participants may require less leadership to meet their self-directed leisure needs.

In conclusion, leaders must be able to adjust their methods of working with groups to adapt to the continuum of the beginner who is both chronologically and experiencially immature and the beginner who is chronologically mature but immature in experience. By the same token, leaders may work with groups that are mature in both age and experience or chronologically immature but advanced in terms of skills. Figure 12.1 shows that, basically, maturity in skill, not age, determines the techniques of the outdoor leader. On the basis of a review of the literature on adult education, we recognize that adults:

1. Are capable of change at any age;
2. Seek fulfillment or happiness; (Learning experiences can be an avenue for achieving self-fulfillment.)
3. Are extremely capable and become frustrated unless they are given the opportunity for self-direction;
4. Have developed "mind sets" based on past experiences that have much to do with how they react to a particular learning situation;
5. Are capable of learning from personal experience but need help in determining a logical process for analyzing those past experiences;
6. May be quite mature in relation to one set of standards and quite immature in another; (In cases where the learners are still immature, more guidance may be required from the instructor.)
7. Have periods in their life which make them more receptive to learning certain subjects and give them blocks against other subjects until that problem is solved or that phase is past;
8. Are uniquely different based on aims, values, social habits, and experience; therefore, each learner should be treated with respect for his/her individuality.

FIGURE 12.1

Relationship of Leader Techniques to Chronological Maturity and Skill Maturity

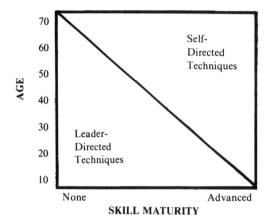

The following guidelines are offered for leaders who work with adults:

1. Adults expect to be treated with dignity and respect. They want to feel valued as individuals and have their opinions respected and given credence.
2. Leaders should recognize the value of the uniqueness of each individual. It is important to remember that each adult in the group will bring unique skills, experience, and knowledge to the group environment.
3. The leader should attempt to determine both individual and group goals since individual goals within adult groups can vary tremendously. Some attempt should be made to identify and respond to individual desires and expectations expressed by group members.
4. Leaders should work to create a supportive social climate. This is important to build a relationship of trust and openness that facilitates positive communication.
5. Adults find leisure experiences more personally meaningful if they are actively involved in the decision-making process.
6. Adults respond to personally relevant leisure experiences; that is, outings that draw upon the participants' meaningful past experiences are often more successful than those that deal in abstractions.

7. Adults respond to leaders who are genuinely concerned about their welfare, needs, interests, and desires.
8. In developing relationships in groups of adults, the leader should work to create trust between group members and between him- or herself and the group.
9. The leader should attempt to interact with participants in a parallel fashion rather than in a superior/subordinate way. Respect for the leader should be based on knowledge and skills rather than solely on his or her position within the organization.
10. The leader should be able to adjust the goals of the activity or program, where appropriate, to meet the needs of group members. It is not unusual for the goals of the group to be different from those of the leader, and some modification may be necessary.

Making Decisions

The basic process of decision-making boils down to knowing when to say "yes" and when to say "no," when to say, "go on," "stay put," or "go back." A program without safety controls is one that has hazards, and leaders of these are either unaware of the accidents that could occur, or are aware of them and make no decision or the wrong decision. The program *with* safety controls calls for decisions based on external factors and caution.

The most important part of outdoor leadership is this decision-making process. Unfortunately it entails the elusive skill of judgment, which varies with each situation, and there is no way of measuring a leader's judgment ability in advance. Further, good judgment in one situation does not guarantee good judgment in another or even in a second similar situation. However, it is generally understood that, in outdoor settings, the decision-making process should be the result of conscious assessment of five external forces. Usually when a decision must be made by the leader it relates to changing the route, aborting the climb, getting of the water, evacuating the injured, or treating hypothermia. (Or any immediate action because of potential danger or risk.) The leader must be able to support this judgmental decision as being the same one that would have been made by other reasonable and prudent professionals.

Technical, socio-psychological, safety, physiological, and environmental forces should all be analyzed and evaluated before a decision is made (illustrated in Figure 12.2). *Technical Forces,* often referred to as Equipment Forces, cause the leader to analyze what equipment is necessary for each decision. Are there enough ropes, stoves, clothing, food, or whatever is needed to carry out the action? What is their condition? *Socio-Psychological Forces* are those that affect the group itself. Peer pressure, individual and group expectations, personality differences, mental preparedness for emergencies, and individual and group ethics all have an impact on the decision, as do knowledge, common sense, fear, the will to live, and the openness of communication. *Physiological Forces* are the fitness levels of the individuals, the fatigue factor, nutritional levels, and the participants' awareness of their own stamina and strength. *Environmental Forces* to be considered include the weather, altitudes, snow, ice, rock, rapids, waterfalls, vegetation, animals, terrain, time of day, and even aesthetics. *Safety Factors* relate to pre-trip planning, first-aid supplies, the number of first aiders, and contingency and alternate plans.

The Decision

Making a decision should be an act based on a step-by-step process of rational action, not precipitous action. These logical steps are as follows:

1. Consider the task. What is the situation and what must be done?
2. Consider the resources. These are the five external factors listed above.
3. Consider a range of alternative actions, then evaluate each in respect to the five external factors. For example, you could go on, but how does each external factor affect this decision? What are the effects of each if you stay? If you go back?
4. Write down all possible ideas and pick the best one. That is your decision. If you can't write them down, discuss them and then pick

one, remembering that the responsibility rests with the leader. You can't pass the buck and say, *"They* told me to do it that way."
5. Put the decision into action positively and emphatically. Don't waste time discussing or thinking, What if? "What if," is out of the picture. Stick to your decision.
6. In the end, evaluate the results of your decision. It might influence future ones.

Hopefully, a leader is aware of dangers and potential decision-making situations before they happen. Like the "defensive driver," the defensive leader tries to anticipate. In some cases, the decision may even be made before the actual danger occurs.

FIGURE 12.2

Factors Contributing to the Decision-Making Process

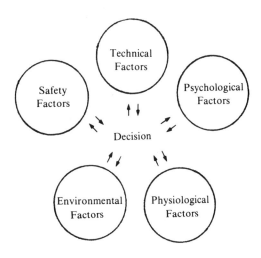

243

LEADER POSITIONS

There are some simple techniques that make all the difference between a good and effective leader and a leader in name only. Leaders should have well-modulated voices and clear enunciation so that no words are slurred or lost to the listener. Your voice must carry in storms and above the sounds of rushing water. An alert leader will not attempt to talk next to a waterfall or in a gale or blizzard without trying to move the group to a quieter, sheltered location.

Listeners should have their backs to the wind, the sun, or anything that might be a distraction. On hillsides, it is usually best for the instructor to face uphill toward a group, especially if the terrain forms a natural "amphitheater." If the leader stands above the group, participants may see him or her silhouetted against the bright sky and may have to maintain awkward head positions to see clearly. The resulting strain on the back of the neck will preclude many from watching the leader at all.

Leader positions on the trail are also important, as illustrated and discussed in Figure 12.3. Note that, in some cases, the group may be separated if the leader is in the wrong position. In such cases, no leadership exists at all.

SUMMARY

Leadership techniques should vary according to the experiential maturity of the group. Adults expect to learn in a more self-directed manner while children expect a leader-directed technique. There are times when experience level does not coincide with the chronological maturity of the participant and teaching methods must change.

Regardless of style, the final responsibility for decision-making rests with the leader. Decisions should be made only after considering technical, socio-psychological, environmental, physiological, and safety factors.

BIBLIOGRAPHY

Edginton, Christopher and Ford, Phyllis, *Leadership of Recreation and Leisure Service Organizations,* New York: John A. Wiley and Sons, 1985.

Knowles, Malcolm, *Self-Directed Learning,* Chicago: Association Press, 1975.

FIGURE 12.3 Examples of the Effects of Leader Position(s) on Group Control

Pattern	Advantages	Disadvantages
A Leader Follows	The leader "sweeps" the trail and so in theory can attend to slow or disabled participants.	The leader has limited or no control over the pace or route decision of the lead walker.
B Leader Moves About	The leader is able to walk with each participant, sharing skills or knowledge.	Control of the lead walker and or security at the end of the line are compromised.
C Leader goes first	Pace can be controlled effectively and decisions about the route are made by the leader.	There is no sweep or "back-up" at the end of the line, and communication with individuals may be different.
D Leader-Caboose System	Two leaders, or one leader with a qualified participant appointed as "caboose" provides good confinement.	No functional disadvantages, though some participants may feel regimented or confined.
E Very small groups, each with a leader	With care a leader can keep track of and communicate effectively with 2-3 participants while walking. Speed is also enhanced by traveling in small groups.	None *if* each party is fully equipped for emergencies and *if* each leader is aware of and capable of following the agreed-upon route.

There are four basic rules which, if adhered to, could reduce the chance of losing a participant to near zero.

1. The slower people go first, just after the leader;
2. No passing is allowed;
3. Always stop at any decision point or point of possible confusion;
4. Every person is responsible for the person *following*.

FIRST AID CLASSES FOR OUTDOOR-ORIENTED PEOPLE SHOULD INCLUDE SPLINTING AND LITTER CONSTRUCTION USING MATERIALS LIKELY TO BE AVAILABLE
A single rope stretcher can be constructed in minutes and reinforced by poles, skis, ice axes, or pack frames.

CHAPTER 13

FIRST AID

Outdoor leaders need first-aid skills and knowledge beyond the scope of most Red Cross, St. John's, or other courses designed for urban dwellers. Even the E.M.T. (Emergency Medical Technician) courses generally fail to provide information on improvisation and long-term care since there is little need for these skills in proximity to sophisticated medical treatment. The purpose of this chapter is to provide a review of basic first-aid techniques in terms of the needs of outdoor leaders. The material provided here is intended only as a supplement to Red Cross, E.M.T., or other standard training, however, and cannot replace hands-on experience in a comprehensive outdoor-oriented course. Anyone planning to lead outings in wilderness or back-country areas should invest in a course and also seek out good supplementary study in back-country first aid.

Outdoor-oriented courses are available in most major cities through parks and recreation districts, departments and universities, or outdoor clubs. Check with your local Red Cross office since they are usually aware of these and may even sponsor one. Local sporting goods stores are also a good place to inquire.

Why go to all the bother? Is all the training *really* necessary? The point is somewhat more complex and interesting than one might think. For many people the answer is simple: someone might be injured and need care, and furthermore, the treatment of an injury in a back-country setting can require more advanced "second aid" skills. This is certainly true, yet while many find this reason to be sufficiently motivating, many others do not. We each have different perceptions of the level of risk inherent in outdoor pursuits and this, of course, varies widely with the particular activity, time, and place. Given an accurate objective estimate of the danger, individuals respond differently and may be more or less willing to accept the risk depending on the particular circumstances. Many leaders don't see the risk of injuries as sufficient justification for an investment of time and money in first-aid training, and in at least one limited sense they may be correct!

Outdoor pursuits, taken as a whole, are *not* particularly risky. For example, outdoor-pursuit activities in the mountains claim 400-600 lives per year in Japan, a similar number in the combined Alps of France, Switzerland, Germany, Austria, and Italy, and about sixty lives in the United States. These figures, especially those for the Alps, seem extremely high, yet when viewed in the context of the tremendous number of participant days, the death rate (and presumably the injury rate) turns out to be not far above normal rates for the population. Hour for hour, ice climbing may not be much more hazardous than driving, and backpacking is no doubt safer than life in many urban areas! Some people simply don't see this level of risk as warranting a special effort. Nevertheless, leaders do need first-aid training for reasons that transcend their perceptions of and attitudes toward risk.

Leaders are responsible for the well-being of others. As has been explained earlier, the leader is both morally and legally bound to provide certain basic forms of care, and adequate response to injuries is perhaps the most basic of all. While it is certainly true that all adult participants in an outing *should* know first aid, the leader can be assured that such will almost never be the case. He or she is expected to provide all necessary care, which in all likelihood will exceed the capabilities of any member of the group unless the injury is very minor. Furthermore, the provision of such care requires skills and knowledge beyond that taught in "urban" first aid courses. Our legal system tends to support the expectations of participants, and competence in first aid is widely acknowledged as a basic requirement of outdoor leadership, professional or otherwise. It isn't "reasonably prudent behavior" to go beyond the rapid availability of professional medical care and facilities without sufficient means to take care of yourself and your party members.

Thus, it should be agreed that competence in first aid is necessary. The material presented from here on will assume familiarity with current practices and procedures at least to the level of the American Red Cross Advanced First Aid course. The intent here is to 1) highlight certain aspects of basic first aid that are especially important in outdoor situations, 2) provide information not adequately covered in standard courses, and 3) provide a list of resources for further study.

INITIAL RESPONSES TO EMERGENCIES

Most first-aid books give advice for the "critical response" period, the critical interval between first awareness of an accident or injury and direct "hands-on" contact with the victim. Nevertheless, we are going to review the main concerns and options in initial response because this period is especially important in outdoor situations. In town, a would-be rescuer or first aider can make repeated mistakes or even become a victim, yet the situation is usually remedied quickly by others. Assistance and expertise are never far away in or near cities in the United States and in most developed countries. Out of town the situation is very different, and mistakes can be far more costly. Sophisticated support systems are generally not available, and the prognosis for the injured patient can be profoundly affected by the quality of care by the first aider. Too often, an urgent but non-critical situation is turned into a nightmare by errors in initial response!

Let's work through a possible situation. Since the transportation phase of any outing is where you are most likely to encounter a major accident, imagine yourself driving down the highway with a van full of clients, enroute to the trailhead for a day of hiking. You're a couple of hours out of town and a half hour past the last telephone. There is not much traffic. As you round a corner you see a pickup truck on its side in the ditch on the outside of the next curve, its wheels still spinning. No other cars have stopped yet. What do you do? You want to help, of course. You're tempted to pull up close to the pickup, leap out and run over to check on the occupants, knowing that saving lives may depend on speed if by chance there are breathing or other time-critical problems. Before you slam on the brakes, hesitate for a second! Think very carefully and clearly at this point. Don't panic, and most importantly don't fix your attention too quickly on that pickup in the ditch.

There are many factors to consider here, and your action will affect you, your passengers, and other motorists, as well as the occupants of the pickup. Take in the *whole* scene and the whole context of the accident. Your actions should reflect concern for the welfare of *all* of the people potentially involved. Usually this means that you have to spend precious time finding a safe place to park and making sure that no further accidents occur. In many situations the placement of flaggers, flares, or other warning systems can be more valuable to the victims than anything else you can do since secondary accidents are all too common. Assume you have stopped your van in a safe place and that traffic is adequately warned. Now what? Your options depend a lot on the capabilities of your passengers. Let us assume you have a mixture of children and adults, and can leave the youngsters confined to the van supervised by an adult while you and the others go to the wreck, taking whatever blankets and first-aid supplies that can be grabbed without delay. A word of caution here — don't allow members of your group to just wander around and watch! People should have something constructive to do or stay well away from the scene. Unnecessary people at the site of an accident are distracting, get in the way, and not uncommonly dilute your efforts by becoming victims themselves. It is common for some to faint while watching, especially if blood is visible. Be firm in your control of onlookers. You can explain your actions later.

As you approach the vehicle, keep looking around. Don't fix your attention on one thing to the exclusion of the rest of the scene! Are the flares slowing traffic safely? Was another car involved? Look around! Was anybody thrown out? What about across the road? Once at the pickup, announce your arrival but don't risk a costly mistake by diving into the cab too quickly. Is the vehicle stable? What about gasoline? *Look around!* This may be especially difficult at this point, since your pumping adrenalin is now surely accelerated by the sight and sound of the victim(s). Keep calm! Make sure that you, your assistants, and the victims aren't endangered by movement of the vehicle, by fire, or by an explosion from the gasoline. Turn off the ignition key if you can and *give clear directions to your helpers.*

At this point you may encounter ambulatory and concerned companions of the injured parties. (This is usually the case, since most people travel with friends or relatives.) Just as with your own party, you have to take care not to compound the situation by allowing well-meaning but non-productive people on the scene. Usually these companions want to help, can assist in meaningful ways, and may have a right to stay at the scene. Nevertheless, it is sometimes necessary to remove individuals physically who are so upset or distraught that they compromise treatment of the victims. After taking care of them, you are ready to render direct aid to the injured.

The next stage will be discussed in the next section. Meanwhile, think through some other scenarios, this time in the back country. The same careful, eyes-wide-open approach is just as essential in a hiking, climbing, skiing, or water accident as on the highway. Don't fail to protect yourself and the healthy members of your party as well as the victims from environmental hazards. Rockfalls, avalanches, and lightning *do* strike twice! Remember that the best final resolution of the situation will depend upon how well you are able to control all of the variables in this critical interval. You want to employ all of your resources to assist the victims, not compound the problem by adding more victims!

DIRECT CARE OF THE VICTIM

Once the total context of the accident allows you to deal directly with the patient, make your approach as quickly as possible but with care that you don't cause further injury. It is a good idea to talk to the victim as soon as voice contact is possible, and the very first communication should be a request for the victim to stay still or "hang on" — whatever is necessary to keep the person from moving until you can assess the nature of his or her situation and injuries. Reassure the person that help is coming, but be sure not to cause the person to move. As you approach, be careful not to slip or trip, causing you or some object to slide into and move or injure the victim. On a hill, try to approach from the side or from below if you can do so safely. It is also a good idea, when possible, to approach from a direction or manner that won't elicit undesirable movement by the victim. As you approach, the victim will naturally try to turn to face you, which could cause major complications in the event of spinal injury or a precarious position. Coming in from the front of the patient may help prevent spontaneous turning.

At this point it is important to scan the victim quickly for those injuries or conditions that can be immediately life-threatening. *Avoid fixation on any one injury!* Check quickly for adequate respiration, cardiac function, major bleeding, and any sign of spinal injury. These concerns, along with a very few others (certain poisons, diabetic conditions, etc.), can cause death or serious long-term disability if not treated promptly and correctly. Once they are dealt with, the time element becomes far less critical. Shock, fractures, and other injuries must be attended to promptly, but in a time frame of minutes, not seconds. It is most important to remain calm and assess the victim from head to toe with great care. Major injuries are easily hidden by clothing, and victims often are unaware of or even strongly deny serious injuries. Outdoor clothing can be especially concealing; too often major injuries are not discovered because they are hidden underneath costly ski pants or rain wear. Yet consider the cost of one day in the hospital!

So far, only the physical care of the victims has been addressed. While essential, this is only part of the challenge. Don't forget that the psychological well-being of the patient can affect the final outcome profoundly. This is an even greater concern in wilderness and back-country situations due to added stress and prolonged treatment. Put yourself in the victim's place. How did you feel the last time you were hurt in an accident? Chances are, you were responsible for what happened, you knew you were pushing your luck a bit, and afterwards you felt rather embarassed. You may also have felt foolish, guilty, and concerned about the future. Victims begin to worry about the consequences even in the midst of the accident. "What are the injuries?" "How long will they take to heal?" "What will the cost be?" "What about loss of employment?" "What will so and so think?" resolve. The physical outcome for the patient is significantly affected by his/her mental state,

and these situations give him or her a lot of time for worrying and sometimes a lot to worry about. When you were last injured, what sort of financial help did *you* want? What sort of help did you seek, or if you weren't able to go for help, what sort of help did you want or expect? Most likely, if your injuries were major, you wanted someone who *looked* and *sounded* competent. One of the best ways to improve your ability to help others is to spend a few minutes thinking of first aid from the victim's point of view, and working through some scenarios.

In the back country or on a country road, no ambulance is going to whisk away the victim within minutes. Establish a rapport with him or her as quickly as possible, and *stay in communication* throughout the incident. Establishing a trusting and comfortable rapport can be difficult, and requires a degree of self control and maturity on the part of the first aider. Try to keep your voice calm, and try using the victim's name in conversation. Even if that is not your usual style, give it a try. When you are really hurting, it feels good to hear your own name. Be careful in your use of humor; what may work for a small child with a cut finger may not be appropriate for the injured adult. Honesty goes a long way toward establishing credibility and in virtually all circumstances you should keep the victim informed of what's happening and of what you are going to do. Still, simple kindness and your sense of the danger posed by psychogenic shock may limit your options. If the victim asks "What are you doing," it might be best to think of an alternative reply if in fact your answer could cause the victim to be even more concerned about the seriousness of the injury. Be sensible, and be honest unless good reasons support a lie. The most difficult situations are those involving deaths of family or friends. Usually there is no life-threatening reason to stop you from telling the truth. Just be careful to assess the implications of such a disclosure vis-a-vis the entire period of care and transportation to medical facilities.

Another important aspect of victim care is record keeping. Circumstances may not allow note taking during the first few minutes, especially if you are alone, but some time should be allocated for this chore. At the very least, check and record your time of arrival on the scene and the times of critical events. Better yet, assign a person to this task. The final outcome for the patient may depend in large part on accurate diagnoses upon arrival in the hospital; accurate records can provide clues to the nature and extent of injuries or illness. Good notes should include clear and detailed commentary on the patient's condition, treatment and care administered, and vital signs. Changes or events should be noted even when they don't seem important at the moment, and vital signs registered at frequent intervals. Seriously injured patients should be monitored *continually*, with notes taken at least every half an hour.

LONG-TERM CARE AND IMPROVISATION

Standard first-aid courses assume access to professional care and facilities within minutes, or at most within an hour or so. While the same initial treatments are generally appropriate in back-country situations, some conditions and injuries need special attention if access to a hospital or another specialized care facility will be delayed.

The following advice is intended only as a supplement to a thorough understanding of Red Cross, St. Johns, EMT, or other standard procedures.

Respiratory Problems

The concern here depends upon the cause of the distress, so let's review some of the implications of conditions one is likely to encounter in a back-country setting.

Altitude-Related Problems. As elevation increases, air pressure decreases. The body, finely tuned to near sea-level air pressure, responds poorly to pressure reductions, and several effects combine to create problems for mountain travelers and pilots. First, fluid balance becomes more difficult to maintain because water evaporates from the body more rapidly under lowered pressure, and because high-elevation air tends to have a lower relative

humidity. In addition, high elevation causes some poorly understood shifts in fluid distribution in the body. Of course hypothermia is often a threat in such environments, and can result in serious fluid disturbances. Increasing elevation can also result in hypoxia, since oxygen is not picked up by the body at low pressure as efficiently as it is at normal pressure. This oxygen deficit can usually be felt at elevations as low as 5000-6000 feet (less than 2000 meters), even by perfectly healthy, fit people. The brain is one of the first organs affected by an oxygen deficit, which is why many people feel a bit exhilarated, giddy, or "high" when moving quickly to such elevations. While most healthy people will experience no worse than a little shortness of breath when exercising at 2000 meters, those with compromised cardiovascular systems may experience significant distress even at rest.

Above 8000 feet (2500 meters), some people may begin to experience some of the symptoms of Acute Mountain Sickness. "AMS," as it's called, is actually a complex of symptoms that is just now beginning to be understood. These range from mild headache, insomnia, loss of appetite, nausea, vomiting, periodic breathing, lassitude, and ataxia (loss of coordination) to very serious life-threatening complications such as pulmonary and cerebral edema. At 10,000 feet (3000 meters), AMS symptoms become quite common.

For practical purposes, the AMS complex can be divided into three categories: mild, moderate, and severe. In mild AMS, the symptoms are limited to a slight headache, perhaps some insomnia and loss of appetite, and shortness of breath when exercising. While these conditions alone usually aren't terribly uncomfortable or limiting, they should be taken as an indication of a need to rest and perhaps take an extra day to acclimatize before going up to a higher elevation. Moderate AMS is indicated by such symptoms as a bad or severe headache, lassitude, nausea, and loss of coordination. Not all of the symptoms need be present to warrant concern because this level of AMS is very serious, and clearly indicates that you need to descend. Simply stopping the ascent is usually not sufficient therapy. A descent of 1000-2000 feet (300-600 meters) is often necessary.

Ataxia (loss of coordination) is worth checking for if its presence is suspected. Common "sobriety" tests work well; ask the suspected AMS victim to walk heel to toe in tiny steps on a ten- or fifteen-foot-long line scratched in the soil or snow. Any abnormal difficulty should be considered a sign of ataxia and cause for concern. Another good test is the Romberg: have the patient stand as if at attention. Place your arms on each side of him or her and reassure the person that you won't let them fall. Then ask the person to close his/her eyes. Most people can stand quite still with almost no swaying, while an ataxic will, within ten to fifteen seconds, sway back and forth and even fall into your arms. Failure of either test should be taken seriously as an indication of possible moderate AMS.

It must be remembered that the various degrees of AMS are only convenient subdivisions of a progressive condition; a person with moderate symptoms is likely to develop severe symptoms soon, if therapy is ignored. Severe AMS includes a number of life-threatening conditions such as pulmonary edema and cerebral edema. Even if these don't develop, the ataxia detected in the above tests can progress to complete inability to stand up in just a few hours. Anyone planning to travel at elevations above 8000 feet (2500 meters) should invest in a good treatise on the topic of altitude-related problems and study it thoroughly. Peter Hackett's "Mountain Sickness" is a small, concise, and easily read resource highly recommended for this purpose.

Asthma. Many of the factors that may contribute to asthmatic symptoms are common in outdoor settings. Dry air, heavy exercise, and a wide range of allergies can bring on an attack The initial attack can often be controlled through medication if appropriate drugs are available. Often the individual will be carrying an inhaler or antihistamine, or these may be included in the first-aid kit or carried by another participant. As with all drugs, prescription *or* over-the-counter types, take care in prescribing their use. Unless you feel the situation is truly desperate, it is always best to allow the individual to make the decision to use the drugs and to avoid putting yourself out on a legal limb by stating or implying that the drug is safe and will help the person. In any case, read the label carefully and see that directions are followed explicitly.

Another helpful technique for asthmatics is to provide warm moist air. This can be done by guiding steam towards the person's face with a piece of cloth. Be careful, however, not to construct a device that is too efficient, since hot steam and the gases given off by stoves can profoundly complicate your dilemma. A backpacking stove or a fire can be used to boil water, and the steam guided by the sleeve of a coat or shirt. A hot steaming towel can often provide enough relief by resoaking often in very hot water. Once the initial attack has ended, give the individual plenty of time to rest, and avoid further exposure to the conditions that brought on the initial attack. As with most respiratory problems, it is a good idea to go down in elevation. Generally, however, there is little concern below 9,000-10,000 feet (2700-3000 meters).

Bronchitis. Bronchitis is an infection of the trachea and the major air passages of the lungs. Although it may occur independently and may be caused by a virus, most typically it occurs during or after a viral cold, and is caused by a bacterial infection. The symptoms usually include a frequent cough that after a day or two begins to produce thick greenish or yellowish sputum. The person usually doesn't appear to be very ill otherwise, and may or may not have a slight fever. The treatment consists of moderate rest, avoiding prolonged or hard exertion, general TLC, and antibiotics.

Antibiotic therapy is something rarely attempted on outings since success depends upon having a sufficient quantity of the proper drug to attack the infection, and the drug must be one that the patient has no adverse reaction to. Antibiotics need to be given in specific doses in a certain pattern designed to raise the level of the drug in the body to a high one very rapidly, and maintain it there throughout the course of treatment. Failure to maintain a high enough drug level can allow the still-living bacteria (presumably the most resistant) to multiply. For these reasons, carrying "just a few" of one or two kinds of antibiotics is probably a waste of time in most cases. If the outing is so lengthy or remote as to preclude escape to medical care in a day or two, then a substantial quantity of antibiotics might be brought along, with types and quantities worked out in consultation with a physician.

Pneumonia. Pneumonia is an infection of one or both lungs. The disease varies considerably according to the nature and extent of the infection. Viral pneumonias tend to be less severe than bacterial pneumonias, yet either type can be extremely disabling and even fatal if not properly treated. The symptoms including coughing, a fever of 102° or higher, weakness, and a general appearance of being quite ill. If the infection is bacterial, chills and a very high fever may be present.

Even though coughing can sometimes be extremely painful in these cases, the patient must be encouraged to cough deeply at least several times a day to minimize fluid build-up in the lungs. Antibiotics and rest are also very important. The fever and infection increase the body's demand for oxygen while the latter and fluid buildups reduce the oxygen-transfer capabilities of the lungs. This alone can be life threatening. High elevations can tip the balance, so get the patient down to low elevation as quickly as possible.

Dehydration. Even in the absence of general systemic dehydration, the lungs can become dry and irritated due to dry air. Low pressure, as at high altitudes, contributes by increasing the evaporation rate. A hacking dry cough may result, which is usually alleviated by a night of rest, especially if humidity in the tent can be raised by periodically boiling a pot of water outside and letting it cool off in the tent. This problem is most common among ski tourers and climbers in cold, dry conditions, and usually isn't particularly serious unless the irritated and vulnerable lungs become infected.

Hyperventilation. Hyperventilation is a fairly common occurrence in outdoor activities. Most standard first-aid texts refer to the problem of accidental hyperventilation by swimmers attempting to load up on oxygen before a dive. Another common cause is anxiety. The ski run or the next pitch of the climb may not produce anxiety in the leader, but may well terrify a beginner. Watch participants before particularly

challenging events and you may well see forced and rapid breathing. Yet another common cause is improper breathing while hiking or climbing. Too often hikers or climbers are told to breathe and step in a certain pattern, a counter-productive method of breathing control at best that all too often overloads the system with oxygen. Better to let people find a comfortable need-determined breathing rate. Usually the adverse symptoms can be easily resolved by breathing in a sack, the paper bag recommended by the Red Cross text replaced by a stuff sack or plastic bag. Ten minutes of this followed by a half hour of rest and relaxation will usually restore a normal carbon-dioxide reflex, and reduce the anxiety level. A much reduced pace for an hour or so can help avoid relapses, which are common.

Respiratory Arrythmia. While uncommon below 6000 feet (1800 meters), Cheyne-Stokes breathing (respiratory arrythmia) is fairly common above 10,000 feet (3000 M.). It is unnerving to experience since its pattern is a minute or two of very heavy breathing followed by up to several minutes of no breathing at all. Waking up in the non-breathing phase is quite an experience, usually resulting in a quick review of your day for any cause of death since both breathing and the desire for breath are absent. In a tent partner, it can be equally distressing. Normally the person draws your attention by the heavy breathing cycle, which then declines to no breathing at all. This can be a source of much concern (depending upon one's attitudes toward the tent partner). Fortunately, this odd pattern does provide adequate oxygenation, even if it causes loss of sleep. Sometimes getting up and moving around a bit, or even taking a short walk and having a bite to eat, can help; otherwise the problem usually resolves itself in a few hours. Going down in elevation by a few thousand feet (1000 M. or so) usually ends the problem.

Respiratory Arrest. Whatever the cause of cessation of breathing, great care must be taken to constantly observe the victim once breathing is restored because relapses are likely. Traumatic events such as blows to the chest may result in fluid accumulation or swelling of the lungs over time. Drowning in salt water has a similar effect, in that fluid from the body enters the lungs to dilute the salt water since its concentration of salts is higher than that in bodily fluids. Victims can then drown in their own fluids long after being resusitated initially. Fresh-water near-drowned victims must also be watched carefully, since fresh water is absorbed by the lungs and can cause dangerous shifts in blood chemistry. Any case of respiratory arrest should warrant immediate evacuation by the most expedient means, despite evident initial recovery. These cases usually warrant a helicopter evacuation if such can be arranged.

A question that is often heard is "how long do you give mouth-to-mouth resuscitation?" Certainly, if the victim's heart is still beating, mouth-to-mouth should be continued until professionals can take over. It is possible to imagine a situation where one must choose between giving mouth-to-mouth and going for help. There is no answer to that dilemma; it simply reinforces the argument for leaving detailed plans with responsible people at home, and especially for travelling with three or more people. Leaders should keep such grim scenarios in mind when planning an outing. Even on a day outing, you should have an assistant leader and adequate clothing and equipment to allow simultaneous long-term care of the patient and evacuation of the remainder of the group while going for help.

Cardiac Problems

There are several types of cardiac problems of concern to an outdoor leader.

Arrythmias. Most arrythmias are not especially dangerous. Extra systoles are common, and while alarming to the patient should not be a source of great concern if the condition is sporadic and short term. These "extra beats" are sometimes associated with heavy consumptions of caffeine, though many other causes are possible. Tachycardia, a very rapid heartbeat that may last up to an hour or more, is very distressing yet usually not life threatening. Forced breathing against a closed glottis or painful pressure on closed eyes can sometimes provide the electrical stimulus necessary to reverse the condition. Bradycardia, or a reduced heart rate, may be more serious and related to the use of certain drugs or to cardiac disease.

Angina Pectoris. The best treatment for sufferers of angina is usually complete rest coupled with the use of nitroglycerine tablets. These tiny white pills are taken under the tongue where the nitroglycerine is readily taken up. The result is dilation of the coronary arteries and rather rapid relief. Unfortunately, cerebral vessels are also affected, and rather severe headaches can accompany use of this drug. Patients may be able to walk out under their own power, though not without risk. Ideally, the patient should be flown or carried out, yet this may not, in all cases, be possible without prolonged delay. Chances are the attack is not the first, and the person, usually a middle-aged or older male, will know how much rest is needed before proceeding. Certainly one should in no case subject these patients to stresses anywhere near as great as those that overtaxed the coronary blood supply. The plan should be to head for the car at a leisurely pace after an extended period of rest.

Heart Attack and Heart Failure. Patients surviving the initial episodes of either a heart attack or heart failure condition need to be handled with great care. As with respiratory arrest, helicopter evacuation is warranted if it can be arranged. If not, these patients need plenty of rest. Rough or primitive evacuation should be put off for at least several hours unless a good litter and plenty of carriers are available. The patient will want to sit or lean up slightly to minimize respiratory difficulty, making carrying still more difficult. Thus rest may be better than a traumatic and lengthy evacuation. After several days, the person may be able to walk very slowly out or down a trail, with no pack on and plenty of rest stops. This isn't ideal, but in a party of two or three it may be necessary, especially if food or water supplies or foul weather make waiting for help impractical.

Head Injuries

Standard first-aid texts say little about head injuries other than to suggest rest, treatment of symptoms as they appear, and careful observation of the patient. One of the major concerns in head injuries, as explained in most standard tests, is the development of sub- or extra-dural hematomas over time. Another concern is hematoma from secondary bleeding, that is, bleeding not from the original wound but caused by stress on weakened or damaged vessels. The latter concern reinforces the importance of observing the patient for days and even weeks following any serious blow to the head. One of the authors, despite having taught this for many years, ignored his own advice after knocking his head on a heavy oak beam in a hut in the Japanese Alps. Days later, secondary bleeding caused by a strenuous climb resulted in headache, nausea, double vision, and a lot of concern.

A good rule of thumb might be that if the blow raises an "egg" or causes any unconsciousness, rest for an hour or so and then head for civilization if it can be reached in a few hours over safe and easy ground. Otherwise, a few days of *complete* bed rest are in order, followed by very slow and easy travel. The danger lies not only in causing damaged vessels to rupture; clots will form early, in the first hours, yet may not fully adhere for a couple of days. Clots breaking loose can travel through the vascular system and lodge elsewhere, causing blockage of arteries in the heart, lungs, brain, or other body parts. Another general rule of thumb is that blows causing unconsciousness for less than thirty minutes *usually* don't result in long-term consequences. Blows causing longer periods of unconsciousness probably will have more serious results. This rule may offer encouragement in cases where a person is unconscious for only a short time, but should not be used to avoid treatment. It is better to be conservative here.

Fractures

There are two major differences between town and back-country treatment of fractures. One is splinting, and the other is the greater likelihood of having to move or manipulate the injured

part. Outdoor splinting is complicated by the lack of conventional materials and devices, yet the splint must usually be far more secure, with better support and padding than in town. The patient will probably either walk out or be carried out, and in either case the limb will have to withstand far more than the amount of abuse typically given an in-town injury. The basic principles of splinting still apply — immobilization of the joints above and below the fracture site, and ample padding.

While these skills seem quite straightforward, the authors have yet to see an adequate splint applied by a first-aid class student on the first try. Probably the only way to fully appreciate the amount of padding and the proper method of securing a splint for a back-country evacuation is to participate in a rescue practice, preferably as the victim. Failure to splint adequately can result in very serious loss of function of a limb, in bedsores (in this case caused by death of tissue due to pressure of the hard parts of a splint), or at the very least in lots of unnecessary wasted time and distress for the patient as splints are readjusted.

There are plenty of excellent splinting materials available in a typical backpacker's kit. Foam pads make excellent padding, and the stiffer foams can add rigidity to splints. Stuff sacks can be filled with various substances or clothing to provide padding. Tent poles and pack-frame parts are good stiffeners, as are walking sticks, ice axes, ski poles, and skis. When you're looking for splints, pads, and ties, keep in mind that it now costs about $450 per day to stay in a hospital. Don't hesitate to "modify" some gear to suit the purpose; in economic terms alone it is a bargain, not to mention the value of reducing further pain and injury. Traction splints, almost always essential for femur fractures, can be constructed from ski poles, skies, ice axes, or pack frames (see Figure 13.1 for an illustration of several improvised traction splints). Evacuation devices (litters, sleds, etc.) will be discussed in the chapter on Search and Rescue). It cannot be overemphasized that hands-on practice is absolutely essential. The first time you really need to treat a fracture is *not* the time to learn.

The other major concern vis-a-vis fractures is the occasional need to move or manipulate a limb. If the part of the limb distal to the injury

FIGURE 13.1   Improvised Splints

A

B

C

A few of the possibilities for improvising a traction splint for a femur fracture (fracture @ X).

A. An ice axe can be bound to the good leg, with the axe held away from the foot by any solid means, such as a stack of carabiners carefully taped in place. A single harness and tensioning system can then be rigged to

the pick.

B. The straps of two ski poles can be interlocked, forming a skier's version of a "D" ring splint. As in all splinting, *lots* of padding and *lots* of good secure ties are essential.

C. A pack frame can be used, if it has an extension far enough to provide the needed fixation and tensions.

shows signs of lack of circulation or of compromised nervous function, and if several hours will pass before the victim can be seen by a doctor, there is a good chance that permanent loss of function might occur. Careful manipulation of the part may help. Keep in mind that a nerve or a vessel is probably already being compressed, or may have been cut by the broken ends of the bone. Movement may relieve the pressure, or it may cause irreparable damage. The danger of further injury is reduced somewhat if the movement is made soon (within

thirty minutes at least), gently, and with respect for the victim's sense of pain. Gentle traction can help relieve pressure between bone ends on arm as well as leg fractures. The direction of motion should be toward the position of function, that is, toward the position the limb would normally assume when relaxed. Another reason for moving a limb may be to allow for transportation. A person with a broken arm whose bone is sticking straight out to the side will make a very awkward passenger on a litter, and will probably develop a bad attitude toward the otherwise beautiful brush and trees along the trail. The same principles apply to movement of the limb. Check periodically to be sure that the parts distal to the fracture continue to have adequate circulation and nervous function. With this in mind, see that the splint allows sufficient access to the limb so you can check on its condition.

Dislocations

Dislocations are among the most common injuries in outdoor activities. Skiing and off-trail hiking and climbing contribute substantially to the number of these injuries. Before discussing treatment, a few words on prevention are in order. In skiing there are three common causes of dislocation. The first is bindings that don't allow lateral release. While uncommon in properly adjusted Alpine bindings, several ski-mountaineering bindings, such as the older Silvretta models, and some touring and cross-country downhill equipment, such as heel locators, greatly increase chances of serious injury. Many ski schools, for example, won't allow students to use heel fixation devices for this reason. Most three-pin bindings will release the boot under heavy stress, though some of the new stiff boots and bindings may be capable of holding on beyond the limits of human joints.

Another common dislocation is caused by falling forward onto the knees when using cross-country gear (in Alpine gear the toe piece and/or heel would release first). This fall can jam the knee into the snow, causing a posterior dislocation of the hip joint. The solution is to practice falling by sitting backwards and to the side, extending the legs together just as the snow is contacted by the upper thigh. This fall is relatively graceful, easy to recover from, and isn't likely to abuse the body.

The third skiing concern is the use of pole straps in downhill travel on Alpine or cross-country skis. There are several ways in which pole straps can contribute to dislocations. First, if the strap is used it has to be used properly (hand up through the loop). In the typical beginners' "grab-the-pole-through-the-loop" position, a rolling fall can dislocate either the thumb or the arm, depending on the direction of the roll. Second, when straps are used and the pole is planted ahead to slow down, it can either slide up the rib cage or jam against the collarbone and break it, or pass over the shoulder, dislocating that joint since the pole can't be quickly released. Yet another hazard is catching the basket on something while skiing downhill. Some baskets and straps are designed to release, and some actually do. But why risk it? Straps aren't very useful in downhill skiing anyway!

With regard to treatment, the same concerns prevail here as with fractures, especially vis-a-vis impairment of vessels and nerves. The problem is that in every case except finger and chronic shoulder dislocations (wherein the problem has occurred repeatedly), reduction of the dislocation can be extremely dangerous. If vessels or nerves are pinched already, it is very hard to get the joint back in working order without doing irreparable damage. For this reason, dislocation involving loss of nervous or circulatory functions are very serious and warrant the expedition's evacuation to medical facilities. If the impairment is severe, the evacuation method will be primitive, and medical treatment will be delayed for many hours, then it is probably worth attempting to relocate a shoulder in the field. (Again, if the shoulder dislocation is a repeated event, and if nerves or vessels are not pinched, reduction is far safer and can proceed with the consent and help of the patient.)

There are standard ways to move a shoulder back into place, and any good first-aid book will discuss these methods for both anterior and posterior dislocations. In the field the "dirty sock" method may be used, wherein a foot is placed in the victim's armpit to allow the first aider to pull and rotate the arm gently back into place. The key here is to apply a gentle steady pull to gradually fatigue the spasming muscles, and to rotate and guide the arm back into the socket. It is essential to look carefully at a skeleton or good anatomical drawings to see this technique demonstrated. Another method is to have the patient stretch out face down on a log or similar support and then hang a padded weight (a stuffsack of snow or dirt will do) on the wrist. About four or five pounds should suffice to turn the muscles in ten or twenty minutes and allow the area to relocate.

Relocations of a hip, knee, ankle, or thumb are difficult and dangerous at best, and require a steady pull as in the case of the shoulder-reduction techniques. While this can be attempted it should only be done when the situation is so dire as to warrant the very high risk of serious damage that accompanies field relocation of these joints. In all cases, icing can reduce swelling, and immobilization of the part is invaluable.

Sprains

A sprain that is only an annoyance in town can be a serious impairment five miles up the trail. When a sprain occurs it is best to ice it immediately, unless it is obviously trivial. Too often a "minor" sprain of the ankle is followed soon after by a major injury, when the stretched tissues yield under a second rolling. Cooling reduces both swelling and the long-term consequences of the injury. Cold water or snow are ideal for this, and chemical ice packs also work well but are a bit heavy to carry in a back-country first-aid kit. The icing process should be continued for as long as possible through at least the first day, keeping the part chilled but not devoid of circulation. It should be obvious that care must be taken to avoid freezing or overcooling the part, causing systemic hypothermia. But even many days after the injury, periodic icing can help speed recovery. Cooling at night can also help.

In the case of a sprained ankle, wrap it in wet cotton cloth and let it hang out of the bottom of a sleeping bag, elevated on some soft gear. Elevation in general can help reduce swelling, in conjunction with icing or in place of it if coolants can't be obtained. Elastic bandages or tape also give support. Elastic bandages are the easiest to use, usually in figure-eight patterns around the ankle or knee. (It helps to know enough anatomy to be able to visualize the primary structures surrounding these joints.) The elastic bandage is most useful when stretched tightly over the damaged area, then moderately over the rest of the joint. Be sure to check for adequate circulation distal to the wrap, and monitor the part to see that circulation continues.

Taping is by far the most secure and supportive technique for the ankle, and always preferable in wet conditions. All leaders should have immediate recall of taping patterns. Prewrapping with non-adhesive gauze makes later removal of the tape less painful; however, taping directly to the skin and hair is far more secure. Shaving the part first is a good idea, as half of the hair will be pulled out by the tape anyway. The knee can also be taped, although an elastic bandage allows easier walking. Leave the tape or wrap on for several days. Icing can be done over the tape, though it is best to remove the elastic wraps since they lose their elasticity when wet. Have the patient walk very carefully for a week or so after the tape is removed — the supporting structure will still be quite weak, and relapses are common. Most people can walk out of the back-country on a sprained ankle or knee, if necessary, using a combination of careful taping, elastic wraps, and improvised crutches. A reduction of the pack load helps, especially on downhill portions of the route. On skis, wrapping them in cord makes for slow but much safer progress downhill.

Contusions

Contusions (bruises) are frequent injuries, and are usually of no great consequence. Keep in mind, however, that major bruising can be very serious and even life threatening. For example, a heavy fall such as a slip on an icy trail can cause rather massive bruising of the thigh and buttocks, not to mention the elbows and ego. There are two major concerns in such an injury. First, if the victim rests for awhile, perhaps camping for the night, he or she may be very nearly immobilized by morning. Swelling, pain, and muscle spasms make future travel painful and slow at best. The second and more serious concern is that within a few hours clots will have formed internally, yet they will not have had time to firmly anchor. Walking may well cause these clots to break loose and travel, and they may possibly lodge in vital organs, causing major disability or death. In such cases, then, three choices exist: 1) walk out immediately, 2) stay put for at least two and one-half days until the clots have stabilized, then walk *slowly* out, or 3) carry the person out.

258

Nicks and Bashes

Minor cuts, nicks, scratches and abrasions are almost everyday occurrences. Generally speaking, treatment consists of cleaning and protection from contamination. Ordinary soap does a good job, although one of the medicated soaps is preferable. Betadyne is a good choice since it is effective and its reddish-brown color stains the skin and makes it easy to see what parts have been cleaned. Wounds to the palms of the hand, lower legs, and feet are particularly hard to keep clean; they heal slowly and may require frequent washing. Gauze pads or Band-aids usually suffice for protection.

Deep cuts present more serious concerns. Gross contaminants should be washed out with clean if not sterile water, and then you have to choose whether or not to close the wound. Closing the wound has several advantages, including controlling bleeding, looking better (a real psychological advantage in some cases), and sometimes facilitating mobility. In some cases closing the wound may also reduce further contamination, and in the unlikely event that infection should *not* occur, it may reduce scarring. Leaving the wound open, on the other hand, reduces chances of anaerobic infection. Besides, the first thing the doctor will do to any major wound is open it up for a good scrub anyway. If you decide to close the wound, a commercial "butterfly" can be used or made from adhesive tape. Suturing is rarely needed in the field. It has certain advantages, especially in wet weather, but good butterflies suffice in most every case. Bandages should be changed every few days, and if signs of infection appear the wound should be opened, soaked in warm sterile water, cleaned, and then left open. Wounds that are left open can be packed with vaseline-impregnated gauze or non-stick gauze, and bandaged. Some infection is almost unavoidable. The dressing should be left in place for a few days, then changed as necessary. The wound may need to be soaked and probed to insure drainage each time the bandages are changed.

Blisters

No doubt the most common injury by hikers, blisters are often not even mentioned in many standard first-aid courses. At best a blister is an annoyance; at worst it can ruin a trip and even lead to serious infection. Prevention of blisters is relatively easy for some people and nearly impossible for others. Some can slip into a poorly fitting pair of stiff boots and walk all day with no problems, while others blister at the slightest new rub. Participants should be advised of the importance of appropriate footwear that fits well and is well broken in, and of the value of a sheer inner sock, preferably of a fabric such as polypropylene that wicks water away from the skin. Your first-aid kit should contain Betadyne or other cleaning soap, a needle, adhesive tape, Band-Aids, moleskin (a thin adhesive padding), and molefoam (a thick adhesive padding).

It is always best to prevent blisters by noticing sore spots early. Leaders should enforce careful foot checks very early on any beginners' hike, and help identify incipient blisters. Beginners often don't recognize the significance of minor irritations. Treatment prior to development of a fluid-filled area may consist of changes in the footwear or socks, or application of tape or moleskin. A molefoam donut applied early may prevent injury at the back of the heel or on top of the toes, where pressure is often too great for tape alone to provide protection.

Once a blister is formed, repair is somewhat more time consuming and tedious. If the blister is large or tall, and therefore likely to tear, it is best to drain it. Clean the area (Betadyne works well) and insert a sterile needle into the fluid, passing first through some healthy skin that will help keep contaminants out of the affected area. Contamination can easily lead to infection, since it is essentially like a little nutrient-filled greenhouse just waiting for innoculation. Cut out a donut of molefoam or several of moleskin big enough to miss the blister by about $\frac{1}{8}$ of an inch. The top of the blister will need to be protected from the tape or moleskin which will eventually cover the whole area, so cut a piece of sterile non-stick (Telfa tape) pad the size of the donut hole. Then the non-sticky side of the plastic covering the molefoam donut hole can be cleaned and used instead.

Now apply the donut(s), which should be sticky enough to keep all pressure off the blistered area. Place the blister-top protector over it, and put moleskin or tape over the area to secure it. It also helps to angle off the corners of the molefoam to prevent formation of a blister around the edge of the donut. The patch covering the blister and donut will stay in place much longer if the corners are rounded. Square corners, edges, or points will roll up, causing more sore spots or blisters.

Blisters shouldn't be ignored, once treated, since infection can go from slight redness and tenderness to the touch to a grotesquely swollen foot and high fever in just a couple of days. Most professional outdoor leaders can site examples of such incidents. It doesn't happen often, but when a serious infection does occur the speed of onset can be astounding. In an attempt to minimize the risk of such infections, many schools and programs require footwashing and a change to clean socks every day, and do not allow any barefoot walking or wading.

Grand Mal Seizures

Grand Mal or Major Motor seizures are characterized by a loss of consciousness, followed by muscle rigidity, especially in the limbs. Flailing or jerking of limbs come next, after which the entire body becomes limp. Grand mal seizures are often accompanied by salivation and a loss of bladder and/or bowel control. Upon regaining consciousness, the person may be headachy, tired, and somewhat uncoordinated.

An "aura" such as an unexplained fear, unpleasant odors, odd sounds, nausea, etc., acts as a warning of an impending seizure to some persons. Approximately one half of the persons with epilepsy experience an aura.

The following measures should be taken when a person is having a grand mal seizure:

1. Do not try to restrain the individual's movements or place anything between his teeth. Do not give him anything to drink or he may strangle.
2. Try to prevent the person from striking his head or body against any hard, sharp, or hot object by moving such objects out of the way and placing a pillow under his head.
3. When convulsive movements have ceased, turn the body and head to one side. This will assure unobstructed breathing. Do not be frightened if the person having a seizure appears not to be breathing momentarily.
4. Do not try to revive the individual. Let the convulsion run its course.

5. Carefully observe the details of the seizure for a subsequent report to a medical person. Such information as time of onset, presence of fever, duration of seizure, seizure activity, etc., may be important.
6. When the person recovers consciousness, he may be incoherent or very sleepy. He should have the opportunity to rest.
7. Should a grand mal seizure last more than ten minutes, or should a person begin to have a series of seizures, emergency attention is vital.

Burns

Minor burns are adequately discussed in standard texts. Figure 13.2 gives one way of estimating the seriousness of a burn injury, and keep in mind that the chart is based on the actual extent of the injury. Be conservative (i.e., pessimistic) in estimating the degree and extent of a burn! Major burns can be life threatening under the best of circumstances.

Here are some points to consider when treating a burn injury in the back country. First, it is very hard to determine the extent and degree of a burn on inspection. The prognosis depends upon a number of factors, including the amount of damage to structures beneath the epidermis. Second, "burn shock" is a serious concern largely due to the very large amount of fluid that will be lost through anything greater than a first-degree burn. This problem is compounded by the inability of many victims to tolerate water taken orally after the first thirty minutes or so following the accident. With this in mind, burn victims should be given large quantities of water immediately, and allowed to drink as much as can be tolerated over the next day or so. Significant amounts of water may be consumed if taken in tiny swallows, and it can also be administered by letting the patient chew on a wet rag or washcloth frequently resoaked. The water should contain one teaspoon of salt and one-half teaspoon of baking soda to one quart (approximately one liter) of water, although plain water is better than nothing and may be critical in saving the patient's life. If the patient is unconscious, little can be done in the field without apparatus for IM or IV administration of fluids. Retention enemas are a possibility if tubing is available.

FIGURE 13.2 Seriousness of a Burn

In the adult, most areas of the body can be divided roughly into portions of 9 percent, or multiples of 9. This division, called the rule of nines, is useful in estimating the percentage of body surface damage an individual has sustained in a burn. In the small child, relatively more area is taken up by the head and less by the lower extremities. Accordingly, the rule of nines is modified. In each case, the rule gives a useful approximation of body surfaces.

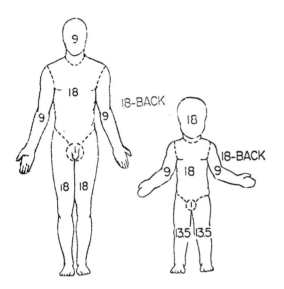

Critical (Severe) Burns - This category includes:
1. All burns of whatever degree and extent they are complicated by respiratory injury and other major injuries or fractures.
2. Third degree burns involving critical areas such as the face, hands, or feet.
3. Third degree burns which involve more than 10 percent of the body surface.
4. Second degree burns which involve more than 30 percent of the body surface.

Moderate Burns - This category includes:
1. Third degree burns of 2 to 10 percent of the body surface which do not involve the face, hands, or feet.
2. Second degree burns which involve 15-30 percent of the body surface.
3. First degree burns involving 50 to 75 percent

of the body surface.

Minor Burns - This category includes:
1. Third degree burns of less than 2 percent of the body surface if no critical areas are involved.
2. Second degree burns involving less than 15 percent of the body surface.
3. First degree burns of less than 20 percent of the body surface.

In evaluating a patient who has sustained a burn, age and general condition must also be considered. A moderate burn in an aged patient who is chronically ill should be classified critical in terms of the immediate treatment required because of the patient's general condition apart from the burn.

Third, assume infection. The process of cooling the burn should remove most gross contaminants, yet infection is almost inevitable in burns where the epidermis is not intact or is badly damaged. Even the cleanest spring water will add some contaminants, and many more will be captured from the air before the wound is bandaged. The use of plastic wrap or other impermeable covering will ease pain, reduce additional contamination, and slow fluid loss from major burns, and a compression wrap using stretchy gauze can reduce swelling. In back country situations it is probably best to leave this wrap on for several days. Second-degree burns begin to heal after this time, and third-degree burns will inevitably be infected and require careful cleaning and redressing.

Elevation can also reduce swelling and help minimize loss of circulating fluid volume. Be sure to check for adequate circulation distal to the wrap, and check frequently as long as the wrap is in place. Remember that the combination of wrapping pressure, pressure from swelling, and the effects of cooling, elevation, dehydration and shock may result in inadequate circulation, requiring a frequent adjustment of wrapping tension to maintain good circulation.

Hypothermia

'Hypothermia' has become a well-known word in outdoor pursuits in the last decade. Even the news media occasionally use it, though the old catchall "exposure" still remains popular. Hypothermia is discussed briefly in most first-aid books, although these discussions fall far short of the needs of outdoor leaders.

There are two types of hypothermia, commonly known as "systemic" and "immersion." Together they are a major cause of death in outdoor pursuits, second only to drowning. As will be obvious in the discussion of field treatment, this is a condition that is almost invariably the result of poor planning and inadequate preparation. Most of the fatalities involve poor judgment with regard to clothing and equipment. Fall and spring are the worst seasons in terms of mortality, probably because the weather may seem to be fine yet can quickly turn wet, cold, and windy. During the winter the weather is sufficiently intimidating to inspire caution. In the summer, experienced mountain hikers and climbers generally understand the danger and equip themselves appropriately in higher country, although less-experienced people sometimes succumb to the weather. A mid-August snowstorm at 6000 feet is no surprise to an experienced person, but an amazing and too-often fatal surprise for the novice.

Leaders can no longer plead ignorance of hypothermia or of its prevention or treatment. It is also common knowledge that the majority of participants in beginning classes in outdoor pursuits know little or nothing about this condition. Given this fact, the leader has to assume responsibility for assessment of the environment, the route, and the intended activities; for the determination and enforcement of minimum clothing and equipment standards; and for the education of the participants. The treatments given below are by no means 100% effective in saving lives, yet even these sometimes inadequate measures depend upon some extra resources of clothing, shelter, cooking equipment, and food. These resources are not necessarily expensive or hard to obtain, and are not very heavy if distributed among the leaders or participants.

Successful treatment of a hypothermia patient in the field requires knowledge, skill, luck, *and* the foresight to have included certain group gear items. In maritime mountains, the absolute minimum group gear for day hiking or climbing would include a tarp shelter, fire-making tools or a stove with fuel, a sleeping bag or half bag, a pot for heating water, and extra food. Above the timberline a stove becomes essential. Most leaders consider a stove mandatory in *all* terrain

since the weather that causes hypothermia makes for difficult fire building, and speed is essential. Insulating pads are also often considered necessary.

Hypothermia is a condition in which the core or internal body temperature is reduced. The body can withstand only a very slight reduction in core temperature without significant impairment of function. When it declines over a period of hours, as is typical in mountain or back-country situations, the condition is known as systemic hypothermia or often simply hypothermia. In cold water the rate of heat loss is so great that severe suppression of body temperature can occur in minutes. Since such rapid cooling almost invariably requires immersion in water, this condition is known as immersion hypothermia. Table 13.1 gives the progressive symptoms of hypothermia. Figure 13.3 explains the effect of cold on the body's surface and core temperatures.

Stick your finger in an icy cold stream for a few seconds, then pull it out. Chances are that it will turn red; your system is doing its best to keep the finger warm by adding circulation. Put your finger in the water again for about thirty seconds, and the result will be an ashen, almost numb extremity. What is happening, of course, is that your system is protecting itself from excessive heat loss through the finger. The functioning of vital organs and processes is quite efficient at about 98.6° F (37° C). The body will tolerate a 3 or 4° F increase in temperature but responds poorly to suppression of the temperature by only 2° F or so. One of the primary heat-regulation mechanisms is the surface blood flow. That transfer is proportional to the difference in temperature between two objects or substances. For example, heat is lost more readily by 90° F skin than by 80° F skin. By controlling blood flow to the surface, the body partially moderates the amount of heat lost to the environment. On a fifty-degree day a person at rest with light clothing would need to conserve heat. Skin temperature might drop to 70° F or so in light clothing, while the core would exhibit almost no shift in temperature. On the same day while exercising hard the skin may be maintained at a toasty red 98° F to help radiate unneeded excess heat. The body is capable of great variation in blood flow to the surface and can change blood-flow volume quite rapidly, as in the earlier example case of the finger in the creek. In this case, the extremity was in a sense sacrificed to save vital core organs. In systemic hypothermia, all of the body surface and all of the major extremities may be similarly compromised in order to maintain the temperature of the vital organs. Unfortunately, the head is treated as an extremity, so that loss of mental acuity is an early result of the body's response to cold stress. Ironically, the victim quickly becomes unable to manage his/her own treatment!

The body maintains a nearly constant internal temperature by balancing heat production and heat loss. In the case of cold stress, and thus potential hypothermia, maintenance of a viable temperature depends upon 1) adequacy of heat production and 2) adequacy of heat conservation. Heat production depends upon the metabolism of foods. Heat gains from external sources (the sun, fire, hot food, and drink, etc.) can add to this side of the balance, yet in actual field settings these factors rarely provide more than a small percentage of the caloric energy necessary to maintain viable core temperatures.

The easiest way to review the major concerns vis-a-vis heat production is to list those factors that inhibit metabolic processes. Metabolic heat production is inhibited by hypoxia (inadequate oxygen uptake), dehydration, inadequate diet (too little, improper, or poorly timed food intake), fatigue or exhaustion, most illnesses, stress or anxiety, and, unfortunately, by hypothermia itself. Table 13.2 lists these concerns and suggested remedies, but let's look at these concerns in greater detail here.

Hypoxia. Metabolism requires oxygen, and it is harder for the body to obtain adequate oxygen at higher elevations. While rarely a significant factor by itself below 10,000 feet (3000 meters), hypoxia can be a major factor on high-altitude climbs, and can contribute to difficulties at lower elevations.

Dehydration. This is a common and significant factor. The body cannot metabolize foods effectively without an adequate supply of water. Even moderate activities can greatly increase the need for water, and if this is not replaced promptly the efficiency of metabolism declines. The result is weakness and an inability to produce heat, and the situation is unfortunately most common and most problematical in cold weather, where water is difficult to obtain (due to access in deep snow or the need to melt ice or snow) and may be unappealing (who wants

TABLE 13.1 Symptoms of Hypothermia

HYPOTHERMIA

Inevitably, if heat loss continues, the temperature of the body's inner core will begin to fall below 99 degrees. As the core (rectal) temperature drops, symptoms are as follows. There may be some variability in the degree and the order of appearance of these symptoms in different individuals; note especially that shivering does not always occur and cannot therefore be counted on as a sign of cooling.

99 TO 96 DEGREES: Shivering becomes intense and uncontrollable. Ability to perform complex tasks is impaired.

95 TO 91 DEGREES: Violent shivering persists. Difficulty in speaking, sluggish thinking, and amnesia start to appear.

90 TO 86 DEGREES: Shivering decreases and is replaced by strong muscular rigidity. Exposed skin may become blue or puffy. Muscle coordination is affected, producing erratic or jerky movements. Thinking is less clear; general comprehension of the situation is dulled and may be accompanied by total amnesia. The victim is generally still able to maintain posture and the appearance of psychological contact with his surroundings.

85 TO 81 DEGREES: Victim becomes irrational, loses contact with environment, and drifts into stupor. Muscular rigidity continues. Pulse and respiration are slowed.

80 TO 78 DEGREES: Unconsciousness, the victim does not respond to spoken word. Most reflexes cease to function at this temperature level. Heartbeat becomes erratic.

BELOW 78 DEGREES: Failure of cardiac and respiratory control centers in the brain cause cardiac fibrillation, probable edema and hemorrhage in lungs, and death.

The frequency with which pulmonary edema is present in fatal cases of acute hypothermia is a new finding in the medical literature on this subject. Often one of the terminal events before death is labored breathing, and whitish froth may well into the mouth from the congested lungs.

FIGURE 13.3   Effect of Cold on Body Core Temperatures

EFFECT OF COLD on the body's surface and core temperatures, shows decline of temperature of the skin and extremities while inner core maintains its warmth. Figure at left represents comfortable warmth; at center, mild cold; at right, severe cold. Right-hand figure will soon experience a significant drop in core temperature unless he is immediately re-warmed. (Based upon a schematic drawing in "Death from Cold" by Marlin B. Kreider, *Appalachia,* June 1960).

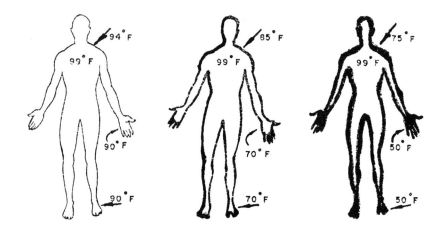

TABLE 13.2   Concerns and Remedies of Hypothermia

Predisposing Factors -
- Poor condition
- Inadequate nutrition and hydration
- Thin build
- Non-woolen clothing
- Inadequate protection from wind, rain, snow
- Getting wet
- Exhaustion

Signs (observed by others) -
- Poor coordination
- Slowing of pace
- Stumbling
- Thickness of speech
- Amnesia
- Irrationality, poor judgment
- Hallucinations
- Loss of contact with environment
- Blueness or puffiness of skin
- Dilation of pupils
- Decreased heart and respiratory rate
- Weak or irregular pulse
- Stupor

Symptoms (felt by climber) -
- Intense shivering *
- Muscle tensing
- Fatigue
- Feeling of deep cold or numbness
- Poor coordination
- Stumbling

TABLE 13.2 CONT'D

- Poor articulation (thickness of speech)
- Disorientation
- Decrease in shivering, followed by rigidity of muscles
- Blueness or puffiness of skin
- Slow, irregular or weak pulse

* NOTE: Don't count on shivering as a sure warning of hypothermia. It doesn't always occur!

Prevention -
- Good rest and nutrition prior to climb
- Continued intake of food
- Waterproof-windproof clothing (some woolen)

- Emergency bivouac equipment
- Exercise to keep up body's heat production (isometric contraction of muscles)

Treatment -
Reduce Heat Loss:
- Shelter the victim from wind and weather
- Insulate him from the ground
- Replace wet clothing with dry
- Put on windproof, waterproof gear
- Increase exercise level if possible
Add Heat:
- Put naked or nearly naked in warmed sleeping bag (with another naked climber)
- Hot drinks
- Heat from hot stones or hot canteen of water
- Huddle for body heat from other climbers
- Immerse in tub of hot water (110° F)

to drink a liter of nice cold water on a cold and windy day?).

Compounding the situation still more is the fact that hypothermia itself results in increased blood circulation to the vital organs, resulting in extra pressure on the kidneys in increased elimination of fluid *and* the elimination of the feeling of thirst. The best remedy is careful attention to fluid intake and output; maintain a "clear and copious" outflow by consuming about three liters or so per day when exercising moderately outdoors. This is often most conveniently done by seeing that everyone in the party consumes one liter in the evening, one liter in the morning, and at least one liter during the day. Also, pay attention to the quality and quantity of urinary output, prescribing copious water intake for anyone producing darkened urine. (This would be a good time to review the sections on water needs in Chapter 2.)

Inadequate Food Intake. It would be wise at this point to reread the section on food and nutrition. While the human digestive system is amazingly tolerant of variations in diet, individuals subject to a cold and hostile environment cannot afford to compromise the body's ability to produce heat. Leaders should consider the caloric requirements of an outing, being especially careful on trips of more than two or three days. Consider, also, what these needs would be in the event of an unexpected extra day or so due to injury or other mishap. Participants should be given lists of suggested

foods or even complete menus, and food consumption should be monitored during the outing. While there are several possible reasons why someone may not feel hungry on an outing, lack of hunger may be a symptom of beginning hypothermia. This is one of the several ways in which hypothermia tends to accelerate itself.

Other causes of inadequate food intake may include dieting (some people see outings as a great opportunity to lose weight), illness, unappetizing foods brought along, or not enough time to eat. Leaders should provide ample time for food preparation and eating; an experienced person might arrive at camp at 8 p.m. and hit the sack at 9 p.m., fully fed, while the beginner may still be struggling with his or her tent! This problem can be minimized by careful attention to the camping process, so that all participants are ready to begin cooking and eating as soon as possible. If care is taken to provide many short snack breaks during the day, the evening meal can be small and simple.

On an outing where the environment is cold but not extremely hostile, an argument can be made for meal planning based on no cooking at all, except for the occasional hot drink or soup. This saves a lot of time and fuel. At high elevations (above about 12,000 feet or 4,000 meters) the provision of adequate palatable food becomes both more critical and more difficult. Hypoxia and stress reduce appetite, making it important to provide appetizing foods, yet cooking is exceedingly time consuming at best — even with a good pressure cooker. (Any group planning more than a few days at such elevations should consider the advantages of a pressure cooker, which may actually save weight in some cases due to fuel savings.)

Fatigue. Have you ever noticed an increased sensitivity to cold when a hard day or lack of sleep have left you very tired? Fatigue reduces the amount of heat generated by the body, and this factor alone can tip the critical balance to a net heat loss. When it is well rested, the body can withstand a remarkable amount of cold stress, at least for a few hours. (The exception to this, of course, is immersion hypothermia.)

Again, planning and good group management can all but eliminate the problem. One of the key responsibilities of a leader is to plan an outing within the limits of his or her group. Unless a leader has many years of extensive experience with groups in the back country, the best advice is to be extremely conservative in evaluating the ability of an individual or group, to monitor the situation continually, and to plan alternative plans and escape routes. The difference between a mild degree of tiredness and complete, stumbling exhaustion can be amazingly little, measured in meters or in minutes.

Illness. Most illnesses drain the body's energy reserves. While the specific mechanisms vary, any current or recent disease should be a matter of concern for the leader. A participant may not want to miss an outing despite an apparently minor illness, or may even participate shortly after recovery from some ailment. On easy outings in fair weather, this may not represent any significant liability, except for the risk to party members who might contract the disease. On longer, more stressful outings where cold may be significant, such individuals should be strongly urged to reconsider or not be allowed to participate, at the option of the leader.

Anxiety. Studies of real-life survival situations have shown that anxiety reduces an individual's survival time in a cold environment. In two well-documented cases, each involving several individuals with nearly identical clothing and equipment, the body temperatures of the survivors were ordered in a way that corresponded perfectly with their experience levels (measured objectively) and the low levels

of anxiety exhibited (as derived from interviews). While the mechanisms at work here are not well understood, at least part of the negative effects of anxiety are probably due to earlier onset of fatigue, because of extra mental activity, less efficient muscular activity, and loss of sleep. To use a simple example, consider the effect of a 3000-foot-high (1000-meter) angle ski run on cross-country skiers. For the confident expert, the only aftereffect may be momentary shortness of breath. For the novice at the limit of his or her ability, the result can be severe physical and mental fatigue.

Leaders need to pay careful attention to the emotional state of participants, and keep in mind the effects of anxiety on the level of fatigue and on resistance to cold. Remember that for many people just being away from the road and out in the woods can be highly stressful! This is not to imply that mental stress is to be avoided at all costs; it is, in fact, an inherent and valuable component of all outdoor activities. Anxiety alone is unlikely to be a significant suppressor of heat production, yet it can compound existing heat-balance deficits. Leaders in programs such as Outward Bound, wherein mental stress is intentionally induced, need to be especially aware of this possibility, maintaining ample compensating reserves of energy, clothing, and equipment. Leaders should also bear in mind that *they* are not immune to the same effects!

Hypothermia. No doubt the most dangerous factor contributing to hypothermia is hypothermia itself; it reduces metabolic efficiency, causing a rapid increase in the rate of cooling. Figure 13.4 shows a dotted curve representing a constant rate of cooling, as would be expected with a constant rate of heat production and a constant rate of heat loss in a constant environment. In theory, the curve might even tend to become more level at lower body temperatures, since heat loss is roughly proportional to the relative temperature of the body and the environment. The solid curve illustrates the actual case, the difference between the two being the effect on metabolic heat production of a lowering of body temperature. The cooler the body, the less heat is produced. As a result, the condition of a hypothermia patient worsens at an accelerated rate towards disaster. Hypothermia also has a prolonged aftereffect, leaving an individual predisposed to the condition for many weeks at least. Some studies indicate decreased resistance to cold stress for a year or more.

Table 13.1 shows the likely signs (effects visible to others) and symptoms (effects felt by the victim) of systemic hypothermia at various temperatures. It is important to keep in mind that each case will manifest itself in different ways. The exact order of appearance of effects and the absolute temperature at which they appear will vary. Some effects may not appear at all! Shivering, for example, cannot be relied upon as a warning, as it often does not occur.

Treatments for Hypothermia

There are several possible treatments for hypothermia, though the options available in the field are usually limited and unfortunately often inadequate. Ideal treatment in a hospital setting may involve the use of sophisticated support systems and techniques such as peritoneal dialysis or the use of a kidney dialysis machine. These have a high success rate provided the condition of the victim is not too dire. Such treatments are sadly unavailable to most patients within a reasonable time span. And many hospitals do not have the expertise or experience to carry out such treatments.

More commonly, and in any case where the patient's condition is not critical, hospital treatment consists of immersion in a warm-water bath. Initial water temperature is usually about 80°F (27°C), raised as rapidly as the patient can safely tolerate to about 110°F (43°C). Care must be taken throughout this process to avoid too-rapid mixing of core and shell blood. The blood in the extremities is cold and has undergone chemical shifts so that the effects of premature mixing may be intolerable. Mixing can be forced by rough handling, by the injection of certain stimulants, or by tricking the body into dropping its defenses and allowing more normal circulation. Care must be taken, for example, to avoid warming the wrists or the back of the neck. Warmth at these sites can trick the body into thinking that the environment is no longer hostile, resulting in elimination of the protective shunting mechanism.

In the field, options may be extremely limited

if the leader's planning was inadequate. At best, the field treatment of anything beyond the early stages of hypothermia carries a very high risk of mortality.

There are two basic options available. The first assumes the patient's condition is diagnosed very early, before the core temperature has dropped more than a few degrees, and certainly before any late-stage signs or symptoms have appeared. This option also assumes that the patient has significant reserves of energy and that dry clothing, food, and water are available.

The key here is to act quickly and aggressively, despite the objection of the patient. It is vital to remember that the patient will almost undoubtedly be suffering from a loss of at least high-order reasoning. Denial of need and resistance to care are normal, and must be overriden by the first aider. In the course of at most five minutes, get dry clothing on the patient and provide (force feed if necessary) as much readily digestible food as possible, ideally a mixture of sugars and complex carbohydrates like bread. Give the patient water (warm is good but warm water is not worth wasting time building a fire for), and begin to walk at a rapid

FIGURE 13.4 Loss of Body Temperature in Three Hours of Hypothermic-Causing Exposure. (Note dip after treatment when symptoms are irreversible.)

1 - Immersion hypothermia

2 - Long-term hypothermia

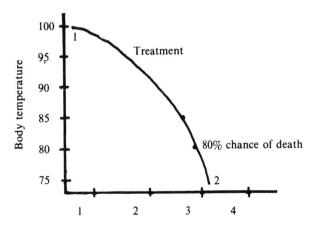

pace, preferably toward the trailhead, for at least 45 minutes until the patient has been perspiring lightly for at least one-half hour and appears fully normal. If travel toward the trailhead is not practical, consider heading toward a sheltered campsite or perhaps walking in a circle, around the lake, or in whatever direction provides heavy exercise and an option of shelter. A good plan, if time, distance, or other considerations preclude leaving the area, is to have the group set up a good camp and prewarm a sleeping bag for the patient while at least two assistants walk the patient on a closed route.

If the patient exhibits more than just early signs of hypothermia or is tired, ill, injured, or otherwise unable to exercise, then the only option is to attempt treatment in place. In this case no more than a couple of minutes should be spent seeking an ideal campsite unless the weather is extremely bad or the shelter marginal. Even in the worst site or weather, minutes count! Set up a tent or substantial tarp to provide complete wind and rain protection while others huddle tightly around the patient, giving sugary foods if the patient is sufficiently conscious. Be extremely careful about handling the patient if his/her condition has reached the point of stumbling and collapse. Patients in the later stage can be killed easily by rough handling, and should be treated as gently as someone with a spinal injury.

As soon as the tent or tarp is in place, add a couple of sleeping pads and a sleeping bag, and while the poles, stakes, cords and other finishing touches are underway, get a healthy person, naked, into the bag. If a choice is available, choose a big bag or one that is part of a zip-together pair since this will make things more comfortable and even allow a third person in the bag. While this is being done, someone should be setting up a stove and getting a big pot of hot water ready. As soon as the sleeping bag is warm (aggressive isometrics help), the patient should also be stripped and slipped into the bag with the valiant bag warmer. Most people have had to put up with sharing their bed with someone with cold feet or hands, and most experienced outdoor folks have on occasion warmed a friend's numb feet on their bellies. Few, however, have experienced the delights of being squashed up against someone

with a cold, a *very* cold, whole body. Expect the bag warmer's eyes to cross and teeth to rattle!

Many novices do not understand why it is necessary for a naked individual or even two naked individuals to be in the sleeping bag with the naked victim. A sleeping bag does not warm a person; it retards cold air from entering the bag and warmth generated by the sleeper from leaving. In the case of hypothermia, there is no warmth being generated and just being inside a sleeping bag will not change that condition. However, the warmth from naked bodies will pass to the cold body of the victim, and, because all are within the confines of the insulating material of the sleeping bag, that warmth will leave the bodies slowly. In damp conditions, where down may get wet and soggy, a sleeping bag lined with synthetic material works best.

Resist the temptation to rub the patient's arms and legs. Don't forget the danger of premature mixing of the shell and core blood. At this point it is probably best to just be still for a few minutes, to let the patient recover from the inevitable stresses of being moved into the shelter and bag. Soon, however, extra heat can be added, using hot water bottles in the groin and armpits and taking great care to protect the skin by wrapping the bottles in light clothing. If the patient is fully conscious, feed him or her warm sugary drinks, keeping in mind that caffeine and alcohol should be avoided, and that the sugars, other nutrients, and the water itself are far more important than the heat in the drink. So long as the drink is not much below body temperature it should do no harm, and will provide needed fuel and hydration. Hot drinks are psychologically beneficial, but sugary fluids should not be delayed if a source of heat is not readily available to warm them up.

A common and unfortunate effect of hypothermia is an exhanced desire to urinate, a voluntary matter in the early stages that becomes involuntary in later ones. Field treatment in a sleeping bag is often complicated by urination, which can make things miserable for all concerned; however, there are several ways of dealing with this problem. A wide-neck bottle (for males) or a pan (for females) can be held in place, again taking care to avoid excess motion. In the absence of such containers, it is possible, especially with sleeping bags with full zippers, to open them and let the patient urinate through an appropriately placed hole in the tent floor (easily patched, by the way, if made at a right-angle cut). If those solutions are not possible, and the patient's temperature or the conditions outside preclude getting out of the bag, simply change to another prewarmed bag. Accidental urination is, in fact, so common that it is probably a good plan to keep a spare bag warm with this in mind. Most sleeping bags will accommodate two people, not comfortably but adequately for survival, so the rest of the group can usually double up. If the incident occurs on a day hike or climb, then extra care must be taken to prevent soaking of the sleeping bag since only one is usually carried as group gear. The patient should be kept in the bag until he or she appears fully normal and has an oral temperature of near 98.6°. Given the best and most aggressive field treatment, this may take many hours, and will probably commit the party to an extra night out.

Would-be rescuers must be prepared for the possibility of failure, even in moderate cases of hypothermia. If the patient's temperature was very low when treatment in the field was started, the odds are stacked dramatically against survival. Patients with hypothermia beyond the very early stages often die despite competent and aggressive field treatment, and in fact have a good chance of dying even when hospital water-bath therapy is available!

All this simply amplifies the importance of prevention.

The key is, of course, adequate planning, and planning is a responsibility resting solely on the shoulders of the leader. Leaders are expected by participants, by the public, and by the courts to understand and act responsibly vis-a-vis significant risks to health and safety, and no leader can claim ignorance of hypothermia. Prevention depends upon care in the overall planning of the outing. It is up to the leader to determine what the basic elements of the outing will be — who, when, where, and what; and furthermore to see to it that adequate margins of safety are maintained at all times. By margin of safety we mean in this case those factors that act to limit the possibility of, or consequences of, hypothermia.

The most important of these are:

1. **Participant awareness:** Every participant should be aware of the risk of hypothermia and should become familiar with significant signs, symptoms, treatments, and preventive measures.
2. **Health and fitness:** The leader needs to be aware of the state of health, the fitness level, and the energy reserves of each member of the party. Most important elements for these are adequate rest, food, and water, and all must be continually monitored. No activity should be of such difficulty or duration that less than several hours of reserves remain in each person. Leaders with extensive experience in stressful outdoor programming can sometimes cut this margin to perhaps two hours, but the difficulty of estimating these limits is so great that even experts sometimes miscalculate. Be conservative here!
3. **Alternative plans:** The leader must, in the initial planning of the outing, consider the possible consequences of changes in the weather, unexpected variances in the rate of travel, accidents, injuries or health patterns. Alternative plans must be continually updated and reviewed throughout the outing.
4. **Equipment and clothing:** The leader must let only adequately equipped individuals take part in an activity. It is the leader's responsibility to specify this gear or to accept or reject items brought by participants. *The minimum allowable gear must be sufficient to allow survival in the event that the individual is lost alone in the worst weather reasonably foreseeable. The leader must also see to it that the group has sufficient gear to treat hypothermia (as well as any other reasonably foreseeable injury or illness) in the field.*

Given adequate planning, hypothermia is both less likely to occur and less consequential if it does occur. The majority of fatal incidents involve individuals or groups venturing into the back country in fair or moderate weather, unprepared for climatic changes and lacking the knowledge and equipment to prevent, diagnose, and treat the condition. Unfortunately, the majority of participants on outings have little or no understanding of hypothermia, so the leader must assume responsibility for minimizing the risks and consequences of this condition. Viewed positively, they can constitute an interesting and valuable educational component of the experience for both participants and leaders.

The negative reinforcement for care in preparation and planning rests on the basic legal assumptions that leaders must perform in a manner consistent with that of others in the profession. Leaders should always consider the possibility of having to explain every action or lack thereof in court, and a lack of adequate prevention measures or insufficient means of treating hypothermia in the field would be extremely hard to defend. In such cases the court would probably base its decision on the opinions of experienced outdoor leaders who have worked under similar conditions. No two outings are the same, and no one set of rules or lists of equipment can adequately cover all of the possibilities. It is vitally important, however, that the leader understand the standards of practice among established outdoor leaders in the area, and maintain standards at an equivalent level or be prepared to justify variances. This is not to say that the way something has always been done is necessarily the best or safest way. Clearly this is not always the case. Nevertheless, the leader is expected to understand accepted practices and is responsible for any variance.

Heat Stress

The outdoor traveler is often led to believe that exposure to cold is the only concern in outdoor recreation activities. This isn't necessarily true, as heat exposure is also of major importance. In terms of physical response, we find that heat stress presents far more problems than cold since the human body is designed to produce heat far more efficiently than to get rid of its excess. The body's cooling system (blood circulation coupled with the evaporative cooling of perspiration) is much like the cooling system in an automobile — its ability to function properly is directly related to the physical condition and capacity of the cooling system

and the demands made upon it. Consequently, with the self-contained cooler in the human body, the ability to get rid of excessive heat is limited to such factors as water and salt intake, intensity and duration of exertion, cardiovascular fitness, and prior acclimatization to the heat. A rise in normal body core temperature (98.6°F) of only six degrees renders the person incapable of providing for his or her immediate needs of water, shade, salt, and rest. A prolonged body core temperature of 106°F usually results in death. It's interesting to note that in a hypo-thermic condition (exposure to cold and lowering of the core temperature) death occurs at a core temperature of about 78°F — that's *20* degrees below normal. Therefore, it is easy to see that excessive body-heat gain is of far greater danger than an equal amount of body-heat loss. Ironically, a winter skiing or snowshoeing trip on a clear, sunny day can create problems with heat stress through sunlight reflected off the snow and the subsequent possibility of hypohydration (extreme dehydration) and sunburn.

An understanding of how the body gains heat can be important in preventing and dealing with heat-stress problems. Essentially, the body gains heat through two mechanisms (often simultaneously!): 1.) *Absorption:* Heat gain from the warm air, radiated and/or reflected sunlight, and direct contact with warm objects and 2.) *Internal:* Heat produced by working muscles and normal body metabolism.

By an examination of these two mechanisms, we see that heat-gain problems are primarily "two-pronged" in nature. Both require your attention and preventative measures.

It normally takes the human body two or three days to adjust to the additional cooling and metabolic requirements of a hot climate. The following are suggested as ways of allowing the body to adjust and still have a good time:

1. Be sure to drink plenty of water whenever you feel the least bit thirsty. Thirst is one of the body's early warning signals that you are becoming dehydrated. In hot weather, your body will need a *minimum* of 2-3 quarts of water per day to maintain normal body functions.
2. Don't hesitate to add extra salt to food, water, and drinks. If the water goes in fresh

and sweats out salty, where do you suppose the salt came from?

3. Realize that salt tablets are *not* substitutes for proper acclimatization.

4. If you minimize perspiration and drink whenever you're thirsty, your body water level will remain high. Remember: *Ration sweat, not water.*

5. Stay out of the direct sunlight as much as possible.

6. Keep your clothes on. Sunburn is not only uncomfortable, but is a skin injury which *will raise* the body-core temperature. Also, exposed skin loses water faster than covered skin and results in less cooling.

7. Wear a hat that will shade the head, neck, and face.

8. Slow down your activities to minimize body-heat production. Pace yourself — and increase your pace slowly.

9. Eat only as much as necessary for the activity. Eating increases body-heat production through the digestive process.

10. Rest the cooling system, as well as arm and leg muscles, frequently. If cramps develop in the extremities, it's probably from salt and/or water depletion in overworked muscles. Sit in the shade and drink water with salt added. (Beware — too much salt will cause nausea). About one (1) tablespoon per quart will do just fine.

11. Realize that body water lost through both perspiration *and* breathing must be replaced or the body's mental *and* physical efficiency will suffer. Anytime the body's cooling system is over exerted, very definite mental and physical side effects appear. If the cooling system runs out of water and can't cool the body, core temperature will begin to rise along with a definite decrease in the person's ability to deal with the impending emergency. The *American Red Cross Advanced First Aid Manual* is an excellent source of information on the symptoms, care, and treatment of many heat problems. Because of the severity of heat stroke and heat exhaustion, the following excerpts from the *Advanced First Aid Manual* are presented.

HEAT STROKE *(This is an immediate life-threatening emergency.)*
Signs and Symptoms
High body temperature
Hot, red, and dry skin
Rapid, strong pulse
Possible unconsciousness
First Aid
Cool the victim using any means available (avoid overchilling). Undress the victim and sponge bare skin with cool water or rubbing alcohol, or place victim in a tub of cold water (a stream or lake would be okay), or, apply ice packs to the body. Fan the victim. Don't give any stimulants, i.e., coffee, iced tea, soft drinks, etc. If victim's temperature begins to rise again, repeat the cooling process.

HEAT EXHAUSTION
Signs and Symptoms
Approximately normal body temperature
Pale, clammy skin
Profuse perspiration
Tiredness and weakness
Headache
Nausea (possible vomiting)
Dizziness (possible fainting)
First Aid
Lay victim down and give sips of salted water.
Elevate feet 12-18."
Loosen clothing.
Apply cool, wet cloths, and fan victim.
Don't give additional fluids if victim vomits.
Protect victim from further exposure to warm temperatures during the rest of the trip.

The film *Thermal Wilderness** offers good guidelines to activity planning and conduct in the hot weather. And remember that the time to deal with hot-weather problems is before you leave home, by deliberately planning to regularly replace body water/salt and to adjust your activities to the weather and personal/group physical condition. The heat can be more of a threat than you may realize since it affects you very slowly, and emergencies caused by heat stress can occur quickly and without warning.

Thermal Wilderness is available free through Associated Films, Inc., Portland, OR.

First-aid Kit

A first-aid kit should be a basic part of everyone's gear. It is important for persons venturing into the outdoors to be as self-reliant as possible. In the event of an accident, help is often many hours or days away, and you will probably have to personally deal with any emergency situation. Listed below are just a few of the problems you should be prepared to deal with when you are miles from "civilization" and professional help.

Strains
Sprains
Sunburn
Burns
Blisters
Bloody nose
Infected scratches and bites
Hypothermia
Food poisoning, upset stomach
Headache
Dehydration
Muscle cramps
Heat stroke
Heat exhaustion
Chapped hands and lips
Poison oak
Bee stings, insect bites
Shock

Fortunately, most trips will be uneventful as far as injuries are concerned. But often a minor injury, if not treated properly, can end up causing major problems.

The items listed below, along with knowledge of their proper use, are a good starting point in handling common first-aid problems. Additional materials should be included as your particular needs and experiences dictate.

2 @ 40" triangular bandages
2 @ 2-3" roller gauze (conforming)
6 @ 3x4" telfa pads (non-adhesive)
1 @ 8x10" surgi-pad
6 @ 2" gauze compresses
12 @ 4" gauze compresses
12 @ 1" Band Aids
2 @ 3x4" moleskin (molefoam)
1 roll 1-2" athletic (adhesive) tape
1 pair of good quality tweezers

6 salt tablets (with dextrose)
6 antacid tablets
1 pair small good-quality scissors
1 sewing needle and heavy-duty thread
6 large safety pins
12 acetaminophen and/or aspirin tablets
6 antihistimine tablets (for mild allergic reactions)
1 elastic (ace-type) bandage (3" size handy)
1 tube antibiotic ointment (Neosporin, mycitracin, or similar types)
any personal medications (know side effects)
small container of antiseptic
cleaning solution (like betadine or small bar of soap)
2 dimes and 2 quarters for emergency phone calls
paper and pencil for rescue information/message
a good first-aid manual or guide — someone may have to treat *you*

Under no circumstances should you carry prescription drugs without first conferring with a physician. Many drugs can cover up important symptoms and hinder effective treatment or evacuation, and serious side effects which you cannot foresee or treat can also occur. Know the side effects of drugs prescribed for yourself, and be aware you assume a tremendous risk giving drugs to others (and it is also illegal). Good first-aid treatment is your first and primary concern.

In an emergency situation do not expect that you will be calm, cool, and collected, and will immediately remember what to do. Try to have a first-aid manual handy, and after treating life-threatening problems, take some time, read, and above all *think. Have a definite reason for everything you do.*

A very useful exercise in preparing yourself and companions for that serious injury or accident is the following. Each time you take a trip, at some point in your travels simply assume that a specific person has had a certain injury and plan what you and the group would do. "What would we do if Bob just slipped on that rock and broke his leg? We are eight miles from the nearest road and help is at least 24 hours away. We can't carry him and we've got two hours before dark."

One thing to remember is that in wilderness areas helicopters are used *only* in life-or-death situations since they are considered motorized vehicles and thus banned under normal circumstances. And before you and your friend try to carry Bob out, remember it takes a minimum of ten to twelve people to effectively carry one person out of the woods.

HELPFUL READING

Advanced First Aid and Emergency Care, The American Red Cross, 1973.

Medicine for Mountaineering, The Mountaineers, J.A. Wilkerson.

Emergency Medical Guide, McGraw Hill, John Henderson, M.D.

Mountaineering First Aid, The Mountaineers, Dick Mitchell.

Mountaineering Medicine, Skagit Mtn. Rescue Unit, Fred T. Darvill, M.D.

Emergency Care and Transportation of the Sick and Injured, American Academy of Orthopedic Surgeons.

Freedom of the Hills, The Mountaineers, ed. Peggy Ferber, 1973.

Surviving the Unexpected Wilderness Emergency, Survival Education Association, Gener Fear.

Hypothermia, Killer of the Unprepared, The Mazamas, Theodore G. Lathrop, M.D.

Frostbite, Museum of Science, Boston, Bradford Washburn.

It is often helpful to read more than one text. Many books are not specifically oriented towards the outdoors, and you may find that treatments suggested in one book differ from those suggested in another.

For information on first-aid classes, contact your local chapter of The American Red Cross.

Share your knowledge with your friends. They may end up being the ones who will have to save *your* life. Knowledgeable friends are a good form of health insurance.

BIBLIOGRAPHY

American Academy of Orthopedic Surgeons, *Emergency Care and Transportation of the Sick and Injured*, American Academy of Orthopedic Surgeons, Menasha, Wisconsin, 1977.

American National Red Cross, *Standard First Aid and Personal Safety, and Advanced First Aid and Emergency Care*, Doubleday and Company, Garden City, New York, 1980.

American National Red Cross, *Advanced First Aid and Emergency Care*, Doubleday and Company, New York, 1973.

Clarke, Ward and Williams, *Mountain Medicine and Physiology*, Reprint by Mountain Safety Research, Seattle, Washington, 1975.

Committee on Injuries of the Academy of Orthopedic Surgeons, *Emergency Care and Transportation of the Sick and Injured*, George Banta Co., Menasha, Wisconsin, 1970.

Darvil, Jr., Fred T., M.D., *Mountaineering Medicine*, Skagit Mountain Rescue Unit, Mt. Vernon, Washington, 1969.

Forgey, William W., M.D., *Hypothermia - Death by Exposure*, ICS Books, Inc., Merrillville, Indiana, 1985.

----------, *Wilderness Medicine*, Indiana Camp Supply Books, Pittsburg, Indiana, 1979.

Gross, Harms Post and Mitchell, *Mountaineering First Aid and Accident Response*, The Mountaineers, Seattle, Washington, 1975.

Hackett, Peter H., M.D., *Mountain Sickness*, The American Alpine Club, New York, 1980.

Houston, Charles S., M.D., *Going High*, Charles S. Houston, M.D. and The American Alpine Club, Burlington, Vermont, 1980.

Lathrop, Ted, M.D., *Hypothermia: Killer of the Unprepared*, D. Mazamas, Portland, Oregon, 1972.

Mitchell, Dick, Mountaineering First Aid, The Mountaineers, Seattle, 1975.

Washburn, Bradford, *Frostbite*, Museum of Science, Boston, 1970.

Wilkerson, James A., M.D. ed., *Medicine for Mountaineering*, The Mountaineers, Seattle, 1975.

Wilkerson, James A., M.D. ed., *Hypothermia and Frostbite*, The Mountaineers, Seattle, 1982.

USING A MAP IN THE FIELD
Classroom study of maps and compasses can be highly efficient in conveying basic concepts, but there is no substitute for hands-on field experience.

CHAPTER 14

MAPS, COMPASSES AND NAVIGATION

Participants in backpacking, mountaineering, cross-country skiing or any other wilderness or back-country pursuit need to learn how to interpret maps and charts, use compasses, and enjoy techniques of navigation. Those who navigate rivers and lakes need to understand land navigation for emergency uses as well as for following tributaries and meanders. No other set of skills is so vital in terms of safety, since the level of risk in these activities is largely dependent upon an understanding of terrain and location.

Leaders have to be especially adept in these skills. Effective planning requires thorough knowledge of the resource, which almost invariably requires a combination of map interpretation and input from other sources such as guide books, local experts, and land managers. Reasonable control of risk while in the field may depend upon the leader's ability to maintain a constant awareness of position. Clearly, the leader has to be competent in order to provide participants with quality instruction.

Teaching the use of maps and compasses is not difficult, but can be frustrating. The most common pitfalls for the instructor are 1) lack of skill, knowledge, or experience in navigation (it's hard to teach what is not known, and hard to be convincing if there is a lack of reinforcing experience), 2) trying to teach to an unreceptive audience (do the participants want and believe they *need* the information?), 3) trying to teach, even to the most eager audience, in the face of significant environmental or other distractions (the beginning backpacker facing another two miles to camp, the climber anxious about the next pitch, or the cross-country skier pondering survival on the next hill), and 4) assuming that participants understand basic concepts of mapping and/or the measurement of angles (trying to teach too much, too fast).

Let's look at these concerns more closely. What constitutes adequate competence for an instructor? The answer clearly depends upon the nature of the activity, the terrain to be covered, and the program itself. At the very least, the leader should be able to 1) interpret a topographic map accurately, 2) use a compass to measure bearings on the map, measure bearings in the field, plot bearings on the map, and follow bearings in the field, 3) determine location in the field by resection and triangulation, and 4) compute and employ trail gradients. In addition, the leader should at least understand the basics of orientation by the sun and stars.

The second concern deals with motivation. It is well worth considering whether or not the participants really *need* map and compass skills. Usually the answer is yes, emphatically. If they will be backpacking, mountaineering, ski touring, or otherwise conducting themselves through the back country, they will need these skills. There are exceptions, however. Lots of people employ the service of guides or leaders on *all* of their outings, not uncommonly for the specific purpose of avoiding the need to learn how to navigate, or at least the need to worry about it if they are already skilled. While it is always tempting to force self-sufficiency on such people, success is likely to be limited. Besides, insofar as they continue to use guides, they may not *need* to know much about navigation. Another reason for reduced need by participants is because their activities may take place in a part of the world where map and compass skills are not essential. For example, hikers in the Kita Alps of Japan or perhaps in the Berner Oberland in Switzerland will find clearly marked trails on sharply defined ridges and often in populated valleys, with huts at half-day intervals. This is not to say that maps are not useful to these people — far from it! Yet in these areas all that is needed is a *very* basic ability to read maps. Compasses are rarely ever used by hikers in such areas, and only climbers and others venturing well off maintained routes need these and topographic maps. In summary, the leader should attempt to understand how and

where the participants may find a reason for employing these skills, and, if a need is seen, try to develop their interest in learning.

The third concern has to do with the setting in which learning takes place and the receptivity of the prospective students. Our experience has proven to us that most people find maps and compasses puzzling, to say the least. The average beginning backpacker needs to focus just about all of his or her wits on those little squiggly lines and on that spinning needle. The instructor, on the other hand, can stride along comfortably in sophisticated high-tech clothing, feet toasty-warm and comfy, not a sore muscle or strained breath, watching the scenery with one eye while rattling on about the fine points of correcting to declination in areas of local magnetic disturbance. The poor beginner, limping from blisters and out of breath from the pace, tries to glance on his map while hiking and does a face plant in the next mud hole. Even stops at short rest breaks can be poor teaching settings, since most of that time is spent resting, treating sore feet, putting on and taking off clothes, finding, eating, and repacking snacks, and making frantic dashes into the bushes for elimination. Too often the instructors, needing little time for maintenance, try to include too much teaching too soon or too late on a cool day when the whole prospective class is shivering convulsively and eager to move. A common frustration is trying to teach navigation while ski touring. It is a fine and even enjoyable thing to do during a long lunch stop on a warm spring day, but doomed to failure in wind, snow, or rain unless the participants are exceptionally motivated. That mile of ten-percent slope that the instructor eagerly awaits may inspire ever-increasing anxiety in the students all day. They may be envisioning teeth marks in the lodgepole pines while staring with eager and apparently receptive eyes at the instructor.

A closely related concern is the "sheep syndrome." While not like stress per se, it just as surely limits learning ability and resembles environmental stress, a greater problem for beginners than for experienced participants. The "sheep syndrome" is the tendency of people to stop orienting themselves when following another person. We follow in sheep-like (or lemming-like?) order, finding it almost painfully difficult to keep our minds on where we are and on our direction of travel. This tendency, coupled with tiredness, discomfort, or anxiety, usually results in little or no capacity for learning or refining navigation skills. Thus small groups that frequently rotate with the lead person are essential in virtually any attempt at teaching navigation in the field.

The key, then, is to appreciate the physical and mental stress on the group, and modify instructional patterns accordingly. Try to do most teaching in pleasant, non-threatening settings at times when the students or participants are comfortable, relaxed, well-fed, and watered. This points to a rather obvious alternative, that of classroom or at least in-town teaching. In fact, classroom settings can be nearly ideal since a variety of media can be used to illustrate points or to replicate certain elements of the terrain depicted on the practice maps. Some specific examples will be discussed later.

Last but not least is the mistake of trying to teach too quickly or to convey too much information. The instructor may well overwhelm even the most eager, receptive, and intelligent student if this happens. In any group situation some individuals will have special needs, and maps and compasses present problems for a surprisingly large number of people.

One common difficulty has to do with understanding the view of the land's surface as represented on a map. For most of us, it is easy to understand the concept of a vertical view; the explanation that most maps are bird's-eye views (actually closer to the simultaneous sight of an infinite number of birds!) is usually sufficient. Others, however, have difficulty in shifting perspective. Look at a child's "map" of a city street — all of the building *fronts* are visible though tilted back and distorted. Some people never do become comfortable with conventional mapping systems, and will require considerable extra instructional activities. The use of compasses, for instance, requires a basic understanding of angles; many people have little idea of what an angle is, much less a bearing, and need assistance in the form of definition and simple examples and analogies. Since it is difficult to quickly assess the particular needs of everyone in the class, and since basic concepts

of geometry and perspective are so crucial to the entire realm of navigation, it is usually a good idea to begin such lessons with at least some review of these topics. Don't forget that many people also have a long-standing anxiety about *anything* that sounds "mathematical." This alone can be extremely limiting, and if the difficulties are compounded by specific learning problems or by any of the concerns discussed earlier, both the instructor and the student are in for a frustrating experience!

Let us assume that teaching basic navigation is included in the program objectives, and that the leader is fortunate enough to have eager and receptive participants combined with appropriate resources and good weather. What should be taught? Again, it is necessary to carefully assess the needs of the students and the limits set by constraints of time. Planning is important here, since an adequate segment must be allowed for this as for any other aspect of a program. The following progression includes most of the basic navigational concepts and skills useful for hiking, backpacking, and mountaineering. While the relative importance of these concepts and skills will vary for each group (and perhaps for each individual), care should be taken not to skip those steps upon which later ones depend. It is assumed here that the reader already understands navigation by map and compass and wants to know how to teach others. The progression also takes for granted that you are using an orienteering style compass (see Figure 14.1). While other types of compasses are acceptable, they are generally more difficult to operate, especially in measuring or plotting bearings on a map.

BASIC NAVIGATION

No one will find a map or compass useful unless basic navigation skills are understood. If people don't know where they came from, no map or compass will help them understand where they are or where they are going.

Staying Oriented

Keeping oriented is essential to maintenance of position awareness, and students need to be reminded of the need for continual attention to

FIGURE 14.1   Orienteering Compass

THE PARTS OF AN ORIENTEERING COMPASS

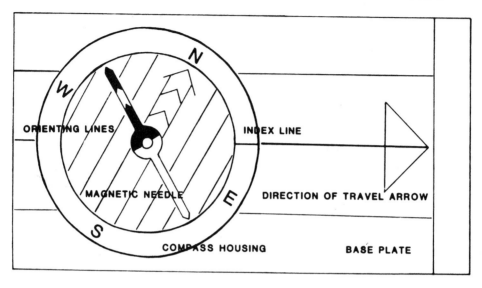

this. We all tend to follow blindly, leaving ourselves at the mercy of the leader or just plain luck. Discuss how to understand the relative position and orientation of major natural and man-made features of the area to be traversed. Most students will be able to recall hiking or traveling in situations wherein they had no idea of their location or direction. Offer suggestions for keeping track of where they are such as 1) carefully reviewing maps of the area beforehand, 2) frequently comparing one's "mental map" with both the observed terrain and the "paper map," and 3) assuming some personal responsibility for orientation. It is usually worthwhile to emphasize the basic simplicity of the process since they *can* learn how to avoid becoming lost, yet it is also necessary to stress the importance of methodical and conscientious attention as they navigate. Remind them that if position is verified by comparing the map and the observed terrain every quarter of an hour, they will be less likely to be off by more than half a mile or so (a kilometer or less); backtracking then remains an option.

Solar Clues. This section may have to be preceded by a brief explanation of direction and cardinal versus bearing systems (see compass use). Remember, especially if you are working with very young people or big-city residents, that they may be remarkably unaware of natural patterns. A quick review of planetary mechanics is useful here to establish the regularity of apparent solar motions and to explain seasonal variance in the sun's elevation in the sky. Tell them that, while only a crude approximation, the sun moves from east to west at about 15° per hour (remind them of sundials). At the very least they should understand that at noon, Standard Time (at least if one is near the center of the time zone), the sun is at its highest point (shadows are shortest) and that these shadows point north for observers in the northern hemisphere and south for those in the southern hemisphere. This gives students at least one way of roughly approximating direction by the sun if they know what time it is and which way the shadows point.

A useful related fact is the near symmetry of the day around the noon hour. If, for example, it gets light five-and-a-half hours before noon, it will get dark five-and-a-half hours after noon — *Standard* Time of course. They should also be reminded of the effect of Daylight or summer time; noon, or Standard Time, becomes eleven o'clock on Daylight Time. (See Figure 14.2)

Stellar Clues. As with solar navigation, few people need, want, or will retain more than very basic concepts. Often the only nighttime references that need to be explained are the Big Dipper and Polaris (see Figure 14.3), or directions to the more illusive sigma octans for Southern Hemisphere residents. The nearly due-east rising of the star in the center of Orion's Belt is a point of interest as well, but perhaps best left for an evening of stargazing.

MAPS

What is a map? Use the bird's-eye-view analogy. Models, globes, and sketches can help explain perspective. A good exercise with children (and sometimes with adults) is to have them draw maps of small areas. For example, have children draw a picture of the top of their own desk and explain that it is a map. Then have them draw a picture of all the desks in the room as seen by someone peering through a hole in the ceiling (another map). Then have them draw the playground, the neighborhood, and their route to school. This progression will help children as young as age six understand the meaning of maps.

What kind of maps are available? Show planimetric and topographic maps using highway, USGS, or other topographic expressions ideally of the same area. (Overheads or slides of these are handy in the classroom.) The simplicity and low cost of planimetric maps can be contrasted to the greater amount of information but commensurate increases in cost and complexity of topographic images.

How are they made? Explain aerial photographs and the use of overlapping photos to allow interpretation of topography. (See Figure 14.4) Explanations of various mapping projections and parallel effects will be interesting to a few people, but aren't necessary. It is important to

note that the process involves a combination of human and machine work, and that the map is thus just an approximation of reality and will contain errors. Common errors should be mentioned, such as out-of-date or incorrectly placed roads and trails and frequent inaccuracies in coloring designated vegetation, ground cover, and bodies of water. These points are best illustrated by overlaying our examples on maps of the same local areas.

Which way is up, and what do all those symbols and colors mean? Explain that on most maps true north is toward the top of the map; that is to say, any vertical line on the map is approximately true north/south. Every country has its own conventions for symbols, and the more common ones should be explained. Most use green to designate contiguous vegetation, and it is sometimes of interest to explain the standards used. In the U.S., for instance, areas are colored green on USGS topographic quadrangles if the map maker estimated that an acre of such vegetation would be adequate to hide a squad of Marines! Aerial photos, especially low-vegetation oblique ones of terrain or practice maps, are valuable aids here.

Scale. Explain the idea of ratios and proportions, and show examples of maps on different scales, ideally of the same area. Derive some easily understood equivalents for common map scales such as 1 cm. = ½ kilometer on a 1:50,000 map; 1 inch = 1 mile for 1:62,500 maps (62,500 is close to 63,360, the number of inches in a mile); or ½ inch = 1,000 feet for 1:24,000 map. (See Figure 14.5.)

Contour lines. Classroom presentation of sketches, overheads, and other visual aids is especially useful here. (See Figure 14.6.) Suggest that participants imagine the successive shorelines created by placing a large lump, a little "mountain" of clay, in a bathtub, then raising the water level one inch at a time. This idea can be extended to explain the behavior of contour lines on gentle and steep slopes, ridges, and valleys. Other effective techniques include the use of topographic mock-ups made by layering sheets of cardboard cut on "contour lines," examples on the chalkboard wherein a simple conical expression is modified

FIGURE 14.2 North by Sun and Wristwatch

FIGURE 14.3 Dippers and Polaris

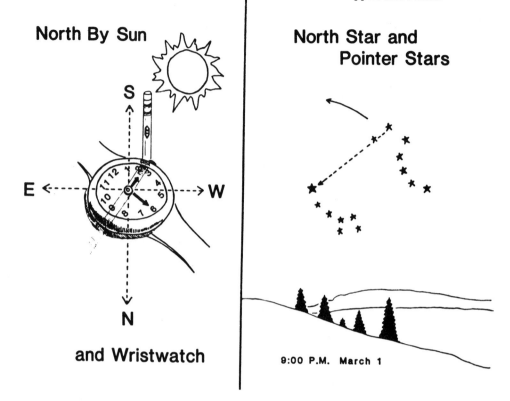

North By Sun

North Star and Pointer Stars

and Wristwatch

9:00 P.M. March 1

FIGURE 14.4 How Topographic Maps Are Made

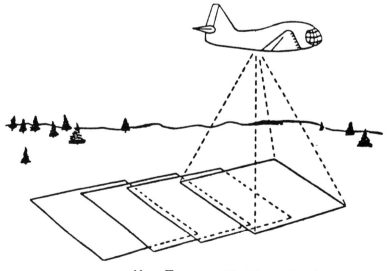

How Topographic Maps Are Made

FIGURE 14.5 Map Scales

TOPOGRAPHIC MAP SERIES

7.5 – minute

1:24,000 scale,

1 inch = 2,000 feet,

Area shown, 1 square mile

15 – minute

1:62,500 scale,

1 inch = about 1 mile

Area shown, 6 3/4 square miles

U.S. 1:250,000

1:250,000 scale

1 inch = about 4 miles

Area shown, 107 square miles

FIGURE 14.6 Contour Intervals

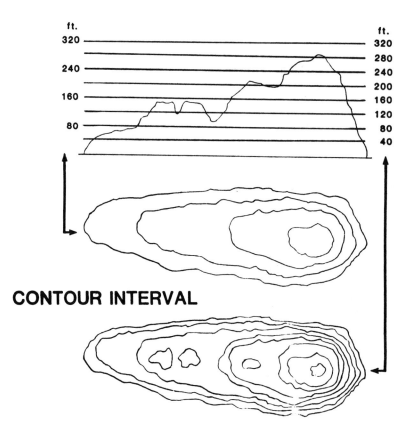

CONTOUR INTERVAL

to show how various shapes might be expressed, and slides showing terrain identical to that on topographic maps in the hands of students. This use of slides can be very effective if such are available. A set taken from a high point on the students' maps can be used to approximate the effect of actually sitting on the point with the class, identifying and relating the real perspective view with the topographic map expression.

A valuable exercise at this point is to "take a hike" on the students' maps. Fifteen-minute (1:62,500 scale) USGS maps, USFS wilderness maps, 1:50,000 metric maps, or others of a similar scale are good to use as examples since they are in common circulation and are intermediate in scale to the other maps often available for back-country use. Select a route of about ten miles (1.6 km.) or so that includes

uphill and downhill portions and a range of landforms and features. Follow the route, discussing and describing the trail, terrain, vegetation, and other features one would encounter if actually walking along the route.

Beginners should at least learn to identify uphill and downhill portions and to read elevations of selected points. More advanced groups should learn to total vertical gains and losses, to check their figures against the overall difference between the start and end points, and to compute trail gradients.

Trail gradients are extremely easy to figure (they are simply the vertical gain or loss divided by the horizontal distance travelled), yet an amazing number of people have trouble with even primitive mathematical calculations. A diagram or "cross-section" of the trail helps here to show that the slope of a line (trail) can be simply expressed as a percentage by dividing the rise or fall by the length of the trail and multiplying by 100 (add the contour intervals crossed in the segment of trail in question). Obviously the units have to be the same (feet or meters are usually best). In practice, since most people can't accurately picture 100 feet or meters, it is usually best to scale it down to ten feet or meters. For example, a 15% slope (fifteen units of vertical change per 100 units of horizontal change) is the same as 1.5 units of vertical change per ten units of horizontal change. Knowing that the trail climbs (or drops) 1.5 feet for every ten horizontal feet of trail (or 1.5 meters for every ten meters of trail) is a lot more meaningful and thus useful than trying to picture what a rise of fifteen feet in 100 feet will look like. Again, beginners won't find this necessary or useful at first, though for others it is a simple way of understanding what a trail will be like. It is easy to misread the steepness of trails, especially if one is relatively new at map reading or has to use maps of many different vertical and horizontal scales.

Angles. Too often we leap into discussions of bearings, resection, and triangulation without defining basic concepts. Unfortunately a lot of adults are no better off than young children in terms of their understanding of basic geometric concepts. Any discussion of angles should include the idea of a reference line and of the use of a 360-division "circle." Since we are teaching map and compass use, not geometry, keep it simple and right from the start use examples of vertical lines (up and down the chalkboard, if that is the medium of choice) that are consistent with maps. Angles, for the same reason, should be shown to be measured only in clockwise directions for the vertical (on the chalkboard) line, which should be identified as the "reference line."

Directions. Once the concept of angles is adequately understood, it is time to introduce directions. Most people know the cardinal points (N, E, S, W, plus intermediates NW, SE, etc.), though there is usually someone in any large class who has east and west reversed. A useful diagram consists of a circle with a center point showing the cardinal points indicated,

along with a standard 360° scale expressed as key figures corresponding to the cardinal points (See Figure 14.7). Students must understand that the degree figures define the various lines one could draw from the center of the circle to points on the circle or "scale," and that these lines represent directions. "Bearings" can then be defined as equivalent to these lines of direction and designated by reference to the scale number, which in turn gives the angle between the reference line and the line of travel. Once this is understood, have the students imagine themselves standing in the center of the circle. "Following a bearing" can then be explained as walking from the center straight out toward the appropriate point on the scale. Bearings from one place to another on the map can be shown by extension of this idea; have students imagine the starting place to be at the center of the circle. At this point it is worthwhile to note that the reference line is due north (true versus magnetic north will be discussed later).

COMPASS USE WITH A MAP

Strange as it may seem, the first thing to teach beginners — and even some who claim to be experts — is how to hold the compass. Many people hold the compass flat on one palm and face the direction in which they are headed. Little do they realize that the hand holding the compass is *not* pointing in the same direction as the body but at an angle of ten to fifteen degrees right (if they're right-handed) of where they are headed.

The best way for beginners to hold a compass is with both elbows tucked in tight against the body (as if to hold the pants up) and the hands held palm upwards one on top of the other. The compass should rest on the top hand with the base plate parallel to the waist and the direction of the travel arrow pointing directly forward.

The second thing to teach about the compass is how to recognize the north or magnetic end of the needle. Some beginners, in their confusion, do not realize that one end of the needle points to the *south* and that following it is disastrous. These two items may seem overly simple or even ludicrous, yet one of the authors has seen well-educated men following the wrong

FIGURE 14.7 **Bearings and Cardinal Points**

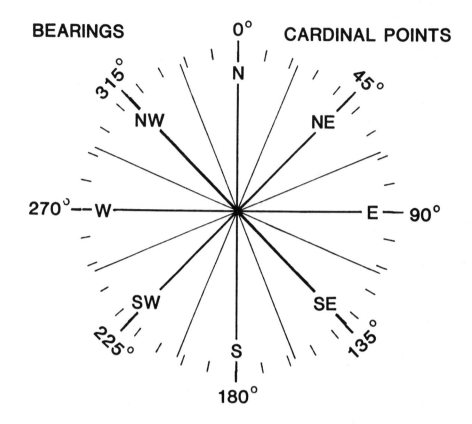

end of the needle because no one bothered to point out the way to tell the north end from the south.

The compass is best introduced as a device for measuring angles first. Have students just ignore the needle for now, for the scale can be equated to the circle used to illustrate the concept of direction. It probably speeds the learning process to have the students see the scale as fixed and the rectangular base as movable to continue the comparison to the circle of directions.

Perhaps the most important idea to be introduced here is orientation of the scale using the "orienting lines" visible within the compass housing. Sample points can be drawn on the board and/or on the maps to illustrate and practice measuring bearings. Once students can measure these accurately, have them reverse the process and plot bearings on the map. This is usually best accompanied by several procedures such as measuring the distances between points, so that in plotting bearings from a given point a combination of bearing and distance can be used by the student to locate the new end point.

True north can be defined at this time as a direction straight toward the North Pole. A simple sketch (Figure 14.8) shows that the North Pole is at the axis of the earth's rotation, and that longitudinal lines converge at that point. (Magnetic north can be discussed soon; however, its introduction here will only add unneeded confusion).

Most beginning students need to learn nothing more than how to measure bearings on the map; more advanced students will find resection and triangulation interesting and useful. Resection is best illustrated by using a blackboard sketch (illustration) or simple map example wherein students imagine themselves walking along a ridge, creek, road, trail, or other linear feature. The first imaginary situation should be simple, for instance a nearly straight east/west feature from which a certain other feature (say a peak) appears to be due north of the observer.

Later situations can be as interesting as class ability, interest, and time allow, including twisting or switchback trails wherein a bearing line drawn back from the sighted features may define several possible locations. Once this "point-line" method is in hand, two point fixations (triangulation) can be illustrated and practiced, again starting with a simple case (if you can see Spire Peak due north and Red Bluffs due east, where must you be?"). As with all compass use, lots of practice is essential.

Magnetic North. About the most one can hope for in most classes is that some of the students know that there is a north magnetic pole and that it isn't the same as the "real" North Pole. Since the concept may be a new one, it is usually best to refer to the diagram used to illustrate the North Pole and longitudinal lines (Figure 14.9), adding terms like "magnetic field" and illustrating the location of the North (and perhaps South) magnetic poles. While avid geographers in class will enjoy knowing that the pole is near Bathurst Island, that fact is meaningless to most people.

For practical purposes, knowing that the pole is in far northeastern Canada is much more valuable and will be retained far longer. A simple sketch on the expanded original illustration can show that while maps are usually drawn so that a vertical line is parallel to meridians (lines of longitude) and points North, compass needles point toward the magnetic pole. (See Figure 14.10.) It is appropriate here to define true north and magnetic north as the directions toward the true and magnetic poles, respectively. The difference between the two, called the declination, will of course vary with location, and local declination should be given and illustrated ("if we face true north, this is the direction toward the magnetic pole and the way our compass needles will point"). If local topographic maps are being used, true and magnetic north will usually be shown in the legend of the map, along with other "norths" less useful in recreational outdoor activities. In any case, students should be appraised of the best way of finding out the declination for their particular area, region, or country. (See Figure 14.11.)

COMPASS USE IN THE FIELD

The concept of orienting the scale should be discussed here in detail because it is so crucial to effective use of the compass. Remind students that all a compass is is a tool for measuring angles, and that angles are always measured from a reference line. For convenience and to be consistent with map conventions, this reference line is the true-north direction line. Orienting the scale to true north on a map means lining up the orienting lines in the housing with any map or imaginary "vertical" (up-and-down) line on the map, while in the field the magnetic needle gives us a clue to the direction of true north. The key to the simplicity of this system lies in letting the north end of the compass needle point to the declination figure on the scale! If this is done, then the scale (and its orienting lines) are oriented to True North. This one simple step, usable anywhere in the world, of allowing the needle to point to the declination figure, eliminates all of the confusing and rarely retained mumbo jumbo of adding and subtracting to convert map to field or field to map. (See Figure 14.12.)

It should be noted that some compasses have a feature that allows the orienting lines to be mechanically offset, thus allowing "boxing" of the needle parallel to the orienting lines in field use. This, however, disallows easy use of the compass on the map unless this compass is reset in normal position for map use. Students are often confused by this feature, intended to make things easier. Another important reminder relates to orienteering as a sport in itself; in orienteering, magnetic lines are often drawn on maps so their measurements can be quickly made in magnetic. Thus the compass needle can be allowed to orient with the orienting lines in field use, an advantage when you're trying to read the compass quickly while scrambling through the woods. The addition of magnetic lines to one's backpacking map seems

FIGURE 14.8 Parallels of Latitude and Meridians of Longitude

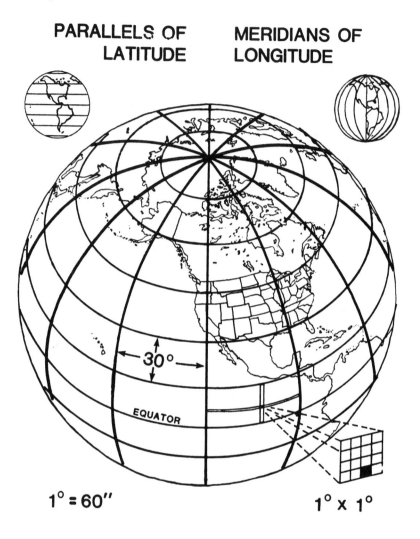

PARALLELS OF LATITUDE

MERIDIANS OF LONGITUDE

30°

EQUATOR

1° = 60''

1° x 1°

unwarranted, however, since the few additional seconds needed to locate the declination point on the scale aren't likely to be significant.

In summary then, one measures the bearing point by lining up the edge of the compass (or one of the scribed parallel lines) with the two points, being sure that the "direction of travel" arrow is pointing toward the destination. The scale is then oriented to true north by rotating the housing and thereby lining up the orienting line with any real or imagined north-south (up-and-down) line on the map (be careful to put

north "up"). Following the bearing in the field is easy. Simply let the north end of the needle point to the declination figure on the scale, thus orienting it, and sight along the centerpost directions of the travel arrow line. (See Figure 14.13.)

There are several sources of confusion for students once they actually get out in the field, so remind them of a few even before they give it a try — not to confuse them but to prevent frustration. The most important are:

FIGURE 14.9 Magnetic Declination

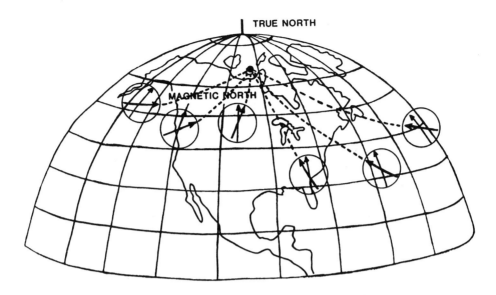

MAGNETIC DECLINATION

1. *How* to sight; compare the advantages and disadvantages of holding the compass at eye level versus the waist-level position. In particular, point out the problem of rotating the compass between orientation of the needle and sighting in the eye-level position, and rotating the eyes or head instead of looking *straight* out in the waist level position.

2. *What* to sight at; too often the target object is too close, or not visible as it is approached. Grade-school kids are likely to sight on the cow or the brush with the raven on it. Encourage long sights when feasible.

3. Poor estimation of distance; once in the field, set up a pace line! Have the line set up on a gentle slope, so students see the effect of stride-lengthening in downhill walking.

4. Sidehills; note the tendency on steep, slippery, or intimidating terrains to creep up, and on modest terrains to creep down if one is tired.

5. Obstacles; note that all that is necessary is to keep track of where the line is! You don't have to thrash through the dense blackberry patch or build a raft to cross the lake! Explain simple ways of dodging obstacles and of returning to the line. Figure 14.14 also illustrates simple rectilinear- and alternative-calculated offsets. These are rarely useful for beginners, though of some value to more advanced students.

6. Magnetic aberration; ask even a college class what elements are likely to be magnetic and the answer is likely to be "uh — steel? brass?". (It is best here to assume that students have not had more than grade-school science and have forgotten most of that.)

Start with basics and don't give more information than will be useful. It is usually adequate to just mention iron and its alloys and compounds, as other materially magnetic elements are not usually a problem in practice.

FIGURE 14.10 **The Earth's Magnetic Field**

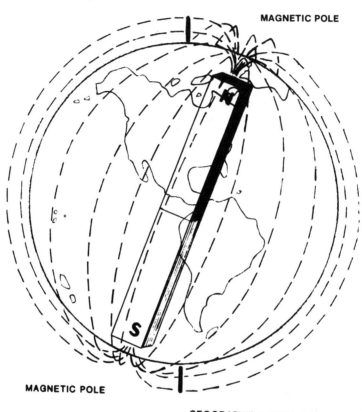

THE EARTH'S MAGNETIC FIELD

FIGURE 14.11   Lines of Declination

LINES OF DECLINATION

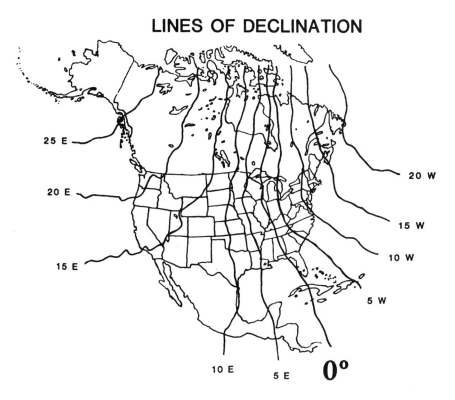

Point out the obvious effects of some iron-bearing alloys, and mention that copper, brass, aluminum, etc. are not problems unless they are carrying an electric current. At about the time that you are showing an example of electric current (like the effects of wiring), someone is likely to assault your theory with a large brass belt buckle that grossly deflects the compass needle. Even if no one does, it is worth pointing out this possibility since brass-plated iron-alloy belt buckles are such common ornaments. The instructor might also explain that aluminum pack frames so often set aside before using a compass are not likely to be a problem unless the frame is struck by lightening, in which case deviation of the compass needle assumes a somewhat diminished significance.

Natural causes of local variations in the magnetic field are very common and can add considerable confusion. Iron-ore deposits (various iron oxides) are often magnetic, as are

fine-grained, dark-colored intrusive volcanic rocks. Dark color generally means high iron mineral content, fine-grained means rapid cooling, and intrusive means that the molten rock sat in place as it cooled. The result is that iron-bearing minerals, which tended in their molten state to orient with the magnetic field of the earth, were fixed in place so that the entire rock mass now acts as a giant magnet. In coarsely crystalline rock the process of crystallization effectively randomizes the orientation of the magnetic minerals, and in lava flows the continual motion through the solidification process has a similar effect in greatly reducing the magnetic influence of the rock mass.

Students should be reminded of the need for caution in areas of known iron deposits and on or near rocky outcrops that look suspicious (i.e., meet the above criteria). Intrusive volcanic masses are often exposed at the tops of hills and

FIGURE 14.12   Finding a Bearing from the Map

FINDING A BEARING FROM THE MAP

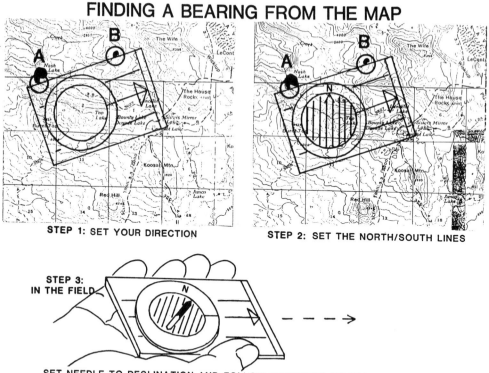

STEP 1: SET YOUR DIRECTION   STEP 2: SET THE NORTH/SOUTH LINES

STEP 3:
IN THE FIELD

SET NEEDLE TO DECLINATION AND FOLLOW DIRECTION OF TRAVEL ARROW

ridges since this type of rock tends to be highly durable and thus forms such features.

Suggest ways in which the students might be able to detect such problems. In many cases the effect can be dramatically illustrated by moving the compass near the rock — causing movement or even reversals of the needle. Show how to test for local effects by sighting on a very distant feature, moving, and sighting again. (If the feature is very distant, no change occurs; a change means something is amiss.) This test is based on the usually valid assumption that such distances vary widely in short distances. Show how to measure and correct for such disturbances by comparing the bearing of a feature measured on the map to the bearing measured by direct field observation.

COMPASS PRACTICE COURSE

Once the basic idea is understood, get out and try it! Have students take bearings on distance features and compare them to those measured by others. Compare map and measured bearings. Call out a bearing and ask what feature is at that point. Follow preset courses; good ones can be set up quickly even in small areas such as a field or school campus.

It is usually easiest to simply locate the pointer by walking around the area, if it is small. Bearings can then be directly measured on a second round through the course. If the area is larger, maps and/or aerial photos can be used to locate approximate prime locations; then points can be fixed on site and bearings determined by measurement on the map,

FIGURE 14.13 Finding a Bearing in the Field

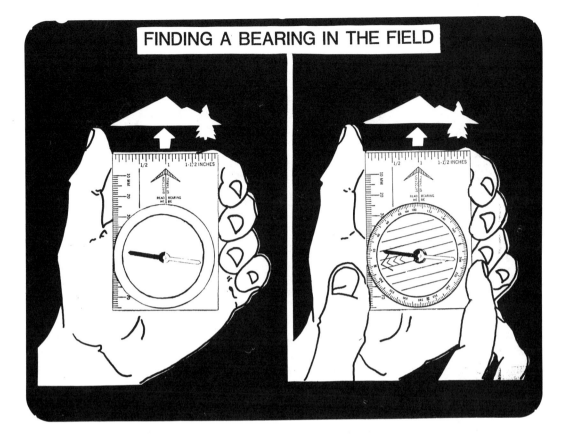

FINDING A BEARING IN THE FIELD

confirmed by walking at least key legs between points. The value of this confirmation will be explained a bit later when we discuss local distortions of the magnetic field.

A flat area can be used to practice finding points using bearings only, if the points are obvious enough that they won't be missed by a person walking on the proper bearing. If bearings are the only clue, be sure to establish clear boundaries for the course, so individuals or groups know when to stop if they miss a point! Otherwise, you may have people wandering all over the countryside looking for and using that illusive point nineteen.

All manner of games and systems for verification have been devised. These can add interest and excitement for certain groups, and

the most popular ones involve complex riddles or codes solved by clues formed at each point. Verification systems may require the participant to record a code number, take a coded tag, or even photograph the point. All of this complexity can be avoided if participants are already motivated to find points and to improve their skills.

In actual back-country travel, destinations are seldom found solely on the basis of directions. Land forms, roads, trails, signs, and, of course, distance all provide valuable additional information. Distance can easily be added to any course by measuring each leg of the route and providing bearing data for it. On a simple short course, bearing and distance clues are often given to participants either completely at

FIGURE 14.14 Making a Detour

MAKING A DETOUR

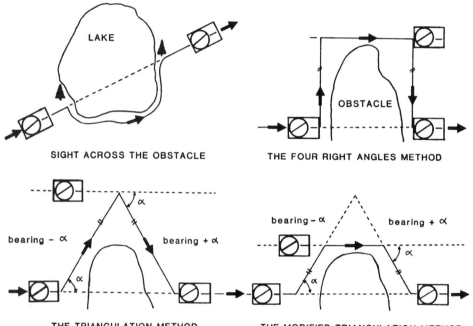

SIGHT ACROSS THE OBSTACLE

THE FOUR RIGHT ANGLES METHOD

THE TRIANGULATION METHOD

THE MODIFIED TRIANGULATION METHOD

the start or by posting directions along the route.

Since participants need to learn how to read and measure bearings and distances on maps, the best way to preserve the information is on a map! Having to determine direction and distance from one is a realistic and excellent practice.

If the purpose of learning to use a map and compass is to facilitate back-country travel, practice should, if possible, be on terrain that resembles the intended area of use. Such terrain may not be available in or near town, in which case even a small flat bearing or bearing and distance course is certainly better than nothing. The ideal, however, is to at least approximate the "real thing." This means finding an accessible park, farm, or other piece of land for which one can obtain a topographic map with

some terrain variations and interesting land forms but no significant hazards.

Such sites, though not always easy to find and gain access to, can provide opportunities for half-day or full-day outings and the development of a range of skills. Most urban or suburban sites or local parks will be a mile or less in each dimension. An area of a square mile (two or three square kilometers) is large enough to allow challenging and rewarding practice, yet small enough to control if adequate barriers define the site. Clear definition of the site is especially important with beginners or if confusing or hazardous terrain borders it.

It is essential to bear in mind what might happen if an individual or group should miss a point on the practice course. What may seem an obvious corrective action to the leader or individual familiar with the area may not be so to the confused beginner. The nature and extent of barriers (limiting features) necessary for safety depend on the likelihood of error (someone becoming lost and confused) and upon the consequences. Young beginners need more protection than well-prepared groups of college students; sites surrounded by undeveloped land are more hazardous than parks or other places surrounded by populated areas.

Clear instructions should be provided both verbally and on the map vis-a-vis the outer limits of the site if any significant hazards exist. Even in areas of only a square mile, the risks usually warrant allowing only small-group travel. Two or three heads are (usually) better than one, and from the standpoint of the leader a small group is easier to find (while at the same time causing quite a bit less anxiety!).

Certainly careful check-in and check-out procedures are called for on any such course, and clothing requirements and safety instructions play a significant role in reducing real risk and might well alter the legal outcome for the instructor should an injury occur. Waiver forms should be utilized as on any outing, unless the course is very small and highly controlled.

AN EXAMPLE OF A MAP-AND-COMPASS COURSE

Figure 14.15 illustrates a sample course layout. The map is a seven-and-a-half minute series NSGS map, copied in black and white and plastic coated to resist the elements. The course illustrated is very nearly ideal in several respects. Control is relatively easy since it lies almost entirely on the west half of an isolated hill circled by farmland and bounded closely on one side by rivers. No cliffs or major hazards are in the area. Confused or lost participants simply need to be reminded not to cross the roads or rivers at the base of the hill. This course is run every few months by thirty to sixty university students and on several occasions during the year by Parks and Recreation, military, and other groups, as well as by many past participants brushing up on skills. Climate and elevation allow year-round use and adequate regrowth of protective ground cover.

The points on this course are three-foot-long natural Douglas fir poles that are four to six inches in diameter and sunk eighteen inches in the ground. Creosote or oak wood would have greatly prolonged the life of these posts; however, they were donated. Labor was provided by local military reserve units and the Sheriff's Office Search-and-Rescue Team.

Once the points were in place and mapped, routes were determined. Each one includes a variety of challenges, including easy and hard points, brushy-forest and open-meadow travel, and a range of terrain features. Some points are more easily found by direct bearing lines, some by following contours, and some by landform or vegetation patterns. Each route is of approximately the same length in terms of time, not distance needed to complete it. Since it is also important to avoid all unnecessary contacts between groups, routes are laid out to minimize common points.

Operation of the course is relatively simple if planning has been adequate. It is designed to be used by up to sixty students (and an additional ten or twelve staff) at one time. Ten stakes, lettered "A" through "J," are set out near the start point. Students are organized into groups of three, each group with a watch. One group stands by each post, and the letter of the post defines the route to be followed. Thirty students can thus be accommodated on the first "wave."

Each group is issued up to three maps, three compasses, and one three-by-five card to keep track of attendance and to sign out maps and compasses. Staff assistants see to it that each card is filled out with the students' names, route letter, and waive number and that compasses and maps are assigned to individuals. Collected and used to verify roll at the lunch stop or midpoint of the course, the cards check people out and map and compasses in at the end of the day.

An additional two stakes are set out to use as a pace line, separated by 100 feet or fifty meters, depending on the scale of the map. (Students are encouraged to use this before setting out.) After a brief review of techniques, safety procedures, and assembly times and places, the first wave is sent out. The course is designed so that there are five initial points sought by two groups each. This is usually necessary in terms

FIGURE 14.15   Sample Course Layout

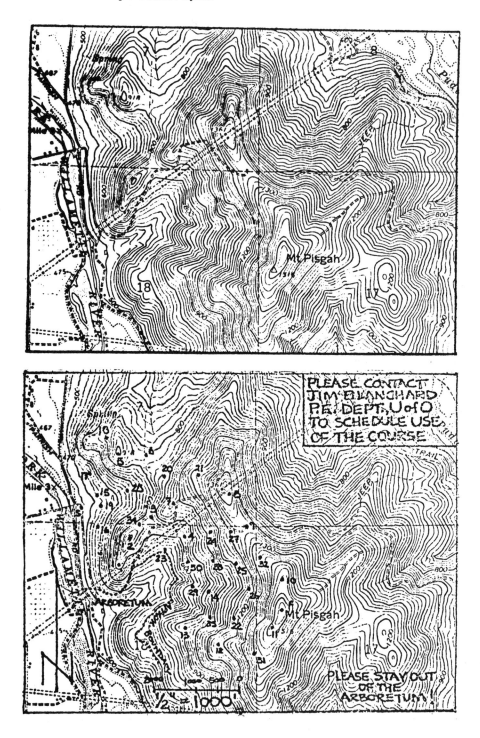

ROUTE													ALT.
A	S	15	5	6	20	21	8	9	32	10	F		G
B	S	16	1	2	4	24	27	32	10	F			H
C	S	19	28	3	7	21	8	27	25	26	F		E
D	S	15	28	20	7	24	33	25	32	F			F
E	S	16	34	3	4	30	29	14	26	11	F		C
F	S	19	3	2	23	30	24	25	10	F			D
G	S	34	23	4	30	14	22	12	31	11	F		A
H	S	17	28	7	24	33	14	22	11	F			B
I	S	17	18	5	20	3	4	33	25	26	F		J
J	S	1	23	29	13	12	22	31	11	F			I

ROUTE												

of course layout and geometry, and has the distance advantage of allowing only five staff people to assist the entire group through the first and thus most critical leg of the course. The two groups on the first leg can also offer some mutual aid. After the first point, the routes all separate, and the leaders have to rabbit around in pursuit of everyone.

Interesting variations on the course include not allowing compasses or night work. While the course can be run without maps by giving students pre-measured distances and bearings, this approach is not usually worth the effort and is not very realistic. Since the eighteen-inch-high wood posts are only visible, in some cases, from thirty feet or less, and since distances between points average about 800 feet, the course is probably just a bit harder than most "real" back-country navigation challenges. Simple trigonometric calculations show that the accuracy needed to find the points should allow you to hit or at least pass by close to a football field a mile away, if it were approximately broadside.

MAP-AND-COMPASS PRACTICE IN THE FIELD

Map-and-compass teaching in the field can be highly rewarding or incredibly frustrating. As mentioned earlier, the primary issue is the willingness and ability of the students to pay attention to the subject at hand. This will not occur if the student is cold, tired, or under stress. Who cares about compass use when the next piece of ski trail looks like the north face of the Eiger! If the student has to spend significant physical or psychological energy just surviving, little or no attention can be focused on "extraneous" learning. So don't set expectations too high unless the terrain, weather, and activity are well within the fitness and skill limits of the participants. Be patient, and expect some difficulties in transferring concepts from the classroom or the in-town practice course to the field. The vastness of the terrain and the "reality" of finding their way in an uncontrolled environment is unsettling for many people.

Rest stops, if they are unhurried and participants remain warm and comfortable, can provide opportunities for viewing the terrain

and comparing it to the map. A most valuable practice is to have every participant carefully review the last part of the hike, relating each detail to reality, then predicting the hike to the next rest stop and so forth. This is well worth the time and essential if they are to gain the ability to travel safely without the assistance of guides and teachers. Nothing beats sitting on top of a hill or ridge, looking out on terrain depicted on your map. Features can be related to the map and vice versa, and bearings measured, sighted, and plotted. Triangulation can also be practical.

One of the best ways to avoid the sheep syndrome is to assign a participant to the navigator's position at the head of the line, and to rotate the position at intervals of perhaps a mile or so. People tend to pay attention best if they are responsible, and if the regular staff allow the practice navigators to make errors, the rest of the participants will often be made sufficiently anxious to "back-seat drive."

Extreme care must be taken when letting individuals or small groups travel alone (without staff) to practice reaching destinations. This is a most valuable teaching method *if* safety issues are adequately dealt with. Usually, a staff person should "tail" each independent group or individual. If this cannot be safely done (it's tough unless snow cover or open terrain facilitates it), then the route must 1) be very short, 2) be surrounded by safe and unmistakable terrain barriers, 3) traverse terrain that is well within the skill limits and fitness of the participant, and 4) must be free of significant hazards. In addition, such independent participants must have adequate equipment and clothing and be given clear and concise directions as to what to do and how to survive a night should they become disabled or lost.

SUGGESTIONS AND GUIDELINES FOR SUPERVISING THE MT. PISGAH MAP-AND-COMPASS COURSE

The Mt. Pisgah (Buford Park) course consists of 32 numbered points, plus start and finish lines, located on approximately 700 acres of partially wooded hillside. Given careful attention to the concerns listed on the student handouts, up to ninety participants can practice in this area with minimal risks of injury or damage to the environment (provided the course is run only two or three times per term). Following the suggestions below should result in an optimal experience for both students and staff.

1. At the class meeting prior to the trip, distribute the Pisgah handout and request that students carefully read the directions, the warnings, and the clothing requirements for the outing. Also suggest methods of getting to Mt. Pisgah, including car pooling (but do not get directly involved in the pooling yourself!). Be sure to explain directions to Mt. Pisgah.

2. Assemble the following items to take to the site:

36 plasticized maps	2 felt pens
36 plasticized route cards	1 tape measure
	1 set of roll sheets
12+ compasses	2 first-aid belts
40 blank 3 x 5 cards	2 foam pads
6 clipboards	2 blankets
2 topo maps (Spfd., Quad)	1 tarp
	1 stokes litter
12 stakes (10 lettered A-J)	
12 wire wands	
2 rolls flagging	

3. Meet with the staff (ideally at least four or five people counting yourself) at 7:30 sharp at the starting point.

4. Put out the ten lettered stakes parallel to the fence and about 60-70 feet east of it consecutively at six-foot intervals.

5. Put the yellow flags (wire wands) on lines perpendicular to the line of stakes from "A" to "J" to help guide the formation of the waves of participants, if you choose to have all the waves form up simultaneously.

6. Just north of the end of the stake line, and perpendicular to it, place the two extra stakes 100 feet apart, with one stake near the fence. This gives a slightly slanted calibration line for pacing.

7. As soon as cars begin to arrive, assign one student to parking (keep cars well to the side of roadway and parked close together,

expecting perhaps thirty to forty of them), one student to roll keeping, and one student to keeping all other students on the west side of the steps over the fence (to save the grass and isolate the staff).

8. Review all plans with the staff.

9. If desired, plot and place a short (three-to-five point) practice course in the adjacent field area.

10. At the starting time (whatever the handout says, usually 8:30 a.m.), assemble the students below the steps. In this discussion you should:
    — Explain the overall procedure (briefly!);
    — Remind them to sign the roll;
    — Explain times for lunch at the top, and implore their cooperation!
    — Review the environmental concerns (as on the handout);
    — Review the hazards (as on the handout);
    — Remind them of the need for raingear, warm clothing, food, and water;
    — Emphasize staying in groups and checking in at lunch and at the end of the day;
    — Discuss the poison oak. Tour the pacing line and the practice course;
    — Direct those needing tour or practice courses to the proper place;
    — Give basic instructions for using maps and compasses to locate points (quick review);
    — Direct others to line up in groups of three with a watch and at least one compass by stakes "A" to "J." This will be "wave one."

11. At the stakes, have a staff person hand out one map, one route card, and one 3 x 5 card to each group.

12. Instruct each group to write the day in the upper left corner of the card, the wave number in the middle of the top, and the route ("A"-"J") in the top right corner. Have them sign their names on the lower portion of the card.

13. Check to be sure each group has a watch, but do not become directly involved in loaning or borrowing one, or directly ask a student to loan or borrow a watch (liability!).

14. Insofar as the compass supply allows, try to equip each group with at least two

compasses by loaning out the University ones. Loan the compass to an *individual* and note this on the 3 x 5 card.

15. Collect the 3 x 5 cards and arrange for a staff person to take them to the top for lunch.
16. Remind the groups to:
    — Stay together;
    — Arrive on top before _____ or later than _____;
    — Stay on the trail between points nineteen and fifteen (arboretum land);
    — Contact a staff person if they need assistance;
    — Move quickly away from points so that other groups will not have unfair advantages in locating these;
    — Cross fences with care (note that they are *not* limits of the course!).
17. Ask the groups to move away from the stakes, check their paces, and proceed from point "S" near the steps.
18. Begin assembling "Wave Two," and repeat steps 11-17. Allow at least fifteen minutes (twenty to twenty-five is ideal) between waves to avoid conflicts at the points.
19. Repeat, if necessary, for "Wave Three."
20. Dispatch staff, making sure that the north and south flanks and major center routes are covered, with one person assigned to be on top at least thirty minutes prior to the lunch deadline.
21. Follow the routes, giving advice as needed.
22. At lunch take roll by groups, using the 3 x 5 cards.
23. Review techniques for increasing accuracy in map reading and compass use, and discuss triangulation and methods of detecting, qualifying, and correcting for magnetic aberration and solar navigation.
24. Explain the procedure for descending, including how to determine the "alternate" route. (Emphasize practice in pure topo, pure compass, and combination of the two.)
25. Emphasize the need to check out, not before _____ or later than _____ .
26. Dispatch groups by waves, with at least fifteen minutes between waves.
27. Dispatch staff to follow groups fifteen minutes or so after each wave, being sure to cover all areas of the hill. Assign one staff person to be at point "S" with the

3 x 5 cards by the beginning of the check-out period defined in 25 above, to check out groups and collect maps, route cards, and compasses.
28. Police the lunch area for litter.
29. Be at the bottom by the final checkout time and hold all staff until *all* groups are in.
30. Remove all materials (except point S), police the area thoroughly, and depart.

MT. PISGAH MAP-AND-COMPASS OUTING AGENDA

08:30
Meet at Buford Park at Seavey Loop Road *(No later)*.
08:30-09:00
1. Make sure that you have your rain gear, extra clothes, pack, lunch and water (and watch, pencil, and compass, if possible).
2. Sign in on the roll sheet (indicate your vehicle license number if you brought a car).
3. Form a group of the size indicated by the instructor (usually two to four people).
4. Be sure at least one person in the group has a watch.
5. Obtain a clipboard, map, route card, blank 3 x 5 card, and (if needed) one or two compasses from the instructor(s).
6. You will then be assigned to a specific route. Stand, as a group, by the appropriate stake.
7. List, on the blank 3 x 5 card, your names and route number or letter.
8. Review the environmental and safety concerns on the other outing handout.
9. Carefully note the procedures and sugges-tions for following the route (to be given by the instructor[s]).
10. Be sure to ask the instructor(s) if you have any questions.
09:00-12:30
1. Follow your route according to the instructions.
2. Meet at the summit of Mt. Pisgah at 12:30.
12:30-13:15
Lunch
13:15-15:45
Mt. Pisgah Map-and-Compass Outing

Mt. Pisgah, located in Buford County Park, is an excellent area for map and compass practice. The park is located at the east end of Seavey Loop Road, just east of the Coast Fork of the Willamette River, five miles east of Eugene and two miles south of Springfield. The class meets at the park, not on campus. Students are responsible for their own transportation. Your careful attention to the following points will help us provide a worthwhile experience with minimal danger to yourself and to the environment.

Environmental Concerns.

1. Watch where you walk! Try to avoid unnecessary trampling of vegetation, and avoid single-file walking in meadow areas (a plant may survive one, but not three or four boots).
2. Don't harass the wildlife! If your course is going to spook the deer or cattle, compute and follow an offset line to go around them.
3. Absolutely no littering! (And please, if you see any litter, pick it up.)

Safety Concerns.

1. Poison Oak is *everywhere* on Mt. Pisgah. Learn to identify it, be extremely cautious all day, and don't drop your guard until *after* a soapy, cool shower and clothes laundering. Remember to clean your boots, too!
2. Rattlesnakes are not uncommon. Watch your step and don't put your hands or feet anywhere that a snake might hide. You are likely to see rattlesnakes — just give them plenty of room to escape. If bitten, don't panic! Stay put or move slowly, and seek assistance from the instructors.
3. Watch out for the barbed wire! Many routes cross old fence lines.
4. The weather may vary from very warm to quite wet and cold in a short time, and you will be out all day. All participants must have warm clothes (including a hat), raingear (head to toe), water, lunch, and a day pack. Take the time to regulate your body temperature; heat exhaustion and hypothermia, at least in their beginning stages, are real possibilities.
5. Stay with your group! *DO NOT* separate without the specific consent of the instructor(s), except to report an emergency.

6. Don't fail to sign out! Failure to do so will result in a search.

General Concerns.

1. Please pay careful attention to the instructors. It's hard to speak to a large group outdoors without wearing out your voice.
2. You will be assigned to a small group. Be sure to share responsibility for navigation to give everyone an equal chance to learn.
3. Note the *time* and the *place* of assemblies and *be on time*.

BIBLIOGRAPHY

Brower, David, Editor, *The Sierra Club Wilderness Handbook,* Ballantine Books, New York, 1971.

Disley, John, *Orienteering,* Stackpole Books, Harrisburg, Pennsylvania, 1967.

Hart, John, *Walking Softly in the Wilderness,* Sierra Club Books, San Francisco, California, 1977.

Kjellstrom, Bjorn, *Be Expert with Map and Compass,* Charles Scribner's Sons, New York, 4th edition, 1976.

Merrill, W.K., *Getting Out of Outdoor Trouble,* Stackpole Books, Harrisburg, Pennsylvania, 1965.

The Mountaineers, *Mountaineering the Freedom of the Hills,* The Mountaineers, Seattle, Washington, 1960.

Owendoff, Robert, *Better Ways of Pathfinding,* Stackpole Books, Harrisburg, Pennsylvania, 1964.

Province of British Columbia, *Outdoor Safety and Survival,* Information Branch, Ministry of Forests, Victoria, B.C., 1976.

Riley, Michael J., and Robert Cremer *Contemporary Books,* Inc., Chicago, 1979.

RAISING A CLIMBER IN AN IMPROVISED "ROPE BASKET"
Leaders conducting groups in rugged terrain should know how to carry out such rescues unless specialized rescue teams are immediately available. High-angle rescue can be complex and dangerous and should not be attempted without proper training.

CHAPTER 15

SEARCH AND RESCUE

Much of the excitement and value of outdoor pursuits stems from the uncertainty inherent in activity in an uncontrolled natural environment. No one wants to eliminate this uncertainty (and it is not an option), yet with it comes real risk to our well-being. Every year hundreds of people die while engaged in outdoor recreation, and many more survive everything from survival scenarios to minor cuts and bashes. One result of these unpleasantries can be search-and-rescue (SAR) missions, the formal or informal seeking or extrication of people in distress. People get themselves into all sorts of trouble outdoors. They fall into crevasses or get stuck on rock faces, they wrap their watercraft around midstream boulders, and most of all they get lost. The possibilities and permutations are endless.

When emergencies occur in a group with a designated leader, he or she is almost always expected to save the day. While a host of legal and moral factors may modify the formal responsibility of a leader in a given situation, in practice the leader usually has the greatest amount of experience and is expected to know what to do. Unless clear and specific agreements to the contrary have been reached with the participants, the leader(s) of an outing should expect to bear full accountability for resolution of emergencies.

Leaders should understand that good planning and effective field leadership are essential to the conduct of a reasonably safe outing and that both depend on awareness and conscientious action. Prevention is always best, and a good planning process can reduce the chance of major mismatches of terrain, weather, activities, and people. Qualified leaders, using state-of-the-art techniques and maintaining high standards in terms of equipment and clothing, can keep the real risks extremely low. Nevertheless, mishaps will occur and this must be considered in the planning process.

Planners need to consider all reasonably foreseeable problems, and see to it that reasonable alternatives or remedies are available. Unexpected changes of weather or mobility might necessitate a change in route or a need for escape to civilization. Any number of events might cause a group to be delayed significantly, and this requires extra food or water. Injuries or accidents might require technical apparatus or skills in order to gain access to, extricate, and transport the victim. Thus planners need to be sure that 1) alternative routes, known as "escape routes," exist and are known to the field leaders of any land- or water-based outing away from civilization; 2) enough supplies of water, food, gear, and clothing are carried by the group to meet any reasonably foreseeable need, and 3) that the group has sufficient expertise on search-and-rescue techniques appropriate to the activity and site.

Field leaders shouldn't expect, or be expected to, avoid all problems, but they should maintain the options, skills, and equipment necessary to resolve any reasonably foreseeable emergency situation. Lack of foresight or unsupported optimism are no excuse, morally or legally, for allowing an outing to proceed without adequate preparation for emergencies.

"Contingency planning" is no less important than any other aspect of the planning process. Some suggestions for gear and clothing are given in the section on specific activities. The "group gear" portions of these lists contain items included primarily for their value in the event of an emergency.

One more point needs to be made before getting into the nitty-gritty of SAR strategies and tactics. Even though the leader may at the bottom line have to orchestrate group response to an emergency, participants should continue to bear some responsibility. Every effort should be made by the leader to explain clearly the risks and specific hazards of the activity as well as what is being done to control risks or provide options in the event of an accident. Participants deserve to know what they are getting into, need this information to be able to respond appropriately when at other times they are not accompanied by a leader, and should be expected to maintain some significant portion of the duty for their own well-being. Besides, there is no better defense against unforeseen happenings than an alert, informed group.

What happens when something goes wrong? Let's limit our concerns here to situations involving lost persons or the problem of access, extrication, and transport. First aid has been dealt with in another section.

In town, it's a whole lot easier. In most urban areas a phone call brings a quick response to virtually any emergency, thanks to nearly instantaneous communication and high-speed transportation systems. Out of town, response time elongates in proportion to distance all the way to the end of the road, then takes a flying leap upwards. Any emergency more than, at most, about a half mile away from a road is usually considered to be beyond the reach of conventional emergency service personnel. Their footwear, clothing, equipment, and sometimes fitness simply aren't compatible with back-country travel. Snow, steep terrain, wild water, or severe weather can further limit the range of effectiveness of conventional fire departments, police, and ambulance services.

Coverage of areas beyond the road heads is typically the responsibility of some government agency. In the United States, the legal burden for search-and-rescue operations generally falls to the sheriff of the county in which the incident occurs. Every country has its own hierarchy, however, and it is important that leaders know who is in charge and how to contact this agency or individual. The cost of services varies widely depending on the jurisdiction. In some cases the individual may be held liable for all of the cost of an SAR mission, and in others the cost is minimal or there is no charge at all. There is a good deal of difference between the various countries of the world, and in many, like the United States, the situation varies from region to region and is complex and constantly changing. SAR liability insurance is available in Europe and elsewhere. In any case it's always worth asking about in advance since the answer could affect the manner in which the leader chooses to resolve an emergency.

There is a great deal of variability in the quality of assistance one can expect from SAR groups, depending on where you are. Just about the only thing one *can* count on is that a call for help will eventually bring someone to the scene. How much this improves the situation is another story. Quality SAR response is very, very costly. Be quality response we mean prompt response by enough properly qualified and equipped personnel to maximize the chance of finding, gaining access to, extricating, or transporting the victim to safety. A top-notch SAR team supported by aircraft and a sophisticated communication system is a luxury enjoyed by very few places on earth. Switzerland is one such example, where they can rightfully claim a fifteen-minute response time to any point in the country if the weather cooperates. This sort of assistance doesn't exist anywhere else outside of the movies. Only a few places come close, including some popular coastal and Alpine regions of the Soviet Union, Western Europe, the United States, Australia, New Zealand, and Japan.

Leaders should find out just what sort of outside assistance is available in the event of need, and do so early in the planning phase. The quality of SAR services is an important factor in determining routes and activities. Any group has to be capable of at least stabilizing an accident scene, and both groups and *individuals* should always be prepared to survive for an unplanned night or two, even when quality SAR services are available. The reasons for this should be obvious: theoretical response times don't consider the time it takes to get to a telephone or radio, delays caused by weather, and the often considerable time required for searches, rescues, and transportation of victims. If efficient SAR services are available, then the group itself will have to assume greater portions or even all of the responsibility for all aspects of SAR, including carrying any disabled people to the road head.

One might anticipate differences in services between two separate countries, yet be surprised by differences across county, state, provincial, or other divisional lines within one country. The fact is that great contrasts may exist. For example, in the Oregon Cascades the county lines run along the crest of the range. If an accident occurs, the quality of the response has much to do with what county the accident occurs in. Here the western counties with big populations, relatively high incomes, and a lot of outdoor-recreation activity can and must maintain substantial SAR capabilities. The eastern counties with smaller populations and budgets are in no position to maintain equivalent resources. Mutual-aid agreements help, but the service still suffers. Similar disparities exist elsewhere in the United States and throughout the world. In many places SAR services are all but non-existent.

There are two general scenarios in SAR. Let's work through a couple of examples before getting into specific strategies and tactics. The two typical cases are 1) help from the outside is solicited and 2) the operation is carried out by members of the group, possibly with some assistance by passersby. The purpose of these examples is to illustrate the amount of time it takes to resolve a typical SAR situation, and to point out certain advantages of self-help over the use of outside help.

We'll use as an example a minor climbing accident, wherein the victim will have to be carried to the road. Let's assume that the accident occurs at 75,000 feet only a mile above a major trail, and that the terrain between the accident site and the trail is moderately steep and partly snow covered, but doesn't require any special skills to traverse. Let's further assume that it's five miles to the trailhead on an easy downhill grade, an hour's drive to a telephone, and another hour's drive to town and hospital. The victim's two climbing partners are with the victim, who appears to have a fractured lower leg. The climbers were smart enough to carry a foam pad, sleeping bag, tarp, stove, and extra food and water with them, so they are capable of huddling through at least one night if need be. The weather appears to be fairly stable.

Note that the scenario we've depicted isn't at all extreme. It's not at all uncommon for hikers, hunters, fishermen, skiers, or climbers to spend a good portion of their outing time at least this far from the road. We'll look first at the options of calling for help, and see how this might go. We'll be optimistic as to the times required at each stage, except that we won't assume the help of helicopters. Why? Helicopters are wonderful tools, and although every attempt is made to use them, many things can get in the way. They cannot be taken for granted, as we'll explain later.

Let's assume that the injury occurs at about 2 p.m., when our victim takes a short but fast slide down an unexpected slick little snowpatch and into a rock. The process of assessing and treating the injury, then getting the victim into a sheltered and reasonably comfortable place will take at least half an hour. It will usually take at least another few minutes to decide on the best course of action, which we are assuming in this case to be for one person to stay with the victim, and one to go for help. This isn't ideal;

it would be much better to have two people stay with the victim to insure continual observation and assist in nursing and camp chores, and for safety it would be better for two to go for help. Nevertheless, if it's decided that help is needed, little recourse is available. Signalling might be effective, but the best result would probably be to catch the attention of others elsewhere on the mountain, and waiting for more manpower might delay the call for help for hours.

Since the party was small enough to carry survival gear, and the weather and route out aren't likely to present problems, it's probably best to send one person out. First, however, a note should be written to be sure that all important details are communicated to the rescue group. The note should include all the information that the rescue group will need to do an efficient job. Think about what you would want to know if called upon in town to go rescue a person on a mountain! Essential data would include a description of the victim (name, age, sex, approximate height and weight, address, and names of physicians and relatives or contact persons. Police agencies also sometimes appreciate a driver's license number from which they can access more information on the individual), the nature of the injuries (include the signs and symptoms as well as your opinion, and be sure to note the time the incident occurred and any changes in signs or symptoms), treatments administered (what, when, and with what response), others on the scene (names, affiliations and qualifications in subjects like first aid and SAR), available gear and equipment (can the party survive the night?), and a very specific and detailed account of the location (*exact* location by reference to the map and local features, ground cover, and terrain) and the weather (exactly what's happening and what you predict). It is also important to note any changes that might occur in the location of the victim if the party is larger and might attempt to move. In addition, if there is any chance of using a helicopter, possible landing sites should be carefully described.

All of this will take a while to write down, yet the time is usually well spent. Taking a few extra minutes to make sure of locations and note the other details suggested above can save hours at the other end of the SAR mission. By now it will be at least 3 p.m. The person going

for help will need at least two and a half hours to get to the trailhead, especially since time must be taken to mark the cross-country portion of the route out. Care and caution are essential here; this is not the time to run madly down the trail!

By about 5:30 p.m., the messenger should be at the trailhead, having, we hope, remembered to bring along the car keys. An hour of driving — safely — is required to get to the phone, so at about 6:30 p.m. the SAR agency is finally contacted. If the person taking the call is efficient, the messenger will be pumped for all manner of details, even beyond the limits of the notes made on the hill. Usually the messenger will also be asked to stay at the phone or at an agreed-upon contact point until someone can meet him or her. What happens now depends upon the structure and resources of the agency and upon the availability of personnel. Typically, since we are assuming a ground operation here (and it's getting close to dark anyway, so we might as well), it will take at least an hour to organize a quick response team. This will consist of either volunteers or professional rescue workers equipped with basic first-aid equipment and radios. The party is usually small and its purpose is to get in to the accident scene as quickly as possible, to locate and stabilize the victim, and to provide by radio any information needed to fine tune the major effort to follow.

If all goes well in this case, the quick-response people should be heading out of town by 7:30 p.m. or so for the two-hour drive to the trailhead. By 9:30 they should be there, and by 10 p.m., in the company of one very tired messenger, they should head back up the hill. Six miles of uphill travel under heavy loads, at a time when the body was all ready to hit the sack, is not easy and may not be very fast. The mile of off-trail travel may be tedious or nearly impossible depending upon how well the route was marked and the memory of the messenger. Five hours may seem like a long time, but experience has shown the need to allow at least that much. This means that it will be 3 a.m. or so when the victim and companions are reached.

Meanwhile, back in town, a large party may have been organized that will arrive at the site perhaps two hours later. We'll be optimistic and assume this here, although in common practice this large party is sometimes withheld until first light in the morning. An even larger back-up and transportation group will usually bring with them an array of equipment, ranging from medical supplies to litters and technical hardware, to facilitate moving the victim. This group may consist of members of "search-and-support" groups, "technical rescue teams," or both, depending on the anticipated mission needs. By about 5 a.m., all of the help has arrived, and by perhaps 6 a.m., the no-doubt tired rescuers might begin the six-mile carry out. On the average this should take about seven hours, though it can vary a lot either way, depending on the type of stretcher, the trail characteristics, amount of snow, and strength and number of rescuers. By about 1 p.m., then, the victim should be at the trailhead, and in another two hours, at 3 p.m., in the hospital.

Compare that scenario to what we've come to expect in town! Twenty-five hours is a long time, and sometimes that length of time can seriously affect the prognosis in injuries. What if the group hadn't had the basic equipment needed to survive a night out? What if the weather had been worse? It's also worth considering the costs of the rescue, not just in terms of possibly having to pay the bill (you *may* have to pay, and costs of $10,000 or more aren't uncommon) but also in terms of costs to society and to the rescuers themselves. If the victim doesn't pay the bill, taxpayers have to. Some rescuers are professionals; it's part of the job. Most mountain search-and-rescue personnel are volunteers, however, and a mission can cost heavily in terms of time lost from work and wear and tear on equipment.

Perhaps most important is the risk factor. Rescues can be hazardous. It's not possible to move parties of people into back-country terrains in a hurry, often at night or in foul weather, without risk. Every year some rescuers die in attempts to locate or rescue people in the outdoors. But rescuers don't complain this necessary cost must be paid if service is to be rendered, and every effort is made to be as safe as possible. Those who would call for help need to consider these matters, though, and not take a call for SAR assistance as lightly as one might take a call for assistance in town. At the same time, don't hesitate to call if help is truly needed, and don't delay calling if doing so might only make things worse in the long run.

SAR teams are there to help, and they want to help — just keep in mind the cost.

In some cases there may be an alternative to calling for help. It may be possible for a group to evacuate the injured party using only its own resources. Again, let's assume an injury at 2 p.m. among a group of five or more members. If party members know enough about first aid to assess the injury accurately, stabilize it effectively, and predict its response to transportation stresses, and if party members know how to construct or devise a means of transporting the victim, then movement without outside aid might be possible. Any improvised transportation system is probably going to be a lot harder on the victim than a professional litter, especially since the victim's splint will be improvised and there will be few carriers. Consider, too, that going only part way and running out of energy or being otherwise stopped could be worse yet.

Nevertheless, the advantages may outweigh the disadvantages. Getting a top-quality improvised splint on the victim and constructing a good, comfortable sturdy litter can take a full two hours. Maybe instead a rope-seat "piggyback" could be used, or one of the two-man carriers could be improved by ice axes or poles. In any case let's allow two hours to get ready to move. Under these conditions, carrying the victim out could easily take twelve hours, and even that figure might be low unless a bit of help was obtained from others in the area. This approach, however, gets the victim to the trailhead at 4 a.m. and to the hospital at 6 a.m., nine hours ahead of the outside-help alternative. The advantages are many: 1) the group stays together, a real psychological boon; 2) the group gets off the mountain quickly, a possibly lifesaving move if the group wasn't prepared to survive the night or if foul weather hit; 3) group members learn a lot; and 4) everyone feels good — it's a good feeling to do something on your own.

Leaders of organized groups are in a slightly different position than members or leaders of private parties, mainly because of fear of liability. For them the advantages of self rescue are many, yet the risk to the victim may be somewhat higher. Barring overriding concerns over group survival or need for haste in getting the victim to a hospital, the very safest course may be to call for assistance. In real life the number of possibilities and variables is enormous, and the decision will always be a judgment call. The more the leader knows and has experienced in the realm of first aid and SAR, the better that decision will be.

It was mentioned earlier that helicopters, while potentially valuable, often can't be used. This is contrary to popular notions about SAR operations, which probably stem from film or television productions in which helicopters invariably play a major role. When they can be employed, helicopters are a tremendous aid, saving rescuers or searchers a lot of work and making the evacuation a lot faster and more pleasant for the victim. But the drawbacks include:

1. A helicopter capable of doing the work must be available. Not all of them, in fact relatively few, can carry significant loads at higher elevations and fly safely in the mountains. At lower elevations and in less rugged terrain, more options exist.
2. Qualified pilots who are willing to undertake the risk are not easy to find. Helicopter rescue work can be extremely hazardous and requires exceptional skill.
3. Fuel supplies and maintenance for the helicopter must be obtained if the mission is prolonged.
4. Flying conditions must be safe. Visibility, amount and type of precipitation, air temperature, air pressure, and wind velocity all have to be within the limits of the aircraft.
5. A safe landing site near the scene, or winch capability, is usually required unless the helicopter is being used only for observation or communication.
6. In many areas permission has to be obtained from government agencies before using and/ or landing aircraft. Policies vary widely but in many cases disallow air support. In the United States, for example, there are strict policies regarding the use of helicopters in wilderness areas. Here it is often impossible to use them unless the emergency is truly life-threatening.
7. Someone has to pay for the helicopter. This cost is sometimes absorbed by military units or government-funded emergency services, so the burden is spread out among taxpayers. In other cases, individuals may have to pay

for the rescue helicopter and pilot, which can be very costly. Typical rates range from $200 to $1200 or more per hour for the kinds of helicopters commonly used in rescue work.

All told, helicopter assistance is often unavailable. In most cases, SAR agencies begin and maintain a ground-based operation regardless of whether or not a helicopter may be employed, knowing that the chopper could be delayed or cancelled for any of the reasons listed above. In addition, there is always the possibility of an accident or mechanical failure. Leaders should nevertheless be prepared to work with helicopters, which means learning basic rules for entering and exiting and understanding the general specifications of landing sites.

Most of the time, however, the leader will have to assume ground-based assistance only, and will have to make strategy choices on that basis. One of the major decisions to be made is whether or not to call for outside help. As the earlier illustration pointed out, there are a number of things to consider before making this verdict. Intermediate solutions may be possible and desirable, like sending out for help and also saving emergency service personnel a lot of work by having the group begin the transportation or search process. This is a common practice, though it has also caused a number of frustrating situations where rescuers and the distressed party passed in the night, each laboring for many needless extra hours due to poor communication, or where well-meaning searchers became lost themselves.

The most important thing a leader can do in any emergency is maintain control of the group so that any group actions do not further aggravate the situation. In the event of any emergency, from the point of first awareness, the leader should fight to maintain internal calm and perspective on the situation, resisting the urge to respond emotionally or irrationally. Stabilization of the accident scene and concern for the welfare of uninvolved people are both essential. In back-country settings it is vital to avoid additional victims or missing people. Manpower is always in short supply in these cases, and the last thing needed is one less helper and one more victim.

Often the very first task of the leader has to be directed toward the unaffected part of the group. Whether hiking or running a river, the order to stop or return to the scene of the incident must be conveyed quickly and effectively unless previously established plans will automatically return the other party members to the scene in time to help. In the case of situations requiring access, extrication, and improvisations of transportation, urgent priorities might include getting someone safely to the victim to provide first aid and stabilization and getting the group assembled, organized, and protected. If a person is missing, group control is just as important yet often much more difficult. The most effective strategy in a search depends on many variables, including the likely behavior of the missing person, the urgency based on the victim's projected survivability, the terrain, and the number of searchers available. For victims lost in the back country, current theory and practice favor the earliest possible use of confinement and of trail, road, and likely route and site searches. (Confinement refers to the blocking or continual observation of every possible way out of an area.)

In practice, this usually has to be limited to key points on roads, trails and possibly ridges and valleys. Searching means sending individuals or pairs of searchers along every man-made or natural route within the area. Both techniques are valuable, and they are usually used simultaneously if enough manpower is available. However, the leader trying to organize a search for a missing participant has to be extremely careful in using these methods since they involve loss of contact with the searchers. No one should be dispatched unless the leader is absolutely sure that the individuals know their routes and instructions. In every case, it's essential that the leader establish cut-off times for returns to some fixed and well-known assembly point. Too often, searchers leave with no fixed time of return, so that it becomes impossible to control the operation effectively.

Leaders may have to contend with any number of situations requiring skills in searching, extrication, or transportation. Each type of outdoor activity has its own special set of potential problems and solutions. Leaders have an obligation to themselves and their clients or students to know and to be able to employ effective SAR methods. There are many excellent books available giving detailed information about these methods for virtually every specialty in the realm of outdoor pursuits. These texts provide a valuable foundation of knowledge and reference, yet cannot be substituted for practice. There is no reasonable alternative to hands-on experience in rescue techniques and search tactics.

While an ability to carry out self-rescue is essential, leaders also need to understand the specific capabilities of the agencies upon which they may have to call, and must know how to contact these agencies. It also helps a lot, should a real need arise, to have had some personal contact with those who might come to your aid. This isn't always practical or possible, but put yourself in the shoes of the rescuer or searcher and the value becomes clear. The organization and executions of an effective SAR operation depend in large part on the information the organizers have about the emergency situation. This information is almost never complete and is always subject to question and interpretation. The more the organizers know about the people at the scene, the better they can interpret and predict from the information on hand.

SEARCH-AND-RESCUE INFORMATION FORM

Please fill out both sides of this form *clearly and completely,* and give the form to the authorities responsible for search and rescue (this is usually the County Sheriff). If more than one person is lost or injured, attach a separate sheet with all subject data. BE SPECIFIC.

SUMMARY.

Date: _____ Day: _____ Person Reporting: _____

Time of Incident: _____ AM PM Time of Report: _____ AM PM Address & Phone of above: _____

If Organized Group, give Name of Organization: _____ City, State: _____

Name of Leader(s): _____ Trip or Course Title: _____

Agency Contact Person (name): _____ Phone(s): _____

What Happened? (Describe *incident* in detail. Victim data section follows.)

_____

_____

_____

_____

_____

What Assistance Do You Need?   (Personnel, equipment)

_____

_____

What Are Your Plans? (What *exactly* are your plans?)_____

_____

_____

What Personnel Are on Site? (Names, experience, associations) (Attach separate list if necessary.)

_____

_____

What Equipment Is on site? (Shelter, sleeping bags, lights, food and water, stoves, fuel, etc., with *quantities)*

_____

_____

If a Helicopter Might Be Used, give: best landing sites (Detailed location, dimensions and obstructions, distance to victim).

_____

_____

LOCATION. A precise location is extremely important. Describe location of all significant points by as many methods as possible.

Location of Trailhead (Name of trail, number of trail, road name and number, etc.)

_____

Location of Victim or Party (Use legal description *and* relationship to major features.)

_____

_____

Where Will You Meet Search-and-Rescue Team? (and *when*. How long will you wait, and then what will you do?)

_____

_____

To Find You, What Should Searchers Look For? (Colors, markings, signals at meeting point)

_____

_____

WEATHER. This information will help search-and-rescue personnel conduct an efficient operation.

Current Temperature (estimate degrees F.): _____, windspeed: _____ steady or gusty: _____

Wind Direction (wind is out of the . . .): _____ Visibility (specify feet or   miles): _____

Clouds, Fog (describe): _____ Precipitation (amount, type): _____

Describe Snow Cover, if any: _____

Weather Summary, Past Day (include max/min temp.): _____

_____

Weather You Predict, Next Day: _____

_____

INJURED OR LOST SUBJECT DATA. (Name: _____ Age: _____ Sex: _____

Address: _____ Phone(s): _____

Height: _____ Weight: _____ Hair: _____ Eyes: _____

Driver's License Number: _____ State: _____

Person to Contact: _____ Relationship: _____

Address of Above: _____ Phone(s): _____

Alternate Person to Contact: _____ Relationship: _____

Address of Above: _____ Phone(s): _____

IF LOST, GIVE: Footwear type (Describe shoes, boots, skis, snowshoes, etc., including size & tread pattern.):

_____

Coats & Rainwear (Color, size, type, brand): _____

Pants (as above): _____ Hats (as above): _____

All Other Gear (As above for all equipment, shelter, clothing; be complete & include colors):

_____

_____

Is Subject Alone or in a Group? (Explain): _____

Place Last Seen (Exactly): _____

Time Last Seen (Exactly): _____ AM PM Day & Date: _____

Direction of Travel (And trail, road, etc.): _____

Subject's Plans at Last Contact: _____

_____

Physical Condition of Subject: _____

IF INJURED, GIVE:

Time of Injury: _____ AM PM Time of Report: _____ AM PM

Can Victim Walk Safely? _____ Ride Sitting Up? _____

Nature of Injuries (Give full details of *all* signs and symptoms.): _____

_____

_____

Treatment Given (When?): _____

_____

A LONG-DISTANCE SKI TOUR ACROSS THE OREGON CASCADES
Combining ski touring and backpacking can allow access to magnificent terrain normally reached only during the summer months.

CHAPTER 16

STEP-BY-STEP PLANNING

The very first step in planning is the initial idea. Most ventures begin with a relatively simple notion, usually in response to some construed need. "Let's see if we can get the group out backpacking one of these days," or "maybe people would sign up for a canoe lesson!" are typical beginnings. However, there are at least three things to be done before committing lots of time and energy to the plan.

First, rough out the goals and objectives of the outing to clarify just what sort of experience is intended. This doesn't need to involve formal documentation at this stage, though in many institutional settings it will be necessary later in the organizational process.

Second, with the intent of the outing clearly in mind, take a good look around the community to see if similar programs are being offered. There are several reasons for this: 1) it may save a lot of time and expense if your efforts can be combined with the other program, or if your participants simply enroll in the other program. At the very least there may be much to learn from those who have already developed one. 2) If two programs are to be developed, this is the time to check out potential conflicts over the use of land or water resources, rentals, lodging, and potential staff. 3) Viewed positively, it is common courtesy to locate and contact those who have already invested time and energy in developing similar programs, and 4) viewed a bit selfishly, it is simply good politics to do so. Private and public sector organizations struggling to fill their rosters may not appreciate more competition. A friendly contact can usually at least minimize the problem.

Finally, see whether or not the outing is in fact feasible. Outings can be thought of as consisting of several key elements and can be schematically displayed as follows: participants — money — transportation — clothing and equipment — lodging or shelter if needed — participant preparation — leadership skills and knowledge — resource-owner or manager permission — land or water resources. (All or most of these connecting elements also involve money, which for clarity we will consider as an additional element.)

The trip simply isn't possible unless some way can be found to bring the participants, properly clothed, equipped, and skilled or lead, to an appropriate resource. In most institutions there is yet another critical element — authorization. Generally speaking, authorization, the "go ahead" from the powers that be, is much more likely to be forthcoming if the basic feasibility of the outing is determined in advance, and if a clear rationale can be given for it. Thus whatever the purpose of the outing, it should be clearly thought out, with supporting arguments in mind. The decision to go ahead will probably be based on some form of cost/benefit analysis. The greater the apparent benefits, the greater the chance of approval of the program so long as costs remain within the norms and potentials of the institution. Too often, potentially valuable experiences are "shot down" due to insufficient management awareness of the virtues of outdoor activities. Managers may not be or even know active participants in outdoor pursuits, and may see such activities as unreasonably costly and hazardous. So don't fail to couple your request and feasibility assessment with a substantial dose of praise for the attributes of the program. Ideally you want the support and encouragement, not just the passive nod, of the institution.

Is the resource suitable for the activity in mind? Is it accessible? Access to an area usually depends upon at least four factors: 1) distance to the site, 2) condition of access roads, 3) condition of trails or routes, and 4) permission of the land manager or owner. It is not at all uncommon to find that the site isn't accessible due to snow, blocked roads, or problems in obtaining permission to use the site. The best and easiest way to clarify these issues is to simply call the managing agency or the landowner and discuss the possibilities directly. If this contact provides reasonable assurance of

clear access and site suitability, the next step should be to locate 1) good maps (topographic and current, and with a scale of at least 1:62,500 or 1:50,000 if possible) and 2) a person thoroughly familiar with the area.

While the managing agency or owner can usually be located easily in the phone book, finding a person who knows a particular site can be more of a challenge. It may well be that the instigator of the idea knows the area well. Managing agencies, land owners, local sporting goods shops, outing clubs, or parks and recreation districts may also be able to help. Colleges and universities usually have outdoor programs or classes, and can often provide access to information, maps, and expertise. Ideally, you want to find someone who knows the site well no matter what time of year you want to use it, and who also understands what it is you want to do. A person who has never led a group similar to yours may not be very useful in assessing the appropriateness of the site. In case the person you find knows the site but isn't familiar with either the participants or the activity, then it will be essential to also find someone who is.

Now it's time to sit down at a table with the maps and experts on hand and rough out a plan. Sketch out some possible routes and work through some time sequences in sufficient detail to convince yourself that the general idea is feasible. Decide on trailheads, alternate and escape routes, vehicle shuttles, group sizes, and leadership requirements, as well as desired routes and activities. With this information in hand, it is possible to assess other basic needs like transportation, clothing, equipment, leadership, and training. Once these are established compute the total cost of the program.

There are many possible ways of transporting participants, though usually only a few practical options available to a given program. The pros and cons of various systems have been discussed in the section on transportation. All that is necessary at this stage is to find out whether or not transportation is available and to estimate the costs. Knowing the approximate group size and intended trailheads and shuttle distances provides a starting point for cost estimates, but don't forget to allow some margin for error, including enough leeway in the budget for unexpected mileage and less-than-efficient vehicle use. (Filling 80% of the seats is often the best one can expect.) In cases where institutional vans or buses are to be taken, reservations must be made weeks or months in advance, so be sure to confirm them later. Once the route and the activity are established, lodging needs can be determined and costs and reservations obtained quite easily.

A complete individual and group clothing and equipment list should also be generated. The spectrum of possible gear requirements is very wide, from shorts and a sack lunch for a picnic at the beach to nearly a hundred items for a winter high Alpine adventure. It is always best to separate absolute requirements from options when making these lists. Look carefully at the minimum needed and be sure everything is 1) adequate to protect individuals lost alone and 2) adequate to protect the group in case of emergency in any reasonably foreseeable weather. When the list is completed, the important but difficult task of determining if all of the gear can be obtained begins. Do not compromise on basic safety items; list essentials separately from the "nice but not absolutely vital" ones. Ask yourself, do the participants have the essentials? Does the institution have them? If not, can they be obtained on time? What will the cost be, and will the items be purchased by individuals or by the institution? Are low-budget/army-surplus, used or rental options available? Can your institution borrow from another?

Sometimes participants can make their own gear, adding to the value of the program while cutting costs. Often the money needed for buying or renting appropriate clothing and equipment is simply too great! If so, go back to the drawing board to see if costs can be cut by simplifying the activity or perhaps by moving to a site requiring less gear. For example, the chosen route may reach elevations that demand stout boots and heavy sleeping bags, while a much lower route in the same area may be safely traversed in tennis shoes and sleeping done in inexpensive "car-camper"-style sleeping bags.

Given the purpose of the outing, the number of participants, the route, and the intended activities, what prior knowledge or skills should the participants have? There are at least three areas of concern here: 1) participant and staff safety, 2) the ability of participants to enjoy the activity and to approximate program objectives, and 3) environmental impact; the safety of the resource itself. Some activities require little or no skills or knowledge beyond the ordinary, others very extensive safety training prior to participation. The amount of necessary basic training is determined by the inherent characteristics of the activity, the site and potential weather, the amount and type of equipment to be used, and the program goals and objectives, all moderated by funds and time. As with equipment, it is best to specify minimum pre-activity training and preparation requirements separately from extras so that minimal costs can be calculated. Here, of course, the charge may be measured both in time (for staff and participants) and instruction (staff, facilities, and equipment).

The most problematical and costly item on any outing is leadership. The number of required leaders depends upon age, skill, and number of participants, the nature of the activity, and the environment in which the activity will take place. Commonly accepted minimal requirements vary for from one leader for every twelve to fourteen adults on short, easy close-to-the-road summer hikes, to one leader for every two or three students in advanced mountaineering classes. For example, a typical summer three-day backpacking outing with a dozen teenagers would require at least one leader and one assistant for an on-site 1:6 ratio. On wilderness or back-country outings on land or water, both common sense and common practice dictate no fewer than two leaders with each independent field group. Suggested qualifications for leaders are given in the appendix at the end of this book. Its essential concern is to find out if enough qualified leaders are available for the program.

At this point an estimate of the total cost can be calculated by adding the prices of permits, rental fees, or other charges for accessing the resource lands; transportation; lodging, if needed; clothing and equipment; pre-trip training or meetings; leadership; and other fees. In most cases the minimum number of participants needed to justify a program is a compromise between program ideals and economic realities. Vehicle capacities, shelter or lodging space, and instructor ratios usually result in a step sequence, where actual expenses move up in increments as additional vehicles, shelters, or instructors are added. The result is fluctuation in the real cost of the outing per participant that may, for example, drop with each additional person seated in a van until the van is full, then rise dramatically as the next person is added, requiring a second vehicle.

One more element remains — the participants. The best-planned outing can fail due to lack of participation since people are not much easier to predict than the weather. All too often a lot of time and energy is put into developing what seems like a fantastic outing or class, only to have three people sign up and two arrive at the meeting point. There is no sense in continuing to develop a program or even submit it for the approval of one's employer unless enough people justify its existence. This may be any number, but let us assume that in this case we will need twelve participants to sustain the time and effort required to develop and operate the program. Let's also assume that twelve participants are enough to either cover the cost of the program or to justify institutional costs. Experience has shown that getting twelve people to show up for any voluntary activity usually means that at least fourteen or fifteen must sign up. A decrease in the rate of attrition can sometimes be obtained if the organizer has some leverage (like grades or non-refundable deposits), yet even then some inevitably drop out due to illness or unavoidable time conflicts. Since outdoor activities are often pursued with friends or relatives, the loss of one person not uncommonly results in the loss of several others as well. Now look carefully at the event in terms of the appeal you envision for participants. It is certainly not too late at this point to make adjustments as needed so that timing, duration, and resultant costs look as appealing as possible. The best advice here, as stated above, is to be very conservative in estimating the actual participant tally.

As elaborated on here, the entire initial phase of planning may seem quite ponderous yet can usually be completed in a few hours. The length of time needed depends a lot on the experience of the planners and also on luck in making

contact with resource managers and others with needed information.

If the program has to be approved at some higher level, then the plans need to be scraped off the table and arranged in some convincing form. Assuming approval, it is time to start promoting the outing!

Staffing and Final Planning. It's time now to begin to pull all of the loose ends together. The most important and difficult task is hiring the staff. This should be the first item attended to since major modifications in the program may be necessary due to the qualifications and/or availability of leaders. The primary task is, of course, to determine minimal qualifications for the job. Generally this will include expertise, leadership experience, first-aid and other relevant skills, and familiarity with the area and activity coupled with maturity, responsibility, and an agreeable personality. In the appendix we provide some specific additional guidelines for a number of popular activities. Hiring is never an easy task, even for the simplest of tasks, and hiring outdoor-pursuit leaders is especially difficult since the chosen individual must be responsible for participant welfare in potentially hazardous and remote settings well beyond the limits of direct supervision and control by management. The choice is critical yet the task is extremely complex, and the situation is often compounded by a lack of expertise in the activity among managers responsible for hiring. For this reason we have included in Chapter 7 sample questions and guidelines for assessing the qualifications of potential leaders.

Finding applicants is relatively easy in a large urban area; a few phone calls can usually locate a number of them. Good places to start are also local city and county parks-and-recreation districts and/or departments, college and university outdoor-program/physical education departments, and stores selling the equipment used in the activity. Even private guides and outfitters often provide direct service or help locate candidates. In areas with fewer resources of this type, it may be necessary to advertise, in which case it is probably best to limit the description of the task to the bare essentials (for example, "experienced backpacking instructor needed for one weekend outing"). This will likely inspire a few calls from some who can't work on the preferred weekend, but if a shortage of potential candidates is a problem, these same people may become accessible by changing the outing dates.

Ideally, candidates should be reviewed using an application form and references. But references should be looked at skeptically, and personal discussions about them are almost almost always best. Be careful about recommendations from past students or participants in the leader's outings; participants, especially beginners, may have little way of knowing how good a job was done. This review should be followed by interviews with the best of those who evidently meet all of the preliminary qualifications.

Still speaking ideally, the best of the interviewed candidates should then be observed actually working in the field, perhaps as assistant leaders on a short outing similar to the one for which they will be responsible. The reason for such a thorough assessment process should be clear; while the objective qualifications of a leader can be measured at least tolerably well on paper, subjective factors such as maturity, common sense, good judgment, personality, and ability to communicate are exceedingly hard to evaluate. Large organizations such as the major private outdoor-oriented schools, many recreation districts and departments, and many colleges and universities *do* go to such lengths to gain confidence in their choices. The institution is, after all, responsible for the consequences of its choices.

Small operators and institutions seeking only occasional part-time help may not have the means to conduct such a thorough search. As a result, the program is often poorly staffed with a resultant reduction in program safety and quality. This tarnishes the image of the institution and greatly increases the risk of injury to participants and financial disaster via litigation. Unfortunate and in every case unnecessary, the situation can be avoided through at least three reasonable alternatives:

1. If funds don't allow for a complete and thorough search, hire a leader who is currently doing similar work for an established and credible organization, and for whom good references are available. This may require adjusting the scheduling of the outing, but may be well worth it.
2. Modify the outing so that the leadership requirements are well within the apparent abilities of the better candidates. By this we mean allow a wide margin of error; be highly skeptical of the actual ability of leaders until they have proven themselves in the field.
3. Cancel the program. This may seem drastic, but it is often the only responsible choice — morally, ethically, and legally.

It is now time to finalize the tentative agreements established in the initial feasibility survey. If an adequate job was done at that point, the tasks remaining should be relatively straightforward. First confirm and, if necessary, sign contracts for transportation, lodging, and any rentals that may be needed. The paperwork for land-access permits can sometimes take a while to complete, so if the land manager or owner requires this, do so immediately.

This is also a good time to go visit the area. Certainly at least one of the leaders should know it well, and it is better yet if all or as many of the staff as possible have at least visited the area once. A typical two-day backpacking route can usually be checked out by a small, fast party in just one day.

This is also the time to make up handouts for participants. There are several examples of these in the appendix, and the most important is the gear list. Keep in mind 1) that the leader and the institution are responsible for the consequences if someone is allowed to participate without adequate gear, 2) that the leader and the institution are responsible for determining what that gear is, and 3) that the majority of participants on any outing will arrive at the meeting point missing one or more significant items unless the requirements are very clearly and emphatically stated. Even so, some people will arrive without proper items.

For now, remember that participants must arrive at the meeting point with what the leader considers minimal equipment, and that the gear list is the primary tool for inducing this response. The list must be clear in specifying what is required (i.e., absolute; participation is not allowed without it) and what gear is nice but not absolutely essential. The amount of descriptive detail depends upon the extent of contact with the participants prior to the trip. When no pre-trip meeting is planned, the word "boots" may be quite insufficient. Even "experienced" participants can be counted on to misinterpret ambiguous requests or orders. If any footwear possibly resembling "boots" won't be acceptable, a lot of annoyance and wasted time can be avoided by including a more complete description. If minimal footwear consists of medium-to-heavy-weight Vibram lug-sole climbing boots, then *say* so. Don't expect participants to read your mind. Instead, expect a literal and minimal interpretation of the list.

It is important to specify clearly and unequivocally what will happen if required items are not brought to the outing, and note that all items will be checked by the instructor at the meeting point. The appendix includes a number of examples of gear lists, as well as examples of several additional "helpful hints" lists that can be duplicated or modified as desired.

Important data sheets include a health form, a waiver form, and a detailed description of the potential hazards of the trip. (Examples of these are included in Chapter 8.) The health form provides insights into the current and past health status of the individual, while the latter two tend to reduce the likelihood of litigation and can serve to the leader's advantage should litigation occur. These are discussed at length in the section on liability.

Another important form, examples of which are included in the appendices, gives the time and place of pre-trip meetings, assembly time for the outing, and return time from the outing, as well as any basic rules that participants should be aware of. When deciding on a time to meet, be sure to think carefully and somewhat pessimistically through morning events. For example, if you need to be hiking up the trail by 10 a.m., that means arriving at the trailhead by at *least* 9:15. Forty-five minutes is not much time to stretch the legs and get everybody saddled up and ready to go; an hour is more realistic for most groups. If, for example, the drive to the trailhead will take two hours, that

means driving away from the assembly point at 7:15 or 6:45 if a "fifteen-minute stop for a donut and coffee" is planned. "Fifteen-minute stops," especially in the morning, take at least thirty minutes. And this assumes no vehicle troubles, no stops for gas, and no need to stop and put on chains, etc. Leaving at 6:45 means getting everybody together by at least 6 a.m. or earlier if equipment is to be checked! What happens if the form says "meet at 6 a.m. sharp, and plan to leave by 6:45."? Most people will arrive, of course, between 6:30 and about 6:50. Thus it will save a lot of unnecessary delay if the form simply says "meet at 6 a.m. *sharp*."

In terms of participation, the success of an outing depends largely on care in scheduling. Care must be taken to avoid unnecessary conflicts with other activities of interest to the group, like sports events, concerts, similar outings by other organizations, and some holidays. All can cut into attendance figures. Weekends are usually the best time to schedule day or overnight trips for obvious reasons. Thursdays, however, are popular days off for many physicians and professionals working weekends, and other weekday trips may appeal to housewives, students and others not obligated to a forty-hour Monday-through-Friday schedule. As every outdoor enthusiast knows, weekdays are also the best on which to avoid crowds, and rental rates, ski-lift rates, and lodging rates are often much lower than on weekends. When scheduling three-day trips, remember that Fridays seem slightly easier for most people to take off than Mondays.

Pre-trip Meetings. Pre-trip meetings should be held about two weeks prior to the outing, ideally. A common and convenient format is to use the two preceding Tuesday evenings; the first meeting allows enough time to acquire equipment, reserve rentals, or whatever, and the second gives you a couple of days to get things in order, yet is close enough to the outing itself so that important points aren't likely to be forgotten by participants.

All pre-trip meetings should be scheduled early, that is, far enough in advance of the outing to allow participants to gather, make, purchase, or rent necessary equipment and clothing. A typical session runs from one to two hours on an evening early in one week followed by one on the same night in the next week, as mentioned above. Pre-trip contacts are extremely valuable and can, along with a post-trip meeting, contribute very substantially to the value of an outing program. They can significantly reduce risk and enhance the quality of the experience for participants, while rewarding leaders with a great reduction in the number and severity of delays, equipment failures, and problems caused by misunderstood expectations.

The first problem, however, is getting people to attend the meeting, and the usual ploy, which may or may not be effective, is to require attendance. When a good deal of information critical to safety or to the efficient operation of the program will be conveyed, such meetings are often required and considered a prerequisite to the outing. In other cases it may be up to the instructor to see to it that everyone who misses the initial meeting is thoroughly informed later.

Given a roomful of eager prospective participants, what should be covered? Whatever the activity, the following items and issues are important at a pre-trip meeting.

1. **The General Introduction.** The first item on the agenda is to briefly identify yourself, your assistants, and the organization, then explain the intent and length of the meeting, the nature of the outing, and the time, duration and cost. If the outing has fitness or skill prerequisites likely to be beyond those of anyone in the audience, make them clear now. The best way to do this is to compare the activity requirements to something known to the participants. Skiers may be able to assess themselves against some verbal descriptions of skiing skills, for example, and climbers or river runners may be able to understand a comparison between the intended activity and a few well-known local examples. If only general fitness is required, try to determine a very simple standard, like "If you can run a mile without stopping, you'll get by but be a bit tired. If you can run five miles, the trip will be easy for you." The purpose of this brief introductory statement, which should take no more than five or ten minutes, is simply to orient people and allow those who may be in the wrong place to leave. It's important to

provide a comfortable escape for these people at this point.

2. **Introduction of the Staff.** There are at least two goals here: 1) to give the participants an idea of who the leaders will be and to instill a sense of confidence in the qualifications of those leaders, and 2) to instill in the participants an awareness of the *fallibility* of the staff. The first step is usually easy and amounts to a brief listing of pertinent experiences. The second point comes a little harder for some leaders, yet is at least as important.

One good way to do this is to be blunt, explaining that one leader cannot possibly be in all places at all times, cannot solve every possible problem, and can make mistakes. Any leader with even a very small amount of experience can surely think of a few errors he or she has made, and one or two of these might be useful as examples. To keep things on a positive note, it is sometimes a good idea to mention that leaders are still learning, too, and hope to gain skills and experience right along with their students.

3. **Introduction and Assessment of Participants.** There are several schemes for this, but the easiest is usually to have people introduce themselves and answer a few easy questions, such as where they are from and what their experience in the activity has been. With larger groups, it may be best to just direct questions to everyone at once. Experience level is probably the most important single concern. Once a sense of this is gained the leader can quickly make the needed adjustments in his or her perceptions of what will happen on the outing.

4. **Attendance and Fee Collection.** Having started the meeting, the next thing on the agenda is usually the business of taking attendance and collecting any fees, if necessary. It is always a good idea to obtain a list of addresses and phone numbers as well, since one or more people will inevitably have to be contacted by phone at a later date, and phone numbers can allow fairly rapid communication of last-minute changes in plans. It is usually best to hold back the

gear list and other handouts until later, as these tend to absorb attention and reduce the value of spoken comments.

5. **Detailed Outing or Program Description.** The next step is to present, as clearly as possible, a description of what will take place on the outing. It is important here to be as accurate as possible so that participant expectations closely approximate leader expectations and, hopefully, the real event.

Slide shows can be very useful in portraying the events to come, especially when the slides of the intended site are current. Pictures are especially valuable for beginners, and can be used to begin familiarization with new concepts and words.

When selecting slides, be sure to choose only the kind showing behavior that will be expected of participants, unless there is a specific hazard or fault that must be emphasized. The reason for this is that in any visual presentation most people retain the images. It may matter little what is *said* if the audience *sees* mostly a certain kind of behavior. An example, if you're backpacking, would be to use only pictures of camps in appropriate places. No matter how emphatic the dialogue, if the slides show tents placed right next to lakes and streams, the participants will retain this as a model for behavior. They will see *themselves* in those tents, and will eventually turn these images into reality. The same thing is true in terms of technique. It has been shown that skiers, for instance, learn by looking at other skiers or by photos of other skiers. If the audience sees only proper technique and body position, their performance on the snow will likely be improved. Slides showing poor technique can create significant learning barriers.

Maps can be very useful in explaining routes and plans. Considerations here are to:

a. Remember that many people, including a surprising number of well-educated adults, have a great deal of difficulty reading maps.

b. Try to provide a large-scale map that includes both the starting point of the trip (the city or town) and the area of the activity. All too often people don't know where they are; they may be able to locate themselves on the map of the activity site, but don't know where the site is in relation to town or other major features. This is in part due to the tendency of everyone but car, van, or bus drivers to completely ignore distance and direction.

c. Try to provide one map per person. Photocopies are sometimes useful if a good clear original and well-inked machine are used. These aren't very useful in the field, but are adequate for explaining routes and plans.

d. Use opaque projectors to project maps sometimes.

e. When possible with school classes or groups of especially devoted participants, use a worksheet to stimulate careful study of the route. If independence is a goal of the program, their competence in map reading is an essential objective.

One important caution here: uncertainty is inherent in outdoor activities. The trip may, for any number of reasons, turn out to be much more difficult than the leader intends. Be sure to explain that extremes of weather, accidents, or other major mishaps, while unlikely, could occur. If these could result in an extra night out or in some other inconvenience, cost, or risk, be sure to make that clear. The point here is to be sure all participants are fully aware of what they are getting into and are fully prepared for what might happen. It is better to have most trips turn out to be easier than participants expect than to subject them to stresses and hazards they hadn't anticipated. Taking care to forewarn of hazards and stresses 1) reduces the likelihood of mishaps by increasing participant attentiveness and 2) puts the leader in a somewhat better position should an injury result in litigation.

One of the best ways to warn of hazards is to illustrate them with slides. Show a few pictures of nasty weather, people slogging in knee-deep slush, kayaks wrapped around rocks, or skiers practicing linked face plants — whatever is appropriate to the activity.

6. **Equipment Requirements.** The next step is to review in detail all clothing and equipment requirements. It is usually best to discuss the reason for these imperatives before handing out the list. (If the list is handed out first, people will be too busy reading it to pay attention.) You can also write down each of the required items one at a time on the blackboard, explaining and giving suggestions for making, borrowing, buying, or renting. Leaders should be aware of the availability of any item needed by the participants — especially in beginning classes or for outings where people may find themselves lacking something that presents a significant cost barrier. You should be able to assist participants in locating acceptable low-budget alternatives; too often leaders display only high-tech, state-of-the-art equipment and discuss only rental or purchase at a specialty store. Certainly for some items this may be the only reasonable course, yet many things can be made or bought secondhand at a surplus store or better yet, borrowed.

Beginners should not be expected to go out and invest a lot of money in new equipment for an activity they may not decide to pursue later. It is better to encourage minimal investment, borrowing, making, renting, buying at a discount, or visiting surplus or used-equipment stores. Gear swaps can be another inexpensive source of gear, but borrowing is still the best option for most people. While an argument can certainly be made for buying high-quality goods at a reputable store, this option should be exercised mainly by those who have a confirmed interest in the activity and have had enough experience to know exactly what gear meets their needs.

Good-quality state-of-the-art equipment for outdoor pursuits is not only expensive, it is addictive! Too many people fall into the trap of equating the experience with the equipment, and leaders can help offset this tendency by concentrating on basic essentials and functions rather than form. A ragged old wool sweater scavenged from a garage sale may be just as warm and comfortable as the hundred-dollar high-fashion ski sweater. The old one may even be more enjoyable to use,

since inevitable wear and tear won't be a matter of concern.

After explaining the various gear requirements and reviewing suggested options, leaders should go over food requirements for the trip if participants are expected to provide their own. Specific suggestions are invaluable, including sources, types, brands, quantities, and packing techniques. Handouts are also useful here.

When beginners are involved, it is a very good idea to have everyone bring their packs or gear bags, fully loaded and ready to go, to the last pre-trip meeting. A complete gear check at this time can save frustration on the morning of the outing. On some school trips, it is a good idea to keep the packs or bags locked up until the actual outing to ensure that everything stays in order. With most groups, however, this would be insulting to say the least, and would also involve responsibility for equipment security. The usual plan is to have participants bring their gear to the meeting point where it will be checked just prior to departure. The success of this plan depends almost entirely upon the ability of the leader to convey the importance of obtaining and packing *all* required equipment. If *any* ambiguity is expressed, participants can be counted on to omit or ignore some required items. The following three suggestions can help minimize these last-minute problems.

a. Strongly urge participants to pack at least a couple of days prior to the outing. This is another advantage of requiring participants to bring their gear to the final pre-trip meeting.

b. Remind participants that if the gear list is used as a checklist, and that if all of the required items are carefully checked off as they are put in the pack, that there is no need to worry about missing items. Since some may still worry, suggest a pad of paper and pencil near their beds so at least a quick note can relieve their minds and allow sleep.

c. Remind participants that required items are just that — *required*. Explain in clear terms that their comfort and safety and the comfort and safety of the other participants are the responsibility of the leaders, and that the sponsoring agency does not permit exceptions.

d. Unless the program has some form of special insurance coverage, remind people that items left in vehicles are not covered.

7. **Program Goals and Objectives.** Review the goals and objectives of the program. Participants have a right to know what outcomes are expected, as well as the means by which they will be achieved. For instance, a goal common to the great majority of outdoor classes and outings is to gain enough skill and knowledge for independent participation in the activity. If this is a goal of the program in question, it should be emphasized. In attempting to force participants to think for themselves, it is common, in fact, for leaders to intentionally err or avoid giving assistance. If you use this strategy, however, be sure to explain what you are doing.

Once the outing has been described and participants know what has been planned, it is always good to encourage their input. Find out if any changes or modifications are desired by the group, for it is important to have participant and leader expectations closely correspond. Unless some external constraints are in place, this can be achieved by changing participant or leader expectations. It does not really matter what is altered, however, so long as everyone has the same sort of experience in mind.

8. **Explain the Responsibilities of the Participants.** Regardless of the nature of the trip or the anticipated relationship between participants and staff, it is vital that the group develops, from the beginning, a sense of responsibility for what is going to happen on the outing. Everyone's overall safety depends very much on their alertness and concern.

The worst thing a leader can do is to allow the group to believe that he or she is an absolute master of the craft, willing and able to provide an absolutely safe trip. This may seem a preposterous assumption, yet most participants are predisposed to this sort of thinking. There are several reasons for this.

One is that people sometimes develop an image based on past experiences wherein the all-powerful leader seemed capable of anything. There is also a tendency for people to assume that any activity sponsored by a reputable institution — i.e., any large, well-known, or simply publicly funded organization, *must* be safe. There is a feeling that somehow, if the program were not really, truly safe (despite the warnings of the leader) that it would not be allowed to operate, that some imaginary all-knowing legal or insurance system would cancel the unsafe activity. Clearly this isn't true, yet it is a common belief. While most people would maintain a certain level of skepticism when participating in a small, low-budget private class activity that seems potentially hazardous, the same individuals are likely to blindly follow the leader in a similar class sponsored by a large and "credible" organization. In reality, of course, there is a low correlation between program quality and institutional size. This digression is intended only to remind leaders of the importance of suppressing the "lemming" response. It is not easy, but it is morally, ethically, and legally essential.

9. **Final Business.** The final item on the agenda for the first meeting is to set a time and place for the second, or for the outing itself if only one pre-trip meeting is held.

The second meeting is usually somewhat shorter than the first, and serves primarily as a last-minute opportunity to make sure that everyone is still planning to go, has adequate gear, and knows exactly when and where to meet for the outing. This is also a good time to begin teaching skills if they are a program objective. Films, demonstrations, and practice can be used to advantage to teach and/or to develop interest and excitement.

When setting the time for group assembly on the morning of the outing, be sure to allow ample time for late arrivals, gear checks, filling out of waiver forms, and all of the other inevitable little delays. It is rarely possible to depart from a meeting point in less than a half hour from the stated time, and an hour or so is common. Also allow a while for driving and stops for gas, coffee, or whatever, and assume thirty minutes to an hour at the trailhead or put-in spot before heading up the trail or onto the water.

All this usually adds up to a fairly early hour for assembly. For example, to leave the trailhead at 10 a.m. after a two-hour drive means the group must assemble at 5:30 or 6 a.m. This, in turn, means that people have to get up at 4 or 5 a.m. Keep in mind that 4 a.m. is for many people a very strange concept. They may have heard rumors that such a time exists, yet may never have been awake at such an hour. Even people used to getting up fairly early may find it hard to break old patterns, especially if the night's sleep was less than satisfactory, as is all-too-often the case. The typical participant begins to pack at about 7 or 8 at night on the evening before the outing, and at midnight is still trying to find the last critical item, repair the just-discovered hole in the hiking shorts, or figure out how to get everything in the pack. Sleep is likely to be interrupted frequently by concerns over forgotten items, dreams caused by anxiety about the outing, fears of oversleeping, and fears of not getting enough rest. These problems can be minimized by attention to the following points:

a. Try to reduce excessive anxieties by reminding the group that everyone will have an opportunity to participate in decision-making, and that no one will be required to do anything against their will. If skills or techniques are to be taught, remind people that you will progress one step at a time, with personal improvement and enjoyment, not competition, as a goal.

b. A lot of sleep is lost over fears of not getting enough sleep, thus two points seem worth making to outing groups; first, most people can miss an occasional complete night of sleep yet function quite well all day, and second, just being perfectly still and relaxed results in about half of the rest of actual sleep. Even a whole night of sleeplessness, then, can still provide the equivalent of several hours. While such a night may not be very restful psychologically, the body will usually feel fine. Furthermore, just keeping these thoughts in mind is often enough to reduce tensions and allow sleep.

c. When the alarm is set for an earlier hour than usual it is easy to sleep right through it. Suggest that participants either set two alarms or, better yet, that they exchange phone numbers and arrange to call one another at a certain hour, usually ten or fifteen minutes after the alarms are supposed to go off. This system has at least two advantages: first, there is no worry about hearing the alarm, and second, if one of the people is ill or will be late in arriving at the meeting point the leaders can be given this message by the other person. Since, in most cases, leaders will be away from their phones and on the way to the meeting point before the participants are up and about this is especially helpful.

Final Assembly of the Group. When selecting a meeting point from which to depart for the outing, try to find a site with adequate parking, toilet and telephone access, and at least some shelter. While parking space is usually the only essential, the other features are often convenient and can sometimes save delays. Trying to check and load equipment in the rain is hardly pleasant, and there is always a need for toilets and/or telephones.

If the information given the participants is clear and unambiguous, and if a good wake-up system is set up, most participants will be assembled at the requested time. (Although someone will *always* be late.)

As soon as possible, leaders should get things organized and underway. If several staff members are available, then it may be possible to complete several chores simultaneously and save a good deal of time. The following is a list of those chores common to most outdoor-pursuit activities.

1. Take roll. If necessary, also collect fees or recheck registration and fee-payment records.
2. Call and check on missing participants, unless, by virtue of the "phone-buddy" system, absences are already explained.
3. Check all gear. Be sure that everybody has all required items. With beginners it is also wise to ascertain total pack weight to be sure that no unreasonable excess is carried. When checking gear it is generally a waste

of time to simply ask, "Did everybody bring sunglasses?" The person who forgot his sunglasses, if he even heard the question, isn't likely to want to step forward and admit it, especially when they are required items. This tendency is increased when the item seems trivial to the participant; many also tend to assume that the leader(s) will somehow save the day, so the only effective way to check gear seems to be through an item-by-item inspection. One staff member can check the gear of ten participants in about twenty minutes if the process is carried out efficiently. Be careful not to cut corners here by simply asking, "Did you bring X item?" It is far better to say either "Let me see your _____," or at least "What sort of _____ did you bring?" The latter system is usually adequate for an experienced adult group, though in all other cases the only foolproof system is direct visual inspection. Beginners may in good faith arrive with items that are totally inadequate. In any case, it is good to see what each person has along so that mental note can be made of any marginal items.

What happens if required items are missing? It is best to think this through carefully, since it is bound to occur. It should be clear that letting people participate without required items is not a viable option in most programs. If the list was conscientiously constructed and is in fact what the leader considers a reasonable minimum, then he or she should not hesitate to insist on compliance. If a person is allowed to participate without a completely adequate set of gear, the results may include increased risk, degradation of program quality due to substitutions for the missing items, increased environmental impact, and serious legal jeopardy for the leaders and program administrators.

Another concern is that the participant may come to see required items as not really important! If someone gets by without raingear on a mountain hike once, he or she may well fail to carry it on the next private outing. "So what," say the proponents of this philosophy. "Think of the quality of the experience for the individual." Except for the leader's legal concerns, one could take the position that it is best not to enforce such requirements, but this argument ignores the interests of the group and focuses on the nature and quality of the learning experience for the individual. Leaders should be aware of this and should expect to encounter people who feel very strongly that strict gear requirements infringe upon their individual rights. (This is a particularly common attitude in the United States, where individual rights are something of a cultural obsession.) While the leader is not likely to significantly change deeply engrained beliefs in a couple of minutes of discussion, a few points are worth keeping in mind for such occasions. First, discovering by trial and error and thus experiencing directly the results of one's decisions is probably the best way to learn anything. The problem is that this method is inefficient; it may take a lifetime before an individual "reinvents the wheel" and through enough experience realizes the value, to go back to our concern here, of carrying certain items on an outing. This process of learning will also take a lot more time, expose the individual to more risk, likely endanger or at least inconvenience companions, and almost surely result in greater impact on the environment.

Okay, so a person does not have the gear, and you are committed to the requirements. Now what? Many leaders bring a sackful of the more frequently forgotten items to the meeting place. It only takes a few trips to convince them that a small investment in some used but adequate gear saves lots of hassles. However, this kit must be kept a secret prior to the outing. If people know that gaps in the list will be filled by the instructor, he or she had better arrive with a van full of gear.

The only other alternative, short of denying participation in the outing, is to let the person return home or go to a store to obtain the item. If the gear requirements were made clear prior to the trip then the leader should not feel obligated to delay the group. If anyone feels the delay would be unreasonable, simply send the person home. When young people are involved, though, it is important to make sure that parents or others are aware of this change in plans.

4. Sign out any items for which the participants will be personally responsible. It is common for programs to provide such things as compasses or lifejackets. Some programs provide a large number of them. In any case, experience has shown that the only way to recover everything is to sign each item out. Clearly number and label items, too, so that they cannot be interchanged. When a set array of gear is to be checked out, it also saves a lot of time if the staff makes up the appropriate number of full sets in advance and uses a standard form. In this way all you need to do is note the identification number of each item as it is handed to a participant, then have the participant sign the form.

5. Collect and review all health forms. These should be taken along on the outing, carried by the appropriate group leaders.

6. Have the students sign and return waiver forms and others that explain the hazards of the outing. (See the section on liability.) The waiver form should be signed as closely as possible to the start of the outing itself, while health and hazards notifications may be signed earlier. All of these should be stored in town, not taken on the outing. They may be of little value if the vehicle they are carried in is the one that goes in the lake, or if a back-country accident results in their loss.

7. Be sure the vehicles are available or are being delivered. (Reservations should be checked out at least a week prior to the outing and again a day or two before.) Unless the entire transportation phase has been contracted out, that is, unless both vehicles and drivers are being provided, the leader has to assume responsibility for checking them over. This is true even for rental equipment, and, in fact, is not a bad idea even when contracting for full service. Look at the tires, check the headlights, taillights, turn signals, and other safety-related equipment. (A checklist is provided in Chapter 7.)

In vans and cars, one of the first things to do is to get all of the seat belts up and in usable positions. Bear in mind that even in jurisdictions where use of the belts is not required by law, failure to wear them is still just plain stupid. The tremendous value of seat belts in minimizing injury and saving lives in accidents has been more than adequately proven. Common sense alone ought to provide enough incentive, yet many people seem lacking in that regard, and don't realize that only vehicles have brakes; passengers are connected only by friction on the seats, which is next to meaningless in even a low-speed crash. Any leader reluctant to require seat belts should also consider that virtually every major outdoor program in the U.S.A. requires that all participants and staff be buckled up at all times when the vehicle is moving.

8. Assemble the group gear.

9. Assemble the group, and check to be sure that everyone is ready to go, feels well, and knows the overall plan.

10. Check on road and weather conditions, and get the latest weather forecast.

11. Meet with the driver(s). Be sure that each driver knows the destination and route, the plans for handling delays or emergencies, and the basic "rules of the road." Minimum rules usually include a strict compliance with traffic laws and speed limits (55 means 55, not 57, etc.); b.) absolutely no consumption of intoxicants before or during driving; and c.) strict enforcement of seat belt use.

12. Load the gear. Take care to secure it in such a way as to prevent flying forward in an accident. This means that no equipment should ever be stacked higher than the back of the seat, and even then should be secured. Also, be careful not to block escape from the vehicle by blocking exits.

13. Load the people. Given the reluctance of some to buckle up, check carefully to be sure that seat belts are in use, and remind people that they must remain on whenever the vehicle is moving. It is also a good idea to instruct people not to slouch down in the seats with the belt above the hips. This is a sure way to suffer a spinal fracture in a crash, so insist that those who want to doze do so sitting up; it is not that much less comfortable.

Transportation. There is little doubt that transporting participants to and from the outdoor-activity site constitutes the greatest part of the overall program risk. People worry about climbing a mountain or skiing down a mogul-ridden hill; then when the day is over they relax and career down the highway at high speeds, completely oblivious to the consequences of either mechanical failure or of a split second of human error.

Here are some suggestions for decreasing risk during the transportation phase of an outing:

1. Use seat belts all of the time for all passengers. No other single action is as important.
2. Engage competent, experienced adult drivers with excellent traffic records. All must be familiar with the type of vehicle to be used under the conditions expected, such as snow or ice. Many organizations require chauffeur's licenses and/or special driver-training courses.
3. Do not allow drivers to operate a vehicle when under the influence of any intoxicating substance, when tired, when ill, or when upset or distracted for any reason.
4. Do not allow drivers to go for more than two hours without a break, and, if possible, provide competent relief drivers more often.
5. Provide at least one relief driver for each vehicle. These individuals must be as qualified as the primary chauffeur.
6. Inspect the vehicle before use for proper functioning of safety features. Even when vehicles are borrowed from an agency motor pool or are maintained by institutions, this responsibility cannot be overlooked. It only takes a few seconds each to check headlights, taillights, brake lights, turn signals, tires, and brake fluid, and to be sure the spare tire has enough air in it. A quick check should also be made to be sure flares, fire extinguisher, jack, and tire-changing tools are in good order. Many organizations also insist on a good first-aid kit in each vehicle.
7. Make sure that at least one person in each vehicle is qualified in first aid. At best, this individual should *not* be a driver since drivers and front-seat passengers, even in seat belts or harnesses, are more likely to be incapacitated in an accident.

8. Be sure that each driver and/or person assigned as "navigator" in a vehicle knows the destination, route, and stopping or meeting points along the way. Usually the safest and most convenient plan when using several vehicles is to designate meeting points at one- to two-hour intervals at specific points with telephones. No one should leave these areas until all vehicles are accounted for, and the leader should go *last* so that any problems along the way — flat tires, break-downs, or accidents — will be seen and dealt with. This can save a great deal of anxiety and time in resolving such situations since the leader can simply phone ahead to the assembly point and notify the rest of the party. When going to a back-country trailhead or put-in point, the group should be sure to assemble at the last telephone enroute. Back-country roads can be very confusing, so it is best to explain them here, then leave behind a lead car containing someone most familiar with the correct route. Avoid using convoys in town or on a busy route, and keep the leader near the rear. It is dangerous to split a driver's attention between the task of driving and the task of keeping track of cars ahead or behind. This danger is increased by the tendency of drivers to perform heroic feats in order to catch the vehicle ahead or allow a slower vehicle to catch up.
9. Be sure that all drivers are clearly and firmly told to obey all traffic regulations. Most people seem to think that speed limits apply to everybody else and not to them. Remind drivers that when responsible for program participants and vehicles, 55 miles per hour means, amazingly enough, 55 miles per hour.

The conscientious application of all of these suggestions should significantly reduce the risk of the transportation phase of the program. Applying them as firm policy can also benefit the leader and the institution in a legal sense, showing good intent and good planning on the part of staff. Anything less, by the way, would be considered dereliction of duty in the eyes of many professional outdoor leaders and administrators.

On the topic of liability, consider the following additional points:

1. It is best not to assign passengers to specific vehicles or seats, except when needed for safety as in the assignment of drivers. Even then the driver should be given a clear option.
2. If money or a promise of money is given to chauffeurs by riders prior to a trip, the recipient of the money has just assumed the responsibilities of a commercial carrier. In addition, this may invalidate his or her driver's insurance for the duration of the trip.

At the Trailhead or Starting Point of the Activity. There are a number of chores that must be done once the group is assembled on the trailhead or starting point. Concerns common to most activities are, in the usual time sequence, the following:

1. Be sure that the group understands the need to meet upon arrival. This means that if more than one vehicle is used, instructions for when and where to meet must be made clear before the last leg of the journey. Otherwise the leader may arrive to find participants scattered and have to spend a lot of time just getting everybody together. This may sound trivial, but somehow morning hours zip by at a lightning speed! It is also a good idea to get in the habit of announcing plans and requests before the vehicle stops. Especially if it has been a long drive, the load of passengers will otherwise be halfway to the outhouse or the bushes before the dust settles. It is always easier to exercise control from the start than to try to gain it later.
2. Assemble the group and set a time and place for reassembly. Ten minutes is plenty of time. Have participants use the time to visit the restrooms or outhouses. If no facilities are available, give advice as to where to go. If beginners are involved, be sure to give basic instructions in sanitation and the proper disposal of human waste.
3. Assemble the group again and supervise the unloading of the vehicles, placing group gear and personal items in separate places. Insist that *all* items be removed from any vehicle to be left parked and unattended. Have the participants get into proper clothing, including enough extra warmth to allow a bit more standing around, and then

get all of their gear ready to go. Remind everyone to leave room for group gear if this will be necessary, then give a specific time and place for reassembly. (About twenty minutes is usually enough.)
4. At this point the staff should be moving quickly to pack up and change clothes if needed, and to circulate among the participants to provide assistance in getting them ready.
5. Sort out the group gear. Every activity has its own requirements, but in most cases there will be substantial amounts of group equipment. If more than one group is being outfitted, each should have a separate array of gear. This is needed, for instance, when there are two or more rafting, hiking, or climbing units which, though perhaps on the same route, will travel independently. Separate equipment simplifies and speeds the process. Each set of gear, first-aid kits, ropes, rafts, or whatever, can then be easily checked for completeness and turned over to each group leader.
6. Distribute the group gear. It is often necessary for participants to help carry communal equipment. In fact, a good case can be made for requiring this whenever possible since it makes participants more aware of the equipment requirements of the activity and promotes a feeling of full participation.

Probably the fairest and fastest system is for the staff to make an appropriate number of nearly equal piles, letting participants then choose whatever items they prefer or those that will fit in their packs. This system works well if supervised thoughtfully to see to it that no one ends up with an unreasonable load. Children, for instance, should be given little or nothing to carry, except perhaps token items, until they are big enough for adult loads. Men can be a problem here when, through youthful exuberance or attempts to project a macho image, they insist upon carrying far more weight than others in the group. Strength, skill, experience, and the quality of each of the backpacks are appropriate criteria for distributing loads — age and gender are not. Remember that excessively heavy loads are dangerous, and a big athletic person is not immune to a sprained back or ankle. Also, a person carrying too much of the group gear disallows others. from accepting their responsibility, which can be a valuable part of the experience and provide a sense of contribution. Overweight men can be a special problem. There seems to be a tendency for these people to want to carry great loads as though the fat were muscle, only to risk exhaustion if not cardiac problems. Women can also be hard to deal with when it comes time to distribute gear. First, many women insist upon carrying loads fully equal to those of the men, thinking this is in fact a fair and equal sharing of the responsibility. It may be fair in a limited sense, but weight should be distributed according to *ability*, not by equal shares.

A larger, stronger, and more fit person can carry a given load more easily, with greater speed and fewer risks than someone smaller or less fit. (By fit we mean not only in the cardiovascular sense but in conditioning to the activity as well.) A light but strong and fit woman can sometimes carry a bigger load than a larger unconditioned male, yet this is the exception in our society. Usually, men can carry more due, at least, to strength and body mass, and so the weight should be divided accordingly. The other concern is that some women expect the men to carry the majority of the weight, and resist carrying a fair share based on health and size. The leader should, in any case, lift all of the packs and keep a mental note of how much group gear each person is carrying.

It is also important, when backpacking, to check the lay and design of packs. A poorly designed, fitted, or sized pack can necessitate a much lighter load. Also take note of each person's health and degree of fatigue. Those who were up half of the night won't be as able to carry a load. Remember, too, that beginners are much less efficient than experienced participants and will have a far harder time just keeping up, much less lugging great loads. (This is especially true in skiing and climbing.) Sometimes the inequities are so small as to not be worth trying to rectify. Usually small shifts can be made without objection, and arrangements

can often be made to shift at least group, if not personal, gear at rest breaks, lunch stops, or with each day's travel.

7. Make sure that the group leader or a qualified first aider carries the first-aid kit.

8. Once group gear is distributed, check every participant's pack to be sure everything is adequately (i.e., very securely) fastened and that rain protection is adequate if this seems necessary. Note who has what items. A written list can be a real time-saver later in the trip when searching for things. Many programs formally sign out gear to students.

9. Recheck vehicles to be sure that absolutely no gear or clothing is visible from the outside. Cars and trucks are broken into for very small items. The simple precaution of hiding everything left in the vehicle can greatly reduce the chance of break in. The rules are simple — if *you* can see it, so can anyone looking for things to take. Keep in mind that break ins for items like an old pair of tennis shoes are common. Leave *nothing* visible if the vehicle will remain unattended.

10. Decide on a system for hiding and storing the keys. It is common to use tires, fenders, some place on the engine, or the tailpipe. A thief wouldn't take long to check all of these common hiding places, so be creative! First, let several other people, including your staff, know where the keys will be hidden. Then remember that a few places that may not be so obvious attract pack rats and some birds that love little shiny objects and are amazingly good at finding them. (Human thieves may also be even smarter than the rats.) Finally, don't forget that rain or snow can alter a landscape and make it hard to find that flat rock with the odd shape next to the riverbank. It's better yet to carry keys with you.

11. Meet with the staff to finalize plans for the day.

12. Meet with participants and get ready to head up the trail or out to the water. There are several important points to be covered in a brief talk before starting. It is usually easiest to do this as a large group.

    a. Review the plans for the day. This means that everyone should have access to a map unless the route is extremely simple and well-understood already (like a few miles of river already driven past). Go over the route and encourage the frequent use of the maps during the day. If, as in most programs, independence is a goal, then this is essential. Map reading is a basic and necessary skill in most outdoor activities, and is learned *only* by repeated chart prediction, observations of reality, and subsequent chart review. Participants should also be made aware of the timing of rest breaks, lunch, and alternatives in the event of unexpected changes in the weather, etc.

b. Explain the method to be employed for keeping track of everybody. Whether you're on a trail or on a river, this usually involves staying between a lead and a tail and being responsible for those *following* (the hardest point to get across). The specifics of these plans are important and will be discussed in detail in sections on each activity.

c. Explain what to do if anyone becomes out of contact with the group for more than the specified time. This is usually five minutes (which in practice usually turns out to be ten or so). The usual directions given participants are to simply stay put and wait for the group to return. Again, be sure to review specific advice regarding the type of activity in question.

d. Explain how to deal with sanitation concerns. If outhouses or toilets will be available, say so at your time of arrival. Otherwise explain the accepted procedures for minimizing the social and environmental impacts of human waste. In sensitive areas, even experienced people need reminders, and beginners may need some very basic advice.

e. Suggest the appropriate clothing at the start of the activity, and then break into travel or task groups. If this hasn't already been done, it is usually easiest to have individual group leaders stand as far apart as possible to completely separate the units.

13. Head up the trail, cursing to yourself and trying to figure out how to get started *next* time in less than an hour!

Procedures and Concerns when Returning to Vehicles. The period from perhaps one or two hours of travel until arrival at the vehicles tests the skills of any leader. No matter how much fun the group is having, and even if it has only been a one-day trip, the "smell of the barn" syndrome takes over. People lead with their minds, and by the time you get to the cars and vans you are already mentally engrossed in whatever awaits in town. It is essential that the leader anticipate this and gain firm control before there is a mad dash for the vehicles. Usually this requires that one of the leaders move to the front of the group, holding the lead to a reasonable pace whether walking, skiing, boating, or biking. Innumerable search-and-rescue operations have resulted from inadequate control during this period. A little extra speed and lack of attention greatly increase the risk of missing a trail or making a technical error. Usually people are at least a little bit tired, which makes a slow pace and caution even more important. Without emphatic reemphasis, most people tend to forget all about whoever is following, even when the habit seemed well-engrained after a long trip. A good plan is to stop perhaps three hours before the end of the day and explain the need to "run a tight ship" all the way to the vehicles.

Procedures and Concerns on Return to Vehicles. People are almost always happy to get back to their cars. Even the most ardent mountaineer, canoeist, or nature lover usually savors this transition to "civilization." If time is short and there is a concern for efficiency in returning to town, the leader needs to maintain control from the moment of arrival at the trailhead. Once relieved of packs or watercraft, people who are not tired will have a tendency to scatter, and anyone who is tired is likely to be found snoring in a back seat of a van if he or she is not put to use getting gear quickly stowed away.

Take roll carefully to be sure that everyone is accounted for. When group gear has been issued, it is best to collect it at the trailhead, especially when darkness, rain, or other inconveniences are expected back in town. This can be a fast and efficient process. The leader should assemble the group and have each person extract all group gear from his or her pack or gear bag. A little forethought in camp on the last morning can result in most of this being right on top. If forms were used to sign out equipment, it is a simple matter to check items back in. The entire process takes just a few minutes and saves inevitable hassles in trying to gather gear back in town. In town people will be even more tired and eager to get home, resistant to having to empty a pack or gear bag to find some missing items, and very likely to vanish before the leader is ready to let everyone go.

Again, the gear must be loaded in such a way as to preclude the possibility of it falling forward in a collision or flying about should the vehicle roll. Equipment inside vans may sometimes be secured with seat belts. Anything stored inside must not be placed in a manner that could limit escape from the vehicle; roofs or other outside racks are always preferable on vans.

Once the gear is completely loaded, take a careful look around the parking area for items left behind. This is a very common occurrence and worth a special effort. As a last chore, it is a good idea to spend just a few minutes cleaning up the area. Whether it is a trailhead or a landing, inconsiderate people have probably left at least some litter. Picking it up as a group is very easy, takes very little time, does a valuable community service, temporarily reduces the amount of litter that will be dropped (clean sites tend to stay clean), and perhaps, most important of all, is very good for the participants. People, even sloppy people, are much less likely to litter if they have actually had to pick up after others. Besides, if the leader has been conscientious in the field, participants should already be inclined to pick up litter without being urged to do so.

Transportation Back to Town. Transporting participants to and from the activity site is no doubt, as stated earlier, the most dangerous part of any outdoor-pursuit program. The return trip is, in most cases, far more hazardous than the outbound one. There are several reasons for this increased risk. First, drivers are not as well rested. Second, return trips often involve night-time driving. Third, drivers may be anxious to return home, and, finally, the group is likely to be either asleep and not supportive of the

chauffeur or awake and excited, laughing, joking, and distracting him or her. On trips to the site the group is usually awake but not yet cohesive and not so likely to be rambunctious.

The most important points to consider when getting ready for the trip home are:

1. Be sure that the driver(s) are fit to drive, not too tired, and in a good frame of mind.
2. Check the vehicle safety features again: headlights, taillights, brake and turn signals, and tires. This takes one or two minutes — a cheap investment.
3. Be firm about the use of seat belts, and check to be sure they are in use. Remind people again not to slouch down in the seats. Remember that it is not just a matter of individual freedom; an unbelted person is a liability to all of the other passengers since everyone pays extra insurance premiums because of the far higher costs of repairing the average unbelted accident victim.
4. Once everyone is belted down, it is easier to count, so now is the time to confirm that the correct number of people are on board, and that no one is left sitting in the outhouse.
5. Use a series of intermediate meeting points on the return. Usually drivers should have a break or be replaced every hour on the return trip, instead of every two hours as when travelling *to* the site.
6. Again, it is usually best for the leader's to be the last vehicle on the road so that any problems can be known and handled efficiently. There is a potential problem, however, in that just as in the field, the party may try to go too fast in their eager-ness to get home. It may be best to put another staff person or at least the most trustworthy driver in the lead to keep speeds down. Remember that many return trips are downhill, and that downhill driving can be much more dangerous than uphill. A stretch of road safe at 55 miles per hour uphill may have to be driven downhill at 40 miles per hour or less to maintain the same braking distance and control.

Procedures at the Return Point. Remember that by the time people arrive back in town they won't want to stand around and listen to any discussions. Before the vehicle stops, be sure to explain any final procedures. Usually this is a matter of checking in gear (if not done at the trailhead or landing), helping return group gear to storage, distributing personal gear, and setting a time and place for the post-trip meeting.

Remember that the journey is not yet over for participants. The leader has to be sure that everyone has a way to get home. Anyone too tired to drive safely or without a ride should be assisted in finding one or be given one.

The staff usually have a number of chores remaining to keep them amused until long after the participants have gone home. Gear needs to be cleaned, dried, counted, and stored; vehicles need to be cleaned and parked or returned to the supplier.

Post-trip Meetings and Procedures. What happens after an outing activity can be extremely important in terms of the value of the experience for both participants and staff. Post-trip contacts with participants provide an opportunity to review the experience, reinforcing the positive aspects of the trip and minimizing the effects of any negative ones. If the outing was skill oriented, this meeting provides an opportunity to clarify techniques, answer questions, and provide guidance for continued development. Personal and social benefits are included in the objectives of many programs and are, in fact, inevitable on virtually any outing. These areas can be explored as well, often to great advantage if the leader is skillful in bringing out participant comments.

Staff also invariably benefit from a thorough critique of the experience by participants. A technique of special value is to have participants direct comments and suggestions to each staff member. The discussion can be initiated by first eliciting general ideas about what the participants expected of the staff, and then thoughts about what actually happened on the outing. Staff find this extremely useful with regard to future outings, and participants learn something about the demands of leadership.

Scheduling the meeting well in advance is a good idea, so it can be announced along with the pre-trip meetings. After a weekend outing, the following Monday or Tuesday evenings are usually best in terms of attendance. A meeting a week later will likely attract fewer people, but

has the advantage of allowing enough time for them to relax, think things over, and show photos.

Evaluation forms can also help the leader and the institution responsible for the program. These give the institution at least a limited form of feedback as to the qualities of the program and the staff, and provide helpful information for the leader. It is almost always best to have participants fill them out at the post-trip meeting. Unless some sort of control over the participants is available, the return rate is likely to be low for any take-home form. (Examples of evaluation forms are included in Chapter 10.)

Staff post-trip meetings should always be conducted. All too often a great deal of useful feedback and constructive criticism is never received by leaders or assistants following a trip. Hindsight is always best, and yet the advantages of this perspective are often lost. The following format works well: 1) Review the overall achievements of the program. Were goals approximated? Were specific objectives met? Is it worth trying again? Would a different site, different timing, or different route help? What about gear? Were the participants physically and mentally prepared for the experience? Were they well equipped? What can be construed from student evaluations and comments? 2) Review each staff member's performance. All should be given an ample opportunity to comment both objectively and subjectively on the performance of every other staff member. This works best if everyone is strongly urged to give absolutely candid comments, whether or not they may personally have done a better job or know of a better way. Too often leaders shy away from making comments that may be construed as critical, not wanting to offend someone or perhaps not wanting to inspire negative remarks about their own performance. The staff head should make it clear that this is a rare and valuable opportunity for open and constructive feedback among friends and colleagues all trying to do a better job. He or she can also lead the way by encouraging direct feedback about his or her own behavior and by responding to all comments in a positive and appreciative way, avoiding any hint of defensiveness. This is not easy, and perfection probably is not possible, yet the benefits of honest evaluation by fellow leaders is well worth the effort.

Finally, the program should at least be summarized in writing so that leaders of similar future outings may take advantage of the experience. Usually there will be some additional required paperwork relating to expenses, inventory control, and staff evaluation and compensation.

Appendices A through L are examples of various outdoor pursuits with recommended instructional materials and equipment lists.

BIBLIOGRAPHY

Angier, Bradford, *Skills for Taming the Wilds,* Stackpole Books, Harrisburg, Pennsylvania, 1967.

Bridge, Raymond, *High Peaks and Clear Roads,* Prentice-Hall, Inc., Englewood Cliffs, New Jersey, 1978.

Brower, David, editor, *The Sierra Club Manual of Ski-Mountaineering,* The Sierra Club, San Francisco, 1962.

Buell, Larry, *Leader's Guide to the 24-Hour Experience,* Environmental Awareness Publications, Greenfield, Mass., 1978.

Cardwell, Paul, *America's Camping Book,* Charles Scribner's Sons, New York, 1969.

Fear, Gene, *Surviving the Unexpected,* Wilderness Emergency, Survival Education Association, Tacoma, Washington, 1972.

Fleming, June, *The Well-Fed Backpacker,* Victoria House, Portland, Oregon, 1976.

Fletcher, Colin, *The Complete Walker,* Alfred A. Knopf, New York, 1970.

Glass, Walter, *The Key to Knots and Splices,* Key Publishing Company, New York, 1959.

Gormley, Chuck, *Group Backpacking, A Leader's Manual,* Groupwork Today, Inc., So. Plainfield, N.J., 1979.

Howard, Gordon E., "Hiking and Mountaineering" in *Safety in Outdoor Recreational Activities.* AAHPER, Washington, D.C., 1977.

Hurley, William Osgood, and Hurley, Leslie, *The Snowshoe Book,* The Stephen Greene Press, Brattleboro, Vermont, 1971.

Lathrop, Theodore G., *Hypothermia: Killer of the Unprepared,* Mazamas, Portland, Oregon, 1972.

Malo, John, Malo's *Complete Guide to Canoeing and Canoe-Camping,* Collier Books, New York, 1969.

Malo, John, *Wilderness Canoeing,* Collier Books, New York, 1971.

Mandolf, Henry I., editor, *Basic Mountaineering,* Sierra Club, San Francisco, 1967.

Manning, Harvey, *Backpacking One Step at a Time,* The REI Press, Seattle, 1972.

Meier, Joel; Morash, Talmage; and Welton, George, *High Adventure Outdoor Pursuits,* Brighton Publishing Co., Salt Lake City, 1980.

Mendenhall, Ruth Dyar, *Backpack Cookery,* LaSiesta Press, Glendale, California, 1966.

Mendenhall, Ruth; and Mendenhall, John, *Introduction to Rock and Mountain Climbing,* Stackpole Books, Harrisburg, Pennsylvania, 1969.

Merrill, Bill, *The Survival Handbook,* Arco Publishing Company, New York, 1972.

Miracle, Leonard, *Complete Book of Camping,* Harper & Row, New York, 1961.

Peterson, Gunnar A.; and Edgren, Harry D., *The Book of Winter Outdoor Activities,* Association Press, New York, 1962.

Rethmel, R.C., *Backpacking,* Burgess Publishing Company, Minneapolis, 5th edition, 1974.

Risk, Paul H., *Outdoor Safety and Survival,* John Wiley & Sons, New York, 1983.

Rohnke, Karl, *Cowstails and Cobras,* Project Adventure, 1977.

Rustrum, Calvin, *The New Way of the Wilderness,* The MacMillan Company, New York, 1958.

Shanks, Bernard, *Wilderness Survival,* Universe Books, New York, 1980.

Sierra Club, *Belaying the Leader,* The Sierra Club, San Francisco, 1956.

Sussman, Aaron; and Goode, Ruth, *The Magic of Walking,* Simon & Schuster, New York, 1967.

Tejada-Flores, Lito, *Backcountry Skiing,* Sierra Club, San Francisco, 1981.

USFS, *Backpacking,* Superintendent of Documents, U.S. Government Printing Office, Washington, D.C., 001-000-04075-8, 1979.

Van Lear, Denise, editor, *The Best About Backpacking,* Sierra Club, San Francisco, 1974.

Wood, Robert S., *Pleasure Packing for the 80's,* Ten Speed Press, Berkeley, California, 1980.

APPENDIX A

HIKING

A. General Description

1. What It Is; What Is Done. When does a walk become a hike? It probably isn't possible to say, and really doesn't matter. Hiking *is* walking. In common usage the term implies that the walking is for pleasure, is of significant length, occurs in a natural setting, and lasts for less than a day. The range of possibilities includes anything from relatively short and easy trail strolls to rugged, limit-testing adventures. Multi-day travel is regarded here as trekking or backpacking, and will be considered separately.

2. Hazards in the activity. Hiking is probably one of the safest of all recreational pursuits so long as participants exercise good common sense. This activity — walking — is rarely hazardous by itself. If the planning process includes a thorough assessment of potential environmental risks and if these are acknowledged in route and equipment selection, then serious mishaps are unlikely.

3. Who Participates. Hiking is no doubt the most popular of all land-based outdoor pursuits. In many cases there are essentially no barriers to participation. Most paths and trails are free, and you need no special skill, fitness, or equipment to begin. For these reasons hiking is an option for people of all ages and fitness levels.

4. Resource Requirements. All that's needed for a hike is the freedom to walk. Great hikes are possible in any terrain and in almost every conceivable setting. Many cities have urban or suburban parks large enough to allow long, all-day hikes. A surprising number of major metropolitan areas adjoin relatively natural lands. Hong Kong is one such city where you can begin a hike from a downtown hotel and walk all day in monkey-inhabited semitropical forests, wandering back into town in the evening. Most hiking utilizes trails, paths, and back roads, sometimes linked by cross-country travel across hills and fields. The popularity of hiking has resulted in an abundance of guidebooks in most parts of the world. If you read with all due caution in translation and attention to accuracy and currency, these guides can provide a survey of local options. Other good sources include land-management agencies, local parks-and-recreation districts and departments, and local suppliers of hiking clothing and equipment. It's always important to check with the resource manager as soon as possible to find out about policies, regulations, and hiking permits.

5. Equipment and Clothing Requirements.

Hiking in its simplest and least ambitious form may require very little equipment or clothing. An all-day summer hike in a large suburban park might require nothing but comfortable loose clothing and enough cash to buy lunch and bus fare home. On the other hand, a hike of a few miles into a wilderness area, even in the same season, might require some more essential gear. Common sense dictates that on a hike of several miles it's not possible to call a cab if the weather turns rotten or if walking becomes difficult due to blisters. And what about a sprained or broken ankle? What about getting lost? Neither misfortune is likely to occur, but they are always possibilities and have led to many fatalities over the years when overconfident hikers have treated wilderness travel as casually as strolls in the park. Paranoia isn't called for here, just good sense. Think about what would be needed if it became necessary to treat and stabilize an injured participant overnight, and consider the minimum training, skills, and equipment an individual needs to have a reasonable chance of surviving a night lost in the environment of the hike.

A good compromise seems to be to carry sufficient group equipment to treat any reasonably foreseeable injury, and to stabilize and protect an injured person until outside help can be obtained. This means bringing sufficient first-aid supplies (and expertise!) plus insulation, shelter, and food and water appropriate for the terrain and season. Most organizations also feel that individual participants should also carry sufficient equipment and clothing in case they become separated from the group and lost.

This seems more than reasonable, since the best of group-control systems can fail, and participants' lives shouldn't depend totally on luck and direct contact with the group. Therefore, every hiker needs to carry enough insulation and wind and rain protection to sit out at least one night in the worst weather likely to be encountered. The exact items that should be required on a hike depend upon the climate, season, terrain, and skills of the participants. (Weather forecasts should be interpreted with great caution.) When in doubt, it's always best to opt for more extensive gear requirements, within reason of course.

Participants on hiking outings are often naive and trusting, and used to being protected from natural hazards. Leaders have to be aware of this, and set and enforce standards based on their best judgment. Consider the leader who allows a person to participate on an outing without some item or some bit of information or skill considered important for survival. What happens if that person gets lost and doesn't survive until found by search teams? How might the leader feel? How will the leader fare when his or her actions are compared by a judge or jury to the "standard of the trade?" What about the liability of the sponsoring agency? Leaders would be well advised not to compromise on any safety-related issue.

The following list is an example of what to carry to prevent such liability. The group list includes items carried by each independent group in the field and the individual list includes items that every individual, including instructors, need to carry. Required items mean just that — required. No individual participates without all of the required personal items, and no group goes out without the required group items. Note that the optional lists contain some items which may, under certain circumstances, be necessary. For example, you should insist that sun hats be brought along in certain hot and sunny environments.

Both lists were designed for a specific environment with the potential for cool wet days and cold nights even in mid-summer. Few environments require more clothing and equipment, so the gear shown here should be adequate for at least three seasons in the mountains, forests, and deserts of the mid latitudes of either hemisphere.

Leaders of any outdoor pursuit should be aware of the costs of the necessary gear and be prepared to assist participants in locating reasonably priced and low-budget alternatives. Function rather than form should be emphasized, and participants should be made aware of local options for making, borrowing, or renting gear.

SUGGESTED MINIMUM GEAR REQUIRED FOR HIKING

Individual Gear

Required Items (*Certain synthetics may be substituted at the discretion of the instructor.)

1. Boots (weight and type specified for each outing)
2. Wool* sox (1 or 2 pair to wear)
3. Wool* sox (1 or 2 pair for complete change)
4. Wool* layers for the legs (large pants, knickers and sox, or long johns)
5. Long pants (if long-johns option is chosen above)
6. Wool* layer for the top (shirts and/or sweaters)
7. Warm parka or vest (down or synthetic)
8. Raingear (substantial fabric, hood-to-ankles; may be jacket or poncho plus pants or chaps, or may be cagoule and high gaitors)
9. Wool* hat (must cover ears)
10. Gloves or mittens (wool preferred)
11. Sunglasses (especially necessary in snow or at higher elevations in sunny weather)
12. Sunscreen (15 or higher rating preferred)
13. Water bottle (1 liter or more, plastic; bring full)
14. Matches (12 or more, waterproof or in watertight container)
15. Pocket knife (a multi-tool "Swiss Army" type is nice but not essential)
16. First-aid kit (small, including Band-Aids and moleskin)
17. Whistle
18. Flashlight (alkaline or lithium batteries preferred)
19. Map(s) (protected in plastic bag)
20. Compass
21. Candles (1 or 2 votive type work well)
22. Cup (metal, to melt snow or boil water)

23. Food (the appropriate edibles for the hike plus the equivalent of at least one full extra lunch as emergency food)
24. Emergency shelter and ample cord to set it up (small tarp, "space blanket," or large poncho, with 15 meters of parachute cord)
25. Day pack (large enough for all carried gear plus some group gear)

Optional Items (All are recommended and may be required at the discretion of instructor.)

1. Light shoes (sneakers)
2. Liner sox
3. Gaitors
4. Shorts
5. Light cotton shirt(s)
6. Windshell (top and pants)
7. Sun hat
8. Handkerchief
9. Umbrella
10. Watch (leader should consider this essential)
11. Nylon cord (15 ft. or 15 meters, multipurpose)
12. Insect repellent
13. Personal medications and toiletries
14. Toilet paper
15. Binoculars
16. Camera and film
17. Notebook and pencil (leaders should consider this essential)
18. Extra clothing, food, and water (to be left in the vehicles)

Group Gear

Required items for each independent field group.

1. Insulated pad(s) (approximately 1 for every 12 participants on dry ground, and 1 for every 2 participants on snow)
2. Sleeping bag(s) or equivalent insulation (approximately 1 for every 12 participants in warm weather and 1 for every 8 participants in cold weather)
3. Tarp(s) (adequate to cover and block wind flow for the entire group. A 3-x-4 meter tarp will suffice for at least twelve people if used effectively)
4. Container for heating water (at least one liter volume, to process drinking water and

to make hot-water bottles of liter-water
bottles)

5. First-aid kit (see suggested contents in the
first-aid section)

Optional Items.

1. Portable stove and fuel (required in areas
where natural fires would be impractical)
2. Extra food (such as a bag of candy or some
soup mixes)
3. Extra clothing (a complete change of clothes
can be valuable, especially in wet weather
or where falls into water are possible)
4. Wire saw (to facilitate use of small trees or
limbs for splints, litters, or emergency fires)
5. Nylon cord (20 meters)
6. Nylon tubular webbing (6 meters; many uses
including security tie-in to assist participants
on steep, slippery, or intimidating terrain)
7. Climbing rope (may be useful in steep,
hazardous, or intimidating terrain and can
be used to construct a litter)
8. Headlamps and extra batteries (especially
valuable if flashlights are not required of
individuals)
9. Plastic flagging (very helpful in the event of
a search for a missing person)
10. Watch (if not required of individuals)
11. Insect repellent (if not required of
individuals)
12. Sunscreen (if not required of individuals)
13. Toilet paper (if not required of individuals)

6. Leadership Requirements and Qualifications.
The minimum qualifications for a hiking-group
leader depend largely upon the environment in
which the hike is to be conducted. A short
summer walk in a large suburban park might
demand no more than reasonable maturity,
common sense and responsibility, and an ability
to find the route through signs or maps. On the
other hand, even a modest wilderness adventure
may require a leader with highly specialized
skills and extensive experience, able to inspire
group attitude and action while remaining
constantly alert to conditions in the environment.
The bottom line is the same in either case; either
outing must be conducted in a manner
consistent with participant expectations and
accepted leadership practices. Meeting
participant expectations results in satisfied

"customers," while compliance with accepted
standards and practices provides substantive
support in the event of a mishap resulting in a
lawsuit against the leader or his or her
employer. Any hiking leader should have at
least the following attributes:

A. Maturity consistent with the responsibility
of the job;
B. Evident intelligence and common sense;
C. An ability to relate to the employer and the
participants in a friendly and personable
manner;
D. An ability to assess the psychological and
physical needs and limits of the participants
with reasonable accuracy;
E. An ability to communicate ideas and
instructions effectively and appropriately
(This includes an awareness of the
importance of the setting in which the
communication is being attempted, of
physical appearance, timing and the use of
gestures and eye contact.);
F. An understanding of teaching methodology
as required by program objectives (This
includes an effective balance of verbal
instructions, demonstration, and practice.);
G. A willingness and ability to exercise control
over the actions of the group in conformance
with the standards and policies of the
employer;
H. Driving ability and a satisfactory driving
record, plus ample experience in similar
vehicles and road and weather conditions as
required by the program;
I. First-aid skills appropriate to the situation
(This must include experience and training
in improvisation and long-term care if any
back-country or wilderness travel is planned
since any injury help is at *least* many hours
away. First-aid training must also include
substantial emphasis on the recognition and
treatment of immersion hypothermia and
hyperthermic conditions and means of
preventing these.);
J. Search-and-rescue training appropriate to
the program (This must at least include an
awareness of the capabilities and limits of
local search-and-rescue services and an
understanding of how to control and use
these services effectively.);

K. Knowledge of the area in sufficient detail to allow effective planning of the field portions of the program (This almost invariably requires a high level of competence in map reading, good maps, and at least some firsthand knowledge of the area.);

L. Specific outdoor skills and knowledge sufficient to conduct the program safely (This includes an ability to deal effectively with any foreseeable natural hazards such as steep terrain, rockfall, stream or ice crossings, insects or animals, or adverse weather, and may include advanced navigational skills.);

M. Leadership and organizational skills sufficient to conduct a safe program (This includes an ability to maintain control of the group at all times under any reasonably foreseeable condition. In turn, this implies an ability to utilize buddy systems, leader-caboose systems, or other appropriate control techniques, and to maintain an awareness of and concern for the well-being of all participants at all times.);

O. Special skills and knowledge as necessary to meet the specific objectives of the program (This could include, for example, skills or knowledge in counselling, local history, natural science, or any other topic relevant to program objectives.);

P. An awareness of local environmental concerns and a willingness and ability to set an example for participants and to conduct an environmentally sound program;

Q. An awareness of and willingness to conform to the rules and regulations of holders or managers of the resource lands on which the activity is to take place;

R. Substantial hiking experience in an environment similar to that of the intended program.

An individual with all of the above attributes should be able to do an adequate job of leading a hike. Those listed above are common to virtually every outdoor pursuit, and will be referred to as basic leadership requirements in the sections on other activities. They are intentionally generalized in this section because hiking is such a varied activity.

7. Leadership Ratios. Hiking, because of its inherently low risk and slow pace, requires fewer leaders for a given group than most other outdoor pursuits. With the exception of back-country travel or experiences with special objectives requiring a lot of teaching, one leader can usually handle at least a dozen participants. Common sense dictates the bottom line here. It is generally easier to maintain supervision over adults than children and control on trails is simpler than in unconfined or rugged off-trail travel. Special program objectives may necessitate higher leadership ratios. In an urban or suburban setting, for example, a single leader may be sufficient if the participants are mature and can cope temporarily with his or her absence or incapacitation. In a back-country or wilderness setting one leader is almost never sufficient since group control is more difficult and any number of events could result in participants having to fend for themselves.

There are few situations, in either case, where a single leader can provide reasonable service to more than twelve-to-fifteen participants. In any significant back-country travel, this ratio should not exceed one instructor for every eight-to-ten participants, with at least two leaders on site. This puts an upper limit on a group size of over twenty people, which is very large and unwieldly, likely to provide less than a satisfactory experience for participants, and may well infringe on the enjoyment of other users of the area. Such a large group may also exceed the group-size limits of resource-management agencies. Many organizations set an upper limit of twelve-to-fifteen people, including at least two leaders, for any back-country hiking.

B. Course Conduct

1. Common Formats. Most hikes are conducted in a relatively informal manner, since in most cases there is little that the participants need to know prior to the outing and equipment requirements are minimal. Easy hikes in the summer may require only a pre-trip information sheet specifying the nature of the outing, fitness and equipment standards, and the time and place of start and return. (This can be distributed at the time of registration.) More extensive or rigorous outings may require more pre-trip meetings to allow for elaboration of the above information and, most importantly, to enable leaders to assess the participants and adjust the program (or participant expectations) accordingly. If only one pre-trip meeting is planned, it should be several days prior to the outing, especially if gear acquisition may be a problem.

Weekends are the most popular times for hikes, for obvious reasons. Saturdays or Sundays may be the only free days common to a group of people. A surprising number can also get away on weekdays as well, and this population is by no means limited to housewives. Many students, shift workers, retirees, and self-employed or professional people can do this. Weekdays offer great advantages in many areas where trails are congested on weekends, so a rewarding three- or four-hour hike can be scheduled after school hours during much of the year and after normal working hours in late spring and early summer — especially on daylight or summer time.

2. Objectives (When Possible As Progressions).
The objectives of hiking are often limited to simple relaxation and exercise, but may extend to any number of areas. In fact, it probably isn't possible to go on a hike without gaining at least fitness, relaxation, a sense of perspective, social skills, and greater awareness of the natural world. The following objectives are common to most hiking programs and are, in fact, common to most outdoor-pursuit activities. Typically the participant should:

A. Enjoy the experience and want to pursue the activity further;
B. Gain in physical fitness and in awareness of the fitness requirements of hiking;
C. Develop an awareness of and sensitivity to the environment;
D. Gain in walking skills, including pacing, the rest step, and other skills as appropriate to the terrain and route (Safety skills such as techniques for maintaining contact with group members also develop.);
E. Be aware of the major hazards inherent in the activity and ways of reducing or eliminating risks;
F. Understand the clothing and equipment requirements of hiking (This includes

selection, acquisition, maintenance and packing.);
G. Understand the major types of environmental damage that can result from human usage, and the ways in which such impacts can be reduced or eliminated;
H. Be aware of the principle landholders and/or agencies responsible for managing local recreation resource lands, and of the policies and regulations that relate to hiking on these lands;
I. Understand the basic principles of survival and the specific techniques needed to assume a reasonable chance of survival in the local environment;
J. Understand how to provide basic first aid for injuries and conditions likely to occur in a back-country setting (This includes improvisation and long-term care and a thorough understanding of hypothermia and hyperthermic responses, which in turn implies needs that are beyond the scope of most outdoor-pursuit outings or classes.);
K. Be aware of the capabilities and limitations of local search-and-rescue services, and of how to obtain and facilitate such assistance;
L. Be able to interpret both planimetric and topographic maps (This includes an ability to measure distances and to interpret contour lines to determine elevations, elevation differences, and land forms.);
M. Be able to identify and assess potential hiking areas, trails, and routes using maps, guides, and other resources (This includes probable travel times and potential hazards, camping or bivouac sites, water sources and alternate or "escape" routes.);
N. Be able to follow marked routes in the field using maps, guides, and other resources;
O. Be able to measure bearings on a map and follow bearings in the field;
P. Understand and be able to use resections and triangulations to determine field locations;
Q. Develop the skills necessary for safe and environmentally sound off-trail travel;
R. Acquire the knowledge, skills, and experience necessary to independently plan and carry out a successful hiking outing;
S. Develop a level of understanding and concern for the environment that results in responsible actions on behalf of the environment.

3. Levels (Easy, Moderate, Difficult; Beg., Int., Adv.) — Contents. Hikers can be loosely categorized on the basis of overall difficulty, as is usually the case with purely recreational hikers, or on the basis of the array of objectives for the outing. For our purposes here, we'll use the terms easy, moderate, and difficult for levels based on difficulty, and beginning, intermediate, and advanced for levels based on the objectives of a program. It's important to keep in mind that while beginners usually need or seek out easy ventures and advanced-level participants often seek harder challenges, any combination is possible. The label "easy" implies hikes that stick mostly to trails and involve limited distances and elevation gains. Ventures labeled this way shouldn't exceed distances of six or seven miles (ten or eleven kilometers) or elevation gains of more than 1000 feet (about 300 meters), even on a full-day outing. Rough trails, steep terrain, or snow cover might reduce these figures considerably, and a "moderate" hike can cover up to twice the distance and elevation gains, including segments of off-trail travel. Any hike covering more than twelve to fifteen miles (nineteen to twenty-four kilometers) or more than 2500 feet (800 meters) of elevation gain is probably best labeled "difficult" unless the route is exceptionally forgiving.

Objectives "A" through "F" are appropriate for any hike and should be the central focus of "beginning" level outings. Objectives "G" through "M" might be considered reasonable targets for "intermediate" level experiences. The remainder, while very much worthwhile, are probably attainable only after repeated experiences at the intermediate and/or "advanced" levels.

APPENDIX B

TREKKING AND HUT-HOPPING

A. General Description

1. What It Is, What Is Done. Trekking and hut-hopping are terms sometimes used interchangeably to refer to overnight travel involving hiking. The term trekking is usually used in the context of international or exotic travel, and may involve anything from city sight-seeing and hotel stays to rugged backpacking. Trekkers may also travel by any conceivable form of transport. In this context, however, we're concerned with the most common format, which involves walking or hiking between established accommodations. This type of trekking, often called "hut-hopping," is far more popular than backpacking in many, if not most, parts of the world. The term "hut" is used loosely here to include any suitable lodging providing bedding and, usually, meals. Many countries have extensive systems of mountain huts, varying from cabin-sized structures housing perhaps twenty guests and a resident arranger/cook to huge storm-proof full-service mountain hotels housing 2000 guests.

Hiking from hut to hut has distinct advantages over backpacking in terms of the loads that must be carried, allowing relatively small packs and commensurate comfort and freedom of motion. The disadvantages compared to backpacking include higher daily costs, less freedom of choice in choosing where to spend the night, and less privacy. Depending on the circumstances, these advantages may be offset by reduced expenditure on equipment (shelter and cooking supplies, large packs, etc.), dense arrays of huts, and opportunities to escape the crowds given the much lighter loads that need to be carried. Another strong argument in favor of the use of huts is that while the impact on the hut site itself is usually heavy, the overall impact of human use is reduced since the vicinity is not subjected to the abuse of many small camps, each adding cumulative damage through fuel use, soil compaction, and pollution.

2. Hazards in the Activity. Trekking is similar to hiking in that walking, the essential activity, is rarely hazardous in itself. As in hiking, an awareness of the natural hazards of the area, including the weather, is essential. The primary danger is poor planning and inadequate preparation for unexpected extra time exposed to the elements. Unlike backpackers, hikers and trekkers don't carry complete lodgings on their backs. Too often lives depend upon reaching the shelter of the hut, so carrying basic survival gear and knowing how to use it can reduce risks to a very low level.

3. Who Participates. Trekking or hut-hopping requires little or no more skill or fitness than basic hiking, but does present some barriers in terms of lodging and meal costs. These activities, as in backpacking, also involve larger blocks of time away from home and work. The result is a smaller potential clientele for this type of outing than for hiking.

At the same time, many public and commercial purveyors of outdoor activities find it easier to attract participants to trekking or backpacking than to hiking. One likely explanation is that hiking may sometimes be, and almost always at least appears to be, an activity not warranting the services of a leader. Domestic hut-hopping trips involving little transportation cost and reasonably priced lodging and meals appeal to a broad range of people, including teenagers, young adults, and young families. Extra foreign travel, which typically involves substantial costs in time and money, appeals to many but is affordable by a relatively small segment of the population. Therefore clientele for these services have in common a strong spirit of adventure plus substantial financial resources and/or a willingness to make the necessary adjustments in lifestyle to afford the trip.

4. Resource Requirements. Hut-hopping implies the availability of accommodations. These may be any form of shelter acceptable to leaders and participants, but some provision must be made to provide food. A few lodgings include full meal service and snack lunches, while others provide only cooking facilities. In the latter case

the food has to be carried or purchased along the way.

It's also important to check with each proposed lodging well in advance to be sure that the facility will be open, available to the group, and have enough room. Private operators sometimes limit usage to certain clubs or organizations, and reservations (with deposits) are often required. It's often possible to obtain substantial discounts on housing and/or meals by joining the appropriate organizations. Extensive public and private hut systems exist throughout the mountainous portions of Eastern and Western Europe and Japan, and in some mountain regions of Australia, New Zealand, Great Britain, Canada, the United States, the Soviet Union, and many other countries. In many cases, especially in areas of extensive hut development, there is little choice but to use the system since virtually every place suitable for camping has become a hut site. Not uncommonly, camping is prohibited in such areas anyway for economic or environmental reasons.

5. Equipment and Clothing Requirements. The equipment requirements of trekking don't vary significantly from hiking; basic needs remain essentially the same because the dangers are the same, namely unexpected injury, accident, or loss of way preventing access to lodgings for the night. Even on long trips, little extra clothing is needed since most huts often have a water supply ample enough to allow washing and a place to dry clothes in wet weather. Many huts require you to use slippers or sneakers inside, though if this is the case they are usually provided.

The hiking list should serve the trekking party well if attention is paid to the social, if not real, survival value of some of the optional hikers' gear like toilet paper and a clean shirt.

6. Leadership Requirements and Qualifications. Hut-hopping or trekking instruction may require no more than the attributes suggested for the hiking leader. This is especially true on short domestic trips where the only additional requirement may be an ability to sustain good relations with the group for the length of the trip. Longer trips or foreign travel can be far more demanding; the process of scheduling transportation, lodging, and meals can become quite complex and difficult, and may require the handling of substantial amounts of money. The leader of a domestic trip can often rely on telephone communications and well-established credit systems, while the leader on a foreign trip may have to solve problems without recourse to the employer's advice, negotiate prices and make payments using foreign currencies and credit systems, and often do all of this in another language.

The leader of a trek or hut-hopping venture therefore needs all of the attributes of a hiking leader plus:

A. An awareness of available lodgings, accommodations, and procedures for securing access to needed facilities;
B. In the case of foreign travel, an ability to efficiently conduct the group through such bureaucratic and urban delights as passport controls, currency exchanges, and chaotic mass-transit systems enroute to the trekking area;
C. An ability to conduct whatever financial affairs may be necessary (This may in some instances require a willingness and ability to carry large sums of money, establish pricing agreements, pay bills, and keep acceptable records of transactions.);
D. An ability to respond effectively to the psychological and physical stresses of extended travel (This includes personal stresses as well as those of participants.)

7. Leadership Ratios. As in hiking, acceptable ratios vary considerably. One leader may be able to supervise twelve to fifteen participants on a popular well-marked path in good weather; however, higher leadership ratios generally improve program quality and safety. Each case has to be assessed separately, as in hiking, and it is vital to consider the potential consequences should a leader become incapacitated or out of touch with the group. Just as in hiking, a strong case can be made for two leaders on any wilderness or back-country trek, and many people feel that most foreign treks warrant this. In any case, the total party size has to be consistent with available space in lodgings since

large groups may have considerable difficulty finding space, even with advance notice.

B. Course Conduct

1. Common Formats. Most overnight programs involve only one night, since a two-day weekend is by no means universal. Even in the developed countries and even where it's the norm, household chores and other obligations often put a high price on non-working time. Three-day formats, while more difficult for participants to arrange, offer distinct advantages. Though the first and last days are partly consumed by travel to and from the site, you have an entire day free of concerns about getting back home. Psychologically and in terms of available program time, this is a great advantage. Some resorts and huts also offer discounts for two nights of stay, or even limit reservations to two nights during weekends, another argument for three-day formats.

Domestic trips are sometimes run on a one- or two-week basis, usually during the summer months when kids are out of school and vacations are commonly taken. These trips are best planned with work schedules in mind, since vacations most often involve taking full workweeks off. Foreign treks are usually scheduled as two-, three-, or four-week adventures, largely because of the high cost of air transportation. Longer trips are rare since few people can obtain or afford longer vacations and the shorter formats allow them to fit the trip into shorter vacation periods or to travel on their own during the remainder of available vacation time.

In any case, pre-trip meetings are valuable. Longer domestic trips usually warrant at least two of these, perhaps ten and three days prior to the outing. Foreign trips require substantial contact with participants, by mail and/or pre-trip meetings well in advance of the excursion, to insure that passports, visas, tickets, innoculations, and all necessary gear is in order well in advance of the departure date.

2. Objectives. The objectives listed for hiking, specifically "A" through "G," are appropriate for trekking and hut-hopping. The longer lengths of such ventures usually result in more progress in hiking experience and more opportunities to pursue any number of additional specific interests. (Among the more popular are photography and various aspects of nature study.) Foreign treks are characterized by less emphasis on skills and greater emphasis on historical and cultural understanding. An objective specific to trekking and hut-hopping is the development in participants of an awareness of and an ability to use systems of back-country lodging and accommodations.

APPENDIX C

BACKPACKING

A. General Description

1. What It Is, What Is Done. Backpacking is a popular activity in most economically advanced countries, especially in the United States, Canada, and Australia, which have relatively large expanses of roadless land and relatively few huts. Backpacking is different from hiking or trekking in that all necessary provisions are carried in the pack. The result is larger loads and a slower pace but a greater sense of independence. Backpackers can set up camp on almost any small flat piece of ground rather than having to return to the roadhead or to a hut at night. Under most weather conditions, modern gear provides a high level of comfort plus a good deal more privacy than that attainable in most huts.

2. Hazards in the Activity. The hazards encountered in backpacking are similar to those in hiking. Greater loads slightly increase the possibility of strains and sprains. Backpackers also travel farther into the back country than hikers, especially on multi-day outings, increasing the significance of any given mishap by lengthening the distance to outside services. On the other hand, backpackers are relatively independent in terms of shelter and provisions, so the dangers inherent in getting lost or becoming stranded are far reduced. Overall, backpacking is probably safer than hiking or hut-hopping, and no doubt ranks as one of the safest of all recreational pastimes.

3. Who Participates. Backpacking has advocates and committed participants of all ages. While many are young adults, typically middle- and upper-middle-class students and professionals, no demographic category is unrepresented.

4. Resource Requirements. Backpackers need trails or other walkable routes and places to camp. Some areas have an abundance of freely accessible resources, while in others these may be limited by road or trail conditions, steep or densely vegetated terrains offering few campsites, climate or weather, insect pests or animal hazards, or limits on travel and/or camping. Limits on access or camping privileges are common for a variety of reasons, ranging from politics to economic, safety, and environmental concerns. Local resource managers are a good source of information about potential backpacking sites, along with local providers of goods and services related to backpacking, guide books, and hiking or backpacking clubs. In any case it is important to check with the resource manager to find out about regulations, policies, and any permit requirements. Resource managers can also provide current information about the condition of access roads, trails, and campsites, and can usually give you accurate maps.

5. Equipment and Clothing Requirements. The basic essentials for backpacking are few and simple, and include little more than adequate footwear, enough shelter and insulation to allow a good night's sleep, and some provisions for food and water. When constructing a list of minimum required clothing and equipment for a backpacking outing, it is important to include all items necessary for safety and to reduce impact on the land. At the same time you should keep in mind the basic objectives of backpacking, which can be rendered unattainable by excessive gear. Too much equipment means too much weight, and too much weight decreases the enjoyment of walking while increasing the chance of injury. Pack weights of twenty percent or less of a person's body weight can be carried comfortably for long periods by adults in reasonable condition, assuming a well-constructed and well-fitted backpack. At thirty percent, all but the very tough or masochistic sorts will begin to suffer, and for most purposes this should be taken as an upper limit for backpack weights. At forty percent the risk of injury to the unconditioned carrier begins to rise dramatically, and travel becomes an ordeal for everyone. Few situations justify loads of fifty percent of the body weight, even for those tough enough to attempt it.

Even more serious degradation of the experience can result from the use of gear that does more than is necessary. For example, a good mountain tent, which may be a necessity on a high Alpine climb or a winter backpack trip, can be an expensive, heavy liability on a summer low-elevation outing. When a simple tarp provides more than ample protection, why isolate participants from the wilderness, blocking the breezes, the moon, and the stars with a high-tech little mobile home?

The following suggested equipment list is based, like the hiker's and trekker's lists, on travel during the spring, summer, and fall in mountainous regions of the Pacific Northwest of the United States. Note that the individual list is identical to that for hiking except for items 24 through 26 on the individual required list and item 19 on the individual optional list. Group requirements vary from the hiking list in that only item 5, the first-aid kit, is listed as required since individuals each carry sleeping bags and some form of shelter. The optional group list remains the same except for item 14.

Participants should understand that function is more important than form, and should be made aware of low-budget sources of gear, including homemade, borrowed, or rented items.

SUGGESTED MINIMUM GEAR REQUIRED FOR BACKPACKING
Individual Gear

Required Items - Items 1 through 23 are the same as those for hiking (Appendix A).

24. Large pack (to carry all of the above plus some group gear)
25. Shelter (may be shared, however, each individual should carry a part, such as a fly or groundsheet, as an emergency shelter)
26. Stove, fuel, and cooking utensils (may be shared and listed as required only because this is often the case due to environmental concerns.)

Optional Items - Items 1 through 18 are the same as those for hiking (Appendix A).

19. Repair kit (sewing supplies, extra buttons, wire, clevis pins, split rings, ripstop nylon-cloth repair tape, duct tape, and glass fiber tape are especially useful components, along with miniature scissors and pliers and a small screwdriver and awl)

Group Gear

Required items for each independent field group.

1. First-aid kit (see suggested contents in the first-aid section)

Optional Items - Items 1 through 13 are the same as those for hiking (Appendix A). Item 14 is required group gear.

15. Snow shovels (can be invaluable at high-elevation trailheads in early and late season to dig out cars)
16. Snowshoes (a small pair can be a great help in breaking trail in the event of unexpected snowstorms in early or late season)
17. Water purification system (this is necessary and should be required unless required of individuals; possibilities include provision of appropriate chemicals, stoves, fuel, and containers for boiling, or filtration devices such as Katadyne filters.)

The following lists are consistent with the foregoing suggestions, and are based on many years of experience by the author. The items listed in the left-hand column below are for multi-day hikes in the fall and spring in the mountainous parts of the Pacific Northwest of the United States and similar maritime climates. Winter activities may require slightly more insulation, though the list includes sufficient clothing and gear for most winter outings at moderate elevations. Both skiing and mountaineering require additional specialized equipment. The left-hand column of items should total about fifty-five pounds, including camera, film, tent, and three days' food supply. Sharing tents, stoves, food, cooking gear, and other "group" items can reduce the weight to thirty pounds or less. A similar reduction can result from replacing items in the left-hand column with the corresponding mid-summer alternatives listed in the right-hand column. The weight estimates assume care in selecting lightweight versions of each item on the list, but do not assume use of superlight high-tech gear.

Clothing worn

Undershorts
Wool* pants or knickers & sox
Medium-weight wool shirt
Medium-to-heavy hiking boots
2 pair of wool sox

Possible Alternatives for mid-summer

Light wool pants or 60/40 knickers
Light wool shirt
Light trail boots

Clothing carried

Wool hat
Cotton sun hat
Wool mittens
Leather gloves
Light glove liners
Cotton shirt
Polypropylene turtleneck
Wool turtleneck
Wool sweater
Synthetic vest
Light down parka
Wind shell, light nylon with hood
Cagoule, coated nylon with hood
Spare undershorts
Wind pants, light nylon
Rain pants or chaps, coated nylon
Polypropylene long johns
Medium-weight synthetic (pile) pants
Sox, wool (at least one complete change)
High gaitors
Plastic bags for feet, four camp shoes

Possible Alternatives for mid-summer

Leather gloves & liners only
Polypropylene turtleneck only
Wool shirt *or* vest
Pile jacket only
Omit wind shell
Poncho, full size
Omit wind pants
High gaitors with cagoule or poncho
Long johns only
1 pr. wool sox only
Low gaitors
Two camp shoes
Sandals instead

Gear Carried

Large (10 x 12 foot or 3 x 4 meter) tarp
Light ground sheet
Sleeping bag with 3 in. (7 cm.) top loft

Insulated sleeping pad
Gas or kerosene stove, fuel, & large pot
Headlamp & small flashlight
Cord, 50'x ⅛" (15 x 3 mm.)
Plastic flagging, 1 roll
Plastic water bottle, 1 liter
Cup and spoon
Sunglasses
Maps
Pack cover
Umbrella
Kits (detailed below)

Possible Alternatives for mid-summer

Smaller tarp
Bivouac sack
Elephant's foot and parka
Light closed-cell pad
Alcohol stove, fuel, & small pot
Two small flashlights

Repair and small-item kit

Compass
Pocket knife
Whistles — 2
Extra batteries — alkaline, 4
Flashlight bulbs
Wire saw
Plastic or duct tape
Candles (votive type)
Pitchwood fire starter
Matches
String or cord, 20 ft. (7 m.)
Ripstop tape
Wire, 6 in. (2 m.)
Sewing kit
Assorted safety pins
Insect repellent
Sun-block lotion (15 rating)
Small flashlight
Small notepad
Pencil
Pen

Toilet kit

Washcloth
Comb
Mirror
Toothbrush
Toothpaste

Dental floss
Razor
Toilet paper, in plastic with matches

Personal first-aid kit

Betadyne
Elastic bandage, 4 in. (10 cm.)
Kling roller gauze, 3 in. (7-8 cm.)
4 x 4 in. (10 x 10 cm.) pads, 12
Moleskin, 20 sq. in., (150 cm.^{2})
Band-Aids — 12 assorted
Butterfly closures, 6
Aspirin
Tylenol
Antihistamine
Salt tablets
Oil of cloves
Soap (tiny bar)
Tweezers
Thermometer
Adhesive tape, 1 x 12 in. (2½ cm. x 4 m.)

Optional three-season additions

Extra sweater
Extra wool hat
Handkerchief
Camera and film
Binoculars, miniature
Two-person tent

Optional mid-summer additions

Cotton shorts
Cotton pants

6. Leadership Requirements and Qualifications.
A backpacking leader should possess all of the attributes of a hiking leader and have in addition:

A. Substantial experience in backpacking in an environment similar to that of the intended program;

B. Knowledge of the area beyond that specified in item "K" of the hiking list, to include locations of potential campsites and water supplies as well as natural hazards;

C. An awareness of and ability to respond effectively to the safety concerns related to camping in the environment in question (This should include such hazards as wildfire, treefall, wind or storm damage, insects or animals, and water pollution.);

D. An awareness of the potential for human impact related to camping and a willingness and ability to organize an environmentally sound program.

7. Leadership Ratios. Leadership ratios in backpacking can at least in theory be the lowest of any outdoor pursuit if safety alone is considered. The closest comparable activity is hiking, where in ideal conditions two leaders might be able to handle up to twenty participants. In theory, two backpacking leaders might be able to handle even more adult participants, simply because each individual is self-contained and in far less danger should he or she become separated from the group.

In practice, however, such group sizes and leadership ratios are rarely seen because of several problems with such large parties. First, many land managers will not allow parties of twenty or more due to concern about environmental impact and degradation of the experiences of other users. Limits as low as twelve people per group, including leaders, are widely recommended and occasionally mandated by managers. These are valid concerns and should be respected. A party of more than a dozen people may encounter a scarcity of suitable campsites or end up spread over a number of widely scattered ones. Larger numbers tend to overcrowd sites, expanding compaction and abrasion damage and overstressing delicate local ecosystems. Few private users like to encounter large groups, and one of the best ways for an organization to get a bad reputation among the locals is to field large groups in popular areas, especially in "high season."

In practice, most organizations limit groups to twelve to fifteen people, including two leaders. These ratios are typically increased to one leader per three or four participants, again with a minimum of two leaders per group for "outer-limits" activities such as rugged off-trail adventures. The reasons for having two are the same as those for hiking. Any number of situations can result in the incapacitation of one leader, or in the need for a leader to be in two places at one time. Beyond the safety advantages, any teaching objectives and the general comfort and satisfaction of the group

are enhanced by having two along. Another distinct benefit not mentioned earlier is the potential for training leaders by employing those with less experience in assistant or apprenticeship roles.

B. Course Conduct

1. Common Formats. The most common backpacking format is an overnight, two-day excursion, primarily because most participants have difficulty obtaining more free time. Certainly a two-day outing can be a pleasant and rewarding experience, yet the advantages of longer trips are so great as to warrant careful attention. Even one additional half day provides a disproportionate increase in the potential satisfactions of the outing. The extra part or full day allows two nights' stay rather than one, opportunities for travel much farther into the back country, and/or much more time for attainment of other objectives. Participants on three-day or longer outings appreciate having a full day untainted by the need to travel to or from the trailhead. Many people feel that three-to-five-day outings are optimal since they allow attainment of the principle objectives of backpacking yet don't require extremely heavy pack loads. But even in summer conditions, the food and sometimes extra gear requirements of longer ventures can result in uncomfortably heavy loads. While there are more potential recruits for two-day outings, leaders and managers can still look carefully at the advantages of longer outings and consider adding such programs.

Whatever the trip length, backpacking outings usually warrant at least one pre-trip meeting. Two are better, with one perhaps ten days and one about three days prior to the outing. The first meeting can be used to introduce participants to the nature and content of the activity and to establish correspondence between participant and leader expectations. Gear requirements can also be detailed, allowing plenty of time to locate appropriate items. The second meeting allows for last-minute adjustments and directions to participants, facilitating a smooth departure on the outing day.

2. Objectives. As in any outdoor pursuit, participants gain from the experience in many ways. Specific goals and objectives of an outing are usually decided by the manager and/or leader(s), and are determined in part by the overall aims and directions of the sponsoring agency. The following list of objectives includes those appropriate for advanced-level outings, as well as for intermediate or beginning ones. Some are listed with those common to all backpacking outings first, followed by others in the order in which they might be approached in the field. More specific and advanced objectives are thus grouped toward the end of the list.

No two leaders will agree on the exact ordering of objectives, and every leader will want to make certain additions, subtractions, or modifications to the list. It is valuable, however, to review the list carefully and to establish a similar set of objectives before leading any outing. If the activity is part of a class, especially a class in an educational institution, then it may be necessary to construct a formal written list. In any case it's often useful to carry a few notes into the field to help insure that key topics are addressed.

Typical objectives for backpacking are that the participant will: A through E are the same as those for hiking (Appendix A).

F. Understand the clothing and equipment requirements of backpacking (This includes selection, acquisition, maintenance, and packing.);

G. Understand the major types of environmental damage that can result from human usage, and the ways in which such impacts can be reduced or eliminated;

H. Be able to identify potential campsites and assess the site for natural hazards and potential for environmental damage;

I. Be able to set up a safe, comfortable and environmentally sound campsite, use the site effectively, and leave the site clean and undamaged (This implies an understanding of how to set up tents and/or tarps, how to use tents, pads, sleeping bags, stoves or fires, how to cook, and other skills as appropriate.);

J. Be aware of the principle landholders and/or agencies responsible for managing local recreation resource lands, and of the policies and regulations that relate to backpacking on these lands;

K. Understand the basic principles of survival and the specific techniques needed to assume a reasonable chance of survival in the local environment;

L. Understand how to provide basic first aid for injuries and conditions likely to occur in a back-country setting (This includes improvisation and long-term care and a thorough understanding of hypothermia and hyperthermic responses, which in turn implies needs that are beyond the scope of most outdoor-pursuit outings or classes.);

M. Be aware of the capabilities and limitations of local search-and-rescue services, and of how to obtain and facilitate such assistance;

N. Be able to interpret both planimetric and topographic maps (This includes an ability to measure distances and to interpret contour lines to determine elevations, elevation differences, and land forms.);

O. Be able to identify and assess potential backpacking areas, trails, and routes using maps, guides, and other resources (This includes probable travel times and potential hazards, camping or bivouac sites, water sources, and alternate or "escape" routes.);

P. Be able to follow marked routes in the field using maps, guides, and other resources;

Q. Be able to measure bearings on a map and follow bearings in the field;

R. Understand and be able to use resections and triangulations to determine field locations;

S. Develop the skills necessary for safe and environmentally sound off-trail travel;

T. Acquire the knowledge, skills, and experience necessary to independently plan and carry out a successful backpacking outing;

U. Develop a level of understanding and concern for the environment that results in responsible actions on behalf of the environment.

3. Levels. A successful outing depends upon meeting participants' needs and expectations. Dividing outings into levels based on difficulty or objective contact can assist participants in selecting appropriate experiences. The following suggestions for categorizing outings are consistent with common practice, yet are subject to considerable variations. It's also important to remember that uncertainty is inherent in all outdoor pursuits due to the complexity of the activities and the unpredictability of the weather and other factors. Outings are often described in terms of both difficulty and objective content, though the latter system is primarily associated with classes or outings within educational settings. Describing them in both ways is always a good idea since beginners don't necessarily want easy outings and advanced practitioners don't necessarily want the challenge of a difficult trip.

Many factors affect the difficulty of an outing. A backpacking experience is a complex event affected by terrain, ground cover, trail conditions, the length and specifications of the route, the nature and condition of campsites and water supplies, the type and amount of gear carried, the weather, and, of course, the fitness, experience, and attitudes of the participants. An "easy" backpacking trip seldom involves trail distances of more than four to six miles (six to ten kilometers) and total elevation increases of more than 1000 feet (300 meters) per day on a two-day trip, since, presumably, much of the first and last days will be spent in getting to and from the trailhead. On easy hikes it is best not to assume travel rates in excess of two miles (three kilometers or so) per hour of walking, which will result in only about one-and-a-half miles (about two-and-a-half kilometers) per hour of travel when rest stops are included. An additional hour is usually required for every 1000 feet (300 kilometers) of elevation gain.

On longer trips the distances might be increased by days other than the first and last. For example, an easy three-day backpacking trip might involve four to five miles (six to eight kilometers) of moderate uphill travel on day one, six to ten miles (ten to sixteen kilometers) of relatively level travel on day two, and six to eight miles (ten to thirteen kilometers) of gentle downhill travel on day three. These suggestions assume reasonably fit and well equipped adult participants in good weather and walking conditions. When planning an easy trip it is usually best to be conservative and opt for the shorter, gentler alternatives since any number of factors can increase travel times and difficulties.

A "moderate" trip might involve longer distances (perhaps six to eight miles on first and last, or ten to twelve miles on middle days), or greater elevation gains (up to 2500 feet or so) on portions of rugged, snow covered, or off-trail travel not exceeding twenty percent of the total distance. Trips longer than three or four days are often labeled "moderate" due to the inevitable extra stresses and pack weights associated with them.

Any backpacking trip covering more than eight to ten miles (thirteen to sixteen kilometers) on first and last days, and twelve miles (nineteen kilometers) on middle days is usually considered "difficult" even if the route follows easy trails. This label is probably appropriate for any backpack route involving elevation gains in excess of 2500 feet (800 meters), major sections of snow-covered or very rough trail, or off-trail travel other than in easy fields or meadows.

Objectives "A" through "H" are appropriate for a beginning-level backpacking outing, and can often be attained on a two-day trip with good planning, experienced leaders, and a bit of luck. A pair of two-day outings or one three-day outing is usually ample to meet these objectives under most conditions. Objectives "I" through "O" are appropriate for intermediate outings and usually require at least a couple of weekends or an additional three-day outing beyond the beginning level. Intermediate courses are designed to give participants the ability to do some trail backpacking on their own with little outside assistance. Much of the basic information necessary to attainment of these objectives can be taught very effectively in a classroom setting, thus accelerating the progress on outings. This is especially true of first aid and some aspects of map and compass use. Objectives "P" through "U" are typical for advanced outings. The main differences between intermediate and advanced levels, as defined here, are the emphasis on off-trail travel and the focus on complete independence. The final objective in the list transcends all of the others in that it's the only one not centered on the individual; it could be attained at any point on the progression or never at all. Perhaps more than for any other objective in the list, leadership by example is critical.

4. Sample Itineraries and Instructors' Guidelines.
The following "Planning Guidelines for Instructors" and "Recommended Daily Agendas" illustrate one way in which the recommended objectives might be attained for advanced groups.

Leaders may find that it is useful to transcribe notes similar to those on the "Recommended Daily Agendas" to file cards for use in the field.

BEGINNING BACKPACKING OUTING PLANNING GUIDELINES FOR INSTRUCTORS

Length of Outing (days): 3
Departure Time: 7 a.m.
Meeting Place:
Transportation Method:
Days of Week: Friday-Sunday
Return Time: about 5 p.m.
Student Gear and Equipment Requirements (refer to gear lists): All required items on standard equipment list, plus maps of the area. Emphasize minimal nature of the list and suggest extra insulation.
Instructor and Leader Gear and Equipment Requirements (additional): One *extra* clothing layer to share, one small first-aid kit, and repair items for stove and packs.
Group Gear and Equipment Requirements (per independent field group): First-aid belt, tarp. Depending on site and season: snow shovels (for vehicles), stoves, extra fuel, rope & slings (to protect gear on river crossings), snowshoes (to break trail).
Specification of the Location and Route(s): The site should enable several groups to travel independently during the day but meet on at least one night. Routes should allow easy-to-moderate trail hiking of four to five miles on Day 1, six to ten miles on Day 2, and four to five miles on Day 3. Off-trail hiking in easy-to-moderate terrain for one to three miles should be included for Day 2 or Day 3. Snow cover should not exceed one-half of the total distance. A minor peak or scenic viewpoint should be included to facilitate map-and-compass training. Whenever possible, select the lowest and least-used site to minimize physical and social impacts.

BEGINNING BACKPACKING OUTING RECOMMENDED DAILY AGENDA

DAY 1

Business at Meeting Point

1. Take attendance
2. Distribute and collect waivers
3. Return waivers to store room
4. Assemble group gear (sign it out from the gear room)
5. Provide cleared driver *and* relief driver for each vehicle
6. Recheck all student gear
7. Check *all* vehicles for proper condition of lights, seat belts (*1 per passenger!*), horn, tires (including spare and chains)
8. Make sure each driver has clear directions and emergency instructions and knows the rules about speeding, seat belts, and drugs.
9. Check road conditions and weather forecast

At the Trailhead

1. Recheck the attendance
2. Obtain permits if required
3. Form groups and assign group gear
4. Shuttle vehicles as needed
5. Discuss staff course objectives and specific plans with students
6. Discuss group and individual procedures for injury, being lost, sanitation, minimizing environmental impacts while hiking, rest stops, pacing, lead trail people, hydration, and specific hazards of the site.
7. Show all staff where car keys are hidden

During the Day

— Frequent stops to check clothing and feet and to interpret the area (history, geology, plants, and animals);
— Emphasize trail etiquette and safety and practice proper trail techniques.
— Encourage study of the map (relating the map to reality through predictive observation and review);
— Point out examples of environmental impact and campsites along the way;
— Emphasize general (campsite) and specific (tent site) selections as you approach and set up camp.

In the Evening

— Assist students in locating safe, low-impact, comfortable sites;
— Check for proper function and use of tents, tarps, stoves, and other gear;
— Be sure that all students know the rules about leaving the campsite and are comfortable with their eating and sleeping arrangements;
— Have a meeting to discuss the day, answer questions, monitor attitudes and health, and plan the next day. Appropriate topics include a detailed review of the route, including travel rates, terrain interpretation, prediction of the next day's route based on this experience, a discussion of local history (man's use of the area and natural science), and techniques for staying warm and dry overnight.

DAY 2

In the Morning

— Wake the students at least two full hours before you plan to be on the trail;
— Before breaking camp have a "Tour of Homes" to let everyone share information about their sites and shelters, sleeping gear, stoves, and food;
— Before leaving, emphasize *complete* restoration of the site;
— Also before leaving, make sure everyone has looked *carefully* at the map and understands the route and plans;
— Allow students and staff to adjust groups if desired and reasonable.

During the Day

— Keep reviewing the basics covered on Day 1, and monitor hydration and nutrition carefully;
— Re-emphasize *frequent* prediction, observation, and review as a means of learning to interpret maps (Allow time for this!);
— Get up on a high point, and thoroughly review map interpretation and compass use — ideally, it is good if you can see most of the terrain you have been and will be hiking in;
— If possible, select a campsite that varies

significantly from that of the first day in terms of aesthetics, exposure, potential for damage, and safety characteristics, then discuss necessary precautions to avoid impact and hazards.

In the Evening

— Check, as on Day 1, to be sure all students are well sheltered and fed, and in safe, low-impact sites;
— Meet, as on Day 1, adding to the contents of that day's meeting an assessment of the students' interests with regard to the next day's program;
— A short night hike (trails only) can be fun and worthwhile.

DAY 3

In the Morning

— Repeat Tour of Homes, again allowing about two hours from wake-up time to departure time;
— Discuss timing as an important part of planning;
— Carefully review the route;
— Tour the site with the group to see if the site was properly restored.

During the Day

— Allow more student leadership, under supervision of the staff;
— Consider routes of varying lengths and difficulty to accommodate student interests;
— Given the proper stream, expertise, equipment, and interest, try a major stream crossing;
— Review techniques for safety and comfort in downhill travel if the route allows (as it usually does on the last day);
— Plan to be at the trailhead between 2 and 3 p.m.

At the Trailhead

— Collect *all* group gear;
— Remind drivers of the rules and plans, and check the vehicle (all as in Day 1 at the meeting point!);
— Carefully check the roll once everyone is in the vehicles;

— Allow no vehicle to leave without the instructor's consent;
— Before leaving, have a short debriefing/ evaluation of the trip and arrange the post-trip meeting.

At the Return Point

— Check in all group gear;
— Clean the vehicles of litter and any excessive mud on the inside;
— Be sure the drivers know the check-in procedure for the vehicles and have rides home;
— Be sure that all participants have rides home, and be especially careful to provide a safe trip for individuals who are very tired or not feeling well;
— Check the return point *carefully* for items left behind;
— You are not done yet! Fill out a trip-record form and a list of the total mileage for each vehicle;
— Go home and *relax;*
— Conduct the post-trip meeting. This is a most valuable part of the course, and should include: 1) a detailed review of the route to compare the students' pre-trip predictions to their field experiences, 2) a chance for students to critique the planning and leadership of the trip, 3) a chance for the instructor(s) to emphasize or reinforce important concepts and to add material not covered in the field, and 4) a discussion of the types of outings or further training that the trip has prepared the students for, with examples of local options;
— Conduct staff evaluations in cooperation with the coordinator.

INTERMEDIATE AND ADVANCED BACKPACKING OUTINGS PLANNING GUIDELINES FOR INSTRUCTORS

Length of Outing (days): 3
Days of Week: Friday-Sunday
Departure Time: 7 a.m.
Return Time: about 6 p.m. (varies)
Meeting Place:

Transportation Method:
Student Gear and Equipment Requirements (refer to gear lists): Same as beginners', but with at least one item of extra clothing to share (sweater, coat, vest, etc.), a small first-aid kit, and a repair kit.

Group Gear and Equipment Requirements (per independent field group): First-aid kit; large tarp. Ropes and hardware for protection on stream crossings will usually be needed, as will snowshoes if the route is high and the trip is planned early or late in the season.

Specifications of the Location and Route(s): There are several possible ways to achieve the objectives of these courses. Route length and difficulty will vary depending on the fitness, skill level, and interests of the group. Each route should be interesting and challenging and include 1) opportunities for several miles (four or more) of moderate-to-difficult off-trail navigation, 2) a viewpoint for map interpretation and triangulation, 3) a long (1500-3000 foot) steep area (thirty percent grade or more with cliff bands) for steep terrain practice, and 4) an opportunity, preferably near the final trailhead, for stream-crossing practice (which must be *protectable* and should involve knee- to waist-deep water).

INTERMEDIATE AND ADVANCED BACKPACKING OUTING RECOMMENDED DAILY AGENDA

DAY 1 - Same as Beginning Backpacking Outing.

At the Trailhead - Same as Beginning Backpacking Outing.

During the Day - Same as Beginning Backpacking Outing plus new activities.

— Emphasize student responsibility for control of the group, including the necessary additional procedures for off-trail travel.
— Discuss travel rates as they relate to snow cover, steepness, vegetation cover, angle of travel on a slope (up, down, diagonal or

across), pack weights, pack types, fitness, and agility;

— Demonstrate and have students practice techniques for minimizing rockfall hazards and environmental impacts on steep off-trail slopes using both controlled and random zigzag patterns;
— Discuss methods for improving rates of travel through route selection, alternative types of navigation, and effective trail and off-trail walking;
— Point out examples of environmental impacts and campsites along the way;
— Emphasize general (campsite) and specific (tentsite) selections as you approach and set up camp.

In the Evening

— Assist students in locating safe, low-impact, comfortable sites;
— Check for proper functions and use of tents, tarps, stoves, and other gear;
— Be sure that all students know the rules about leaving the campsite and are comfortable with their eating and sleeping arrangements;
— Have a meeting to discuss the day, answer questions, monitor attitudes and health, and plan the next day. Appropriate topics include a detailed review of the route, including travel rates, terrain interpretation and prediction of the next day's route based on this experience; a discussion of local history (man's use of the area and natural science); and techniques for staying warm and dry overnight.

DAY 2

In the Morning - Same as Beginning Backpacking Outing plus new activities.

— Allow students and staff to adjust groups if desired and reasonable;
— Arrange to travel in small groups (with two staff members each if separations may exceed two to three hours at a time);
— Be sure that each independent group has adequate shelter, first-aid supplies and first-aid expertise (at least one individual with at least a current American Red Cross Advanced card or equivalent certification).

During the Day - Same as Beginning Backpacking Outing plus new activities.

— Practice resection and triangulation;
— Plan and carry out a one- to three-mile cross-country hike. (*If* a safe, "bombproof" barrier is available, consider dispatching students in small groups, shadowed by staff.);

In the Evening - Same as Beginning Backpacking Outing plus new activities.

— A discussion of outdoor leadership roles, responsibilities, and concerns can be valuable;
— A short night hike (trails only unless the terrain and vegetation allow safe travel with flashlights and headlamps) can be fun and worthwhile, especially in conjunction with a stay of a few hours at a site to simulate bivouac conditions.

DAY 3

In the Morning - Same as Beginning Backpacking Outing.

During the Day - Same as Beginning Backpacking Outing, plus:

— Try to incorporate a two- or three-thousand-foot descent on steep terrain to practice route selection and techniques for negotiating cliff bands and other obstacles with maximum safety and minimum environmental impact;
— Given the proper stream, expertise, equipment, and interest, try a major stream crossing;

At the Trailhead - Same as Beginning Backpacking Outing.

At the Return Point - Same as Beginning Backpacking Outing.

APPENDIX D

MOUNTAINEERING

A. General Description

1. What It Is, What Is Done. Mountaineering encompasses all of the elements of hiking, trekking, backpacking, and often snow camping, as well as the climbing activities central to the popular image. High-angle rock and ice climbing and summit attempts are often part of the experience, but aren't an essential part of this activity. The typical trip begins with a period of travel via trails and off-trail routes to the point where climbing skills become necessary, then centers on some form of snow, ice, or rock climbing until the return trip back down to the realm of hikers and backpackers.

2. Hazards in the Activity. Mountaineering is no doubt more dangerous than backpacking; however, the exact nature of the risks is extremely hard to pin down. There are some natural hazards in mountainous terrain, including steep slopes of snow, ice, and rock, crevasses, avalanches, rockfall, and raging streams. But these present little danger to people who follow accepted mountaineering practices and good common sense. Just as on the highway, virtually all accidents are the result of poor planning and/or poor judgment. The frightening numbers of mountain fatalities in Japan (about 500 annually) and in the Alps of Europe (another 500 annually) are attributable to the very large numbers of inexperienced people who have access to very steep terrain in these areas. In the United States, where only about sixty people die each year in the mountains, getting to such terrain usually requires considerable time and effort, which greatly reduces the total number of inexperienced people involved in this activity. U.S. attitudes toward safety are also much more conservative than in Europe or Japan and may contribute to the low fatality rate. In any case, serious accidents are rare in organized mountaineering outings employing qualified leaders and instructors who adhere to modern teaching standards and practices.

3. Who Participates. Mountaineering, like all outdoor pursuits, attracts avid participants of all ages and demographic backgrounds. Enthusiasts tend, however, to be older and to have even higher incomes and educational levels than those of backpackers. Also, the need for backpacking experience and the higher risks, fitness requirements, and equipment needs in mountaineering combine to reduce the number of potential participants to well below that for other outdoor pursuits. A few programs reduce entrance barriers by providing some of the needed equipment, including fitness training, and reviewing backpacking skills. Giving "mini-lessons" in climbing skills while backpacking can encourage participants to move on to mountaineering classes as well.

4. Resource Requirements. Almost any moutainous area has something to offer, and specific resource needs will depend upon the nature of the outing. If the trip is purely recreational and the participants are experienced, then the possibilities are nearly unlimited for anyone living near the mountains. Outings with specific objectives may require special types of terrain such as steep slopes of rock, snow, or ice, crevassed glaciers, or accessible summits. When you intend to teach skills to groups, site specifications can be critical, further limiting the options. While the ideal mountaineering course should include a range of techniques for rock, snow, and ice climbing, the realities of terrain, season, and weather often require either additional outings or a compromise of objectives. Maps, guidebooks, and local expertise often provide all the information necessary for planning a modest recreational venture with experienced participants. But when teaching is intended, secondhand knowledge of the resource is rarely adequate. Leaders of such outings should make every effort to personally scout the area to determine the series of sites best suited for learning the various skills. Snow slopes for self-arrest practice, beginning belay practice, or any activity where an uncontrolled slide could occur should have good gentle run-outs. Rock-climbing practice sites should be free of rockfall and allow upper belays.

5. Equipment and Clothing Requirements. Gear requirements for mountaineering vary widely.

Most outings involve some back-country hiking, and overnight trips require backpacking gear unless huts or accommodations are available. In some cases the climbing portions of the outing may require no special equipment or clothing, while in others these may be extensive. Items commonly needed for climbing include helmets, ice axes, crampons, ropes, slings, harnesses, various kinds of anchors, and specialized footwear. Along with highly specialized clothing, a vast array of technical hardware and devices may also be essential for some types of climbing.

The following gear lists assume that the outing involves hiking, trekking, backpacking, or snowcamping, and that the appropriate equipment will be carried for these activities. The array of required items assumes that the climbing portions of the outing include glacier travel and basic Alpine rock climbing at middle latitudes from early spring to late fall.

SUGGESTED MINIMUM GEAR REQUIRED FOR MOUNTAINEERING IN ADDITION TO REQUIREMENTS FOR HIKING, TREKKING, OR BACKPACKING

Individual Gear

Required Items:

1. Suitable boots (this implies relatively stiff lug soles, plus stiff leather or plastic uppers if crampons are to be used. Fit, durability, waterproofness and insulation are also critical);
2. Gaitors (high type is necessary if deep snow is expected or if pants are used rather than knickers);
3. Additional insulation (two layers rather than one layer of wool or better fabric, and neck covering such as a turtleneck);
4. Dark, full coverage sunglasses (side shields are sometimes useful);
5. Ice axe (axe specifications should be set by the instructor and all axes carefully inspected before taking on the outing);
6. Crampons and straps or attachment system (Specifications should be set by the instructor.

Crampons' crampon fit and attachment security must be carefully checked before the outing.);

7. Helmet (to instructor's specifications);
8. Prusik loops (to instructor's specifications).

Optional Items (may be required at option of instructor)

1. Carabiners (often required) Two locking types and one non-locking type meet most needs. Many may be required for some technical routes;
2. Harnesses (often required) Many types of seat, chest and combination harnesses are available commercially. Inexpensive versions suitable for basic glacier travel and climbing can be made from tubular webbing;
3. Climbing slings (often useful and sometimes required of individuals) Careful inspection of sling fabric and construction is essential;
4. Skis, ski boots, ski poles, or snowshoes (often necessary);
5. Avalanche beacons or avalanche cords (rarely essential though always an advantage in avalanche terrain. The beacons serve no purpose unless participants are trained in their use, and neither device should be allowed to induce a false sense of security.);
6. Headlamps (extremely useful for the night travel common in mountaineering, almost essential for night climbing or skiing, and often required. Alkaline or other cold-resistant batteries are needed as normal cells are useless in temperatures below about freezing.);
7. Wind protection (Wind-resistant parkas and pants that don't trap moisture are valuable for hard work in cool, windy environments.)

Group Gear

Required Items

1. Tarp or bivouac shelter (Any group traveling above timberline needs to be able to shelter an injured party member and one or two companions for extended periods until outside help can be obtained. Failure to carry such shelter has resulted in many fatalities.);

2. Sleeping bag or equivalent extra insulation (A half bag or elephant's foot plus a vest and parka might suffice. This is an essential adjunct to the above shelter.);
3. Foam pads (at least enough for an injured party and companions. In snow above timberline one three-quarter length sleeping pad for every two party members meets the basic needs and also provides comfortable seating during breaks.);
4. Stove, pot, and fuel (These are considered a basic requirement for groups on Alpine climbs because they provide access to water if ice is available and can provide essential warmth in the form of hot drinks and hot-water bottles.);
5. Avalanche probes (These should be considered a required item at any time that avalanches are possible, which is most of the time in the mid-latitude mountains assumed in this list. Ideally, each person should have a four- to eight-foot [1½ to 2½ 3534 m.] good-quality probe.);
6. Shovels (Portable folding shovels are invaluable should an avalanche bury a person or gear, and should, like the probes, be considered required items in any situation where avalanches might occur. One shovel for every six climbers is probably adequate for rescue work.);
7. Climbing ropes (The type, quality, and condition of the ropes is critical and must be reviewed carefully by the instructor. "Perlon" or kernmantle ropes are the easiest to handle and provide safety advantages in certain technical climbing applications, but are costly and hard to assess for damage. "Goldline" and other laid or braided ropes provide adequate security for most purposes and are less costly and easier to inspect for damage; thus they are generally more suitable for use with classes and large groups. In most cases it's sufficient to provide one rope for every three climbers. Larger parties often carry a spare rope as well, and still others may be required by climbing schools or classes.);
8. Hardware (The exact needs depend upon the route and conditions during the climb. Often-needed items include pickets, flukes, and other snow anchors, screws and other

ice anchors, and pitons, nuts or other rock anchors, as well as belay devices, rappel devices, pulleys, rope-ascending devices, specialized hammers, and tools for steep ice work.);

9. Software (Various-sized loops made from different diameters of rope and widths of webbing are used to secure anchors such as tie-ins and for a multitude of other purposes. As with hardware, group needs must be carefully assessed to avoid over as well as undersupply, and communal needs may be partly met by gear carried by individuals.).

Optional Items

1. Wands (Especially useful when changing conditions or poor visibility might make route-finding difficult. They are used most often on glaciers and snowfields.);
2. Altimeter (sometimes useful for route finding, especially for poor-visibility or night travel. Rarely essential.);
3. Aerial photographs and guidebooks (Especially useful if the outing has specific objectives that require efficient use of the terrain and exact locations of certain routes and areas.)

Remember that the above suggestions are based on mixed glacier and rock climbing at mid-latitudes in situations requiring access to the mountains by foot. You must review the gear suggestions for hiking, trekking, backpacking, snow camping, and rock climbing as well as the items suggested here before specifying the gear requirements for a mountaineering venture. Consider both the dangers of being caught with inadequate gear and the penalties that accrue from carrying too much. Concerns about comfort, safety, and liability are also valid and must be addressed. Nevertheless, unneeded extra gear can easily overburden the pack, drain the wallet, and degrade the experience by clouding the relationship between the participant and the environment. Cost and inconvenience is no excuse for not carrying and using high-quality basic mountaineering safety gear; "Winnebago Fever" is no excuse for stuffing packs with every aid and comfort produced by our society.

6. Leadership Requirements and Qualifications.

A mountaineering leader should possess all of the attributes of a backpacking leader, as well as the ability to conduct the climbing portion of the outing.

Specific additional attributes include:

A. Substantial general mountaineering experience in terrain and climate conditions similar to those in the area of the intended outing (Mountain conditions are complex and variable, and many outings are necessary to build an adequate depth of experience.);
B. An ability to select and assess climbing routes based on direct observation, maps, photographs, and guidebooks, including estimation of hazards, gear needs, best approaches, safest conditions, timing for ascents and descents, total time required, and suitability for various party sizes and ability levels;
C. Training and competence in estimating avalanche and other snow structures and hazards, in selecting safe routes, and in avalanche rescuing under back country, as opposed to ski-area, conditions;
D. An understanding of rope and climbing fabric strengths and characteristics;
E. An ability to tie all of the basic mountaineering knots, including at least the figure eight on a bight, the figure eight follow-through, the single bowline, the bowline on a coil, the double fisherman's (grapevine), prusik knots, and the Muenter hitch;
F. An ability to use ropes, slings, and hardware effectively in establishing both natural and artificial anchors in snow, ice, and rock using pickets, flukes, screws, pitons, nuts, bolts, bollards, and other means;
G. Competence in belaying, using both manual and device-assisted techniques in snow and on rock (This should include the use of standard signals, sitting hip- and boot-axe belays, and belays using belay rings, descenders, and Muenter hitches.);
H. Competence in the use of the ice axe, including the various positions of the French technique, step cutting, and self-arrest on a variety of snow surfaces;

I. Experience in glacier travel, including route selection and the use of accepted techniques for roping up and roped travel on glaciers;

J. Competence in crevasse-rescue techniques, including hands-on practice with 2:1, Bilgeri, and 3:1 "Z" systems, prusik and mechanically assisted rope-climbing techniques, and the construction of rope litters;

K. Competence in rappelling using at least the Dulfersitz, carabiner and figure-eight systems, and the lowering of others using the figure eight and Muenter hitch;

L. An understanding of mountain weather and the weather patterns peculiar to the site of the intended outing;

M. An understanding of altitude-related stresses and physiologic responses, including hypoxia, AMS, HAPE, CE, and retinal hemorrhages, and the recognition, treatment, and prevention of these conditions;

N. An understanding of the effects of cold, wind, exhaustion, and anxiety on the mental and physical conditions of climbers (This includes an awareness of how these stresses affect the learning process, and of techniques for maximizing receptivity and communication.);

O. Fitness and climbing ability exceeding the demands of the route to be led or of the class to be taught;

P. Snowcamping skills and snowshoeing or ski touring ability appropriate for the terrain, climate and season of the intended outing.

7. Leadership Ratios. Mountaineering outings generally require high leadership ratios. Recreational ventures following standard routes well within the abilities of the participants are sometimes led by one fully qualified leader assisted by an assistant who has similar skills but less experience. In this case the pair of leaders may be able to handle as many as 16-20 participants if there are no technical "bottlenecks" on the route. There are several possible objections to this size of a party. First, it may be disallowed by resource managers. Such parties have the potential for substantial overuse of campsites with resultant environmental damage, and can seriously interfere with other parties attempting the same route. Safety is also a concern, because a large party kicks loose a lot of rock, inevitably

bombing itself, and is usually so slow as to greatly extend the time spent on the mountains. This in turn increases dangers. The only substantive counter argument is that large groups can, in theory, carry out their own wounded. Large parties can be reasonable, but only if travel, especially camping, is largely on ground protected by snow, and if the season, timing and route preclude conflict with other climbing parties. The route itself needs to be relatively non-technical, since belays, rappels and even the use of fixed lines can require incredible patience and long delays. Consider that a group of five people can usually rappel off a cliff in about twenty minutes while a group of twenty would require an additional full hour!

Any outing attempting a challenging route or wherein teaching is intended should be limited to about a dozen participants and two leaders. Many organizations attempt to provide a leader or an assistant leader for every three or four participants. This is ideal, though probably not essential in most cases.

B. Course Conduct

1. Common Formats. There are many possible formats for mountaineering trips and classes. Two-day or larger outings and classes are the norm since considerable time is usually required just to access mountainous terrain. When difficult routes or summit attempts are intended, mountaineers usually try to begin climbing very early in the morning, often well before sunrise. This almost always requires travel to a high base camp or hut on the preceding day, and makes for a very long second day if a return to town is necessary by that evening.

Some mountaineering programs that emphasize teaching break up the activity into component parts, offering single-day or evening courses in knot-tying, rock climbing, and other skills that can be taught in or near town, followed by one or more extended outings to teach snow climbing and glacier travel and to integrate various activities. Such a series might include courses covering the mountain environment, a review of backpacking skills, knot-tying and rope use, map-and-compass use on- and off-trail, basic rock climbing. mountain-rescue skills, and first aid for mountaineers, followed by a two- or three-day glacier school and a two- or three-day summit attempt combining glacier travel, snow climbing, and rock climbing.

Pre-trip meetings are essential. When the outing has educational objectives at least two are usually required to allow time to describe the outing, assess the participants, review basic skills (knots, rope handling, and belaying), and explain the gear requirements. The first meeting should be held at least ten days prior to the outing to allow time for the participants to acquire the necessary gear. The second should be held just a few days before the outing, close enough in time so that directions will be remembered and commitments upheld, yet allowing a few hours for last-minute adjustments. Time always flies by at an incredible speed when you're trying to get out of town with a group, and a lot can be saved by checking participant gear at the last pre-trip meeting or perhaps at a special meeting on the evening prior to the outing. Missing items or misfitted crampons are far easier to deal with prior to the time of departure, after which the only option is often to leave the person behind.

2. Objectives. No two mountaineering outings are identical, no matter how hard leaders may try to conform to plans. Nevertheless, it's always worthwhile to set forth principal objectives. Without a clear understanding of these, it's difficult to plan effectively and impossible to present potential participants with a clear picture of what goals to attain. At the same time, it's probably more important in mountaineering than in any other outdoor pursuit to elaborate on the uncertainties inherent in the activity. The alpine environment changes constantly, for example, and the conditions necessary for safe travel and for conduct of many of the component activities of mountaineering may or may not exist on a given outing.

Some outings have very few objectives. This is especially true of casual recreational events with experienced participants. Others have many, as is usually the case in mountaineering classes and schools.

The following list includes only those objectives not suggested earlier for hiking, trekking, backpacking, snow camping, and rock

climbing. These activities are included in the broad definition of mountaineering, and skill in these areas is usually considered a prerequisite to participation in mountaineering. In those cases where prior skill development is not required, the mountaineering course has to be extended to cover them before you move on to more advanced topics. All of the objectives of the prerequisite areas are therefore potentially valid for mountaineering outings and should be reviewed carefully. The reader should review objectives for backpacking, which include those for hiking, then read the objectives for snow camping and rock climbing.

When selecting goals for a specific outing or program, it's important not to overestimate participants' abilities and to choose objectives that are reasonably attainable. As stated above, it's also important to have alternatives in mind for any alpine adventure. Common objectives specific to mountaineering are that participants will:

1. Be able to identify potential sites for mountaineering, using maps, guides, and other resources;
2. Understand the fitness requirements of mountaineering, and prepare with appropriate conditioning exercises;
3. Understand the gear requirements for mountaineering and be able to construct an appropriate list of equipment and specifications given a description of the location and route;
4. Be aware of the physiological effects of altitude and extreme cold, including the recognition, treatment, and prevention of resulting medical problems;
5. Understand avalanches and snow-structure hazards, including basic avalanche predictions, route finding, and avalanche rescue in back country settings;
6. Understand the special hazards and elements of mountain weather, and be able to predict and respond appropriately;
7. Understand the environmental concerns characteristic of alpine and sub-alpine regions, and the ways of minimizing or eliminating impacts in these zones;
8. Be able to select and assess climbing routes based on direct observation, maps, photographs, and guidebooks, including

estimation of hazards, gear needs, best approaches, safest conditions, timing for ascent and descent, total time required, and suitability for various party sizes and experience levels;

9. Be able to tie the most important knots used in mountaineering, including but not limited to the figure eight on a bight, the figure-eight follow-through, the single bowline, the bowline on a coil, the double fisherman (grapevine) and prusik, and the Muenter hitch;

10. Be able to use the ice axe effectively and safely to cut steps, to provide balance and security using the French technique positions, and to engage in self arrest up to and including arrest from a head-first, on-the-back position;

11. Understand the strengths and limits of ropes and the other fabrics used in slings, harnesses, and carabiners, and be able to tie in ways appropriate for climbing on snow and glaciers;

12. Understand the strengths, weaknesses, and proper use of follards, flukes, prikets, ice axes, ice screws, pitons, nuts, bolts, and other anchors used in mountaineering;

13. Demonstrate competence in setting up, securing, and carrying out sitting hip, foot-axe, and friction-device-assisted belays;

14. Be able to select, adjust, fit, and securely attach crampons effectively and safely on a variety of snow and ice surfaces using appropriate French and Austrian techniques;

15. Understand the techniques for crossing glaciers, including route selection, roping up, and ways of reducing the chance of falling into a crevasse;

16. Be able to respond effectively if another party member falls on a cliff or into a crevasse (This includes an ability to set up appropriate systems for accessing and extricating the victim.);

17. Be able to respond effectively after falling while roped (This includes an ability to utilize slings, prusik knots, and mechanical ascenders.);

18. Acquire the skills and knowledge necessary to independently plan and carry out a safe, environmentally responsible, and enjoyable mountaineering outing, integrating all aspects of the sport.

3. Levels. Like other outdoor pursuits, mountaineering trips can be described according to level of difficulty, objectives, or both, and several standard systems describe the difficulty of climbs and climbing routes. Detailed comparisons of these systems can be found in some mountaineering texts though some refer only to the technical difficulty of individual pitches while others attempt to include consideration of distance, time, and necessary effort. One serious drawback to any such system lies in the fact that even minor changes in the weather or the ground or snow surface can profoundly affect the difficulty of the route.

Here we'll define levels of difficulty in very general terms and remind leaders to be prepared to adjust routes and activities as necessitated by unexpected conditions. An "easy" mountaineering trip, while almost always involving more expertise and skills than an easy backpacking trip, should not assume far greater fitness or immunity to intimidation by heights. Most easy trips involve two- or three-day outings unless the high country can be reached in just a few hours. Even when access is not difficult, however, the benefits of acclimatization may make two- or three-day trips more enjoyable. Outings that take longer than three days can be wearing on people not used to the stresses of higher elevations.

"Easy" mountaineering trips usually peak at 5000 feet (1600 meters) or less, with highest elevation well under 12,000 feet (4,000 meters). This should involve no more than about 4,000 feet of gain on the climb itself, assuming good conditions, fit participants, and few delays caused by roping up or belaying. Typically, an easy trip covers some sections of scrambling or climbing where ropes may be needed for psychological if not real security, and very limited sections requiring belays, rappells, or other techniques.

A moderate outing might involve more difficult access to the mountain, slightly greater elevation gains on the climbing route, and more sections requiring technical climbing skills and techniques. Routes that might be easy under good conditions may well be called moderate or even difficult in different seasons or bad weather, or when attempted within a shorter time frame. A route that requires very high levels of fitness, mastery of basic climbing skills, total elevation gains of more than 7000 feet (2300 meters), or maximum elevations of over 14,000 feet (4600 meters) should be listed as "difficult."

Planners of mountaineering outings may find it difficult to keep program objectives within realistic limits. Outings and classes for beginners usually need to cover or at least review many of the basic skills associated with hiking, trekking, backpacking, snow camping, and rock climbing before addressing specific mountaineering topics. As a result, little time may remain in beginning-level outings for more than cursory review of a limited number of topics and skills. This is an argument for extensive use of pre-trip meetings or multiple outings at the beginning level in any mountaineering program. When planning beginning programs, it's often necessary to decide between non-technical ascents and the inclusion of more skills training. Even basic lessons in knots, ice-axe use, crampon use, glacier travel, and the many related skills and topics can gobble up days on the mountainside, leaving little time for summit attempts unless planners compromise on content or depth of instruction, or add additional outing time.

Intermediate-level experiences typically assume that participants already have basic back country and mountaineering experience and have at least a limited ability to utilize the tools and techniques of the sport. Some programs devote all of the attention in beginning classes to skill development and reserve the label "intermediate" for easy to moderately difficult teaching outings wherein the participants integrate their knowledge and skills in a summit attempt. In other cases, the intermediate level may involve skills training in any number of specialized activities for participants with basic experience or training. Popular topics include snow or ice climbing, rock climbing in Alpine settings, or rescue techniques. Some review of basic concepts is invariably required in these courses.

Advanced-level outings probably vary more in content than those of any other level due, in part, to widely varying conceptions of what constitutes advanced skills; it also takes many years of experience and practice to attain anything approaching mastery of any of the several activities that constitute mountaineering.

Most mountaineering programs are designed to introduce participants to the sport, and these tend to label as "advanced" any outings for which a few basic or intermediate ones are prerequisites. Such "advanced" trips are similar to those at the intermediate level in that a review of basics is usually necessary, from in-depth training in specific topics to routes requiring the use of intermediate or higher skills. A few programs offer truly advanced experiences involving participants in lead climbing, outing planning, group leadership, and other areas necessary for full mastery of all the suggested objectives, including independent participation in the sport.

4. Sample Itineraries and Instructor Guidelines. The following "Planning Guideline for Instructors" and "Recommended Daily Agenda" are intended as examples of aids to instructors. They are based on materials issued to instructors and leaders in the Outdoor Pursuits Program at the University of Oregon in Eugene, Oregon, and relate to the three-day outing portion of a beginning mountaineering sequence. Students in this program receive substantial pre-trip knot-tying and rope-use training, including belaying, avalanche, and related safety techniques, and are required to have substantial training or experience in backpacking and related basic skills. As a result, more topics can be covered in greater depth than if only limited pre-outing education is provided.

Documents of this type, perhaps transferred by leaders to notes on file cards, can be real assets in the field.

BEGINNING MOUNTAINEERING OUTING PLANNING GUIDELINES FOR INSTRUCTORS

Length of Outing (days): 3
Days of Week: Friday-Sunday
Departure Time: 7 a.m.
Return time: About 5 p.m.
Meeting Place:
Transportation Method: Vans and pickups, State Motor Pool.

Student Gear and Equipment Requirements (refer to gear lists): All required items on the standard equipment list. Skies or snowshoes and appropriate accessories may be required at the option of the instructor.

Instructor and Leader Gear and Equipment Requirements (additional): One *extra* clothing layer to share, small first-aid kit, repair items for stoves and packs, extra slings and carabiners and climbing harness (seat and chest, or combination).

Group Gear and Equipment Requirements (per independent field or climbing group): First-aid belt, tarp, 1/2 bag or sleeping bag, foam or ensolite pad, stove and fuel, one rope per three people, extra hardware as needed (pickets, flukes or other anchors, descending devices, ascending devices, pulleys, slings, carabiners, etc.).

Depending on site and season: snow shovels (for vehicles), snowshoes (to break trail).

Specifications of the Location and Route(s): The site should allow several groups to camp below the timberline on durable sites well away from popular zones, yet be within one to two hours of the climbing-practice area(s). Usually one campsite will be used for two nights, with the first and second days spent practicing glacier travel and the last on an easy climb. Practice sites for self-arrest must be safe (with good snow run-outs), and should include headwall slopes grading up to 45 degrees or so. Crampon practice areas should be easily protected and provide varied slopes, with short sections of very steep (sixty-degree) angles. If possible, the surfaces should vary from soft snow to ice. Glacier travel (rope team) practice sites must be well scouted and provide gentle slopes for team-arrest practice. The summit route should not exceed a I-2 in difficulty. (Most used by the Beginning Mountaineering class are I-1. Especially competent Mountaineering I sub-groups may attempt I-2 routes.) No route or practice area may be used during periods of significant avalanche danger, and every effort must be made in planning sites to avoid conflict, however minor, with other user groups.

BEGINNING MOUNTAINEERING OUTING RECOMMENDED DAILY AGENDA

DAY 1

Business at Meeting Point - Same as Beginning Backpacking Outing.

At the Trailhead - Same as Beginning Backpacking Outing.

During the Day

— Make frequent stops to check clothing and boots (Climbers may have to carry unusually heavy loads and may wear very stiff boots, so foot care is essential.);
— Encourage early preventive foot care and a slow pace;
— Discuss and demonstrate the rest step;
— Plan to be at campsite by 2 p.m. or sooner if possible;
— Review basic trail etiquette and safety;
— Take the time to study the map, and provide the students with time to predict from it, observe the terrain, and review what they've seen (Repeat this often.);
— Assist students to locate safe, low-impact, comfortable campsites in small groups or singly, but in an area small enough to allow assembly of the entire group;
— Before leaving the students to set up your camp, be sure that they have adequate gear and knowledge to set a good camp, have adequate food and water, know the rules about leaving camp, know where staff are camped, and know exactly where and when to assemble for the evening meeting and practice, as well as what to bring with them. Effort at this point saves much delay later in the day.

In the Evening (or as early in the afternoon as possible!)

— Assemble as planned;
— Review knots (Teaching should be done initially in the pre-trip meetings since conditions in the classroom make concentration on the knots far easier. All

students need to be able to tie *at least* the figure eight on a bight, figure-eight follow-through, grapevine, bowline, bowline on a coil and prusik knots. Usually students are also asked to learn the fisherman's, water, bowline on a bight, and butterfly knots. Another useful knot is a bowline *with* a bight. All bowlines must be tied with the working end in the center, and must be tied off with an overhand knot. The usual test of proficiency will be tying the knot in reasonably good time *behind the back*. Doing so insures good understanding of its shape.);

— Practice belaying, using standard techniques (Using trees or rocks as anchors, clip belayers to their harnesses and have "climbers" tie in directly using figure-eight follow-throughs. Practice standard body (hip) belaying until all students have acted in both roles. Evaluate staff if in doubt of their skills. Be sure that *all* students are belaying efficiently and know the standard signals.);

— If time allows, have students practice prusik knots and practice climbing on ropes suspended from or between trees;

— Also, if time allows, demonstrate roped climbing and the use of prusiks (Time can be saved on the next day if students practice roping up at this session. Ideally they should rope up twice, once in the middle and once on an end, then put on prusik slings.);

— *Any material not covered at this time must be covered at the beginning of the second day!*

— Following the practice session, assemble staff and students to go over the plans for day two (Plan to get up early, usually up at 5 a.m. with assembly at 6:30 a.m. This is necessary to allow adequate practice time and helps adjust sleep schedules to facilitate the *very* early start on the following [climb] morning. Be sure that all students know when to get up and have some wake up system, and know when and where to assemble. Be clear as to what they must bring with them: specify what personal and group gear. Considerable time can be saved if students and staff pack *before* retiring.);

— Have a brief staff meeting to finalize the plans for the practice sessions.

DAY 2

In the Morning

— Make sure all students are awake *at least* 1½ hours prior to assembly;

— Depending on circumstances, a brief "Tour of Homes" may be worthwhile (The students are backpackers, not climbers, and may benefit from discussions and observation of camping techniques and equipment suitable for higher sites and more extreme weather.);

— Check all camps to be sure all gear is stored properly before leaving;

— Make sure all students carefully review the map and understand the plans for the day;

— Assign group leaders and have them check group and personal gear.

During the Day

— Hike to the practice site and assemble (Several instructional formats are possible. A recommended system is to have an assistant leader assigned to a squad of four to six students, with the instructor, and, if possible, one or two very experienced leaders, free to supervise. The instructor or a designated leader can demonstrate a skill or sequence to the assembled squads, after which they should separate for practice on adjacent slopes. *Hardhats must be worn* at all times by students *and* staff on glaciers and potential rockfall areas. Note that accomplishment of all of the topics on today's agenda require very efficient use of time!);

— Practice walking on snow and ice (*gentle* slopes) and carrying the ice axe;

— Demonstrate and practice self arrest (Begin on gentle slopes and work up to steep [thirty-five degrees +] slopes, *always* with a good run-out. All students should progress in an orderly sequence from simple sitting slides on gentle slopes to head-first dives on their backs. Instructors *must* test all runs prior to any student use, then repeat test runs as conditions change during the day. All practice slopes must have safe runouts that slow down students out of control on the steepest runs in slick raingear.);

— Demonstrate and practice basic crampon technique (Begin on easy gentle snow slopes.

Care must be taken to follow a logical progression so that students do not exceed their capabilities. The goal should be to cover the basic French positions and front pointing, with appropriate use of the ice axe, on everything from soft snow to moderately hard ice and on slopes from gentle to about sixty-degree grades. [This variety may or may not be possible depending on the season.] Students should learn and practice *pied marche, pied en canard,* and *pied a plat* positions with the appropriate *canne, panne, manche,* and *ramasse* ice-axe positions. *Piolet appui* and *rampe* should be shown as descending techniques. More advanced students can be introduced to *pied troisieme, piolet poignard* and *ancre,* as well as to front-pointing [Austrian] techniques, though these are usually reserved for the last day of the outing should weather keep the class from a summit attempt.);

— Demonstrate and practice glissading, including sitting, crouching, and standing techniques. As in all of the techniques and skills taught this day, discuss the advantages and potential hazards of each. Staff must test each run, and run-outs are required as in self-arrest practice;

— Demonstrate and practice roped climbing for crevassed areas, team arrests, and basic crevasse rescue (Have each team simulate a crevasse rescue if an appropriate and safely protectable site can be located.).

In the Evening

— Before sending students to their camps, be sure to arrange a time for the evening meeting;

— Check to be sure that students are well-sheltered, hydrated, and fed, do a thorough "health-and-attitude" check, and remind them of the meeting;

— Have a meeting with staff to plan the last day, which usually involves a summit climb (Form plans that allow ample time for practice en route, return to camp, breaking camp, hiking to the trailhead, and driving to town *before* the group becomes too tired to drive safely. Usually this means returning to camp at 1 p.m., the trailhead at 5 p.m., and

home at 8 p.m. Understand that all decisions are to be *very* conservative with regard to hazardous snow, ice, crevasses, and avalanche potential! Decide on student and staff groupings and gear needs. *No* group is to leave base camp for home until *all* groups are in camp, and no group is to leave the trailhead until *all* groups are out of the woods.);

— In a general meeting, discuss and finalize plans with students, being sure that they are privy to the *process* of planning and have adequate input (*Planning* is perhaps the most important subject to be taught on the outing!)*;

— Be sure that all students know what to bring and what to wear in the morning, and have arranged a reliable wake-up and assembly system.

*The overall goal of the program is the development within participants of an understanding of and ability to care for themselves, other people, and the environment. Skills are necessary, but are viewed as no more than a means to this end. Planning is, in a sense, the single most important skill in an activity such as mountaineering that involves a potentially hazardous complex of terrain and weather.

DAY 3

In the Morning

— Assemble (usually at 3:30-4 a.m.) and thoroughly check student health, amount of rest gotten, and equipment (personal and group) (This task may be delegated to group leaders.);

— Review plans briefly in light of the current and likely weather, snow, and, especially, avalanche conditions;

— Depart as early as possible.

During the Day

— *If climbing,* travel as independent groups (with two leaders per group), meeting at key points along the route (Plan to review safety skills en route prior to potential needs for them! This means that an hour or more should be added to normal climbing times for self arrest, team arrest, and belaying review. Navigation and route finding are of great importance and should be given emphasis at every major rest stop and key geographical transition. If, for any reason, anyone cannot proceed, does not wish to do so, or is not, in the opinion of the staff, able to do so safely, that person must be allowed to remain at a safe location. Usually this means that the group will return to camp. Occasionally a safe resting place on the return route can be found, but under no circumstances can an individual be left in camp or on the mountain with fewer than two accompanying persons and ample bivouac gear. Exceptions to this policy are to be made only by the instructor or the coordinator of the outdoor-pursuit program. On routes in use by other climbers, our groups are to defer to them as much as possible. Every effort must be made to avoid any adverse contact with small private parties. Descent must be begun at a time that allows a safe rate of descent without compromising the time of arrival at the trailhead. The risk of pushing tired drivers is not worth the pleasure of making the summit. Students and staff should understand this during the planning phases, especially vis-a-vis the determination of wake up time for the climb!;

— *If not climbing,* the reason is usually foul weather, and under these conditions an extra hour or two of sleep is usually warranted with a new plan formulated by staff at an early meeting (Worthwhile alternatives include foul-weather navigation, more advanced crampon technique, crevasse-rescue practice, avalanche seminars, and climbs of lesser peaks or of local ridges.).

At the Trailhead - Same as Beginning Backpacking Outing.

At the Return Point - Same as Beginning Backpacking Outing, plus:

— Conduct the post-trip student meeting. This is a most valuable part of the course, and should include:

1. a detailed review of the route to compare the students' pre-trip predictions to their field experiences,
2. a chance for students to critique the planning and leadership of the trip,
3. a chance for the instructor(s) to emphasize or reinforce important concepts and to add material not covered in the field, and
4. a discussion of the types of outings or further training that the trip has prepared the students for, with examples of local options;

— Conduct the staff evaluations in cooperation with the coordinator. Staff training and your own development are as important as any aspect of the outing, and are well worth the effort.

APPENDIX E

ROCK CLIMBING

A. General Description.

1. What It Is, What Is Done. Rock climbing is a common outdoor pursuit. Originally part of the broader sport of mountaineering, it has for many become a specialized activity. Devotees usually begin climbing with top belays on small cliffs or bounders, or even on artificial walls, before graduating to lead climbing on major cliffs and mountain peaks. Some continue to focus on certain aspects of the sport such as "bouldering," developing the skills needed to scale routes of ever-increasing difficulty.

2. Hazards. There are several potential hazards in rock climbing. These include falls, injury from falling rock, and a range of general environmental perils related to the weather and risks inherent in accessing and leaving the site. Minor injuries such as bashed knuckles and scraped elbows are fairly common, especially on certain types of rock and in more advanced climbing. The chance of major injury can be eliminated or reduced to an extremely low level if participants and leaders use common sense, standard safety procedures, and top-quality equipment.

3. Resource Requirements. There are very few areas without good natural rock-climbing sites nearby, and indoor or outdoor artificial climbing walls and structures can meet a wide range of needs. Belaying and rappelling practice require only walls and appropriate anchor points, and basic skills can be taught even on low walls. Climbing techniques are best taught on rock inclines and cliffs, though primary moves, balance, and conditioning can be replicated on man-made surfaces using wood, metal, concrete, and plastic to simulate natural handholds, footholds, cracks, and corners. (Some of the publications in the bibliography include designs and suggestions for artificial climbing-practice structures.)

Natural sites range from large boulders to great cliffs or mountain peaks. Accessibility is a

ROCK CLIMBING
This site, in an abandoned quarry, provides solid, safe rock with good access to top anchors. Many such small areas, in or near town locations, are ideal for teaching beginning techniques.

key concern, including distance, time, and permission to use the site. Land managers in both public and private sectors may have legitimate concerns about safety and liability, environmental damage to the site, and access routes or campsites. Private owners may be concerned about privacy and security compromises caused by the presence of strangers on their property; thus it's important to identify these areas and contact other user groups to avoid conflicts.

Most practice areas have a limited number of good sites for teaching certain skills, so coordination can be essential. Rock types are important as well. Granite, limestone, dolomite, basalt, and certain sandstones and welded tuffs are among the better known and most popular climbing surfaces, yet many of these outcrops are unfit due to local peculiarities in composition, structure, or weathering. The rock must be tough and hang together well, not subject to excessive rockfall. Quarries, road cuts, sea cliffs, and fault zones can offer superb climbing but need to be carefully checked for instability caused by blasting, earth movement, and rapid erosion.

Except in the case of very advanced programs, it's also vital to have easy access to the top of the climbing face and some means of placing anchors. Common anchors include substantial, healthy, well-rooted trees or solid rock suitable for bolting, but the best of cliffs may be useless if topped by sloping soil or loose rock. Some marginal sites can be improved by removing loose material, though this process should be avoided until the environmental implications have been carefully considered.

Except for advanced classes focusing on multipitch climbs, there is no need for great height. Routes of thirty to sixty feet (ten to twenty meters) allow easy communication from top to bottom, bottom belays using standard climbing-rope lengths, and a change of direction pulley or carabiner on top, plus enough height to provide excitement and challenge. Local equipment stores, guidebooks, and climbers can usually provide an inventory of local options.

4. Equipment and Clothing. The requirements for rock climbing vary tremendously, from no more than shorts and sneakers to hundreds of specialized items. The following list is a compromise, assuming a one-day program at a natural outdoor rock-climbing site in town or very near the road.

SUGGESTED MINIMUM GEAR REQUIRED FOR ROCK CLIMBING IN ADDITION TO THE REQUIREMENTS FOR HIKING, BACKPACKING, OR MOUNTAINEERING

Individual Gear

Required Items

1. Suitable footwear (There are many possibilities. Beginners may find that sneakers are adequate so long as the soles don't protrude further than the uppers. It is important that the weight be placed directly above the edge of the sole, and some new running shoes, designed with broad soles to increase stability, make it almost impossible to stand on narrow ledges. Lug-sole hiking or climbing boots may also be used, although Norwegian welts should be avoided for the same reason as running shoes are. A host of highly specialized rock-climbing shoes, most resembling beefed-up high-top sneakers, are available but rarely needed by beginners.);
2. Helmet (specifically designed for climbing. Most bicycle and motorcycle helmets are not appropriate.);

Optional Items

1. Harnesses (Many types of seat, chest, and combination harnesses are available commercially, and acceptable alternatives can be made from tubular nylon webbing. Designs and specifications must be very carefully assessed — a well-designed and well-made harness can provide a considerable margin of safety if used properly, yet some commercial and many popular "homemade" types have serious flaws.);
2. Carabiners (For beginners one or two locking types and one or two non-locking types are usually plenty, if not included as group gear.);
3. Slings (A variety of sizes and types are sometimes useful as personal gear, though

again these may in many cases be considered group gear.);

4. Hardware (More advanced climbers sometimes carry rappell devices, chalk bags, and other tools as personal gear, though in most class or program settings these items are considered a group responsibility.).

Group Gear

Required Items

1. Climbing rope (For most instructional purposes relatively short ropes of 120 ft. [35 meters] in length are adequate. Eleven mm. "Perlon" or kernmantle ropes are the easiest to handle and provide several safety advantages in lead climbing, yet are expensive and hard to assess for damages. 7/16 in. "Goldline" and certain other laid or braided types offer more than ample strength for upper belays, are cheaper, and are much easier to inspect for damages. The number of ropes needed for a rock-climbing session depends upon the skills to be taught, the number of available anchors and routes, the number of students, the number of routes or positions that can be supervised at one time, and the need for additional ropes to establish anchor points. Typically, one instructor can only supervise one or two routes (each with a belayer and climber) at one time. Therefore it's usually sufficient to allow one rope per two students up to the total that can be supervised, plus any extras needed. Ropes have a limited safe life span, must be carefully checked before each use for any signs of damage, and should not be expected to last more than a few years even with the best of care.

Optional Items

1. Software (There seems always to be a need for slings and loops of various sizes tied from pieces of rope or nylon webbing. Exact needs depend on the site, route, and techniques employed. It's important to date all slings and to inspect them carefully before, during, and after use. Webbing fabric is especially vulnerable to weathering and abrasion, and knots in such fabric tend to loosen easily. Webbing should be marked or cut up, then discarded if any doubt exists as to strength. It should not be expected to last as long as rope.);

2. First-aid kit (sufficient for conditions. Size and contents will depend on distance from medical assistance.);

3. Hardware (This may include carabiners, rappell devices, ascenders, pulleys, bolts and bolting tools, pitons, nuts and high-tech anchor devices, hammers and extraction tools, and a host of other specialized items.).

Remember that the above suggestions assume a site close to the road or even in town. Review hiking, trekking, backpacking, or mountaineering lists for suggestions about trips away from the road, overnight, or in mountainous terrain. To teach knot-tying, it's a big help to have a supply of twelve to fifteen ft. (four to five meter) ropes. These can be anything from old cotton clothesline to sections of old climbing rope.

6. Leadership Requirements and Qualifications. The keys to safety in a rock-climbing program are awareness, preventive actions, and constant alertness. Rock-climbing instructors have to be able to assess potential hazards and design, implement, and reinforce safety procedures and policies. They must also instill a sense of personal responsibility in participants. The nature of the risks in rock climbing is such that there are seldom second chances; if rocks or people fall, there are no extended periods to ponder alternatives or seek advice. Prevention is the only good alternative, and adequate prevention may depend on the technical skills and group leadership ability of an experienced leader.

The minimum attributes of a rock-climbing leader include:

A. Items "A" through "Q" on the hiking-leader list;

B. Applicable items from the trekking, backpacking, or mountaineering lists if rock climbing will take place in the context of these activities;

C. Rock-climbing experience and skill at a level well beyond that to be taught in the program;

D. A thorough understanding of rope and other climbing-fabric strengths and characteristics, including maintenance;

E. An ability to tie all of the basic rock-climbing and mountaineering knots, including at least the figure eight on a bight, figure-eight follow-through, single bowline, bowline on a coil, double fisherman's (grapevine) knot, prusik knot, and Muenter hitch (The leader should be able to tie any of these quickly and perfectly behind the back.);

F. An ability to use ropes, slings, and hardware to establish anchors in rock and other natural features (This includes a thorough understanding of the effects on system strength of angular stresses within knots, in bending ropes around objects, and in the positioning of knots and anchors.);

G. Competence in belaying, using both manual and device-assisted techniques (This should include the sitting-hip belay and the use of belay rings, descenders, and Muenter hitches, as well as standard signals.);

H. Competence in rappelling using Dulfersiz, Carabiner, and descender systems;

I. Competence in rescue techniques, including hands-on practice in self rescue, prusik and mechanically assisted rope-climbing techniques, lowering systems, construction and use of rope-and-sling-assisted piggy-back carries, rope-basket litters, and stretchers;

J. Familiarity with the proposed site, including the characteristics of the rock, the routes, the potential for rockfall, and the potential or existing anchor locations.

Leaders of rock-climbing programs need to be exceptionally alert and conscientious about detail, and willing and able to maintain close, ongoing supervision of myriad details. Every knot, every anchor, every tie-in, and every move is significant in this activity. There is no room for "Space Cadets" among the ranks of rock-climbing instructors.

7. Leadership Ratios. Safe and efficient rock-climbing instruction usually demands a high ratio of staff to participants. It's hard for one instructor to adequately supervise more than two climbing routes at one time, and this is possible only if the routes are short, close together, and relatively uncomplicated. This means that one instructor can rarely handle more than four active participants (two belayers and two climbers) at one time. The overall ratio can be expanded by including other participants who might watch, practice knots, or participate in some safe, unsupervised alternative activity, although this is generally not a good idea since it can lead to distractions for the instructor and the belayers. A counter argument is that one onlooker per route can gain from observation and provide assistance should some mishap require the instructor to focus on one climber or belayer; thus some programs allow up to six participants per leader or qualified assistant. There are exceptions, of course, as in knot-tying and belaying practice where no one is actually exposed to danger and can be supervised at a ratio of perhaps a dozen participants per leader. Lectures on theory also have no real upper limit.

In any case, the rock-climbing leader should always be assisted by at least one other person so that fast and safe rescue of an injured individual is possible. Minimum qualifications of assistants vary according to the nature of the site and routes, and may range from a competent program graduate to no less than a fully qualified leader.

B. Course Conduct

1. Common formats. If adequate artificial or natural practice sites are available nearby, rock climbing can be one of the easiest activities to schedule. Many of the basic skills can be taught in a classroom setting; knot tying, for example, is probably better taught indoors than out since participants can focus on learning the complex movements and patterns undistracted by weather and terrain. Once in the field, you'll find it can be harder to focus participant attention on details.

Most rock-climbing programs begin with one or more indoor sessions that serve as pre-trip meetings and an opportunity to discuss ropes, slings, hardware, and basic climbing techniques and to practice knot tying and belaying. The length of time necessary for actual climbing practice depends upon access, set-up and take-down times. Some indoor facilities require only a few minutes to set up and take down, so that significant progress can be acheived in an hour or perhaps even less. Most field sites, however, require substantial time to get ready even when top anchors are in place. It's usually necessary to allow about half an hour to get a few top anchors in place for belay stances or change of direction pulleys, and as much time at the end of the session to remove the slings and hardware and coil ropes. Add to this the time needed to sign out and distribute equipment (if, as is usually the case, helmets and other items are provided by the program) and the time needed to collect, sign in, and return the equipment to storage. In some cases leaders or assistants may be able to set up and take down equipment before and after the scheduled program; however, this isn't always possible and may not be desirable. The placement of anchors and other systems and the proper dispatching and care of equipment are important components of any instructional program. As a result, sessions of less than two hours may allow little actual climbing time. If the routes are relatively short (half a rope length or so), an hour of actual climbing time is usually sufficient to allow two or three climb cycles. If two or three participants are assigned to a route and rotate the roles of climber, belayer, or observer, all should be able to climb once in an hour.

Whatever the length of individual sessions, it's important to develop skills and techniques in a logical progression. Each session should somewhat overlap the contents of the prior session, and leaders should make sure that every participant has prerequisite skills and knowledge before proceeding to the next level of skill.

2. Objectives. The following suggested objectives should be valid for most rock-climbing programs, and are listed here in the order in which the subject matter is usually addressed. On completion of the program, participants should be able to:

A. Identify potential sites for rock climbing using maps, guides, and other resources;

B. Understand the fitness requirements of rock climbing and appropriate conditioning exercises;

C. Understand the basic gear requirements of the activity and construct an appropriate list of gear needs given a description of the site and routes;

D. Tie the more important knots used in rock climbing, including at least the figure eight on a bight, figure-eight follow-through, single bowline, bowline on a coil, double fisherman's knot, prusik knot, and Muenter hitch (Ideally, participants should be able to tie these knots quickly behind the back. This requires a greater comprehension of the knot but insures far longer retention of the skills.);

E. Understand the strengths and weaknesses of ropes, slings, carabiners, and any other hardware used in the program;

F. Be able to locate, adequately assess, set up, and utilize natural anchors and pre-set artificial anchors without causing environmental damage;

G. Demonstrate competence in setting up, securing, and carrying out sitting-hip and friction-device-assisted belays using standard signals (This includes proper tie-in to the belay using both rope only and rope-and-harness system in upper belay climbing);

H. Demonstrate an understanding of the three-point rule and of basic climbing techniques including friction climbing, slab climbing, face climbing, mantling, and jamming, stemming, bridging, lie-backs, and other counterforce moves, as well as traverse and down climbing;

I. Set up and safely use at least the Dulfersitz, carabiner-seat, and figure-eight or other friction-device-assisted techniques;

J. Respond effectively after falling while roped (This includes the use of slings, prusik knots, and mechanical ascenders.);

K. Respond effectively to assist a fallen climber on belay;

L. Select, place, and utilize artificial anchors such as nuts and pitons (This includes an awareness of safety concerns and potentials for environmental impact.);

M. Set up and employ appropriate anchors, belays, and other techniques in lead climbing;

N. Acquire the skills and knowledge necessary to independently plan and carry out a safe, environmentally sound, and enjoyable rock-climbing outing.

3. Levels. Rock-climbing outings and programs can be described by reference to the technical difficulty of the climbs or the objectives of the program. The technical difficulty of a climb is usually expressed in terms of numbers or letters in a rating scheme, but there are several problems inherent in such systems, including lack of uniformity among the dozen or more "standard" ones. These schemes have evolved over the years in several countries, and are based on various criteria such as individual move difficulty, overall technical difficulty of the route, strenuousness of the route, or the equipment needed. For our purposes here, it will suffice to describe outings according to course objectives, grouping outings into beginning, intermediate, and advanced levels.

Beginning outings start with no assumptions about climbing or rope handling ability, and focus on orienting oneself to the sport, knot tying, belaying, and basic climbing skills. Climbing activities at this level are always top roped if more than a few feet off the ground, and objectives 1 through 8 are reasonable for beginning programs. Rappelling, the subject of objective 9, is often included in beginning programs because it's flashy and fun, though given time constraints the session might better be spent practicing down climbing. Intermediate programs might, after careful review of basic skills, attempt to achieve objectives 9 through 12. Much of the intermediate class time is usually spent on skill development with top ropes. Advanced programs are usually designed to meet objectives 13 and 14, with at least initial experience in leading belayed from above. Advanced programs also include exposing participants to state-of-the-art techniques and equipment and assume that they will pursue the sport independently of leaders.

APPENDIX F

SNOWSHOEING

A. General Description

1. What It Is, What Is Done. Snowshoeing is fun, practical, and relatively easier and safer than skiing. Where skiing guarantees thrills and spills, snowshoeing offers peaceful, if sometimes strenuous, enjoyment of the winter back country free of anxiety over high-speed collisions with the scenery. Snowshoes have distinct advantages over skis on certain terrains. On a long, fairly steep slope with abundant trees or other obstacles, the snowshoer can usually just plod straight up or straight down, while the skier may have to traverse back and forth on the way up, and choose between very long traverses or linked face plants on the way down. In such terrain the snowshoer, much to the frustration of the skier, usually covers the ground faster and with somewhat less expenditure of energy. Little skill or balance is necessary to snowshoe on gentle slopes, and nothing beats snowshoes when you're carrying large, heavy, or awkward loads or pulling hard on sleds. Skis do have an advantage over snowshoes on steep side hills, especially on hard or slick surfaces, and under good ski conditions on slopes well within the ability of the skier.

Snowshoe outings may simply be hikes, treks, or backpacking ventures on skis, or may focus on the specific skills and pleasures of snowshoeing. Travel over snow on snowshoes (or skis) is rarely as fast as travel over the same terrain by foot on bare ground in mid summer. Routes tend therefore to be relatively short, especially in mid winter when daylight is limited.

2. Hazards. Snowshoeing itself isn't inherently hazardous; the dangers in this sport are related to the weather and snow cover. Hypothermia, frostbite, avalanches, and a variety of snow formations can cause grief for the unaware traveler. Ice- or snow-covered water can often be crossed more safely on snowshoes than on foot, yet real danger still exists and great care is essential. Safety in such environments depends upon a combination of knowledge, alertness, a willingness to modify plans to maximize safety margins, proper equipment, and the skills necessary to respond to mishaps. Becoming lost or injured in a winter environment is generally more serious than similar events in the summer. Communications are impaired, and travel and transport times are all lengthened dramatically in the cold season. For missing persons, both search efficiency and survival times are reduced. Nevertheless, snowshoeing is probably the safest of all winter outdoor pursuits if the activity is conducted well.

3. Who Participates. Snowshoeing has advocates throughout the snowy parts of the world. There is good evidence that this activity was pursued as far back as 4000 BC, and all manner of foot-surface-expanding contraptions have been used ever since. Because snowshoeing requires little balance, almost anyone can do it, at least on gentle terrain. Before the advent of modern ski equipment, snowshoeing was enjoyed by a larger proportion of winter recreationists; however, the absolute number of snowshoers is probably higher now than at any time in the past. Many people, attracted to winter sports by skiing, turn occasionally to snowshoeing for relaxation or for the several practical advantages of this activity for special purposes. Rescue groups often find snowshoes superior to skis since "shoes" assure steady travel relatively unaffected by snow conditions, terrain, loads carried, or the ski skills of participants, and because they are uninterrupted by waxing stops. Snowmobilers and pilots often carry snowshoes for emergency use.

4. Resource Requirements. The requirements for good snowshoeing are minimal, and are in most cases similar to those for hiking with, of course, the addition of enough snow to justify their use. Walking on foot is usually the best option in soft snow depths of up to about one foot on the level and two feet on hillsides. Beyond these depths snowshoes usually provide an advantage unless the snow surface is very firm; it's not unusual in the winter for conditions to change rapidly from a solid surface suitable for boots and difficult, on side hills, for snowshoes, to conditions impossible to negotiate on foot due to softening or the addition of new snow. Late-spring snow packs

usually don't require snowshoes early in the day, though they may be required in the afternoon. Routes should insofar as possible avoid lengthy sidehills and need not be long since travel is generally slower than on bare ground. Great care must be used in selecting terrain and routes to allow options in the event of avalanche conditions or unsafe snow bridges. Parking can also be a problem since trailheads are not always plowed in the winter, and, even if they are, may be full, require permits, or limit parking times.

5. Equipment and Clothing Requirements. The essentials for snowshoeing are relatively simple, the same as those for hiking, trekking, or backpacking with a bit of extra insulation, warmer footwear, and snowshoes required. One or two ski poles are handy options, and there are hundreds of snowshoe and snowshoe-binding designs that use just about every imaginable material and configuration to provide support and control under different conditions of snow and terrain. Wood-and-gut or rawhide snowshoes, the "state-of-the-art" for centuries, now compete with an array of modern designs in steel, aluminum, magnesium, and a host of plastics. Rentals are available in most cities in snow country.

SUGGESTED MINIMUM GEAR REQUIRED FOR SNOWSHOEING
Individual Gear

Required Items (*in addition to* those for hiking, trekking, or backpacking)

1. Snowshoes and bindings (type and fit specified by the instructor);
2. Warm boots (There are advocates of everything from high-top moccasins to mountaineering boots. Ski boots, snowmobile boots, and shoe-pacs are also popular.);
3. Extra insulation (Two layers of wool or better for the legs and the top, two pairs of gloves or mittens, and a total top insulation of at least one inch should be adequate in most climates, though local adjustments will be necessary.).

Optional Items (again, in addition to the requirements for hiking, trekking, or backpacking)

1. Shovels (always useful for making emergency shelters and invaluable in avalanche rescue. A ratio of one portable snow shovel per six participants is probably sufficient for most purposes.);
2. Repair items for snowshoes (cord and whatever pieces, parts, and tools may be necessary in the event of breakage).

Optional Items - None beyond those of hiking, trekking, or backpacking although attention should be paid to the greater importance of insulating pads, insulation, and strong, weatherproof shelter.

6. Leadership Requirements. The general requirements for leading a snowshoeing activity depend upon the nature of the outing. Typically the trip will be similar to a hiking, trekking, or backpacking one. If so, the leader should possess at least the qualifications suggested for the closest summer equivalent, plus specific snowshoeing and winter-travel skills and experience.

Specifically, the leader should have:

A. Substantial experience on snowshoes, preferably on snow conditions and in terrain similar to that of the intended site;
B. Experience in travel on snowshoes or skis in weather similar to that of the intended site;
C. Training and competence in estimating avalanche and other snow-structure hazards, safe route sections, and avalanche-rescue under back country as opposed to ski-area conditions;
D. Familiarity with the intended site and route sufficient to allow safe and effective utilization of the resource under winter conditions (Knowledge of an area under summer conditions may not be adequate.);
E. An understanding of snowshoe and binding types sufficient to assist participants in using, maintaining, and repairing their equipment;
F. An understanding of the recognition, treatment, and prevention of hypothermia, frostbite, and other cold-related injuries.

7. Leadership Ratios. The risks of travel in winter are somewhat higher than in summer. Journeys themselves are more difficult, slips and falls more likely, and a variety of snow-related hazards may exist. Visibility is impaired by bad weather, and snow muffles sounds, impairing verbal communication and the range of audible signals; thus participants may be distracted or less attentive than when basking in summer warmth. Also, any mishap that occurs may have far more serious consequences than in the summer due to decreased survival times and protracted SAR times.

These considerations must be kept in mind when establishing minimum leader ratios, and suggestions for the closest summer activity (hiking, trekking, or backpacking) should be reviewed carefully. In most cases somewhat higher ratios will have to be maintained for snow travel if the same level of risk is desired. The value of a second qualified leader or qualified assistant for each independent field group should be obvious.

B. Course Conduct

1. Common Formats. Most snowshoeing involves single-day outings, although any length of time is possible. The inherent slowness of winter travel, combined with short days, the need to carry greater weights of equipment, and less appealing camping conditions, tends to shift winter travelers away from long outings and toward short or single-day experiences. Most of what has been said here about hiking, trekking, and backpacking formats applies to snowshoeing, but pre-trip meetings should be extended in length or number to allow thorough pre-outing discussions of snow and cold-related safety topics.

2. Objectives. Any of the objectives suggested earlier for hiking, trekking, or backpacking could be applied to similar outings or snowshoes. Typical additional objectives specific to snowshoeing are that the participant will:

A. Learn how to use at least one type of snowshoe and binding combination to travel (This includes maintenance, adjustment, and repair in the field.);
B. Understand clothing and equipment

requirements specific to snowshoeing and winter travel, as well as clothing and equipment requirements of the general type of activity;

C. Understand the recognition, treatment, and prevention of hypothermia, frostbite, and other cold-related conditions;

D. Understand basic avalanche theory, avalanche-hazard estimation, route selection in snow-covered terrain, and avalanche rescue in back country settings;

E. Understand the various types of snowshoes and bindings that are available, and be able to select the appropriate types for any specified combination of terrain, snow conditions, and intended use;

F. Be able to travel on snowshoes efficiently (smoothly and with minimal energy) and be able to kick steps, traverse, stem turn, kick turn, and descend using good technique in a wide range of snow conditions.

3. Levels. Snowshoe trips, like hikes, treks, or backpacking outings, can be described by level of physical difficulty (easy, moderate, or difficult) or by objectives and prerequisites (beginning, intermediate, and advanced). Since winter travel is by nature either slower or more strenuous than walking on bare ground, snowshoe trips need to be considerably shorter than summer equivalents. For example, where an easy summer hike might cover six or seven miles, an easy snowshoe hike might be limited to three or four miles (five to six-and-a-half kilometers), with elevation gains of 1000 feet (about 300 meters) or less even on a full-day outing in good snow conditions and good weather. If a "full day" is defined by daylight, then the number of hours available for travel during winter months may be extremely limited. On shorter days and/or in difficult snow or adverse weather, a trip of even half this distance may not be easy. It's difficult to be precise since so much depends on conditions and the efficiency with which the group is able to break and pack their trail. "Moderate" day trips might double these, and estimates for almost any snowshoe trip covering more than eight miles or 3000 vertical feet (600 meters or so) probably ought to be called "difficult."

Overnight trips also need to be shortened compared to summer backpacking or trekking ventures. On these longer ventures, the difficulty of any given route becomes harder to assess. Although snowshoeing is basically easy to do, the addition of a backpack is enough to topple many people over, at least occasionally, and everyone travels quite slowly compared to travel without a load. While an easy backpacking trip on foot might cover four to six miles on a first day delayed by travel to the trailhead, an easy backpacking trip on snowshoes might only cover one or two miles (about one to one-and-two-thirds kilometers) on the first day. "Easy" winter backpacking trips rarely include climbs of more than 1000 vertical feet (about 300 meters). A "moderate" outing might cover twice as much mileage and elevation gain, so "difficult" trips include any snowshoe backpacking venture of more than four miles (about six-and-a-half kilometers) or so on short days, six to eight miles on full travel days, and elevation gains of more than 2000 ft. (about 600 meters) per day.

"Beginning" trips are designed to meet the needs of those who haven't snowshoed before. Objectives "A" through "D" are appropriate for these, while objectives "E" and "F" are appropriate for "intermediate" and "advanced" trips. In any case, goals for the appropriate level of hiking, trekking, or backpacking should be reviewed carefully and incorporated into the program.

APPENDIX G

CROSS-COUNTRY (NORDIC) SKIING

A. General Description

1. What It Is, What Is Done. "Nordic skiing" is skiing on gear that allows the heel to be lifted. The term is often used to differentiate this type from "Alpine" skiing, which involves the use of equipment designed to provide maximal control on downhill runs. Nordic skiing gear allows a wide variety of activities, from walking and gliding on flats to uphill and downhill travel in almost any terrain, and its increased popularity has led to the development of highly specialized equipment and techniques for at least five kinds of "loose-heel" sport. Ordered according to type of skiing and equipment used, these activities generally focus on horizontal travel in tracks (walking or gliding), best done on the lightest and narrowest of skis and with very low boots that allow a great deal of forward flex, or skiing on untracked terrain, load carrying, or downhill turning, best conducted on wider, stronger skis and in stiffer, more supportive boots. Thus nordic skiing progresses from cross-country racing on very light, narrow skis in sneaker-like shoes through non-competitive cross-country skiing, ski touring, and nordic downhill to ski-mountaineering, the descent from peaks using wide skis and high, stiff boots almost identical to those used by Alpine skiers.

The most popular types of nordic skiing are here termed "cross country" and "ski touring," although there are local differences in the definition of these. By "cross-country" or "XC" skiing we refer to the most popular of all nordic skiing specialties, the use of relatively light, narrow skis and light, flexible boots to walk and glide on roads, easy trails, and tracks. Much of this activity is limited to single-day outings near the roadhead or even within ski areas and resorts, many of which now feature systems of groomed tracks. Participants typically seek exercise and devote much of the day to skill development.

"Ski tourers," on the other hand, engage in back-country travel, following roads, tracks, and off-trail routes on single- or multi-day tours.

"Ski touring" is essentially a winter or snow-covered terrain version of hiking or backpacking and "nordic downhill" is simply skiing downhill on nordic skis. While some downhill skiing is always involved in this sport, the nordic downhill enthusiast focuses on the excitement and challenge of turning "skinny skis" on downhill slopes using parallel and telemark techniques. Even within this seemingly narrow focus, however, there are clusters of specialists who seek mastery of packed or unpacked snow, ice or powder or racing, on everything from light racing skis (the greatest challenge) to nordic downhill skis that are essentially narrowed versions of the conventional ones.

Nordic skiing is an extremely valuable form of exercise, particularly in the form of cross-country skiing or ski-touring. The typical XC skier or ski-tourer exercises upper and lower muscle groups at a modest level for many hours during a day of activity, while the typical downhill skier may actually exercise only one-and-a-half to two-and-a-half hours each day.

2. Hazards. It's difficult to make a general statement about the safety of nordic skiing because of the wide range of activities encompassed by this term. Cross-country skiing on moderate-to-flat terrain is inherently safe. Speeds tend to be low, and the lightweight, flexible gear make fall-related injuries unlikely. Certainly track skiing in and around ski areas is far safer by the hour than the Alpine variety. On the other hand, ski tourers and ski mountaineers may be subject to significant danger from avalanches and other snow- and ice-related hazards, from the perils of getting lost, and from injury due to the greater dangers of skiing with substantial packs on ungroomed surfaces. Nordic downhillers face risks similar to those of Alpine skiers, making this a relatively high-risk activity in terms of fractures, sprains, and strains. The consequences of such injuries are substantially controlled, however, when the activity takes place within Alpine ski areas and resorts due to the availability of ski-patrol services.

3. Who Participates. Like Alpine skiing, nordic skiing appeals to people of all ages. While many participate in both sports, though, there are substantial differences between the typical

Alpine skier and the typical nordic skier: Alpine skiing has a socially oriented, flashy, high-risk, challenging but not physically demanding image; nordic skiing connotes individuality, utilitarianism, and strenuous exercise despite the reality of the sport and industry attempts to lighten up this impression.

4. Resource Requirements. If there's snow, nordic skiing is at least a possibility. Some basic rules of thumb are that it takes about an inch (two-and-a-half cm.) of snow to "ski" a lawn or golf course, a foot (thirty cm.) of snow to ski roads (especially unpaved roads), two feet (sixty cm. or so) of snow to ski most hiking trails, and three feet (ninety cm. or so) of snow to ski off-trail in most terrain. Clearly, it's necessary to assess each site on its own; these figures assume fairly dense snow — not fluff.

Cross-country skiers often enjoy skiing in the prepared tracks found in many Alpine ski areas and winter resorts. Fees are usually charged to use these tracks, which are often scoffed at by skiers until they try them once. In fact, a well set track is a delight to ski on and can greatly improve technique for even the most hardened back-country skier. Nordic downhillers also tend to favor Alpine ski areas since groomed slopes, like prepared tracks, speed the learning process. Ski lifts are a real asset, too, especially once basic skills have been mastered; with marked roads, tracks or routes on mixed terrain you can ski many miles without having to walk uphill.

The popularity of nordic skiing has resulted in an abundance of maps, guides and other information on facilities and resources in most areas. Ski shops and public and private land-management offices can usually provide these materials, and local advice and expertise is often available from clubs, the outdoor programs of recreation departments and schools, and private-sector ski schools.

5. Equipment and Clothing Requirements. Specific gear requirements for nordic skiing depend on type and setting. When activity will take place entirely within the confines of a ski area or resort and on well-marked trails that form a closed and limited system, it's usually reasonable to ski without survival equipment, just as Alpine skiers do. In this case gear requirements depend solely on the type of skiing to be done. Those who travel outside of developed areas need additional gear for the same reasons that hikers do, and have some special needs as well. First, it's easy to get lost while ski touring, despite the popular myth that one can always turn around and follow the tracks back. Whoever invented that idea apparently never tried to follow tracks on an icy or wind-packed surface, through a maze left by others, or after a half an hour of windblown new snow! It's not only easy to get lost; the consequences are far more serious when it does occur. Winter days are short, temperatures are low, and SAR response times are lengthened. Still another concern is the increased likelihood of being forced to spend an unplanned night out due to injury or gear failure. And a relatively minor injury can also make skiing difficult or impossible. Certainly the chance of incurring one is high when compared to summer hiking. Breaking a ski or binding or even a ski pole can slow progress to a snail's pace — a *cold* snail's pace. Still another possibility is reduced speed due to such delights as ice, breakable crusts, and deep new "mashed potato" snow.

Skis, boots, and poles are constantly evolving, with new models on the market every year. Participants are often confused by the vast array of options and combinations, and all too often buy before they understand their needs. Encourage participants to borrow and use rental gear, and make consumer education a part of every beginning course. Many combinations of equipment can suffice for any one individual, and the quality and durability of most modern products is very high. On the other hand, enjoyment of the sport can be enhanced by carefully matching gear to the particular needs of each participant. Factors to consider include the type(s) of activity, current and projected skill level, aggressiveness, physical strength, and weight, as well as the amount of money the individual can afford to spend.

From a top view, skis vary from slightly "boat" shaped to slightly "hourglass" shaped. This shape is called "sidecut," and is one of the factors that determines how easily the ski turns. Boat-shaped skis and skis with parallel side walls tend to stay in tracks and run straight, while skis with a lot of sidecut (hourglass) shapes tend to turn more easily. Good skiers can make any type of ski go straight or turn,

but shape does make a difference, especially for beginners trying to learn and experts pushing the limits.

Ski length is also an important and often misunderstood dimension, and instructors would do well to pay careful attention to the length of participants' skis — especially in *advance* of outings when adjustments can be made. While it is true, in a limited sense, that short skis are easier to turn than long ones, much more is involved. Ease of turning is also affected by the shape of the ski, its flex pattern, tortional rigidity, bottom-surface qualities, and other factors. Ski length, the primary and often only variable in selecting cross-country and touring skis, is too often determined solely by the height of the skier. While most ski shops have charts relating height to ski length, the skier's total weight is in fact the issue. A slender or overweight person or anyone who will be carrying a large pack, fitted using standard charts, may be given skis too short or long that can seriously impair progress and enjoyment. Skis function best when they are loaded or pressed onto the snow with the correct amount of force, and that force is determined by the weight of the skies, the pack, and the skier's strength and technique. Some shops have weight charts, but even these must be used carefully. A good test that has become popular in recent years is to have the skier stand squarely on both skis on a smooth, perfectly flat surface. (A short-fiber indoor-outdoor carpet seems to work well.) In this condition, XC or touring skis should not touch the floor for at least two feet (sixty cm. or so) on 205 cm. skis. Test this by slipping a small card or piece of paper back and forth between the ski and the floor. As a rule, the better, stronger skiers will want even more clearance to insure they'll be gliding on tip and tail surfaces, not the surface underfoot. No-wax skis should, in general, be fitted with more clearance. Those that are too short or not stiff enough are easy to detect; the gripper pattern drags, producing friction and noise. There is also a second part to the test: Have the person put all his or her weight on one ski to see if it can be depressed enough to grab a piece of paper. Beginners should be able to do this just by standing still, while experts may want to find a ski requiring a slight downward push, especially if a pack will be carried. The "paper test," as it's commonly known, doesn't apply to skis designed strictly for downhill skiing since there is no need to maintain a "wax pocket" on such skis.

To wax or not to wax? This is an area of rapidly evolving technology wherein any specific recommendations would be quickly out of date. Without a doubt, waxed skis are still delightful to use in temperatures below about 25°F (approximately 4°C). On the other hand, the simple patterns of no-wax ski bottoms insure forward travel in temperatures near freezing, and in many cases smooth and pleasant skiing in an even wider temperature range. Nevertheless, there are plenty of "purists" who decry the no-wax bases as being too "high-tech" while fumbling through tubes and sticks of incredibly complex compounds developed by the chemical industry to deal with the myriad texture and temperature conditions of the snow surface. Instructors should by all means discuss and, if possible, demonstrate the virtues of both systems, but should consider using no-wax skis for beginning classes and for any other class or outing where snowfall will vary or temperatures will hover near the freezing mark. Under these conditions, waxing may consume a substantial amount of time. It is a valuable skill, but having to devote a lot of time to the process can be frustrating for those who have no-wax skis and would prefer to be skiing.

The value of metal edges is often debated among nordic skiers. Metal edges grip better on very hard surfaces and may be essential on truly icy slopes, and some nordic downhillers and ski mountaineers prefer them since such conditions are common in Alpine ski areas and on the high peaks. Even in these areas, however, skis without metal edges work perfectly well most of the time, and ski tourers and cross-country skiers rarely need them. When conditions are so icy that metal edges are really essential, it's probably best to pop the skis off and walk! Metal edges are expensive, can add to maintenance problems, add weight, modify flex patterns, mutilate the opposite ski, chop up ski poles, and can be dangerous in a fall. Any instructor can recall having students ski over his or her skis, and if the student's skis had metal edges can still point out the grooves. It's also worth noting that the most skilled of instructors will eventually hit a participant's ski or pole,

and the damage (and potential obligation) will be far greater if the instructor uses metal edges.

Bindings are important as well, and should be suited to the activity. As with skis, almost any type can be used, but maximal enjoyment depends upon a good match of equipment. Narrow racing or track-type binding systems are ideal for use with light boots and shoes in tracks and for gentle turns in good conditions. Seventy-five mm. three-pin types are designed for use with substantial boots on back-country trails and in untracked off-trail areas, as well as for turning on downhill runs. Either type of binding can be used for either set of activities, though with less ease and efficiency. Beginners usually prefer the relative stability of the wider (75 mm.) types — even in track skiing — until enough confidence has been developed to move to the narrower binding/boot combinations. More advanced skiers tend to have a strong preference for the light gear used in track skiing, and wider bindings and tortionally stiff boots for back-country use. Boots are also extremely important. Participants who will be renting should be given clear directions as to how to fit them, how to check for tortional rigidity and proper fit in the bindings, and how to contact the heel plate or "pop-up."

Ski poles vary in length, basket design, and grip style. Racers and cross-country track skiers favor relatively long poles (a tight fit in the armpit is a common measure), and small, sometimes wedge or "half-moon" baskets. Ski-tourers usually prefer slightly shorter poles with full, round baskets, while Nordic downhillers often use the shorter Alpine style. Grip and strap design is also very important and often overlooked. Efficient technique depends in part on an ability to relax the hand without losing control of the pole, and this requires adjustable straps and at least an inch or so (two to three cm.) of pole top to protrude above the point where the strap enters it. Beginning participants often come to an outing with poles that don't have this "top knob," in which case adhesive tape can be used to bind down the top part of the strap.

Waxes are another essential part of the system common to all types of nordic skiing. Even when "no-wax" skis are used, "running," "glide," or "speed" waxes are needed to provide fast tip- and tail-gliding surfaces. Also useful for reducing snow build-up on the kicker surfaces of no-wax skis, wax kits can be complex sets of waxes and klisters or simplified systems using only two or three waxes or waxes and klisters.

There is much more to be said about skis, boots, and poles, and every season brings advances in technology and technique. It's difficult to stay abreast of every new advance while maintaining a sense of perspective on the relationship between skiing and ski equipment. On one hand, matching individuals with the best possible types of ski gear for a given activity can make a big difference in terms of ease of learning and avoidance of frustration. On the other hand, it's very easy to become overly concerned about gear. Almost any type of skiing *can* be done on almost any type of gear. The importance of having the equipment well matched to the activity increases when skill development is the central focus of an outing.

SUGGESTED MINIMUM GEAR REQUIRED FOR NORDIC SKIING DAY TRIPS WITHIN DEVELOPED AREAS

Individual Gear

Required Items

1. Skis and bindings, boots, poles, and waxes (see above discussion);
2. Two pair of wool or better sox plus spares;
3. Light clothing (light breathable clothing for the torso and legs of fabrics such as wool, nylon or polypropylene that maintains warmth when wet; the layer should provide neck cover);
4. Warm clothing (at least an inch [2½ cm.] of insulating layers for the torso);
5. Windproof clothing (for torso and legs);
6. Gloves (at least one pair of warm gloves);
7. Hat (substantial ski-type cap to cover the ears);
8. Sunglasses (dark tint with full coverage);
9. Sunscreen (preferably 15 or better rating);
10. Safety straps (for nordic downhill skiing only; required by many ski areas and always a good idea).

Optional Items

1. Raingear (this may be a required item in some climates, and is always a good idea);
2. Gaitors (the low type are usually adequate in tracks and on groomed slopes, while nordic downhillers often prefer the high type if unpacked slopes will be skied);
3. Whistle (always a good idea);
4. Belt pack or small day pack (handy for small items, lunch, and water);
5. Climbing skins (nordic downhillers sometimes find "climbers" useful even in Alpine ski areas).

Group Gear

Required Items

Since these activities take place in developed areas which usually have ski shops and emergency facilities, there may be no essential group gear. If such facilities are not available, appropriate gear should be taken. (See the ski touring and ski mountaineering group gear list for suggestions.)

Optional Items

1. Tool kit (screwdrivers, extra screws, binding and pole parts, tape, scrapers, file, and other maintenance and repair items.

SUGGESTED MINIMUM GEAR REQUIRED FOR SKI TOURING AND SKI MOUNTAINEERING

Individual Gear

Required Items

1. All of the items listed as required and optional for cross-country or nordic downhill skiing, plus:
2. Additional insulation (extra clothing beyond the requirements for XC skiing sufficient to allow the skier to survive an unplanned night out even if one layer is soaked by rain or sweat; this usually requires two layers of

light-to-moderate thickness for both torso and legs, plus a combination of torso-insulating layers such as vests or parkas totalling more than an inch (2½ cm.) in thickness);

3. Items 13 through 26 from the minimum gear list required for backpacking.

Optional Items

1. Avalanche cords or beacons (may be required; useless without training);
2. Extra gloves and mittens;
3. Insulating pad (small seat pad or, better, a 2/3 length pad; far superior to bough beds in survival situations, required if boughs unavailable, and easier on ecosystem);
4. Extra batteries (alkaline, lithium, or other cold-resistant types);
5. Climbing skins (many ski mountaineers and some ski tourers prefer "climbers" to waxes when using waxed skis in certain types of snow and terrain);
6. Pack cover (almost essential for keeping gear dry in rain or very wet snow, and always handy. Large plastic bags can be used, though fitted covers of coated nylon are preferable.);
7. Sun hat (preferably with visor or brim).

Group Gear

Required Items

1. Tool kit (screwdrivers, extra screws, binding and pole parts, tape, scrapers, files, and other maintenance-and-repair items);
2. Insulating pads (at least one 2/3 length pad for every two or three people unless carried by individuals);
3. Sleeping bags or half bag (essential in the event an injured person must be stabilized until SAR assistance can be obtained);
4. Tarp or small tent (adequate to provide shelter for an injured person and one to two attendants; Tarps are usually more versatile. Don't forget sufficient cord to set up the tarp!);
5. Stove, fuel, and pot (in a survival situation, a portable backpacking- or mountaineering-type stove with plenty of fuel and at least a two-liter container can provide drinking

water and water for hot-water bottles);
6. Shovels (one for every 3-6 people, for avalanche rescue and to aid in shelter construction in unplanned bivouacs);
7. Plastic flagging (to mark routes in the event of emergencies; ski tracks *cannot* be relied upon);
8. First-aid kit (substantial kit; see first-aid section).

Optional Items

1. Avalanche probes (may be required; should be carried if *any* avalanche danger exists, at a ratio of at least one six-foot (two meter) or longer probe per two participants. In situations where substantial avalanche danger exists, beacons or at least cords should be carried and used by all participants. Training in avalanche rescue is essential for this equipment to be of value);
2. Extra food (a supply of high-energy foods can be very helpful, at least in terms of maintaining positive attitudes in emergency bivouacs and unexpectedly extended outings);
3. Sled or pulk (This can be useful for hauling group gear and, if large enough, for use as a rescue sled; can be a great asset in the event of an injury).

Note that the above suggestions are for day trips only, and do not include gear for overnight travel. For extended ski tours or ski-mountaineering outings, consult the backpacking, snowcamping, and mountaineering lists.

6. Leadership Requirements. Nordic skiing is an immensely varied realm. The reader should review the suggested qualifications of hiking leaders, as all are appropriate for nordic leaders (or instructors) except item R, which is phrased in terms of hiking. Certainly the nordic leader should be familiar with the site to be used when the activity will take place outside of developed areas. Even within developed areas though, familiarity is a great advantage. While it's clear that activities held strictly within the confines of a developed area may relieve the leader of some portion of the responsibility for certain aspects of emergency response, care should be taken to assess each situation carefully. Ski-patrol services are not able to prevent injuries and cannot resolve all situations effectively. The speed and quality of response by such services varies greatly between areas, too.

The reader should also review the suggested qualifications for snow-camping and/or mountaineering leaders if these activities may be part of the program. Additional attributes for instructors of cross-country or nordic downhill outings within developed areas include:

A. Familiarity with the techniques to be taught, including an ability to perform the maneuvers or skills with a high degree of expertise, since modeling is the key to instruction, and a thorough understanding of the physical and biomechanical aspects of the maneuvers;

B. A knowledge of both modeling and step-by-step analytical approaches to instruction. This includes a thorough understanding of effective progressions, an ability to identify errors, and an ability to formulate constructive, positive comments and strategies leading to improvements in participant skill levels. Leaders should also know how to recognize and to minimize the effects of cold weather and anxiety on the teaching process;

C. An understanding of ski clothing and equipment, including waxing and skis, binding, boot and pole design, function, maintenance, and repair;

D. An understanding of cold-related traumas, including the recognition, treatment, and prevention of hypothermia and frostbite;

E. An understanding of avalanche and other snow- and ice-structure hazards, including rescue techniques and methods of reducing risks.

Ski touring and ski mountaineering leaders should possess at least the last three attributes listed above (items C, D, and E) and may need attributes A and B if ski-technique instruction is part of the program. In addition, ski-touring or ski-mountaineering leaders need:

A. Skiing ability well beyond the minimum requirements of the outing;

B. An understanding of the effects of cold,

anxiety, and physical stress on communication, and how to reduce or overcome these effects;

C. A thorough understanding, backed by practical experience, of cold-weather survival. This includes snow-shelter construction as well as the special physical and psychological demands of cold weather.

7. Leadership Ratios. Cross-country and nordic-downhill instruction within developed areas are among the few activities in the realm of outdoor pursuits wherein one leader is sufficient for each group. In such closed and relatively protected areas, the consequences of an incapacitated sole leader are seldom dangerous to participants. Additional leaders or assistants can, however, be useful and can enhance program quality while allowing beginning leaders to gain experience. Most ski instruction for beginners is actually better performed in small groups than individually. A group of three or four students is probably ideal, allowing plenty of individual attention while moderating the stress on each person. On the other hand, group control becomes difficult and individual attention inadequate if group size exceeds about ten participants. For example, modeling is extremely important and requires frequent reinforcement of images, so the instructor usually needs to demonstrate frequently. If demonstrations follow every third student's attempt at a maneuver, the instructor will be performing at a pace near the limits of his or her endurance in a class of nine. Even at this ratio, the instructor will be skiing three times as much as any one student, and probably having to stride, herringbone, or side-step to the starting point at least two extra times.

On ski-touring or ski-mountaineering outings, a second leader or assistant is necessary for the safety reasons expressed in earlier discussions of back-country experiences. Groups of more than a dozen can be awkward since safety and the inherent variability of skiing paces extends the distance between skiers on a trail. Group control is often more difficult than in backpacking, while the consequences of inadequate control are often more severe. Two leaders can supervise five or six participants each and journey in semi-independent groups. This mode of travel increases overall speed, and safety isn't greatly reduced *if* each group has a complete set of group gear and *if* the groups meet at frequent intervals. Minimum requirements for these activities should thus be two leaders for up to twelve participants, plus an additional leader or qualified assistant for each additional unit of up to six participants.

B. Course Conduct

1. Common Formats. Cross-country and nordic-downhill classes are often taught as a series of short lessons. The one-and-a-half hour format seems to be about ideal for periods of direct instruction since attention spans, limits of endurance, and the stresses of winter weather make longer sessions relatively unproductive. A full-day format involving three one-and-a-half hour segments separated by one-hour breaks for practice and lunch fills most of the available daylight in midwinter and pushes the patience and interest limit of the most earnest student. The use of one-hour teaching segments is not recommended unless utilized in sequence form during a day. Such short sessions actually provide only about fifty minutes of instructional time, and initial sessions may be largely consumed by attempts to assess the skills of participants. Whenever the total time is limited, session objectives should be narrowed appropriately; it's far better to make substantial progress on a small point than to overwhelm and frustrate participants with unrealistic and unattainable expectations.

Ski-touring outings are usually confined to one day, and can be thought of as a winter equivalent of hiking. These outings typically involve fewer hours of travel than equivalent summer activities because of protracted travel times, greater amounts of time needed to get ready to ski from the trailhead, and shorter days. Except for ideal gentle downhill runs well within the ability of all participants, travel rates will also be much less than for hiking. While it often feels as though skiing is faster than walking, this is rarely the case. Overnight ski tours are discussed under snowcamping.

Ski-mountaineering outings are usually conducted as overnight or multi-day ventures, though in some cases mountainous terrain is accessible within the limits of a single-day

outing. Since extra distances, elevation and obstacles are characteristic of day outings, they often require pre-dawn starts and late-night returns.

Pre-trip meetings are valuable for any nordic ski outing. Beyond the values of these meetings discussed for hiking, backpacking, and other activities, they can provide opportunities to discuss and explain gear requirements and teach technique in ski classes. Very substantial improvement in skills can result from studying films and videotapes of skiers demonstrating techniques. Pre-trip meetings should occur far enough in advance of the outing to allow participants to arrange for rentals or to borrow ski gear. One session two weeks prior to the outing and one session just a few days prior to the outing work well.

2. Objectives. Some nordic skiing classes have very limited objectives. An example is a nordic downhill class which might focus on one specific aspect of the sport, such as deep-snow skiing or a particular turn. Ski-touring and ski-mountaineering outings may have very broad objectives similar to those of hiking, backpacking, snowcamping, or mountaineering. Thus the suggested objectives for these activities should be reviewed carefully.

Typical objectives for skills-oriented cross-country and nordic-downhill classes are that the participant will:

A. Enjoy the experience and want to pursue the activity further;
B. Gain a fitness and an awareness of the fitness requirements of the activity;
C. Develop an awareness of the hazards inherent in the activity and of ways of reducing these risks. This includes hazards related to cold and to avalanches;
D. Understand the clothing and equipment requirements of the sport, including selection, maintenance, and repair;
E. Be able to identify potential resources and facilities for the activity. This includes an awareness of managing agencies or landholder policies and regulations;
F. Improve in skiing ability. This objective is often expressed in terms of specific skills or maneuvers. Specification is useful in certain educational settings wherein grading is based

on attainment of objectives, and in most cases can help in clarifying leader and participant expectations with regard to course direction and content;

G. Develop an awareness of and sensitivity to the environment (This objective is too often forgotten in skills-oriented classes!)

Typical objectives of ski-touring and ski-mountaineering outings include, in addition to those suggested above, that the participant will:

A. Be able to navigate under winter conditions, which implies an ability to use maps and compasses effectively;

B. Be able to identify potential sites for emergency bivouacs, and construct adequate shelters using the minimal equipment carried;

C. Be aware of the capabilities and limitations of local SAR units under winter conditions;

D. Acquire the skills and knowledge necessary to independently plan and carry out a successful ski-touring or ski-mountaineering day outing.

3. Levels. The terms "easy," "moderate," and "difficult" apply to back-country ski-touring or ski-mountaineering outings but have little application to activities within developed areas, where physical stress can usually be adjusted to meet the needs of individuals, and where technique rather than strength or endurance are required. An "easy" ski tour rarely involves more than three or four miles (five to six-and-a-half km.) of skiing, with elevation gains of less than 1000 feet (about 300 meters). Ski ability and ski conditions can, however, vary this considerably. "Moderate" outings may double these limits, and any outing covering more than eight miles (thirteen km.) or 2000 vertical feet (about 600 meters) is usually best described as "difficult" unless the route and conditions are exceptionally favorable or the participants are exceptionally fit and skilled.

The terms "beginning," "intermediate," and "advanced" are usually applied to technique-oriented classes. "Beginning" outings typically address the needs of those who haven't skied before, haven't skied on nordic gear even though experience has been gained on Alpine

gear, or have limited nordic experience. The following maneuvers or techniques are generally considered appropriate for beginning courses. All might be included in a two-day format, while only selected portions of the progression should be attempted in more limited blocks of time:

Equipment Review:

Safety discussion	Uphill stride
Tip paddle turn	Herringbone
Tail paddle turn	Straight running
Sidestep	Step turn
Kick turn	Single plow
Tip/tail crossover	Snowplow
turns	Snowplow turn
Falling	Traverse
Getting up	Stem turn
Walking	Telemark Bumps
Basic diagonal	Basic telemark turn
Double poling	
One-step	

"Intermediate" outings typically involve review of beginning maneuvers, followed by instruction in part or all of the following maneuvers:

Skating turn	Unweighting
Advanced diagonal	Uphill christie
Traverse sidestep	Christie garland
Sideslip	Stem christie
Forward sideslip	Parallel turns
Pole use	Advanced telemark turns

Advanced outings also typically begin with review of the basics, then focus on some selected interest such as specialized turns, deep snow, ice, crust and crud skiing, skiing with packs, steep terrain, or polishing of parallel or telemark-linked turns.

While the terms "easy" and "beginner" are useful and fairly well understood by most skiers and potential skiers, there is often a lot of confusion over what constitutes an "intermediate" or "advanced" level of competence. For these, it's usually best to combine the term with a statement or two about the skills people need before participation. "An intermediate level outing for those who can make basic snowplow turns" helps clarify what is required and offered.

Back-country outings are sometimes described by a combination of difficulty level and prerequisite skiing ability. This provides a range from "easy" trips for "beginners" to "difficult" trips for skiers with "advanced" skills.

4. Sample Itineraries. The following "Planning Guidelines for Instructors" and "Recommended Daily Agenda" provide an example of one possible format for a beginning course. Such materials, used in conjunction with specific lists of objectives and progressions, can be of great value to instructors in the field and help insure that the outing is carried out in reasonable correspondence to the plan.

BEGINNING SKI-TOURING OUTING PLANNING GUIDELINES FOR INSTRUCTORS

Length of Outing (days): 3
Departure Time: 7 a.m.
Meeting Place:
Transportation Method:
Days of Week:
Return Time: about 6 p.m.
Student Gear and Equipment Requirements (refer to standard gear lists): All required items on standard equipment list, plus maps of the area. Emphasize minimal nature of the list and suggest extra insulation.

Instructor and Leader Gear and Equipment Requirements (additional): One *extra* clothing layer to share, small first-aid kit, repair items for skis and bindings; a small snow shovel; substantial headlamp; and a pack large enough to carry a complete winter camping kit (in case a student is unable to proceed and supplies must be carried in).

Group Gear and Equipment Requirements (per independent field group): First-aid belt, tarp, foam pad(s), and sleeping bag or half bag, and, in the vehicles or in the cabins, at least one complete kit of extra clothes, extra food, stove, fuel, pots, tent, foam pads (2), avalanche probes and snow shovels (2), with a suitable pack.

Specifications of the Location and Route(s): Beginning ski touring is best carried out using cabins or other "civilized" lodging. Winter camping at best consumes a great deal of time and energy, greatly reducing the amount of ski technique that can be taught. Exceptions might be considered for special groups having substantial winter camping experience. The site should offer immediate access to ski patrol or other rescue services. If this is not possible, a suitable sled *must* be taken to the site and stored in the vehicles or lodging. The site must provide 1) flat, open areas and flat or *gently* rolling terrain for beginning exercises and for track skiing, 2) easy access to gentle to moderate ($\leq 20°$) slopes for downhill practice, 3) a few short steep hills ($\leq 40°$) for the better students, side slipping and other technique practice, and safety discussions, and 4) possibilities for several levels of beginning tours.

All use must be planned to minimize conflicts with other users. This means scheduling track and practice areas at times of low use by the public and planning tours that avoid very popular places (at least at popular times, i.e., weekends). All decisions must carefully consider the avalanche danger, and must be extremely conservative in this matter. If there is any doubt, find another route or stay off the hills!

Typical Agenda: As detailed in the recommended agenda, Day 1 usually consists of the drive to the site, getting settled in the lodging, beginning practice on nearby flats and tracks, lunch, and practice on the tracks until dinner. Talks and moonlight skiing are fun and useful evening events. Day 2 is spent revising basics on the tracks for an hour or so, moving to an area for downhill practice, lunch, and a four-hour tour. Day 3 is spent on an all-day tour with instruction in technique, navigation, and survival skills, with return to the lodging at about 3:30 and departure for home at 4:30.

BEGINNING SKI-TOURING OUTING RECOMMENDED DAILY AGENDA

DAY 1

Business at Meeting Point - Same as beginning backpacking outing, plus a first-aid kit and snow shovel for each vehicle.

At the Lodging Site - Same as beginning backpacking outing plus:

1. Collect *all* lodging fees *before* moving in!
2. Set meeting time and place (usually within the hour), and move into the lodgings.
3. Meet with students and staff to review course objectives and specific plans for the day. Also emphasize rules for behavior.

During the Day

— Prepare good training tracks near the lodging;
— Meet the students near the lodging for beginning practice;
— Have them leave their skis *off* until shown how to put them on properly;
— Cover safety items first. Do so thoroughly but quickly (falling, pole straps, not wandering off, etc.);
— Go through basic progression (attached) as a large group, if possible, to allow efficient grouping into ability levels. This large group teaching/sorting process seems to work best when carried through the "walking" maneuver;
— Divide the groups by ability/interest levels;
— Move to the tracks before lunch if time allows;
— After lunch, continue to work in tracks, with occasional relief via *short* tours and/or obstacle courses. Try to get through the basics of diagonal stride, double poling, and "one-step" (single kick w/double poling);
— Videotaping can *sometimes* be useful. Be careful not to intimidate students or take away significant amounts of ski time.

In the Evening

— Make sure that rules about skiing outside the lodging area are clear;
— Clarify plans for Day 2 and specify gear requirements. For the half-day tour, ask them to pack *tonight;*
— Have a brief meeting to answer questions;
— Arrange a moonlight tour if conditions allow;
— Show videotapes.

DAY 2

In the Morning

— Wake students at least two hours before you plan to be out skiing;
— Explain the waxing and gear needs of the day in light of weather changes;
— Be sure day kits are packed.

During the Day

— Review and practice, with slow warmup, obstacle course and track skiing (about an hour total);
— Move to gentle slopes (safe, unintimidating runouts!) for uphill stride through beginning snowplow (an hour or so);
— Move to moderate slopes for snowplow through basic telemark turns (an hour or so);
— Have lunch;
— Go on a short tour, teaching as you go (*reviewing* techniques rather than adding at this point) A tour of two hours and an hour of practice works well.

In the Evening

— Check health and attitude and equipment;
— Specify and have the student pack gear and clothing for day tour;
— Be sure students are part of the process of route selection (The planning process is probably more important than anything else we teach, including technique, in terms of the potential for affecting student enjoyment and safety);
— Show videotapes.

DAY 3

In the Morning

— Again, allow two hours from wake-up to departure time;
— Leave a "flight-plan" with a responsible party at the lodging;
— Carefully review the route, timing, contingency plans and other details with students in small groups;
— Be sure all staff know *all* routes and contingency plans.

During the Day

— Review basic techniques as needed, having an instructor follow and then lead each student in rotation, to work on individual problems;

— Stop at appropriate places to introduce, if possible, skating turns through forward sideslip. The lockstep turn is also valuable. Fancy moves and turns can be demonstrated provided care is taken to prevent injury to students who may fearlessly but clumsily follow you and to prevent losing ground by confusing students with too much material;

— Try to reach a pretty lunch spot, but keep students informed of the hazards of returning tired down a packed-out, hard, frozen trail as the daylight fades, and of the reasons for the decisions you make about timing and routes;

— Discuss "what-if's," such as ski, binding, pole, or boot breakage, injury, making snow shelters, escape routes, foul weather, and avalanches. These are vitally important, so allow plenty of time!

— Get the students involved in navigational decisions. (Navigation is also vital, but very hard to teach to *beginning* skiers, who have too much to consider already. Emphasize importance of developing these skills).

At the Lodging

— Be sure that the accommodations are left in perfect shape, and check out with the manager;

— Collect *all* group gear;

— Remind drivers of rules and plans, and check the vehicle (all as in Day 1 at the meeting point!);

— Carefully check the roll once everyone is in the vehicles;

— No vehicle is to leave without the instructor's consent;

— Before leaving have a short debriefing/ evaluation of the trip and arrange the post-trip meeting.

At the Return Point - Same as beginning backpacking outing.

SNOW CAMPING

APPENDIX H

SNOW CAMPING

A. General Description

1. What It Is; What Is Done. Snow camping by its broadest definition includes *any* camping in the snow, though to some the term connotes only the use of igloos, snow caves, and other shelters made of snow. We'll use the broader definition here while acknowledging the importance of snow-shelter construction and use. Camping in the snow, especially in snow shelters, seems to many non-participants to be an intrinsically miserable activity to be avoided at all costs. In fact, with proper equipment and a few skills beyond those of ordinary backpacking, it can be amazingly comfortable. As advocates quickly point out, there are even a few advantages over summer camping, including little or no competition for campsites (due to far fewer users and far more potential sites), a guaranteed soft or at least adjustable surface, no distance to water (just melt the snow), no dust,

no mud, and no bugs! Many snow campers use some form of shelter excavated or constructed from snow blocks, though almost all of them carry fabric shelters as well as insurance against collapsed, inadequate, or incomplete cover, poor construction conditions, or rain. Snow campers use skis or snowshoes, transporting their somewhat heavier than bare-ground loads in backpacks or on sleds (pulks). Distances are usually fairly short due to the inherent slow pace of winter travel, short days, and the extra time needed to construct snow shelters. Camping in the snow extends the backpacking and mountaineering seasons, allows skiers access to remote sites, and is an exciting and thoroughly enjoyable activity in and of itself.

2. Hazards. As in snowshoeing or ski touring, the greatest concerns are medical problems related to prolonged exposure to cold and the dangers of avalanches, snow-bridge collapses, and weak ice or snow surfaces on bodies of water. Travel itself isn't necessarily hazardous if conducted on snowshoes; however, slow travel with a large pack or a sled in tow can be risky. The best initiated turn on skis can literally turn

393

into disaster if the skier doesn't precisely compensate for the momentum of the pack or if the sled decides to make the turn somewhere else. There is also a special kind of "double whammie" face plant peculiar to ski travel with loose-heel bindings and a large backpack, wherein the skier unfortunate enough to make a conventional face plant is, milliseconds later, smashed another several inches into the snow by the backpack. A more common occurrence, potentially dangerous on hard or crusty surfaces, is the sudden planting of rear and elbows from backwards lean. Finally, the dangerous knee-in-the-snow forward fall on skis is far more dangerous with a large pack since the momentum of the extra mass can easily overtax the bones and joints of the leg.

There are also a few hazards associated with the camping process itself. Especially when using tents, you must avoid camping beneath snow-laden branches or trees likely to be overloaded during the night. In relatively warm maritime climates, snow accumulation in the trees can be extremely heavy and capable of developing devastating energy in a long fall. The best of tents can be crushed by such "tree dumps," which may contain branches as well. Snow caves, igloos, quinzes, and other shelters may also collapse, though this is a rare event and the dangers are usually more from unplanned lack of shelter than from burial. The greatest danger in caves and igloos, and tents for that matter, are poor air quality due to inadequate ventilation and the build-up of toxic fumes due to stove use within the shelter.

Snow camping, despite all of the potential hazards, can be conducted safely. Virtually all risks can be avoided by careful planning and by utilizing common sense and accepted practices.

3. Who Participates. Snow camping isn't nearly as popular as backpacking or ski touring, yet a surprising number of people do camp in the snow, at least occasionally. Most participants are experienced backpackers or mountaineers who do it to extend the hiking or climbing season, to gain access to the peaks (which may require camping on snow well into summer in some areas), or simply to experiment with the intriguing notion of sleeping in snow shelters.

Because of the need for, or at least desirability of, previous backpacking experience and the need for extra gear, there are relatively fewer potential candidates for snow camping than for backpacking programs. Kids and adults alike are usually fascinated by the concept of the igloo, so that single-day or carefully controlled near-the-road overnight experiences may appeal to relative camping newcomers as well as to backpackers.

4. Resource Requirements. All that is really needed for snow camping is a little snow and an attractive site. The earlier suggestions for backpacking sites apply here, though in general smaller areas are better due to the shorter distances that must be travelled under winter conditions. Parking can sometimes be a problem, too, since some trailheads aren't plowed, limited to day use, or require permits.

Little snow is needed since many types of shelters can be constructed from snow gathered and piled or processed into blocks. Depending on the ground surface, six inches (about thirteen or fourteen centimeters) of snow may be enough to make good pile shelters, while three feet or so (about one meter) is sometimes enough for snow caves if wind action has created deep drifts.

5. Equipment and Clothing Requirements. Snow camping requires basic backpacking gear, some additional clothing and insulation, somewhat warmer footwear, ski gear, or snowshoes, and, if snow shelters are to be constructed, certain tools. None of the required equipment is highly technical or sophisticated, and most can be obtained at a reasonable cost. The backpacking list and discussion should be reviewed carefully since only additional needs or specifications will be covered here. It should also be noted that, as in summer or "high season" travel, there are penalties to be paid for carrying excessive gear. No essentials can be left behind, yet care should also be taken to avoid adding superfluous items to loads necessarily large due to tools and extra insulation. The difficulties of travel over snow compound the usual penalties of extra weight, and the advantages of simplicity are no less valid in winter than in summer.

SUGGESTED MINIMUM GEAR REQUIREMENTS FOR SNOW CAMPING

Individual Gear

Required Items (in addition to the requirements for backpacking):

1. Extra insulation (This usually includes two layers of wool or better fabric for the legs and torso, instead of the one layer needed for three-season backpacking.);
2. Turtleneck or other neck covering (A wool scarf will suffice, but zippered turtlenecks are especially versatile.);
3. Extra hand coverings (At least two layers, including substantial wool or better mittens. Wool or polypropylene glove liners and leather work, and ski gloves are useful.);
4. Warm footwear (There are many possibilities, including mountaineering boots or insulated hiking boots, snowmobile boots, shoe-pacs, some types of ski boots, and various insulated overboots. Snowcampers often bring two pairs of footwear — one to travel in and one to wear around camp.);
5. Gaitors (The high type are usually best.);
6. Warm sleeping bag (Depending on the area, the two-inch minimum suggested for backpacking may need to be increased to three inches or more.);
7. Warm sleeping pad (Closed-cell pads of three-eighths inch or greater thickness are usually needed on snow. Air mattresses are not recommended.);
8. Substantial shelter (Tarps work very well. As to many types of tents, however, fabric types, construction quality, and design are more critical in snow and winter weather.);
9. Skis, boots, and poles or snowshoes (Modern light touring skis are strong enough for winter backpacking. Seventy-five millimeter three-pin bindings and substantial boots with tortionally stiff soles are desirable unless the route follows prepared tracks or gentle roads.).

Optional Items

1. Avalanche cord or beacons (may be required);
2. Extra water bottle (Hot-water bottles in sleeping bags are especially nice in cold weather, helping to drive excess moisture out of the bags and greatly increasing comfort. When water must be provided by melting snow, the increased storage volume is also very useful.);
3. Insulation for stove bottom (A small square of asbestos or foil-covered ensolite is needed for some hot-bottomed stoves, while for others an unprotected square of ensolite is adequate.);
4. Sleeping-bag covers for bivouac sacks (For use in snow caves and igloos. Note that these may inhibit the escape of vapor from sleeping bags, causing loss of insulation, and should be unnecessary in well-constructed shelters in temperatures well below freezing.);
5. Additional candles (Winter nights are long, and candles work very well in caves and igloos.);
6. Sieve or screen for water (Melting snow for water often results in a thin soup of pine or other tree needles, mosses, and other vegetable matter. Coffee strainers, tea strainers, or simply a small square of plastic window screen can quickly remove most of this.);
7. Ski poles (If snowshoes are elected on required list.);
8. Shovel (Almost essential for excavation of snow caves or construction of pile or mound shelters, and useful in building igloos. Large grain-scoop types are useful for most work; however, smaller portables are far superior for work inside caves and in hardened snow such as in avalanche-rescue work.);
9. Snow saw or knife (The snow saw is usually considered the more valuable tool.);
10. Sled or pulk (This is a great way to transport gear over snow on certain types of terrain. Like skiing, the basic idea is simple, but proper gear and a certain amount of technique are essential for enjoyment and safety!)

Group Gear

Required Items (in addition to the requirements for backpacking!):

1. Snow shovels (If not carried by each individual, at least one for every six party members for avalanche-rescue purposes, and at least one for every shelter to be constructed.);
2. Snow saws or knives (Saws usually preferable at a ratio of one for each snow-block shelter to be constructed.);
3. Repair kit (In addition to the contents suggested for backpacking, the kit should contain any pieces, parts, or tools needed for maintenance and repair of snowshoes, snowshoe bindings, skis, ski bindings, or ski poles.)

Optional Gear

1. Snow-removal tarps (Old tarps or sheets of plastic, nylon, or other strong, slippery material are useful for dragging snow out of insides and entranceways during construction of caves and mound structures. Good tents, tarps, or ground sheets can be used but are likely to be damaged.);
2. Sled or pulk (There can be a great safety advantage to having a substantial sled along, especially if it's long enough to use as an emergency transport device for injured group members. On trips that will push more than a few miles into the back country, this can greatly shorten rescue times. Such a sled can also be used to haul group gear, thus reducing pack weights and possibly the risk of ski injuries caused by travelling with extra-heavy loads. It's also useful to have a way of transporting all of a participant's load in the event of a minor sprain or strain that would otherwise slow or stop the group.)

One more reminder; the above list only covers suggestions beyond those given earlier for backpacking, so those lists must be reviewed carefully. Everything on the backpacking list is appropriate for snowcamping with the exception, of course, of insect repellent.

B. Course Conduct

1. Common Formats. Snow camping outings, like backpacking outings, are usually conducted as two-day overnight excursions. While there are many advantages to longer trips, the average outing length on snow tends to be less than for similar dry-land excursions. Snow travel is potentially more tiring, the cold weather adds a certain amount of stress, and pack loads are usually fairly heavy even without additional food. It's often useful or even necessary to have several pre-trip meetings instead of the one or two recommended for backpacking. Even though participants in snow camping are presumably experienced in backpacking, all of the gear requirements for this activity need to be reviewed in addition to the special needs related to snow travel and camping. Time spent in chalkboard discussions of shelter construction can reduce frustrations and speed construction in the field. And a comprehensive avalanche-safety lecture is always a very worthwhile addition to snow camping courses and an essential component of any program that will involve the use of avalanche-prone areas.

2. Objectives. The objectives suggested for backpacking also apply to snow camping and should be reviewed before compiling another list for a particular program. The objectives listed below are specific to travel and camping in the snow and typically require that the participant will, in addition to meeting the appropriate goals of backpacking, be able to:

A. Understand the special equipment and clothing requirements of snow camping;
B. Understand the special hazards of travel in snow-covered terrain (This includes avalanches and hazards related to cornices, snow bridges, and other snow formations.);
C. Recognize, treat, and minimize the risks of hypothermia, frostbite, trenchfoot, and other cold-related conditions and injuries;
D. Locate safe and environmentally sound campsites, and find safe tent or shelter sites within the campsite;
E. Set up a safe and comfortable camp using tents or tarps, and use sleeping bags, stoves, and other gear effectively;

F. Construct safe and reasonably comfortable snow shelters (This should include at least two types of shelters selected from mound types, snow caves, and block houses or igloos, and at least one survival-type shelter such as kick-holes or tree-well caves.);

G. Develop the skills, knowledge and experience necessary to independently plan and carry out a successful snow camping outing.

3. Levels. An "easy" snow-camping outing rarely involves travel distances of more than a few miles (up to five km.) with little elevation gain. When shelter construction is a primary goal and the group is made up of beginners, a mile of travel may be pushing the limits of "easy" since so much time will be needed to build the shelters. A "moderate" trip might involve considerably more distance, though even with experienced participants a lot of time has to be allocated for shelter construction. In most cases it's necessary to allow at least two hours for experienced individuals and three hours for beginners to build snow shelters. Setting up tents, by comparison, takes about thirty minutes at most, and fifteen minutes is usually sufficient for experienced backpackers if the snow surface needs little packing. A moderate trip might, therefore, cover up to five or six miles (eight or ten km.) on tenting days but only three or four miles (five to six-and-a-half km.) on shelter-building days. Shorter distances may be required if significant elevation gains are included.

Snow travel is so variable in speed and efficiency that it's very difficult to give specific guidelines here, and on the best planned outing variances from predicted paces can be anticipated. Snow conditions in some areas can vary in hours from a firm boot-walkable surface as fast to traverse as a bare summer trail to deep snow that forces a snail's pace on skis or snowshoes. Any trip covering more than about seven miles (eleven kilometers or so), or elevation increases greater than 2000 ft. (600 m.) probably ought to be labeled "difficult" unless the travel conditions are exceptionally good.

A "beginning" snow-camping outing can be "easy," "moderate," or "difficult" in terms of the effort needed, though most beginning trips are "easy" since "beginners" need to devote most of their attention to developing skills and

techniques. If participants have limited backpacking experience prior to the outing, it may be necessary to limit the objectives of the outing to "A" through "E" suggested above for snow camping, and an appropriate selection from those suggested for backpacking. With substantial prior backpacking experience, objective "F" can usually be attained partially on a two-day trip and wholly on a two-night, three-day trip. "Intermediate" experiences may focus on construction techniques, adding new shelter types, and improving efficiency. Some intermediate groups use the available time to travel greater distances, utilizing tents or very basic snow shelters. "Advanced" outings might also focus on shelters, stressing speed of construction or construction in shallow snow, ice, or other difficult conditions. They might additionally take the form of long-distance adventures. One good advanced snow-camping activity is to follow popular summer hiking or backpacking routes while moving participants toward attainment of objective "G."

4. Sample Itinerary. The following agenda is an example of one way to conduct a three-day, two-night beginning snow-camping outing.

BEGINNING SNOW-CAMPING OUTING RECOMMENDED DAILY AGENDA

DAY 1

During the Day

— Make frequent stops to check clothing, feet, and response to the cold;

— Observe and give appropriate suggestions on snowshoe and ski techniques (Don't spend unnecessary time on this since the first order of business is to get shelters built.);

— Be sure students know the general lay of the land, their route, and the reasons (practical, environmental, and safety) for selecting the particular site and route;

— In camp, help student groups (usually in two's, three's, and four's) select their sites (One instructor can usually supervise two or three areas, and should be assigned to do so.);

— Each student should build at least one type

of full shelter selected from snowcaves, igloos, blockhouses, burial mounds, or quinzes, and construct one survival trench, pit, or kick-hole;
— Each student should spend one night in a full shelter and the second in another or (ideally) survival-type shelter;
— All sites should be frequently checked to be sure that proper safety precautions are being taken with regard to tool use, roof thicknesses, venting, and student physical condition;
— Before it begins to get dark, gather *all* students and staff for a *brief* "Tour of Homes," to provide ideas and locate all sites (Be sure that locations of all snow caves are well marked. A quick freehand map and wanding of the hard-to-find sites can help if new or blowing snow covers caves and wipes out tracks.).

In the Evening

— Be sure all students have adequate shelter, food, and cooking capabilities, and know the locations of instructors (Wand lines to instructor sites if at all questionable.);
— Identify a time and place for morning assembly, with instructions not to dismantle the shelter before meeting;
— Make at least one "Mother Hen" tour after dinner.

DAY 2

In the Morning

— At the morning assembly, discuss plans for the day, check on student health and attitude, and conduct a "tour of homes" (Visit each site to let everyone share construction ideas and their evaluations, personal clothing, sleeping gear, food, and cooking gear.)

During the Day

— Take a short tour (two hours) to find 1) sites for camps, 2) sites for bivouac (survival) shelters, and 3) areas and slopes useful in

discussions of avalanche-hazard evaluation;
— Have lunch, at which time, visibility permitting, some topo map interpretation can be done;
— After lunch, have the students build at least one more kind of full shelter, plus one survival type if this hasn't been done on the tour.

In the Evening

— Same as evening of Day 1, but if possible include a night (ideally moonlight) tour or ski lessons.

DAY 3

In the Morning

— Repeat the "Tour of Homes" again, allowing two hours from wake-up to departure time (This time have each camp destroyed by the *group*, which 1) saves time by spurring on the slow folks, 2) lets everyone discover the strength of igloo walls, and 3) is good, clean, destructive fun;
— After inspecting the sites, assemble the groups to explain and discuss routes for the tour (Usually two or more options are necessary, one for good skiers or snowshoers, and one for beginning skiers.).

During the Day

— Carefully supervise the tour since this has not been a course in snow travel, and the loads will be heavy and awkward;
— Depending upon routes and upon the likely interests and motivations of the students, survival shelters, avalanche studies, or mock evacuations can be worthwhile if time allows. Be sure to get to the trailhead early enough so that drivers are alert and capable. *(NOT everyone sleeps well in snowcaves!)*

At the Trailhead - Same as Beginning Backpacking Outing.

At the Return Point - Same as Beginning Backpacking Outing.

RAFTING
Rafting provides thrills and spills at a relatively low risk if (and only if) common sense and accepted safety procedures are conscientiously applied.

APPENDIX I

RAFTING

A. General Description

1. What It Is, What Is Done. Rafting has been with us since the first person wobbled out across the water on a drifting log. It probably wasn't long before several logs were lashed together, a sophisticated design that has continued to this day. The simplicity and inherent stability of rafts is appealing enough to offset their characteristic lack of maneuverability relative to canoes, kayaks, and other solid-hull crafts. Rafts are either paddled or fitted with oarlocks and/or frames and rowed. Most rafting is done in rivers with fast currents and obstacles that insure an exciting ride, but outings vary from an hour or less of leisurely drifting to ambitious multi-day white-water runs.

2. Hazards. Rafting, as a watercraft activity, has certain inherent hazards caused by proximity to water. The precise level of risk is dependent upon the nature of the body of water, the kind of activity, the type and condition of the craft, and the extent to which the participants employ common sense and adhere to safety rules and procedures. Raft stability is an advantage in that it is all but impossible to sink most of them (though swamping and rollovers are common). The same physical characteristics that lend stability to the craft also, unfortunately, increase resistance to turning and movement, so to a certain extent rafts are at the mercy of the currents — at least much more so than canoes or kayaks. Getting tossed overboard is a common event in all but the mildest white water, and it is often impossible to maneuver the craft to facilitate a quick retrieval. Perhaps the greatest danger specifically attributable to rafts is their apparent stability; they lull users into believing that it would be almost impossible to fall overboard. Another danger that is sometimes greater in rafting than in other watercraft activities is entanglement in lines and gear. Rafts have great load-bearing capability, and it's common for lots of equipment to be lashed and stowed on board on multi-day trips. Rafters have to be careful to avoid entrapment in this cargo, however, or its securing ties may flip the craft over.

A hazard common to all watercraft activities is hypothermia. Rafters may be particularly vulnerable to both the systemic type, if the air is cool, and the immersion type, if the water is cool. Cool, remember, doesn't necessarily mean cold, and wind or current speeds dramatically drop the effective temperature for either condition. Paddling a raft is often an intermittent process; a little fast water is likely to result in wet clothing from paddling and or sweat, while the period of relative inactivity may result in insufficient metabolic heat production to sustain a healthy core temperature. If someone falls in, immersion hypothermia is a possibility whenever water temperature is much below body temperature, and very likely if the water temperature is below about 60°F. A rafter experiencing mild hypothermia from prolonged chilling prior to going overboard may be especially vulnerable to the far greater rate of heat loss characteristic of water immersion. An often-heard suggestion is that rafters and others exposed to such conditions should always wear wet suits if the combined air and water temperatures total less than 120°F (49°C, sometimes rounded up to 50°C). Many programs require participants to pass a swim or survival swim test, or to possess current certification in basic swim skills from an organization such as the Red Cross.

Rafting is a favorite recreational pursuit, sufficiently popular, in fact, to support substantial manufacturing and commercial guiding industries. Almost anyone can participate, given a suitable choice of craft and site. Rental options can reduce the cost barrier, and inflatable rafts, now standard in the sport, make transporting relatively easy. Since many of these have large capacities, rafting is somewhat more suitable for group or family activities than canoeing or sail-powered boating.

3. Resource Requirements. Beginning trips require no special body of water on which to practice paddling. Soon, however, even novice rafters seek rivers with sufficient current to provide exciting action. The popularity of

rafting has led to the publication of guidebooks for most regions, and, combined with attention to changes in river levels and other river characteristics, they can provide the beginner with many options. Rivers, unlike most trail systems, are linear. As a result, all usage is concentrated into one narrow zone, making management of the resource somewhat more frustrating for user and manager alike. Both private and public landholders have often had to resort to some form of vigorous control in order to maintain the long-term quality of these limited resources. so users should always check well in advance to determine who manages the stream, then contact the manager to find out about rules, regulations, and permit requirements. Some rivers are so popular that permits must be obtained a year or more in advance! Beleaguered managers of these usually set aside some permits for private parties and a larger number for commercial operators, since they can usually take people down a river with a somewhat less-than-average environmental impact per person. However, the balance of commercial vs. private "sport" never seems to please either group. Those sincerely interested in the environment have to at least applaud the efforts of the managers, but since demand exceeds supply on certain popular rivers, plan ahead! There are many, many fine rafting rivers for which no permits are required or for which they are easy to obtain.

4. Equipment and Clothing Requirements. As in any outdoor pursuit, specific gear and clothing requirements vary depending upon the demands of the particular activity, its duration, the site, and the qualifications and abilities of the participants. Clearly a raft is required, but the possibilities are almost endless, from one-person general-purpose models to immense craft with highly specialized designs. New designs and construction materials evolve each year, as a review of current magazines relating to the sport will show. Most are inflatables made of neoprene-coated nylon or other abrasion and salt-water-resistant fabric. All but the simplest small models have several air compartments that provide security should one section be punctured or otherwise lose air. Rafts can be purchased outright or rented. The latter option has some distinct advantages for those who don't raft often, want to learn more about the sport or certain raft types before purchasing, or want to eliminate overhead and maintenance costs.

Life jackets (personal flotation devices or "PFD's") are also an essential item common to all water activities. The American White Water Affiliation recommends a minimum flotation weight of fifteen pounds (6.8 kilos) for adults and twelve pounds (5.5 kilos) for children under 100 pounds (45.5 kilos). PFD's are rated in the United States by style and function as Type I, II, III, IV, and V. Types I and II are efficient and usually large types that all but guarantee a face-up floating position, but they are somewhat restrictive for rafters or others needing to paddle or work while wearing the devices. Type III's are less effective in that they don't, in their simplest form, automatically bring the face out of the water. However, because of their slim, vest-like fit, they do allow easy paddling and so are very popular with rafters, canoers, and kayakers. Type IV's don't really count in activities like rafting; they are only intended to be tossed, like life rings. Type V refers to all sorts of highly specialized devices, and some new versions are essentially Type III's with flotation collars, a distinct advantage for anyone whose swimming ability is low for any reason, or for any very rough water. Most organizations offering rafting excursions or classes require that all participants wear a Type III or better PFD at all times. Common sense dictates that the only way to reap the benefits of a PFD is to wear it and to wear it properly fitted and secured. Planning to put it on if you have an accident is just as inane as planning to buckle a seat belt before a car crash. Just as in driving, the statistics verify a tremendous reduction in mortality rates when these simple measures are taken in advance.

What else needs to be taken? This depends on the river and the weather, and, of course, on the length of the trip.

The following lists are based on single-day outings in cool water in the Pacific Northwest of the United States during the warmer six months of the year. Throughout this period the river water temperatures are low, ranging from 34°F (1°C) to perhaps 60°F (16°C) in rare cases. Daytime maximum air temperatures range from a little below freezing to 100°F (38°C) or more, with quite cool evenings and nights in canyon bottoms.

SUGGESTED MINIMUM GEAR REQUIRED FOR RAFTING

Individual Gear

Required Items (*certain synthetics may be substituted at the discretion of the instructor)

1. Shoes (sneakers with wool* sox, or wet-suit boots, preferably with wool sox);
2. Light clothes to wear (preferably polyprop or nylon T-shirts and shorts work well);
3. Wool* layer(s) for the legs (The instructor may require additional layers, and must require a wet suit if the combined air and water temperatures are less than 120°F [49°C]);
4. Rainwear for the legs (if wet suit not worn. Leg bottoms must not be sealed with elastic or snaps.);
5. Wool* layers for the torso (two or more if specified by the instructor. Again, the instructor must require a wet-suit top [at least "Farmer John" style] if the combined air and water temperatures are less than 120°F [49°C]. Short-sleeved wet suits don't replace wool layers);
6. Rainwear for the torso (even if short-sleeved wet suit is used, to protect wool layers and to reduce convective and evaporative heat loss. Garments must have either a tight neck or loose cuffs and bottom to avoid water build-up when swimming.);
7. Wool* hat (tight knit, to cover ears);
8. Sunglasses (with retaining strap! The glare from rivers can be intense.);
9. Water bottle (plastic with "leash" attached, one liter or more. Bring full!);
10. Lunch (preferably durable items or in a sturdy plastic box to withstand the abuse of being mashed into a dry bag!)

Optional Items (All are recommended and may be required at the discretion of the instructor.)

1. Helmet (Usually considered a device for kayakers, this item is valuable in wild-water rafting in Class III or higher-rated streams.);

2. Whistle (commonly required and useful for signaling);
3. Knife (A small, fixed-blade knife in a sturdy locking sheath can be useful in an emergency for cutting away tangled ropes or cords. Often required);
4. Cap (light color with a bill for sun protection);
5. Sunscreen (Obviously something with water repellency is best.);
6. Windshell (*not* in place of a rainsuit, but in addition to the waterproof option. A windsuit "breathes" and may be more comfortable in some conditions.);
7. Dry clothes and a towel (to leave at the car. It's common to return to the vehicle soaking wet, so bringing a change from head to toe is a good idea.);
8. Dry bag (if not carried by the group or if extra room is needed).

Raft Gear

Required Items (to be carried in each raft. Also see Group Requirements if group consists of only one raft.)

1. Throwline (a standard sack type using 50-100' [15-30 meter] 3/8" [9 mm.] nylon);
2. Knife (as above if not carried by individuals);
3. Whistle (as above if not carried by individuals);
4. Dry bags (as needed for gear);
5. Bailing can (One or two plastic "bleach bottle" types attached by cord are useful).

Optional Items

1. First-aid kit (carefully sealed to avoid water damage. Often required, it should be carried in each raft unless the group is always moving together.);
2. Emergency kit (see group gear below);
3. Spare PFD (in case of lost or damaged PFD).

Group Gear

Required Items (for groups of up to three rafts. *Note that these items must travel in the last raft!):*

1. First-aid kit (if not carried in each raft);

2. Emergency kit (if not carried by each raft, to contain 120 feet [about 36 meters] of strong nylon or polypro rope [three-eighths inch or nine mm. or larger diameter], two carabiners, two pulleys [or two additional carabiners], a repair kit for patching leaks, a pump with appropriate fittings, a backpackers' style stove, pot and fuel and/or fire-starting materials, a tarp or other shelter, an ensolite or other insulating pad, and a sleeping bag or half bag)

Optional Items

1. Comealong (This can be a useful addition to the emergency kit for retrieving lodged rafts, especially in swift currents.);
2. Thermos (Full of hot chocolate, hot soup, or other hot drinks, it can be useful in assisting the warming of mildly hypothermic participants.);
3. Maps and compass (Unless the guides or leaders are intimately familiar with the river, these should be considered required items!);
4. Flashlight(s) (If there is a chance of getting back near or after dark. When selecting gear, also consider a few prohibitions, i.e. no hard-soled shoes or boots, rubber boots with higher than six-inch tops, no cotton long pants or heavy cotton (chamois or flannel) shirts, and no rain ponchos. All can be dangerous to the craft or to the wearer.)

The above suggestions are for single-day outings. Supplementary gear for overnight camping might include shelters, sleeping pads, sleeping bags, and more food, as well as additional clothing, personal toiletries and medications, and flashlights. Dry bags and great care in packing are essential for obvious reasons.

5. Leadership Requirements and Qualifications.
A rafting leader should possess all of the qualifications listed earlier for hiking leaders (except for item "R") since these attributes are no less vital here. *Review these carefully!* In addition, the leader should have:

A. Substantial general experience on and about water and watercraft;
B. Substantial experience in the type of water environment likely to be encountered on the outing in question;

C. Familiarity with the type of craft to be employed, including an understanding of its proper and effective use, legal and practical limits and weaknesses, field maintenance, and proper handling during transportation to and from the site;

D. Familiarity with the proper use of all safety equipment to be taken on the outing in question (PFD's, throw-lines, ropes and pulleys, helmets, etc.);

E. A willingness to enforce the use of personal safety equipment at all appropriate times;

F. Swimming and water-safety skills appropriate to the activity and site (Many employers require certification by the Red Cross or other agencies.);

G. Rescue and recovery skills appropriate to the craft and site (This includes the salvage of overturned or swamped craft and the freeing of craft pinned against obstacles.)

The above qualifications are appropriate for the "captain" of each raft. In addition, the leader of each group of up to three, or in rare cases four, rafts (the usual limits of effective control) should possess:

H. Familiarity with the stretch of river to be run (This normally requires at least *two* recent runs on the section of river in question, including at least one in similar craft and at similar stream-flow rates.)

6. Leadership Ratios. Leadership ratios are largely dependent upon the ability of a leader to control the course of events. Rafts may hold several people in a rather confined space, making control within a craft relatively easy. On the other hand, rafts are to a certain extent at the mercy of the currents, and communication between them is extremely difficult. Travel upstream can be next to impossible; leaders of multi-raft parties have to choose between taking the usually favored position in the lead, which may be necessary for scouting purposes even though the route is well known, and taking the rear position, which allows relatively easy supervision and access to any other raft should a mishap occur. As a result, one fully qualified group leader is usually required for every three (or in rare cases four) rafts. This leader should possess all of the attributes listed above ("A"

through "H"). Each raft needs a leader or "captain" with qualities "A" through "G" at least, since it's entirely possible that any one raft could have serious problems and be inaccessible to the others for significant periods of time. Good group management (such as having the craft with rescue gear last and *always* travelling so closely that no one is out of sight for more than a few minutes or a few hundred yards, whichever is least) can shorten emergency access times. Yet at best these access times are likely to exceed the survival time of a person pinned under water.

The bottom line then, depends on raft size. If, for example, the rafts hold six people each, then a group leader and two qualified assistants are needed for a total of fifteen participants.

B. Course Conduct

1. Common Formats. Most rafting is done within the limits of a single day for rather obvious reasons. Single-day outings require less time and equipment, and, of course, less planning. Getting rafts to the put-in point, inflating them, making shuttle arrangements, and other logistical concerns make full-day trips more practical than short trips, at least in terms of the labor-to-fun ratio. Overnight trips are also popular, and can extend as long as desired if the time is available. Even on rivers that aren't long enough to allow travel each day of a long trip, one campsite can be used for several days while participants hike, swim, or perhaps use other types of paddlecraft to explore the adjacent stretch of river.

Pre-trip meetings are always valuable and usually essential. It's best to have at least one meeting well in advance of the outing so that people have time to assemble the requisite gear, especially if an overnight adventure is planned. Many programs require participants to pass swim or survival float tests, and this should be held or at least scheduled at an early date. A meeting just prior to the outing (perhaps on an evening two or three days ahead) can fine tune the program, increasing the likelihood of a smooth start on the morning of departure. As in all outdoor pursuits, a post-trip meeting can be immensely valuable in maximizing the value of the experience for both participants and staff.

2. Objectives. Participants in rafting programs gain in many ways from their outing experience. Every program has its own set of general goals and objectives, and these in part determine the specific goals and objectives of the outing.

Typical objectives of a rafting outing are that the participants will:

A. Enjoy the experience and want to pursue the activity further;

B. Develop an awareness of and sensitivity to the environment;

C. Learn how to travel safely by raft, which includes competency in basic paddling and/or rowing techniques, self-rescue techniques, techniques for assisting in the rescue of others, and techniques for avoiding and treating hypothermia;

D. Understand how to minimize social and physical impacts on the river and riverbank environment;

E. Understand river dynamics and develop an ability to read the river by direct observation;

F. Develop an ability to interpret river charts, maps, and guides;

G. Become aware of the capabilities and limitations of local water search-and-rescue resources, and of the most effective means of accessing these resources;

H. Acquire the skills and knowledge necessary to independently plan and carry out a successful rafting outing;

I. Develop a level of understanding and concern for the environment that leads to responsible actions on behalf of it.

3. Levels. As in land-based pursuits, it's useful to categorize rafting outings by both level of difficulty (easy, moderate, or difficult) and by objective content (beginning, intermediate, and advanced). Rating the difficulty of a river isn't easy since it is always based on the opinions of the observers, and water-level fluctuation can dramatically alter the size and energy of rapids.

As in land-based activities, myriad other factors such as the weather, the water temperature, the equipment used, and the overall length of the trip can profoundly influence the overall experience. Still, there are several "standard" rating systems. The most universal of these was derived from the I-VI climbing classification system of Europe, and uses six levels to cover the spectrum from easy, minor riffles barely noticeable in a raft (Class I) to next-to-impossible cataracts rarely challenged even by the lunatic fringe. Runs are often described by overall difficulty, with any tougher exceptions pointed out ("a Class II run with two short Class III rapids"). For rafters, Class I and II rapids are usually considered "easy," Class III "moderate," and Class IV "difficult." Class V rapids are so tough that "difficult" is probably an inadequate term. These are for experienced experts *only,* so Class V isn't worth discussing there!

Another important consideration when describing the difficulty of a run is its length, measured not so much in terms of distance as in time. It's also important to consider whether the raft will be rowed or paddled since paddling usually involves all of the passengers in frequent rotation, while rowing may involve only the leader or perhaps a succession of rowers. River currents and the number and frequency of stops determine the rate of travel.

Beginners usually appreciate easy water at first but quickly develop a taste for Class III rapids. Thus objectives "A" through "C" or "D" are usually appropriate for beginning-level courses. Intermediate-level participants will appreciate Class III rapids and perhaps one or more carefully chosen and scouted Class IV thrills. At this level objectives "D" and "E" through "G" can be added, along with emphasis on greater development of paddling or rowing skills. Advanced classes further refine skills in pursuit of objectives "H" and "I."

APPENDIX J

CANOEING

A. General Description

1. What It Is, What Is Done. Canoeing is an immensely popular activity. The canoe is an elegant and inviting craft, readily available in many parts of the world and easy to handle in a wide range of conditions. Canoes can carry surprisingly large loads and still glide smoothly over flat-water lakes. With a little practice, Class II rapids are no problem, and skilled canoeists regularly run Class III rivers. Beyond this level, however, most people prefer the more stable raft or more maneuverable and water-shedding kayak.

Canoe trips range from short paddles on flat water to adventurous multi-day outings that can include combinations of flat and wild water, sometimes linked by "portages" wherein canoes and gear are carried between bodies of water.

2. Hazards. Most of what has been said about hazards in rafting applies to canoeing as well. Canoes tend to be a good deal less stable than rafts, and generally require more skill in paddling. These drawbacks are, however, largely compensated for by greater control and maneuverability. In most cases canoeists stay drier than rafters — a distinct safety (and comfort) advantage. Most canoes are fitted with flotation devices which, while not equalling the flotation of a raft, do provide enough lift to support two people in a swamped craft. Again, the comments in the rafting section should be reviewed.

3. Who Participates. Whatever the current pastime! Canoeing is a staple activity at many youth camps and outdoor centers, and canoe youth camps and outdoor centers, and canoe lessons are often the first water-based additions to parks-and-recreation or school-based programs. Rental opportunities increase the ease of entry into the sport, which appeals to people of all ages. Since the canoe lends itself to so many types of use, it's found in one form or another in countries around the world.

4. Resource Requirements. Canoes are equally enjoyable on flat water or modest white water, so it's almost always possible to find someplace to go. Beginners tend to favor ponds and lakes — or even swimming pools — in which to practice beginning strokes. Many tend to stay on flat water, perhaps extending their adventures to include multi-day camping excursions. Medium-sized lakes or bays can provide this option, as can some very large rivers where there are no significant rapids. Others prefer the excitement of running rivers, and it doesn't take more than Class II rapids to provide thrills and occasional spills. For most people, Class III rapids are more than tough enough. Since canoes can be shouldered and carried easily by two people and tolerably well by one, it's often possible to get a lot of mileage out of a relatively short stretch of river. In many cases the canoe can even be paddled up through or around rapids, so a full day can be spent in a rather small area. These can be distinct advantages over rafting, depending upon the configuration of water resources in the program vicinity.

5. Equipment and Clothing Requirements. Canoes come in a wide range of sizes, shapes and materials. The selection of a particular model depends upon the intended primary use, alternative uses, and, of course, on the amount of money available. Often the best plan is to utilize local rental options until the possibilities are well understood. Even then rentals are often the best way to go, considering storage hassles, maintenance, and insurance costs.

Transporting canoes can be a problem. Rooftop carriers for cars or vans can be constructed at a low cost, but while appropriate for small numbers of canoes, the rooftop option is inadequate for large groups. Canoe trailers come in a variety of configurations, often homemade modifications of small flat-bed trailers designed to carry up to a dozen. Some canoe-rental businesses also rent such trailers, and this again should be considered if usage will be limited to several times per year.

The Suggested Minimum Gear Requirements for rafting can be used for canoeing outings with just a few exceptions. Since canoes are far more maneuverable, it's not usually considered necessary to carry a throw line on each craft.

One throw line for each group of up to four or five canoes is probably adequate if the canoes travel closely together and the canoe with the throw line stays in a position allowing rapid access to the site. Where rafting groups usually must be limited to three or four crafts, canoe groups can usually consist of up to eight or nine. For obvious reasons the pump isn't necessary in the repair kit.

When portaging is anticipated, some sort of carrying device is needed. Any sort of pack will do, though the favorite for hauling gear is the Du Luth pack or recent super-waterproof alternatives that resemble duffel bags with pack straps.

6. Leadership Requirements and Qualifications. The comments in the rafting section are appropriate here as well.

7. Leadership Ratios. Canoes are far more maneuverable than rafts, which allows the leaders more opportunity to move about at will. This same mobility, however, is also available to participants, so while the leaders are more mobile the task of group control is compounded. Under most circumstances a reasonable level of control can be maintained over a total of nine canoes by two leaders, each in separate canoes. That is, the group consists of seven canoes, each carrying two participants, and two canoes, each carrying a leader with or without a participant. If the leaders are skilled and attentive and maintain themselves at lead and sweep positions, assistance and communication can usually be maintained. This results in a ratio of two leaders per fourteen to sixteen participants, which is slightly greater than for rafting. Certainly this ratio should be increased (another leader added) if outing risks are greater than normal due to more treacherous water, less experienced participants, or any situation that lessens control.

B. Course Conduct

1. Common Formats. Canoeing is a somewhat more skills-oriented activity than rafting after some classroom-theory work. Many paddle strokes can be practiced in swimming pools prior to open-water use. Upstream travel or even portaging allow short segments of river to be used for extended practice sessions, thereby eliminating shuttle problems. Otherwise, the possibilities are, as in rafting, nearly unlimited. Canoe camping is popular, and bodies of water can be linked by portages.

2. Objectives. The objectives suggested for rafting are appropriate for canoeing.

3. Levels. Canoes are somewhat less suited to rapids than either rafts or kayaks. As a result, while Class II rapids may not be too exciting in a raft or kayak, they offer plenty of thrills for beginning canoeists and are good practice grounds even at the intermediate level. Class III rapids, which might be considered "moderate" by rafters, would be "difficult" for most canoeists. Advanced canoe classes, however, might polish technique and play in some Class III rapids.

KAYAKING
Many basic kayaking skills, such as the Eskimo roll, can be taught first in the warm, quiet water of a pool and then in calm, natural water before trying rapids.

APPENDIX K

KAYAKING

A. General Description

1. What It Is, What Is Done. Kayaks probably evolved along the northern sea coasts, where rough water and foul weather demanded covered craft and resistance to swamping. These sleek, fast craft offer great maneuverability and a good deal more stability than commonly attributed to them. True, they aren't as stable as canoes under some circumstances; however, the low body position (relative to the kneeling position of canoeing) improves this, and sitting also allows greater comfort on long trips. Some kayaks are designed to carry large loads, and some can even be fitted with sails. The light weight of modern designs makes transportation by vehicle at least as easy as canoes, and the availability of rentals and instruction have rocketed this sport into widespread popularity within the last decade. No other craft gives such an intimate sense of contrast with the water. Kayak outings range from practice sessions in pools (kayaking is the most skill-oriented of the water-craft activities discussed here) to long-ranging voyages by sea, lake, or stream.

2. Hazards. Kayaking isn't inherently more dangerous than canoeing or rafting if certain precautions are taken. Since the craft are somewhat more likely to capsize, it's important that the spray skirt that seals the kayaker to the craft is instantly removable should attempts at rolling be unsuccessful. Helmets are also more important if the craft is used in rapids. Common sense and good judgment are also critical since the sport typically involves the development of skills and the challenge of even more energetic and difficult rapids. Just as in its closest land-based equivalent, Alpine skiing, most kayaking accidents are related to overly ambitious activities. Serious mishaps are rare if limits of skill and craft design are respected.

Reread the section on rafting hazards, especially vis-a-vis PFD's and hypothermia since these concerns are no less valid here.

3. Who Participates. It's not easy to find a major stream or body of water not bearing at least a few kayaks. Even though the basic craft have been in use by Eskimos for centuries, kayaking as a sport is very young. Participants also tend to be young, although the average age is increasing as people continue to kayak into later years. As mentioned in the canoeing section, studies indicate substantial participation figures; industry figures on kayak sales show continued and growing interest from an ever-broadening demographic segment.

4. Resource Requirements. Like canoeing, kayaking can be enjoyed on any water. Pool practice sessions are especially valuable for kayakers, who find the still, clear, warm water perfect for mastering one or more of the several types of rolls so crucial to successful mastery of Class III or higher rapids. Some people enjoy sea or lake kayaking, and multi-day outings can be made as easily in kayaks as canoes if proper craft are selected. Most people, however, seem to prefer river running, and virtually any stretch is worth considering if it contains enough water flow and challenging rapids. There are shops in most major cities specializing in paddle craft, and these usually stock guidebooks identifying local resources. Clubs, schools, and parks-and-recreation departments can also usually provide information about suitable sites.

5. Equipment and Clothing Requirements. Kayaks come in many specialized shapes, usually constructed of fiberglass or high-tech plastic. Equipment requirements are essentially the same as for canoeing, except that kayakers need a spray screen.

6. Leadership Ratios. Kayaking leadership ratios tend to be greater than in canoeing since control of individual craft is as difficult with single occupation as when each craft contains two participants. Two leaders are still required to supervise six or seven people, but exceptions can be made in pools or perhaps other tightly controlled situations not in moving water. In such cases one leader might be able to supervise eight or nine boats.

B. Course Conduct

1. Common Formats. Kayaking classes are often conducted as a series of shore sessions (one to three hours) wherein participants spend a short time in the classroom and most of the time on the water. Several initial sessions can be spent in a swimming pool, where basic strokes and the roll(s) can be taught most effectively. When possible, a small lake, bay, or other protected body of still water can be used to extend basic skills and practice rolls under more natural (and usually colder and less clear) conditions. Once skills are improved and confidence is up, streams of increasing difficulty can be attempted. These early lessons are usually short since attention spans and energy reserves rarely extend beyond a few hours. Later outings can be of any length, with skills sessions as brief interludes throughout the day.

2. Objectives. The general objectives suggested for rafting are appropriate for kayaking. Specific skill objectives can be extracted from any of a number of kayaking texts.

3. Levels. Kayakers will find Class I and II rapids adequate at "beginning" levels, and should spend most of their initial skill-training sessions in water ranging from flat and still to the upper limits of Class II. "Intermediate" kayakers, those able to do rolls while drifting in a current, will enjoy most Class III rapids but should expect to spend many hours developing skills at this level. Many devotees rarely push beyond this even after years of kayaking. "Advanced" outings might expose participants to carefully selected upper Class III or modest Class IV rapids, though such groups might well focus on perfection of skills in modest Class III or easier conditions.

APPENDIX L

BIKE TOURING

A. General Description

1. What It Is, What Is Done. Bike touring is a popular activity encompassing everything from short day trips to extended world tours. Tourists pack their gear, from basic tools and a picnic lunch to a complete repair-and-maintenance kit and camping equipment, in panniers (special bags suspended from racks over front and/or rear tires), then set out on highways and back roads. Some tourists even take mountain trails, using specifically designed "mountain bikes."

Bike touring offers many of the benefits of wilderness and back-country activities, yet with the exception of some mountain-trail biking, the activity takes place in relatively close proximity to civilization. As a result the tourist is seldom deprived of civilized amenities for more than a few hours at a time.

2. Hazards. If asked to list "high risk" outdoor activities, most people wouldn't think of bike touring, at least not before giving a long list of such activities as skiing or climbing. In fact, bike touring probably ought to be included somewhere near the top. Even at modest speeds, equipment failure, an unexpected checkhole, rock, or slippery spot, or an error in judgment can send the pedaler over the handlebars or into a ditch. Worse yet, most tourists share the road with motor vehicles, and collisions, even grazing sideswipes, can be devastating. Careful attention to safety rules and procedures, the use of high-visibility clothing, gear, and/or flags, and helmets can all help reduce the risk of accident and injury. At best, however, an element of risk remains since falls cannot be completely eliminated and the most cautious biker is subject to danger caused by careless drivers. On the positive side, such incidents don't occur often, and professional care and equipment is often accessible within minutes (in cities) or at least within an hour or so on most country roads. Nevertheless, the overall chance of serious injury or death is probably higher for bike touring than for any other outdoor pursuit unless the activity is very carefully controlled and all applicable safety measures employed.

3. Who Participates. By the broadest definition, just about everyone has at one time or another gone on a bike tour — that is, if packing up a picnic lunch and riding across town to the park is accepted as "touring." On the other hand, full-blown modern bike touring, panniers stuffed and cycle shoes in toe clips, has a relatively limited appeal. Even more than nordic skiing, bike touring has an image of strenuousness. This is unfortunate and generally inaccurate since, as in any outdoor pursuit, the pace is usually self determined and can be as leisurely as desired. Most devotees of bike touring are fit and relatively young, and tend, like participants in wilderness and back-country pursuits, to be well educated and/or well off financially. One clue to the number of potential clients for a bike-touring program, aside from the above demographic considerations, is the abundance of bicycle shops in the community. Many of the bicycles sold for general commuting and recreation are adequate for at least beginning touring, so people with such bikes are at least over the primary hurdle of initial purchase.

Bicycling is currently experiencing a wave of popularity, probably sustained in part by recent high levels of interest in general fitness. This should result in an expansion of interest in touring as some bike owners begin to push the limits of the sport.

4. Resource Requirements. Bike tourists need access to reasonably smooth paths or roads. It's most convenient if you can begin from town or wherever the program would normally meet, though this isn't necessary if vans, pickups, or other transportation can be used to carry tourists and bikes to the starting point. Traffic safety and local regulations may preclude the use of certain roads and highways. On the other hand, many communities have developed extensive pathways primarily for bicyclists, and in some areas special bike lanes have been designated. Guidebooks are also available for many areas, showing recommended touring routes. These can be especially valuable when initially investigating areas with extensive urban and rural road systems since checking out all of the possibilities can be a formidable task.

5. Clothing and Equipment Requirements. The gear requirements for bike touring depend upon the length (in time and in miles) of the trip, where it will take place, the season and likely weather, and the tourists' willingness to face being stranded by equipment failure. For the purposes of this list, let's assume that the outing consists of a long full day, covering perhaps fifty miles (eighty km.) on fairly remote rural roads. Gear requirements might be less in urban areas, but will be greatly increased if overnight camping is planned, in which case the backpacking list should be reviewed for appropriate items.

SUGGESTED MINIMUM GEAR REQUIRED FOR BIKE-TOURING DAY TRIPS

Individual Gear

Required Items

1. Bicycle (in good repair. There are many aspects of frame, wheel, and component design and construction that affect both comfort and safety. Expensive specialized bicycles are not essential to enjoyable beginning touring, and care should be taken to assess all safety related aspects of any bicycle prior to a tour.);
2. Rack(s) (Racks for the front and/or rear are essential since it's dangerous to carry anything on your back while riding. Both front and rear racks may be essential for overnight trips involving camping.);
3. Panniers (Panniers or other containers that can be carried on the rack are essential if any gear is to be carried. A full set of panniers, including a handlebar bag, may be needed for overnight tours involving camping.);
4. Helmet (Investigate each model carefully. Not all available types provide adequate protection.);
5. Water bottle (A pint [500 cc] or larger plastic bottle is usually adequate.);
6. Small tool kit (patch kit, pump, knife, and screwdriver, if not part of group gear.);
7. First-aid kit (adequate personal kit to stabilize broken bones, bleeding, and other possible injuries if it isn't carried as group gear.);

8. Protective clothing (this will vary with locale and season, but may include rain protection, wind protection, and insulation appropriate for the possible weather and temperatures.);
9. Driver's license and/or other identification (required in some areas for operating a bicycle on roadways);
10. Maps of the area.

Optional Items

1. Light and batteries or generator (essential if any night riding may be done);
2. Rear and side reflectors (also essential if night riding is possible);
3. Warning flag (A bright flag or pennant on a pole is always a good idea and may be especially valuable in rolling terrain.);
4. Full tool kit (In addition to small tool-kit contents, possible contents include two tire irons, Allen wrenches, adjustable wrench, universal wrench, spoke wrench, spokes, "third hand" free-wheel extractor, chain breaker, assorted nuts and bolts, and a spare tube.);
5. Lock and chain (unfortunately essential if the bike is to be left unguarded in some parts of the world);
6. Toe clips and straps (*very* useful and considered essential by some);
7. Cycling gloves (A good pair can increase comfort and reduce damage to the hands.);
8. Cycling shoes (Proper shoes can increase comfort and efficiency.);
9. Sunglasses.

Group Gear

Required Items

1. Small tool kit (unless carried by individuals);
2. First-aid kit (unless carried by individuals).

Optional Items

1. Full tool kit (described above)
2. Warning flag or sign (In traffic it's sometimes worthwhile to use a bright flag or pennant on a pole and/or a sign warning on bikers ahead for the last biker in line.)

Overnight camping is often an important part of the touring experience. If camping is planned each tourist will need to carry a sleeping bag, some sort of pad to sleep on, and cup and spoon, and arrange for shared access to shelter (a tarp and ground sheet or a tent) and cooking gear (a stove, pot, and fuel). Review the backpacking list for other useful items, but bear in mind that unnecessary gear adds complexity, a lot of extra work when climbing hills, and risk, since extra weight reduces stability and control.

6. Leadership Requirements. Most bike-touring programs either include overnight camping or focus on the skills necessary to begin this type of touring. Leaders and instructors therefore usually need skills and experience in camping, especially bike touring and camping, as well as substantial skill and experience in riding, bicycle maintenance, and repair. Any bike-touring leader should have at least the following attributes:

A. Maturity consistent with the responsibility of the job;
B. Evident intelligence and common sense;
C. An ability to relate to both employer and participants in a friendly and personable manner;
D. An ability to assess the psychological and physical needs and limits of participants with reasonable accuracy;
E. An ability to communicate ideas and instructions effectively and appropriately;
F. An understanding of teaching methodology insofar as required by program objectives;
G. A willingness and ability to exercise control over the actions of the group in conformance with the standards and policies of the employer, highway and traffic safety rules, and any other applicable policies, rules, or laws (This includes an ability to organize the group, employing leader-caboose or other appropriate control situations effectively in any reasonably foreseeable weather and traffic conditions while maintaining an awareness of the well-being of all participants at all times.);
H. If driving is required by the program, appropriate licenses and a satisfactory driving record;

I. Appropriate first-aid skills (This must include training and experience in long-term care and improvisation if the route includes areas where professional care and emergency equipment are not readily accessible. Leaders should be especially well versed in hypo- and hyper-thermic conditions and on the importance of hydration and nutritional considerations — especially if the tours will be long or strenuous.);

J. An awareness of emergency services available throughout the program area, including procedures for obtaining such assistance in emergencies;

K. Expertise in the skills and techniques of bike riding, including pacing and rhythm;

L. Expertise in touring-bike evaluation, maintenance, and repair;

M. Special skills and experience as needed for the program (This usually includes overnight camping, which requires experience in gear selection, packing, riding with full camping gear, site selection, and camping.);

N. Substantial bike-touring experience in the area to be used by the program, or at least some familiarity with the area backed by substantial experience under very similar conditions.

7. Leadership Ratios. The number of leaders required on a tour depends upon the nature of the tour, its setting, and the age and number of the participants. Since most tours operate on or near roads and not distant from "civilization," at least in the form of telephones, the incapacitation of a leader is unlikely to be a serious threat to the security of adult participants. One leader can usually supervise about ten adults though this can be difficult in certain traffic situations and results in very long spreads when riding single file with safe spacings between riders. Five to seven riders per leader are usually easily manageable and should be considered the maximum if the participants are young or require closer attention or supervision. A second leader or qualified assistant is necessary if the group might be unable to respond safely and responsibly to an accident involving the leader or to some other situation in which the leader may become unable to supervise the group.

B. Course Conduct

1. Common Formats. Most bike-touring programs consist of one or more pre-trip meetings and one or more outings. Outings may be as short as an hour or two or may extend to multi-day tours. At least two pre-trip meetings are usually necessary, even on relatively short single-day tours since the first meeting needs to be well in advance of the outing to allow participants to get bikes and gear organized and in good working order. A later pre-trip meeting a few days prior to the outing provides opportunities for more instruction and final plan resolution to insure that all participants arrive at the outing on time and with all necessary gear. Bike maintenance, safety issues, and other topics can easily fill a number of additional pre-trip sessions. A post-outing session is, as with all outdoor-pursuit activities, of great value to both staff and participants. In this session the overall value of the program can be enhanced by reviewing the experience and reinforcing important issues. Post-trip meetings also allow you to cover material that wasn't adequately addressed on the outing, provide guidance to participants with regard to future involvement in the activity, and gain formal or informal evaluative feedback leading to improvement in future programs.

2. Objectives. As in any other outdoor pursuit there are many inherent benefits which may or may not be specifically addressed in a list of objectives. On virtually any bike tour, for instance, participants gain in fitness, self awareness, social skills, and appreciation of the natural world while gaining the benefits of relaxation and an enhanced sense of perspective on everyday life. Typical objectives specific to bike touring are that the participant will:

A. Enjoy the experience and want to pursue the activity further;

B. Gain an awareness of the fitness requirements of bike touring;

C. Understand the hazards inherent in bike touring and basic safety procedures to reduce the chance of accidents or injuries;

D. Understand the equipment and clothing requirements of bike touring (This includes the selection, maintenance, and repair of bicycles and other gear.);

E. Develop skills in bike riding and touring, allowing more efficient, comfortable, and safe travel by bicycle;

F. Understand sufficient first-aid and emergency care to stabilize injuries until professional assistance can be obtained;

G. Be aware of the resources available for bike touring in the area;

H. Acquire the knowledge and skills necessary to independently plan and carry out a successful bike-touring day outing;

I. Acquire the knowledge and skills necessary to independently plan and carry out a successful bike tour involving overnight camping.

3. Levels. Like hiking or backpacking, bike touring can proceed at almost any pace, so virtually any distance or type of terrain can be negotiated with ease, given enough time. It is, however, convenient when describing outings to assign adjectives such as "easy," "moderate," or "difficult." If a full-day tour is planned, it may well be possible to include six to eight hours or more of riding. Beginners, however, will find so much time "in the saddle" tiring and likely to result in sore limbs and seat. Since most programs deal with beginners, three hours or so of actual riding should be considered maximal for an "easy" tour, and distances on flat roads should rarely exceed thirty miles (about fifty km.). Hills, rough pavement, head winds, foul weather, or substantial gear loads may substantially reduce these limits. A "moderate" tour may involve twice as much distance and four to six hours of riding, while any tour covering more than sixty miles (about 100 km.) should be called "difficult" — especially if the loads are heavy and/or the route is anything less than ideal.

Objectives "A" through "D" or "E" are usually appropriate for "beginning" classes, while "intermediate" classes typically reinforce objectives "D" and "E" and move participants toward objectives "F," "G," and "H." "Advanced" classes often focus on objective "I." At every level considerable review is usually necessary, and integration of all basic skills should accompany attempts to attain more objectives.

APPENDIX M

WATER: THE KEY TO STAYING COMFORTABLE IN A COOL, WET ENVIRONMENT

Staying comfortable on an outing is largely dependent upon maintaining your body temperature within a very narrow range. Your temperature can go up a few degrees or down several degrees without long-term damage, but variation of more than one degree in either direction can be most unpleasant. Maintaining a comfortable temperature requires that heat gains equal heat losses, and that's where water becomes an important factor. Heat *gains* come primarily from metabolic heat production, and that process is very sensitive to the body's level of hydration. Good health, plenty of rest, and a proper diet are important and not to be ignored, but don't forget to drink water! (Some specific concerns and suggestions are included below, in the section labeled *"Hydration."*) Most heat *losses* occur through radiation, conduction, convection, evaporation, and respiration. The level of humidity in the environment profoundly affects at least the last four of these factors since air, the real "insulator" in most types of clothing, is a very poor one when it's wet. This effect is best minimized by keeping your body and clothing as dry as possible, as explained in the section "Staying Dry." The following information should help you maintain heat production and control heat loss, thus increasing your comfort, safety, and enjoyment of the outdoors.

Hydration

You need to maintain adequate hydration in order to produce heat (and power your body) efficiently, yet many outdoor activities involve both accelerated water loss (high respiration rate, heavy perspiration, and perhaps a high evaporation rate due to elevation or dry air) and difficult access to drinking water (potentially polluted sources or below-freezing weather). So what can you do?

1. Recognize your body's need for water! The "average" person will need anywhere from one-and-a-half to six liters or more per day depending on the level of activity and myriad environmental factors. Three liters per day is a common figure for daily needs on a typical backpacking or ski-touring venture. *Remember,* thirst is a very poor indicator of need. You can satisfy your thirst at each "water stop" but gradually become seriously dehydrated. Long before you develop that "human raisin" look, you will suffer unnecessary weakness from lessening metabolic efficiency.

2. Control your need for water! Pace yourself *and adjust your clothing* so you don't lose excessive amounts through perspiration and heavy breathing. Drink small quantities frequently so you don't trigger your body to eliminate the excess through urination. Don't rely on consumption of salt tablets to "hold onto the water;" it doesn't work that way despite the popularity of the process.

3. Drink enough! A good rule of thumb is to drink what you feel like at rest stops (which should be each hour or so), *then drink another equal quantity.* Adding flavorings may increase palatability in case you've used water purification chemicals or aren't a water lover, but do be sure to consume plenty! (Understand that while you may avoid major debilitating symptoms on a one- or two-day outing, a daily deficiency of a pint or two will build to serious levels in about three days.) A good though somewhat delayed sign to monitor is urine color. Darkened (more intense) color or a burning sensation is usually a sign of having consumed too little. Women prone to bladder infections should be extra careful to maintain a high fluid flow.

4. Think about your sources! Be prepared to purify any questionable water (and nowadays, unfortunately, most is). Be sure to keep plenty of it on hand for those times of the day when the inconvenience of purifying it on the spot might result in going without or risking water-carried disease. It is a good idea to drink a liter of water in the evening and another in the morning, then leave camp with yet another liter to consume during the day. In this way the

water can be boiled or treated beforehand, and you will be less likely to be tempted by marginal sources during the day.

Staying Dry

The surface of your skin is never completely dry because small amounts of moisture constantly pass from it into the air. This evaporative process cools the body (the vapor state producing higher energy than the liquid state) and is one of your body's primary heat-loss mechanisms. An increase in environmental temperature or metabolic heat production (i.e., more rapid exercise) increases the fluid flow and this, ideally, returns your temperature to normal. In a cool, wet environment it is easy to end up with *too much* water on your body surface. The result is that cool, wet, thoroughly unpleasant feeling we experience all too often in the northern latitudes. Water also affects the efficiency of insulation since it has about 240 times the thermal capacity of air. Dry air is a very good insulator, and most inner and outer wear relies on trapped "dead air" spaces to prevent heat from travelling efficiently from your body outwards.

Clearly, staying comfortable requires some control over the amount of moisture on your skin and in your clothing. Here are a few ideas and "tricks of the trade" that I've gathered in more than twenty-five years of roaming the often cool and wet Cascades, Sierras, and Alps of Europe and Japan:

1. Consider the need to stay dry! This may seem obvious, but considering the substantial difficulty sometimes encountered in actually doing so, it's worth thinking about. Clearly, you would not want to find yourself "in the bush" (that is, without benefit of "civilized" accommodations) with no adequate dry clothing. Sometimes, though, escape to a warm shelter with drying capabilities is *absolutely* certain, or you may find that you can sacrifice one outfit and still have plenty of dry clothes left. If your activity level will remain high for the duration of the wet-clothes episode, then you may also be able to stay reasonably comfortable. Just remember that even the amazing new synthetics are pretty miserable for sitting still or sleeping in if they are soaking wet.

2. Control your perspiration rate by adjusting your pace and, most importantly, your clothing. Using thin layers will allow cooling, which may keep your body from pumping out excessive moisture, and using permeable layers may allow excessive moisture to evaporate before humidity gets too high.

3. Control your perspiration, and thus both evaporative cooling and water loss, by using a vapor barrier. This means wearing a totally *impermeable* layer next to your skin or over any clothing you don't mind getting wet. Your skin-surface humidity won't get much above eighty percent, so you won't be swimming in sweat. This system also works well in sleeping bags, adding quite a bit of warmth by minimizing evaporation from your skin, keeping body moisture out of the bag, and at the same time helping conserve water (you don't wake up thirsty!).

4. Plan your route and your schedule to correspond to places and times of drier weather. Sometimes you can alter your route to an area of less rainfall, or go to a higher elevation where there is snow instead of rain. This will generally help *if* you can get high enough to reach temperatures below 26° or so since warmer snow can be as soaking as rain. Travel during morning hours maximizes your chance of drizzle and stratus-type rains, but minimizes chances of thunderstorms. Morning travel also ups the chances for light, dry, cold snow as opposed to the warmer snow of the afternoons. (Don't *count* on any particular kind of weather. You will find these patterns to be generally valid though many meteorologic processes can override them!) Additionally, avoid wet, grassy meadows until the sun has baked the dew off, and watch out for snow-covered trees on sunny days — it might as well be raining snowballs. The frozen snow crust is dry and pleasant to walk on during the early morning hours of spring and summer, but walking through the slush from midday on is tiring and bound to soak your boots.

5. Camp out of the rain! A favorite trick of mine is to put up a large fly or tarp as soon as I select a campsite, then pitch my tent (or just a ground sheet) under the shelter. It's great to be able to move about, touching tent walls all I like, and to get up and out comfortably (out of the rain!) and pack up a dry tent. The wet fly is quick and easy to roll up, and you get to set up a dry tent the next night. Substituting a large, light tarp for a tent fly doesn't add much weight to your pack.

6. Keep your stuff dry! For me, success in this requires no less than putting my goods in plastic bags (stout, not produce), then putting these inside "waterproof" stuffsacks, and finally packing everything in a large garbage bag inside of my "waterproof" nylon pack, all under a coated nylon pack cover. (Pack covers are great, almost essential in really wet conditions. Only then can you take a nice *dry* pack inside your shelter.) Humidity is incredibly insidious, and will eventually permeate *everything* unless it is kept *sealed* in totally waterproof material. (Coated nylon is very repellent but not totally waterproof.)

7. Hike out of the rain! Try an umbrella! In other parts of the world, umbrellas are a common sight on trails. People laugh a lot at mine when I use it around here, but only until they see how well it works . . . no raincoat, no drips down the back of the neck, no hat. A little collapsible businessman's model works fine, even in all but the worst-off trail conditions. And a model with a hook-shaped handle can be used with no hands; the pack supports it, and the handle hooks on your shirt or pack strap to hold it in place. Of course, it is not a solution in windy conditions (or for skiing!) and cannot be relied upon as a survival tool.

8. Use insulation materials and fabrics that don't "hang on" to water! Cotton is the worst, being extremely hard to dry and next to worthless when wet. It is amazing how many people venture back into the woods in sweatshirts and Levis or cords. Experienced Northwest hikers call such outfits "idiot" or "suicide" suits, for good reason. This is not to say that cotton can't be used, but if you choose to you would indeed be considered foolish not to have a substantial set of wool or synthetic clothing stashed in your pack. The reason for using this or other fibers is that wool (and the new "pile" and other synthetic fabrics) repels moisture rather than holds onto it, maintaining trapped air spaces despite the presence of dampness. A wet wool or pile garment will lose much of its water by dripping and draining in a short while, and much of what's left can be wrung or spun out, then easily moved away from your body by a modest thermal gradient. This is not so with cotton. (Why do you think cotton, not wool, is used for towels?) So always have a clothing layer of wool or of one of the synthetics (polypropylene is one of the best) with you.

In sleeping bags, down is analogous to cotton in that it soaks up water. It also is *very* hard to dry in wet weather (impossible is probably more accurate), and the better-quality downs are fluffier and *more* vulnerable than the cheap ones. (The only down bag I ever had that was any good in wet conditions was made, I think, of whole ground robins. At least the quills and feet kept the bag layers from matting together.) Many new synthetics, modeled on Dacron-like fibers, provide very high resistance to moisture and relative ease of drying at a much lower cost (and slightly greater bulk and weight).

9. Select and invest in top-quality rainwear! My experience and that of most professionals and "heavy users" I know is that Goretex isn't an acceptable fabric for coats and jackets. It seems tolerable for rain pants and fine for tents (my favorite tent is Goretex), but jackets must pass lots of perspiration, which always eventually fouls the fabric's ability to shed water. Thus jackets work fine *until* you need them, then leak massively. Most of us have given up tedious cleanings after every hard use, and have gone back to urethane-coated nylon or similar highly repellent fabrics. I prefer high quality, well-seam-sealed (or taped) but very lightweight fabric, since rain gear spends most of its time in your pack. Heavy, fancy raingear with lots of reinforcing and pockets and flaps to seam-seal just adds weight, bulk, and needless cost. Rainchaps are light, compact, and easy to make, but rain pants are nice for skiing or other snow play. Ponchos are fine on trails out of the wind, but umbrellas are almost as effective. Plastic raingear is usually a waste of money since it almost always tears and breaks apart in the cold, wind, and brush. Whatever you choose, put on a cotton T-shirt, cotton pants, and the raingear and stand in the shower before going on an outing. Any leaks will then show up as wet spots on the water-grabbing cotton layer.

10. Keep your feet dry! A basic rule is, of course, to wear wool or synthetic socks and be sure to bring spares. Don't forget extra insoles, too, if yours can soak up water. (Otherwise, changing socks won't help.) Socks can get wet from the outside or from the inside (perspiration), and damp socks are poor insulators, so your feet can get cold. To keep them dry, use plastic bags (*tough* ones). Put on a light pair of socks, a plastic bag, your heavy socks, and another plastic bag. This way your boots will get wet, but your socks will stay dry — it really works!

Another rule is to expect your boots to leak profoundly after a day or two of wet-weather travel (or travel on wet snow or ground, or in wet grass or brush). Careful sealing with one of the better wax or silicone preparations will do a fine job for a day or so in moderate conditions or with stiff new boots, but don't expect any treatment to keep water out of leather ones. In wet weather the surface of your boots is always moist, and no treatment will allow you to flex the leather indefinitely without some (usually *much*) leakage. I've tried new plastic boots and despite the aesthetics and some lingering engineering problems, they seem to offer welcome relief from wet feet and should be considered an alternative to leather boots for wet-weather travel. Meanwhile, plastic bags will have to do. I've also tried the new Goretex lined boots, and so far have been quite amazed at how well they've worked. Shop carefully, of course, as some models apparently leak badly.

11. At night, try to control the humidity in your tent or shelter by maintaining adequate ventilation! Be especially careful to avoid adding unnecessary moisture by keeping wet items of gear and clothing outside and by not boiling water inside. It's important to keep the tent fly away from the tent to prevent seepage through walls.

A sleeping bag can get quite damp even without any outside wetness. You lose a pint or more each night of insensible water, and much of this is trapped. At some point in its travel through your bag, the water vapor will condense and/or freeze. The only outward sign may be some surface moisture, usually near or at your feet where your body-heat output is not great enough to force the water completely out. One way to help increase the thermal gradient and keep the bag drier is to take hot-water bottles to bed with you at night; you keep your bag drier and toes warmer. Another solution is the vapor-barrier system mentioned earlier, especially in conjunction with a vapor-proof cover. Goretex or *any* material that impedes the passage of vapor (yes, Goretex does slow it down, even if it doesn't stop it completely) should *not* be used as a cover for a bag without an *internal* vapor barrier. Anything that gets in the way of vapor exit will just increase the amount of moisture captured in the bag. In wet climates, the best solution is often a combination of careful attention to keeping water off the bag, hot-water bottles, and the use of synthetic fill materials.

12. Once your clothing or gear is wet, you may want to try to dry it. If so, your task may be formidable unless you are lucky enough to have sunshine and/or dry air. Try wringing out items or spinning them (tied on a cord or put in a netting sack and whirled around to throw out the water). Drying clothing by wearing it at night in your sleeping bag is rarely worth the trouble. You will be chilled by the evaporation, and most of the moisture will end up in the bag's insulation. A hot-water bottle can provide enough heat to dry socks, gloves, or a hat wrapped around it.

13. Know when to give up and go home! Unless you are quite sure of your capabilities, it's usually a good idea to head for civilization when your last reserve layer of dry clothing is compromised. Survival, not just comfort, may be at stake. Don't be afraid to turn around — you can always come back in better weather!

CREDITS

Copyrighted works, listed in the order of appearance, are printed by permission of the following:

Chapter 1, page 1. Jensen, Clayne, *Outdoor Recreation in America,* Burgess Publishing Company, Minneapolis, MN, 1970, pp. 8-9.

page 6. Table 1.2 from Brown, Christopher, "New Handshake: Management Partners Along the Appalachian Trail," *Parks and Recreation,* National Recreation and Parks Association, June, 1982, p. 37.

page 7. Table 1.3 from Nash, Roderick, *Wilderness and the American Mind,* Yale University Press, New Haven, CT, 1967, p. 271.

page 12. The Athletic Ins.

Chapter 2, page 17. Maslow, Abraham, *Toward a Psychology of Being,* D. Van Nostrand Company, NY, 1980, p. 25.

page 27. Ibid., p. 26.

Chapter 3, page 49. HUG-A-TREE c/o Mrs. Jacqueline Heet, 6465 Lance Way, San Diego, CA 92120. Copyright 1981, Thomas R. Jacobs and Ab Taylor.

Chapter 4, pages 55-62. Reprinted with permission of Macmillan Publishing Company from *Principles and Practices of Outdoor/Environmental Education* by Phyllis Ford. Copyright 1981 by John A. Wiley & Sons.

Chapter 5, page 85. Nash Roderick, *Wilderness and the American Mind,* Yale University Press, New Haven, CT, 1967, p. 255.

page 87. Ibid., p. 267.

Chapter 6, page 105. Nash Roderick, *Wilderness and the American Mind,* Yale University Press, New Haven, CT, 1975, p. 273.

page 112. From: *Outdoor Recreation* by Douglas Knudson, p. 256. Copyright 1984 by Macmillan Publishing Company. Reprinted with permission of the publisher.

Chapter 11, page 226. Figure 11.4 from Paul Hershey, Kenneth Blanchard, *Management of Organizational Behavior: Utilizing Human Resources,* 3rd edition, 1977, p. 170. Reprinted by permission of Prentice-Hall, Inc., Englewood Cliffs, NJ.

Chapter 12, pages 237-238. Reprinted with permission of Macmillan Publishing Company from *Leadership in Recreation and Leisure Service Organizations* by Christopher Edginton and Phyllis Ford, pp. 204-212. Copyright 1985 by John Wiley & Sons, Inc.

INDEX